Communism in America

A HISTORY IN DOCUMENTS

Communism in America

A HISTORY IN DOCUMENTS

Albert Fried

COLUMBIA UNIVERSITY PRESS
NEW YORK

Columbia University Press

Publishers Since 1893

New York Chichester, West Sussex

Copyright © 1997 Columbia University Press

All rights reserved

Library of Congress Cataloging-in-Publication Data

Communism in America : a history in documents / [edited by] Albert Fried.

   p. cm.

  Includes bibliographical references and index.

  ISBN 0-231-10235-6 (pbk. : alk. paper).

  1. Communism—United States—History. 2. United States—Social conditions—20th century. 3. United States—Intellectual life—20th century. I. Fried, Albert.

HX83.C63   1997

335.43'0973—dc20   96-34561

Printed in the United States of America

c 10 9 8 7 6 5 4 3 2 1

p 10 9 8 7 6 5 4 3 2 1

This book brings to a close a plan I conceived a long time ago to provide what was then unavailable to the interested public, accounts of the Socialist and Communist experiences in America through original sources, in the words of their participants. A commercial publisher, persuaded by the insurgent mood of those days, agreed to do them.

Socialism in America, which came out in 1971, sought to inform, or remind, readers that Socialism was an integral part of American life from the first Shaker experiments on, that remarkable men and women were drawn to it throughout each stage of its evolution, reflecting as it did America's development into a mighty industrial nation, and that it affected society at large in ways that mainstream historians had neglected to acknowledge. The book ended in 1919, the year the Socialist Party, still potent, still fearsome, split in twain, its "left wing" gravitating toward the revolutionary model embodied in Russia's new "Communist" government. Hence the subtitle: "From the Shakers to the Third International" (perhaps a better one would have been "*Communist* International"). The volume on Communism was going to carry the story to its melancholy conclusion—the demise and fall of a movement that was once so prosperous, influential, and full of optimism.

But I laid the project aside and after a while gave it up altogether. Then, in 1993, Columbia University Press reprinted *Socialism in America*. My interest reawakened, I was surprised to discover that there was still no book on Communism of the kind I had conceived, even though American Communism was by now something of a rage among scholars. I found myself picking up where I had left off, rummaging through library stacks and gathering documents old and new, a fair number of them excerpts from memoirs recently written by ex-Communists. And so the process thus set in motion has eventuated in this attempt to satisfy a need still unmet by the ever-burgeoning literature on the subject.

This is a book very different no doubt from the one I originally had in mind. Before the rebellious 1960s I saw Communism from a Cold War angle, refracted through left-liberal lenses. Caught up in the ensuing turbulence, I abandoned that species of liberalism, though a remnant of the old anti-Communist animus survived; a glance at *Socialism in America* will confirm this. Since then I have come to look upon American Communism more benignly and, I trust, more objectively, to value its achievements, such as they were, without minimizing the gravity of its defects, and to regard it as no less an authentic and legitimate expression of our native radical tradition than the Socialism that preceded it. I came to focus my attention not so much on how and why Communism brought about its own demise but on what sort of movement it was, on the details of what it did, especially during the momentous decades of its apogee—the 1930s and 1940s—and on what hostile forces overwhelmed it and consigned it to the outermost margins of the polity.

Before going further, I should clarify exactly which Communism the book deals with. There were, after all, three Communisms by 1930, each claiming to be the true legatee of Bolshevism, the sole keeper of the Marxist-Leninist flame. There was the Communist Party of the United States, there was the Communist League of America (later the Workers Party and finally the Socialist Workers Party), and there was the Communist Party (Opposition)—or, respectively, Stalinists, Trotskyists (followers of Leon Trotsky, Stalin's exiled rival, killed by Stalin's agents in Mexico in 1940), and Lovestonites (after Jay Lovestone, who had been dismissed as head of the Party because he sided with another of Stalin's rivals). Trotskyists and Lovestonites consisted of extremely talented Communists, but both were sects because of their tiny numbers, their inbreeding, their tendency to produce schisms. Stalinists, on the other hand, constituted a mass organization, a broad-scale movement of some consequence, with a bewildering complex of auxiliaries, affiliates, and fronts and the active support or encouragement of thousands upon thousands of fellow travelers, associates, sympathizers, and well-wishers. This explains why the Communist Party of the United States occupies the relatively privileged place in history that it has; why, accordingly, it has continued to receive so much notice, even though it long ago ceased to be taken seriously; and why it is the subject of this book.

To do justice to American Communism in a single volume of documents has been a daunting task, not that I had any illusions that it would be anything less. I was no stranger to such collections. The problem (as usual) was which documents to include and which not from a source so rich and multifarious and laden with controversy. In other words, which issues should get how

much coverage, what weight should be given in particular to culture and art,
on what basis should specific individuals qualify for admission? Readers
familiar with Communism may quarrel with the choices. But they will realize that such a work cannot be an omnium gatherum, that to touch on every
question that engaged Communists and their friends, even space permitting,
is to shortchange the important and fascinating ones, that every addition
requires a deletion. To these critics I say in the spirit of collegiality: There is
ample room for other anthologies.

I cannot conclude these prefatory remarks without thanking several of the
people and institutions who helped me to complete the book, or at least rescued me from doing a worse one. My wholehearted gratitude goes to
Columbia University Press, and editor John Michel in particular (his considerable virtues I had already come to know), for taking a chance and being so
gracious about it. The great New York City libraries—Columbia University's, the New York Public Library, and New York University's Tamiment—
were indispensable. Buried in their enormous archives are just about all the
materials I wanted and much I had not been aware of.

Worthy of special mention, too, are the books that provided information
and leads found nowhere else. (To value their scholarly contributions is not
necessarily to accept their interpretations.) Theodore Draper's witty and
elegantly written volumes on the Party organization and its intramural conflicts—*The Roots of American Communism* (New York: Viking, 1957) and
American Communism and Soviet Russia (New York: Vintage, 1986)—alas, go
only up to 1929. Harvey Klehr's *The Heyday of American Communism: The
Depression Decade* (New York: Basic Books, 1984) takes his very thorough survey of that organization and its extraordinary ways to the eve of World War
II. Daniel Aaron's *Writers on the Left* (New York: Columbia University Press,
1992) is an exhaustive study of the vagaries of Communist literary politics in
the same period. Maurice Isserman's *Which Side Were You On?* (Middletown,
Conn.: Wesleyan University Press, 1982) traces the Party's career from the
war to its collapse in the 1950s and beyond. Finally, two first-class pieces of
scholarship, which saved me countless hours of labor, I enthusiastically recommend to anyone who wishes to learn of America's radical inheritance: For
tracking down the lives of even the most obscure Communists, *Biographical
Dictionary of the American Left* (Westport, Conn.: Greenwood Press, 1986),
edited by Bernard K. Johnpoll and Harvey Klehr, and, for its comprehensive
and scrupulous objectivity, *Encyclopedia of the American Left* (Urbana:
University of Illinois Press, 1992), edited by Mari Jo Buhle, Paul Buhle, and
Dan Georgakas.

Communism in America

A HISTORY

IN DOCUMENTS

CHAPTER ONE

Summary and Overview

I

In March 1919 the Bolshevik regime, which had seized power in Russia sixteen months earlier, launched the Third or Communist International (Comintern, or CI for short) in the name of proletarian and peasant revolution everywhere, chiefly in the Western nations, the United States included, because they were the most advanced, the most proletarianized. And indeed the prospects for revolution were auspicious. The barbarous war that had just ended left behind a deepening malaise that affected the victors almost as much as it did the vanquished. Violent strikes broke out across the Continent. Mini-civil wars raged in German and Austrian cities. The Hungarian and Bavarian revolutions, though short-lived, were regarded as harbingers of things to come. Nor was the United States immune from the contagion. Never, in fact, had the country witnessed such labor unrest. No major industry escaped protracted, angry, often bloody showdowns between workers and employers, this after years of wartime calm. One can see why Lenin, Trotsky, and the other Bolshevik leaders acted as they did, why they felt they could not let down their fellow revolutionists, especially now that imperialist capitalism seemed on the verge of disintegration.

The establishment of the Comintern was the move that America's left Socialists had been waiting for. Tensions between them and moderates had been building ever since the Socialist Party became a force to reckon with, certainly since 1912. That was when its leader, Eugene V. Debs, on his fourth try as presidential candidate, received nearly a million votes and many

Socialists were elected or appointed to local office. With Socialist publications reaching a huge audience, Socialists, confident as never before, bodied forth their answer to the question that increasingly disturbed America: What should it do about the tremendous concentration of private economic power that was enthralling it? Despite the Left-Right tensions—the Left believing in revolutionary change, the Right in piecemeal change within the system—the Socialist Party had managed to hang together. During World War I some members angrily left because the overwhelming majority opposed American participation in it. For their opposition, many Socialists suffered grievous persecution, Debs among them. Tensions resurfaced the moment the war ended in November 1918, and with a severity that nothing could assuage. For one thing, the foreign-language associations within the Party, always left-leaning, had by then attained numerical superiority. For another, the Bolshevik Revolution had driven them even further to the Left. Why this occurred is obvious from their origins: most of their members had emigrated from the subject nations of the tsarist empire—Ukraine, Lithuania, Latvia, Poland, the Jewish pale—to all of which the Bolsheviks promised liberation. And so America's left-wing Socialists, like their counterparts everywhere else, enthusiastically lined up with the Comintern and founded what they had no doubt would be a brave new Socialist—that is, Communist—beginning.

As long as the left wing was only a faction within a broad-based party, its own internal differences remained more or less hidden from view. But no sooner did it break free of the old restraints in the late summer of 1919 and adopt the name "Communist" than those differences emerged full-blown and with a rancor hitherto reserved for moderates. Two Communist parties vied for legitimacy, each claiming exclusive kinship with the Comintern. Reluctantly at first but inevitably, the Comintern was thus drawn into America's political thickets, its task to bring about Communist unity if not harmony.

Just then the red scare went into its most virulent stage, marked by thousands of Gestapo-like arrests and detainments and expulsions from the country, as well as the establishment of police apparatuses at federal, state, and local levels charged with investigating, identifying, and punishing radicals, no matter what their persuasion. To protect themselves the Communists went underground. This was fine with the authorities because it compounded the difficulties Communists faced in getting their revolutionary message across; without their leadership, the masses, however discontented, were inert. These obstacles notwithstanding, unity was at last achieved through Comintern intervention; that is, the conflicting groups—Communist and Communist Labor Parties—kept their animosities within the bounds of a single organization. For any individual or faction to refuse to do so was to incur Comintern displeasure, to be left high and dry, alone without destiny. At the same time Communists, again at Moscow's behest (Moscow was

Comintern headquarters), abandoned the underground life, where apocalyptic illusions too often enabled the faithful to avoid the pain of brute reality, and, with the formation of the Workers Party in 1921, agreed to play by
the rules of the capitalist system and so take advantage of its politics, trade
unions, and social institutions, abhorrent as these were. The change in tactics
corresponded to the change in Communist tactics everywhere now that the
revolutionary fervor had died down and conservatism was in the ascendance.
The measure of a movement's ability to prevail in the long run, said Lenin
repeatedly, was how well it took its losses and how orderly its retreats were.

The Workers Party, if it was to be a bona fide Communist organization, a
member in good standing of the international Communist community,
needed to go an important step further. It needed to properly "Bolshevize"
itself—to make the transition from a typical bourgeois party, its leaders chosen by geographic districts, to a truly Communist Party based on factory and
neighborhood constituencies, from the unit or cellular level to branches and
districts up to the Central Executive Committee and, at the summit, the
Political Committee, which answered to the Comintern on general policy.
By Bolshevizing itself (by 1925), the Workers Party believed it had also
democratized itself in the process of being immediately available for mass
action should the masses demand it. That it was scarcely democratic in practice goes without saying, if *democratic* means free-wheeling debate and criticism before the participants come together and vote on decisions. Debate
and criticism there were, to be sure, but within the limits of, and in strict
conformity to, programs laid down from above. Rank-and-file Communists,
however, accepted the Bolshevik definition of democracy; in fact they
proudly embraced it. Nor did they doubt in the least that history would ultimately vindicate them.

Such, in brief, was the structure of the American Communist Party as it
developed in the early 1920s. And so it has remained down to the present,
even as the world that called it forth, whose values it reflected, has disappeared entirely.

2

Why, it might be asked, did so many people—hundreds and hundreds of
thousands, perhaps millions, of them over the decades—join the Communist
movement not only as card-carrying Party members but as fellow travelers,
sympathizers, and apologists? For besides physical persecution by the state,
which might descend on them at any time, they faced a public that more or
less reviled them and everything they stood for. Americans sanctified private
property, religion, family, self-reliance, small-scale government, and low
taxes, and by and large felt comfortable with existing—that is, discriminatory—racial, ethnic, and gender arrangements. Fear that Communists

would if they could overthrow these civilized norms and replace them with an unspeakable tyranny, a fear easy for the Right to exacerbate, automatically made them "un-American," the catchword that, having come into vogue with World War I, attached itself to them like the mark of Cain, generation after generation. Yet Communism, we repeat, grew into one of the important insurgencies of American history. And so again the question arises: What did its adherents find in it?

Here we can only sketch in some of the obvious reasons. We will omit the characterological one which tells us that individuals with a certain character formation, certain psychological predispositions or needs were attracted to Communism or other "extremist" movements or ideologies. True or not, what then? The statement is ad hominem and reductionist; beyond the utterance, it advances our understanding not a whit. We still want to know why those individuals ended up joining this specific movement and no other. To thus lump antithetical movements and ideologies together under the "extremist" rubric is to trivialize them, denying to their partisans the reality that defines their lives, making them into psychopathological case studies. We will avoid such a dead end, such an act of bad faith, by asking what they saw in Communism, and only in Communism, to justify the sacrifices they made in its behalf.

At the rudimentary level, Communism meant to them taking sides with the poorest, most vulnerable, most exploited people against the ruling elites who thrived on their suffering. But this kind of moral solidarity with the wretched is too abstract, too all-encompassing, too rudimentary—applying as it did to radicals in general, anarchists, Socialists, left-liberals, et al. What distinguished Communists was their commitment to Marxism-Leninism, their conviction that industrial capitalism as such was for them the root cause of the injustice. The central task for Marxist-Leninists, it followed, was to organize the main victims of capitalism, the working class, into a force sufficient to replace it with a system under which they, the workers, would take possession of the instrumentalities of wealth, the means of production, and, reaping the full rewards of their labor, inaugurate the epoch of economic and social freedom for themselves and for all of humanity. The victims of capitalism, however, were not necessarily aware of their latent power; part of their victimization lay precisely in their lack of class-consciousness. And so, according to Marxism-Leninism, those who understood where capitalism was headed—toward greater concentration and increasing unemployment on the one hand and fiercer exploitation of the employed on the other—constituted the vanguard of the working class. Communists arrogated to themselves the responsibility of being that historic vanguard. Upon them fell the burden of living their lives as if the revolution were imminent, however far-off it might in fact be, as if the future were present in the here and now and embodied in *them*.

It is therefore no huge insight to observe, as so many have, that

Communism was akin to a religious vocation, offering to its apostles the liberty that comes with willing obedience to exacting discipline. Oliver Cromwell would have been proud of this New Model army, whose Bolshevik table of organization and rules of engagement his descendant, Lenin, had first outlined in 1902. This was why, compared to other radicals, Communists were so formidable, so eager to serve the cause to which they committed themselves, whatever the cost. They went where the normally prudent feared to tread, acting with great courage when tested. Communists welcomed martyrdom as their occupational hazard. Who else would dare to organize Alabama's black workers and sharecroppers, Imperial Valley fruit and vegetable pickers, North Carolina textile workers, starving coal miners abandoned by their union? Who else would dare to lead unauthorized, hence violently resisted, protest marches in cities across the country calling for more home relief, for rent freezes, for jobs? And on and on. The number of causes were legion that only Communists, or Communists above all others, took up. And although they usually lost, they also scored impressive victories, as we will see. Indeed the futilities, the failures, the martyrdoms prepared them for the many successes that did come their way, that they, more than anyone else, had earned.

They were notorious as well for exemplifying the vices of their virtues, and of this too much has been written. They paid quite a price for their solidarity, discipline, and courage. If their movement was the consummation of history, morally perfect in its essence, what did that make their adversaries? Communists inhabited a Manichean universe, full of drama and surprise, in which they played the lead. In such a universe, where so much was asked of them, personal feelings and loyalties yielded to the larger good. So did consistency and conventional ethical norms. With little compunction, they could, when required, do a 180-degree turn in policy, the transcendent cause of the Party being the standard of morality. By the same token, they could embrace old ideological enemies and even form alliances with those once condemned as irredeemably evil. With them, as with the righteous at all times, their faith gave them a tactical advantage, a freedom to maneuver that the morally inhibited lacked. The means/ends conundrum did not especially trouble them.

I am drawing a rather unlovely portrait of Communism, one familiar to students of the subject, to those who had any idea of the animosities it aroused. My intention here is not to justify those animosities, still less to add to them. Both the vices and virtues of Communism reflected the tremendous sense of urgency in a movement that rested on the certitude of a revolution that might arrive at any moment. The locomotive of history waited for no one. There were individuals who joined up thinking that it was nothing more than a band of do-gooders, paracletes who sought to help the insulted and injured. To be sure, without these rudimentary principles, as I said, there would have been no movement, no Party. But it could not have taken such compassionate individuals long to realize where they were. Rare, even in the lowest echelon, was the Party member or seasoned fellow traveler whose illusions or innocence did not soon give way under the Party's stern tutelage. That was one reason it continued to experience such a furious turnover: many times more members left after a few years or months or even weeks than stayed on. Unlovely as Communism may have been then—who will gainsay the fact?—the realities it addressed were a thousandfold unlovelier. So its partisans argued, and a powerful argument it was.

The Communist Party and the broader movement associated with it laid itself open to the most withering criticism of all, that it was subservient to, if not the mere plaything of, the Soviet Union. The criticism covered the ideological spectrum. Fierce conservatives regarded Communists as traitors pure and simple, literally and metaphorically, for not only did they owe their loyalty to a disgusting foreign power, they were bent on destroying America's most cherished values. They were the Huns within the gates. At the opposite end were the liberals who rejected such a patently simple-minded view but who decried the Communists' slavish attachment to and imitation of a totalitarian system. Nor could Communists themselves deny the liberal critique. The Party was, after all, the American section of the Communist International (until the latter was disbanded in 1943) and did of course defend the Soviet Union uncritically, anything less being anathema within the ranks.

But even here, where Communism seems most susceptible to criticism, there is more than meets the eye. Here the equation can be reversed, the Party exemplifying the virtues of its vices. To anyone lending an interested ear, it proudly affirmed its Bolshevism and its special relationship to the Soviet Union, where economic insecurity was banished along with ignorance and obscurantism and racial, ethnic, and gender discrimination (easy divorce, abortion on demand, etc.) and where access to high culture was a right. Valid or not, the claim, by the very fact that it could be asserted, made the Soviet Union the moral exemplar of mankind and put the United States especially to shame, given its pretensions to democracy. Thanks to the Communist International, which is to say the Soviet Union, Communists could also claim that among radicals they alone belonged to a movement that transcended national frontiers and parochial concerns, that united them in struggle with comrades everywhere on earth, that raised their consciousness as citizens of the world.

The American Party obeyed policy from on high, but it hardly follows that it did not also act on its own, freely and spontaneously, with wide tactical latitude in its everyday functioning, when dealing with local issues. No institution, however hieratic its structure of organization, however centralized its bureaucracy, is as tightly controlled as the Party was alleged to be. At the lower levels, in the units and branches, the faithful exercised a greater degree of individual initiative and tended to be more principled, ingenuously so,

than the leaders. It is a mistake, then, to ascribe the sins of the Party officials
to the rank and file who fought in the trenches. Moreover, like institutions in
general, the Party experienced deep factional and personal conflicts at the
topmost echelons throughout its career, conflicts that the Kremlin might
keep in check but could not resolve.

An obvious fact cannot be emphasized enough: expulsion of errant members was the sole punishment available to the American Party. Being voluntary and private, it lacked what the Soviet model possessed, namely, the ability to coerce, to use the power of the state. However authoritarian the
American Party was, or tried to be, it cannot therefore be confused with its
Soviet counterpart and held responsible for what happened there in the
name of Communism. The Party may have apologized for Stalin's crimes, but
it committed no crimes of its own. Peculiar as it may have been and, for most
people, distasteful to boot, it was no less legitimate than any other party that
ever existed in America.

3

The destiny of American Communism—and of Communism in general—
was inextricably bound up with world-historical forces. Communism presumed to be the master of these forces. In fact it was dependent on them
from start to finish.

The Bolshevik Revolution was itself a response to the moral and spiritual
as well as the economic and political catastrophe that overwhelmed the West
during and after World War I. Communist Russia held out the promise of a
new order to replace the murderously corrupt imperial capitalist system that
subjugated the peoples of the world. But the Communist regime spent its
first ten years attending to its own desperate needs, surviving one trauma
after another: civil war, famine, brutal power struggles following Lenin's
death in 1924. Meanwhile, imperial capitalism stabilized and the fear of
Communism diminished correspondingly. The promise seemed remote.

The Communist alternative certainly had little impact on Americans.
They were no more concerned about the fate of the Soviet Union than they
were about the rest of the world. With a vengeance they repudiated the
Wilsonian vision, articulated during and immediately after the war, of a
nation willing to lead humanity in the quest for international law, and they
returned to the isolationism of their fathers. Moreover, an alternative of any
sort, much less one so inimical to traditional values, scarcely seemed necessary to Americans given the rampant prosperity most of them enjoyed, and
with no end of it in sight. Communists themselves in the 1920s talked of
"American exceptionalism," the belief that thanks to its natural resources,
industrial capacity, and absence of rigid class distinctions, America might for
a long while avoid the crisis that must eventually befall every capitalist soci-

ety. American exceptionalism explained to Communists why their movement, like the rival Socialist movement, fared so poorly here in the most advanced capitalist country on earth.

To everyone's astonishment the crisis did come, suddenly and with unprecedented ferocity. And, by a quirk of serendipity, Communists found themselves better positioned to react to it than anyone else on the Left. That was because the Communist International—that is, the Soviet government (i.e., Josef Stalin)—had ordered a tactical about-face in 1928 and called on Communists throughout the world to engage in class warfare. Moscow claimed that the "imperialist" powers were preparing to attack the Soviet Union. How it arrived at that conclusion is still unclear. At any rate, it had the effect of gearing American Communists for action before the 1929 Wall Street crash and well before the nation realized just how serious the "downturn" was. The period of confrontation that Communists thus launched proved to be a creative one, if by *creative* is meant the extent, variety, inventiveness, and audacity of the things they did, the insurgencies they organized. They suffered for their troubles, too, as was mentioned, but their suffering only deepened their commitment and earned them the respect, often grudging, of those they sought to help.

Communists began to benefit at the same time from their identification with the Soviet Union, which had just embarked, again serendipitously, on a totally new economic course marked by the rapid buildup of industry and the collectivization of agriculture. So it was that the Soviets counterposed their massive development, accompanied by guarantees of full employment and comprehensive social security, to the unrelieved disasters of capitalism. While they recruited American skilled workers and engineers, the jobless rolls in this country broke all records. Who would not choose Communist planning and humanitarianism over capitalist anarchy and contempt for life? That question the American Party exploited for all it was worth.

Yet Americans still failed to join the movement in anything like the number that the economic breakdown and Communist sacrifices justified. Party membership tripled between 1929 and 1934, but only from the low figure of about ten thousand, scarcely a triumph. A further measure of the relative indifference was the abysmal vote that the Party's presidential candidate received in 1932, the nadir of the Depression. The Socialist Party's candidate, Norman Thomas, did much better, but his numbers were no less disappointing if compared to previous Socialist performances. Perhaps Americans were willing to give the system one more try in the person of Democrat Franklin D. Roosevelt. Should he fail, the crisis would enter the acute stage.

The crisis did not become acute; New Deal reforms saw to that. But it persisted nonetheless, and Communists were hardly alone in assuming that the New Deal was wrong-headed or insufficient. Then, just as suddenly as before, decisions of world-historical import compelled the Party and movement to make another amazing tactical switch, one that turned out to be even more portentous than the last.

The cause this time was the immitigable evil of Fascism. More exactly, German Fascism or Nazism.

Fascism had been around since 1919, when Italy's Mussolini invented the doctrine. By means of it (with the support of the ruling elites) he seized power three years later. Fascism presented itself as the answer to the fractious Left, Communism in particular, which Mussolini, true to his promise, went on to crush while installing himself as dictator (*Il Duce*). This was a blow to the Comintern but no perceptible danger to Soviet security. Besides, Soviet theoreticians wrote off Fascism as a transient phenomenon, predicting that the class conflicts that had called it forth would soon reassert themselves, and more virulently than ever. Fascism, according to the official Communist view, represented the death throes of capitalism.

Meanwhile, in the Far East, something of a danger to the Soviet Union did loom up, and it too could be defined as a kind of Fascism. The Japanese military, concerned about the decadence in their society—labor troubles, leftist opposition, student unrest, and so on—decided to act against the Bolshevik-inspired demon and in 1931, in the name of greater Nippon, took Manchuria, which bordered on the Soviet Union. Neither the League of Nations nor the Western democracies opposed Japanese aggression; after all, it was not directed at their colonies.

Two years later Germany's President Hindenburg appointed Adolf Hitler chancellor. This certainly should have worried Soviet leaders. No one on the world stage hated Bolshevism more violently than Hitler, hatred his Nazi Party, the country's largest, fully reflected. Germany, moreover, was a great power that lay within easy striking distance of European Russia, as World War I had demonstrated. But here again prevailing Comintern dogma got in the way of an objective assessment, an accurate appraisal. It should have given Stalin and company pause, for example, that Mussolini was more entrenched than ever. But they continued to assume that Nazism was the final, degenerate form of capitalism, that Hitler would fail just as miserably as his predecessors had, and that the Communist Party, Germany's third largest, would then pick up the pieces. So the German Communist Party went to its doom, joined soon enough by the Socialists and all other anti-Nazi parties. For not only did Hitler not fail, he succeeded brilliantly. He established a New Deal of his own—albeit a military-industrial one—to end Germany's enormous unemployment and gave most Germans the leadership they craved; the Führer was their man of the hour. By mid-1934 it had become clear, even to the Kremlin, that he was going to preside indefinitely over a strong and unified nation—despite Versailles Treaty restrictions, the German military buildup went on relentlessly (England and France turned a blind eye)—bent on destroying Bolshevism root and branch. Soviet statesmen did not need to consult maps to notice the cordon sanitaire forming around their country.

Hitler's incredible rise sounded many alarms: not only Communist bells but liberal and democratic and some conservative ones too, and Jewish loudest of all, for he was also the greatest anti-Semite on the world stage. Nazism routinely conflated Jews and Bolsheviks, scarcely uttering one of those curses without the other. And so when, finally, the Comintern mounted its campaign against Fascism, essentially "Hitlerism," it welcomed all who wished to join up, without regard to their ideological proclivities. The twofold object of this "Popular Front" was to prevent Fascism from gaining control over any other government and to mobilize people against Fascist aggression or expansion of any kind.

Little could the American Communist Party have known as it embarked on its Popular Front strategy what advantages would accrue to it because of its special identification with the Soviet Union and Soviet foreign policy. From 1935 on, the existing international order disintegrated as the Fascist powers, Japan among them, invaded one country after another (Ethiopia, China, Austria, Czechoslovakia, Albania) while brazenly helping Fascist rebels overthrow the democratically elected Spanish government. The only nation to oppose the aggressors consistently and actively was the Soviet Union—Communist international brigades fought in Spain against the rebels—while England and France appeased them and the United States withdrew ever more deeply into its carapace of isolationism. And so, the American Communist movement flowered as more and more non-Communists went over to the Popular Front because of their anxiety over advancing Fascism, their fear of Hitler in particular. By 1939 American Communism was a significant factor in the life of the times. No radical movement in American history, it is safe to say, had come along so far, had accomplished so much in such areas as trade unionism, civil rights, and popular culture, its accomplishments being attributable in large measure to its intimate association with the Soviet Union.

It was during the Popular Front that the most grotesque of the Moscow show trials took place. Stalin, quite paranoid by now, had gotten it in his head that leading Bolsheviks, among them Lenin's closest comrades (Zinoviev, Kamenev, Bukharin, Rakovsky, Rykov, Tomsky, et al.) were conspiring with arch-villain Trotsky and the German and Japanese military command to seize control of the Soviet government and kill him and his lieutenants. The severely tortured victims confessed, some pleading for their own execution, at the series of show trials held between 1934 and 1938. That the American Party defended the trials went without saying. Yet the public in general, or that portion of it sympathetic to Communism, however skeptical or even critical it might have been of what was transpiring in Moscow, still considered anti-Fascism the overriding issue. The movement kept gaining support during the period of the trials. Of course, scarcely anyone then had an inkling of the enormity of Stalin's purges, of how many millions he sent to die in the gulags.

America's Communists discovered that the advantages they enjoyed from their ideological kinship with the Soviet Union rested on shaky foundations indeed. Just as they were reaping the benefits of the Popular Front strategy, the success of which resulted from the broadly accepted assumption that the Soviet Union stood as a bulwark of rectitude and hope in a world that was succumbing to Fascism, they also discovered a savage truth: the Soviet Union was not only the Communist homeland, it was a nation engaged willy-nilly in the deadly game of might over right, in which ideological consideration yielded before the imperative of self-interest. With breathtaking surprise came the news—no serendipity here!—on the eve of World War II that Stalin had made a deal with Hitler, had signed a nonaggression pact that allowed Germany to concentrate on fighting England and France. It even seemed for a while as if Hitler and Stalin had actually teamed up: that was when a mini-war broke out between the Soviets and gallant little Finland after Finland refused to cede to them a piece of land they demanded. For liberal and progressive Popular Fronters, and not a few Communists, the perfidy was complete, especially when Hitler's Wehrmacht proceeded to conquer or otherwise dominate all of Europe except England, alone, beleaguered, obviously finished. The weight of national enmity thus fell on American Communists. New laws were passed to expedite their prosecution; a major red scare was getting under way. But even as they prepared to go underground again, they continued to denounce the Roosevelt administration—once such a resolute Popular Front ally—for attempting to keep England alive through vast amounts of economic and military assistance. Taking the same position were America's many Fascist grouplets plus the Socialists and the Trotskyists and the millions of isolationists, most of them Republicans from the mid- and far West. The vagaries of international politics had made strange bedfellows!

Hitler's betrayal of Stalin, his unannounced invasion of the Soviet Union on June 22, 1941, produced yet another astonishing reversal in the fortunes of American Communists. For them it was now back to the Popular Front, back to the love affair with Roosevelt and other anti-Fascists and the American people. Love affair it certainly was on both sides after the United States entered the war: though attacked by Japan, it fought Hitler as the main enemy. But without the Soviet Union his defeat was problematic and in the effort millions of American lives would have been lost. The country's appreciation of Soviet heroism and suffering translated into goodwill for Communists, their fronts and affiliates, whose ranks rose again, reaching almost the halcyon levels of prewar days.

Readers can now see the approaching denouement, tragic or poignant or happy, depending on their point of view.

At war's end, the Party and its numerous friends were at the top of their golden hours. No longer was Communism feebly knocking on the door of history. Thanks to Soviet armies it was not only inside the house, it occupied an important section of it, that is, from the Elbe River to Vladivostok, along with all of Southern Europe except for Greece and Turkey. (Communists probably could have taken over Greece too, but Stalin held them back for reasons of his own.) Mighty Communist parties flourished in Italy and France and participated in their postwar governments. Another mighty one controlled much of China and was growing by the day. Still others were rising up in part of colonial Asia, in French Indo-China, the Dutch East Indies, Malaya, and Singapore, and, for that matter, the Philippines. This extraordinary movement of world-historical forces obviously heartened and inspired American Communists. They were riding the wave of the future.

Many of them hoped that the Popular Front, as it were, might continue, that the Soviet Union and the United States, the only superpowers, might remain partners, or at least collaborators, and jointly guarantee the success of the United Nations. That hope of course died with the onset of the Cold War, as each side demonized the other and prepared itself for armed conflict, a condition that only heightened their insecurity. The Cold War was a self-reinforcing system. Providence played a dreadful trick on American Communists, proving again that what it gives with one hand it may take away with the other. In other words, the tremendous Communist expansion abroad in which they rejoiced was their undoing here. Convinced that the Soviet Union and Communism was a mortal threat to their existence, the vast majority of Americans turned in fury on the Party and anyone associated with it; they bought the argument, long propounded by the Far Right, that Communists (loosely defined) were traitors and should at a minimum be treated as pariahs and outcasts. The red scare of the Cold War era was much more pernicious than the relatively lambent one of 1919–20: it went on for decades, cut a wide swath across American life, and left in its wake an immense apparatus of repression. By the time it more or less ran its course—by the 1970s, say—the red scare had done its job. It had contributed immensely to the fall of American Communism, so much so that its privileged relationship with the Soviet Union had by then ceased to interest anyone, obsessive anti-Communists included. Nor did anyone care, or notice, when that relationship ended altogether, seventy years after it had begun with such a flourish, such enthusiasm, following the collapse of the Soviet Union and most of the other Communist states. Pitiless are the forces of world history when they turn against you.

CHAPTER TWO

The 1920s: Birth, Insurgency, Retrenchment

I

One can understand why American Socialists, and above all the left-wingers among them, were so elated after Germany signed the armistice that ended the Great War. For a whole painful year they had been unable to openly express the feelings that the Bolshevik Revolution inspired in them. It had struck them with the force of an epiphany. Until then, like much of the Left throughout the world, they had been enveloped in thickening gloom ever since the war began. Because they opposed America's participation in it, American Socialists (along with such other recusants as pacifists and members of the Industrial Workers of the World) had suddenly found themselves in a very hostile environment; a wrong move on their part and they might have received a twenty-year jail sentence; quite a few of them had. And beyond their personal troubles had been the deeper ones arising from shattered ideals. Instead of the ineluctable progress of humanity, on which those ideals rested, with Socialism to be its next stage, there was the reality of the war, with its hideous, unrestrained barbarism, its astonishing love of death. Understandable, then, was the joy the war's opponents had felt when they learned of the Russian miracle. But while the war continued, during which time American soldiers had played an increasingly important role, they had had to keep their feelings to themselves and bide their time. But peace having arrived at last, pro-Bolshevik Socialists could come out and proclaim the restoration of the old ideal, but only under the new revolutionary dispensation, only after the old order was swept away, as surely it would be.

Events seem to confirm their reading of the future. From coast to coast, Boston to Seattle, in textiles, steel, railroads, coal, and public service occupations, workers struck, often using tactics and language borrowed from the Bolshevik experience. Postwar inflation, coupled with unemployment, exacerbated the growing sense of unease over the Versailles Treaty and the foreign commitments in which it threatened to entangle the country. To make matters worse, random acts of violence broke out in several big cities, New York in particular, perpetrated by no one knows who and for no discernible purpose. That did not stop the authorities, the press, and much of the public from blaming the "Reds," a catch-all term signifying agents of disorder, usually foreigners who would, if permitted, impose their foreign views on blessed America. "Reds," in fact, eschewed terrorism, even when it was less wanton and irrational than the sort that killed so many people at the New York Stock Exchange, but nice distinctions meant little to a fear-ridden populace.

Meanwhile, as though to reinforce the point, Bolsheviks seemed to be sweeping across Europe. Revolution was the order of the day, and even if the uprisings failed, having succeeded for a moment (as in Bavaria and Hungary), nothing could quell the euphoria of the Far Left, the assumption that imperialist capitalism was doomed, tomorrow if not today. That euphoria, that assumption, animated the group of revolutionaries from various countries who met in Moscow in March 1919 at the behest of the Communist regime there to launch a Third International. It was to be the Communist or revolutionary answer to the Second International, which, in the name of the Socialist parties it represented (chief among them the German), had disgraced itself by collaborating with imperial capitalism in the recent slaughter of millions of workers and peasants—so the Communist International, or Comintern, argued in its appeal for mass uprisings everywhere and its virtual declaration of war on traitorous Socialism.

America's left-wing Socialists were thus emboldened to take the step which so far they had avoided and, breaking with the moderate wing, which ran the Party, strike out on their own. Their main support came from the growing ranks of the foreign-language associations, most of whose members—Jews, Finns, Letts, Ukrainians, Poles, Serbs, Croats, Hungarians, et al.—had emigrated from the oppressed nations of the tsarist and Austrian empires, to which nations the Bolshevik Revolution held out the prospect of freedom at long last. The establishment of the Comintern brought the irrepressible conflict to a head. The left wing conceived American Communism in April 1919 when it put out its "Manifesto," setting forth the reasons for its irrevocable move. The official birth of Communism in Chicago that September was therefore something of an anticlimax, despite the Sturm und Drang that attended it.

The two parties that emerged, Communist and Communist Labor, pretty much reflected the dual character of the left-wing coalition. (Theodore Draper gives a hilarious account detailing their simultaneous conventions, their squabbles, their contretemps with the police.) The Communist Party was larger because it had the bulk of the foreign-language association members, but the Communist Labor Party had a larger proportion of native-born radicals, notably John Reed, the great political journalist (author most recently of *Ten Days That Shook the World*, his minute-by-minute eyewitness description of the Bolshevik Revolution). A cursory review of both party programs reveals how similar they were, even in the phrasing. But the differences, trivial to the innocent eye, took on gigantic significance to these revolutionaries. This may explain the animosity they felt toward each other. For them every point had the status of a principle, and to compromise a principle was to betray the working class in its hour of opportunity, when the hammer was lying on the anvil. As it was, each of the Communist parties had all it could do to maintain its own integrity against the centrifugal energy that brought it into existence. The danger of revolutionists without power is sectarianism; hence the tendency to keep splitting in the search for the precisely right formula. The danger of revolutionists with power is the inclination of one sect to lord it over the others, consuming itself in the process. In any case, the divisiveness and ill-will among Communists at the start of their career set an uninspiring example for the masses they presumed to lead.

On another front, however, left Socialist or Communist artists and intellectuals came up with *Liberator* magazine, successor to the *Masses*, that ornament of the movement since it first appeared in 1912. And a worthy successor the *Liberator* was, beginning with its March 1918 inaugural issue. (It survived the remaining months of the war by the skin of its teeth, the government having tried, unsuccessfully, to imprison its editors for sedition.) Under Max Eastman and his remarkable sister, Crystal Eastman, the *Liberator* was quite as open, irreverent, outrageous, and witty as its predecessor. Nor did it make hard-and-fast distinctions between political and social commentary on the one hand and fiction, poetry, criticism, and satire on the other, between revolutionists and bohemians. Its illustrators graced its pages as they had the *Masses*: Art Young, Stuart Davis, Reginald Marsh, William Gropper, Hugo Gellart, Robert Minor, all were masters of agitprop (agitation and propaganda) art, descendants all of Daumier and Thomas Nast. And among such featured poets as Carl Sandburg, Arturo Giovannitti, and Eastman himself, one, Claude McKay, deserves special mention. Having recently arrived from the West Indies, where he was already known, McKay became an editor of the magazine, its voice of black protest, and was at the same time a prime mover of the Harlem Renaissance, which was then getting under way. The *Liberator* attained an incredibly high circulation for such a publication, eighty thousand (approximately three times that of the *Masses*) according to some estimates, before it fell to a more normal, if still respectable, level as the decade wore on.

Communists should have anticipated a concerted assault against them and the Left in general. They should have realized that the guardians of the status quo would sooner or later strike back with the considerable might at their disposal. No Communist could have been so Panglossian as to think that the revolution would advance upward and onward along a straight-line trajectory. Not that they should be taken to task for their misreading of the times. What could they have done, short of ceasing to be Communists, even if they had made an accurate analysis of the situation? In truth, what happened surprised just about everyone, Communists and non-Communists alike.

The so-called red scare was actually the last phase of the great repression that began when the United States declared war on Germany back in April 1917. Only now, some three years later, following a brief postwar hiatus, it was directed with a vengeance against the Reds, or "Bolsheviki," indeed against those who bore a tincture of that dread coloration, even if they were anti-Bolshevik (e.g., such famous anarchists as Emma Goldman and Alexander Berkman). Suspected aliens of incarnidine hue were jailed or deported en masse (among them Goldman and Berkman). Others deemed a threat to established order—strike leaders, trade union militants, outspoken advocates of radical reform, not to mention professed revolutionaries— were routinely harassed and had to worry about getting arrested on the merest pretext. To the numerous victims of what amounted to a sweeping purge by federal, state, and local authorities, the courts were practically mute and often complicitous.

In response, the Communist parties went underground. They may have been justified in doing so, given the danger at hand, but the move worked out badly for them. Institutionalized paranoia—fear of government spies (legitimate to be sure)—permeated their upper ranks. They were less than skilled in the arts of concealment and subterfuge, in adopting duplex identities, secret codes, and the like. Demoralization inevitably set in. Membership dropped sharply, from a combined total of about fifty thousand in 1919 to about a third of that number within two years. Worse still, the underground life fed the sectarian tendencies afflicting both parties, the Communist Party especially, dominated as it was by the more doctrinaire foreign-language associations.

By the time the red scare petered out in the spring of 1920, the strikes had been badly defeated and the labor movement had lost much of its militancy. Not that any of this displeased trade unions in general, members of the American Federation of Labor (AFL), for they were ideologically aligned with business interests. And as we noted, the retreat of the Far Left was part of a worldwide phenomenon. Lenin and Trotsky and their Bolshevik confreres had looked to the industrial West, Germany in particular, to save the revolution by broadening it, by replicating it in societies where the proletariat comprised the majority; Russia was backward by comparison, hardly the ideal testing ground for Socialism, a fact no one knew better than Lenin, Trotsky, et al. The general retreat of the Left compelled them to make a major retreat of their own. They settled for a consolidation of the gains already achieved,

Communist Russia having beaten back the counterrevolutionaries in a horrible civil war and gone on to recapture most of the lands it had given up when it had signed a separate peace with Germany in March 1918. They also adopted a tactic of accommodation to reality. Soviet Russia accordingly embarked on a New Economic Policy (NEP) to encourage private enterprise and foreign investments and parcel out the land taken from the gentry to small farmers who would sell their goods to the free market for a profit. As for Communists elsewhere, America's included, they would have to shed their revolutionary image, take part in the bourgeois political process and the existing trade unions and such other equally conservative institutions as might be susceptible to their influence. Now the turnabout, as Lenin himself asserted in his great essay on the "disorder" of left-wing "infantilism," was only a temporary expedient, a tactic in the unceasing war against imperialist capitalism.

In the United States, the tactic took well over a year, and increasing Comintern intervention, to accomplish. Persuading Communists who had spent a good deal of their lives in fierce combat against "misleaders" of AFL unions and moderate Socialist advocates of obedience to capitalist laws and procedures was hard enough. Much harder was the Comintern demand that all Communists, whatever their differences, form form a single party. And so out of the Communist and Communist Labor Parties emerged the United Communist Party. But the foreign-language stalwarts still refused to accede, until, again at Comintern insistence, and with its representatives present during the deliberations, a new all-embracing organization at last crystallized in December 1921. The Workers Party, as it called itself, was conspicuously legal and aboveboard—banished forever was the underground life!—and thus eager to appeal to an electorate fed up with the status quo enough to vote for a Communist alternative. American to the core the Workers Party aimed to be, or appear, but how thoroughly the foreign-language associations still dominated it, numerically at least, is evident from the astonishing fact that Finns alone accounted for more than half of its twelve thousand members.

But for Comintern intervention, it is worth emphasizing, American Communism might have expired at infancy in a congeries of warring sects. Nor, as we said, was it an alien body that did the intervening. American Communists of every persuasion, regardless of what they thought of one another, thought of themselves as an organic part of the Third International. No greater honor could be conferred on them than an invitation to attend a Comintern conference in Moscow or, better yet, to work for a Comintern agency. That the Soviet Union was the Comintern's permanent host, its financier, and its directing authority only redounded in their view to the Soviet Union's further credit.

By 1925 the Workers Party was ready for the next phase of its metamorphosis. It was ready to integrate itself more fully into the Comintern system by following the Soviet Union's sacrosanct model of a party—in a word, by

Bolshevizing itself. No longer would its officials get elected according to the usual geographical constituencies, local to national, a cumbersome structure if the chief desideratum was immediacy of action and unity of purpose. Refashioning itself along Bolshevik lines meant planting the basic units or cells in neighborhoods and factories, having the units or cells elect delegates to the branches, the branches to elect their delegates to the districts, and the districts theirs to the Central Committee, in theory the Party's sovereign body, which decided finally who should execute its policies, that is, sit on the Political Committee and serve as Party Secretary.

"Democratic centralism" was the name given to this concept of organization, which Lenin had invented decades earlier and Stalin perfected following Lenin's death. Touted as a superior form of democracy to the bourgeois kind, democratic centralism specified that each constituency, from the merest unit or cell to the Political Committee, should encourage intense and vigorous debate, giving amplest room for minority opinions, until the majority decided on a course of action, chose its leader, and so on. Then unanimity must prevail; there could be no dissent. The penalty for refusing to acquiesce was expulsion. In most instances, as we said, expulsion was unnecessary, refractory individuals having dropped out of their own volition. And as many have observed, even within its terms, democratic centralism in practice was very different from the theory. On important issues the range of debate was narrowly defined from above. The upper reaches of the organization consisted of a self-perpetuating oligarchy, approved by Moscow. The Bolshevized Party was certainly centralized but hardly democratic in the usual acceptation of the term. The provisos discussed earlier should be kept in mind, however. Anyone who disliked the Communist way of running things was free to leave the Party—difficult as that was for those with strong attachments to comrades of long standing—or keep a sympathetic distance from it. As for the true believers, the dedicated Marxist-Leninists who looked to the breakdown of capitalism, with all its apocalyptic consequences, or who, out of moral outrage, were eager to do battle with it here and now against this particular injustice or that—for them, only such an organization, which made such extravagant demands and required such wholehearted obedience, could rally the masses when the time came, enabling them to achieve the greatness of which they were capable.

2

As the 1920s unfolded, conditions in America justified the quite unrevolutionary tactic that the Workers Party adopted under Comintern pressure. The economic crises, which had seemed so promising in the immediate aftermath of the Great War, had given way to booming prosperity, as the "second industrial revolution"—the mass production of consumer goods and

ancillary trades (advertising, public relations, popular culture, etc.)—came
into its own and Wall Street began its vertiginous climb beyond all limits.
Depressed sectors there were, in agriculture, garment manufacturing, coal
mining, among others, but in general living standards rose steadily for most
Americans. Many companies were even willing to share their largess with
their employees through higher wages, shorter hours, and other amenities—
anything to keep the unions and the "Reds" at bay. President Harding was
prophetic when he ushered in the overwhelmingly Republican, overwhelmingly conservative era: the country wanted "normalcy" rather than nostrums.
And whose nostrums were further removed from normalcy than those
advanced by Communism? And the things that gripped the public mind—the
wonderfully buoyant spirit of fun and gaiety, the sense of happy release, personal and cultural, the preoccupation with scandal and crime and corruption—amounted to a gigantic diversion, so far as the Left was concerned.
So it was that Communists now referred to "American exceptionalism,"
arguing that American capitalism was unique in its capacity to put off its final
crisis. How to maintain their revolutionary optimism in the teeth of this
uncomfortable fact was the challenge they set for themselves.

The Workers Party sought out alliances with farmer-labor groups, centered mostly in the Midwest, who kept the progressive hope of prewar days
from being totally extinguished. Communists even negotiated with Senator
Robert M. ("Fighting Bob") LaFollette, Wisconsin's great progressive leader,
when he ran in 1924 for President on a third-party line. But these efforts
failed, not least because Communists had not yet learned the subtle art of
political give and take and ended up denouncing, as only they could, what
they failed to control. That was why in that election the Party offered its own
presidential candidate—William Z. Foster—rather than support its enemy
LaFollette. Foster received an embarrassing thirty-three thousand votes. But
then again, given the public temper, whatever the Communists did, even if
they had played the acquiescent junior partner, would have been for naught.
LaFollette got five million votes, until then more than any third-party candidate in history, yet nothing came of his extraordinary showing. His
Progressive Party was soon gone (he died shortly after the election) and its
cohorts returned to the Republican fold, while, undaunted, the Workers
Party soldiered on.

3

It was in 1926 that American Communists left the wilderness and served
notice that henceforth they would have to be reckoned with.

For years they had been making inroads among needle-trade workers. The
industry as a whole was severely depressed, and Communists, preaching militant resistance, found an attentive audience among men and women whose

income had been steadily eroding. They scored a major victory when, after a long struggle, culminating in a four-month strike, they wrested the Furriers Joint Board from the old-line AFL leaders who had neglected rank-and-file interests. Special credit for this success went to Ben Gold, chief organizer and head of this, the first Communist-run international union in America. And Communists almost took the powerful International Ladies Garment Workers Union from the Socialist old guard. They had managed to gain control of the ILGWU's New York Board and therefore a large numerical majority of the union whose many locals, most of them tiny, were scattered hither and yon outside New York City. Weighted voting (which favored these locals) gave the old guard a solid advantage at convention time. The old guard nonetheless had to support the strike of cloak[coat]makers called by the New York Joint Board to protest a savage wage cut. And a brutal strike it was, thanks largely to the tacit understanding between employers and ILGWU leaders that a Communist triumph would result in a complete Communist takeover. Sure enough, after nearly six grueling months, the strikers threw in the towel, the old guard intervened to settle it, and the Communists were purged or humbled into submission. They remained confident that in time the ILGWU majority would turn to them again, but the defeat was permanent.

Valiant, and also abortive, was the Communist effort in the bituminous and anthracite coal fields, where conditions were desperate beyond belief. The United Mine Workers and their redoubtable boss, John L. Lewis, were in full retreat before the owners' onslaught; "sauve qui peut" should have been their slogan. But while the union melted away as bargaining agent of the rank and file it fought with every weapon in its armamentarium of violence to ward off any challenge to its authority. And that meant the Communists, whose Progressive International Committee won enough of a following among disaffected miners in the 1924 union elections to frighten Lewis. At the 1926 United Mine Workers convention, he waged war without quarter against the Communists and their allies. For all their valor, they proved no match for his ruthless machine, and they were driven from the fields. The hundreds of thousands of jobless and unrepresented miners had to fend for themselves, literally to scavenge for their survival.

And then there was "Passaic," shorthand for the interminable strike that roiled the New Jersey industrial town of that name and caught the public's attention well beyond its precincts.

During that generally quiescent decade the Communists were proudest of their role in that strike: it allowed them to justifiably boast of their kinship with the old Industrial Workers of the World (Wobblies), the defenders of the most ill-used, despised, and abandoned workers. This would be an accurate description of the Eastern and Southern European immigrant men and women who were shut out of the small, exclusive AFL union, the United Textile Workers. The affair started in October 1925 when the textile mill owners imposed a 10 percent wage cut. In their anger at this latest outrage the workers began listening to the Communists, whose United Front Committee demanded restoration of the cuts, extra pay for overtime, and no firing of union militants. Rising above the din was the eloquent voice of one Albert Weisbord, a remarkable young man—he was all of 24!—who had graduated from City College of New York and Harvard Law School. It was Weisbord who, with consummate skill, led the walkout of fifteen thousand. Amazingly their ranks held for a year in the face of the harshest adversities, not least of them constant police intimidation. And while the Communists could not claim total victory—in the end, Weisbord and the United Front Committee withdrew from the negotiations so that the AFL union could handle them—the mills yielded to the Committee's original demands. The Communists received the applause they deserved for having seen the victory through. It came a few weeks after the collapse of the cloakmakers' strike.

The year 1926 also marked a cultural event in the history of American Communism. Replacing the *Liberator*, which had just expired, was another "revolutionary magazine of art and literature," the *New Masses*, whose name suggested the tradition it promised to uphold. By now, however, Max Eastman, who more than anyone else embodied the adventurous spirit of the old *Masses* and the *Liberator*, both of which he edited, was breaking with the Party, and he refused to participate in the new venture. Control of the magazine fell to two talented young protégés of his, Mike Gold and Joseph Freeman, each a dyed-in-the-wool Communist, whose intention nonetheless was to keep alive the latitudinarian ethos of its predecessors, to reaffirm their rebelliousness, their zeal for dissent, their passion for novelty. But from the first issue of the *New Masses*, we detect a subtle difference that would grow more pronounced with time. Latitudinarian and audacious it still was, but less so. Why is no mystery. By 1926 the American Party could not help but reflect the struggles agitating the Soviet hierarchy, struggles between the "left opposition" and the "right opposition," with Stalin, who commanded the state and party bureaucracies, playing off one side against the other. We detect a tremor of cautiousness in the magazine, a tightening sense of limits, an increasing tendency for politics to encroach on literature and the arts. These caveats aside, the *New Masses* was then—and remained well into the 1930s—one of the best publications on the cultural Left. Its illustrators, the same ones who had worked for the *Liberator*, were certainly the best to be found anywhere. It spoke well for the Party that it was willing to subsidize the magazine with so few strings attached.

An interesting Communist publication of a very different sort came out that year too. *Labor Defender* specialized in publicizing egregious crimes against workers, strikers, political dissidents in general, which it accused the authorities of committing in the course of protecting big business, the beatings and jailings in Passaic being a case in point. In sharp, pungent language, the language of agitprop at its most effective, and accompanied by eye-opening photographs—being in these respects miles ahead of the tabloids that were then beginning to make their mark—*Labor Defender* proved to be an excellent vehicle for what it tried to do: provoke indignation in fellow Communists and win support from liberals with a heart. It was the organ of the International Labor Defense (ILD), a Party auxiliary that had just come into existence with a mandate to fight the kinds of legally sanctioned crimes the *Labor Defender* was highlighting. Founder and head of the ILD and editor of its publication was thirty-five-year-old James P. Cannon, like so many Communists originally a Wobbly. Under his aegis the ILD deployed a battery of outstanding lawyers, not all of them Communists, who learned how to navigate the legal system in behalf of clients no one else would take. The ILD went where even the American Civil Liberties Union, for all its good works, dared not go.

The Sacco-Vanzetti case dominated the ILD's first year. Not that Nicola Sacco and Bartolomeo Vanzetti lacked defenders (although one might not know that from the pages of the magazine). By the time the ILD and *Labor Defender* arrived on the scene the case was an international cause célèbre. These Italian immigrant workers, both avowed anarchists, whose hatred of capitalism matched that of the Communists, had been convicted and sentenced to death in July 1921 for killing two guards during a robbery in Braintree, Massachusetts. Whether or not either or both of them were involved in the crime—four or five men drove away with the loot—is still debated, few cases in American history having generated more controversy; what is beyond doubt, however, was the injudiciousness of the proceedings, from the misbehavior of the trial judge and prosecutor to the rubber stamp appeals court, the cowardice of the governor, and the bigotry of other establishment figures. Palpable was the hostility of these Brahmins toward the two lowly, heavily accented anarchists and what they symbolized. While the case made its way back and forth through one tribunal after another, and as sensational new evidence came forward only to be dismissed, Communists did not try to outdo the Socialists and liberals and even some conservatives who joined in support of Sacco and Vanzetti. But now, with the appearance of the ILD, and with the case approaching its denouement, the Party took the lead in organizing public demonstrations against what it decried as a capitalist assault on the working class. And intellectuals who were eager to participate looked to the ILD for guidance and discovered much to sympathize with in Communism, increasingly so in the harrowing weeks and days leading up to the execution on August 23, 1927.

This much had become clear to American Communists as the Sacco-Vanzetti affair drew to its sad close. Though they lost most of the battles they had fought in the past year or so, the important thing was that they had fought them. They were becoming a factor to contend with, small as they were, now that dissatisfaction was endemic among groups left behind and with nowhere else to turn in a society otherwise so ebulliently prosperous, so indifferent to their fate. Communists felt that the "united front" tactic of providing a radical and combative alternative within the system, wherever possible in concert with non-Communists, was a success, laying the basis as it did for the revolutionary response when, one day, that system could no longer cope with its crises.

4

But then the Party succumbed to internal perturbations so serious it had to set everything else aside for the rest of the decade in order to deal with them.

The time of troubles can be traced back to the death, in March 1927, at the age of forty-five, of Charles E. Ruthenberg, the Party's General Secretary. Ruthenberg appears to have been a very good leader indeed; that is, he held the factions in check even though he himself belonged to one of them. His opponents respected him for his fairness and for his administrative abilities as well—he had been a successful bookkeeper and manager in Cleveland before devoting himself full time to the Socialist, then Communist movements—and because the Comintern bosses liked him. That was why he received such a lavish funeral in Red Square and was buried in the Kremlin Wall, alongside John Reed.

With Ruthenberg gone, hostilities heated up. Roughly speaking, two main factions competed for advantage. One came out of the labor side of the movement and counted among its adherents several impressive men. Besides Cannon, they were William P. Dunne (plus his four brothers), veteran of the labor wars and radical politics of Minnesota and Montana before joining the Party; Earl R. Browder, a Kansas City ally of Cannon (and incidentally a bookkeeper too) who at the moment was on detached duty to the Comintern, which honor would serve him well someday; and, above all, William Z. Foster, at forty-six an elder among the hierarchs, who was famous for having led the great steel strike of 1919, at which time he fol-lowed the syndicalist path—he believed that all power, political and eco-nomic both, should go to organized labor—but turned to Communism a few years later when the Party allowed him to remain head of the Trade Union Education League (TUEL), an organization he created to fight for militant, even revolutionary trade unionism, but within existing (AFL) institutions, hateful as they might be; under TUEL auspices, Communists conducted their horrific strikes in New York City, Passaic, and elsewhere, but always, it will be recalled, inside the union structure whose conservative leadership they sought to replace.

It requires little imagination to appreciate how such strong-willed indi-viduals who had gone through so much felt when Ruthenberg's baton went to his twenty-nine-year-old executive assistant, Jay Lovestone. That Lovestone was a prodigy of vaulting ambition they quickly realized if they did not already know it. Born in Lithuania and raised in New York, Lovestone graduated from City College, where he demonstrated his organizational talents as a left-wing Socialist, which talents he used both in Ruthenberg's behalf and his own. After serving as interim Party Secretary, he garnered an overwhelming majority to retain the post—given his youth, in perpetuity—effectively marginalizing his rivals, led by Foster.

By then the Party had expelled James Cannon and several of his associates for grand heresy. The genesis of this conflict brings us back to the Soviet Union, where Party disputes, bound up as they were with state power, had taken an ugly turn.

After Lenin's death in 1924, Soviet leaders, as we noted, divided into right and left factions, while Stalin, his control growing by leaps, cleverly mediated between them. He sided with the right faction, represented most conspicuously by Nikolai Bukharin, which favored continuation of the New Economic Policy (NEP) and therefore unflagging support for a free market in which small farmers and entrepreneurs could thrive. The left faction, led by the titanic figure of Leon Trotsky, wanted to move the revolution forward in behalf of the working class by stimulating industrialization, reducing the swollen state bureaucracy, and doing more to bolster Communist insurgencies abroad. By the time of Lovestone's ascent in 1928, not only was the left opposition defunct, but Trotsky had been thrown out of the Party and exiled to Alma Ata (and before long to Turkey), and Trotskyism, the ideology of the left opposition, anathematized as treasonous. That was precisely when Cannon, while attending the Sixth Party Congress in Moscow in the summer of 1928, went over to Trotsky. Cannon of course waited until his return to America before declaring where his allegiance lay. Thus was born the American Trotskyist movement, a movement first of tens, then of hundreds (including three of William Dunne's brothers), but never much more than that, though the exceptional abilities of its votaries often belied its numbers. And a heresy Trotskyism was in the theological sense, since it professed to be truer to Bolshevik ideals, truer to Communism, than the "Stalinists" were, Stalinism being its expletive for the Party and whoever traveled or sympathized with it. Here in America Stalinists and Trotskyists only cursed each other, in the Soviet Union (and later wherever Communists controlled the state) Trotskyists paid with their lives; nor did Trotsky himself, exiled now in another hemisphere, escape Stalin's monstrous retribution.

Meanwhile, bitter irony awaited Jay Lovestone. Though he had proved his fealty to Stalin by the zeal with which he had Party toughs bully Trotskyist dissenters, Stalin, it happened, detested Lovestone; exactly why is still unclear. For one thing, Lovestone had made a tremendous miscalculation. He sided with Bukharin and the right opposition in the belief that they not only had the correct policy but would triumph in the end, with Stalin in tow. In fact, no sooner had Bukharin helped Stalin defeat the left opposition than Stalin turned against him; thus began Bukharin's slide to oblivion.

Lovestone's fate was settled as well. Despite Stalin's insistence that he step down, he refused to surrender the chair to which the Party had elected him virtually without demur. No matter. To make a very long story short, it unceremoniously dumped him, at most only a few hundred of its ten thousand members departing with him to form their own sect. And, like Trotskyists, they, the Lovestonites, claimed to represent authentic Bolshevism, the Soviet Union, and the Comintern, as they should be under Bukharin's leadership. Never more than a corporal's guard, they disbanded shortly after Stalin had Bukharin executed in 1938. Jay Lovestone then underwent a complete transformation. He and several of his coadjutors were shadowy operatives of some value to the United States in its Cold War with the Soviet Union. Not to his dying day sixty years after his fall did he let his enemies forget what they had done to him.

So it was by chance rather than design that William Z. Foster in 1929 got his wish and became de facto Party Secretary. But for him and the movement these were hardly the best of times. The Party was at its nadir, to judge from its membership rolls. Though its internal problems undoubtedly contributed to its decline or stagnation, they did not cause it. The lamentable truth was that the economy continued to move upward and onward, stimulated by a booming stock market. In Herbert Hoover the nation had a president who as man and politician exemplified the virtues that contented Americans celebrated. If asked, they would have enthusiastically agreed with the Communist view (provided they did not know who said it) that their way of life was exceptional among the peoples of the earth.

BIRTH OF THE MOVEMENT

1
REVOLUTIONARY SOCIALISM
Louis C. Fraina

Fraina, born in Italy and brought to America as a boy, was a committed Socialist of the Far Left by his teens; he was by then a talented polemicist, too. The Bolshevik Revolution was his epiphany, as it was the Far Left's in general. His book, Revolutionary Socialism, *which came out only months after the Revolution, was a rallying cry of those in the Socialist Party who would soon break away and launch the Communist movement. Fraina himself would become a Communist leader for a while. He disappeared from view, emerging in the 1930s as a well-known radical intellectual under the name Lewis Corey.*

The world war has brought Capitalism to the verge of collapse. It has compelled the state to lay a dictatorial hand upon the process of production, and the nation to negate its own basis by striving to break through the limits of the nation. It has compelled industrial necessity to subordinate itself to the overwhelming fact of military necessity. The debts of the belligerent nations are colossal, and they will fetter the nations, constitute a crucial problem in the days to come. The war has weakened Capitalism while it has strengthened a fictitious domination of the capitalist class. Contradictions and antagonisms have been multiplied. War has become the normal occupation of Capitalism, and the transition to peace will shake Capitalism to its foundations, posing new and more acute problems for solution. Industry will have to adjust itself to a peace basis, and it will be a herculean task; the proletariat will have to adjust itself to the new conditions, new struggles and new problems, and the experiences of war are not calculated to make it submissive.

The proletariat will find upon the conclusion of peace that all its sacrifices have availed it naught, and that the old system of exploitation persists in intensified form. Capitalism will equally find that war has availed it naught: its old economic problems will not have been solved and new problems will have been created. Will Capitalism answer with a feverish era of industrial expansion? But war debts will weigh upon the nation, and an era of expansion will simply hasten the new crisis and a new war. There is a point where Capitalism comes up against an impasse in the industrial process. The forces of production inexorably generate new contradictions and crises. Capitalism verges on collapse. . . .

The immediate objective of the proletarian revolution is the conquest of the power of the state; and this means the annihilation of the bourgeois state, its parliamentary system and bourgeois democracy, and the introduction of a new "state" comprised in the dictatorship of the proletariat. In his "Criticism of the Gotha Program" Marx projected this phase of the proletarian revolution: "Between the capitalist and the communist systems of society lies the period of revolutionary transformation of the one into the other. This corresponds to a political transition period, whose state can be nothing else than the revolutionary dictatorship of the proletariat."

The alternative to this dictatorship of the proletariat is the bourgeois state, its democracy and parliamentary system. To compromise with this system is to yield up the revolutionary task and to allow Capitalism to dominate. The parliamentary bourgeois state must be destroyed not simply because it is the ultimate purpose of Socialism to do away with the state as constituted in bourgeois society, but because it is immediately necessary in the process of disposing of the old society and introducing the new. It is a tactical necessity. The dictatorship of the proletariat is a revolutionary recognition of the fact that the proletariat alone counts, and no other class has any "rights." The dictatorship of the proletariat places all power in the control of the proletariat, and weakens the bourgeoisie, makes them incapable of any concerted action against the Revolution. Organized in a dictatorship of the proletariat, the Revolution unhesitatingly and relentlessly pursues its task of reconstructing society on the basis of communist Socialism.

The parliamentary regime is the expression of bourgeois democracy—each equally an instrument for the promotion of bourgeois class interests. Parliamentarism, presumably representing all classes, actually represents and promotes the requirements of the ruling class alone. Its trappings of army, police and judiciary are indispensable means of repression used against the proletariat, and the proletariat in action annihilates them all: in place of the army, the armed proletarian militia, until unnecessary; in place of the police, disciplinary measures of the masses themselves; in place of the judiciary, tribunals of workmen. The bureaucratic machinery of the state disappears. The division of functions in the parliamentary system into legislative and executive has for its direct purpose the indirect smothering of the opposition—the legislature talks and represents the pretense of "democracy," while the executive acts autocratically. The parliamentary system is a fetter upon revolutionary class action in the epoch of the final struggle against Capitalism. The proletarian revolution annihilates the parliamentary system and its division of functions, legislative and executive being united in one body—as in the Paris Commune and in the Russian Councils of Workers and Peasants.

The dictatorship of the proletariat, moreover, annihilates bourgeois democracy. All democracy is relative, is *class* democracy. As a historical category, democracy is a form of authority of one class over another: bourgeois democracy is the form of expression of the authority and tyranny of Capitalism. Authority is an instrument of class rule, historically: Socialism destroys authority. The democracy of Socialism, the self-government of the proletarian masses, discards the democracy of Capitalism—relative democracy is superseded by the individual and social autonomy of communist Socialism. The proletarian revolution does not allow the "ethical concepts" of bourgeois democracy to interfere in the course of events: it ruthlessly sweeps aside "democracy" in the process of revolutionary transformation. Capitalism hypocritically insists upon a government of *all the classes*; the Revolution frankly and fearlessly introduces the government of *one class, the proletariat*, through a proletarian dictatorship. The proletarian revolution is inexorable; it completely and ruthlessly annihilates the institutions and ideology of the regime of communist Socialism.[*]

This problem of democracy is crucial in the proletarian revolution. Democracy becomes the last bulwark of defense of Capitalism, an instrument used by dominant Capitalism and the *petite bourgeoisie* in a last desper-

---

[*]During the course of events in Russia, democracy was a fetter upon the development of the proletarian revolution; once this revolution was accomplished, democracy became a counterrevolutionary instrument used by the petty bourgeois Socialism of the Mensheviki and Social-Revolutionists of the Right through the Constituent Assembly. If the Soviet government had not dissolved the Constituent Assembly, it would have stultified itself and the Revolution. The Revolution, declared the decree of dissolution, created the Workers' and Soldiers' Council—the only organization able to direct the struggle of the exploited classes for *complete* political and economic liberation; this Council constituted a revolutionary government through the November

ate defense of private property. Any compromise on the issue of democracy compromises the integrity of the Revolution, stultifies its purposes and palsies its action: it is an issue pregnant with the potentiality of fatal mistakes. And yet it is all simplicity itself: in the revolution, the proletariat may depend upon itself alone; it alone is necessary in the process of production; it alone is a revolutionary class, implacably arrayed against all other classes; it alone counts as a class in the reconstruction of society, and, accordingly, the dictatorship of the proletariat refuses political "rights" and recognition to any section of the bourgeois class.

Through its dictatorship, the proletariat organizes itself as the ruling class, acquires social supremacy. The basis of the new "state" is not territorial, but industrial: its constituents are the organized producers. The other elements of the people function in this proletarian government in the measure that they are absorbed in the new industrial scheme of things, become useful producers. The process of transformation into communist Socialism is a process of the organized producers, and of these alone. . . .

2

MANIFESTO
Left Wing of the Socialist Party

Consisting of delegates from twenty states, the National Council of the Left Wing of the Socialist Party met in New York City on June 21, 1919, and drew up the following statement. If the language reminds one of Fraina it is no coincidence; he wrote most of it.

The world is in crisis. Capitalism, the prevailing system of society, is in process of disintegration and collapse. Out of its vitals is developing a new social order, the system of Communist Socialism; and the struggle between this new social order and the old is now the fundamental problem of international politics.

The predatory "war for democracy" dominated the world. But now it is the revolutionary proletariat in action that dominates, conquering power in some nations, mobilizing to conquer power in others, and calling upon the proletariat of all nations to prepare for the final struggle against capitalism.

Revolution, after perceiving the illusion of an understanding with the bourgeoisie and its deceptive parliamentary organization; the Constituent Assembly, being elected from the old election lists, was the expression of the old regime when authority belonged to the bourgeoisie, and necessarily became the authority of the bourgeois republic, setting itself against the revolution of November and the authority of the Councils; the old bourgeois parliamentarism has had its day and is incompatible with the tasks before Socialism, and that only such institutions as the Workmen's and Soldiers' Councils are able to overcome the opposition of the ruling classes and create a new Socialist state; "the central executive committee, therefore, orders the Constituent Assembly dissolved."

But Socialism itself is in crisis. Events are revolutionizing Capitalism *and* *Socialism*—an indication that this is the historic epoch of the proletarian revolution. Imperialism is the final stage of Capitalism; and Imperialism means sterner reaction and new wars of conquest—unless the revolutionary proletariat acts for Socialism. Capitalism cannot reform itself; it cannot be reformed. Humanity can be saved from its last excesses only by the Communist revolution. There can now be only the Socialism which is one in temper and purpose with the proletarian revolutionary struggle. There can be only the Socialism which unites the proletariat of the whole world in the general struggle against the desperately destructive Imperialisms—the Imperialisms which array themselves as a single force against the onsweeping proletarian revolution. . . .

POLITICAL ACTION

The class struggle is a political struggle. It is a political struggle in the sense that its objective is political—the overthrow of the political organization upon which capitalistic exploitation depends, and the introduction of a new social system. The direct objective is the conquest by the proletariat of the power of the state.

Revolutionary Socialism does not propose to "capture" the bourgeois parliamentary state, but to conquer and destroy it. Revolutionary Socialism, accordingly, repudiates the policy of introducing Socialism by means of legislative measures on the basis of the bourgeois state. This state is a bourgeois state, the organ for the coercion of the proletarian by the capitalist: how, then, can it introduce Socialism? As long as the bourgeois parliamentary state prevails, the capitalist class can baffle the will of the proletariat, since all the political power, the army and the police, industry and the press, are in the hands of the capitalists, whose economic power gives them complete domination. The revolutionary proletariat must expropriate all these by the conquest of the power of the state, by annihilating the political power of the bourgeoisie, before it can begin the task of introducing Socialism.

Revolutionary Socialism, accordingly, proposes to conquer the power of the state. It proposes to conquer by means of political action—political action in the revolutionary Marxian sense, which does not simply mean parliamentarism, but the *class action* of the proletariat *in any form* having as its objective the conquest of the power of the state. . . .

Moderate Socialism refuses to recognize and accept this supreme form of proletarian political action, limits and stultifies political action into legislative routine and non-Socialist parliamentarism. This is a denial of the mass character of the proletarian struggle, an evasion of the tasks of the Revolution.

The power of the proletariat lies fundamentally in its control of the industrial process. The mobilization of this control in action against the bourgeois state and Capitalism means the end of Capitalism, the initial form of the revolutionary mass action that will conquer the power of the state. . . .

The old machinery of the state cannot be used by the revolutionary proletariat. It must be destroyed. The proletariat created a new state, based directly upon the industrially organized producers, upon the industrial unions or Soviets, or a combination of both. It is this state alone, functioning as a dictatorship of the proletariat, that can realize Socialism.

The tasks of the dictatorship of the proletariat are:

a. To completely expropriate the bourgeoisie politically, and crush its powers of resistance.

b. To expropriate the bourgeoisie economically, and introduce the forms of Communist Socialism.

Breaking the political power of the capitalists is the most important task of the revolutionary dictatorship of the proletariat, since upon this depends the economic and social reconstruction of society.

But this political expropriation proceeds simultaneously with an immediate, if partial, expropriation of the bourgeoisie economically. The scope of these measures being determined by industrial development and the maturity of the proletariat. These measures, at first, include:

a. Workmen's control of industry, to be exercised by the industrial organizations of the workers, operating by means of the industrial vote.

b. Expropriation and nationalization of the banks, as a necessary preliminary measure for the complete expropriation of capital.

c. Expropriation and nationalization of the large (trust) organizations of capital. Expropriation proceeds without compensation, as "buying out" the capitalists is a repudiation of the tasks of the revolution.

d. Repudiation of all national debts and the financial obligations of the old system.

e. The nationalization of foreign trade.

f. Measures for the socialization of agriculture. . . .

The acceptance of the Communist International means accepting the fundamentals of revolutionary Socialism as decisive in our activity.

The Communist International, moreover, issues its call to the subject peoples of the world, crushed under the murderous mastery of Imperialism. The revolt of these colonial and subject peoples is a necessary phase of the world struggle against capitalist Imperialism; their revolt must unite itself with the struggle of the conscious proletariat in the imperialistic nations. The Communist International, accordingly, offers an organization and a policy that may unify all the revolutionary forces of the world for the conquest of power, and for Socialism.

It is not a problem of immediate revolution. It is a problem of the immediate revolutionary struggle. The revolutionary epoch of the final struggle against Capitalism may last for years and tens of years; but the Communist International offers a policy and program immediate and ultimate in scope, that provides for the immediate class struggle against Capitalism, in its revolutionary implications, and for the final act of the conquest of power.

The old order is in decay. Civilization is in collapse. The proletarian revolution and the Communist reconstruction of society—*the struggle for these*—is now indispensable. This is the message of the Communist International to the workers of the world.

The Communist International calls the proletariat of the world to the final struggle!

3
PLATFORM AND PROGRAM
Communist Labor Party

On August 31, 1919, eighty-two delegates from twenty-one states met at Machinists Hall, Chicago, and established the Communist Labor Party. Led by John Reed, they had just walked out of the Socialist Party convention that was taking place nearby. Elsewhere in Chicago meanwhile another Communist faction was holding its convention. Even to insiders, the situation was confusing to say the least.

PLATFORM

1. The Communist Labor Party of the United States of America declares itself in full harmony with the revolutionary working class parties of all countries and stands by the principles stated by the Third International formed at Moscow.

2. With them it thoroughly appreciates the complete development of Capitalism into its present form of Capitalist Imperialism with its dictatorship of the capitalist class and its absolute suppression of the working class.

3. With them it also fully realizes the crying need for an immediate change in the social system; it realizes that the time for parleying and compromise has passed; and that now it is only the question of whether all power remains in the hands of the capitalist or is taken by the working class.

4. The Communist Labor Party proposes the organization of the workers as a class, the overthrow of capitalist rule and the conquest of political power by the workers. The workers, organized as the ruling class, shall, through their government, make and enforce the laws; they shall own and control land, factories, mills, mines, transportation systems and financial institutions. All power to the workers!

5. The Communist Labor Party has as its ultimate aim: The abolition of

the present system of production, in which the working class is mercilessly exploited, and the creation of an industrial republic wherein the machinery of production shall be socialized so as to guarantee to the workers the full social value of the product of their toil.

6. To this end we ask the workers to unite with the Communist Labor Party for the conquest of political power to establish a government adapted to the Communist transformation. . . .

RECOMMENDATIONS

We recommend the following measures:

1. That all Locals shall elect Committees on Labor Organization, composed so far as is possible of members of Labor Unions, whose functions shall be:

a. To initiate, or support, the creation of Shop Committees in every industry in their district, the uniting of these Committees in Industrial Councils, District Councils, and the Central Council of all industries.

b. To propagandize and assist in the combining of craft unions, by industries, in One Big Union.

c. To bring together in the centers of Party activity—Locals and Branches—delegates from factories and shops to discuss tactics and policies of conducting the class struggle.

d. To propagandize directly among the workers on the job the principles of Communism, and educate them to a realization of their class position.

e. To find a common basis for the uniting of all existing economic and political organizations based on the class struggle.

f. To mobilize all members who can serve as organizers to fill the demand for men and women who can organize bodies of workers along the lines indicated above.

g. To direct the activities of local Party organizations in assisting the workers wholeheartedly in their industrial battles, and making use of these battles as opportunities for educating the workers.

2. That a National Committee on Labor Organization be elected by this Convention, which shall cooperate with the local committees above mentioned. In addition, the National Committee shall be charged with the task of mobilizing national support for strikes of national importance, and shall endeavor to give these a political character.

a. It shall collect information concerning the revolutionary labor movement from the different sections of the country, and from other countries, and through a Press Service to Labor and Socialist papers, shall spread this information to all parts of the country.

b. It shall mobilize on a national scale all members who can serve as propagandists and organizers who cannot only teach but actually help to put into practice the principles of revolutionary industrial unionism and Communism.

4

Manifesto
Communist Party

The other left-wing faction, almost all of whose 128 representatives came from foreign-language groups, convened at Chicago's Russian Federation building ("Smolny") and called itself the Communist Party. It will be obvious to the reader that Fraina had a hand in writing its fiery manifesto.

DICTATORSHIP OF THE PROLETARIAT

The proletarian revolution comes at the moment of crisis in Capitalism, of a collapse of the old order. Under the impulse of the crisis, the proletariat acts for the conquest of power, by means of mass action. Mass action concentrates and mobilizes the forces of the proletariat, organized and unorganized; it acts equally against the bourgeois state and the conservative organizations of the working class. Strikes of protest develop into general political strikes and then into revolutionary mass action for the conquest of the power of the state. Mass action becomes political in purpose while extra-parliamentary in form; it is equally a process of revolution and the revolution itself in operation.

The state is an organ of coercion. The bourgeois parliamentary state is the organ of the bourgeoisie for the coercion of the proletariat. Parliamentary government is the expression of bourgeois supremacy, the form of authority of the capitalist over the worker. Bourgeois democracy promotes the dictatorship of capital, assisted by the press, the pulpit, the army, and the police. Bourgeois democracy is historically necessary, on the one hand, to break the power of feudalism, and, on the other, to maintain the proletarian in subjection. It is precisely this democracy that is now the instrument of Imperialism, since the middle class, the traditional carrier of democracy, accepts Imperialism. The proletarian revolution disrupts bourgeois democracy. It disrupts this democracy in order to end class divisions and class rule, to realize industrial self-government of the workers. Therefore it is necessary that the proletariat organize its own state *for the coercion and suppression of the bourgeoisie*. Proletarian dictatorship is a recognition of the fact; it is equally a recognition of the fact that in the Communist reconstruction of society the proletariat alone counts as a class.

While the dictatorship of the proletariat performs the negative task of crushing the old order, it performs the positive task of constructing the new. Together with the government of the proletarian dictatorship, there is developed a new "government," which is no longer government in the old sense, since it concerns itself with the management of the production and not with the government of persons. Out of workers' control of industry, introduced by the proletarian dictatorship, there develops the complete structure of Communist Socialism—industrial self-government of the communistically organized producers. When this structure is completed, which implies the complete expropriation of the bourgeoisie, economically and politically, the dictatorship of the proletariat ends, in its place coming the full, free social and individual autonomy of the Communist order. . . .

THE PARTY CONSTITUTION

I. Name and Purpose

Section 1. The name of this organization shall be The Communist Party of America. Its purpose shall be the education and organization of the working class for the establishment of the Dictatorship of the Proletariat, the abolition of the capitalist system and the establishment of the Communist Society.

II. Emblem

Section 1. The emblem of the party shall be a button with the figure of the earth in the center in white with gold lines and a red flag across the face bearing the inscription, "All Power to the Workers"; around the figure of the earth a red margin shall appear with the words "The Communist Party of America" and "The Communist International" on this margin in white letters.

III. Membership

Section 1. Every person who accepts the principles and tactics of the Communist Party and the Communist International and agrees to engage actively in the work of the party shall be eligible to membership. It is the aim of this organization to have in its ranks only those who participate actively in its work.

Section 2. Applicants for membership shall sign an application card reading as follows:

The undersigned, after having read the constitution and program of the Communist Party, declares his adherence to the principles and tactics of the party and the Communist International; agrees to submit to the discipline of the party as stated in its constitution and pledges himself to engage actively in its work.

Section 3. Every member must join a duly constituted branch of the party. There shall be no members-at-large.

Section 4. All application cards must be endorsed by two persons who have been members for not less than three months.

Section 5. Applications for membership shall not be finally acted upon until two months after presentation to the branch, and in the meantime the applicant shall pay an initiation fee and dues and shall attend meetings and classes. He shall have a voice and no vote. Provided that this rule shall not apply to the charter members of new branches nor to the members who make application to newly organized branches during the first month.

Section 6. No person who is a member or supporter of any other political organization shall be admitted to membership.

Section 7. No person who has an entire livelihood from rent, interest or profit shall be eligible to membership in the Communist Party.

Section 8. No person shall be accepted as a member who enters into the service of the national, state or local governmental bodies otherwise than through the Civil Service or by legal compulsion.

Provided, that the civil employment by the government is of a non-political character.

Section 9. No members of the Communist Party shall contribute articles or editorials of a political or economic character to publications other than those of the Communist Party or of parties affiliated with the Communist International. (This clause shall not be considered as prohibiting the contribution of articles written from an economic or scientific standpoint to scientific or professional journals. Permission to answer an attack upon the Communist Party in the bourgeoisie press may be granted by the Central Executive Committee.) . . .

5

ZINOVIEV LETTER

The antics of America's two Communist parties puzzled the Russians. Here is the secret letter that the head of the Comintern, Gregory Zinoviev, a close associate of Lenin, sent on January 12, 1920, urging them to reconcile and change their tactics. The letter figured in the red scare, which was then in progress, because The New York World *got hold of a copy. How the public interpreted it can be imagined.*

To the Central Committees of the American Communist Party and the American Communist Labor Party

Dear Comrades:

From the reports of comrades who arrived from America and who represent both tendencies of American communism, the Executive Committee of the Communist International has the opportunity of acquainting itself with the differences between the American comrades; differences which have led to an open split and to the formation of two communist parties. . . .

This split has rendered a heavy blow to the communist movement in America. It leads to the dispersion of revolutionary force, to a harmful parallelism, an absurd partition of practical work, senseless discussions and an unjustifiable loss of energy in interfactional quarrels. A concentration of American bourgeois forces has increased to an unprecedented extent, while the class struggle is becoming more acute every day and demands unprecedented sacrifices from the American proletariat. The world revolution is inexorably growing; great possibilities and brilliant perspectives are opening up before the American proletariat! This is not the time for division of communist forces.

In addition to this we must assert that the split has not been caused by any profound differences of opinion as regards program. At bottom there are but certain disagreements on the question of tactics, principally questions of organization.

Under such circumstances this split has not the slightest justification and should be liquidated at all costs. In so far as both parties stand on the platform of the Communist International—and of this we have not the slightest doubt—a united party is not only possible but is absolutely necessary, and the E. C. [Executive Committee] categorically insists on this being immediately brought about.

The necessity for immediate unification is imperatively dictated by the further fact that the two parties represent, as it were, varying sides of the communist movement in America. The American Communist Party is principally a foreign party embracing so-called "national" federations. The American Communist Labor Party chiefly represents American or English speaking elements. If the first is more developed theoretically and is more closely connected with the traditions of the revolutionary struggle of the Russian working class, it is on the other hand more isolated from the mass movement and mass organizations of the American workers who are gradually entering the broad path of the struggle between the classes. The second party which has not passed through a similar revolutionary school has received less training in the subtleties of Marxist theory and is in need of a certain intellectual guidance, nevertheless has the advantage that it may much more easily influence American labor—which is to play the most important part in the coming decisive battles of the class war. Thus both parties naturally supplement each other, and only by their unification is it possible to create in America an efficient Communist Party which must take the lead in the mass movement, and in the oncoming communist revolution. . . .

The party must take part in the everyday incidents of the class war. Up until now the American left wing socialists devoted most of their attention to agitation and propaganda and in this direction did important work. But confined in a more or less close circle of comrades all thinking alike, they, to a large extent, stood aside from the every-day class struggle of the proletarian masses which is flowing in broad streams throughout the country; at any rate they did not play the leading part in the greater conflicts between capital and labor. It is particularly necessary to remember that the stage of verbal propaganda and agitation has been left behind, the time for decisive battles has arrived. Uniting in its ranks all the class conscious and most active elements of the working class, and developing the widest propaganda of communist ideas, the communist party must at the same time strive to become the leader in the proletarian class struggle in all its various aspects, from separate economic strikes, demonstrations, mass meetings and election campaigns, to general political strikes and armed insurrections of the proletariat. The most important task confronting the American communists at the present moment is to draw the wide proletarian masses into the path of the revolutionary class struggle. . . .

The Executive Committee urges the American Comrades immediately to establish an underground organization even though it is possible for the Party to function legally. This underground organization shall be for the purpose of carrying on direct revolutionary propaganda among the masses, and, in case of violent suppression of the legal Party organization, of carrying on the work. It should be composed of trusted comrades, and kept entirely separate from the legal Party organization. The fewer people who know about it the better. For the formation and control of this underground organization, a small sub-committee of the National Executive Committee can be appointed. An underground printing plant and distribution machinery should be established.

We remain, Yours fraternally

President of the Executive Committee of the Communist International

Zinoviev

6

UNITY CONVENTION
The United Communist Party

Under pressure from the Comintern, and after tortuous negotiations, the United Communist (UCP) and Communist Parties merged at a "joint unity convention" held in

Woodstock, New York, in May 1921. How the delegates finally came to terms was candidly summarized in the first issue of the new party's magazine Communist.

After two more days of caucus meetings, the convention met to hear the report of the Committee on Constitution. The clauses upon which the committee had split three to three deadlocked the convention by a vote of thirty UCP delegates to thirty CP delegates. The clauses agreed upon by the committee were adopted with little debate. At eleven o'clock at night the Committee on Constitution had finished its report. No constitution had been adopted. The convention was hopelessly deadlocked. Neither side left their seats. No motions were made; no one took the floor. The chairman announced that he would entertain a motion to adjourn. This was answered by the humming of the "Internationale." The chairman waited and then declared the session adjourned, and left the chair. But both delegations remained in session. The situation was tense. After a while the chairman announced the re-opening of the session and introduced the representative of the Pan-American Agency, who proposed the settlement of the deadlock on the constitution by the negotiation between the separate caucuses. A delegate from the UCP side moved that a recess be taken which was unanimously voted. Both caucuses then met and negotiations were carried on between them during the night. It was finally agreed to elect a committee of ten, five from each caucus, who were to bring in recommendations on each clause of the constitution upon which the convention could not agree. This committee met during the following day. Each caucus confirmed the compromises reached upon each clause and the convention in joint session rapidly adopted them with very little discussion. The principle points at issue and the decisions regarding them have been already described in detail in No. 1. of the "Official Bulletin."

With the adoption of the Constitution the party lines melted away. Comrades who after having been separated for years embraced each other; hands clasped hands; the delegates sang the "Internationale" with as much energy as could be mustered after the trying 48-hour continuous sessions. Unity had almost been achieved.

Almost—because, while the convention had decided upon a CEC to be composed of nine members, another deadlock occurred over the election of the ninth CEC member. Two names were proposed as the "impartial" ninth man. These were voted for by secret ballot, with the result that both received thirty votes. Neither side was quite prepared to trust to the complete impartiality of the other. After further caucus meetings it was agreed to reconsider the clause in the Constitution providing for nine members on the CEC. A CEC of ten members was accepted. Both "impartial" candidates were then unanimously elected. It was agreed to elect the delegates to the Third

Congress of the Comintern at the convention, and the Joint Unity of the UCP and CP wound up its work and adjourned.

The delegates, exhausted from the strenuous activity of two weeks, but happy at having successfully accomplished their difficult task, formed little groups regardless of former party lines, and left for their homes.

Of the many conventions held by the Communists in this country, the Joint Unity Convention just ended will prove to be the most momentous and the most far-reaching in its effect upon the communist movement in the U.S.

With the unity of the former UCP and CP accomplished the Communist Party in America enters upon a new period. Many comrades may deplore the long factional fight in this country, and the resultant splits within the movement, as a dead loss and waste of energy, but the clarification of Communist principles and tactics which resulted from these splits are a distinct advantage which more than compensates for the apparent loss of revolutionary energy.

The experience gained will be felt when the Communist Party enters the period of revolutionary activity, such as now prevails in Germany. But these factional controversies, when carried beyond the point necessary for the establishing of communist understanding, tend to become barren and may easily result in sectarianism.

For after all, the test of our principles lies in action, in the application of the tactics and principles of communism to the needs of the exploited masses in the class struggle. From now on the Communist Party of America must bend all its energies to bring its program into life; to achieve and maintain that contact with the masses without which there can be no powerful and effective communist movement in this country.

The Joint Unity Convention has produced a program of action sufficient for the requirements of the class war in America. Every member of the Communist Party (formed at this Unity Convention) has behind him the necessary training to make of the CP the revolutionary vanguard of the working class.

All the problems arising out of the unity of the two former factions are by no means settled. There yet remains to be consummated the physical union of the separate units of both the former parties. To this task every comrade must bend his or her energies. The bitterness engendered by two years of factional strife cannot be expected to disappear overnight, but these will wear off as our comrades fight shoulder to shoulder within the unions and elsewhere in carrying out the party's program.

Let every comrade resolve to support the new CEC in its difficult task of bringing into life the new program and constitution of the C. P. of A.

Long Live the Communist Party of America.

Long Live the Communist International. . . .

PROGRAM AND CONSTITUTION
Workers Party of America

Only seven months after its establishment the Communist Party had to change again. It had to end its underground life and appeal to the electorate at large rather than wait for the revolution. Meeting at New York City's Star Casino in late December 1921, its delegates rechristened it the Workers Party. Eight years later it was re-rechristened Communist.

ELECTION CAMPAIGN AND AMERICAN DEMOCRACY

While recognizing the impossibility of the workers winning their emancipation through the use of the machinery of the existing government, the Workers Party realizes the importance of election campaigns in developing the political consciousness of the working class. The first step toward revolutionary political action by the working class must be made through independent political action by the workers in election campaigns. The Workers Party will therefore participate in election campaigns and use them for propaganda and agitation to develop their political consciousness of the workers.

It will endeavor to rally the workers to use their power to make real the rights which the fraudulent American democracy denies them. It will use them to carry on the struggle for the right of labor to create a revolutionary political party and for such an organization to function openly in the political life of the country.

The Workers Party will also nominate its candidate and enter into election campaigns to expose the fraudulent character of capitalist democracy and to carry on the propaganda for the soviets. It will use the election campaigns to rally the workers for mass political demands upon the capitalist state. Its candidates, when elected to office, will use the forums of the legislative bodies for the same purpose. . . .

The division of the organized workers into craft unions is one of the greatest obstacles to the progress of the workers in this country against capitalism.

During the past two years organized labor has been dealt many heavy blows by the employers, who are bent on destroying or at least weakening so as to make ineffective the organization of the workers. In spite of this desperate struggle, each craft has fought alone. There has been no united resistance, no solid united front against the industrial kings, who are striving to reduce the wages and make worse the working conditions of the workers. The example of the seven railroad shop unions striking while nine other railroad unions continued to serve the railroad kings and help them to whip their fellow workers is but one striking example of a situation which exists everywhere in the ranks of organized labor in this country.

In addition to the weakness of the craft form of organization the labor unions suffer from a fundamental error of policy. In place of waging a class struggle to free themselves from the grip of the capitalists they have pursued the policy of attempting to come to an agreement with the capitalists on the basis of "a fair day's pay for a fair day's work."

No such compromise with capitalism can be permanent. The hunger of the capitalists for greater profits drives them to seek to lower the standard of living of the workers when they have the upper hand. On the other hand when the workers are in a strong position their need and their desire for more of the good things they produce results in greater demands upon the capitalists.

The gain of the workers during the wartime scarcity of labor and their present losses indicate the futility of the hope that the class struggle can be settled through a compromise.

The labor unions must be revolutionized; they must be won for the class struggle against capitalism; they must be inspired with a new solidarity and united to fight a common battle. The existing craft unions must be amalgamated and powerful industrial unions created in each industry. The reactionary official bureaucracy of the unions must be supplanted by the shop delegates system.

The Workers Party declares one of its chief immediate tasks to be to inspire in the labor unions a revolutionary purpose and to unite them in a mass movement of uncompromising struggle against capitalism. It will use all the resources at its command to educate the organized workers to an understanding of the necessity of amalgamation of the craft unions into industrial unions.

This end cannot be achieved if the revolutionary workers leave the existing unions to form feeble dual organizations. The work of transforming the labor unions must be carried on inside the existing unions. The members of the Workers Party will carry on their work within the existing unions to awaken the spirit of class struggle and to bring about a reconstruction of the organization form so as to make of the unions powerful organized centers of the workers' struggle against capitalism. . . .

THE DICTATORSHIP OF THE PROLETARIAT

The existing capitalist government is a dictatorship of the capitalists. Today in the United States a comparatively small group of capitalist-financial and industrial kings, with headquarters in Wall Street, control the government of the United States, of the states and municipalities. Through the capitalist government this group of financial and industrial kings enforce their will upon the thirty million workers and their families.

While part of the workers are granted the hollow mockery of voting, they find that whether they vote for the Republican or Democratic candidate, in time of struggle the government is always on the side of the financial and industrial kings.

The Soviet government of the workers will, because of the same necessity—the necessity of suppressing the capitalists—be a dictatorship of the workers. The government expressing the will of the thirty million workers will openly use its power in the interests of the workers and against the capitalists.

THE GOAL OF THE PROLETARIAN DICTATORSHIP

It will be the task of the government of the thirty million workers of this country to take from the capitalists the control and ownership of the raw materials and machinery of production upon which the workers are dependent for their life, liberty and happiness and to establish collective ownership.

Together with this collective ownership the Workers' Government will as quickly as possible develop the management of the industries by the workers.

Through the establishment of this Communist system of industry the exploitation and oppression of the workers will be ended. As the power of the capitalists in industry wanes and Communism is established the struggle between the classes will disappear and the dictatorship of the Proletariat will become unnecessary and will cease to function. The government will become an instrument for administration of industry and the full, free Communist society will come into being.

8

CONVENTION AND RESOLUTIONS
Workers Party of America

This convention, which met in Chicago in late August 1925, is notable for having restructured the Party. It was now a full-fledged organization on the Soviet model, truly the American section of the Communist International.

1. The process of Bolshevizing the Party implies a reconstruction of the Party organization in such a way as to render it adaptable to the requirements of Communist activity. Without a truly centralized organization, based on the workshops, the Party cannot be mobilized for action and the Party decisions cannot be carried out with unanimity and effectiveness.

2. The present structure of the Party is incompatible with Communist organizational principles and, consequently, with the proper execution of Communist policies. The English-speaking territorial branch is a relic carried over from the socialist party which concerned itself chiefly with election campaigns. The foreign language branch tends greatly to isolate the activity of the Party members belonging to them into the channel of propaganda only among the workers of their own nationality and to deflect them away from active participation in the general class struggle which embraces the workers of all nationalities. Neither the English-speaking territorial branch, nor the foreign language branch offers the medium for mobilizing the workers for the struggle in the places of employment. Despite the wishes of the Federation members to the contrary, the Language Federation form of organization, by its very nature, militates against the necessary centralization of the Party. Moreover, the Federation form of organization is a most fertile soil for factionalism and for the sharp division of the Party members according to nationality. The historic reasons for the present form of Party organization have been, in a large measure, outlived and the conditions now exist for a progressive step forward. The Party must take this step resolutely and energetically in spite of the enormous difficulties.

3. The need of adapting the structure of the Party to its task demands a complete and speedy reorganization. The Party must supply the cohesive force which will unite the many individuals and groups of proletarians into a class. The Party must at the same time unify the activities of this class into a purposeful and decisive struggle against capitalism and finally must lead the working class in this struggle. . . .

7. The Central Executive Committee accepts in its entirety the special letter to the Party from the Organization Department of the Communist International and declares its opinion that this letter, which was drawn up with the cooperation of the American delegation, lays down the correct line in regard to the reorganization of the Party structure. . . .

11. Reorganization shall be commenced from below, approximately as follows:

a. The larger cities shall be divided into sections and sub-sections and these sections and sub-sections organizations constructed. Membership meetings shall be called in the sections and sub-sections at which executive committees for the sections are elected. Complete registration of all the Party members, according to residence and place of employment, shall be taken.

b. Wherever three or more members, regardless of their nationality or present federation membership, are found to be working in the same shop, they shall be organized into a shop nucleus. The nucleus collects the Party dues and takes over all the functions of a Party unit.

c. Members living on a given street or in a given neighborhood, who are not employed in any shop or who work in shops where there are no other Party members, shall be attached to other nuclei within the section or shall be organized into International branches. All Party members in the given neighborhood, regardless of nationality or present affiliation of language branches, who are not members of shop nuclei, are to be organized into these branches, pay dues there and carry out all Party functions.

d. After this organization takes place, the present existing English and foreign language branches cease to function as units of the Party. The latter, however, should not be disrupted or dissolved. They shall be reconstructed as Workers' Clubs admitting to membership not only Party members but also non-Party workers of the same nationality who accept the platform of the class struggle.

e. Membership in these clubs will not constitute membership in the Party. Only those belonging to shop nuclei or International Branches will have Party rights.

f. Party members in these Workers' Clubs shall form themselves into factions in the same manner as in all other non-Party organizations for the purpose of exerting the maximum influence over the non-Party workers and drawing them close to the Party.

g. These factions in the Foreign Language Workers' Clubs are to be united locally, by districts, and on a national scale, for the purpose of coordinating and centralizing the Party work in them.

h. Local and District conferences of the representatives of the factions in these clubs shall elect the local and district faction bureaus to lead the work under the direction of the respective Party Committees.

i. National Conferences of the representatives of the factions elect the National Fraction Bureau to lead the work on a national scale under the direction of the Central Executive Committee. . . .

17. The Bolshevization of our Party must accomplish four general purposes:

a. It must establish among its members a fundamental theoretical understanding of the forces of social development and a knowledge of the conditions and the mechanics of realizing the dictatorship of the proletariat.

b. It must develop within the Party and its membership an ability for maneuvering and campaigning in accord with the momentary needs and the possibilities of the class struggle.

A Communist Party must be able to maneuver and to adapt its tactics at all times to changing conditions. Changing conditions in the proletarian struggle for emancipation must not bring confusion into the ranks of the Party but must be met by a Leninist appraisal of the new facts and if necessary by a speedy change of the methods of struggle.

In order to increase the ability of our Party to maneuver it is necessary to establish a close ideological relation between the Party and its leading committees. The Party must not only be required to campaign and maneuver, but it must also be made acquainted with the character and the purposes of all maneuvers.

c. It must adapt the structure of the Party to its task of penetrating and dominating all manifestations of life of the working class and of leading the workers in their struggle for emancipation.

d. It must establish a harmonizing unity of theory, action and structure of the Party which will secure a full use of all available energies of the Party and also insure the Party against fundamental mistakes.

National and local Party leaders must regularly lecture in the Party school and before the membership in general about current events and the Party's judgment of them. The political committee of the Party must furnish the Party press and all educational institutions at least twice a month with an official analysis of political events and the official Party reaction to them.

18. "Without a correct theory there can be no correct practice—theory is concentrated practice," declared our greatest leader, Lenin. The slighting of the value of theory too often noticed in our Party leads necessarily to a complete lack of unified concept for Party activities. Without a unified concept the Party activities become sporadic, disconnected, planless and purposeless. Waste of energy and fruitless efforts are the result. The Party must therefore apply itself to the task of systematic theoretical education of its members.

9

THE COMMUNIST PARTY, A MANUAL OF ORGANIZATION
J. Peters

Even though the tract from which this selection is taken appeared in 1935, here is the appropriate place for it because it details, with extreme lucidity—too extreme perhaps— the Bolshevik conception of the Party. Who was J. Peters? He was a shadowy figure whose real name most likely was Alexander Goldenberg and who belonged to the Hungarian foreign-language affiliate before becoming a Comintern official. He thus spoke with authority on the subject of Bolshevik organization.

II. BASIC PRINCIPLES OF PARTY ORGANIZATION

The Communist Party is organized in such a way as to guarantee, first, complete inner unity of outlook; and, second, combination of the strictest discipline with the widest initiative and independent activity of the Party membership. Both of these conditions are guaranteed because the Party is organized on the basis of democratic centralism.

Democratic Centralism

Democratic centralism is the system according to which:

1. All leading committees of the Party, from the Unit Bureaus up to the highest committees, are elected by the membership or delegates of the given Party organization.
2. Every elected Party committee must report regularly on its activity to its Party organization. It must give an account of its work.
3. The lower Party committees and all Party members of the given Party organization have the duty of carrying out the decisions of the higher Party committees and of the Communist International. In other words, decisions of the CI and of the higher Party committees are binding upon the lower bodies.
4. Party discipline is observed by the Party members and Party organizations because only those who agree with the program of the Communist Party and the CI can become members of the Party.
5. The minority carries out the decisions of the majority (subordination of the minority to the majority). Party questions are discussed by the members of the Party and by the Party organization until such time as a decision is made by the Party committee or organization. After a decision has been made by the leading committees of the CI, by the Central Committee of the Party, or by the National Convention, this decision must be unreservedly carried out even if a minority of the Party membership or a minority of the local Party organizations is in disagreement with it.
6. The Party organizations, Units, Sections, and Districts, have the full initiative, right and duty to decide on local questions within the limits of the general policies and decisions of the Party.

Decisions of Higher Bodies Binding on Lower Bodies

On the basis of democratic centralism, all lower Party organizations are subordinated to the higher bodies; District organizations are subordinated to the Central Committee; Section organizations are subordinated to the District Committee; Party Units (shop, street and town) are subordinated to the Section Committees.

All decisions of the World Congress and committees of the CI must be fulfilled by all parties of the CI. All decision of the National Convention and the Central Committee must be fulfilled by the whole Party; all decisions of the District Convention and Committee must be fulfilled by the Section organizations of that District; all decisions of the Section Convention and Committee are binding on the shop, street and town Units in that Section.

A Party committee or Unit Bureau, throughout the whole of its activity from Convention to Convention, from Conference to Conference, from Unit meeting to Unit meeting, is not only under the control of the higher Party committees, but also under the control of the whole Party membership in the given organization. In cases where the elected Party committee is not capable of carrying out its task and the correct Party line, this committee can be changed through the calling of an extraordinary Conference by decision of the higher committees, or by the initiative of the lower organizations with the approval of the higher committees.

The Communist Party puts the interest of the working class and the Party above everything. The Party subordinates all forms of Party organization to these interests. From this it follows that one form of organization is suitable for legal existence of the Party, and another for the conditions of underground, illegal existence. Under conditions where there is no possibility of holding open elections or broad Conventions, the form of democratic centralism necessarily has to be changed. In such a situation, it is inevitable that co-option be used as well as election. That means that in such a situation the higher committees will appoint the lower committees (for example, the Central Committee may appoint the District Committee; the District Committee may appoint the Section Committee, etc.). Or, in very exceptional cases, when the lower committee is to act quickly, this committee has the right to co-opt new members to the committee from among the best leaders of the organization; and this co-option must be approved by the higher committee.

But even in the most difficult situation, the Party finds ways and means of holding elections. The Conventions or Conferences under such conditions will necessarily be smaller. The organization will be tighter so as to eliminate as far as possible the danger of the exposure of delegates to the class enemies. Under conditions of extreme terror, open election of committees would endanger the elected leaders and make it possible for the bourgeoisie and their police agents to capture the leaders of the Party, and in this way cripple the revolutionary movement. Therefore, such a method is used by the Party in electing leading committees during such a period which eliminates the danger of exposure.

Democratic centralism therefore represents a flexible system of Party organization which guarantees all the conditions for combining the conscious and active participation of the whole Party membership in the Party life together with the best forms of centralized leadership in the activity and struggles of the Party and the working class. . . .

Why Do the Communists Attach So Much Importance to Discipline?

Because without discipline there is no unity of will, no unity in action. Our Party is the organized and most advanced section of the working class. The

Party is the vanguard of the proletariat in the class war. In this class war there is the capitalist class with its henchmen and helpers, the reformist leaders, on one side, and the working class and its allies, on the other. The class war is bitter. The enemy is powerful; it has all the means of deceit and suppression (armed forces, militia, police, courts, movies, radio, press, schools, churches, etc.). In order to combat and defeat this powerful enemy, the army of the proletariat must have a highly skilled, trained General Staff (the Communist Party), which is united in action and has one will. How can an army fight against the army of the enemy if every soldier in the army is allowed to question and even disobey orders of his superior officers? What would happen in a war if, for example, the General Staff orders an attack, and one section of the army decides to obey and go into battle; another thinks that it is wrong to attack the enemy at this time and stays away from the battle; and a third section decides to quit the trenches and retreat to another position instead of going forward? . . .

Forces—Cadres

One of the main conditions for developing the initiative of the Units is the systematic development of *forces, cadres, leadership*. We must realize that without good leadership in the Units and Sections the Party cannot function properly. We must have in each Unit of our Party a core of comrades who are politically developed, capable of making, quickly and boldly, responsible decisions in the most intricate situations—comrades who are experienced, steeled, stable, who will not be weakened under any circumstances, who will follow the line of the Party.

Where are these forces trained? They are trained in militant actions of the masses. These militant, courageous members are our future leading forces. We must help them, encourage them, school them in action, teach them in training schools, persuade them to study and read fundamental Marxist-Leninist classics. We need thousands upon thousands of such forces, in order to be able to give leadership to the Leftward moving masses.

There are other important problems to be considered in connection with the question of forces:

First, the development and proper utilization of the old and new forces. We have spoken already about the necessity of developing forces, about building up a mighty force of new cadres. This is done in our Party by the following methods:

1. Conferences of functionaries, where discussions about basic problems help to develop our cadres; 2. Regular meetings of Unit and Section functionaries, where the decisions of the Party committees are clarified through discussion; 3. Workers' schools; 4. Section schools; 5. District schools; 6. National schools; 7. Study circles composed of promising comrades; 8. Individual study with the help of a more developed comrade.

It should be emphasized that in discussing the question of training forces, we have in mind not only the new forces, but also the old forces who need further training, and in some cases re-education.

The Party, in selecting the members for further training, examines the comrade for the qualifications needed for leadership—not only reliability, loyalty, capacity for development, but also whether he is a mass worker, or capable of being one. Our Party emphasizes the need of American, proletarian elements, the need of Negroes and women in the leadership.

The Party leadership must know its forces, must be able to assign each one to the place where he is most suitable and most needed.

Comrade Lenin, dealing with the problem of the proper utilization of forces, gives a splendid example. To enable the Party leadership,

> not only to advise (as this has been done until now), but really conduct the orchestra, one must know exactly who is playing first or second fiddle, and where, what instrument he was taught, where and how, where and why he plays out of tune (when the music begins to be trying to the ear), and what changes should be made in the orchestra so as to remedy the dissonance.

The systematic control of the carrying out of decisions and the proper application of Bolshevik self-criticism will help the Units and Sections to discover who is occupying a position which suits him, and who is in the wrong place, or who has no business to have any responsible position in the Party. We must know our forces. We must know who we can rely on, who can and who cannot, who will and who will not carry out decisions.

The second problem is the continuous control of the existing forces. We are conducting today, and will lead on a much larger scale tomorrow, mighty battles. In these struggles we are in the forefront. The fighting masses follow us, because they have confidence in the Party, because the Communists are brave, self-sacrificing. But if the workers see that one of the Communist leaders is a coward, or unable to lead them, this will have serious consequences. We cannot have in our leadership members who cannot stand up before the class enemy, who get panicky, who lose their heads in a serious situation. We must know whom we can trust under any circumstances, who will be shaken. . . .

RED SCARE

1

GITLOW'S TRIAL

Benjamin Gitlow, a leader of the Communist Labor Party, was among scores suddenly arrested on November 8, 1919, under orders of the New York State Senate's infamous Lusk Committee, which was investigating "seditious activity." Gitlow and three others were indicted for having published the left-wing "Manifesto" and "Program" (see above) a few months earlier. Following are excerpts from his trial. Gitlow v. New York became a celebrated one in American constitutional law. For in upholding his conviction, the Supreme Court inadvertently struck a blow for civil liberties: it asserted, in passing, that the First Amendment did apply to the states under the Fourteenth Amendment's due process clause. Gitlow's lawyer, incidentally, was the renowned Clarence Darrow.

COURT: Mr. Gitlow, you are not permitted to state what your views are or what you are, or what you think. You must confine yourself to an argument based upon the testi mony in the case.

GITLOW: Well, I will try to make it an impersonal argument. The socialists have always maintained, and the manifesto that has been printed in the Revolutionary Age maintains, that capitalism as it developed would be unable to solve the contradictions that spring up in the body politics of capi talism. What is capitalism? Capitalism is that system of society in which the means of production and distribution are owned by a few individuals for their own profit. You take the United States, for example. You take the large industrial plants. You take the land, you take the banks, you take the railroads, you take all of the factories that have to do with production, take all the means of distrib- ution, and you will discover that they are owned by a few individuals or corporations, by financial institutions, for the profits that can be derived from these institutions. . . .

COURT: I do not like to interrupt you, but there is no evidence presented upon that subject, and you are now referring to something that is not contained in the manifesto.

GITLOW: If your Honor please, the manifesto deals with the Imperialistic war, and this is a phase of imperialism.

COURT: It does not deal with the facts. It deals with assertions. You are attempting to state facts.

GITLOW: Well, in order to dispose of the surplus capital in various countries, the European war broke out, and the European war showed clearly the failure of capitalism to meet the situation in the world. What did we find? We found millions of workers facing one another, and being slaughtered on the fields of battle. They fought for four and a half years, and then a peace was concluded. We were informed that the war was one that was fought for democracy, and when peace was concluded and the Peace Treaty drawn up, we found out that all nations involved desired more territory, desired privileges in mines and ore concessions, desired to expand their territorial con trol, and we found that the question of democracy —

COURT: Again I must interrupt you, because you are stating mat ters which are not facts of this Court, and which the Court has no reason to believe are facts at all.

GITLOW: If your Honor please, the manifesto touches on that very clearly.

COURT: It touches on it, and you may use the language of the manifesto, but you may not make a speech beyond the language of the manifesto.

DARROW: Your Honor, he has a right to explain the meaning of it.

COURT: No, sir, he has no right to explain the meaning of the manifesto, because he is not subject to cross examination.

DARROW: I want to take exception again to the remarks of the Court on that question of cross examination. If he could not explain the meaning —

COURT: (Interrupting) He cannot explain the meaning?

DARROW: Then he can do nothing but read it.

COURT: He cannot explain the meaning of it, because he has not subjected himself to cross examination.

DARROW: I desire to except to the language of the Court and the ruling. . . .

GITLOW: Well, Gentlemen of the jury, I think when you read the manifesto of the Left Wing Section of the Socialist Party, you will understand what the fundamental principles involved in the manifesto are. I want you to realize that I believe in those principles, that I will support those prin ciples, and that I am not going to evade the issue. My whole life has been dedicated to the movement which I am in. No jails will change my opinion in that respect. I ask no clemency. I realize that as an individual I have a perfect right to my opinion, that I would be false to myself if I tried to evade that which I supported. Regardless of your verdict, I maintain that the principles of the Left Wing Manifesto and Program on the whole are correct, that capitalism is in a state of collapse, that capitalism has brought untold misery and hardships to the working men, that thousands of men in this democratic republic are in jails today on account of their views, suffering tortures and abuse, and nothing —

COURT: (Interrupting) Again the defendant must cease from mak ing statements. There is no evidence before the Court that anyone is in jail or suffering tortures and abuse. Proceed.

GITLOW: All I ask of you, gentlemen of the jury, is to consider the language of the manifesto, to realize that the manifesto stands for a new order in society, and a new form of government, and the communists today believe in a new form of society, and necessarily in a new form of government, and that they bend all their efforts in that direction.

JUDGE WEEKS: . . . Now, gentlemen of the jury, the Court must express its thanks to you for your services here. I can only say that I believe that your verdict is a proper and a just verdict, one that reflects credit upon your own sincerity and intelligence, and one which will be of distinct benefit to the country and the State. There must be a right in organized society to protect itself. Its citizens who accept the benefits of organized government, who obtain their education through the taxes collected by means of organized government, who have their opportunity of employment because of the protection given by organized government to the conduct of business, if they do not recognize that the government that fosters them, and which is created by law and based upon law, should only be overthrown by lawful methods, then it is difficult to see where civilization can be maintained and the benefits that come from civilization can be preserved. If there is to be no right of property recognized, except the might of "power to take, and power to keep," it is difficult to see that anything is left but savagery. The savage tribes possessed such property as they were able to retain by force of arms. And it is difficult for the Court to see how absolute destruction of private property can exist in an atmosphere of civilization. . . .

Idealism may be grand, it may be elevating in a sense that a drug that fills the brain with wonderful pictures is elevating temporarily, but idealism without practicality leaves the idealist just where the drug fiend is left when the influence of the drugs has passed. So long as we are on this mundane sphere, the only way that we can stand firm and erect in the sight of God is to keep our feet on the ground, only allowing our heads to be in the clouds. You must have something substantial under you, or you cannot stand, and the substance in this country is the government. If we cannot have a government under us and around us and protecting us, this country, of which we are so proud, is in danger of going where other countries have gone in the past. Gentlemen, your duty has been faithfully performed. I trust that the lesson that has been taught from your verdict is one that will reach out and influence and correct and save these misguided idealists who have allowed themselves to be carried beyond their depth into the stormy waters of a would-be-revolution.

2
AMERICAN LIBERTY
Art Young

In February 1920, at the height of the Red Scare, the following illustration appeared in the Liberator *magazine (about which see below). The artist, Art Young, was one of the great radical illustrators of the time.*

THE *LIBERATOR*

1
THE LIARS
Carl Sandburg

Following are several pieces from the Liberator, *which came out under loose Communist auspices between 1918 and 1925. They give an idea of its range and vitality.*
Carl Sandburg needs no introduction. Before he wrote his many volumes on Lincoln in the 1930s and went on to become a bard of the plain folk, he was a poet who identified with and wrote about radical causes, including the Communist one. "The Liars" appeared in the May 1919 issue.

A liar goes in fine clothes.
A liar goes in rags.
A liar is a liar, clothes or no clothes.
A liar is a liar and lives on the lies he tells
    and dies in a life of lies.
And the stonecutters earn a living—with lies—
    on the tombs of liars.

A liar looks 'em in the eye
And lies to a woman,
Lies to a man, a pal, a child, a fool.
And he is an old liar; we know him many years back.

    A liar lies to nations.
    A liar lies to the people.
A liar takes the blood of the people
And drinks this blood with a laugh and a lie,
    A laugh in his neck,
    A lie in his mouth.
And this liar is an old one; we know him many years back.
    He is straight as a dog's hind leg.
    He is straight as a corkscrew.
He is white as a black cat's foot at midnight.

The tongue of a man is tied on this,
On the liar who lies to nations,
The liar who lies to the people.
The tongue of a man is tied on this
And ends: To hell with 'em all.
    To hell with 'em all.

It's a song hard as a riveter's hammer,
    Hard as the sleep of a crummy hobo,
    Hard as the sleep of a lousy doughboy,

Twisted as a shell-shock idiot's gibber.
The liars met where the doors were locked.
They said to each other: Now for war.
The liars fixed it and told 'em: Go.

Across their tables they fixed it up,
Behind their doors away from the mob.
And the guns did a job that nicked off millions.
The guns blew seven million off the map,
The guns sent seven million west.
Seven million shoving up the daisies.
Across their tables they fixed it up,

The liars who lie to nations.
And now
Out of the butcher's job
And the boneyard junk the maggots have cleaned,
Where the jaws of skulls tell the jokes of war ghosts,
Out of this they are calling now: Let's go back where we were.
    Let us run the world again, us, us.
Where the doors are locked the liars say: Wait and we'll cash in again.

So I hear The People talk.
I hear them tell each other:
    Let the strong men be ready.
    Let the strong men watch.
    Let your wrists be cool and your head clear.
    Let the liars get their finish,
    The liars and their waiting game, waiting a day again
    To open the doors and tell us: War! get out to your war again.

So I hear The People tell each other:
    Look at to-day and to-morrow.
    Fix this clock that nicks off millions
    When The Liars say it's time.
    Take things in your own hands.
        To hell with 'em all,
    The liars who lie to nations,
    The liars who lie to The People.

2

THE DOMINANT WHITE
Claude McKay

McKay was a founding writer of the Harlem Renaissance. He had already made a name for himself in his native Jamaica before coming to America and settling in New York City. Thanks to Liberator *editor Max Eastman, who befriended him, McKay began working and writing for the magazine. He was one of several Harlem intellectuals who belonged to the African Blood Brotherhood before joining the Communist movement. His black nationalist sentiments are reflected in the poem below, from the May 1919 issue. Most of the next fourteen years he spent in Europe, including the Soviet Union; he returned home disillusioned with Communism and politics in general.*

God gave you the power to build and help and lift;
    But you proved prone to persecute and slay
And from the high and noble course to drift
    Into the darkness from the light of day.
He gave you law and order, strength of will

The lesser people of the world to lead;
You chose to break and crush them through life's mill.
  But you've proved unworthy of your trust,
God—He shall humble you down to the dust.

You have betrayed the black, maligned the yellow;
  But what else could we hope of you, who set
The hand even of your own against his fellow,
  To stem the dire tide that threatens yet?
You called upon the name of your false god
  To lash our wounded flesh with knotted cords
And trample us into the blood-stained sod,
  And justified your deeds with specious words:
Oh! you have proved unworthy of your trust,
And God shall humble you down to the dust.

The pain you gave us nothing can assuage,
  Who hybridized a proud and virile race,
Bequeathed to it a bastard heritage
  And made the black ashamed to see his face.
You ruined him, put doubt in his heart,
  You set a sword between him and his kin,
And preached to him, with simple, lying art
  About the higher worth of your white skin!
Oh White Man! You have trifled with your trust,
And God shall humble you down to the dust.

You blinded go, afraid to see the Truth,
  Closing your eyes to and denying Beauty;
You stultify the dreams of visioned youth
  All in the prostituted name of Duty.
You place your Seers with madmen, fools and rogues,
  Their words distort and twist, despise their creed:
You choose instead the little demagogues
  That will uphold you in your shameless greed:
Because you've proved unworthy of your trust,
Oh, He shall humble you—down to the dust.

3

THEORY AND PRACTICE
Stuart Davis

*Stuart Davis was an avant-garde painter in the Cubist mode and a first-rate illustrator for
revolutionary publications. The following excellent example of his talents appeared in the
July 1920 issue of the* Liberator.

Drawn by Stuart Davis.

"My God, this is a free country, ain't it? If a man don't like his job he can quit."

"The dogs ought to be driven back to work at the point of a gun!"

"My God, this is a free country, ain't it? If a man don't like his job he can quit."

"The dogs ought to be driven back to work at the point of gun!" DRAWN BY STUART DAVIS.

4

NOW WE CAN BEGIN
Crystal Eastman

Crystal Eastman, Max's sister and quite as much a rebel (their parents were Congregational ministers of antinomian bent), had been a radical feminist until the Bolshevik Revolution made her a feminist radical. For a while she coedited the Liberator *with Max. She was a fine political journalist, as this remarkably prescient essay from the December 1920 issue reveals. She died eight years later, in the prime of her life.*

Most women will agree that August 23 [1920], the day when the Tennessee legislature finally enacted the Federal suffrage amendment, is a day to begin with, not a day to end with. Men are saying perhaps, "Thank God, this everlasting women's fight is over!" But women, if I know them, are saying, "Now at last we can begin." In fighting for the right to vote most women have tried to be either non-committal or thoroughly respectable on every other subject. Now they can say what they are really after; and what they are after, in common with all the rest of the struggling world, is *freedom*.

Freedom is a large word.

Many feminists are socialists, many are communists, not a few are active leaders in these movements. But the true feminist, no matter how far to the left she may be in the revolutionary movement, sees the woman's battle as distinct in its objects and different in its methods from the workers' battle for industrial freedom. She knows, of course, that the vast majority of women as well as men are without property and are of necessity bread and butter slaves under a system of society which allows the very sources of life to be privately owned by a few, and she counts herself a loyal soldier in the working class army that is marching to overthrow that system. But as a feminist she also knows that the whole of women's slavery is not summed up in the profit system, nor her complete emancipation assured by the downfall of capitalism.

Women's freedom, in the feminist sense, can be fought for and conceivably won before the gates open into industrial democracy. On the other hand, women's freedom, in the feminist sense, is not inherent in the communist ideal. All feminists are familiar with the revolutionary leader who "can't see" the women's movement. "What's the matter with the women? My wife's all right," he says. And his wife, one usually finds, is raising his children in a Bronx flat or a dreary suburb, to which he returns occasionally for food and sleep when all possible excitement and stimulus have been wrung from the fight. If we should graduate into communism tomorrow this man's attitude to his wife would not be changed. The proletarian dictatorship may or may not free women. We must begin now to enlighten the future dictators.

What, then, is "the matter with women?" What is the problem of women's freedom? It seems to me to be this: how to arrange the world so that women can be human beings, with a chance to exercise their infinitely varied gifts in infinitely varied ways, instead of being destined by the accident of their sex to one field of activity—housework and child-raising. And second, if and when they choose housework and child-raising, to have that occupation recognized by the world as work, requiring a definite economic reward and not merely entitling the performer to be dependent on some man.

This is not the whole of feminism, of course, but is enough to begin with. "Oh, don't begin with economics," my friends often protest, "Woman does not live by bread alone. What she needs first of all is a free soul." And I can agree that women will never be great until they achieve a certain emotional freedom, a strong healthy egotism, and some un-personal sources of joy— that in this inner sense we cannot make women free by changing her economic status. What we can do, however, is to create conditions of outward freedom in which a free woman's soul can be born and grow. It is these outward conditions with which an organized feminist movement must concern itself.

Freedom of choice in occupation and individual economic independence for women: How shall we approach this next feminist objective? First, by breaking down all remaining barriers, actual as well as legal, which make it difficult for women to enter or succeed in the various professions, to go into and get on in business, to learn trades and practice them, to join trades unions. Chief among these remaining barriers is inequality in pay. Here the ground is already broken. This is the easiest part of our program.

Second, we must institute a revolution in the early training and education of both boys and girls. It must be womanly as well as manly to earn your own living, to stand on your own feet. And it must be manly as well as womanly to know how to cook and sew and clean and take care of yourself in the ordinary exigencies of life. I need not add that the second part of this revolution will be more passionately resisted than the first. Men will not give up their privilege or helplessness without a struggle. The average man has a carefully cultivated ignorance about household matters—from what to do with the crumbs to the grocer's telephone number—a sort of cheerful inefficiency which protects him better than the reputation for having a violent temper. It was his mother's fault in the beginning, but even as a boy he was quick to see how a general reputation for being "no good around the house" would serve him throughout life, and half-consciously he began to cultivate that helplessness until to-day it is the despair of feminist wives.

A growing number of men admire the woman who has a job, and, especially since the cost of living doubled, rather like the idea of their own wives contributing to the family income by outside work. And of course for generations there have been whole towns full of wives who are forced by the bitterest necessity to spend the same hours at the factory that their husbands spend. But these bread-winning wives have not yet developed home-making husbands. When the two come home from the factory the man sits down while his wife gets supper, and he does so with exactly the same sense of foreordained right as if he were "supporting her." Higher up in the economic scale the same thing is true. The business or professional woman who is married, perhaps engages a cook, but the responsibility is not shifted, it is still hers. She "hires and fires," she orders meals, she does the buying, she meets and resolves all domestic crises, she takes charge of moving, furnishing, settling. She may be, like her husband, a busy executive at her office all day, but unlike him, she is also an executive in a small way every night and morning at home. Her noon hour is spent in planning, and too often her Sundays and holidays are spent in "catching up."

Two business women can "make a home" together without either one being over-burdened or over-bored. It is because they both know how and both feel responsible. But it is a rare man who can marry one of them and continue the home-making partnership. Yet there is nothing essentially different in the combination. Two self-supporting adults decide to make a home together: if both are women it is a pleasant partnership, more fun than work; if one is a man, it is almost never a partnership—the woman simply adds running the home to her regular outside job. Unless she is very strong, it is too much for her, she gets tired and bitter over it, and finally perhaps gives up her outside work and condemns herself to the tiresome half-job of housekeeping for two.

Cooperative schemes and electrical devices will simplify the business of home-making, but they will not get rid of it entirely. As far as we can see ahead people will always want homes, and a happy home cannot be had without a certain amount of rather monotonous work and responsibility. How can we change the nature of man so that he will honorably share that work and responsibility and thus make the home-making enterprise a song instead of a burden? Most assuredly not by laws or revolutionary decrees. Perhaps we must cultivate or simulate a little of that highly prized helplessness ourselves. But fundamentally it is a problem of education, of early training—we must bring up feminist sons.

Sons? Daughters? They are born of women—how can women be free to choose their occupation, at all times cherishing their economic independence, unless they stop having children? This is a further question for feminism. If the feminist program goes to pieces on the arrival of the first baby, it is false and useless. For ninety-nine out of every hundred women want children, and seventy-five out of every hundred want to take care of their own children, or at any rate so closely superintend their care as to make any other full-time occupation impossible for at least ten or fifteen years. Is there any such thing then as freedom of choice in occupation for women? And is not the family the inevitable economic unit and woman's individual economic independence, at least during that period, out of the question?

The feminist must have an answer to these questions, and she has. The immediate feminist program must include voluntary motherhood. Freedom of any kind for women is hardly worth considering unless it is assumed that they know how to control the size of their families. "Birth control" is just as elementary an essential in our propaganda as "equal pay." Women are to have children when they want them, that's the first thing. That assures some freedom of occupational choice; those who do not wish to be mothers will not have an undesired occupation thrust upon them by accident, and those who do wish to be mothers may choose in a general way how many years of their lives they will devote to the occupation of child-raising.

But is there any way of insuring a woman's economic independence while child-bearing is her chosen occupation? Or must she sink into that dependent state from which, as we all know, it is so hard to rise again? That brings us to the fourth feature of our program—motherhood endowment. It seems that the only way we can keep mothers free, at least in a capitalist society, is by the establishment of a principle that the occupation of raising children is peculiarly and directly a service to society, and that the mother upon whom the necessity and privilege of performing this service naturally falls is entitled to an adequate economic reward from the political government. It is idle to talk of real economic independence of women unless this principle is accepted. But with a generous endowment of motherhood provided by legislation, with all the laws against voluntary motherhood and education in its methods repealed, with the feminist ideal of education accepted in home and school, and with all special barriers removed in every field of human activity, there is no reason why woman should become almost a human thing.

It will be time enough then to consider whether she has a soul.

ToWARD PROLETARIAN ART
Irwin Granich

Irwin Granich, better known in the years to come as Michael Gold—he changed his name when the Communist movement went underground—was born to a poor Romanian-Jewish family on New York's Lower East Side (his youth is brilliantly recounted in his fictive memoir, Jews Without Money*), where he imbibed his fierce radicalism. A school dropout, he became a gifted writer in the hard-boiled proletarian mode. The ferocity of his devotion to the Party plus his polemical abilities—no one defended proletarian art with such vehemence and consistency, beginning with this piece in the February 1921* Liberator*—made him an editor and critic to contend with over the next four decades.*

IN THE DEPTHS

I can feel beforehand the rebellion and contempt with which many true and passionate artists laboring in all humility will greet claims for a defined art. It is not mere aristocratic scorn for the world and its mass-yearnings that is at the root of the artists' sneer at "propaganda." It is a deeper, more universal feeling than that. It is the consciousness that in art Life is speaking out its heart at last, and that to censor the poor brute-murmurings would be sacrilege. Whatever they are, they are significant and precious, and to stifle the meanest of Life's moods taking form in the artist would be death. Artists are bitter lovers of Life, and in beauty or horror she is ever dear to them. I wish to speak no word against their holy passion, therefore, and I regard with reverence the scarred and tortured figures of the artist-saints of time, battling against their demons, bearing each a ponderous cross, receiving solemnly in decadence, insanity, filth and fear the special revelation Life has given them.

I respect the suffering and creations of all artists. They are deeper to me than theories artists have clothed their naked passions in. I would oppose no contrary futile dogmas. I would show only, if I can, what manner of vision Life has vouchsafed me, what word has descended on me in the midst of this dark pit of experience, what form my days and nights have taken, as they proceed in strange nebular whirling toward the achievement of new worlds of art.

I was born in a tenement. That tall, sombre mass, holding its freight of obscure human destinies, is the pattern in which my being has been cast. It was in a tenement that I first heard the sad music of humanity rise to the stars. The sky above the air shaft was all my sky; and the voices of the tenement-neighbors in the air shaft were the voices of all my world. There, in suffering youth, I feverishly sought God and found Man. In the tenement Man was revealed to me, Man, who is Life speaking. I saw him, not as he has been pictured by the elder poets, groveling or sinful or romantic or falsely god-like, but one sunk in a welter of humble, realistic cares; responsible, instinctive, long-suffering and loyal; sad and beaten, yet reaching out beautifully and irresistibly like a natural force for the mystic food and freedom that are Man's.

All that I know of Life I learned in the tenement. I saw love there in an old mother who wept for her sons. I saw courage there in a sick worker who went to the factory every morning. I saw beauty in little children playing in the dim hallways, and despair and hope and hate incarnated in the simple figures of those who lived there with me. The tenement is in my blood. When I think it is the tenement thinking. When I hope it is the tenement hoping. I am not an individual; I am all the tenement group poured into me during those early years of my spiritual travail.

Why should we artists born in tenements go beyond them for our expression? Can we go beyond them? "Life burns in both camps," in the tenements and in the palaces, but can we understand that which is not our very own? We, who are sprung from the workers, can we so easily forget the milk that nourished us and the hearts that gave us growth? Need we apologize or be ashamed if we express in art that manifestation of Life which is so exclusively ours, the life of the toilers? What is art? Art is the tenement pouring out its soul through us, its most sensitive and articulate sons and daughters. What is Life? Life for us has been the tenement that bore us and molded us through years of meaningful pain.

THE OLD MOODS

A boy of the tenements feels the slow, mighty movement that is art stir within him. He broods darkly on the Life around him. He wishes to understand and express it, but does not know his wish. He turns to books instead. There he finds reflections, moods, philosophies, but they do not bring him peace. They are myriad and bewildering, they are all the voices of solitaries lost and distracted in Time.

The old moods, the old poetry, fiction, painting, philosophies, were the creations of proud and baffled solitaries. The tradition has arisen in a capitalist world that even its priests of art must be lonely beasts of prey—competitive and unsocial. Artists have too long deemed themselves the aristocrats of mankind. That is why they have all become so sad and spiritually sterile. What clear, strong faith do our intellectuals believe in now? They have lost everything in the vacuum of logic where they dwell. The thought of God once sustained their feet like a rock, but they slew God. Reason was once their star, but they are sick with Reason. They have turned to the life of the moods, to the worship of beauty and sensation, but they cannot live there happily. For Beauty is a cloud, a mist, a light that comes and goes, a vague water changing rapidly. The soul of Man needs some sure and permanent thing to believe, to be devoted to and to trust. The people have that profound Truth to believe in—their instincts. But the intellectuals have become contemptuous of the people, and are therefore sick to death.

The people live, love, work, fight, pray, laugh; they accept all, they accept themselves and the immortal urgings of Life within them. They know reality. They know bread is necessary to them; they know love and hate. What do the intellectuals know?

The elder artists have all been sick. They have no roots in the people. The art ideals of the capitalist world isolated each artist as in a solitary cell, there to brood and suffer silently and go mad. We artists of the people will not face Life and Eternity alone. We will face them from among the people.

We must lose ourselves again in their sanity. We must learn through solidarity with the people what Life is.

Masses are never pessimistic. Masses are never sterile. Masses are never far from the earth. Masses are never far from the heavens. Masses go on—they are the eternal truth. Masses are simple, strong and sure. They are never lost for long; they have always a goal in each age.

What have the intellectuals done? They have created, out of their solitary pain, confusions, doubts and complexities. But the masses have not heard them; and Life has gone on.

The masses are still primitive and clean, and artists must turn to them for strength again. The primitive sweetness, the primitive calm, the primitive ability to create simply and without fever or ambition, the primitive satisfaction and self-sufficiency—they must be found again.

The masses know what Life is, and they live on in gusto and joy. The lot of man seems good to them despite everything; they work, they bear children, they sing and play. But intellectuals have become bored with the primitive monotony of Life—with the deep truths and instincts.

The boy in the tenement must not learn of their art. He must stay in the tenement and create a new and truer one there.

THE REVOLUTION

The Social Revolution in the world today arises out of the deep need of the masses for the old primitive group life. Too long have they suppressed that instinct most fundamental to their nature—the instinct of human solidarity. Man turns bitter as a competitive animal. In the Orient, where millions live and labor and die, peace has brooded in the air for centuries. There have never been individuals there, but family clans and ancestor worshipers, so that men have felt themselves part of a mystic group extending from the dim past to the unfolding future. Men have gathered peace from that bond and strength to support the sorrow of Life. From the solidarity learned in the family group they have learned the solidarity of the universe, and have created creeds that fill every crevice of the universe with the family love and trust.

The Social Revolution of today is not the mere political movement artists despise it as. It is Life at its fullest and noblest. It is the religion of the masses, articulate at last. It is that religion which says that Life is one, that Men are one, through all their flow of change and differentiation; that the destiny of Man is a common one and that no individual need bear on his weak shoulders alone the crushing weight of the eternal riddle. None of us can fail, none of us can succeed.

The Revolution, in its secular manifestations of strike, boycott, mass-meeting, imprisonment, sacrifice, agitation, martyrdom, organization, is thereby worthy of the religious devotion of the artist. If he records the humblest moment of that drama in poem, story or picture or symphony, he is realizing Life more profoundly than if he had concerned himself with some transient mood. The ocean is greater than the tiny streams that trickle down to be lost in its godhood. The Revolution is the permanent mood in which Man strains to goodness in the face of an unusual eternity; it is greater than the minor passing moods of men. . . .

6

EXPLANATIONS AND APOLOGIES
Floyd Dell

Though he had long been connected with left intellectuals, novelist and poet Floyd Dell (he had already written what was to be his best-known book, Mooncalf*) was never really political. He was essentially a bohemian, and it was as a bohemian of the Far Left that he became an editor of radical journals, including the* Liberator. *Inevitably, his approach to art got him into trouble with the naturalist-proletarian school defended by Mike Gold (Irwin Granich), his colleague on the magazine. Dell waited until the June 1922 issue to rebut Gold. He soon after drifted away from Communism and politics in general.*

I have got myself into trouble again. This time it is because I have publicly referred to one of my editorial colleagues, Comrade Mike Gold, as a member of the middle class. . . . Comrade Mike, I think, really cherishes the romantic delusion that he belongs to the working class. But the fact is that Comrade Mike is a literary man, an intellectual, and a member of the salaried middle class. That his literary tendencies are, like Zola's, in the direction of describing the lot of the poor and the oppressed, that his intellectual sympathies are all in favor of the working class in its struggle with capitalism, and that his salary, such as it is, comes from a revolutionary journal, do not affect the facts of the case as I have stated them. The poet Wordsworth was, in his early life at least, a revolutionist, and throughout his life he lived on something like three hundred dollars a year. He was not a workingman for all that. He was a poet, a member of the intelligentsia, and a "boorjooi." And so is Comrade Mike.

And so are we all, in our degree. And, if you ask me, there is nothing to be ashamed of in that. In that fact, it seems to me, lies whatever value we may have to the world, including the revolutionary movement. By a happy accident we have been set free from the necessity of toiling eight to fourteen hours a day with our hands. We are set free—for what? For whatever we choose. If we choose to make use of our freedom—supposing we have abilities of that kind—to exploit our fellows, than our relation to the revolutionary movement is almost necessarily a hostile one. If we choose to make use of our freedom to defend the present system of society, we are active enemies of the revolutionary movement. But we haven't chosen to make such uses of our freedom. We wish the revolutionary movement well. We would like to help it along.

Well what can we do? It happens that none of the group to which I am referring are conspicuously possessed of abilities as organizers, and so are useless in the more immediate and practical way in which we might be of use. What then? We can explain, encourage and teach. We can put in words and pictures, persuasively or eloquently, the thoughts of the workers. We can in some sense be their spokesmen. And if we are really of any use in this direction, it is precisely because we are not workers ourselves. It is because we have had leisure to devote to the art of writing or the art of making pictures, so that we can do such things well. If we can't write better articles or draw better pictures dealing with the miners than the miners themselves can, we have no business writing and drawing pictures. We ought to be in the mines ourselves or washing dishes in a restaurant, or doing something useful.

And what of it? This. That we are, I think—at least I am sure that Comrade Mike is—doing this peculiar task of ours very well indeed. And I think he ought to be proud and not ashamed of himself as a member of the middle class. He can look a striking miner in the eye and say, "The leisure you have given me hasn't been misspent. In fact, if you'd pay more attention to our magazine, and boom our circulation so that I could have a decent salary, it would be money well invested." But Comrade Mike is for some reason ashamed of not being a workingman. At least, I deduce that from his conversation and writings. And so he is in awe of the workingman when he meets him and says extravagant things in praise of him.

It is that I take issue with. If it were as glorious to work twelve hours a day as Comrade Mike appears to think, there would be no revolutionary movement in this country. And if the proletarians before whose working ability Comrade Mike has been rhetorically abashing himself in awe and worship were half as anxious for leisure as Mike and I are, there would be a revolution next week. Comrade Mike has come back from the strike region in a religious mood. He tells us that we are a lot of poor aesthetes, and that our habit of sitting around and talking, talking about ideas, disgusts him. Well, for my part, I want workingmen to have a chance to sit around and talk and talk about ideas. I want them to become aesthetes. I am not in the least awed or worshipful about the strength that can endure twelve hours of hard physical labor. I have done just enough labor to know that the less of it there is, within reasonable limits, the better. I most emphatically do not wish to become like those proletarian heroes that Mike has been telling us about. And I most earnestly do desire that they may become more like me—and Mike.

And—what I think Comrade Mike fails to observe—that is rather what they want too. They are envious, and quite properly envious, of our middle class leisure. . . .

7
EVOLUTION OF THE AMERICAN PEASANT
Robert Minor

Robert Minor, son of Texas, was a very effective cartoonist for the Communist Party. How effective we can see in the following example, from the January 1924 Liberator, *capturing as it does the brutal conditions that faced farmers whom the prosperity of the 1920s was leaving behind. Minor was also a Party functionary. By the end of the decade he had just about given up art in order to devote full time to political affairs. He rose high enough to serve briefly as General Secretary.*

8
AN AMERICAN TESTAMENT
Joseph Freeman

In his mid-teens Joseph Freeman was already a left-wing Socialist, becoming an enthusiastic Communist with the Revolution a few years later. Throughout his Party career he edited several of its publications, starting with the Liberator, *and served as its all-around literary factotum. The selection below is from his first-rate memoir of 1936,* An American Testament *(which has been too long out of print). The Party expelled him a year after its publication because he made the mistake of admitting that he once admired Leon Trotsky.*

The artists and writers who now contributed to the *Liberator* had settled the
problem of art and revolution in a very general way. They thought they had
broken with bourgeois culture and were ready to serve the organized struggle of the working class. But the solution of one problem often means the
creation of new ones. When the Party took over the *Liberator* we felt that one
period in American radical literature had closed, and another had opened.
The *Masses* and *Liberator* as we had known it since 1913 had died. That publication had never been officially attached to any political group. Its contribu-
tors wrote on behalf of socialism, anarchism, syndicalism or communism as
individuals, and the magazine printed their conflicting views. Moreover, its
writers and artists were "universal" men who themselves dealt both with
poetry and with politics. John Reed wrote verses and reported wars; Floyd
Dell did book reviews and defended the Bolshevik Revolution; Max Eastman
tried to interpret politics and composed sonnets; Bob Minor drew cartoons
and commented on current events; Arturo Giovannitti led strikes, wrote
heroic verse and reported trials. There was among the members of the prewar group a division of mind but no division of labor; they wrote on the
assumption that nothing human was alien to them.

Under the aegis of the Party this tradition was of necessity ended. The
new course was symbolized by the existence of two separate groups of "associate editors," whose names appeared in the editorial box in two separate
columns with distinct headings. The "political editors" were for the most part
members of the Central Committee of the Communist Party—among them
C. E. Ruthenberg, William Z. Foster, Ludwig Lore, James P. Cannon, Jay
Lovestone, M. J. Olgin; the "art editors" were for the most part members of
the old *Masses* and *Liberator* group including Floyd Dell, Arturo Giovannitti,
Boardman Robinson, William Gropper, Lydia Gibson, Hugo Gellert, Claude
McKay, Michael Gold. Not all of these were active, however; some were
abroad, others lived out of town. The Party, quite naturally, wished to keep
the direction of editorial policy in its own hands; the realm of art, presumably less serious, was left for the artists. . . .

One of my fellow editors on the *Liberator*, listed in the political group, was
the red-cheeked, dark-eyed, buxom Clarissa Ware. Like Bill Dunne, Foster,
Ruthenberg and Minor, she was an "Aryan" of native American stock, a
descendant of the Pilgrim Fathers. Her family tree went back directly to both
Miles Standish and John Alden. She had come from a well-to-do home and a
university to work in the communist movement. In her presence the "freedom of woman," about which you heard so much in Greenwich Village, took
on new meaning. She flaunted no fantastic symbols—no batik blouses, san-
dals or mannish clothes. She dressed conventionally; even her bobbed black
hair, tousled in thick curls, was heavier than was the fashion. She was a
healthy, handsome, laughing woman full of the charms called feminine, yet
did not burn her candles at both ends. She had a husband and a daughter of

four whom she occasionally brought to Party headquarters. The child was an energetic little devil who crawled across my desk, ruining sonnets, book reviews, and articles on trade-union policy. Once Louis Engdahl looked up at Clarissa Ware and said with his mournful humor:

"Is that steam engine a boy or a girl?"

"Ask her," Clarissa said.

"What are you, darling?"

The kid stopped tearing an editorial I had left in the typewriter. "I'm a communist," she said.

"More truth than poetry!" Engdahl roared, laughing.

At work you did not think of Clarissa Ware's patrician background, or her personal charms, or that she was a woman. In the ranks you were first, last and always a comrade. That was an old tradition of the revolutionary movement, which had set the emancipation of woman as a corollary of the emancipation of labor and of the oppressed races. Before general equality was to be achieved in society as a whole, there was to be equality in the movement itself. We knew the heroic stories of Louise Michel of the Paris Commune, of Vera Figner, Vera Zassulich and Krupskaya in Russia, of Mother Jones and Mother Bloor in America. In the ranks there were no distinctions of race or sex. Differences in position, function or influence were individual. We cited the Marxian aphorism: from each according to his abilities, to each according to his needs. That was meant for the future communist society. Meantime you were supposed to practice it as far as possible within the movement today. The "sex war," of which you heard so much in the Village, and among the bourgeois feminists, and in the novels of D. H. Lawrence, now the rage among the intellectuals, was resolved in Party circles by the common work of men and women for a common cause which transcended sex. Yet communists were neither automatons nor angels. They loved with less fanfare and pretense than Villagers, with less hypocrisy than Babbitts, but they, too, loved.

Occasionally, some functionary would rationalize his male jealousy in political terms. Instead of calling his rival in love a bastard he would call him a social democrat, and with sincere self-delusion would vote against his proposals. In the long run, however, such conflicts had no effect on Party policy. Communism had no Pompadours; the welfare of the movement transcended all personal relations. As might be expected, psychoanalysts of my acquaintance explained this in their own jargon. Power, they said, dissolves love. In warfare of every kind, the libido is diverted from the love object to the leader, who, needless to say, is the father-image.

Because of her special training and education, Clarissa Ware was put in charge of the Party's research department. Her own inclinations impelled her to specialize in the problems of the American foreign-born worker. These inclinations were determined by a need for bridging the gap between her patrician American background and the proletariat with which she identified herself. In the same way Bob Minor, nurtured in the race prejudices of Texas, overcame his "original sin" by becoming the Party's specialist on the Negro problem. My own immigrant background roused my interest in Clarissa Ware's work, and I asked her to do a piece for the *Liberator* which I entitled *Makers of America*. Here she maintained that the core of the American people was the millions of workers who had come from far lands, dug our coal, molded our steel, laid the railway tracks, ran the textile mills; who with their brawn and sweat and blood had built up the gigantic industries of America.

Shortly after this article appeared, Clarissa Ware was operated on for pancreatitis. She died suddenly, in her early thirties. Her last words were:

"I have made a good fight, haven't I?"

To make a good fight for the new society was the pride of the communist; Clarissa Ware's question uttered the attitude of many women in the ranks— the zealous and talented Rose Pastor Stokes; the gray-haired, smiling, enormously energetic Mother Bloor, who organized farmers and workers, yet took time off in Moscow to interview the Danish novelist Martin Andersen Nexö for her "boys" on the *Liberator*; the pale, hard-working, devoted organizers like Rose Wortis, precursors of a new type of woman which Party work was to develop in America.

THE *NEW MASSES*

1
A NEW CONTINENT
Mike Gold

The New Masses *got under way in May 1926. Not until July did editor Mike Gold say what he expected of the magazine, successor to the old* Masses *and the* Liberator. *He did so in response to a piece by John Dos Passos in the same issue stating that he would like to see a* New Masses *"full of introspection and doubt that would be like a piece of litmus paper to test things by." "I don't think it is skepticism to say that November 1917 [the Bolshevik Revolution] is in the past. It shows an incredible faith in the word* New *and the word* Masses."

What is American life like in this hour?

America today, I believe, offers the honest young writers only one choice—Revolt!

No humane and sensitive artist can assent to this vast Roman orgy of commercialism, this wholesale prostitution of mind, this vast empire of cheapness and shallowness and hypocrisy that forms the current America.

No decent creative mind can be permanently happy worshipping the Dollar Bill, or taking "spiritual" commands from Mr. J. P. Morgan, who dictates our American environment.

Revolt is the organ-bass that softly or harshly throbs through the young literature of America today. We are not satisfied. We are not part of this American empire. We repudiate it if only in the name of art. We revolt! . . .

Writers are queer, variable folk; liable to many accidents of the spirit. Yet it is a harsh yet kind mother who keeps these sensitive children in the main path of sanity and greatness—as she kept Walt Whitman.

I want the *New Masses* to explore in this world, not the other. Both worlds exist in America, but one is dying while the other is being born.

How good it feels to be a pioneer in a world so new that even literary men deny its existence. But how can they know it unless they become as little children and learn?

I would like the *New Masses* to be the bridge to this the great part of our lives.

I am an internationalist, but I stand with John Dos Passos in his declaration that American writers in general, and the *New Masses* writers in particular, ought to set sail for a new discovery of America.

Yes, let us explore this continent. Let us lose ourselves in this dangerous and beautiful jungle of steel and stone. Let us forget the past. Shakespeare, Dante, Shelley, and even Bernard Shaw—for here are virgin paths their feet could not have trod in time and space. A gorgeous fresh adventure waits for us—no one has been this way before.

And what is the plan we shall follow? What compass shall we steer by? What North Star shall our eyes study as we move through the storm?

Introspection and doubt, answers John Dos Passos—these will be our stars. Moscow and revolution—these are what he charges I would like to slip into the compass-box.

I deny that that is my answer to you, friend John. . . .

What I deny is that I or anyone else demands of young American writers that they take their "spiritual" commands from Moscow. No one demands that; for it is not necessary. . . . Moscow could not have created John Reed, Upton Sinclair, Jack London, Max Eastman, or Horace Traubel. American life created them. It will create others like them and better. Let us forget Moscow in this discussion. Let us think of America . . . which means it will not be a magazine of Communism, or Moscow, but a magazine of American experiment—only let's not experiment in the minor aesthetic cults.

And I want a conscious exploration—with a compass.

2

LETTER TO THE *New Masses*

Max Eastman

Gold asked his mentor, Max Eastman, who had been abroad for years, to be a contributing editor of the new magazine. Gold's hope was that Eastman remained a loyal Communist, his radical individualism notwithstanding. There were intimations, however, that he had befriended Trotsky, who was rapidly going down to defeat in his struggle with Stalin. The extent to which Eastman alienated the Party and hence the magazine is brought out in this excerpt from his entertaining autobiography, Love and Revolution, *published in 1964, decades after he went over to extreme conservatism, becoming a senior editor of* Reader's Digest.

The active editors in those first issues were: Egmont Arens, Joseph Freeman, Hugo Gellert, Michael Gold, James Rorty, and John Sloan. These names suggested the same mixture of "free expression" with adherence to a program of socialist revolution over which I had presided in the *Liberator*, though here nobody seemed to be presiding. I had received a letter in France asking me to become a contributing editor, and had agreed. Indeed, I had contributed while still in Antibes translations from the Russian of two stories by Isaak Babel, a couple of book reviews, and my rendering in English verse of Pushkin's *Message to Siberia*. And now, on arriving in New York, I attended an editorial meeting at Egmont Arens's penthouse apartment—a rough-hewn penthouse at 120 East Sixteenth Street—and was promoted from "Contributing Editor" to "member of the Executive Board." Most of those present were old friends of mine, and I attended two or three meetings and contributed during the summer three articles made out of chapters of *Marx and Lenin*, which was still unpublished in America.

My theoretical heresies in these articles gave the party heads the pretext they wanted to attack me with intemperate vituperation, and the editors, now dominated by Gold, Gellert and Freeman, made it clear that no more "free expression" on my part was wanted in the *New Masses*. My letter of resignation, dated January 27, 1928, tells the story:

The New Masses

Dear Comrades:

I herewith resign from the Executive Board and withdraw from my association with the *New Masses*, and I want to explain my action briefly.

When I was invited to join the Executive Board, its members were aware of my association with the opposition in the Russian Communist Party. They were also aware of my theoretical position as set forth in my book, *Marx and Lenin: The Science of Revolution*. Their invitation implied that the *New Masses* was independent of the dictation of the Workers (Communist) Party and the International, from which they understood I had been expelled. They had, moreover, from the beginning advertised the *New Masses* as independent of all dictation—a "free revolutionary magazine." It was with this understanding that I joined it.

At the invitation of the acting editor, I published in the magazine, among other things, an article on Sacco-Vanzetti and the relations between anarchism and the science of revolution, and an article called "Lenin Was an Engineer." Although neither of these articles touched even indirectly the questions at issue between the opposition and the ruling group in the Communist parties, they were objected to by the heads of the American Party. I was denounced for my "lies" in large type every day for over a week in the *Daily Worker*. Instead of offering me space to reply, or even to continue explaining my ideas, the *New Masses* gave me to understand that no further contributions entailing any expression of my theoretical position would be accepted.

My offer to explain the conflict between the opposition and the ruling group in the Russian Communist Party, giving some supporter of the ruling group an opportunity to reply to me in the same issue, was also declined. A previous invitation to review the philosophical books of Lenin and Bukharin was revoked. It was suggested that I write an innocuous "literary" book review.

It goes without saying that I am not going to contribute articles without remuneration to a magazine that denies me the expression of my views.

I withdraw from the Executive Board, because I think a magazine with this confused and pussy-footing policy is harmful to the advancement of a genuine revolutionary culture in America. No practical person will deny the value of a party magazine, and no person understanding the present situation in America will deny the value of a magazine of independent expression and criticism. But a magazine which announces itself independent, and then obeys the dictation of the party heads through fear of the loss of patronage or circulation, or through mere fear of stating the facts of life, is worse than useless. A professedly "free" and "revolutionary" magazine which will pass in silence such a historic event as the arrest and banishment under police surveillance of the entire leadership of the opposition in the Russian Communist Party—not through fear of taking sides, but through fear of telling the American workers and radicals about both sides—is merely a new weakness and a new deception.

Yours sincerely,

LABOR

1

ON THE TRADE UNION EDUCATION LEAGUE
William Z. Foster

Foster formed the Trade Union Education League in 1920, following the defeat of the great strikes; the one he led against U.S. steel had been perhaps the greatest of them. Though a syndicalist, a believer in industrial unionism in the Wobbly tradition, he still belonged to the AFL, conservative as it was, because he was dead set against dual unionism. But in 1921, after a long stay in Moscow where he was ardently courted, he entered the Communist camp. He was quite a catch for the Party given his reputation and talents as a labor leader. The Party would henceforth underwrite the TUEL, making his offspring the American section of the Red International of Labor Unions (Profintern). From then until

his death forty years later Foster never deviated from the Party line. The extract below is
from his article in the October 1922 Labor Herald, *the TUEL publication, "Bankruptcy*
of the American Labor Movement."

73

The American labor movement is bankrupt. With its reactionary bureau-cracy and antiquated political and industrial policies and organization, it is altogether unfit to cope with the alert, highly organized capitalist class. Politically it has long been a cipher, and now it is in grave danger of extinc-tion industrially also. During the recent past the capitalist class has discov-ered a new aggressiveness and developed a powerful organization. It is no longer the same class which, before the war, was semi-tolerant of trade unionism. Now it is determined to root out every vestige of Organized Labor. The "open shop" employers have dealt the unions shattering blows in practically every industry, including printing, building, meat packing, steel, railroad, general transport, coal and mining, etc. Consequently the entire trade union movement has suffered disastrously. During the last three years it has lost fully 50% of its entire membership. The whole fabric of Organized Labor is bleeding. The labor movement is in a most critical state. So critical, in fact, that it will never be able to recover unless it quickly and radically changes its policies. The American working class is now immi-nently confronted with the tragic menace of having its trade union move-ment obliterated.

There are still some revolutionaries, unfortunately, who would welcome the elimination of the old craft unions, believing that with them out of the way a new and better movement would speedily take their place. But this is a fatal delusion. We may absolutely depend upon it that should the capitalists, in their great "open shop" drive, succeed in breaking the backbone of the trade union movement they would make all labor organization illegal and repress it with an iron hand. American labor would be reduced to the status of Russian Labor in Czarist days; it would be forced to the expedient of set-ting up revolutionary nuclei in the industries in preparation for some favor-able opportunity when the masses could be stirred to action. Indeed, even as it is, this system will doubtless have to be applied in some of our industries if they are ever to be organized. The mass trade unions are the only protec-tion for the workers' right to organize, the only bulwark against a general flood of capitalist tyranny. They must be defended and strengthened at all costs.

In this grave crisis of the labor movement no relief may be expected from the trade union bureaucrats in high official places. With the rarest of excep-tions, they are dominated entirely by the intellectually dead Gompers. Apparently they would slavishly follow him over the precipice to destruc-tion. They are hopelessly self-lashed to the chariot of conservatism. Even now, in this hour of need, they resist with desperation the mildest reforms in the movement's policies and structure. The further the capitalists push them back the more timid and reactionary they become. They are mentally frozen over solid. If the labor movement is to be saved the regenerating force must come from the organized rank and file militants. They must surge up from the bottom and compel the static leadership into vigorous, intelligent action, or remove it drastically.

It is fortunate, indeed, that just in this critical situation, when their services are so badly needed, the militants are at last freeing themselves from the dual unionism which has cursed them and the whole labor movement for a generation by keeping the reactionary elements in power. They are organizing for action in the Trade Union Educational League, and they are finding the American working class, naturally militant and aggressive, more than eager to accept their program. Now the key to the situation is for the revolutionaries and progressives generally to rally around the League and to carry on a vigorous campaign for its policies of industrial unionism through amalgamation, independent workers' political action, affiliation with the Red International of Labor Unions, and all the rest. If this is done it will not be long until the death clutch of the Gompers bureaucracy is broken and the American labor movement, undergoing a profound renaissance, takes its place where it properly belongs, in the vanguard of the world's workers.

2

ON THE CLOAKMAKERS' STRIKE
Benjamin Gitlow

What follows is a description of one of the important Communist-led strikes of the 1920s—the one by the ILGWU Cloakmakers. Gitlow, who provides it, is no stranger to us. He had gone to jail, it will be recalled, for publishing a Communist document. Now, in 1926, as a top Party official he helped direct the strike. Whether his self-exculpatory account is accurate we have reason to doubt. It appeared in his 1940 memoir, I Confess, *which is to say, long after he had broken with the Party (to go with Jay Lovestone) and become its blood enemy. But his outline of the disaster is accurate.*

Shortly after securing domination of the Furriers Union in 1925, we had succeeded in making considerable inroads elsewhere in the needle trades, and by 1926 we had gained control of the New York Joint Board of the International Ladies Garment Workers Union, which had a membership of about sixty thousand workers. But here the control was not as secure as it was among the Furriers. A number of the large locals—notably the Italian locals 89 and 48, which had a large membership, and the Cutters' local 10, of which David Dubinsky was the manager—as well as several of the smaller ones, were in the hands of the Right Wing. Moreover, the membership outside of New York City, which constituted about two-thirds of the entire

union, was largely controlled by forces in opposition to the Communists.
Besides, we shared our leadership of the New York Joint Board with several
Anarchists and independents. Nevertheless, notwithstanding the precarious-
ness of our control, we did not hesitate to impose our will upon the organization and to use the Joint Board, as much as possible, as a rubber stamp for
our decisions. . . .

On the eve of the Cloakmakers Strike our Party was actively engaged in
two other important labor wars, the Passaic Textile Strike and the Furriers
Strike. For a small Party like ours, with a membership of approximately fifteen thousand, a third strike involving an additional forty thousand workers
would have been a great strain upon our organization even under the most
favorable circumstances, while in this case all circumstances were unfavor-
able. To go into the strike was sheer folly. I personally believed this, and so
did a number of other Party leaders. I definitely knew, as did they, that all the
important leaders of the Left Wing, the Communist and non-Communist
alike, did not favor the calling of a strike. The only one who favored strike
action was Foster, who, in spite of his boasted knowledge of trade union
affairs, never really understood the needle trades or their strike problems.
Though he gained his reputation as a leader of a Steel Strike, he never
assumed responsible leadership in any strike situation for the Party. In my
opinion, he was for a strike of the Cloakmakers for purely factional reasons.
The Ruthenberg group was in control of the Party. To dislodge them, it was
necessary to discredit them in some sphere of important Party activity, and
nothing was more important than trade union work. In favoring a strike he
could speak in a militant manner for uncompromising action against the
bosses and could brand those who opposed strike action as cowardly opportunists who were afraid to fight. . . .

The Cloakmakers Strike was therefore called on July 1, 1926, after the
terms of the Governor's Committee were rejected. A month and a half
before the strike was called the Central Executive Committee's Needle
Trades Committee met and considered the question of the personnel of the
various strike committees. At this meeting, on May 18, 1926, it was decided
that Hyman should be Chairman of the General Strike Committee and
Charles (Sasha) Zimmerman, Secretary; and that David Dubinsky should be
Chairman of the Settlement Committee, despite the fact that he was a leading figure in the opposition to the Communists. Like Dubinsky, a number of
other Right Wingers were given responsible posts in the strike machinery in
order to make them share responsibility.

The main demands of the union were for the forty-hour week, increase in
wages, limitation of jobbers and rejection of the demand of the manufacturers for the right to reorganize their shops by being permitted to discharge 10
percent of their workers at the end of each season. The main objection to the
terms of the Governor's Commission was that it granted the manufacturers
the right of 10 percent reorganization. In September the leaders of the strike

had a conference with the manufacturers for the purpose of reaching a settlement. A tentative basis upon which the manufacturers were ready to settle the strike was handed to the union. It included acceptance of the forty-hour week, an increase in wages and a modified form of reorganization. Following the conferences with the manufacturers, a meeting was held at the District headquarters of the Party, 108 East Fourteenth Street, to consider the terms of settlement. Present at the meeting were our Communist leaders of the strike, Burochovich, Zimmerman, Rose Wortis and others. The party leaders present were Weinstone, Ben Lifshitz, Jack Stachel, a number of members of the New York District Committee, and I.

Burochovich reported. I realized from the way he reported that a basis had been reached by which the strike could be settled. Zimmerman also spoke on the conferences with the manufacturers. He indicated that the terms embodied a compromise settlement which could get the approval of the workers, the obnoxious feature being that, if it were made, the Left Wing would have to take responsibility for inaugurating the principle of reorganization in the industry. It was also clear as the discussion on the proposals proceeded that, if the terms were rejected, the Cloakmakers would have to face a very long and exhausting struggle, the final settlement of which could not be foretold. The discussion went on for hours, but during the entire discussion not one of the strike leaders dared to propose that the strike be settled. They wanted the Party leaders to take the responsibility for the settlement. As the meeting was coming to a close, I turned to Weinstone and whispered, "We have an opportunity of settling the strike. If they would only come out and state that they favor a settlement on the basis of the reported terms, I would support them and move for the settlement of the strike." Weinstone, however, was in a fit of perplexity and afraid to take decisive action. He knew that we were in no position to lead a prolonged struggle. But he did not want to take responsibility for a settlement which would become a football of factional Party controversy, a settlement which Foster would brand as a flagrant sellout. He replied: "Unless Zimmerman and Burochovich definitely come out with a proposal that we accept the terms of settlement, there is nothing we can do." I began to prod the strike leaders with questions, in an effort to make them take a definite stand. They circumvented all my questions. They were determined not to take responsibility. I asked them if they could continue the strike to a successful conclusion. They answered that under certain conditions, which in their opinion could be obtained in cooperation with the Party, they could. Finally, it was decided to reject the terms and to intensify the strike activities in order to get better terms. The strikers never knew the inside story. Had they known, our Communist leaders would have been stoned. The strike, which should have been settled, was not, and the workers were made to pay for it in months of suffering. When the strike was finally settled in December, the terms offered by the manufacturers in September

formed the basis of the settlement and the obnoxious reorganization clause
in a modified form was agreed to.

After this memorable meeting Foster came to New York and received a
report on the situation. When he returned to Chicago he reported to the
Political Committee at its meeting on September 9. But he made no proposal
in the Political Committee that any definite action be taken to settle the
strike on the terms offered. Later, however, as the strike dragged on and it
became clear to the Political Committee of the Party that the Sigman forces
would interfere and take over the strike and the New York Joint Board, it
made desperate efforts to bring about a settlement of the strike, but without
any success. When finances became low, a drive for funds was made, to help
our Communist leadership continue the strike. But not enough money was
collected. Finally, Sigman stepped into the situation and reached a settlement
with the manufacturers. Hyman as Chairman of the General Strike Committee signed it. Following the settlement of the strike, Sigman brought
charges against the leadership of the strike, ousted the Left Wing leadership
and proceeded to reorganize the New York organization. The Communists
fought against his reorganization of the New York organization, but, due to
the protracted unsuccessful strike, they could not rally the workers to their
support. The positions they lost they were never able to regain. The strike
was a very costly affair. For the entire strike period of twenty-four weeks
about three and a half million dollars of union funds were spent. But what it
cost in human suffering and misery, all of which could have been avoided, has
never been estimated. . . .

3

TWO ACCOUNTS OF THE PASSAIC STRIKE
Mary Heaton Vorse

*The following were written by the same person, Mary Heaton Vorse, and taken from her
pamphlets, the first published in 1926 (Passaic), while the strike was still going on, and
the second in 1927 (The Passaic Textile Strike), shortly after it ended. Vorse was one of
the extraordinary women of the age, already known for her novels and short stories and
above all her labor reportage. Born in Massachusetts in 1874, she had led a conventional
life until her marriage broke up, leaving her with young children, and she got involved in
radical causes. In the 1920s she was close to the Communist movement. She remained active
into her eighties. She died in 1965.*

I

The strike of the Textile Workers of Passaic has become one of the classic
industrial struggles in this country.

It will go down in history with Lawrence, Ludlow and the great Steel Strike. It might be said that the Steel Strike closed one era of labor history, that with the Passaic Strike a new era is born. The strike in Passaic demands the organization of the unorganized workers in basic industries.

Labor in this country was asleep—it was at ebb-tide, a time of indifference, of slackness, of reaction. Men seeped away from the Unions. The old militant spirit seemed dead.

Then came Passaic. What happened after the textile workers streamed from the mills on January 25 was like seeing a slow, massive upheaval of Nature, as though a continent had shifted.

The 16,000 textile workers on strike in Passaic represented one million textile workers throughout the country. It was as though the whole body of labor everywhere, a moment before so sluggish, had awakened and moved together, slow, powerful, tremendous.

What has happened during the strike at Passaic has brought the words "Solidarity of Labor" from words into a living fact.

In Passaic the solidarity was manifest to everyone. It was the picket line that showed it. A picket line of two thousand people is an awe-inspiring thing. There is a terrifying quality in its quiet. There is awfulness in its monotony. A slow-moving line as gray as poverty walks back and forth in a long file before the ramparts of the mills. It is not like any other procession. It is like no other thing. It is a picket line—labor showing its power with restraint, Labor with awful quiet showing its force. Monotonous as time passing, the picket line moves on its way. It is so cohesive that it forms a personality of its own. It seems to have more purpose than the marching of armies. It is an army of labor. . . .

. . . Passaic was like an embattled town. The newspaper men came in armored cars. They came in airplanes. The light on Passaic was seen all over the country. All the world got to know what the Passaic workers were fighting for.

In gas masks and helmets they had a procession of six thousand people. At the head of the victorious procession there was a baby carriage, and behind the baby carriage and the boys in their helmets and gas masks and in uniform walked the procession waving and shouting. Thousands upon thousands strode, headed by the baby. They swept past the Botany Mills, laughing and cheering.

The powerful winding picket lines continued, slow and inevitable as the tides, more and more cohesive, until it gave the effect of being a single entity. The weeks that followed the ninth week of the strike when workers usually get tired and discouraged, the workers in Passaic were welding themselves together and making the acquaintance of the workers of America. They did this in the face of continuous and terrible assaults from the police. The breaking up of the picket line, the arrest of girls and women, sometimes for no greater offense than singing, sometimes for no reason at all, was so common that the press ceased to notice it. The brutality of the police and the courage of the workers were two symbols of the two great forces at work in the world, the mighty force of labor and the force of the massed wealth of the country that commands the police powers.

There was never at any time a sag in the spirit of these workers. For this the indomitable will and resourcefulness of the young organizer and the other leaders of the United Front are largely responsible. He never works at random. Long ago he made a far-reaching plan and with the precision of a general he carried out his plan. The fury of the police, the systematic arrests, imprisonments, beatings, the constant need of the work of the ILD increased up to the date of April 4. Then came what was known as bloody Tuesday. That was the day the children were trampled under foot, that screams of women fighting for their children ripped through the air.

Picketing has been the favorite game of the children of Passaic. These mill workers' children have been brought up in a hard school. No mill worker's son will ever wish he were a policeman. He knows the police are his enemies. Children coming from school had joined the afternoon picket line. They taunted and jeered the police. The police revenged themselves with clubs and with arrests.

The children decided to parade in protest against the brutal treatment their parents had received. A permit was denied. They decided to parade just the same. The tension in Passaic had grown with the passing days, with the lines of policemen ever larger opposing the picket line, whose policy was directed by the United Front Committee and Albert Weisbord.

Saturday afternoon while the policemen were breaking up the children's parade, the headlines "Arrest Weisbord" screamed through the strike zone at one o'clock Saturday afternoon, April 10.

It was like the yell of the bosses thirsting for the life of the leader who had held the strikers against them. The air was electric in the mass meeting in Belmont Park. It was the last meeting before Weisbord's arrest. Everyone knew that. But there was no fear. Weisbord came. He was swept from his feet. While the crowd shouted he was carried to the platform on the shoulders of the strikers.

"Stand firm. Carry on the strike as before. Hold the fort while I am gone," were his parting words. The workers saw their beloved leader depart. . . .

All the prominent strike leaders were arrested. Clarence Miller and Jack Rubenstein were held for ten thousand dollars bail. Lena Chernenko was arrested. The most active members of the United Front were locked up for no pretext at all. Albert Weisbord was held for the extortionate bail of thirty thousand dollars.

Then began a week of terror. Sheriff Nimmo of Bergen County came upon the peaceful, tranquil picket line and read the riot act. Allowing not a minute for the picketers to disperse, he cried:

"Clear 'em out, boys." The heavy line of police charged the picketers with their riot clubs. Arrest followed arrest. Esther Lowell, correspondent for the Federated Press, was arrested three minutes after the reading of the riot act for assisting a woman who had been knocked down by a policeman. Robert Dunn of American Civil Liberties Union was arrested while quietly walking down a side street. David Weinstein of the Amalgamated Clothing Workers was another of the out-of-town sympathizers who was arrested for no reason. Deputies patrolled the little town of Garfield. All rights of free speech and free assembly were denied. Sheriff Nimmo acted as though the reading of the riot act were the declaration of martial law. When Norman Thomas attempted to hold a meeting on a rented lot on private property he, too, was arrested and held for ten thousand dollars bail. Strikers were not permitted to go on the streets near the mills, which were now picketed by deputies with guns and police with riot clubs.

The mills' doors were thrown open, but no one walked into them. The workers stood firm. The voice of Albert Weisbord spoke to the workers from jail. The continued arrests, the taking away of their civil liberties, the closing of their halls put iron in their spirits. They streamed into Walling, ten miles away, to hold meetings on the lots provided by Mayor Samuel Nelkin. Their friends from New York streamed out to them. Elizabeth Gurley Flynn, who had been active throughout the strike, now spoke to the strikers daily. The week ended with an injunction more sweeping than had ever been heard of in labor history. This injunction decreed that all the members of the United Front were not even to speak to any of the Huffmann-Forstmann workers. . . .

2

The iron solidarity of the textile strikers, which had defied all the efforts of the bosses to divide them, was at last rewarded when, on December 13, three hundred and twenty-three days after the big strike began, the powerful Botany capitulated to the union and settled on the following terms:

1. Right of workers to organize in a legitimate organization;
2. If a grievance should arise, the right of collective bargaining;
3. Closed shop not demanded;
4. If any other demand made, not agreed on by both parties, the workers to continue working and the question to be arbitrated between these parties: Mill—Workers—Third Party;
5. Help taken back without discrimination;
6. No outside help employed after date of settlement until strikers re-employed. . . .

When the news of the Botany settlement got out, the whole strike area went delirious with joy. The strikers who had stood so solidly and courageously for ten and a half months' grueling struggle against the powerful textile interests, against the mill-dominated courts and police, and even against the constant menace of hunger, gave free vent to their joy. Forstmann-Huffmann strikers and strikers from the Dundee Textile, the United Piece Dye Works, the New Jersey Spinning Company, the Gera mills, all rejoiced with the Botany strikers, correctly reading in the victory of the Botany strikers an earnest of early settlements in their own mills. . . .

Enthusiasm ran high that night. Leader after leader was roundly cheered by that enthusiastic mass whose courage on the picket line and amazing solidarity in the face of all sorts of brutality and poison gas attacks, as well as the loyalty and wisdom of their leaders, had made victory possible. There were cheers for their own Gus Deak, for Francesco Coco, strike leader after Weisbord left, and for those who had been with them from the very first: Alfred Wagenknecht, Lena Chernenko, Thos. De Fazio, Emil Dardos, Ben Levanski, Jos. Magliacano, and the rest. Coco, carrying on his back the marks of police clubs when he was beaten up on Furriers' Sunday, received a thunderous greeting as he stepped forward to address them in English, Coco having, like the strikers themselves, learned to speak English during the strike!

"We have fought for ten and a half months," he told them. "Suffered and fought for what? For a Union!

"Union! That's easy to say. But no settlement will mean anything if you don't use your head. Your brains were asleep ten and a half months ago, but now they are awake, alert. You must keep them so. Constant vigilance is the price you must pay for union, because union means power and the bosses hate to have power in the hands of the workers." . . .

And then came Lena Chernenko. Lena, as she is affectionately known among the strikers. Lena who goes with them at four o'clock in the morning on the picket line, winter or summer, freezing cold or drenching rain, and is with them throughout the day in their various activities, and again in the evenings at their mass meetings. When the cheering had subsided, Lena talked to them briefly and to the point:

"Most of the points have been covered, but I want to take you back ten months ago, eight months ago, with snow on the ground, cold as the devil, and us going on the picket lines in spite of the cold and the clubs of the police which we knew were waiting for us. In those days it was that we began to recognize that what we needed was a union. Not merely the return of the 10 percent wage cut, but a *union*.

"And it is you here in this hall who now have the opportunity to build your union, strong and powerful. It is your chance now to show the bosses whether the clubs of the police have opened your heads."

There were speakers in English, in Polish and Italian, and finally the floor was thrown open to questions and discussion with a lively, intelligent discussion resulting. Then a vote was called, and the settlement terms were unanimously ratified.

Perspectives for Our Party

Jay Lovestone

Here Lovestone, soon to be General Secretary of the Party (he was twenty-eight), gives an example of his "American exceptionalism" views in the June 1927 Communist, *the Party's theoretical organ.*

The present is a very appropriate moment for the Party to review its tasks in the light of the present economic and political situation of the United States. In order to have a correct estimate of the situation confronting the Party and the tasks we are facing we must first of all have a proper evaluation of the general conditions in which capitalism finds itself today.

AMERICAN CAPITALISM ON THE UPGRADE

We will find that it is a basic fact in any analysis to be made of the conditions in this country that American capitalism is still on the upward grade—still in the ascendancy. American capitalism much more than any other capitalism in the world, is on the upward trend. If you take British capitalism, you will find it on the downgrade. In other countries there is a partial stabilization. In still others a very sharp downward trend. In America, much more than in Canada or Australia, the trend of capitalism is still upward. And this can be evidenced very clearly: first, by an examination of the trend of the export of capital from the United States; second, by an examination of the productivity of American industry; third, by an analysis of the trend toward mergers and consolidation in industry and finance. It is not my purpose here to go at length into figures but any examination of the concrete facts of these three expressions of American capitalism will indicate that the curve and development of capitalism in the United States today is still positively and definitely upward.

Some might ask: If it is still definitely upward, does that mean it will continue on the upward trend for some time or is the outlook for a break in the curve? Our answer is that the peak of American capitalism—of American imperialist development—has not yet been reached. America's ability to exploit its colonial resources, America's ability to arm itself for a military struggle with other imperialist powers, America's productive activity, have not yet attained that level to which they can be developed in view of the present potentialities possessed by our bourgeoisie.

When we view this condition we must not view it statically. We must view it dynamically. We must view it in process of change. You will find very deep-going changes occurring in our economic system—changes which express themselves politically and express themselves therefore in changing class relations in the country. Such a change as the industrialization of the South—such a change as the growing power of finance capital and its effect on foreign policy—such changes as are occurring in agriculture as a result of the sharp and positive expropriation of the agricultural masses.

THE IMMEDIATE ECONOMIC SITUATION

But before examining the tasks of our Party in the light of these basic economic features or of the features of American capitalist economy, we should examine the immediate economic situation. What is the immediate economic situation? Have we a depression in America? The answer is: No! Have we had a recession in the so-called last cycle of prosperity? We have had a recession for some months. That recession was evidenced in the steel and automobile industry for a few months toward the close of last year. Are we on the eve of a depression? We are not on the eve of a depression. What is the outlook for an upward swing in prosperity? The outlook is for a sort of even keel in the present economic situation. This means that the peak of the last cycle of so-called economic prosperity has been passed. We have no recession—we have no depression and we are facing a situation which is somewhat lower as compared with the peak of 1925 but is not low enough to give us a basis for saying that we have a depression or we are heading for a depression. You will say that there were certain signs and very definite proofs of depressions in the basic industries. We must here take into cognizance the tremendous reserve power of American capitalism. If a country like France or Italy were to have such depressions—such a recession in the economic and productive relations as we had several months ago—undoubtedly there would be a more harmful effect on the working class of these countries. In the United States, because of the last prolonged period of so-called prosperity and because of the general tremendous reserve power of our bourgeoisie—a power which gains momentum as the curve of imperialist development in the United States continues to go upward—we have not had such political effects. We have not had the economic privations which some might expect on the basis of a mechanical analysis of the economic facts of industry in the last months.

SACCO-VANZETTI

1

AN EVENING AFFAIR

Fred Ellis

Ellis was one of the bumper crop of superior cartoonists who drew for the Party. Here, in the Daily Worker *of August 9, 1927, he deftly brings out the connection between the*

Boston Brahmins and the electric chair with which they will soon kill Sacco and Vanzetti, and the coffins in which they will bury them.

2

Lynchers in Frockcoats

Michael Gold

In this article for the September 1927 New Masses *Gold gives an example of his polemical style—a style entirely appropriate for the Sacco-Vanzetti affair.*

It is August 14th, eight days before the new devil's hour set for the murder of Sacco and Vanzetti. I am writing this in the war zone, in the psychopathic respectable city that is crucifying two immigrant workers, in Boston, Massachusetts.

All of us here fighting for the two Italians are without hope. We feel that they will burn. Respectable Boston is possessed with the lust to kill. The frockcoat mob is howling for blood—it is in the lynching mood.

If the two Italian workers do not die it will not be the fault of cultured Boston. The pressure of the workers of the world will have accomplished the miracle. But I repeat, the handful of friends working desperately here are without hope. The legal procedure in this case is nothing but a bitter joke. The blood lust alone is real.

You can't understand this case unless you are in Boston now. You must mingle with the crowds at the newspaper bulletin boards on Washington Street, hear sleek clerks and ex-Harvard football players and State Street stock brokers mutter rancorously:

"These Anarchists must die! We don't want this kind of people running America!"

They whisper, they fidget, they quiver with nervousness and fear, they jump like cats every time a pin drops. The city has lost its head. The atmosphere is like the war days, when George Creel's skilled literary liars were scaring everyone with the news that the Kaiser's airplanes were about to bomb Chicago, New York and San Francisco.

Those who sympathize with Sacco and Vanzetti in the street crowds keep their mouths shut. They are as unpopular as a Northern friend of the negroes would be at a Southern lynching bee.

Most of the well-dressed, well-mannered Boston bourgeoisie are frank in saying Governor Fuller should not have granted a reprieve. They openly accuse him of being too soft.

The city is under martial law. The entire State militia has been brought into Boston, and is quartered on the alert in the armories. The police are on 24-hour watch, equipped with machine-guns, tear gas bombs, and armored cars. No meetings are allowed on the Sacco-Vanzetti case. If you wear a beard, or have dark foreign hair or eyes, or in any way act like a man who has not had a Harvard education or Mayflower ancestors, you are picked up on the streets for suspicion.

You must not look like a New Yorker. Two New York women, Helen Black and Ann Washington Craton, were arrested and questioned at a police station for the crime of looking like New Yorkers. You must not need a shave. Six Italians in an automobile who had come for the demonstration on August 10th were arrested and held on a bombing charge because two of them needed a shave.

Detectives dog you everywhere; yes, those stupid, criminal, blank detective faces haunt you everywhere, in restaurants, in drugstores while you are having an ice cream soda, in cigar stores, even in toilets. At night you can rise like Shelley from your dreams and stare below into the moonlit street and see a knot of evil, legal detective faces, watching you lest you go sleep-walking.

It is highly dangerous to be out in the streets after midnight. A group of us, after a hard day's work at the headquarters, went searching for a restaurant at 12:30, and were followed, not by four or five of the detectives, but by a whole patrol wagon load of them.

I was one of those who picketed the State House on August 10th, the first date set for the murder of Sacco and Vanzetti. Forty of us marched up and down the concrete walk between the elm trees near the Common, gaped at by a vast curious mob of Bostonians and police and detectives, and from the capitol's ornate balconies, by the official flunkeys of Governor Fuller. . . .

Our picket line was a good cross section of the sentiment that has been aroused in America and the rest of the world. There were sailors, jewelry workers, barbers, bakers, educators, agitators and waiters. There was finally a little fiery Anglo-Saxon aged 62, who made a speech in court affirming that he was opposed to Anarchism, was a Harvard graduate, and wanted justice for the two doomed men, for all of which he was fined $20.

Dorothy Parker and I were arrested by the same brace of iron-handed policemen. As they hauled us off on the long walk to the police station, a crowd followed after us—a well-dressed Boston mob, of the type that lynched Lovejoy during the abolition days.

Some of these respectables booed us, and several of them hooted and howled:

"Hang them! Hang the Anarchists!"

That is the mood of respectable Boston at this hour. A friend of mine who is a veteran newspaperman in this city says he has never seen respectable Boston in as tense a mood as now.

"If this were the South they would not wait for Governor Fuller but would storm the jail and lynch Sacco and Vanzetti," my friend said.

But Governor Fuller is in the lynching mood, though he feels constrained to decorate it with Puritan legalities. And President Lowell of Harvard is in that mood, and all those who have conspired one way or another to execute the two Italians.

They will kill Sacco and Vanzetti legally. They are determined on revenge. For decades they have seen wave after wave of lusty immigrants sweep in over their dying culture. For years these idealists who religiously read Emerson and live on textile mill dividends have had to fight rebel immigrants on strike.

New England is dying culturally and industrially. The proud old libertarian tradition of the abolition days has degenerated into a kind of spiritual incest and shabby mediocre pride of family. The inefficiency of the blueblood factory owners has pushed the textile industry South, where there is plenty of cheap, unorganized and unrebellious native labor.

So these ghosts, these decadents, these haughty mediocre impotent New Englanders have flamed up into a last orgy of revenge. They have the subconscious superstition that the death of Sacco and Vanzetti can restore their dying culture and industry. At last they have a scapegoat. At last they can express the decades of polite frosty despair.

They are as passionate against these Italian workers as white Southerners toward the negro. They know that New England is rotten from stem to stern, and that the slightest match may prove the brand to start a general revolt in the industrial and political field. They will not be moved from their lust for a blood sacrifice—these faded aristocrats. They are too insane with fear and hatred of the new America.

All I can see now to save Sacco and Vanzetti is a world strike. Nothing less stupendous can shake the provincial Chinese wall of this region. Boston is not conducting a murder case, or even the usual American frame-up—it is in the throes of a lynching bee, led by well-spoken Harvard graduates in frockcoats.

A LIVING MONUMENT TO SACCO AND VANZETTI
James P. Cannon

How the Communist Party interpreted the outrageous execution is brought out in this piece, which appeared in the October 1927 issue of The Labor Defender *magazine of the International Labor Defense, one of the Party's best auxiliaries. Cannon was founder and head of the ILD and editor of the magazine.*

After seven years of delay the electric chair has finally claimed its victims. In defiance of the civilized world, in the face of the protest of the world's millions, Sacco and Vanzetti have been executed. This foul murder is the cynical answer of the American capitalists to the people of other countries who appealed to America in the name of humanity and justice. At the same time it is their warning to the protesting workers of America that they are prepared to go to any length to beat down the labor movement, and that legal murder is one of their established weapons.

In this act of assassination the ruling class of America shows its real face to the world. The mask of "democracy" is thrown aside. Judge Thayer and Governor Fuller stand forth not as exceptional officials, apart from all others, but as the authentic spokesmen of American capitalism. The face of Governor Fuller is the face of the American capitalist class. It is this vengeful, cruel and murderous class which the workers must fight and conquer before the regime of imprisonment, torture and murder can be ended. This is the message from the chair of death. This is the lesson of the Sacco-Vanzetti case. . . .

In appealing to the workers for solidarity with Sacco and Vanzetti, and in organizing the protest movement in their behalf, the ILD never considered the case as simply that of two individuals involved in a trial at law. We always pointed out its direct connection with the general issues of the struggle between the classes and endeavored to link up the fight for them with the general defense of the scores of labor prisoners confined in the penitentiaries today and with the broader fight of the toiling masses for liberation from the yoke of capitalism.

Viewing the case always as an issue of the class struggle, we had no illusions about the possibilities of "justice" from the judges or the Governor. Time and again we warned against these illusions, against confining the defense to the task of collecting money for lawyers whose vision did not extend beyond Judge Thayer's courtroom.

The best defense for Sacco and Vanzetti was to concentrate all energies in arousing the protest movement of the masses. Sacco and Vanzetti themselves understood this. These humble workers saw with clear-eyed vision that their hope lay in the masses and not in the courts or the Governor's commission. The contemptuous refusal of Sacco to sign the legal papers brought to him was a gesture more eloquent than all the arguments of all the lawyers. Every utterance that came from them was infused with this spirit. Sacco and Vanzetti were blood-brothers to all labor militants, bound by a thousand ties to the labor fighters in the front ranks of the class struggle and to those languishing in the prisons today for the cause of labor. The deathless heritage of the two great martyrs belongs to the militants and they need no one's permission to carry on their work in the name and spirit of Sacco and Vanzetti. . . .

DISSENSION IN THE RANKS

1

History of American Trotskyism
James P. Cannon

A high-ranking Communist for years—and a charismatic personality—Cannon was the driving force behind the Trotskyist schism that roiled the Party in 1928. The enmity between the two Bolshevik factions reflected the enmity between Stalin and Trotsky, who by now had been exiled to a remote Soviet province. The passage below describing the genesis of American Trotskyism is excerpted from a lecture Cannon delivered in 1942 and published a few years later as a chapter in his history of the movement.

I had smuggled Trotsky's criticism of the draft program out of Russia, bringing it home with me. We came back home and I proceeded immediately with my determined task to recruit a faction for Trotsky.

You may think that was a simple thing to do. But here was the state of affairs. Trotsky had been condemned in every party of the Communist International, and once again condemned by the Sixth Congress, as counter-revolutionary. Not a single member in the party was known as an outspoken supporter of Trotskyism. The whole party was regimented against it. By that time the party was no longer one of those democratic organizations where you can raise a question and get a fair discussion. To declare for Trotsky and the Russian Opposition meant to subject yourself to the accusation of being a counter-revolutionary traitor; and being expelled forthwith without any discussion. Under such circumstances the task was to recruit a new faction in secret before the inevitable explosion came, with the certain prospect that this faction, no matter how big or small it might be, would suffer expulsion and have to fight against the Stalinists, against the whole world, to create a new movement.

From the very beginning I had not the slightest doubt about the magnitude of the task. If we had permitted ourselves any illusions we would have

been so disappointed at the results that it might have broken us up. I began
quietly to seek out individuals and to talk to them conspiratorially. Rose
Karsner was my first firm adherent. She never faltered from that day to this.
Shachtman and Abern, who worked with me in the International Labor
Defense, and were both members of the National Committee, though not of
the Political Committee, joined me in the great new endeavor. A few others
came along. We were doing quite well, making a little headway here and
there, working cautiously all the time. A rumor was going around about
Cannon being a Trotskyist, but I never said so openly; and nobody knew what
to do about the rumor. Moreover, there was a little complication in the party
situation which also worked in our favor. As I have related, the party was
divided into three factions, but the Foster faction and the Cannon faction
were working in a bloc and had at that time a joint caucus. This put the
Fosterites between the devil and the deep sea. If they didn't expose hidden
Trotskyism and fight it energetically, they would lose the sympathy and support of Stalin. But, on the other hand, if they got tough with us and lost our
support they couldn't hope to win the majority in the coming convention.
They were torn by indecision, and we exploited their contradiction mercilessly.

Our task was difficult. We had one copy of Trotsky's document but didn't
have any way of duplicating it; we didn't have a stenographer; we didn't have
a typewriter; we didn't have a mimeograph machine; and we didn't have any
money. The only way we could operate was to get hold of carefully selected
individuals, arouse enough interest, and then persuade them to come to the
house and read the document. A long and toilsome process. We got a few
people together and they helped us spread the gospel to wider circles.

Finally, after a month or so, we were exposed by a little indiscretion on
the part of one of the comrades, and we had to face the issue prematurely in
the joint Foster-Cannon caucus. The Fosterites raised it in the form of an
inquiry. They had heard so and so and they wanted an explanation. It was
clear that they were greatly worried and still undecided. We took the offensive. I said: "I consider it an insult for anybody to cross-examine me. My position in the party has been pretty clearly established now for ten years and I
resent anybody questioning it." So we bluffed them for another week, and in
that week we made a few new converts here and there. Then they called
another meeting of the caucus to consider the question again. By this time
Hathaway had returned from Moscow. He had been to the so-called Lenin
School in Moscow; in reality it was a school of Stalinism. He had been all
smartened up in the Stalin school and knew better how to proceed against
"Trotskyism" than the local shoemakers. He said the way to proceed is to
make a motion: "This caucus condemns Trotskyism as counter-revolutionary," and see where everybody stands on the motion. We objected to this on
the ground—dissimulatingly formalistic, but a necessary tactic in dealing
with a police-minded graduate of the Stalin School—that the question of

"Trotskyism" had been decided long ago, and that there was absolutely no point in raising this issue again. We said, we refused to be a party to any of this folderol.

We debated it four or five hours and they still didn't know what to do with us. They faced this dilemma: if they became tarnished with "Trotskyism" they would lose sympathy in Moscow; if, on the other hand, they split with us, their case would be hopeless so far as getting a majority was concerned. They wanted the majority very badly and they nourished the hope—oh, how they hoped!—that a smart fellow like Cannon would eventually come to his senses and not just go and start a futile fight for Trotsky at this late day. Without saying so directly, we gave them a little ground to think that this might be so. Decision was postponed again.

We gained about two weeks with this business. Finally the Fosterites decided among themselves that the issue was getting too hot. They were hearing more and more rumors of Cannon, Shachtman and Abern proselytizing party members for Trotskyism. The Fosterites were scared to death that the Lovestonites would get wind of this and accuse them of being accomplices. In a panic they expelled us from the joint caucus and brought us up on charges before the Political Committee. We were given a trial before a joint meeting of the PC and the Central Control Commission. We reported that trial in the early issues of *The Militant*. Naturally, it was a kangaroo court, but we had full scope to make a lot of speeches and to cross-examine the Fosterite witnesses. That was not because of party democracy. We were given our "rights" because the Lovestonites, who were in the majority in the Political Committee, were anxious to compromise the Fosterites. In order to serve their purposes they gave us a little leeway, and we made the most of it. The trial dragged on day after day—more and more party leaders and functionaries were invited to attend—until we finally had an audience of about 100. Up until then we hadn't admitted anything. We had confined ourselves to cross-examining their witnesses and tarnishing and compromising the Fosterites, and one thing and another. Finally, when we tired of this, and since the report was spreading throughout the party of what was going on, we decided to strike. I read to a hushed and somewhat terrified audience of party functionaries a statement wherein we declared ourselves 100 percent in support of Trotsky and the Russian Opposition on all the principled questions, and announced our determination to fight along that line to the end. We were expelled by the joint meeting of the Central Control Commission and the Political Committee.

The very next day we had a mimeographed statement circulating through the party. We had anticipated the expulsion. We were ready for it and struck back. About a week later, to their great consternation, we hit them with the first issue of *The Militant*. The copy had been prepared and a deal made with the printer while we were dragging on the trial. We were expelled on October 27, 1928. *The Militant* came out the next week as a November issue, celebrating the anniversary of the Russian revolution, giving our program, and so forth. Thus began the open fight for American Trotskyism. . . .

2

The Crisis in the United States and the Problems of the Party
S. Mingulin

In the June 1930 Communist, *the Party, through one of its spokesmen, tells why it is better off now that it has rid itself of left and right oppositions, Trotskyists, and Lovestonites: It is now free to carry out the demands of Third Period Communism.*

[A] break has occurred in the development of American capitalism and, conforming to that, a turning point has been reached in the development of the class struggle in the U.S. The problem of the building up of a *mass Communist Party* is being solved in the course of the class struggle. Not Europe is being Americanized, but America is being Europeanized. This change did *not* happen suddenly. It seems sudden only to those who acquired a faith in the "permanence of American prosperity," a faith in American "exceptionalism." This change was developing during the last few years, the economic crisis that has broken out in the U.S. has merely *brought it to the forefront* and has given, at the same time, a *tremendous push to the revolutionary development.*

It was precisely the fact that the Communist Party of America was deliberately preparing itself and the masses for the coming change, that it was purging itself mercilessly of a Right (and also "left") opportunism, and because of that, it proved in the main fully equal to the task of meeting the new situation.

The call of the Communist Party met with an enthusiastic response among the broadest masses. By this time it should be clear to all that the Lovestonian leadership was leading the Party directly to ruin, that the ideologic education the Party received at the hands of Pepper was leading it along a path of a "left" Labor Party. At the same time, it is also clear how false were the Trotskyist charges of Cannon against the Party. His policy would have led to a sectarian degeneration of the Party, to the loss of its very loyal Party cadres and to its blissful transformation into the tail end of Menshevism.

However, none of these things have actually happened. In the first place, because both Lovestone and Cannon, have miscalculated things. They didn't realize that the American Communist Party, *the vast majority of it*, is a Party of the *Communist International*, devoted to it, devoted to bolshevism, to the *Proletarian Revolution*. In the second place, because both of them, Lovestone as well as Cannon, miscalculated in another matter. They did not realize that the Communist International and its leadership are the incarnation of the Leninist International and of Leninist leadership. Lastly, because both Lovestone as well as Cannon got fooled by their idol—American "prosperity."

Only a year ago, in fact, even less than that, the subject of the problems and the mission of the American Communist Party was being debated upon. "I think, comrades," said Stalin, in the American commission on 6 May 1929, "that the American Communist Party is one of those very few Communist Parties of the world that are entrusted by history with tasks of decisive importance from the point of view of the world revolutionary movement." Lovestone and Cannon thought differently. They thought that the American Communist Party should act the part of a small chorus engaged in singing panderatory hymns, to the might of American imperialism and to the perspectives "of the proletarian revolution" that "naturally flow" from such might. In contradistinction to the Right (and also "left") revolutionists, the Comintern pointed out, "that the time is not far off when a revolutionary crisis will break out in America. And when a revolutionary crisis will break out in America, it will mean the beginning of the end of capitalism throughout the world" (Stalin).

The revolutionary crisis did not break out in America *as yet*, but the turning point in the development toward that crisis has *already been reached*. The end of world capitalism has not arrived as yet. But does not the turning point in America serve as a starting point for an accelerated development of a growing revolutionary tension into a revolutionary situation? And just because it was basing itself on the above-mentioned considerations did the Comintern emphasize so sharply the importance of the problems of the American Communist Party. "It is necessary that the American CP should qualify for the task of facing the historic moment fully armed and give leadership to the oncoming class battles in America. This task, comrades, requires preparation; you will have to devote all your powers to it, all your resources. You will have to improve and bolshevize the American Communist Party; you will have to work hard and effectively liquidate all kinds of factionalism and all deviations in your Party . . . You will have to apply yourself to the task of forging truly revolutionary cadres and truly revolutionary leaders of the proletariat, capable of leading the many millions-strong working class into class revolutionary battles. Any and all personal and factional considerations must be ruthlessly eliminated and the revolutionary education of the American working class must be made the central point of your problems" (Stalin). . . .

CHAPTER THREE

Militancy and Combat: Third Period Communism, 1929–1934

I

The Sixth World Congress of 1928 was intended to infuse Communism with an energy that it had lacked ever since the revolutionary "First Period" gave way in 1921 to the retreat and consolidation of the "Second Period." The official inauguration of a "Third Period" at the World Congress would enable Communists to again seek through class struggle to rouse the masses from their torpor, to again practice their vocation as history's vanguard, and, if called upon, as its martyrs.

The Soviet Union, which ordered the switch, would, as usual, be the polestar of worldwide Communism. Not only would it materially support Communist-inspired conflicts wherever they broke out, but it would make an even more astonishing switch of its own. It would bring the country overnight to an advanced stage of industrial development, collectivize its capitalist agricultural system at one fell swoop, raise living standards prodigiously, and, to make these possible, build a whole modern infrastructure. Here, then, was a challenge worthy of Communism. Here, in its objective accomplishments, measured quantitatively, would be proof of its superiority over capitalism, America's too.

As for American Communists, no matter how meager their numbers, how bleak (i.e., how healthy) the economic prospects, how reactionary the trade unions, how hostile and impoverished the culture at large, they came alive as never before. They had learned much from their experience in trying to organize disaffected workers and others, even as they had champed at the bit under the constraints imposed on them to get along with their ideological foes. Now, with the constraints suddenly lifted, they could be themselves. They would not wait for the crisis to mature, when the economically and politically disenfranchised—the exceptions to the exception as it were— became a majority and rose up against the powers that be. Quixotic and futile or not, they would do what they must. They were Communists.

Third Period militancy also liberated them from their sometime allies of convenience on the Left and in the labor movement. Probably no constraint bothered them more than their having to seek common ground with Socialists and progressives and union "misleaders." Now they could stake out their own autonomous positions as class warriors, emphasizing their distance from and contempt for these trimmers and sycophants who regularly sold out their constituents. Not surprisingly, Communists saved their choicest epithet, "social fascist," for their Socialist rivals, the opprobrium amounting to all-out war. Those not for us must be against us—this sums up the dogma on which Communists now rested their case. And an adventurous, exhilarating dogma it was, not least because it was so risky. For who could tell how the masses would take to it?

The portents were inauspicious to judge by the first real test of the new militancy, the strike in Gastonia, North Carolina, a signal event in the annals of American labor history.

Its background is the familiar one. The Gastonia textile workers, in particular the thousands of employees of Loray Mills, had grown increasingly unhappy with the "stretch-out" (the speedup), even as their paychecks diminished. Fertile soil for Communist organizers, led by one Fred Beal, a veteran of New England textile mill campaigns. With Communist help of the usual kind—forming a clandestine union, drawing up leaflets, persuading workers to attend meetings, and so on—demands crystallized and were presented to the owners: no stretch-out, a modest wage increase, a forty-hour work week, and union recognition.

So the strike began on April 1, 1929. The consequences were predictable. Local and state police assaulted the pickets, the women and children along with the men. As public interest quickened, the Party sent down more organizers in the hope of provoking a walkout of textile workers throughout the region. Gastonia in the meantime was turning into a charnel house. Vigilantes joined the police in a reign of terror, burning down union headquarters, among other crimes, while the employers were throwing families out of company houses. In early June the Gastonia police chief was killed during an exchange of gunfire. Sixteen of the strikers, including Beal, were arrested for first-degree murder. By now Gastonia was national and international news (thanks largely to the world Communist press), especially after seven of the defendants were convicted, the charges having been reduced to second-degree murder. Out on bail, they promptly fled to the Soviet Union rather than serve long terms in North Carolina jails and chain gangs. Nor was this the end of the affair. One day in September vigilantes slew worker/balladeer Ella May Wiggin, mother of nine children. The jury scarcely deliberated before finding the murderers innocent. By then the strike had dissipated, with little to show for it, the Party having pulled out in a torrent of self-recrimination.

Gastonia failed the test of Communist militancy, but it did generate enormous publicity. Its appeal to sentiment is obvious from the number of novels it called forth in its immediate aftermath. Still worth reading are Grace Lumpkin's *To Make My Bread*, Fielding Burke's *Call Home the Heart*, and Sherwood Anderson's *Beyond Desire*, in all of which, appropriately enough, women were the main protagonists. These marked the rise of "proletarian literature" as a distinct genre promulgated by American Communism (on which more later).

But the drama had one more act to go. Of the seven escapees, three returned from the Soviet Union in the mid-1930s to face the music, one of whom, chief organizer Fred Beal, also wrote a book telling of his disillusionment with Communism, or rather with Stalinism, for he professed to believe still in communism with a small *c*, and attacking the American Party in particular for betraying him and the working class; he served five years. Memories of Gastonia had by then long since faded, to the Party's relief, lost in the whirligig of momentous affairs of state.

Gastonia, however, did nothing to dampen Communist spirits as the Third Period offensive got under way, as Political and Central Committees ordered every district, section, and unit to follow their lead and prepare for direct action.

Their lead took the form of a conference held in Cleveland in late 1929 of the Party's trade union cadre, headed by William Z. Foster, from which emerged the Trade Union Unity League (TUUL), the pivot of its new strategy. The TUUL's specific mission was to unionize the untouchables of American labor—the menial and unskilled, among them immigrants, ethnics, blacks, and women—along lines originally laid out by the Wobblies. Like the Wobblies, the TUUL's set up, on paper, industry-wide unions in the place of privileged and exclusionary AFL crafts, so that, for example, a Needle Trades Industrial Union would embrace women's and men's clothing, hats and caps—each currently represented by separate (and quite anti-Communist) AFL unions: an Agricultural (later Cannery and Agricultural) Industrial Workers Union would include all those in the field, whatever their specializations (cotton, wheat, corn, dairy, fruits, vegetables, etc.); similarly with "marine" workers (stevedores, sailors, warehousemen, et al.), miners (coal, silver, copper, etc.), textile workers (like those in Gastonia), metal workers of every sort, and so on. In thus forming the TUUL—unabashedly the American section of the Red International of Trade Unions—Foster and the Party could not have had any illusion about what they would be up against. They would be taking on the companies, the police, the vigilantes, and the AFL unions as well. But if that was what it took, so be it. And so it was.*

Shop organizing was only one front, albeit the most important, in the Party's general campaign. The others had more flair, more panache, the cultivation of nuclei in mines and mills and offices being a slow and unheralded process. There were the urban marches and demonstrations for jobs and tenant protection and home relief (food and clothing allowances) that began on March 6, 1930, with a good deal of fanfare as "International Unemployment Day." No one was more surprised by the size and anger of the crowds that showed up than the Communists themselves. The police reacted, predictably, with truncheons and mass arrests. (For leading a New York march of thousands from Union Square to City Hall to hand Mayor Walker a petition of grievances, Foster and several comrades spent six months in jail.) Could it be that the recent Wall Street crash signaled a deeper malaise than the experts and the Hoover administration were letting on? The Party suspected so and established neighborhood "Unemployed Councils" to institutionalize the March 6 and subsequent demands. The Councils would supply the shock troops for everyday struggles: boycotts of stores that overcharged and/or hired no minorities, rent strikes, and even more extreme measures in behalf of victimized tenants, food cooperatives, and the like.

Communists also ventured far beyond city precincts, often courting danger to life and limb: policemen on horseback wielding billy clubs were child's play by comparison. Organizers unafraid of martyrdom invaded the feudal sanctuary that was California's Imperial Valley—medieval barons were not more powerful than the fruit and vegetable and cotton growers there—to persuade migrant laborers, who were more ill-treated than serfs, to join the TUUL's Agricultural Workers Industrial Union, an act tantamount to subversion of the whole social order. The Party's reach extended to the South too, where Jim Crow buttressed the feudal arrangement. Only the bravest of the faithful—and there was no shortage of them—volunteered to organize black workers in Birmingham and sharecroppers elsewhere in Alabama and even in Mississippi. Less threatening were the rural fastnesses of Iowa and Minnesota, where farm foreclosures were creating a wasteland, and where

---

*A further word about Foster and the TUUL. It was, in fact, his old Trade Union Education League in new dress. What changed was its mission, and with it its name, the substitution of a single word, *Unity* for *Education*, signifying the direction of the change. True, the TUUL had all along sought to organize workers by industry rather than craft, but, consistent with Foster's principles, it had done so within the established trade union structure. The TUUL would now seek to create unions *outside* that structure and indeed in opposition to it. Whether Foster revised his principles or concluded that the AFL was too hopelessly reactionary to ever work with or could not resist the Party's Third Period mandate to fight alone remains an open question. Not even his recent biographer, a conscientious scholar with no ideological axe to grind, has been able to answer it.

Party functionaries showed up, including the legendary Ella Reeve (Mother) Bloor and one of her sons, Harold Ware, who had studied agronomy in the Soviet Union. In short, wherever Communists detected vulnerabilities in the system, signs of impatience from people who had once been so quiescent— there these New Model warriors went to offer their services in the organization of discontent.

On the cultural front above all the Party, its friends and sympathizers put their enthusiasm and ingenuity on full display and to maximum effect. Just as Communists drew no hard-and-fast distinctions between means and ends, so they drew none between art as a weapon in the class struggle and art as the handmaid of Socialist humanism, between art as agitation and propaganda (agitprop) and art as high culture. Borrowing from the rich "masscult" experiences of the Soviet Union and Germany (whose Communist movement was, until Hitler took over, the West's largest and most innovative), Communists excelled in their ability to introduce ordinary people to the visual arts, literature, theater, dance, music, film, and photography. They subsidized a host of theater groups across the country, many in foreign languages, some radically experimental, along with an astonishing number of dance groups. For those wishing to pursue an interest, or a vocation in film or photography, there was the Film and Photo League (whose magazines, *Experimental Film* and *Film Front*, were well ahead of their time). And in large cities they formed clubs named for John Reed, where people could attend recitals, readings, exhibitions, and book discussions, and where any of them who had a creative bent could get help from professionals in a given field.

There is no need to go on and inventory the number of moves Communists made, the institutions they formed, in furtherance of their Third Period agenda. The undertaking, it is sufficient to say, was as ambitious as it was fraught with uncertainty.

2

To everyone's amazement a depression did come. More than a year passed after the stock market debacle before America realized that the economic downturn, which continued to worsen, might be long-term. Unlike the minions of the status quo and the best and brightest of the experts, Marxists could rightly claim that they alone had predicted what would happen. And of the bewilderment of competing Marxists, moderate to revolutionary, it was the Communists who found themselves in the best position to act on that claim. The Party, it will be recalled, had begun its full-scale assault on the system *before* the Great Depression struck (i.e., before Americans were aware they were in a depression) and had displayed singular commitment, discipline, and boldness. What is more, it possessed an abundance of resources they lacked, thanks in part—but only in part—to Comintern financial aid

("Moscow Gold"), which resources helped launch the theaters and dances and John Reed clubs, the affiliates, auxiliaries, and fronts. Those resources certainly enabled the Party to bring out its vast body of publications— dailies, weeklies, monthlies, many in foreign languages, many devoted to literature and the arts (the John Reed clubs alone accounting for ten of them), some specializing in international affairs, others in trade union issues, still others in theoretical and organizational questions, not to mention the occasional papers distributed in shops and neighborhoods in the name of this or that institution. An impressive apparatus was already in place, ready for duty, when the depression hit home in all its fury.

That is why the Communist movement in general did so well, relatively speaking, during the Third Period, which lasted through 1934. We say movement rather than Party. For although the Party grew considerably in those six years, from about ten thousand to about thirty thousand members, the numbers were still minuscule under the circumstances, still concentrated in a few regions of the country and among the foreign born. And the candidate it ran for president in 1932—who else but William Z. Foster? (whose running mate, James W. Ford, was a black man)—could garner no more than one hundred and three thousand votes, a mere eighth of those of Norman Thomas, the Socialist Party candidate, whose own performance greatly disappointed his followers. But the Communist *movement* was growing by leaps, and by movement is meant primarily the affiliates, auxiliaries, and front organizations. They attracted as many people as they did precisely because the services they offered went beyond politics and spoke to more immediate concerns, though of course politics always hovered in the background; the Party was always in command. Here we will consider only the more notable ones.

There was the International Workers Order (IWO) which the Party founded in 1930 mainly as a way of providing cheap insurance to those who could not otherwise afford any. For about a week's wages per annum, workers could buy fairly comprehensive medical and life insurance policies for themselves and their families. Gathering members by the tens of thousands, the IWO proved to be more than a nuisance to its profit-making (or rather money-losing) insurance industry competitors; it created a yardstick by which to measure their performance. But there was more to the IWO than insurance: it was also a fraternal order that operated schools, camps for children, and recreational facilities for adults, and, utilizing the movement's artistic resources, sponsored plays, concerts, dances, and so on. The IWO was at the center of an emergent Communist subculture in America.

Notable, too, was the American League Against War and Fascism. Its opening convention in 1933 astonishingly attracted some two thousand delegates from all over the country, many of them liberals and radicals representing a broad array of farm organizations, women's groups, labor unions, religious and secular pacifists, and civil libertarians, who had come in response to an urgent call from three of America's best-known social protest writers, Upton Sinclair, Sherwood Anderson, and Theodore Dreiser. Fear brought these Communists and non-Communists of the Left together—fear that the recently installed Roosevelt administration might try to suppress dissent, much as the government did during World War I; the New Deal, after all, was modeling itself on that government. The fear, in other words, was that Roosevelt might take a Fascist turn and do in America what Hitler had already begun doing in Germany. Communists had a more specific fear as well, namely, that Roosevelt might seek to align the United States with those nations, led by Germany, that were committed to the destruction of the Soviet Union and were, by building up their military, preparing for that eventuality.

The Unemployed Councils, mentioned above, were a successful auxiliary indeed. Each new rent strike or hunger march or city hall demonstration added new adherents to their ranks. Politicians and police grew jittery, and concessions followed. Less spectacular but perhaps more important were the gritty things they did at the neighborhood level in behalf of those who had nowhere else to go for relief. The Councils provided an alternative to the failed and corrupt political machines. Nor did it hurt the Communists— quite the opposite—when President Hoover blamed them for leading the 1932 Bonus Marchers in their Washington, D.C., campsite (Anacostia Flats). This canard, this nonexistent threat of revolution—the "Reds" being a marginal presence among those impoverished veterans—justified his sending in the army—tanks, tear gas, and all. The Party did organize its own march on Washington later that year, but little came of it.

By an ironic twist, the Unemployed Councils flourished as Roosevelt's New Deal made its effects felt. That its countless programs for the jobless was to a large extent an attempt to discourage them from taking to the streets served to increase the Councils' leverage. Their national demands for guaranteed full employment, social security, cheap housing, and unemployment insurance would sooner or later get enacted into law.

The Councils' achievements provoked rivals to undertake similar organizing campaigns of their own. By 1932 the Socialist Party had finally authorized its young Turks to compete with the Communists for the support of the jobless, and that they did effectively in a few areas, Chicago and Baltimore in particular. Even more effective were the Unemployed Leagues, which owed their existence to an extraordinary man and his dedicated band of followers. He was Abraham J. Muste, a one-time minister and pacifist who had become a labor organizer and then founder and head of Brookwood Labor College in Westchester, New York, a superb school. He had meanwhile come around to Marxism-Leninism—but a Marxism-Leninism to which he gave his own decidedly non-Communist interpretation—and so left Brookwood for the class struggle. His Unemployed Leagues proliferated in the smaller communities of Pennsylvania and Ohio and West Virginia, where they were every bit as militant as the Councils. They played a central role in the "Republic of the Penniless," the remarkable cooperative and labor barter movement that arose in Seattle and at its height enrolled upward of three hundred thousand citizens, mostly farmers and workers. And in 1934 the Ohio Unemployed Leagues sent thousands to join the striking employees of the Toledo Auto-Lite Company and so helped prevent the company, backed by the police and the national guard, from walking the scabs through the picket lines. The victory—for the company recognized the union—steeled the revolutionaries who later in the year won the great strikes in San Francisco and Minneapolis.

The contributions of the Socialists and Musteites must be acknowledged, but the truth remains that the Communist Party's Unemployed Councils dominated the field, which was why the public and the powers that be correctly held them most responsible for the radical activism that so troubled the authorities.

And then there was the intellectual and cultural life that the Party inspired, encouraged, and underwrote. The times were conducive to the politically charged, class-driven approach that it championed. Those Communists who argued against reducing the arts to a strictly proletarian or agitprop exercise, who valued artists and intellectuals for their independence, whether or not they could be fitted into the Marxist-Leninist worldview—those who took that position were still heard in such outlets as *Partisan Review*, magazine of the New York City John Reed Club. But more and more the art-as-weapon line held sway in movement circles, though unlike the Soviet Union, where state and party administered the line with mailed fist, here its enforcement depended on much less persuasive methods, on the willingness of true believers to accept it.

Proletarian literature, we said, emerged as a distinct genre around 1930–31, the aftermath of Gastonia. It took in an uncounted number of novels, short stories, plays, and poems, not all of them brought out under Party auspices; commercial houses published many of the novels, and commercial theaters put some of the plays on the boards. But the novels did not sell, and the plays had short runs. The genre obviously failed to appeal to the masses, especially at a time when the masses, beaten down by adversity, wanted romance, sentiment, lightheartedness; escape in short. The proletarian genre seemed gloomy by contrast, rooted as it was in the dark inescapabilities of life, the inescapabilities, more exactly, of the work environment that afflicted most people—workplaces, work processes, workers' conflicts with employers, with society at large, with one another and with themselves. It pointedly dealt with women, occasionally with blacks and ethnics and the lumpenproletariat—itinerants, vagrants, hoboes, derelicts, and the like—all of them seeking their freedom, illusory or real depending on the maturity of their class consciousness, on how well they understood why capitalism was victimizing them.

In his classic study on the radical novel (see the Bibliographical Essay), Walter Rideout situates the proletarian literature of the 1930s in the venerable tradition of realism and naturalism that went back to the late nineteenth century and that such writers as William Dean Howells, Frank Norris, Upton Sinclair, and, above all, Theodore Dreiser best represented. Not that the proletarian writers measured up to their standard. To wade through the proletarian oeuvre is to encounter hackneyed plots, stereotypical characters, Manichean tales of courage versus cowardice, selflessness versus greed and ambition, and so on. In the Cold War era especially it became fashionable to dismiss the whole genre as Communist agitprop and little more and have some fun ridiculing it; the abundance of mediocrity made it easy to do so. (See, for example, chapter four ["The Social Muse"] of Murray Kempton's *Part of Our Time: Some Ruins and Monuments of the Thirties*, published in 1955.) But in fact there is much to recommend in the oeuvre, particularly if one judges it by a standard appropriate to its nature and purpose. Much of it was intended to agitate and propagandize by describing a universe that the bourgeois literary and intellectual establishment had neglected and with which working people—an audience that that establishment never addressed—could identify and empathize.

Even within these limits, some very good proletarian novels got written. Edward Dahlberg's *Bottom Dogs* is a travelogue, written in his own stylized language, of the homeless through the nether regions of big cities; Jack Conroy's *The Disinherited* tells a picaresque tale of a coal miner driven from his job and then from pillar to post in industrial America; Robert Cantwell's *Land of Plenty* gives a convincing reconstruction of a lumberman's strike; Grace Lumpkin's *To Make My Bread* is the best of the Gastonia novels; *Jews Without Money* is Mike Gold's account, full of harsh pathos, of his early youth in New York's incredible Lower East Side ghetto around the turn of the century; Albert Halpern provides a harrowing description in *The Foundry* of how, with rebellious dignity, workers endure the assembly line; Josephine Herbst's remarkable trilogy—*Pity Is Not Enough*, *The Executioner Waits*, and *Rape of Gold*—with great skill follows the travails of an extended family from the Civil War to the Great Depression; and, finally, there was another trilogy, James T. Farrell's *Studs Lonigan*, which qualifies as proletarian even though its "hero" and his fellow toughs hardly measure up to the genre's norms, and its exotic setting—the cruel, depraved world of Chicago's shanty Irish—offers scant hope of redemption, but these made it the enormous success and bestseller that it was.

The novels eclipsed the other forms of proletarian literature—short stories, poetry, criticism—that usually got no further than the audiences who read Communist publications. And as with the novelists so with short story writers, poets, and critics, a handful stood out, rose above the bathos and predictabilities to which the genre was susceptible. Among the short-story writers were Meridel LeSueur, who recorded with a sure touch the despair of working women in Minnesota where she grew up and was herself a young mother; and Whittaker Chambers, an urban intellectual who discovered in the rebellious farmers of Arkansas the subject of his best work (before he dropped out to pursue a career in espionage). Among the poets were Muriel Rukeyser who, scarcely out of college, caught the attention of the literary world by her fresh, limpid cry of indignation against injustice; and Kenneth Fearing, whose utterances of protest—spare, elliptical, and witty—could always be heard above the din. And among the critics were *New Masses* editor Mike Gold, who gave up writing novels for the lively, hard-hitting polemics against friend and foe that were his trademark; and ex-professor Granville Hicks, whose *Great Tradition*, a rather schematically Marxist run-through of American literature since the Civil War, became a movement textbook, which, for all its limitations—or because of them—is still worth reading.

The proletarian novel may also serve as a paradigm for the other manifestations of radical culture that sprang up in the Sturm und Drang of Third Period Communism. Strikes, marches, political arrests, martyrdoms, foreign and domestic news events—these and anything else that revealed the corruption of the system and its guardians—supplied the raw material for these insurgent artists. They assumed the task of instructing, raising consciousness, and mobilizing opinion, the task, in a word, of moving people to act—getting them, for starters, to join the movement and, better yet, the Party.

The theater was a prime device for doing so. As early as 1929 the Workers Laboratory Theater was performing on New York streets and soon attracting sizable crowds and imitations galore, many far beyond the city. Joel Saxe describes why the Workers Lab was so influential: "It blended elements of symbolism, realism, vaudeville, dance, music, and mass chants into strident Marxist indictments of capitalism, racism, fascism, and the bourgeois state" (*Encyclopedia of the American Left*, p. 851). Similar theater groups burgeoned across the country, each, it seemed, issuing its own revolutionary manifesto. By the middle of the decade the proletarian theater had begun to flow into the mainstream, all the way to Hollywood in fact, thanks to such playwrights as Albert Maltz (*Peace on Earth* and *Black Pit*), John Howard Lawson (*Success Story* and *Pure of Heart*), George Sklar (*Stevedore*), and of course Clifford Odets, whose *Waiting for Lefty* created a sensation when it was performed (though his *Awake and Sing* is a better play), and thanks to such professional outfits as the Group Theater, which Harold Clurman and Lee Strasberg founded in hopes of doing for the American stage what the great Stanislavsky had long been doing for the Russian; that the Group Theater only partially realized those hopes was accomplishment enough.

Then there were the other manifestations of proletarian culture, an impressive lineup indeed. There was proletarian art, perhaps the most effective of agitprop vehicles, especially so since the Communist movement boasted such brilliant illustrators and caricaturists as William Gropper, Hugo Gellert, Jacob Burck, and Louis Lozowick, such fine painters as Philip

Evergood, Peter Blume, Stuart Davis, Jack Levine, Alice Neel, and the Soyer brothers. There was proletarian dance in abundance too: for example, the Office Workers Dance Group, the Rebel Dance Group, the New Dance Group, the Theater Union Dance Group, each seeking, in the words of the Workers Dance League, the organization to which they belonged, to build "a dance art that is inspired by and useful to workers." And there was even a proletarian music, represented by the Composers Collective of New York, which tried to bring together players and audience and composers—the likes of Charles Seeger, Elie Siegmeister, Alex North, Aaron Copeland, and, most prominently (from a Marxist-Leninist standpoint), Mark Blitzstein— to create and perform works expressing the usual themes: class exploitation, racial justice, opposition to Fascism.

When at the end of 1934 Granville Hicks claimed it had been "a good year, an exceptionally good year," he was referring to the number of young artists and intellectuals who had gone over to the movement and, more specifically, to the distinguished ones who had become fellow travelers. They included the following established writers: John Dos Passos, Edmund Wilson, Theodore Dreiser, Matthew Josephson, Erskine Caldwell, Sherwood Anderson, Lincoln Steffens, Newton Arvin, Lewis Corey, Langston Hughes, Waldo Frank, Malcolm Cowley, and Kenneth Burke—an impressive list indeed. In 1932, as members of the League of Professional Groups, they were among the score who signed the little tract, *Culture and the Crisis*, which supported Foster, the Communist presidential candidate, in the belief that capitalism was doomed and the Soviet experiment the wave of the future.

3

Communists from the start championed the Negro (in those days the honorific term for African-American), but during the 1920s their solicitude bore few results beyond the willingness of this or that individual, a handful all told, to join the Party. The Party thus scrapped the American Negro Labor Congress a few years after its creation in 1925. But, if anything, the prospects for recruiting Negroes looked even bleaker in 1930 when the Party launched the League of Struggle for Negro Rights, whose militancy reflected Third Period confrontationism—to be more exact, the Party's proposal, ordered by Moscow with Stalin's personal blessing, to establish a Negro Zion in America, a republic of, by, and for black people carved out of the black belt states of the deep South (South Carolina, Georgia, Alabama, Louisiana, and Mississippi). Now whatever most or many Negroes thought of the proposal in the abstract they obviously could never act on it. It did, however, convey to them the depth of the Party's commitment to racial justice, a commitment that had little to do with the possibility, immediate or distant, of black self-determination. That commitment enabled the Party to respond swiftly and to good effect when chance situations arose and thus convincingly demonstrate its bona fides to the Negro community.

On March 1, 1931, the New York press carried a strange story, though perhaps not so strange since it involved Communists. The day before, about fifteen hundred people attended a Communist kangaroo court in Harlem, complete with prosecutor, defense lawyer, and jury. The defendant, himself a Party member, was one August Yokinen, caretaker of the Finnish Workers Club, which was located in Harlem (where many whites still lived). For a Communist, Yokinen had committed a grave offense. Months earlier some Negro men showed up at the club dance and were shunned and threatened by the crowd. Instead of interceding in their behalf, he blamed the Negroes for causing the contretemps. The Party called him on the carpet; he admitted his guilt and promised to expiate it. But the Party saw an opportunity to publicize its objections to the "white chauvinism" among the rank and file and its total solidarity with the Negro masses. Hence the mock trial. Before the assembled multitude, Yokinen's lawyer denounced his client's crime but placed it in the broader context of a "vile" and "oppressive system." The prosecutor argued that the crime, which could have damaged the movement and led to riots, demanded expulsion from the Party. The jury (actually the Party hierarchs) rendered a Solomonic decision: expelled he was, but then he could apply for readmission after fighting against discrimination in Harlem. At the close of the proceedings the packed court sang "The Internationale." The press was amused and to the general public amusing it must have been, but what other group at the time would have done such a thing, would have condemned racism so blatantly as the Communists did?

Down in Chattanooga, meanwhile, where the Party had begun a clandestine organizing campaign among Southern Negroes (about which more presently), one of the organizers happened to read that nine black males, ranging in age from thirteen to twenty-one, had been arrested in Scottsboro, Alabama, allegedly for gang raping two white women in a freight car. So began the Communist Party's involvement in the great Scottsboro case. Nothing it ever did yielded it such rewards—such gratitude in the Negro community for single-handedly saving the "boys' " lives, however ineptly it sometimes orchestrated their defense. They had been found guilty with ease, their court-appointed lawyer having gone through the motions, and all except one had been sentenced to die. That was when the Party came in. It employed its whole vast apparatus in their behalf, from protest marches (one of them led by August Yokinen) and clashes with the police, to providing legal counsels for appeals and subsequent trials. Other Communist parties made the case a celebrated international cause. The premier Negro organization, the fiercely anti-Communist National Association for the Advancement of Colored People (NAACP), hardly covered itself with glory; it backed out of the contest altogether. The bewilderingly complex affair dragged on for years and even reached the Supreme Court; not until 1950 was the last of the boys (now a middle-aged man) released from jail. The Party deserves great credit for having kept them from the executioner's block long enough to allow the modicum of due process that would lead ultimately to their freedom. Not that the goodwill Negroes felt toward Communists got translated into political terms; there was no rush of new Party members, for example. That would come later. Saving them was a magnificent achievement in itself.

The affair did give the Party a lift in its Southern campaign which was already under way. It was no coincidence that Alabama emerged as the epicenter of black Communism in the South. More precisely, Birmingham, with its concentration of mills and factories and therefore black industrial workers. Communist organizers, headquartered in Chattanooga, were making headway there even before Scottsboro. The rise of a Communist movement in Birmingham, including some whites (all of which is detailed in Robin D. G. Kelley's masterful treatment, *Hammer and Hoe: Alabama Communists during the Depression*, published in 1990), was, as noted, clandestine. To espouse Communism openly in the land of the Ku Klux Klan and White Legion and monstrous legal repression was, especially for Negroes, to risk one's life. Living underground had terrors of its own, to be sure, and Party leaders rarely stayed in places like Birmingham more than a year or two. Nonetheless, from that beachhead it was able to move out in several directions.

One direction was close by, in rural Tallapoosa County, where discontent among Negro sharecroppers had begun growing in proportion to their indebtedness and hence their fear of eviction. Assisted by Party organizers from Birmingham, these desperate men, hundreds and then thousands of them, would sign up with the Sharecroppers Union (SCU), despite the omnipresent violence arising from the local sheriff's high-handed attempts to forcibly collect debts, that is, their land and cattle. Between 1931 and 1934 several of them were slain in shoot-outs and many more were brutally beaten or sent to jail for long stretches or both (as was SCU member Nate Shaw, whose fascinating life history Theodore Rosengarten recounts beautifully in *All God's Dangers: The Life of Nate Shaw*). And they signed up thousands in other counties, some in Mississippi and as far away as Louisiana. Why they did so, the dangers to life and limb notwithstanding, is explainable too by New Deal agricultural policies, which, from the spring of 1933 on, favored large farmers at the sharecroppers' expense. As their lot steadily worsened, more and more of them turned to the SCU as their sole recourse. The Communist Party provided them with such material and organizational resources as it could in a losing struggle. (For years it supported the families of jailed SCU members.) Its hope, as usual, was that some of them would become tried-and-true Communists, organizing themselves for future insurgencies.

The Party's experience in black-belt Alabama in the early 1930s is a remarkable piece of American history, and only recently have scholars, unaffected by ancient animosities, given the Party faithful their due. That they were decades ahead of their time in matters of racial equality not even their enemies can fail to acknowledge.

Finally, there was the Herndon affair, another drawn-out cause célèbre that worked to the Party's advantage in its appeal to Negroes.

Angelo Herndon was seventeen when in 1930 he joined the Communist Party after taking part in a demonstration mounted by the Birmingham Unemployed Council. A year later the Party sent him to Atlanta, the scene of a good deal of unrest. Before long, he led a hunger march to the city courthouse. The leaflets he distributed asked anyone who was interested in his group to write the post office box he listed. The police were interested and arrested him after ransacking his apartment, where they found plenty of incriminating evidence that he violated Georgia's sweeping anti-insurrection law. The International Labor Defense handled his case, bringing in a lawyer, Benjamin Davis, Jr., with impeccable credentials, among them that he came from one of Atlanta's top black families. The verdict, like the trial, was swift. For distributing insurrectionary literature, young Herndon (he was still a teenager) would have to spend twenty years behind bars. The Party immediately swung into action, making almost as much fuss in publicly defending him as it did with the Scottsboro boys. The injustice was so egregious, "free Angelo Herndon" cries went up in Communist and liberal and other left-sponsored rallies as well. Not until 1937 did the Supreme Court at last hear the case that the International Labor Defense had doggedly pursued through one appeal after another. By the narrowest of margins, in a landmark decision, the court threw out the Georgia law on the grounds that it had abridged Herndon's First Amendment right.

In the fullness of time Herndon and his lawyer crossed paths again. Benjamin Davis became a Communist himself and settled in New York City (Atlanta had declared him persona non grata) where he rose high in Party ranks and was elected to the City Council before bad things happened to him in the McCarthy era for the crime of being a Communist. Herndon did well by the Party, too. Hardly thirty, he was elected to the Central Committee, of which Davis was a member. But shortly thereafter the Party expelled Herndon for espousing the cause of black nationalism. He had by then passed into obscurity.

4

By the end of 1934 Third Period Communism was on the way out, for reasons, however, that had little to do with its failures and successes. An evaluation of those failures and successes reveals the extent to which appearances belied reality, successes being at the same time failures and failures successes.

To begin with, the apparent successes—the sheer number and variety and popularity of Communist cultural activities and Communist affiliates, auxiliaries, and fronts—that these contributed to the Party and movement could not be doubted. But what was the nature of the contribution? The problem for Party officials was this: how to make the consumers of proletarian culture and the beneficiaries of the affiliates, auxiliaries, and fronts—for example, victimized tenants, downtrodden Negroes, the jobless, the uninsured, and so on—how to make them into reliable Party members or at least fellow travelers; how to translate a mood, an attitude, a predisposition into concrete political action; how, in a word, to produce Marxist-Leninist revolutionaries. Judged by hard-nosed criteria, the results left much to be desired. Party membership and electoral performance disappointed the leadership. The Party, it could be argued, was not getting enough of a payoff to warrant the investment of valuable resources.

On the other hand, there were apparent failures, and they were legion. Communists were thwarted in their attempt to organize farmers of the upper Midwest, this despite the impressive regional conferences they held, the informative publications they brought out, and the "penny auctions" they took part in (in penny auctions farmers would get together to save a neighbor by buying his foreclosed farm from the bank for a nominal amount at a public auction—that is, by forcibly stopping anyone else from outbidding them—and then returning it to him). What had seemed so promising at first had fizzled out by 1934, thanks mostly to New Deal measures, from price supports to mortgage guarantees. But these measures would not have been taken were it not for the increasing radicalization of Midwest farmers, the Communists having been only the most radical of the movements that sprang up among them. The government simply adopted many of the agrarian Left (and Communist) demands. And although the effort to organize the Imperial Valley migrant workers also failed—the repression was massive—it did spark uprisings led by alumni of the Agricultural and Cannery Workers Industrial Union that, for the rest of the decade, lit up California's rich valleys, its "factories in the field," from one end of the state to the other, incidentally giving John Steinbeck the material for his best books, particularly *In Dubious Battle*, which turns on a Communist-fomented strike of apple pickers. The fate of the Alabama sharecroppers and their union came closest to being an unredeemed failure, and that was because, by the end of the decade, sharecropping had practically ceased to exist as a way of life, thanks again to New Deal policies (paying farmers to reduce crop acreage).

Certainly the Trade Unity Union League had to be counted as a failure. It hardly got beyond the blueprint stage, even though it carried on many a noble fight, took on many a hopeless cause, some of which we have noted. And even where TUUL organizers signed up disaffected workers, in New England textile mills, say, or among anthracite miners, the effort would usually collapse as soon as it met employer resistance. With such a "reserve army" of jobless Americans, a third of the workforce, how could it have been otherwise?

Only the most highly skilled—and only a minority of them—held on to their unions. The Party could not have chosen a worse time to make good the Wobbly dream of industrial unionism. Yet the experience proved in the long run (within three or four years) to have been no failure at all. Following the defeat of their campaigns, quite a few TUUL organizers ended up in AFL locals, maintaining, surreptitiously, their shop-floor solidarities, thereby planting dragon's teeth for the great challenges to come.

An extraordinary case in point—and an example of what could be expected when those dragon's teeth sprouted—was the Communist Party's 1934 triumph in San Francisco.

For some time the TUUL's Marine Workers Industrial Union had been winning adherents among the longshoremen there. They were being squeezed tighter and tighter between, on the one hand, their employers, the shipping companies (San Francisco was the Pacific coast's main port), and, on the other, corrupt union officials who kept control by means of the shape-up system (by deciding every morning who worked at what jobs). The radicals now belonging to that very union, the AFL's International Longshoremen's Association, headquartered in New York City, were led by an Australian immigrant worker named Harry Bridges. His effectiveness as a leader he demonstrated by the fact that his radical faction took over the local and struck in the late spring of 1934 after the companies refused to replace the shape-up with a hiring hall based on seniority and due process. The San Francisco Longshoremen's strike—actually it was a West Coast strike that extended from Los Angeles to Vancouver—lasted four months, during which time the strikers fought the familiar cohort of adversaries—the business elite, the mayor, the governor, the press, the vigilantes, the ousted union—and suffered the familiar penalties, including the death of two strikers, followed by an elaborate funeral and a general walkout that tied up the city for days. But Bridges and his comrades who ran the union (renamed the International Longshoremen and Warehousemen's Union) held firm and extracted the concession—a hiring hall under its supervision—that meant victory and the consolidation of Communist leadership of a union destined to grow immensely in power and influence. Bridges himself was too shrewd to sign a Party card; had he done so he would have been deported. As it was, the federal government tried three times over the next twenty years to get him; in vain. So it was that the San Francisco economic elites and political establishment simply had to accommodate themselves to a major Communist presence in their midst.

Worth mentioning in this connection are the Minneapolis events of later that year: they replicated those in San Francisco, except that truck drivers comprised the union in question (a local of the International Brotherhood of Teamsters) and Trotskyists—Bolsheviks of a different coloration—comprised its very talented leadership. The Trotskyists won their bloody and protracted strike too, helping eventually to break the stranglehold on the city's economy that its important families (milling, banking, dairy, insurance, etc.) had exerted. Hatred there was between Communists (Stalinists if one prefers) and Trotskyists, but Americans may not have cared and therefore not have noticed what they thought of each other. What they emphatically would have noticed, if they cared, was that in both instances Marxist-Leninists, devotees of revolution, had, against tremendous odds, prevailed over the powers that be.

LEFT TURN

Sixth Comintern Congress: Theses and Program

An air of crisis pervaded the great hall where more than five hundred delegates from fifty-eight parties and numerous youth organizations convened on July 17, 1928. They stayed until September 11. Their task was to legitimate the decisions taken by Stalin and the Politburo to reverse course and resume the class struggle. The Soviet Union was about to expropriate private property, especially in agriculture, as part of its plan to industrialize the nation. The new direction of world Communism—its "Third Period"—was laid down in the "Theses and Program," adopted unanimously on the last day.

After the first imperialist world war, the international labor movement passed through a series of phases of development, reflecting the various phases of the general crisis of the capitalist system.

The first was the period of extremely acute crisis of the capitalist system, and of direct revolutionary action on the part of the proletariat. This period reached its highest point in 1921, culminating on the one hand in the victory of the USSR over the forces of intervention and internal counter-revolution, and in the consolidation of the proletarian dictatorship and the establishment of the Communist International; and on the other, in a series of severe defeats for the Western European proletariat and the beginning of the general capitalist offensive. This period ended with the defeat of the German proletariat in 1923.

This defeat marked the starting-point of the second period, a period of gradual and partial stabilization of the capitalist system, of the "restoration" of the capitalist economy, of the development and expansion of the capitalist offensive, and of the continuation of the defensive battles fought by the proletarian army weakened by severe defeats. On the other hand, this period was a period of rapid restoration in the Soviet Union, of important successes in the work of building socialism, and also of the growth of the political influence of the communist parties over the broad masses of the proletariat.

Finally came the third period, the period in which capitalist economy and the economy of the USSR began almost simultaneously to exceed their prewar levels (the beginning of the so-called reconstruction period in the Soviet Union, the further growth of socialist forms of economy on a new technological basis).

For the capitalist world, this is a period of rapid technical development, and of the accelerated growth of cartels and trusts, one in which a trend toward State capitalism can be observed. At the same time it is a period of intense development of the contradictions in the world economy, operating in forms determined by the entire prior course of the general crisis of capitalism (contraction of markets, the USSR, colonial movements, growth of the inherent contradictions of imperialism). This third period, in which the contradiction between the growth of the productive forces and the contraction of markets becomes particularly accentuated, will inevitably give rise to a fresh era of imperialist wars among the imperialist States themselves; wars of the imperialist States against the USSR; wars of national liberation against imperialism; wars of imperialist intervention and gigantic class battles. . . .

In determining its tactical line, every communist party must take into its calculations the given internal and external situation, the relation of class forces, the degree of stability and strength among the bourgeoisie, the level of militancy and preparedness among the proletariat, the attitude of the middle strata, etc. The party determines its slogans and methods of struggle in accordance with these conditions, starting from the need to mobilize and organize the masses as widely as possible at the highest possible level of that struggle. When a revolutionary situation is developing, the party advances a series of transitional slogans and partial demands corresponding to the given circumstances; these must be subordinated to the principal revolutionary aim, which is the seizure of power and the overthrow of the bourgeois capitalist order. To neglect the everyday demands and everyday struggles of the proletariat is as mistaken as to restrict the party's activities to them exclusively. The task of the party is to use these everyday needs of the working class as a starting-point to lead the workers on to the revolutionary struggle for power.

When the revolutionary tide is rising, when the ruling classes are disorganized and the masses in a state of revolutionary ferment, when the middle strata are inclined to turn toward the proletariat and the masses display their readiness for battle and for sacrifice, it is the task of the proletarian party to lead the masses to a frontal assault on the bourgeois State. This can be achieved by propaganda in favor of transitional slogans on a rising scale (workers' councils, workers' control of production, peasant committees for the forcible confiscation of landowners' estates, disarming of the bourgeoisie and arming of the proletariat, etc.), and by organizing mass actions, to which all branches of the party's agitation and propaganda must be subordinated, including parliamentary activities: among such actions are strikes, strikes combined with demonstrations, strikes combined with armed demonstrations, and finally the general strike, combined with armed insurrection against the State power of the bourgeoisie. This highest form of struggle follows the rules of the art of war and presupposes a plan of campaign, offensive fighting operations, and boundless devotion and heroism on the part of the proletariat. An absolutely essential preliminary to actions of this kind is the organization of the broad masses in militant bodies which, by their very form (councils of workers, peasants, and soldiers, etc.), must embrace and set in motion the largest possible number of working people, and more intense revolutionary work in the army and navy. . . .

By improving the productive forces of the entire national economy, by steadily pursuing a policy of industrialization—the rapid rate of which is dictated by both the international and the domestic situation—the Soviet proletariat, notwithstanding the attempts at financial and economic boycott regularly and deliberately made by the capitalist powers, is increasing the relative share of the socialized (socialist) sector of the national economy in the means of production, in total output, and in trade turnover. Because the land is nationalized and industrialization is going ahead, socialist State industry, State transport and banking, operating through State trading and the rapidly growing co-operative system, are coming more and more to serve as guides for small and very small peasant farming.

In agriculture the improvement in productive forces is occurring in conditions which impose limits on the process of differentiation among the peasantry (land nationalization and the prohibition on the sale and purchase of land, steeply progressive taxes, financial aid for co-operatives and producers' associations established by the poor and middle peasants, legal regulation of the employment of hired labor, restrictions on the political and social rights of the large peasants, special organizations for the village poor, etc.). But since the productive forces of socialist industry have not yet reached that level of development which would make it possible to reorganize agriculture thoroughly on the basis of new agricultural techniques and so facilitate the rapid concentration of peasant farms into large communes (collective farms), the large peasants are also making some progress and uniting with the so-called new bourgeoisie, economically and, in a more gradual way, politically as well.

The proletariat of the Soviet Union controls all the decisive key economic positions; it is methodically squeezing out what remains of private capital in the towns, whose share in the total economy declined very steeply in the last phase of the New Economic Policy; the proletariat is obstructing in every way the expansion of the exploiting strata in the countryside which grow out of the development of a commodity and money economy; it is supporting the existing Soviet farms and promoting the foundation of new ones; it is incorporating the bulk of simple commodity producers among the peasantry into the proletarian system of economy, and so into socialist construction, by means of rapidly developing cooperative organization, which, in a proletarian dictatorship where socialist industry plays the leading part in the economy, is identical with the development of socialism. With the transition from reconstruction to the expanded reproduction of the entire technical basis of the country's production, the proletariat of the Soviet Union faces new tasks, which it has already begun to tackle: the creation of new capital resources (the production of means of production in general, expansion of heavy industry, electrification) and, in addition to the further encouragement of marketing, purchasing, and credit co-operatives, the direct organization of the peasants, on a steadily expanding scale, into collective producers' co-operatives, a task which calls for large-scale material assistance from the proletarian State. . . .

INSURGENCIES

Gastonia

1

IMMEDIATE EFFECTS OF THE GASTONIA STRUGGLE
William F. Dunne

The Gastonia strike was the first test of Third Period Communism. If anyone was qualified to write about it, it was Dunne. He had come out of the bare-knuckles labor and Socialist struggles of Montana, where he had been a rising star. Having joined the Communists in 1919 he became editor of the Daily Worker *and a member of the Political Committee. The extract that follows is from his excellent pamphlet,* Gastonia, Citadel of the South, *published while the strike was still in progress.*

For the first time in the history of North Carolina a fundamental political issue with its underlying economic causes shows itself as an integral part of the ebb and flow of the class struggle in the United States. More than that, throughout the whole South the Gastonia struggle is the center around which social forces—class forces—are crystallizing.

Just as the Haymarket case in Chicago in 1886 symbolized the struggle for the eight-hour day and the emergence of the proletariat in its classic form from the American social structure, so does the Gastonia case symbolize the emergence of the Southern working class as an integral part of the American proletariat.

But the struggle centering around the defense of these 13 workers in the shadow of the electric chair is more than a symbol—it is a dynamic factor molding and shaping the development of the class struggle, not only in the South, but in all America. Around the defense of these workers surge the tides of mighty social forces. The ranks of the Southern proletariat are forming fast and this brings the masses into conflict on issues old as the proletariat itself, but hidden until now in the confusion that has accompanied the development of a modern capitalist system on the base of the old semi-feudal traditions and an agricultural economy.

The right of workers to organize, to strike, to picket, to defend their union, to defend their families and themselves from the armed attacks of the agents of their class enemies—these burning class issues have thrust themselves through the crust of Bourbon prejudices like a giant's fist. These issues will not down. They have come with the Southern proletariat and they will stay until the social revolution resolves them in its fiery crucible.

The *Gastonia Gazette* expresses the policy of the diehards—the remnants of the old landed aristocracy and the new tobacco, textile and water-power capitalists, together with their train of middle-class retainers—the professional and mercantile elements who have been created by the new capitalism and are dependent upon it.

The working class is beginning to emerge as an independent political factor. For the first time the workers speak of working-class needs in connection with politics. The old alignment of democrat and republican has been broken forever. Unions, strikes, wages, hours, conditions of labor, have become political issues. They are no longer divorced from politics in the minds of workers. Among large masses of workers the role of city, county, state and national government will never again be separated from the problems of their daily struggle for a livelihood.

In between the two opposing classes stands a section of the middle class which has derived no benefit from the industrialization of the South and which is consequently in conflict with the textile lords, the power interests, the big tobacco companies and the huge chemical concerns—which together form the basis of Southern industrialization and the new Southern capitalist class. With them are the intellectuals, whose base is the University of North Carolina.

On the question of the right of the workers to organize, the difference that appears in the Southern press is mainly on *tactics*. The diehards of the old regime and the big capitalists *want no unions of any kind*. The smaller capitalists and a section of the middle-class intellectuals are in favor of unions *providing they are properly controlled*.

Militant unionism finds its champions only among the exploited workers—black and white. . . .

That such fierce class battles as that in the Gastonia area should occur in a section of industry—cotton spinning—where the *productive process* is decentralized in an extreme form can be understood only by understanding the manner in which this imperialist period—"the period of wars and revolution," as Lenin characterized it—finance capital, extending its domination over industry and government, creates the condition for mass revolts even in *decentralized* industries. In Gaston County are 114 cotton spinning mills with 1,250,000 spindles—more than one-sixth of the total number of spindles in North Carolina, a state having one-third of 18,000,000 spindles in the South.

The *nominal* ownership of these 114 mills is divided among approximately 85 different companies. The *actual ownership and control*, however, is in the hands of the *big banks and marketing concerns controlled by the New York banks.*

The 25,000 textile workers in the Gastonia area therefore face in the struggles against the stretch-out and for militant trade union organization, *not a collection of small capitalists*, in whose ranks they could count on a certain amount of dissension and division in the pre-imperialist period, but *the ruthless centralized power of Wall Street finance capital and its government.*

The sharp struggle in Gastonia, reaching the point of armed conflict, furnishes irrefutable proof of the process by which the inner contradictions of capitalism in the imperialist period bring on economic struggles which speedily take an a *political* character. The struggle in Gastonia, and throughout the Southern textile industry, is not only an integral part of the international crisis in the textile industry (huge strikes in England, India, etc.) but a symptom of the world crisis of capitalism which leads straight and fast to a new imperialist war, to the direct danger of an imperialist attack on the Soviet Union, the fatherland of the world's working class, as the counter-revolutionary conspiracy in the Far East proves.

The contradictions of capitalism are things these propagandists for American imperialism never heard of or would not and could not understand if they did. A new contingent of the American proletariat was being born, and as it emerged from the countryside and was mobilized in the giant industries of the new South it shed its swaddling clothes and stood forth, freeing itself from the traditions of its rural birthplace.

Today it stands facing its class enemy—the idle owners of the industries which created it and which it in turn created. . . .

The thesis of the new industrial South has its antithesis—the proletariat of the new South. The synthesis is the social revolution of which the present struggles are the preliminary skirmishes. The National Textile Workers Union, affiliated with the Trade Union Unity League, the American section of the Red International of Labor Unions, is in the forefront of these struggles. This is its place. It has won its place by heroic struggle. It has earned the hatred of the mill owners and the loyalty of the mill workers.

The most militant and conscious section of the Southern working class supports it. The National Textile Workers Union will retain this support and enlist new masses in its ranks because its program alone, and its leadership, seasoned in the class struggle, meets the needs of the masses of textile workers in this period when American imperialism drives fiercely at all sections of the working class in its feverish preparations for a new war of world conquest.

The native born American workers of the South are not "free." They are not "unchangeable." They are not "contented." They have given the lie to these three falsehoods, spread by the agents of robber capitalism, in one of the most courageous class battles in American labor history.

The leaders of the National Textile Workers Union whom the ruling class is trying to railroad to the electric chair in a futile but murderous attempt to stem the tide of working class revolt must be restored to the ranks of the proletariat from which they were seized by the government of the mill owners.

Fred Beal, Louis McLaughlin, W. M. McGinnis, K. O. Byers, George Carter, Joe Harrison, J. C. Heffner, Robert Allen, Russell Knight, N. F. Gibson, K. Y. Hendricks, Delmar Hampton, Clarence Miller shall not be done to death. They must be freed together with their fellow-workers.

Support the national campaign for the defense and release of these heroic members of the working class organized by the International Labor Defense.

No more workers' lives to satisfy the vengeance of our class enemies. The heroes of Gastonia shall not die but shall live and be free to carry on their work in the forefront of the class struggle in the new South.

The battle cries of the working class in Gastonia have been heard by the workers in every country. Their appeals for help are likewise heard and answered by the workers of all countries, beginning with the Union of Socialist Soviet Republics, where the workers and peasants rule under the leadership of the Communist Party, to India, where the mass revolt against imperialism grows stronger each day.

With the workers of the world rallying to the call of the Gastonia strikers and organizers, the place of the American working class is in the first line of the struggle for the lives and liberties of our comrades, whose deeds will live long in the memory of the working class.

They struck strong blows for the working class and they did not count the cost. They shall not die—these prisoners of the class war—in the lethal chamber which capitalism keeps for its vengeance.

They shall be restored to the ranks of the working class—unharmed as they were unafraid.

We defend the right of workers to organize unions, to organize to defend their families, their persons and their union against the armed mercenaries of the capitalist class and its government. No compromise on this issue! Fred Beal and his comrades must and shall be freed!

2

Two Ballads
Ella May Wiggins

In an article for the October 9, 1929, Nation ("Ella May Songs"), Margaret Larkin presented a moving portrait of this textile worker and mother of nine (four of her children died of diphtheria the same night) and union militant, whom vigilantes had killed during the Gastonia strike. The article included several of her ballads and this description of her singing: "She had a clear, true tone in her untaught voice. She sang from the chest. Full throated, unmodulated, her voice rang out in simple monotonous tunes. . . . Where the old tune called for it, each line would end with an indescribable upward lift of the note, a kind of yip, like the little yelp with which cowboys vary their riding songs."

THE BIG FAT BOSS AND THE WORKERS
The boss man hates the workers, the workers hate the boss. The boss man
    rides in a big fine car and the worker has to walk.

The boss man sleeps in a big fine bed and dreams of his silver and gold.
The worker sleeps in a old straw bed and shivers from the cold.

Fred Beal he is in prison a-sleeping on the floor,
But he will soon be free again and speak to us some more.

The union is a growing, the ILD is strong,
We're going to show the bosses that we have starved too long.

CHIEF ADERHOLT
Come all you good people and listen to what I tell,
The story of Chief Aderholt, the man you all know well.
It was one Friday evening, the seventh day of June,
He went down to the union ground and met his fatal doom.

They locked up our leaders, they put them in jail,
They shoved them in prison, refused to give them bail.
The workers joined together and this was their reply:
We'll never, no we'll never let our leaders die.

They moved the trial to Charlotte, got lawyers from every town,
I'm sure we'll hear then speak again up on the union ground.
While Vera she's in prison, Manville Jenckes in pain,
Come join the textile union and show that you are the game.

We're going to have a union all over the South,
Where we can wear good clothes and live in a better house,
Now we must stand together and to the boss reply
We'll never, no we'll never let our leaders die.

3
PROLETARIAN JOURNEY
Fred Beal

*Chief organizer Fred Beal's unhappy story after he fled Gastonia for the Soviet Union is
told in his bitter memoir of 1937. His criticism of Stalinism is closely akin to the Trotskyist
position.*

We who consider ourselves class-conscious workers, look forward to and
advocate a system of society without classes, a society in which those who
produce shall be the sole rulers.

My proletarian journey through life, my struggles through strikes, prisons, escapes, and the written word, would be robbed of all meaning if I were to lose my ideal of a classless society. Yet the professed aim of all the liberal and radical groups which worship Stalinism is the same as mine.

But how is one to arrive at this classless goal? At present Stalin has a corner on the class-conscious market. The Stalinists vociferously claim to be the sole custodians of true Communism, the only rightful leaders of the working class. Stalin alone holds the key to the Communist heaven. To enter its Pearly Gates, all must pass through his purgatory. . . .

Did not the Communist Party, with all its liberal and radical subsidiaries and appendages, wage a national campaign in 1929 to keep Fred Beal out of jail? Did not the same *Daily Worker*, on August 27, 1930, when the matter of our escape to Soviet Russia became a national scandal, justify even our bail jumping which I had opposed? Under the caption, "The Gastonia Defendants," the Communist organ then wrote:

> They are quite justified in escaping from the vicious sentence imposed upon them, by placing themselves beyond reach of the Southern capitalist class justice. . . . The working class as a whole should glory in the fact that they got away. The workers should support their escape despite the howls of the bourgeoisie. . . . Let the bosses take the bail; it is better that they have $27,000 than the seven Gastonia fighters serve 117 years in their prison.

Now consider the strange destinies of the seven Gastonia fighters who fell into the Soviet realm.

William McGinnis fought his way out of the Stalin haven, secretly returned to the United States at the risk of being imprisoned, and is reported to have died amidst the silence of his former comrades of the *Daily Worker*.

K. Y. Hendricks also battled his way back to "freedom," to a long prison sentence in America, where he was seized amidst the studied silence of the Stalinist organization, ignored and forgotten in his cell by the brave Communist leaders.

Louis McLaughlin felt the pangs of hunger in Stalin's land of plenty. He was arrested in Moscow for stealing bread. To avoid a scandal abroad, he was shipped off to Odessa.

George Carter was a physical and mental wreck when I last saw him. He was glad to get potato peelings for food when he visited me in Kharkov.

Joseph Harrison was forced to live in an unspeakable workers' barracks, infested with rats and vermin, in a Moscow suburb.

Only Clarence Miller, who was never a worker and whose connection with the Gastonia strike was accidental, blossomed out in Soviet Russia as a "Red professor" and occupied a comfortable apartment in Moscow, enjoying the prosperity of the Soviet bureaucracy.

As for myself, I left Russia with the realization that the radical movement was at the crossroads, and with the determination not to remain silent.

I became convinced that the road taken by Stalin to the goal of a classless society is not the right road. It is advertised as a short cut. It has taken a terrible toll of life. But it has done something even more frightful to the living. And the end is not in sight.

At close range I watched the results of the Stalin drive. I saw the dead and the living. I saw a man-made famine in which millions perished. I stood aghast at murder becoming a normal function of the state—the state of my dreams.

With a twenty-year prison sentence hanging over my head, I made my way back to the United States to speak out somehow, to tell the truth, to call my comrades to take another road for the happiness of the workers.

But my former comrades, my former defenders, indeed, the entire radical-liberal world which took such a seemingly deep interest in the Gastonia case in the name of justice and truth, would not even listen to the truth from Soviet Russia. . . .

The Trade Union Unity League

1

ORGANIZATION AND PROGRAM
William Z. Foster

The centerpiece of the new Communist militancy as prescribed by the Sixth Party Congress was the TUUL, founded in 1929 under Foster. The following is taken from a tract put out in 1931.

The Trade Union Unity League was organized in Cleveland, August 31, 1929. It is a reorganization and expansion of the old Trade Union Educational League, which was organized in November 1920. The old TUEL placed the main stress of its work upon the organization of revolutionary minorities within the conservative trade unions. It led a thousand fights against the AF of L misleaders, mobilizing the rank and file workers to struggle against their disruptive class collaboration policy and for a program of class struggle. The new Trade Union Unity League has as its main task the organizing of the unorganized workers into industrial unions, independent of the AF of L. At the same time it organizes the revolutionary workers within the reformist unions. It unites politically and organizationally the unemployed with the employed.

Nationally, the TUUL is constructed by the affiliation of National Industrial Unions, National Industrial Leagues, the National Unemployed Council, and local organizations that have no other national affiliations. The principal National Industrial Unions are the National Miners' Union, the

National Textile Workers' Union, and the Needle Trades Workers' Industrial Union. These were all born in the heat of the bitterest struggle against the AF of L leaders and the employers. The principal National Industrial leagues are those in the steel, automobile, marine transport, railroad, shoe, food, building, lumber and agricultural industries. These leagues, made up of local groupings in the respective industries, are in process of development into National Industrial Unions. The National Unemployed Council, a dues-paying organization based on individual membership, organizes local unemployed councils, and is affiliated to the TUUL, nationally and locally. The TUUL also organizes Local Trade Union Unity Councils in the various localities, made up by the affiliation of local unions, shop committees, left wing minorities in the conservative unions, etc. State Councils are similarly built. The National Committee of the TUUL, elected in its biennial convention, consists of 53 members. It elects a National Executive Board of 15 members. The TUUL and its affiliated organizations have various departments—Negro, Organization, Financial, Youth, Women, Education, International—and for the various trade sections. The national organ of the TUUL is "Labor Unity."

BASED ON THE UNSKILLED

The TUUL fights for the interests of the workers as a whole and is based primarily upon the unskilled and the semi-skilled masses, the most exploited and militant sections of the working class. The AF of L program of basing the labor movement upon the skilled workers, a policy that was always wrong, is made increasingly disastrous by the wholesale elimination of skill in the industries through standardization, mechanization, and speed-up. The AF of L is founded on the diminishing labor aristocracy. The revolutionary unionism bases itself upon the broad masses of unskilled and semi-skilled, who are the decisive factors in modern industry.

The class struggle unions are industrial in structure. They organize all sections of the working class—Negroes, women, youth, skilled, unskilled, native, foreign. The great consolidation of the forces of capitalism makes industrial unionism imperative for a fighting labor movement. Craft unionism, born in the early stages of capitalism, is worthless in these days of monopoly capitalist organization. In trustified industries, where 90 percent of the workers can learn their "trades" in a week, organization by craft is criminal betrayal of the workers. Even in those industries which are more competitive in character, such as textile, needle, mining, etc., the great banks exert the controlling force, and make necessary an all-inclusive, militant, industrial unionism. Only by great mass movements, drawing in all the workers, and capable of paralyzing whole industries and groups of industries, can the workers make headway against the powerful employers, who are aided by the state and their fascist labor leader allies. The AF of L craft system of one or more "trades" striking while the rest remain at work is a crime against the working class. It must be utterly wiped out.

SHOP ORGANIZATION

The TUUL unions discard the old local structure of craft unionism. They base themselves directly upon the shops, establishing shop committees and the shop delegate system. The building of shop committees, the carrying on of union work directly in the shop, draws the working masses into the life and struggle of the union. The new unions eliminate the autocracy of the craft unions and establish a real democracy among the workers. They wipe out the corrupting high salary practices of the old trade unions and pay their officials only the going wage of the industries. Instead of exorbitant dues and initiation fees, breeders of corruption and reaction, they have union rates within the reach of the lowest paid workers. They systematically carry on a work of education of their general membership as to the real meaning of capitalism and the struggle to abolish it.

STRIKE STRATEGY

The TUUL unions develop a revolutionary strike strategy. They seek, not as the AF of L, ways to surrender to the bosses, but to fight them. They study systematically the strength and maneuvers of the capitalist enemy and calculate the methods which will draw the masses of workers into the struggle, develop their fighting initiative and turn their maximum power against the capitalists at the most opportune moment and in the most strategic place. A correct strike strategy involves a careful evaluation of all the experiences gained by the workers in the class struggle. Especially it requires an attitude of self-criticism regarding mistakes made during the work of the unions. Frank self-criticism is one of the foundation-stones of the revolutionary union movement.

The strike strategy of the TUUL aims to develop the scattered struggles of the workers into the mass political strike. All struggles in the present era tend to take on a political character because the capitalists use the state power more and more aggressively against the workers. It is necessary therefore that the workers bring their fight to a higher political plane, by injecting into it broad political slogans, by widening it to include the masses of workers, by deepening it and giving it more of a class content, by directing its attack against the state as well as against the individual capitalists.

A successful strike strategy requires the adoption of the principles of independent leadership laid down by the Red International of Labor Unions. That is, the setting up of broad rank and file strike committees and action committees, to draw the unorganized as well as the organized workers into the struggle. The organization of Workers Defense Corps against fascist attacks, as at Gastonia, where the workers defended themselves with guns in their hands, is an indispensable part of revolutionary strike strategy. The new unionism in the United States, with its industrial form, militant tactics, etc., is the American expression of the new and higher form of organization and struggle now being developed by the workers all over the world in the present rising wave of struggle.

INTERNATIONAL AFFILIATION

The class struggle unionism is international in character. It recognizes the common class interests of the workers of all countries and the necessity for a united struggle against international capitalism. The TUUL repudiates completely the nationalistic and patriotic stand of the reformist trade unions. It joins hands with the militant labor movement of the world under the banner of the Red International of Labor Unions. The RILU is the only revolutionary world union of workers. It makes war on world imperialism and its social-fascist allies of the Amsterdam International. In every country its unions are to be found in the very forefront of the class struggle. The TUUL is the American Section of the RILU. . . .

THE PROGRAM OF THE TUUL

The Trade Union Unity League bases itself upon the principles of the class struggle. Its slogan is "class against class." It realizes that the interests of the workers are flatly in opposition to those of the capitalists, and that an irreconcilable conflict goes on between the working class and the capitalist class. It rejects collaboration with the employers, the AF of L policy which paralyzes the efforts of the workers to organize and defend themselves. It condemns arbitration, whether voluntary or compulsory, as a method of the employers to defeat the demands of the workers. It rejects social-fascist proposals for the launching of a Labor Party, which would be only another capitalist party. Its foundation working principle is that the workers can secure from the employers only that which they have the power to take in active struggle. The TUUL organizes the workers and aggressively wages the class war, so that their maximum power may be brought into the struggle against the capitalist class. It supports the revolutionary political struggles and the political organization of the working class, the Communist Party.

The TUUL has a revolutionary goal. It points out to the workers the disaster of the capitalists owning the industries and operating them for their own profits. It advocates the overthrow of the present system of capitalist ownership and exploitation and the establishment of a Soviet system in which production will be carried on, not for private profit, but for the social good. Only by such revolutionary action can the American workers, like the workers in other countries, finally free themselves from unemployment, low wages, long hours, the speed-up, gradually worsening conditions, and terrible war. . . .

2
THEM AND US
James Matles and James Higgins

In his autobiography, which came out in 1974, James Matles and his coauthor graphically recount his experience as a TUUL organizer. That experience, plus outstanding talent, later helped make him a leader of the United Electrical Workers, the largest of the Communist-run unions.

For quite a while in the machine industry the Metal Workers Industrial Union had the organizing field all to itself. It did not have to worry about competition from the AFL craft unions. They were in bad shape. The anti-labor offensive of employers through the twenties, and then the Great Depression, had combined to take the steam out of all labor organizations, not only industrial unionism. Most of the AFL membership of less than 2 million was restricted to the building trades and miscellaneous industries, nothing basic.

These were conditions prevailing when a few workers decided in 1930 to found the Metal Workers Industrial Union affiliated with the Trade Union Unity League. Realistically, they had no great expectations. None of them felt that overnight they were going to rebuild the labor movement and enlist masses of working people in the cause of industrial unionism. They were not complete romantics—just romantic enough to believe that somehow, at some future time, they didn't dare to think when, industrial unionism would succeed . . .

All too often, the young activists of the Metal Workers could not escape the vengeance of company-hired spies and goons. For that reason the Metal Workers adopted for the most part the strategy of organizing cautiously and secretly. It seemed to be the only intelligent way of trying to stay alive in the enemy territory of the machine, metal, and electrical shops of the period. The objective was to build union-conscious groups, however small, in these shops and to do it with as few job losses as possible. Some progress in this direction was made in the years 1930 to 1933.

Groups formed in Brooklyn, Manhattan, and Queens. Also in Newark, Harrison, Paterson, and other New Jersey towns. A Metal Workers local was organized in Philadelphia consisting of several tool and die shops. More groups formed at the Yale and Towne Co., Stamford, Connecticut; at Pratt and Whitney Aircraft, and Pratt and Whitney Tool, in Hartford; at a metal fabricating shop in Jamestown, New York. Another local established a base in Cleveland; another in Minneapolis; still another in Chicago. Slowly but surely, the union was putting together a string of component parts here and there.

Most significant, however, in terms of the future of industrial unionism in the electrical manufacturing industry, members of the Metal Workers—mainly skilled mechanics—organized groups in the key plants of the giant corporations of that industry: General Electric in Schenectady, New York, and Westinghouse in East Pittsburgh, Pennsylvania. By the time of the inauguration of Franklin Roosevelt as president in March 1933, when the hopes of working people for recovery from depressed economic conditions could be more and more openly expressed, the young organizers of the Metal Workers Industrial Union had established skeleton crews in dozens of shops in the machine, metal working, and electrical industry.

These active, volunteer organizers were full of zeal and determination but, at the start, very inexperienced. They had to learn the hard way to keep a constant eye out for agents planted by the companies. Soon it came to be taken for granted that in any large shop where union-building was under way, at least one company spy was in the works somewhere.

Nobody, however, knew the extent of this spy operation. It was not until 1936, when the LaFollette Committee of the U.S. Senate initiated a two-year investigation of industrial espionage against labor unions, that it became clear what the industrial unionists had really been up against. A nationwide network of professional spies and strikebreakers, employed by private agencies who sold their services to the most powerful corporations in the land at an annual cost of $80 million, had been operating night and day against union-minded men and women.

There was expectation in the air in those early New Deal months. Workers everywhere were stirred up by the feeling that real political change was about to occur. Nevertheless, it took a while for organizational movement of any size to get under way in larger industry, where fear of the boss had been well implanted in the minds of the workers. Not until the first practical measures of New Deal reform were instituted did these workers, in any great numbers, begin to feel free to let loose their instinctive desire for industrial unionism. . . .

3

THE SPECTER

William Gropper

Gropper was among the best of the proletarian illustrators who flourished in the 1930s. The brutal times were made to order for their style, Gropper's in particular, as the following famous cartoon, which appeared in the January 27, 1933 Worker, *vividly demonstrates.*

4

SEEDS OF REVOLT

Moritz Hallgren

Hallgren was one of the finest political journalists of the 1930s. His book, Seeds of Revolt, *which came out in 1933, is a treasure of valuable information. Here he describes the TUUL's attempt, futile as it turned out, to organize coal miners abandoned by everyone, including their own union.*

The 1931 strike began of its own accord, but the Communists were quick to take advantage of the situation. They made considerable progress as long as their funds held out, for the miners needed no great urging. The radical leaders, as was inevitable, met with bitter opposition from every other quarter—from the Pittsburgh newspapers, particularly from the *Press*, one of the liberal Scripps-Howard chain; from the clergy, the social workers, the UMWA, the coal operators, and the government authorities. Adherents of the

Communist organizers were forced daily to face a silent reign of terror. Strikers were shot at from ambush along lonely roads. In the picket lines the strikers were compelled to walk meekly and silently if they did not want the hickory club of a deputy sheriff brought down on their heads. (A goodly number of the notorious Coal and Iron Police, a ruthless organization which had been formally disbanded, were then working as deputy sheriffs in the soft coal fields.)

The terror did not end there. The nightly attacks on unescorted strikers and workers resulted in several deaths. More than that, a number of Communist organizers and strikers, all proved later to have been unarmed, were killed and wounded in brutal police attacks on the picket lines. In one such attack at the Wildwood mine Pete Zigarac, a picket, was killed by Deputy Sheriff Herbert Reel. For this Thomas Myerscough, a leader of the National Miners Union, was arrested and charged with manslaughter, although he had been taken into custody before a single shot was fired or head cracked by the deputy sheriffs. He sat in the sheriff's wagon throughout the shooting that followed. Myerscough was later convicted on a charge of inciting to riot. Wholesale arrests were resorted to by the authorities in their efforts to break the miners' rebellion. In the first few weeks of the strike 876 men and women were hauled off to the county jail. More than half of them were given jail sentences running from ten to ninety days, while a number of others were bound over for trial on more serious charges.

Some of the Communist followers were demanding action. A speaker at a Fredericktown meeting urged the strikers to "wait for the scabs in front of their homes and bust 'em in the snoot when they come from the mines." Jim Grace, a strike leader from Harlan County, Kentucky, addressing the NMU conference in Pittsburgh the week before, declared: "We must show a united front, and if necessary shoulder arms and fight for freedom." Almost every camp in the Pittsburgh area was literally deluged with copies of the *Daily Worker*. Blood-thirsty headlines were flaunted before the hungry strikers. No other literature or newspapers were to be seen. But it is doubtful whether at that stage anything but the *Daily Worker* would have had a real appeal for the long-suffering miners.

The Communist leaders, on the other hand, sought to check the violent inclinations of their followers and subordinates. Vincent Kemenovich, official of the NMU, had been quoted by the *New York Times* in a dispatch from Pittsburgh as sounding "a warning of impending trouble" and revealing that the "strikers are armed." He denied to me that he had ever made such a statement, pointing out that a threat of this sort would have made him liable as an accessory before the fact in any criminal case arising out of violence on either side. It would have been obvious to anyone who spent a few hours in the NMU headquarters in Pittsburgh that the Communists were not looking for unnecessary trouble. Their war along three fronts in the coal fields—against the operators, the United Mine Workers, and starvation—was altogether too serious a matter for them to allow their adherents to get out of hand. They knew that an invasion of the bituminous country by the state militia or by federal troops would quickly follow a serious outbreak and would just as quickly put an end to their activities. Hence they tried to proceed peacefully, using orthodox strike tactics to further their aims.

The most powerful leaders of the party, among them William Z. Foster and Alfred Wagenknecht, came from New York City to assist in the direction of the strike. Working with them were numerous officials and organizers of the Trade Union Unity League. Lesser tasks were handled by younger members of the party, who received no monetary compensation. They lived off their savings while they did secretarial work, turned out circulars, received visitors, answered telephones, and ran errands. When their money gave out, they left Pittsburgh to return to their old jobs or to find new ones, and other young Communists came in to take their places. The 1931 strike certainly did not fail for lack of organization. Nor was it called off for want of rank-and-file support. It collapsed in the end only because the Communist funds gave out; the party could no longer hold the miners in line by offering them the food that they needed.

But the collapse of the strike did not mean that work was resumed on a generous scale or that starvation decreased in the slightest degree. Conditions remained much the same thereafter. The failure of the Communists to improve the lot of the miners resulted in a marked reaction against radicals of all sorts. However, this feeling did not last long. When I went into the bituminous fields of Pennsylvania the following spring, I found the miners again listening to Communist agitators. . . .

5

THE FORD PROTEST MARCH
Moritz Hallgren

The following is excerpted from Moritz Hallgren's capsule account (in Seeds of Revolt) *of the famous Communist-led march in near-zero weather on the River Rouge plant and what resulted from it.*

On March 7, 1932, with the temperature near zero, some four to five thousand workers marched from Detroit to the River Rouge plant of the Ford Company, where they intended to present a petition asking for jobs and for adjustment of various grievances. At the Detroit city limits they were met by a force of Dearborn police who sought to turn them back. Insisting that they were engaged on a lawful and peaceful mission, the workers refused to comply. The marchers pressed on without regard to swinging clubs or threats of arrest. The police flung gas bombs at them, and the unemployed replied with rocks and jagged chunks of frozen mud. In a few minutes the police, their supply of bombs exhausted, turned and fled before the jobless thousands, who quickly reformed their ranks and marched toward Gate 3 of the Ford plant. There they were met with icy streams of water poured down upon them by engines of the company fire department. Their thin clothes frozen stiff by the water, the enraged workers forgot their plan to send a committee in to the employment office to present their petition, but instead tried to rush the factory gate. A shot was fired from the factory building which seemed to be the signal for a general barrage. Machine-gun and revolver fire swept the ranks of the workers, who had only stones and their bare fists for weapons; and these they had to use in fighting their way through the army of Detroit and Dearborn police, state troopers, and company gunmen, who had closed in on them from the rear. Four marchers were killed; ten were seriously wounded and removed to hospitals under arrest; fifty to sixty were less seriously hurt, or at least managed to escape arrest despite their injuries; fifteen policemen were clubbed or stoned.

The inevitable round-up of known radicals followed. Fifty suspects were arrested. The police announced they were also seeking William. Z. Foster, national leader of the Communists; William Reynolds, district organizer; John Schmies, who had run for mayor of Detroit on the Communist ticket; and Albert Goetz, state organizer. Prosecutor Harry S. Toy made no secret of the fact that he was planning something akin to a grand public festival in connection with the trial of the Reds; it was to be a legal lynching bee on a scale unknown since the Palmer raids of 1919 and 1920. The authorities counted upon the support of an enthusiastic public; but in that they erred. Far from applauding the patriotic efforts of the police and the prosecutor, the people of Detroit turned openly against them. Within two or three days the hostility of the public was so strongly felt that the scheme to railroad the Communist leaders to prison was dropped. Thereafter other attempts were made to indict and bring to trial some of the men who had taken part in the march, but these efforts likewise came to nothing. Even the capitalist press, hostile at first, later joined in the general public condemnation of the police brutality, while the working-class population showed where its sympathies lay when it turned out almost a hundred thousand strong to march in or witness the long parade attending the funeral of the four victims. . . .

The Imperial Valley

<u>1</u>

THE AUTOBIOGRAPHY OF AN AMERICAN COMMUNIST
Peggy Dennis

Helping the wretchedly exploited migrant workers of California organize was on the TUUL agenda. Frank Waldron was one of the main organizers of the Imperial Valley campaign—virtually a suicide mission. What happened to him and others is told here by his widow almost fifty years later. Waldron was badly beaten and arrested again, then broke bail and fled to the Soviet Union. He returned to America in the mid-1930s as Eugene Dennis (which is why she refers to "Gene") and eventually became the Party's General Secretary.

He had gone into Imperial Valley in mid-December [1929] in response to a minor news item about a pending strike among 23,000 Mexican and Filipino lettuce workers.

La Union de Trabajadores del Valle Imperial had led a strike there two years earlier and then disintegrated. The Associacion Mutual del Valle Imperial was organized, with Mexican consulate and U.S. Immigration sanction, to watchdog the work agreements between U.S. labor contractors, the workers, and the Mexican government.

Gene returned from his exploratory trip badly shaken by the inhuman living and working conditions of the field laborers, the prevalence of child labor, and the bitter divisions fostered by the growers between Mexican, Filipino, Japanese, Black and white workers. He reported to the Party and TUUL committees in Los Angeles that a spontaneous walkout was imminent and he urged our active support.

Some were wary of getting involved in a premature strike that in all probability would end in defeat. Gene argued, "We can't sit here and talk our blueprints for struggle. The strike is going to take place, these minority workers are pitted against a Goliath combination of the growers' association, the police and county government. And you are afraid of our contamination with possible defeat!" . . .

On January 6, ten thousand workers walked out of the lettuce fields. With more than 77,000 in the Valley, the massive operations did not close down, but they were badly crippled. Newspaper reports admitted that "California's most valuable single crop dropped to 50 [freight] cars a day as against 100 cars a day earlier this week."

Growers and private guards were deputized. Police enforced a curfew in Brawley and El Centro and warned that white "strangers" seen talking to local farm laborers would be arrested. A migrant camp of Filipino strikers was bombed. Striking families were evicted from company shacks, and when Ida Rothstein of the Workers' International Relief and Leo Gallagher of the American Civil Liberties Union arrived from Los Angeles to set up a tent colony and food station, they were arrested and the supplies were confiscated.

Gene and his small group worked clandestinely with militant contacts among the strikers. They issued leaflets in the various languages, including many Filipino dialects. They helped establish the first united committee in which the many races worked together for the first time. They concentrated on organizing permanent field and shed committees that would outlast the strike itself. They involved women and child laborers in activities.

We learned from the newspapers that 25 Mexican strikers had been arrested, including Gene. A smuggled message told us that the Mexican prisoners had been forcibly deported, and that Gene had been beaten in his cell by deputy sheriffs. The Reverend Clinton Taft, aristocratic-looking chairman of the American Civil Liberties Union, went to the Brawley jail to investigate. He later filed charges of physical assault against Imperial Valley County Sheriff Charles L. Gillette. At the trial in February, Taft told the court:

> When we entered and simply announced ourselves as being down from Los Angeles, interested in the civil rights of three of his prisoners, Sheriff Gillette flew into a rage, using profane and vile language, assaulted us with kicks, attempted to strangle me and violently forced me out of the door.

Gillette testified on his own behalf, saying: "Taft became abusive, I told him to leave and when he persisted, I put him out; if he got hurt it was because the door was too narrow; I did not strike him."

However, within hours of Taft's visit, Gene and the others were released and told:

"Get the hell out of town. We find you here again, you won't walk out of here a second time."

Now in the early morning, as my fingertips lightly traced the hard scabs on his face, Gene whispered, "I'm going back. I have to. They live there. They can't run away to L.A. I've got to go back."

And he did, again and again, secretly slipping in and out of the Valley towns; meeting with strikers in the dark, shades tightly drawn.

The strike was broken through the collusion of the U.S. Immigration Service and the Mexican Consulate. Mexican strikers were rounded-up by the truckload and dumped across the border a few miles away. The Filipino strikers became isolated and could not continue alone. Gene and the local activists concentrated on strengthening the permanent committees which became the Agricultural Workers Industrial League.

A few weeks later the lettuce sheds at Brawley and Calexico were struck solid and R. P. Moore, secretary of the Western Growers' Protective Association, admitted that only 50% of the packers were working in Holtsville and El Centro. This time it was no spontaneous, unorganized walkout, but an action taken by strike vote and one that held firm in face of the grower-shippers' refusal to negotiate. After eight days and during the height of the season, the strike was won and a uniform, Valley-wide wage increase was enforced.

2

THE STORY OF IMPERIAL VALLEY
Frank Spector

In a pamphlet published by the International Labor Defense in 1930, Spector, another Communist organizer, describes a particularly brutal occasion.

A general call was issued by the Agricultural Workers Industrial League for a broad, rank-and-file conference, representative of the masses of ranch and shed workers, to unite the union and to adopt a definite program of strike action. In preparation for this important conference, numerous open-air and indoor mass meetings were held in Brawley, El Centro, Westmoreland, Calexico, Calipatria and other points and also at ranches. They were attended by thousands of workers whose enthusiasm increased with the approaching struggle.

One such preliminary meeting was held in El Centro on the night of April 14 [1930].

Over one hundred Mexican, Filipino, Negro and white workers gathered in a dingy working-class hall in El Centro, the largest city of the Imperial Valley, in California. They had been called there by the Agricultural Workers Industrial Union to discuss their conditions and to prepare to participate, a week later, in a conference of delegates from ranches and sheds. The conference was to weld the ranks of the workers for the coming strike against inhuman exploitation, the contract system, speed-up, and unemployment.

One after another the workers stood up and spoke, each in his own tongue. They told of the starvation and sickness of their wives and children, of the constant wage cuts, and of the long hours of bitter toil under a scorching sun. Each one spoke of the readiness of the workers to fight under their union's militant guidance.

Suddenly the door burst open. Into the hall rushed a mob of policemen, deputy sheriffs and civilians—all armed with revolvers and sawed-off shotguns which they trained upon the assembled workers.

Out of this mob stepped Sheriff Gillette, the chief gunman of the Imperial Valley bosses. Ordering all workers to throw up their hands, he then directed a violent search of each worker, after which every one of the 108 were chained in groups. Then the mob, with a brutal display of force, threw them into huge trucks. The entire one hundred and eight were hauled into El Centro under heavy guard and thrown into the county jail there.

Two months passed. A number of the group, who were Mexican workers, were deported. A number were released.

Following that night of terror the Imperial Valley assumed the appearance of an armed camp. Everywhere, along the railroad tracks, packing sheds, bridges, warehouses, in the fields and on the ranches, before the houses of government officials, were placed guards, armed to the teeth. All the pool-rooms and halls, where workers gather, were closed. Newspapers told fantastic stories of "plots" to blow up bridges, sheds, railroads—"plots" to burn up crops, tear down vines and what not. This hysteria filled the "respectable citizenry" with bitter prejudice and hatred against the workers. Ministers in their churches and the one hundred percent patriotic organizations were frothing at the mouth, denouncing the Communist Party, the TUUL, the ILD, and passing resolutions calling upon the "guardians of law and order" to make "short work" of the imprisoned leaders of the workers. Ugly threats to take the "law" into their own hands were uttered by the frenzied patriots. . . .

The Imperial Valley struggle was seized upon by the bosses in an attempt to strike a death-blow against the hated Communist Party and other militant workers' organizations. Through the criminal syndicalism law they hoped to force underground this militant leader of the California masses. Thirty-two defendants were charged with violating this law, among whom were many leading Communists throughout the state. Bail of $40,000, an unheard-of amount, was set on each of the arrested to insure their remaining in the bosses' clutches.

The International Labor Defense began a determined drive for the release of the workers and succeeded in forcing the reduction of the bail to $5,000 on each. Fearing the rising pressure of mass protests, the bosses changed their tactics. They dismissed the charges against the 32 workers and substituted grand jury indictments against 13 workers. Bail was set at $15,000 for each. The International Labor Defense again fought for the reduction of prohibitive bail, but the same judges, of the Appellate Court, who on the previous occasion were compelled to reduce the bail, now refused to do so.

The indictment returned by the Imperial County grand jury was drawn up on the testimony of three stool-pigeons: Sherman Barber, Charles Collum and Oscar Chormicle—all operatives of the scab-herding Bolling Detective Agency, in the employ of the growers. Notorious spies were employed to procure and manufacture the necessary evidence. Similar creatures were hired to worm their way into the new militant union and [manufacture] frame-up evidence.

Of the 13 indicted, 9 actually faced trial. Two were not found. Two were dismissed on the day of the trial, June 26, in Superior Judge Thompson's court. The trial, lasting 21 days, was conducted with a frenzy of prejudice and hatred, fanned by provocative reports of nonexistent "plots." All attempts to organize protests under the leadership of the International Labor Defense were crushed by the police. . . .

The jury was composed entirely of ranchers and businessmen. Even without a pretense at deliberation, it returned a verdict of "guilty" on all counts against all the defendants. This, of course, was a foregone conclusion.

The most vicious sentences were meted out to Carl Sklar and Tetsuji Horiuchi, serving three to forty-two years in Folsom State Prison; Oscar Erickson, Lawrence Emery, Frank Spector and Danny Roxas, serving three to forty-two years in San Quentin Prison. Eduardo Herera and Braulio Orosco, both Mexican workers, were sentenced to two to twenty-eight years in San Quentin. Originally held for deportation, they were later ordered to jail.

Through the last strike movement the Imperial Valley workers have learned a number of valuable lessons which they will apply in the coming new struggles.

1
MOBILIZING THE POOR
Moritz Hallgren

Hallgren's account speaks for itself.

The Unemployed Councils organized by the Communist Party represented another form of self-help. Instead of waiting hopefully for the government or the rich to help the jobless, the Communists went to work immediately after the stock-market crash in 1929 to persuade the unemployed that they could help themselves only by uniting their demands for work or relief. By street demonstrations held in several industrial cities in December 1929 and in many industrial centers on March 6, 1930, the Communists centered the attention of the working class on the need for such organization. Unemployed Councils (some of which later were captured by the Socialist Party) were formed in every large industrial community and in most of the smaller ones as well. The Communists relied wholly upon mass protests, hunger marches, demonstrations in front of relief centers and municipal buildings. They believed that the capitalist-entrepreneur class had to be thoroughly frightened before it would meet the hunger problem in anything like adequate fashion. This philosophy, as I have suggested in an earlier chapter, was expressed by Herbert Benjamin, national leader of the Unemployed Councils, when he told a Senate committee that no real help would be forthcoming "until every man in Congress is shivering in his very pants because he thinks the unemployed are going to engage in struggle." In this the Communists were more than justified. Social workers everywhere told me that without the street demonstrations and hunger marches of the Unemployed Councils no relief whatever would have been provided in some communities, while in others even less help than that which had been extended would have been forthcoming. There are on record many instances in which public authorities or charitable agencies, having announced that relief would have to be cut down or suspended, quickly reversed their decision and obtained the necessary funds as a result of mass protests in the form of street demonstrations. . . .

2
DANGEROUS SCOT
John Williamson

In his 1969 autobiography, Williamson, a top Communist functionary who, in the McCarthy era, was jailed and then expelled from the country, recounts his experience as a leader of the Chicago Unemployed Councils.

Nowhere was police terror so bad as in Chicago during those years. Corrupt to the core and in alliance with the gangsters, the police arrested hundreds of workers at meetings, demonstrations and strikes and beat them into insensibility in the local police stations. It was the infamous Red Squad, headed by Lieutenant Mike Mills and Sergeant Murphy, who raided party offices, broke up the furniture and brutally beat every Communist they could lay hand on. In 1930, the Communist candidate for Congress, Lee Mason, a Negro worker, was murdered by the police.

It was in this atmosphere that I began my new assignment. While the party district office was in Chicago, the area covered at that time included all of Illinois and Indiana, plus the lower half of Wisconsin, the city of St. Louis and the area around Davenport, Iowa.

Among the unemployed our central demand was for the Unemployment Insurance Bill. While we were getting a tremendous popular response, we still hadn't built a solid enough foundation among the unemployed in their daily fight against evictions, in their demands for relief, for free water, and for gas and electricity, when these were shut off.

We had just developed a program which asserted the right of the Negro people to self-determination in the Southern states and expressed our resolution to intensify our efforts in the struggle for their full political, economic and social equality, with emphasis on the fight against lynching and discrimination. These were the issues around which we hoped to develop the broadest mass struggle of the Negro people in unity with the white workers.

This was a new approach, since Socialists in the past had for the most part ignored the plight of the Negro. Even Eugene Debs was weak on this question. It is doubtful whether he could have attracted such large audiences in his presidential campaigns in the South had he declared for the right of the Negro to vote and enjoy equality.

The wisdom of our conviction on this issue would be confirmed in the months and years to come, as America entered the deepest crisis of its history. The Chicago district, like so many others, was the scene of tremendous struggles, in which Communists displayed high courage and leadership, won support and grew in membership and influence.

At that time we had a membership and leadership in Chicago whose active core was a combination of foreign-born comrades and younger people like myself who had been in the Young Communist League. Bill Gebert and I worked out a rough division of labor whereby he, in addition to his general political responsibility as secretary, gave attention to industrial work and to Southern Illinois, Wisconsin and St. Louis; while I, in addition to party organization and recruiting, devoted myself to activity among the unemployed and the Negro people, and to work in the Chicago, Indiana and Rockford areas.

The daily struggles in those first days of the deepening crisis centered around two issues: the demand for a system of unemployment relief and the prevention of evictions. The local headquarters of the Unemployed Councils were real nerve centers of events affecting the jobless in the neighborhoods. After a while, some of them functioned with military precision in outwitting the bailiffs and police.

In August 1931, the police shot into a crowd on the South Side that was trying to stop the eviction of a 70-year-old widow, Mrs. Diana Gross. Three Negro workers, Abe Gray, John O'Neil and Frank Armstrong, were killed. This aroused the community to seething anger, and brought about a remarkable demonstration of Negro-white unity. From then on, the Unemployed Councils gained strength, and tens of thousands of workers in all parts of Chicago were involved in their common struggles.

During that summer a state hunger march to the capital was organized, with the official support of the party. As it approached Springfield, the state troopers blocked all the highways and the governor threatened to call out the National Guard. The main body of marchers from Chicago, where our party influence was greatest, were corralled into a camp for the night with troopers and police surrounding them.

A committee of which I was a member had been established for the march. Anticipating the moves of the troopers, I had separated from my group in order to be mobile, but now the problem was how to have a committee meeting while still retaining freedom of action.

Runners established contact with me and led me back through bushes and trees, after dark, into the "corral." We had our meeting and worked out a strategy that was successful the next day. In negotiation with the state troopers, who were in touch with the governor and the speaker of the state legislature, it was agreed that if all the hunger marchers were allowed to gather in a meeting outside the state capitol, small delegations would be sent in to speak to the legislature and see the governor. After a last check-up, the committee adjourned and I was taken back through the woods, successfully evading the troopers.

In Chicago a real offensive had been started against the unemployed. Another worker had just been murdered; proposals were being made that all foreign-born unemployed (about 20 percent of the Chicago total) should be deported; and the police force had been increased to deal with the growing crisis.

There was great discontent among Chicago's unemployed and their families. The action that precipitated a great new movement was a 50 percent cut in relief payments to 160,000 family men on October 1, without even a day's notice. The party and those Unemployed Council leaders who were close to the event immediately organized the discontent into the biggest united-front demonstration ever held, under the joint auspices of the Unemployed Councils, the Workers Committee on Unemployment (under Socialist leadership) and the Workers League (led by remnants of the Proletarian Party). The main demands were withdrawal of the relief cut, an end to all evictions and cash relief. To achieve these demands we projected a march through the

Loop and into Grant Park, and opened negotiations with the authorities at city hall. Mayor Anton Cermak emphatically refused our request for a permit.

Our judgment was that the existing conditions warranted our defying Cermak with some hope of success. The unemployed had never been so aroused. Despite the hesitations and sabotage of Socialist leaders like Karl Borders, the Workers Committee branches were enthusiastic for the march. Franklin D. Roosevelt was the Democratic candidate in the November presidential elections, against the infamous Herbert Hoover, and the local Democratic administration would hardly risk a bloodbath on the eve of the elections.

The joint committee announced that the hunger march would take place, as scheduled, without a permit. Its purposes were outlined and responsibility for any trouble was placed on Mayor Cermak and his police. It was also announced that two delegations of 35 each would drop out as the march passed the City-County Building to meet the Mayor and the Cook County leaders.

The newspapers predicted a bloody battle and told of the police preparations. It was with elation that we saw the massive response, estimated at close to 50,000, that formed up into the hunger march. Headed by a phalanx of 45 men and women—15 from each of the sponsoring organizations—we marched through the crowded Loop, stopping all traffic for over an hour.

Among our own group were Claude Lightfoot, Joe Weber, Leonides McDonald, Nick Blattnor, Brown Squire, W. Lamson and myself. While there was great enthusiasm in the ranks of the marchers, among the leaders, especially the Communists who had taken the initiative and bore the chief responsibility, there was great tension. Though our greatest hope for a peaceful demonstration lay in the large number who had responded, one never knew what the Chicago police were planning. We kept certain comrades out of the march in order to assure continuity of leadership, but those of us who were leading the march had little chance of any protection if the police did not back down.

At one point in the Loop we saw a solid wall of police blocking the road with all the top brass in evidence. We slowed down and a small group went forward to talk. The police said we were defying the law by marching in the Loop without a permit. The march leaders stood solidly on their right to peaceful demonstration and placed all responsibility for the consequences of trying to stop the march on the city administration. At a signal from Joe Weber, the leader of the Unemployed Councils, the leaders started forward, with thousands of marchers behind us. The wall of police fell back and joined others on the sidelines. As we passed them we were roundly cursed and threatened with what would happen the next time they had us at their mercy.

Needless to say, everyone was jubilant, although I will never forget the sweat running down my body under the pressure of responsibility. With perfect discipline, the marchers proceeded to Grant Park. I was a member of the delegation chosen to meet Mayor Cermak. He did not appear, but sent a representative. A lot of wrangling took place and we were given no satisfaction.

The next day, however, it was announced that the relief cut had been withdrawn—a great victory with far-reaching effects, arousing new enthusiasm and a consciousness of strength. This was reinforced by a second victory. Growing out of a state conference, a delegation was sent to the state legislature, and after our spokesmen had a heated exchange with the legislature, a $17-million relief appropriation was passed. . . .

3

IN MY MOTHER'S HOUSE
Kim Chernin

As her daughter Kim listened attentively, Rose Chernin reminisced about the time fifty years earlier when she, a militant Communist, led rent strikes in the Bronx.

You know how people lived in that time, in the tenements of the Bronx. There were brick buildings, most of them without elevators, old houses with dark staircases and narrow corridors. There were people in the basement apartments, people crowded into small spaces, living together, sometimes without a bedroom, sharing kitchens and toilets, and afraid to lose the little space they had.

But these places, which no one would call exactly a castle, were better than the street. If a man would lose the job, a week later you'd see his whole family sitting out on the street. So we decided to ask for a reduction. An entire apartment house or a whole tenement would refuse to pay the landlord until the rents were reduced for everyone in the building.

By that time the Unemployed Councils were well known: our workers were everywhere, leading demonstrations, circulating petitions, speaking on street corners. So we would go into a building, introduce ourselves, and ask the people to organize. We said, "As long as we strike we certainly don't pay rent. Let's say we're striking for three months. That rent will never be paid."

The people listened, the idea appealed to them. We promised that we would fight the evictions and help take care of the people who were thrown out. In those days you would walk down the street and see whole families with their children sitting on the sidewalk surrounded by furniture.

When an entire building was organized and willing to participate in a strike, we formed negotiating committees for the tenants, put up large signs in every window facing the street, and picketed the house. The signs read: "Rent Strike. Don't Rent Apartments in this Building."

The landlord, of course, would rather die than give in to the tenants' demands. So the strike began. We knew that one day he would give some eviction notices. But he could never evict everyone. It cost too much.

On the day of the eviction we would tell all the men to leave the building. We knew that the police were rough and would beat them up. It was the women who remained in the apartments, in order to resist. We went out onto the fire escapes and spoke through bullhorns to the crowd that gathered below.

In the Bronx you could get two hundred people together if you just looked up at the sky. As soon as the police came to begin the eviction, we roped off the street and people gathered. The police put machine guns on the roofs, they pointed them down at the people in the street.

We, meanwhile, were standing out on the balcony. I would address the crowd gathered in the street below: "People, fellow workers. We are the wives of unemployed men and the police are evicting us. Today *we* are being evicted. Tomorrow it will be *you*. So stand by and watch. What is happening to us will happen to you. We have no jobs. We can't afford food. Our rents are too high. The marshal has brought the police to carry out our furniture. Are you going to let it happen?"

Or sometimes we would address the workers who had been brought to take the furniture: "We are talking to you, you men who have come here to throw out the furniture of unemployed workers. Who are you? You, too, are unemployed men who have had to take this job in order to eat. We don't blame you. You are one of us. We represent the Unemployed Council and last night we made a collection among the unemployed. We have enough money to pay you off. How much are you going to get for evicting an unemployed worker? Five dollars? Six dollars? We have the money for you. Come up here without the police and without the marshal and we will pay you off. Look at the marshal standing there. Is he working? Let him do the work."

And so we would harangue. We could see the men hesitating. We would continue: "We women are standing here with the furniture that is to be evicted. The water is hot in our kettles. The doors are locked. We're not letting you in."

Often, the hired men would come up anyway. Our doors were locked but they would break them in. We were behind those doors, with our kettles. They would grab a piece of furniture on one side and we would grab it on the other. And both would start pulling. Meanwhile we would say: "Here, here is the money. Leave the furniture."

Some would take the money and go. Sometimes we poured the hot water on the men. Sometimes they would hit us. And then we would run out onto the fire escape, grab the bullhorn, and shout to the crowd: "They're hitting us. They're big men and they're hitting us. But we're not going to let them move the furniture. They can't overcome us. We shall win."

Sometimes, they'd get so disgusted with all this fighting and hollering they'd take the furniture from the apartment but leave it on the landing. That was a victory. We'd stay there and wait for the husbands to return and then we'd put the furniture back into the apartment. We'd put a new lock on the door and the landlord would have to get a new eviction notice. He'd call the marshal and the whole thing would start all over again.

Our fight was successful. The rents came down, the evicted families returned to their apartments, the landlord would stop fighting us. Sometimes we failed and the furniture was carried into the street. Immediately we would cover it with a tarpaulin so it wouldn't get spoiled, and then we'd hold a mass meeting on the furniture, using it as a platform. We were only waiting for the police to leave. As soon as they were gone, the people standing around would pick up the furniture and carry it right back into the building. We'd break the lock, put back the furniture, install a new lock, and the landlord would have to go through the whole procedure another time.

Within two years we had rent control in the Bronx. That's the way it was in those days. . . .

The South

1

THE *SOUTHERN WORKER*

As part of its campaign in the black belt the Party sent its chief authority on the Negro question, James S. Allen, down to Chattanooga to edit its daring newspaper there. This is an extract from the first issue, dated August 16, 1930.

The *Southern Worker* is the Communist paper for the South.

It is being published because the southern workers and farmers need it and want it. The *Southern Worker* is the voice of the Negro and white workers and farmers of the South crying in united protest against the state of starvation, suffering and persecution to which they have been subjected by the white ruling class.

This is the first really workers' paper ever published below the Mason and Dixon line. It is the first Communist publication ever issued in the South. As such it will carry the Communist program to the white and black workers and farmers, pointing out the path to struggle, offering the militant and understanding leadership of the Communist Party to the millions of southern toilers.

The *Southern Worker* is neither a "white" paper, nor a "Negro" paper. It is a paper of and for both the white and black workers and farmers. It recognizes only one division, the bosses against the workers and the workers against the bosses. In this class struggle the *Southern Worker* stands always, without exception, unflinchingly, for the workers. It is a workers' paper. . . .

2

BLACK WORKER IN THE DEEP SOUTH
Hosea Hudson

In his 1972 autobiography, Hudson, a lifelong Communist, tells of his part in the attempt to build a movement in Birmingham, the deep South's only major industrial city.

In spite of the constant battle to make a living, and such racist persecution as I have described, I still remained to some degree a happy-go-lucky sort of guy. I sang in quartets around Birmingham, having the reputation of being one of the best bass singers in that area. I had been singing for seven years and I got used to people following the quartet every Sunday from one church to another to hear my group sing.

So I wasn't at all surprised one day when a man I knew by sight, a Negro worker, named Al Murphy, greeted me warmly. This was around July 1931.

I said, "Where've you been? Ain't seen you 'round in a long time. Still in the shop?"

"I got fired."

"What for?"

He told me he'd been taking part in the campaign for the Scottsboro boys. The company had found out about it and fired him. He said he just got back from a conference in New York where the Scottsboro Case had been discussed.

I asked, "What are they saying about us up there?"

Well, he told me, they wondered why we didn't organize. He had told the conference that Southern Negroes felt they didn't have anything to fight with. They asked him whether it was easier to organize or to fight and he admitted that it was easier to organize.

I met him again in September and he asked me to come to a meeting that week at the home of a fellow named Lee, who worked in the same shop, saying that at this meeting we would organize for action. I thought for a minute of my grandmother saying the Yankees were coming back to finish the job of freeing the Negroes in the South. Every time there was an attack on my people I wondered when that day would come. When the Scottsboro Case was exposed as a frame-up, when telegrams began to pour in from New York and other Northern states, as well as cables from all over Europe, I thought this was the time somebody was coming to help us do something to free ourselves. So when I heard the word "organize" I wanted to join up.

When I got to Lee's house, I expected to see a crowded room but was shocked to see only those I had been seeing every day in the shop or around in the community. There were about eight altogether. What kind of a meeting was this? Al Murphy began to talk about the Scottsboro Case, especially what it meant to the freedom struggle of the Black people. He discussed the jury system in the South, linking it to the fact that those boys had been given a death sentence by an all-white jury.

He said we had to stop the "legal lynching" of the eight who had been sentenced to death (one of them, a 12-year-old had been sent to the penitentiary until he was old enough to be tried). Murphy explained that the Scottsboro Case was only a part of the over-all oppression of our people.

"It's the system itself that brings about these frame-ups and lynchings," and he went on to say he wanted all of us to understand that the kind of society in which we lived robbed the masses of people of a livelihood; that the only way the bosses could prevent the white and the Black masses of people from struggling together was to keep them divided. If they could spread the lie that every white woman was in danger of being raped by some Black man, it helped to spread fear and disunity. He gave us a little pamphlet with a map showing the whole area of the Black Belt. From the beginning, he said, the development of this area was carried on by the slaveholders who raised cotton for the most part. The Black population outnumbered the white. The Blacks built not only the railroads and the factories, they had helped to build the material wealth of the entire South with their toil and sweat and blood.

Yet we Negroes enjoyed practically none of the rights guaranteed American citizens by the U.S. Constitution.

I said to myself, "This man is a Communist!" I was at a Communist meeting and, though nothing sensational was happening, the idea was exciting.

He went on to explain what he meant by "Black Belt." Blacks constituted a majority of the population in many areas of the South. He pointed out that in these areas people like us were kept from voting, from running for public office and from taking part in self-government.

I said to myself, "Yes, when my grandmother, my mother, my brother and I and so many more of us hoped to go to school—and we never stopped hoping—we never did get a chance. Right here and now we Blacks are the last to be hired and the first to be fired. It was we, already existing on the crumbling edge of starvation, who suffered the highest death rate. If we had any medical care at all, it was just a whisper above being nothing!"

When he said that not everybody could be a member of the Party, I wondered if I could be—or who among that gathering of eight Black men from the shop could be. To be members, the man said, people had to be willing to sacrifice a part of their good times; they had to give the time they saved to activity and education among other workers who felt something was wrong with the setup but didn't know what to do about it.

I sat there wondering if I could fit in; then I looked at the other fellows and realized not one of them could read or write. I myself had to spell out every word before I knew what it was.

Al Murphy went on to say Communists spread the Party's message by distributing its leaflets and its newspaper. He said they would hold regular meetings, get to them on time and pay dues regularly. Then he added that the Party would expel members who got drunk or were loose in their moral conduct or careless in handling finances.

After he had made all these points—very calm, quiet and convincing—he stopped. There wasn't much that anybody could fail to understand and there weren't many questions. We all eight signed up, each paying 50 cents initiation fee and pledging 10 cents monthly dues, or more, based on our rate of pay. They elected me unit organizer.

In our brief meeting that night we agreed our main task would be among the workers in our shop. We'd pick out individual workers to make friends with and, in this way, we would be able, we hoped, to build the organization in the Stockham plant. . . .

We held our weekly unit meeting and reported on the conditions in the shop. A Party representative visited each meeting. This time he got us started on a series of actions. "For the next meeting," he said, "sit down and write your complaints just like you are writing a letter—the best you can."

At the next meeting we had our letter telling what the foreman had said to us; how he cussed out John; how one man was doing two men's work and not getting paid for it, and so on. We turned it over to the Party representative and he took it with him.

About two weeks later he brought it back—printed in the *Southern Worker*, weekly newspaper of the Communist Party, published in Chattanooga, Tennessee, with big headlines about conditions at the Stockham Pipe and Fittings Company plant. Our pride and excitement increased when we found out the letter also appeared in the *Sunday Worker*, published in New York. We read the papers as well as we could; we had never before been able to express our anger against these conditions like this, and we were hopeful that the people in the communities would get so indignant that Stockham's would be compelled to do something about them. The Party representative gave us all extra copies to distribute among the people, and one to put where the company stoolpigeon would get to it—actually we dropped it in his yard.

Another few days passed. Then one day the supers, worried-looking, came into the shop and said they didn't want anybody to leave for the bathhouse.

"We are going to have a meeting this evening. Nobody changes until after the meeting."

It was on the right-hand side of the shop, out in the open, in a broad space near a brick wall and the fence. Everybody was out there—Black molders and white machinists, the assistant super, the super himself and other supervisory personnel, including Mr. Nibley, the personnel director, who got up and said that he wanted to tell the men that, "beginning tomorrow, we don't want a man to put his hand on a machine before seven or he's fired. You-all will stop work at 2:45 and clean up your machine by three and be ready to go to the bathhouse."

He went over that again and again. "Times are getting hard," he said, "and we'll have to be cutting wages but I want to tell you men right now we don't want anybody to work more time than you-all supposed to. Stop for lunch when the whistle blows, at 12. Be ready to start work when the 12:30 whistle blows. Stop work at 2:45, clean up your machines, and be ready to get out of here by three o'clock."

I almost burst out laughing when he said, "If any foreman cusses at any man here, he won't have any more job here . . . and the same goes for you fellows." What made it funny, in a crazy sort of way, was his lumping "you fellows"—meaning John Bedell, me, any number of other Black workers in the shop—in the same bag with the superintendents, assistant supers and straw bosses. Suppose one of those white guys did get fired for cussing us—and chances stood a thousand to one against it—he'd have another job before sundown. But let one of us get fired for "standing up" to or "talking back" to a white "bossman" and we might as well decide right then and there to get clean out of the state, because we'd be blackballed at every factory gate for hundreds of miles around.

Anyhow, when the meeting was over, the men all went out full of joy, and some of us said, "Them papers sure did stir things up!" and things like, "If they tell us to strike, I'm ready."

Black workers and white workers—all were openly talking about "this great victory," talking to anyone and everyone who would listen. And among the first talkers were the Communists. The Party put out leaflets calling on workers to organize, Blacks and whites together, for higher wages, job security, unemployment and social insurance for all unemployed. But the inexperienced Party leadership in the South didn't yet know how to guard itself or warn us in the shop unit to watch out for the traps our enemy set. . . .

3

ACHIEVEMENTS AND TASKS OF THE SHARECROPPERS UNION
Al Murphy

The Sharecroppers Union was indeed one of the Party's signal achievements. It began in 1932 in Alabama's Tallapoosa County, not far from Birmingham, where Communist units had already been established. Al Murphy took charge of the union later that year, by which time, in the face of tremendous violence, it was spreading into adjoining black belt communities. This passage is from a speech Murphy gave at a Party conference in New York in 1933. It later came out as a pamphlet.

First I want to say, comrades, next month will mark the first year of the existence of the Sharecroppers Union. During this period we have been able to organize between 2,000 and 3,000 members. Out of all of these members we have not been able to organize one single white farmer and have been able to organize only five Party units, of 30 to 35 members.

Our union has accomplished something; new victories have been won. More victories could have been won with the tremendous possibilities which we have; but the reason we have not spread the union and have not built up a broader and stronger Party capable of leading the masses, the Negro sharecroppers and tenants, and also of mobilizing and leading the broad section of the white farmers, is because the Party is so small. And secondly, it is functioning in a sectarian line and manner. Thirdly, we have not developed local leadership.

What are some of the victories? We were able to force the landlords on three plantations to cancel all debts against the sharecroppers.

We have been able to force from the landlords not only immediate relief in the form of clothes and food, but we have also been able to get cash relief. For example, we had one comrade who wanted some clothes, food and money to buy medicine with. He went to the landlord and asked him for these things. The landlord refused. He came back to the union and asked us what he must do about it. With three or four other comrades we made up a committee consisting of about seven people who went to the office of the landlord who is a gin company operator and asked him for this relief. The landlord immediately saw that there was some organization behind it. At first he refused saying that he didn't have it, that he couldn't get it because he was in debt, but the second time they went to the landlord he immediately instructed the secretary of his firm to write out an order for whatever the cropper and his family wanted.

In addition to that, we have forced the landlord of two plantations to give the croppers the right to sell their own cotton. In the black belt the Negro sharecroppers in particular have not got the right to sell their own cotton. This is one of the main bases upon which the whole robbery system in the black belt is placed. For instance, a sharecropper who works on halves, makes ten bales of cotton. The landlord doesn't allow him to sell this cotton himself, but instead, the sharecropper is forced to turn the cotton and the receipts over into the hands of the landlord and then the landlord puts it in the warehouse; and the croppers are forced to pay for storage on cotton put in the warehouse. It remains there for months and months and the cropper cannot sell it; he has to wait until the landlord takes action. On two plantations we have absolutely destroyed these conditions. . . .

Farmers

FARMERS UNITE THEIR FIGHT
Lem Harris

Lem Harris, one of the Party's agricultural experts—he had studied in the Soviet Union—went out to the Midwest in 1931 to organize rebellious farmers. Out of that rebelliousness came the Communist-led National Farmers Relief Conference, which attracted a surprisingly large number of participants from across the farm belt when it was held in December 1932, the nadir of the crisis. Out of that Conference came, in turn, the Farmers National Committee for Action, of which Harris was executive secretary, as well as a very fine paper, the Farmers National Weekly. What follows is an excerpt from Harris's address, later published separately, to the second Relief Conference. By then—November 1933—New Deal recovery policies were kicking in and the Communist effort was on the wane.

Fellow Farmers, Delegates from all over the country:

We have come here to unite upon a campaign of struggle for winning the most pressing demands affecting all working farmers. At the Washington Conference last year we started our national campaign against forced sales and evictions, for a moratorium on debts, an attack on the swollen profits of middlemen. . . .

Our record during the past year is a struggle to carry out the National Program of Action. In 1929, 123,000 farmers were foreclosed upon or evicted. In 1932, this number rose to 262,100 farms, or one out of every 24 farms. In 1933, the year after the Washington Conference, although farmers are in a worse condition, nevertheless the number of foreclosures and evictions dropped because we made it unhealthy to throw a family out of its home. . . .

Strike is the weapon farmers have been using to force their demands upon the trusts.

We have seen farmers' strikes breaking out two times in Wisconsin, two times in New York and in Iowa and other parts of the country. We find farmers preparing for strikes in Pennsylvania and Connecticut. We also find whenever a strike is planned the enemy makes the most prodigious efforts to get into control and keep it from making much headway. We find in New York, when the farmers came out on strike, that the Farm Bureau and Dairymen's League openly attacked the strike. The New York delegates report that the farmers of New York State are ready to go out on strike again when they get an organization going. . . . In order to win we must have leadership from the ranks of the farmers.

At every step of the way, as we get better organized, we encounter the enemy—the tools of finance capital. We find their courts, judges, sheriffs, legislators, governors and Congress lined up to enforce the ruin of the farmers and workers of the whole country. But we must realize that there are two kinds of enemies: (1) Those who carry bayonets and gas, who arrest, sentence and imprison our farmer leaders; (2) The false friends who get into positions of leadership and talk radically as they betray us.

One example covers the whole situation. In Pennsylvania, soon after the Washington Conference, farmers massed to stop a sale. It was the first time it had happened in that community.

When the sheriff, deputies and lawyer arrived they found children in the lane holding signs: "Save our home," and 300 farmers amassed in the barnyard. The sheriff began by getting tough. "I want you fellows to know this farm is under the jurisdiction of the county. I'm its legal representative and I am in charge of this situation." A farmer who is in this hall right now stepped forward and said: "Wait a minute. This is a farm and this is a manure pile, Mr. Sheriff, and these are farmers and this is a farmers' community." [The lawyer] decided not to bid for the property. The mass power of the farmers was victorious.

One day later on, after many other sales had been stopped, 70 armed deputies were sent to the Pennsylvania village of Red Hill to force through the sale of a farm worked by John Lelko. Faced with this small army, the crowd of farmers refused to accept battle. They had a different plan. A girl speaker got up between the crowd of farmers and the line of deputies: "You have come out against us with arms. . . . We have another weapon. From now on this farm will be a scab farm. We are going to see to it that this owner suffers for this action. We are going to see to it that no new tenant comes on this farm became we are going to inform that tenant that this is a mighty unhealthy place for him and that nobody will neighbor with him and he will find it tough."

In Wisconsin, Iowa and New York this year, soldiers have been called out to stop the farmers from winning their just demands. But did you notice when they call out the militia, they used very young people—practically kids who did not know what it was all about—the ones least likely to turn against businessmen and to the farmers? Is that not true? (Answer from Iowa delegation: "Yes. They were high school kids. Many looked about sixteen.") . . .

When the misleaders find they are losing support they bring in the "red scare." They start a cry: "Look out for the radicals, the reds." Fellow farmers, we most certainly are radical—present distress demands intelligent, radical action. We represent farmers of all views and political opinions.

At our wonderful united front convention in Lincoln, Nebraska, last February, the misleaders tried the red scare and failed. Crocker, the insurance man, and Parmenter, both officers of the National Holiday Association, testified before the Nebraska Senate Committee and broadcast to the state that the 350 farmer delegates assembled in Lincoln were just a bunch of reds. The result must have surprised Parmenter & Co. On the day following the broadcast, 3,500 more farmers came in to Lincoln to join their comrades in a march on the State Capitol. . . .

We are calling on the farmers of America, organized and unorganized, to join forces to win our demands. We are not building an organization but are a united front of all organizations and all exploited farmers.

We have a headquarters, a National Committee and a paper to help direct our national campaigns of struggle. In close cooperation with the National Committee are the hundreds of organizers, speakers, etc., many of whom are sitting in this hall. Perhaps many who have not been out organizing will get vaccinated here at this convention and start some excitement when they go back home. . . .

[We must] get the farm women to participate. . . . I am mighty glad that we have more women delegates than last year. We are counting on them to get more women organized when they go back home. When a woman gets up at a sale and speaks it carries enormous weight. It is the voice of the people speaking. . . .

The Yokinen Affair

The Party published theYokinen "trial" soon after it was held in 1931 under the title, Race Hatred on Trial, *from which the following is taken. The fourteen "jurors" were evenly divided between black and white. Hathaway, the "prosecutor," was editor of the* Daily Worker. *Richard Moore, the "defense attorney," himself a Negro, was a top lawyer for the International Labor Defense.*

1

SPEECH
Clarence A. Hathaway (Attorney for the Prosecution)

I say, never, under any circumstances will we be able to overcome the suspicion, the doubt, the mistrust that every Negro worker has of the whites, as long as incidents such as the Finnish dance are tolerated. Promises, I repeat, mean nothing. Our Party in Harlem must also prove *in action* that we are ready to fight unflinchingly in behalf of Negro rights. If, when these three Negro workers came to the dance at the Finnish club, Communist Party members had come to the defense of these Negro workers, had jumped at the throat of their persecutors and established their right to dance in this hall, to play pool, and even to bathe, Comrade Yokinen, these Negro workers would have known that our promises about equality were not only words. The Negro workers and hundreds more in Harlem, would then have been able to say with conviction: "*The Communist Party, alone, fights for equal rights.*"

Stamp Out White Chauvinism

And now, comrades, especially at a time when the capitalists and landowners are more viciously persecuting the workers than ever before; at a time when great masses of workers, both Negro and white, are actually being forced into starvation; at a time when these same capitalists are feverishly preparing for war, especially against the Soviet Union, the struggle to overcome white chauvinism among the white workers, to overcome the suspicion and mistrust of the Negro workers, to establish a united front of all workers, Negro and white, must be waged more fearlessly and with more energy than ever before. Every manifestation of white chauvinism, no matter how slight, must be ruthlessly stamped out of our own ranks.

The District Committee of the Communist Party therefore proposes that Comrade Yokinen be found guilty of conduct that is detrimental to the interests of the whole working class; that he be found guilty of views and practices which aid the bourgeoisie in bringing about disunity among the Negro and

white workers; that he be found guilty of violating, both in theory and practice, the fundamental laws of the Communist Party.

Find Yokinen Guilty!

We propose that he be found guilty, on all of these counts, and we then propose to the jury, on the basis of this, that they recommend Comrade
Yokinen's expulsion from the Communist Party.

Next, we propose that Comrade Yokinen, as a condition for membership
in the Finnish Workers Club, be assigned to definite tasks which will give him
the opportunity *in practice* to prove that he has corrected the position he previously held, and is now ready to fight for Negro rights.

We propose that he be given the task of calling a meeting of the Finnish
Workers Club, after this trial, and there make a report to the club on this
trial, pointing out the basis for the jury's verdict of guilty, which I am convinced will be given; pointing out his own errors, and taking up in the club
the work of overcoming all remaining chauvinistic tendencies.

We further propose that he be assigned the task of selling a definite number of copies of the paper, *The Liberator*, the organ of the League of Struggle
for Negro Rights, and that generally he be assigned to a whole series of such
tasks as will prove to the working class of Harlem, and to the Finnish workers, that he has corrected his position.

Only by treating this case in such a manner can we help here today to
cement the bonds of Negro and white working-class unity, which is indispensable in our common revolutionary struggle for liberation from capitalist exploitation. (*Applause*) . . .

2

SPEECH

Richard B. Moore (Attorney for the Defense)

We are both in agreement on the guilt of Comrade Yokinen, and Comrade
Yokinen himself admits his guilt. Now Comrade Yokinen must be condemned. This chauvinist act of his must be sharply and severely condemned.
He has forfeited by this act the right to remain in the vanguard of the working class and must be on probation until he proves not only in words but in
his actual practices that he has overcome his chauvinism; and then he takes
his place as a militant class-conscious worker fighting with the Negro workers and with all workers against white chauvinism; then he must be rein-
stated into the Communist Party, the vanguard of the proletariat.

This proletarian court cannot take the attitude of the pious, hypocritical
Jews and Christians, who imagine that they have washed themselves of their
sins when they have killed a lamb or a goat or slaughtered their "savior-gods."
I say, we cannot make and we will not make a "paschal lamb" of Comrade

Yokinen. While we must condemn his act sharply and severely, we must exercise that working-class clemency necessary to win him away from this error back into the ranks of the working-class movement.

Before we come here and yell for the blood of Comrade Yokinen, it would be much better, and far more in keeping with the principles of Communism, to criticize ourselves. Let us examine ourselves, each and every one, and see if we are free from this taint—this vicious influence of anti-Communist, anti-working-class prejudice, of the ruling capitalist class. Nor can we prove ourselves free from this taint of chauvinism merely by clamoring for the expulsion of Comrade Yokinen. We can only prove this in deeds, by the manner in which we actually work and fight side by side with the doubly oppressed Negro masses, against the bosses' Jim-Crow lynch system, for full equality and self-determination.

Disgrace of Expulsion

We must remember that a verdict of expulsion in disgrace from the Communist Party is considered by a class-conscious worker as worse than death at the hands of the bourgeois oppressors. As for myself, I would rather have my head severed from my body by the capitalist lynchers than to be expelled from the Communist International. (*Applause*) And I say, fellow workers, that it will be no part of the actions of a proletarian court to destroy a worker, an honest but unenlightened worker who has fallen a victim of capitalist prejudice. We must not destroy Comrade Yokinen, we must not drive him out of the working-class movement, but we must save him for the Party and the working class.

I say this, fellow workers, as a Negro worker who is conscious of the centuries of brutal exploitation that the Negro toilers have suffered and are still suffering at the hands of the ruling class, at the hands of the brutal, capitalist, imperialist exploiters. But with all this terror and suffering and misery of the Negro workers, I see also the suffering and misery of the workers of the world. I see the Russian workers and peasants bleeding beneath the yoke (in the old days before the revolution), under the terrorist rule of the czars and capitalists. I see the Finnish workers under the lash, under the hammer, under the guillotine of the oppressors, when their revolt was drowned in blood immediately after the last imperialist World War. I see the Chinese workers under the thumb-screw of the brutal European and American imperialist oppressors and of their Chinese tools, the bourgeois nationalist war lords and Kuomintang butchers; I see the masses of workers and peasants in India crushed under the bloody rule of the "socialist" traitor, Ramsay MacDonald, even as the masses of British workers are oppressed by this social-fascist imperialist government, and as the masses in Africa and the other colonies are plundered and massacred under this same British rule. And I realize, comrades, the full significance of what Marx wrote about the American slave system: "Labor cannot emancipate itself in the white skin where in the black it is branded." Just as I also understand that for the Negro toilers, too, emancipation requires the united struggle of the toilers of all races.

With all this clearly before me, I will say to Comrade Yokinen: "You have fallen into a grievous crime against the working class. You have given expression in the working-class movement to this vile boss prejudice, white chauvinism, this vicious force for destroying the working class, for smashing the unity of the working class which is the only hope of our class for emancipation. But you are a worker, you are my class brother. Do not remain in the swamp of white chauvinism. Rise out of it. Correct your error. March forward with the working class. Prove yourself worthy of marching in the army of the proletariat, in the vanguard of the working class. This you must prove by your struggle against the capitalist oppressors, by your fight against white chauvinism, by your sacrifice to build the unity of the workers of all races. Then take your place again in the vanguard of the working class and go forward in the fight." (*applause*) . . .

3

STATEMENT (TRANSLATED FROM FINNISH)
August Yokinen

I admit having been under the influence of white chauvinistic ideology in my activities in connection with the Finnish Workers Club, which led me to manifest open white chauvinism in such utterances as, for example, my statement that I would not care to go into the Finnish bathhouse with a Negro. Also, my attitude supporting the exclusion of Negroes from the Finnish Workers' Club on the basis of fear of financial losses for the institution through the probable decrease of income from the white workers if Negroes are allowed showed plainly that my attitude was chauvinistic.

I now realize that this attitude of mine was a decidedly white chauvinistic attitude and the Communist Party is correct in calling me to trial before the workers. I see now that this white chauvinism is not only an outrage against the Negro workers, but is also a crime against the working class as a whole. Especially at this period, when our class oppressors are sharpening their attack against the workers and are in every way possible trying to divert the working class from struggling against the vicious attack upon their class organizations and their living standard, it is becoming ever more important for the workers to solidify the class solidarity of the Negro and white workers.

The narrow clannishness that has been thrust upon the foreign-born workers of this country by American imperialism, which utilizes the petty-bourgeoisie and its influence upon the minds of many of the workers, has, to a certain extent, led to an isolation of the Finnish as well as other foreign-born workers from the class struggle of the American workers. American imperialism uses this artificial separation of the workers into groups to further split them from each other by spreading its vicious doctrines of race and national prejudices and by playing the Negro and foreign-born and American white workers all against each other. . . .

The Scottsboro Affair

1

SCOTTSBORO'S TESTIMONY

John Dos Passos

Quite to the point is the little piece Dos Passos wrote for the July 31, 1931, Labor Defender. *It is all the more effective because of the distance it keeps from the Party, whose heroic effort it is at the same time defending.*

Our legal procedure is a kind of map of our ruling-class mind. In the South, in a case where Negroes are involved, every white man is given the luxury of being part of the ruling class. You have to realize how physically and emotionally undernourished and starved the small tenant farmers, the small storekeepers, the jellybeans and drugstore loafers who make up the lynching mobs are, to understand the orgy of righteousness and of unconscious sex and cruelty impulses, that a lynching lets loose. The feeling of superiority to the Negro is the only thing the poor whites of the South have got. A lynching is a kind of carnival to them.

Reading the testimony in the Scottsboro case, you feel all that—the band outside the courthouse, the mob starved for joy and sex and power hanging around, passing from mouth to mouth all the juicy details of the raping. You feel that filthy prurient joy in the courtroom, the stench of it is in the badly typewritten transcript of the court procedure, in the senseless ritual, the half illiterate, poorly phrased speeches of the judge and the solicitor, the scared answers of the two tough girls, evidently schooled for days in their story, sometimes seeming to enjoy the exhibitionism of it. *Evidently the court stenographer didn't take the trouble to put down what the colored boys said in their own words; what they said didn't matter, they were going to burn anyway.*

From the testimony you can't make out what actually did happen on that trainful of white and colored boys between Chattanooga and Paint Rock. But you do reach the certainty that it couldn't have happened as told in court and that, even granting that the two girls were forced by some Negroes or whites on the train, there's no particular reason why it should have been the boys who are now held in jail to give the righteous churchgoers of Jackson County, Alabama, the pleasure of legal lynching. Whatever happened, however it turns out, what a pretty picture that case offers (a man has to have a strong stomach anyway to read legal testimony without gagging) of a little corner of civilization in Mr. Hoover's greatest nation on earth. What a story of miserable starved lives, prostitution, rape and sickness comes out between the lines of the courtroom testimony.

Lynching and race hatred, like pellagra, are diseases of poverty and ignorance.

As far as I can see, since the days of the old Abolitionists, no one has had the courage to publicly face the problem until the International Labor Defense and the Communist Party came along with their slogans of equality and cooperation between white and Negro workers. For that reason alone, I think those organizations deserve support, even by outsiders who do not subscribe to their entire creed.

2
SCOTTSBORO
James S. Allen

Here is the Communist Party's take on the affair, presented by its chief expert and strategist on southern blacks, in the May 1933 issue of Communist. *Third Period militancy is evident throughout the piece.*

The main political significance of the earlier stage in the Scottsboro struggle rested in the fight between revolutionary forces led by the Communist Party and reformist forces represented by the National Association for the Advancement of Colored People. The struggle went far beyond the question of who shall carry through the legal defense of the Scottsboro boys. It was a struggle between two opposing class forces. The reformist elements around the National Association for the Advancement of Colored People representing the line of capitulation to the American imperialists, aimed to stifle the mass movement, confining it within the limits of bourgeois legality. The revolutionary forces, under the leadership of the Communist Party, representing the line of relentless struggle against capitalism and national oppression, aimed to weld the unity of the white and Negro masses in a powerful mass movement for the defense of the Scottsboro boys as an integral part of the struggle against the entire system of National oppression. If the NAACP had been the victor in this early struggle—not only in the purely legal question of defense but on the more important point of ideological leadership over the Negro masses—the struggle would have been stifled and its revolutionary potentialities left undeveloped. With the Communist Party registering a decisive victory by establishing its hegemony over the Scottsboro movement, the proletariat had obtained a foothold for establishing its hegemony over the Negro liberation struggle itself. This early defeat of the NAACP—although it was far from destroying the influence of bourgeois reformist elements over the Negro people—removed at least partially one of the main obstacles in the development of the mass movement around Scottsboro. Without having accomplished this preliminary task, it would have been impossible to proceed with the mobilizing of a mass movement.

The fact that the NAACP was forced to practically rescind its statement attacking the Communists, which it had issued on the day following the Decatur verdict, showed how completely the NAACP had been defeated at least temporarily. It recoiled at the realization that to attack the Communists in the face of the seething mass movement would place a rope around its own neck. Its second statement, while containing an underhanded, hypocritical attack upon the Communists, was at the same time forced to announce "cooperation" in the collection of funds for the defense. This was a concrete expression, not only of the effects of the mass pressure, but of the ferment which is taking place within the ranks of the NAACP . . .

The broad strata of the Negro masses who have been activized by the Scottsboro case, bring with them many petty-bourgeois illusions which are the soil in which the reformists implant their influence. That is why the first preliminary setback to the NAACP by no means signifies that nothing more is to be feared from that quarter. If it is not the NAACP, there will be other organizations and individuals to take its place. History by no means guarantees in advance that the broad strata of the Negro population, holding varied and confused views, many dominated by ideas alien to the class-conscious proletariat, will simply fall into the organizations of the Communist movement. In the end they will join the broad stream of the proletarian revolution. But they will arrive via various bypaths and after having passed through varied experiences. They will set up their own organizations, of a non-class-conscious character, which might even be directly opposed to the organizations of the working class. Such, for instance, would be Negro bourgeois nationalist organizations which might crop up on the wave of the Scottsboro case or gain a new lease on life as a result of it. Others of an objectively national-revolutionary character, but strongly dominated by petty-bourgeois ideology and "race consciousness," are even more likely to exert great influence. In any case, while appreciating the broad scope of the Scottsboro movement, we must at the same time realize that a long struggle still lies ahead if we are to establish the unchallenged leadership of the Communist Party in this movement. And when we use the word "struggle" we do not mean it in its narrow sense, but rather in the sense of great flexibility in being able to encompass the popular demands of the Negro masses within the general scope of our program and to channel this popular movement into the general stream of the proletarian revolution. . . .

The Negro misleaders, from Booker T. Washington to DuBois and Garvey, have attempted to indoctrinate the Negro masses with the conception that the white workers and the "poor whites" are the worst and most dangerous enemies of the Negro. This is the pivotal point around which the Negro reformists today build their attack upon the Communist Party and the mass protest movement of the black and white masses.

It would of course be ridiculous for Communists to demand that all those entering upon a revolutionary movement first discard all their illusions. Such illusions can only be dispelled in the course of struggle. The overcoming of illusions among the masses is a process, rooted alike in the stability or instability of the conditions which gave rise to them and in the ability of the revolutionary Party to take advantage of every opportunity to expose them. Events do not of themselves, in some mysterious abstract manner, teach the masses. These events must be underlined and brought home to the masses, by a Party driving persistently toward its goal. This is the role that the Party must play in the Scottsboro movement, at the same time raising the next logical issues inherent in the further development of the movement. . . .

In the further development of the Scottsboro struggle an important task is the winning of the *white workers* and swinging them into action on the specific issues as they are raised in the Scottsboro case. The Negro masses are still to be convinced that the white workers, not singly but in decisive masses, can disassociate themselves from the ruling ideology of "white superiority" to the extent of actually joining with the Negro masses in a fight for Negro rights. This is the kernel around which the Negro reformists have built their whole case against the Communists. The point is not that they are wrong by all the laws of social development. The point is that the Scottsboro case can be made to accelerate this inevitable change in the attitude and actions of the white workers, and to the degree that it does this, will the influence of the Negro reformists and bourgeois democrats be decisively undermined.

The rapidity and the completeness with which the Scottsboro case accomplishes this depends, of course, upon the further development of the movement, the depths of the issues which both the Negro and white workers recognize as their own and act upon. Should the Scottsboro case turn out to be the spark kindling the struggle of the Negro peasantry in the Black Belt, the "poor whites" will be just as vitally concerned with the issue of land and find it necessary to break loose from the ideology of "white superiority" which has chained them to the ruling class. This process will be easier and more rapid for the white workers, especially in the North, but also in the industrial sectors of the South. History has proven and events are proving today that, in any case, the Negroes are the decisive revolutionary force in the South.

The alienation of the white masses from the Negroes, the fostering of enmity between the two, has always been the prerequisite for maintaining the subjugation of the Negro people and, consequently, the very low standard of living of the white toilers in the South. It has been chiefly on the issue of maintaining a "solid white front" against the Negroes, together with certain recompenses granted the "poor whites" in the form of privileges, which are denied the Negroes, that the white ruling class has been able to maintain its domination over the white masses.

The revolutionary Reconstruction governments fell only after the former slaveowners had succeeded in splitting the whites from the Republican Party

and attaching them to themselves on the issue of defeating "Negro domination." The farm revolts of the nineties were appeased in the South by a whole
series of legal discriminations against Negroes culminating in the new state
constitutions of 1900–1901, which replaced those of the revolutionary
Reconstruction days, and granted the white masses those democratic rights
which were by the same act being legally denied the Negroes. Since then
there has been no serious break in this "white superiority" front, notwithstanding the mass migration of over a million Negroes to the North between
1917 and 1924.

The Scottsboro struggle gathering its forces in the milieu of the deep
world crisis, and acting in conjunction with events of a more economically
basic character like the revolt of the Negro share-croppers in Tallapoosa
County, Alabama, might well become the lever for a radical transformation
in the attitude and actions of the white masses in the South.

Appreciating the broad scope of the Scottsboro movement, its popular
mass character, we must develop it from one step to the next, drawing ever
broader masses into motion, to the point where it becomes the rallying center of the struggle for Negro liberation.

3

THE TRIAL
Muriel Rukeyser

*Year after year, trial after trial, appeal after appeal, the affair dragged on, as did the
Party's public protests. Rukeyser, whose talents as a poet were getting recognized beyond the
Communist orbit in which she moved, attended the trial before writing about it. The poem
is found in* Theory of Flight, *her 1935 collection that appeared when she was fresh out
of Vassar.*

The South is green with coming spring; revival
flourishes in the fields of Alabama. Spongy with rain,
plantations breathe April: carwheels suck mud in the roads,
the town expands warm in the afternoons. At night the black boy
teeters no-handed on a bicycle, whistling The St. Louis Blues,
blood beating, and hot South. A red brick courthouse
is vicious with men inviting death. Array your judges; call your jurors; come,
here is your justice, come out of the crazy jail.
Grass is green now in Alabama; Birmingham dusks are quiet
relaxed and soft in the park, stern at the yards:
a hundred boxcars shunted off to sidings, and the hoboes
gathering grains of sleep in forbidden corners.
In all the yards: Atlanta, Chattanooga,
Memphis, and New Orleans, the cars, and no jobs.

Every night the mail-planes burrow the sky,
carrying postcards to laughing girls in Texas,
passionate letters to the Charleston virgins,
words through the South: and no reprieve,
no pardon, no release.
A blinded statue attends before the courthouse,
bronze and black men lie on the grass, waiting,
the khaki dapper National Guard leans on its bayonets.
But the air is populous beyond our vision:
all the people's anger finds its vortex here
as the mythic lips of justice open, and speak.

Hammers and sickles are carried in a wave of strength, fire-tipped,
swinging passionately ninefold to a shore.
Answer the back-thrown Negro face of the lynched, the flat forehead
    knotted,
the eyes showing a wild iris, the mouth a welter of blood,
answer the broken shoulders and these twisted arms.
John Brown, Nat Turner, Toussaint stand in this courtroom,
Dred Scott wrestles for freedom there in the dark corner,
all our celebrated shambles are repeated here: now again
Sacco and Vanzetti walk to a chair, to the straps and rivets
and the switch spitting death and Massachusetts' will.
Wreaths are brought out of history
here are the well-nourished flowers of France, grown strong on blood,
Caesar twisting his thin throat toward conquest,
        turning north from the Roman laurels,
the Istrian galleys slide again to sea.
How they waded through bloody Godfrey's Jerusalem!
How the fires broke through Europe, and the rich and
the tall jails battened on revolution!
The fastidious Louis', cousins to the sun, stamping
those ribboned heels on Calas, on the people;
the lynched five thousand of America.
Tom Mooney from San Quentin, Herndon: here
is an army for audience
        all resolved
to a gobbet of tobacco, spat, and the empanelled hundred,
a jury of vengeance, the cheap pressed lips, the narrow eyes like hardware;
the judge, his eye-sockets and cheeks dark and immutably secret,
the twisting mouth of the prosecuting attorney.

Nine dark boys spread their breasts against Alabama,
schooled in the cells, fathered by want.
    Mother: one writes: they treat us bad. If they send

us back to Kilby jail, I think I shall kill myself.
I think I must hang myself by my overalls.

Alabama and the South are soft with spring;
in the North, the seasons change, sweet April, December and the air
loaded with snow. There is time for meetings
during the years, they remaining in prison.

     In the square
a crowd listens, carrying banners.
Overhead, boring through the speaker's voice, a plane
circles with a snoring of motors revolving in the sky,
drowning the single voice. It does not touch
the crowd's silence. It circles. The name stands:
Scottsboro.

The Herndon Affair

Let Me Live
Angelo Herndon

Herndon got out of jail in 1937 when the Supreme Court struck down the Georgia law under which he was indicted. In that year he brought out the book that described his ordeal. It included his speech to the jury, excerpted below.

On Monday, July 11, 1932, I went to the post office to get mail from this box and was arrested by detectives, Mr. Watson and Mr. Chester. I had organized unemployed workers, Negro and white, of Atlanta, and forced the County Commissioners to kick in $6,000 for unemployment relief. For this I was locked up in the station house and held eleven days without even any kind of charges booked against me. I was told at the station house that I was being held on "suspicion." Of course, they knew what the charges were going to be, but in order to hold me in jail and give me the dirtiest kind of inhuman treatment that one could describe, they held me there eleven days without any charge whatsoever until my attorney filed a writ of habeas corpus demanding that they place charges against me or turn me loose. It was about the 22nd of July, and I still hadn't been indicted; there had been three sessions of the grand jury, and my case had been up before them each time, but still there was no indictment. This was a deliberate plot to hold me in jail. At the habeas corpus hearing, the judge ordered that if I wasn't indicted the next day by 2:30, I should be released. Solicitor Hudson assured the judge that there would be an indictment, which, of course, there was. Ever since then I have been cooped up in Fulton County Tower, where I have spent close to six months—I think the exact time was five months and three weeks. But I want to describe some of the horrible experiences that I had in Fulton Tower. I was placed in a little cell there with a dead body and forced to live there with the dead body because I couldn't get out of the place. The man's name was William Wilson, who fought in the Spanish-American war for the American principles, as we usually call it. He was there on a charge of alimony. His death came as a result of the rotten food given to all prisoners, and for the want of medical attention. The county physician simply refused to give this man any kind of attention whatsoever. After three days of illness, he died, and I was forced to live there with him until the undertaker came and got him. These are just some of the things that I experienced in jail. I was also sick myself. I could not eat the food they gave me as well as hundreds of other prisoners. For instance, they give you peas and beans for one dinner, and at times you probably get the same thing three times a week. You will find rocks in it, and when you crack down on it with your teeth, you don't know what it is, and you spit it out and there it is. They have turnip greens, and just as they are pulled up out of the ground and put in the pot, with sand rocks and everything else. But that's what you have to eat, otherwise you don't live. For breakfast they feed grits that look as if they were baked instead of boiled, a little streak of grease running through them, about two strips of greasy fatback. That is the main prison fare, and you eat it or else die from starvation. I was forced to go through all of this for five months without a trial. My lawyers demanded a trial time after time, but somehow the state would always find a reason to postpone it.

They knew that the workers of Atlanta were starving, and by arresting Angelo Herndon on a charge of attempting to incite insurrection the unity of Negro and white workers that was displayed in the demonstration that forced the County Commissioners to kick in with $6,000, would be crushed forever. They locked Angelo Herndon up on such charges. But I can say this quite clearly, if the State of Georgia and the City of Atlanta think that by locking up Angelo Herndon, the question of unemployment will be solved, I say you are deadly wrong. If you really want to do anything about the case, you must go out and indict the social system. I am sure that if you would do this, Angelo Herndon would not be on trial here today, but those who are really guilty of insurrection would be here in my stead. But this you will not do, for your role is to defend the system under which the toiling masses are robbed and oppressed. There are thousands of Negro and white workers who, because of unemployment and hunger, are organizing. If the state wants to break up this organization, it cannot do it by arresting people and placing them on trial for insurrection, insurrection laws will not fill empty stomachs. Give the people bread. The officials knew then that the workers were in need of relief, and they know now that the workers are going to organize and get relief. . . .

I don't have to go so far into my case, no doubt some of you jurymen sitting over there in that box right now are unemployed and realize what it means to be without a job, when you tramp the streets day in and day out looking for work and can't find it. You know it is a very serious problem and the future looks so dim that you sometimes don't know what to do, you go nuts and want to commit suicide or something. But the Unemployment Council points out to the Negro and white workers that the solution is not in committing suicide, that the solution can only be found in the unity and organization of black and white workers. In organization the workers have strength. Now, why do I say this? I say it because it is to the interest of the capitalist class that the workers be kept down all of the time so they can make as much profit as they possibly can. So, on the other hand, it is to the interest of Negro and white workers to get as much for their work as they can— that is, if they happen to have any work. Unfortunately, at the present time there are millions of workers in the United States without work, and the capitalist class, the state government, city government and all other governments have taken no steps to provide relief for those unemployed. And it seems that this question is left up to the Negro and white workers to solve, and they will solve it by organizing and demanding the right to live, a right that they are entitled to. They have built up this country, and are therefore entitled to some of the things that they have produced. Not only are they entitled to such things, but it is their right to demand them. When the State of Georgia and the City of Atlanta raised the question of inciting to insurrection and attempting to incite to insurrection, or attempting to overthrow the government, all I can say is, that no matter what you do with Angelo Herndon, no matter what you do with the Angelo Herndons in the future, this question of unemployment, the question of unity between Negro and white workers cannot be solved with hands that are stained with the blood of an innocent individual. You may send me to my death, as far as I know. I expect you to do that anyway, so that's beside the point. But no one can deny these facts. The present system under which we are living today is on the verge of collapse; it has developed to its highest point and now it is beginning to shake. For instance, you can take a balloon and blow so much air in it, and when you blow too much it bursts; so with the system we are living under— of course, I don't know if that is insurrection or not!

INTELLECTUAL AND CULTURAL LIFE

Some Intellectuals

1
THE CASE OF THE AUTHOR
Edmund Wilson

By 1932 Edmund Wilson, America's premier literary critic, had come around to supporting Communism, as he explained in this essay from his wonderfully informative and enter-

What has gone before perhaps demands some explanation of the general attitude of the author.

So far as I can see, then, Karl Marx's predictions are in process of coming true. He did not foresee the Russian Revolution; he expected revolution first in some more highly industrialized country like England. But the tendencies he was able to observe in the middle of the last century have gone on just as he said they would, and are apparently producing the results he foretold.

We have had the development of the "capitalist contradictions" inevitable in the competitive system: the stimulation by competition to cheaper and cheaper production and consequently to greater and greater efficiency; the increasing uncertainty of employment due to changes in mechanical methods, and more and more people thrown out of work altogether as it becomes increasingly possible to displace them with machines; with the final consequence that the more cheaply and easily goods can be produced, the fewer people are able to consume them. We have had periodic depressions due to this overproduction and underconsumption, culminating in this abysmal and worldwide breakdown. And with the need for ever larger and larger and more and more expensive plants incurred in the pursuit of efficiency, we have had the accumulation of wealth and power—means of production and natural resources—in the hands of a very few people. We have had the unwholesome separation of the city and the country into "two hostile camps," as Marx, quoting David Urquhart, said, "of clownish boors and emasculated dwarfs," with the city-dwellers cut off from the earth and the farmers caught in the toils of the bankers. And we have the final supreme contradiction of a system which can no longer be run at all except in a strongly centralized fashion and for the benefit of everybody, in the possession of private individuals who try to use it for their own enrichment. Competition produced the great organism and now the organism cannot survive without killing competition. . . .

The great advantage, the great superiority, of Marx over other economists was due not to his being more learned or more expert at managing statistics, but to his psychological insight. People talk about economics as if it were a science of the behavior of money, and as if dollars and cents were entities which had an independent existence and obeyed laws of their own like electrons. The truth is that economics is merely the study of how people behave about money, and Marx, though he possessed the true scholar's temperament and had all the statistics at his finger-tips, never lost sight of this fact. His great strength lay in his imaginative grasp of human history; and the real "laws of capitalist production" of which he writes are merely the instinctive workings of human acquisitiveness, selfishness, and self-deception—the all but universal instinct to sweat, bleed and keep down other people whom we happen to have at our mercy and either to rationalize our predatory acts as policies adopted for the public good or to manage not to know about them at all. This is the kind of idea that one comes by, not by mathematical calculations, but by looking searchingly into one's heart; and this is something that few are able to do and remain to tell the tale. But Marx, like the other great Jewish prophets, was one of those who are able to do it, and it is to this that he owes his great authority.

Was he wrong in the case of America? Is the United States, as many liberals have believed, the great exception which is destined to give the lie to the Marxist assumption of the incurable swinishness and inertia of human nature which automatically creates class war? Is a genuine revolution still possible inside the American middle-class psychology?

Being a bourgeois American myself, I have tried hard since the War to believe so; but I have lately had serious doubts. The place to study the present crisis and its causes and probable consequences is not in the charts of the compilers of statistics, but in one's self and in the people one sees. . . . And though when American capitalism was booming, it was possible to credit it with reasonableness and benevolence—of which it sometimes gave vague signs—in these hard times it looks less reassuring. You can see now that a strong class psychology has been there all the time. . . .

Capitalism has run its course, and we shall have to look for other ideals than the ones that capitalism has encouraged. I don't know where they are coming from. The owning-class Americans seem to me such half-baked and half-educated people that they are no longer capable of giving any kind of leadership. Yet the emergency may produce its leaders, and these may come not out of the world of middle-class psychology at all—not out of business or professional politics or even reform politics, but out of American labor. A new generation of radicals is coming today to reinforce the older men who had gravitated to the left and who had kept the radical movements alive through the post-War period when most people deserted them. These younger men are starting their careers as convinced and cool-headed revolutionists with a clear idea of their relation to American society and of America's relation to the world. There are not many of them as yet, but they are important. They have no illusions about general prosperity based on the present economic system such as sidetracked so many of the Socialists and the AF of L. It is hard to imagine them abandoning their present principles. And as a matter of fact, they are not likely to be tempted to. The longer hard times continue, the more convinced of their position they will be; and the more young men of integrity and intelligence who come to maturity in the working-class world will take the same road that they have.

Such men are not democratic in the old American sense: they do not believe in the ideas of the average man any more than the neo-Nietzscheans do—they do not believe in votes. They look to Russia, in spite of all the differences between Russian and American conditions, as a model of what a state should be—because it is as yet the only example of the communistic society they desire. They want in fact a communist dictatorship. Some of them assume that we shall presently see a business dictatorship when our present breakdown has become complete, and they count on this stimulating a radical reaction even in middle-class-thinking America. And I, though I am a bourgeois myself and still live in and depend on the bourgeois world, have certain interests in common with these proletarians. I, too, admire the Russian Communist leaders, because they are men of superior brains who have triumphed over the ignorance, the stupidity and the shortsighted self-ishness of the mass, who have imposed on them better methods and ideas than they could ever have arrived at by themselves. As a writer I have a special interest in the success of the "intellectual" kind of brains as opposed to the acquisitive kind. And my present feeling is that my satisfaction in seeing the whole world fairly and sensibly run as Russia is now run, instead of by shabby politicians in the interests of acquisitive manufacturers, business men and bankers, would more than compensate me for any losses that I might incur in the process. And I appeal to the other professional theorists and artists to be careful how they play the game of the capitalists. It is bad for their theory and their art to try to adapt themselves to a system which is the enemy of theory and art. Their true solidarity lies with those elements who will remodel society by the power of imagination and thought—by acting on life to make something new; not with those whose work is done and whose grip has failed and who are now being carried along merely by the force of a slackening momentum to which they are unable to supply fresh force. That vision was naive that I had during the War: of science and poetry as great independent entities superior to social institutions—it was the product of having come to know them in the isolation of school and college. I did not understand then how science and art are always entangled with the institutions of the particular social world which, for its good reasons, provides them with leisure; but there was this truth in it—that art and science have been straining since the beginning of civilization to deal not with the individual or the class or the nation or the race but with the whole of human life—with the comprehensive and the universal—and that the true satisfaction of their impulses comes only in proportion as they succeed.

These views do, of course, presuppose certain fundamental assumptions which are not self-evident to many people, which are incapable of being finally proved, and which I can only state here without defending.

I believe then in human evolution: I don't see how it is possible to reject the evidence that contemporary humanity, with all its faults, has developed from beings much lower, or to fail to draw the conclusion that we are to develop into something higher still. I believe in progress as the eighteenth-century people did, and I believe as they did that the development of machinery is part of it. I do not however, believe in progress in the sense in which the nineteenth-century capitalists used the word, taking it over and making it mean mass production, capitalistic profits and the triumphs of colonial trade—a conception entirely different from the visions of the earlier philosophers, who had not foreseen that the rising middle class would be able to seize upon machinery as a powerful instrument for human exploitation. It seems to me as foolish to talk about machines as if they were ogres which had arisen to devour us as to talk about the counters of credit as if they were substances which expanded or contracted in obedience to physical laws or as if they were migratory birds which crossed the ocean at certain seasons. I believe that it is the capitalist use of machinery—its use by a class of owners for private profit—which has made it such a formidable monster. And I should be glad, as I have indicated above, to see a society where this class was abolished. It seems to me plain from my reading of history that the tendency of society is progressively leveling. And with this tendency I am in complete sympathy. I take no stock in the alleged precious "values" cultivated by aristocratic societies and destroyed in democratic ones. Poverty and degradation below and unearned wealth and idleness on top have been implied in all these values. We shan't know what morals or manners or science or art can be until we have seen them in a society of sound people run for the common good. When the middle class upset the feudal landlords and the serfs and the slaves got free, we had the modern bourgeois-governed world; now there is only one more step to go.

It seems to me necessary either to believe something of this kind or to accept the creed of one of the churches. I know that some people manage to combine the two, but for myself, I am convinced that the traditional religions, however valid or inspiring in the past, were made possible only by ignorance, and that all the Western churches are obsolescent—in power over the minds that count if not in actual numbers. I do not believe that there is a hereafter in which what happens on earth will be justified and the whole human situation given a meaning. I believe that any meaning it can have will have to be given to it here by ourselves.

2

FOR REVOLUTION
V. F. Calverton

Calverton (born George Goetz in 1901) was one of the fascinating intellectuals of the twenties and thirties. In 1923 he and a friend published a wonderfully eclectic avant-garde magazine, Modern Quarterly, *which he kept going until he died in 1940. Always a man of the Far Left, Calverton sided briefly with the Communists in the early thirties— the passage below is from a little book he published at that time—and then moved on to other interests. The advice he gives revolutionists here was certainly prescient: the Party was to follow it to a tee three years later, as we will see.*

Objectively speaking, the revolution will result from the contradictions in the capitalist system itself which will make it impossible for it to sustain itself against the forces within, which will tend to break it down, and the forces without, which will tend to overthrow it. The contradictions within, represented by the inherent conflicts of interest on the part of the capitalist class, the impossibility of social cooperation within the framework of a profit economy, the inability to find sufficient foreign markets to dispose of the domestic surplus, the impossibility of solving the unemployment problem intensified by technological advance, combined with the inability to prevent the outbreak of war resulting therefrom—those contradictions, it is obvious, are operative on a more catastrophic scale today than ever before. The contradictions without, represented by the development of the forces of opposition to the capitalist class, the workers' and farmers' movement and all those movements allied to that same base, are just as active and advanced in many European industrial countries as the contradictions within.

It is only in America that the contradictions without have not been paralleled by those within. The workers and farmers in America have not yet developed sufficient class consciousness to constitute an opposition movement to the capitalist system as a whole. In fact, in an important sense it can be said that the American workers even at the present time are on the whole ideologically less advanced than they were some decades ago. Yet it is only such a movement, built about a workers' and farmers' base, that can effect such a revolution as has been described. Any revolutionary movement which does not make its fundamental appeal to the workers and farmers is bound to fail. The dissatisfied bourgeois elements in the population, the declassé intellectuals, may participate in such a movement, may even in certain cases by identification with it become leaders within it, but they cannot be depended upon to form its base. That base must be formed by the disinherited who have nothing to lose by the destruction of an economic system which has been their constant enemy.

The problem that faces us, therefore, is simple in outline but difficult in execution. It is the problem of educating the American workers and farmers to recognize the nature of their own interests, of making them creatively class-conscious. Once that step has been made it will be but one more step to make them revolutionary-minded. It is absurd, however, for us to talk about making a revolution until those steps have been taken—at least by a considerable vanguard of the workers. Indeed, it is absurd for us to talk about taking the second step before we have made the first. The fact of the matter is we have not yet learned how to make the first. . . .

The first part of the problem that confronts us, then, is how to get the American workers and farmers to think in class-conscious terms. In the past, as we have seen, they have thought largely in terms of lower-middle-class aspirations. Today, as we have shown, with the loss of economic stability on the part of the lower middle class, the appeal of the lower-middle-class ideology has begun to lose its vigor. Within the near future the American working class will undoubtedly begin to disembarrass itself rapidly of its former lower middle-class mindedness and develop a radical outlook comparable to that of the European working classes. The task which must be undertaken is that of accelerating the development of that class consciousness, and directing it into revolutionary instead of reformistic or reactionary channels. To undertake that task with success, it is necessary to keep in mind the American masses which have to be dealt with, so as to learn to speak to them in terms of the American tradition which they know. In the effort to radicalize those masses, the revolutionary traditions upon which this country was founded must not be neglected, but utilized in order to give unified and coherent meaning to the struggle that is to be undertaken. Jefferson and William Lloyd Garrison and the importance of what they stood for in their day must not be forgotten; they must be used as symbols of challenge and advance. The American masses must be addressed in terms of that challenge and advance, for it is in such terms that they can understand best the radical rights which are theirs by virtue of their own revolutionary tradition. Revolutionaries must not isolate themselves from the American tradition, but use it to their best advantage, so rich is it in meaning and inspiration. It was no less a revolutionist than Lenin who appreciated the significance of the American revolutionary tradition. Lenin recognized the importance of building upon that tradition. "The best representatives of the American proletariat are those expressing the revolutionary tradition in the life of the American people," he wrote. "This tradition originated in the war of liberation against the English in the eighteenth century and in the Civil War in the nineteenth century . . . Where can you find an American so pedantic, so absolutely idiotic as to deny the revolutionary and progressive significance of the American Civil War of 1860–1865?" The American revolutionary tradition is a tradition which the American masses will quickest understand, and which to neglect, as has been done in the past, is to hinder rather than help the cause of the second American revolution.

While the conditions of the country have changed vastly since the days of Jefferson and Lincoln, and the particular social philosophies which they advocated have been outmoded in terms of their economic applicability, the revolutionary spirit embodied in the challenge which those men addressed to the American people, and which the American masses responded to, constitutes part of the progressive development of the American revolutionary tradition. The objective should be to advance that tradition and not let it rest where it began. In other words, it should be directed into channels which are revolutionary today. Its spirit should be utilized in terms of today and not of yesterday. Few things are more absurd in these days of finance-capitalism, when individualism has been crushed at the root, than to listen to a defense of Jeffersonian individualism and liberalism as applied to the contemporary scene. It is not Jeffersonian individualism and liberalism that must be preserved. They belong to the past; they constitute dead doctrine today. It is the progressive spirit of revolt in the Jeffersonian philosophy which must be salvaged and used. It is not the Lincoln who was the politician who should be defended, but the Lincoln who defended the revolutionary right of the masses; it is not the William Lloyd Garrison who was an enemy of labor who should be extolled, but the Garrison who as a heroic Abolitionist played such a progressive role in the historical advance of this country.

In brief, what must be learned is not to scoff at the American revolutionary heritage but *to build upon it*. If the American workers can be taught to be proud of the revolutionary development of their tradition, they can be inspired with renewed faith in the revolutionary possibilities of the future. There is no reason for Americans to be ashamed of the revolutionary aspects of their past. Parsons, Engel, Frank Little, Bill Haywood, Eugene Debs, Sacco and Vanzetti, and a score of other workers have laid the proletarian groundwork for that past. There need be no fear of nationalistic dangers in building upon such a base. "Are we enlightened Great-Russian proletarians impervious to the feeling of national pride?" wrote Lenin in his essay, "The National Pride of the Great Russians." "Certainly not! We love our language and our motherland; we, more than any other group, are working to raise its laboring masses (i.e., nine-tenths of its population) to the level of intelligent Democrats and Socialists. We, more than anybody, are grieved to see and feel to what violence, oppression, and mockery our beautiful motherland is being subjected by the tsarist hangmen, the nobles, and the capitalists . . . We, Great-Russian workers, filled with national pride, wish by all means to have a free and independent, sovereign, democratic, republican, proud Great Russia, which is to maintain in relation to her neighbors the humane principle of equality, and not the serf principles of privileges that humiliate a great nation."

It is such "national pride," if you will, that must be stirred up in the American workers and farmers—a pride in their revolutionary traditions. Such pride can help inspire them with the fight necessary to overthrow the present ruling class of financiers and industrialists. The American workers must learn to hate the "violence, oppression, and mockery (which their) beautiful motherland is being subjected to" by those financiers and industrialists. Hate and not love is the emotion which they must nurture. The gospel of love belongs to the ruling class; it is its best protection, for by its very preachment it tends to prevent the misery it spreads from volatilizing into violence. The gospel of hate belongs to the proletariat, for it is only by such hate that the energy necessary for its struggle can be engendered. More, it is only by virtue of that hate that a new social world can be created in which the gospel of love can have either place or meaning.

"Between communism with all its chances, and the present state of society with all its sufferings and injustices," John Stuart Mill wrote, "all the difficulties great and small of communism would be but as dust in the balance."

It is that realization which many American intellectuals have already reached; it is that realization which many American workers will reach within this decade if their growing spirit of protest and revolt is not channeled off into futile directions.

It is only by revolution that that realization can be translated into action. Society can be saved in no other way. Our task is to create that revolution, to cultivate the forces that are necessary to its success. It is no little task that confronts us, and it behooves us to gather up all our energies and dedicate all our strength to its achievement. To do less is but to fail. And to fail in that task is to betray the cause of human progress, to sacrifice the future freedom of the human race.

3

Culture and the Crisis
League of Professional Groups for Foster and Ford

In September 1932 Edmund Wilson and fifty-two other intellectuals signed an open letter—published a few weeks later under the title given above—addressed to "Writers, Artists, Teachers, Physicians, Engineers, Scientists, and Other Professional Workers of America," on why they should support the Communist candidates for President and Vice President. Among the signers were Sherwood Anderson, Erskine Caldwell, Countee Cullen, Theodore Dreiser, John Dos Passos, Sidney Hook, Sidney Howard, Langston Hughes, Matthew Josephson, James Rorty, Lincoln Steffens, and Ella Winter.

We of this generation stand midway between two eras. When we look backward, we see our American past like a great tidal wave that is now receding, but that was magnificent indeed in the sweep of its socially purposeless power. When we look ahead, we see something new and strange, undreamed of in the American philosophy. What we see ahead is the threat of cultural dissolution. The great wave piled up too much wreckage—of nature, of obsolete social patterns and institutions, of human blood and nerve.

We who write this, listed among the so-called "intellectuals" of our generation, people trained, at least, to think for ourselves and hence, to a degree for our time and our people—we have no faintest desire to exaggerate either our talents or our influence. Yet on the other hand, we are not humble, especially with respect to the power that measures itself in dollar signs and ciphers, the thought that is not thought, but merely the stereotype of habit, the action that is not will, not choice, but the reflex of fear. Why should we as a class be humble? Practically everything that is orderly and sane and useful in America was made by two classes of Americans; our class, the class of brain workers, and the "lower classes," the muscle workers. Very well, we strike hands with our true comrades. We claim our own and we reject the disorder, the lunacy spawned by grabbers, advertisers, traders, speculators, salesmen, the much-adulated, immensely stupid and irresponsible "business men." We claim the right to live and to function. It is our business to think and we shall not permit businessmen to teach us our business. It is also, in the end, our business to act.

We have acted. As responsible intellectual workers we have aligned ourselves with the frankly revolutionary Communist Party, the party of the workers. In this letter, we speak to you of our own class—to the writers, artists, scientists, teachers, engineers, to all honest professional workers— telling you as best we can why we have made this decision and why we think that you too should support the Communist Party in the political campaign now under way.

There is only one issue in the present election. Call it hard times, unemployment, the farm problem, the world crisis, or call it simply hunger— whatever name we use, the issue is the same. What do the major political parties propose to do about it?

The Republicans propose, in effect, to do nothing whatsoever. Twelve to fifteen million men and women have lost their jobs; twenty-five to thirty-five million people will go hungry this winter; nobody knows the exact figures. The Republican Party, three years after the crash, does not even promise to take a census of our misery. The best its candidate can offer is a pledge to continue the policies which are depriving these millions of work, food and shelter.

Somebody must pay the cost of the depression: will it be the rich or the poor, the capitalists or the workers and farmers? In the battle now raging between them, the Republican administration has taken the side of the rich. To banks, railroads and industrial corporations, it has offered government loans, millions, billions, anything to keep them from going bankrupt. To the Rockefellers and Mellons it has offered a pledge to keep their taxes down— by discharging government employees and refusing government help to the unemployed. It offers nothing to the poor except higher taxes, lower wages and the chance to share their misery. If they ask for more, it gives them bayonets and tear-gas.

The Democrats, in the present election, have tried to appeal to both sides. Their candidate has promised as much as he safely could to as many people as he thought were influential. He has promised progressivism to progressives and conservatism to conservatives. He has promised to lower the price of electric power without lowering the inflated value of power company stock. He has promised more and less regulation of the railroads. He has promised to lower the protective tariff and at the same time make it more protective. He has promised higher prices to the farmers by means of a measure which cannot be put into effect until hundreds of thousands of farms have been sold for taxes and mortgages. He has promised beer to industrial workers, if they have the money to buy it. On the one real issue he promises nothing.

If Roosevelt is elected—and Wall Street expects him to win—there will be changes here and there in the machine of government. The leaks in the boiler will be stuffed with cotton waste, the broken bolts mended with hay wire. A different gang of engineers will run the machine for the profit of the same owners.

The causes of the crisis will be untouched. The results of the crisis—hunger, low wages, unemployment—will still be with us. If there is a temporary return to a limited degree of prosperity, it can only be succeeded by another crisis. The United States under capitalism is like a house that is rotting away; the roof leaks, the sills and rafters are crumbling. The Democrats want to paint it pink. The Republicans don't want to paint it; instead they want to raise the rent. . . .

THE PROFESSIONAL CLASSES WILL BE LIBERATED

Under Socialism science and technology are freed from their dependence upon private profit; their scope and social application are enormously increased. The professional workers, whom capitalism either exploits or forces to become exploiters, are liberated to perform freely and creatively their particular craft function—the engineer need consider only the efficiency of his work, the economist and statistician can purposively plan the organization, management and social objectives of industry, the architect is released from profit and speculative motives and may express his finest aspirations in buildings of social utility and beauty, the physician becomes the unfettered organizer of social preventive medicine, the teacher, writer, and artist fashion the creative ideology of a new world and a new culture.

It is an ideal worth fighting for, and it is a practical and realizable ideal, as is being proved in the Soviet Union. It would, moreover, be much easier to build Socialism in the United States than in Russia because of the infinitely higher development of our technology and our means of production and distribution. . . .

THE COMMUNIST PARTY

The Communist Party stands for a Socialism of deeds, not of words. It appeals for the support of the American working classes, not like the Socialist Party on the basis of broken and unfulfilled promises, but with concrete evidence of revolutionary achievement both at home and abroad.

Already in Soviet Russia, under the leadership of the Communists, unemployment has been wiped out, a gigantic reconstruction of industry to extend a Socialist planned economy has been undertaken, and a cultural revolution of tremendous dimensions has been won on many fronts. The Soviet

Union has freed women from age-old social disabilities and discrimination, provided national and racial minorities with an opportunity to develop their own cultural life, broken down the barriers between city and country and adopted the most advanced system of social insurance in the world. For the first time in recorded history a civilization has emerged unified by a living faith in man's ability to create a classless society in which "the free development of each is the condition of the free development of all," in which every human being is privileged to participate in the collective effort of the whole.

Whatever burdens must be shouldered fall upon all alike. These will be conquered in the future just as famine, blockade, invasion, have been conquered. Until then no one lives in luxury and no one suffers from need. Contrast this with capitalist America in which the luxury of a few is flaunted in the face of hungry and homeless millions.

The Communist Party of America proposes as the real solution of the present crisis the overthrow of the system which is responsible for all crises. This can only be accomplished by the conquest of political power and the establishment of a workers' and farmers' government which will usher in the Socialist commonwealth. The Communist Party does not stop short merely with a proclamation of its revolutionary goal. It links that goal up with the daily battles of the working class for jobs, bread and peace. Its actions and achievements are impressive evidence of its revolutionary sincerity.

The Communist Party is the only party which has stood in the forefront of the major struggle of the workers against capital and the capitalist state. It has unflinchingly met every weapon of terror which frenzied capitalist dictatorship has let loose upon it—clubbings, imprisonment, deportation and murder. It has rallied thousands of workers to resist the onslaught upon their already low standard of living. It has fought the Jim Crow system used by the capitalist class to divide and weaken the working class. It has fought the evictions of the unemployed. It has fought and is prepared to fight in the struggles of every group of exploited workers in the country—the miner, the steel worker, the farmer, the ex-serviceman. It has unmasked the class character of justice dispensed in American courts and led mass demonstrations in behalf of victims of legal frame-ups—notably Tom Mooney and the Scottsboro boys and against the deportations of militant workers. In the present crisis the Communist Party has been the only party which has thrown down a militant challenge to the ruling class and unfolded a program of mass activity. . . .

WHY VOTE COMMUNIST

Why vote for the Communist Party? Because it offers the only practicable solution of the crisis—a workers' and farmers' government. Because it leads in the attack on the capitalist class and its tool, the capitalist state. *Because it is the only organization which can now wring genuine concessions from the ruling classes.*

No ruling class ever surrenders voluntarily a morsel of its power. It must be forced by the threat of the growing power of a militant revolutionary organization to do so. That is why those who are not prepared at the present moment to accept the full revolutionary program of the Communist Party should support it in the coming election. For only if the Communist Party rolls up a strong vote can the capitalist be frightened into acceding to its immediate demands. The capitalist class does not fear the Socialist Party, which it praises for moderation and sweet reasonableness. It fears and hates the Communist Party because it knows it really means to work toward a Socialist State.

The history of the class struggle in America since 1929 proves that it has been the revolutionary demands of the Communist Party which have forced the national and local governments to recognize unemployment and at least make gestures at relief. It was only after March 6, 1930, when Communist demonstrations against unemployment had been broken up throughout the country, and Wm. Z. Foster served six months in prison after his arrest for leading the demonstration, that the country awoke to the effects of the collapse of the previous fall. In New York it was only after a deputation of unemployed under Communist leadership had been clubbed by the police that the Board of Estimate was compelled to make grants for relief. In St. Louis it required a march on city hall by thousands of workers under Communist leadership before the municipal government restored hungry families to the relief rolls. Even where the Communist Party fails to attain its immediate objective, its failure, by bringing into action great masses with potential revolutionary capacities, accomplishes more for the workers than the successes of the capitalist parties.

A vote for any party but the Communist Party is worse than a wasted vote. It is a vote for the class enemies of the workers. A vote for hunger, war, unemployment; for the thousand-fold material and spiritual oppressions which flow from capitalism. A vote for the Communist Party is not a wasted vote. It is an effective protest against a system which permits the necessities of life to be destroyed rather than let them be consumed by those who cannot pay for them.

Why should intellectual workers be loyal to the ruling class which frustrates them, stultifies them, patronizes them, makes their work ridiculous, and now starves them? There are teachers on the bread lines, engineers patching the sheet-iron shacks in the "Hooversvilles," musicians fiddling in the "jungles." The professionals are not yet starving as the proletariat is starving. But since 1929 there reigns a permanent superfluity in the ranks of the professional groups. We "intellectuals," like the workers, find ourselves superfluous. Is that because there is too much civilization, too much "culture"? No, it is because there is not enough.

We, too, the intellectual workers, are of the oppressed, and until we shake off the servile habit of that oppression we shall build blindly and badly, to the lunatic specifications of ignorance and greed. If we are capable of building a civilization, surely it is time for us to begin; time for us to assert our function, our responsibility; time for us to renew the pact of comradeship with the struggling masses, trapped by the failure of leadership in the blind miseries of a crumbling mad house. In a few years dwindling opportunities for employment brought on by progressive rationalization of industry, capitalist economies in the social services of government and the whole anarchistic system of education which prevails under capitalism—will mean the pauperization of the most highly creative groups in society.

What is worse, the spiritual degradation, which every independent intellectual or professional worker suffers when false money-standards are applied to his creative craft, will grow deeper. Today it is difficult for the professional conscientiously to perform his work in the face of demands made by his employers—that he use his art, his science, his skill for ends that are foreign to his professional activity. Tomorrow it will be impossible for the intellectual to function as a free personality under the pressure of vocational unemployment and the necessity of serving those upon whom he is dependent.

It is important that the professional workers realize that they do not constitute an independent economic class in society. They can neither remain neutral in the struggle between capitalism and Communism nor can they by their own independent action effect any social change. Their choice is between serving either as the cultural lieutenants of the capitalist class or as allies and fellow travelers of the working class. That for them is the historic issue which cannot be straddled by the multiform varieties of personal escape or settled by flying to the vantage points of above-the-battle moralities.

The struggle for the emancipation of society from the blight of capitalism is not only an economic question, it is a cultural question as well. Both in theory and in practice, capitalism is hostile to the genuine culture of the past and present and bitterly opposed to the new cultural tendencies which have grown out of the epic of working class struggle for a new society. "The bourgeoisie has robbed of their haloes various occupations hitherto regarded with awe and veneration. Doctor, lawyer, priest, poet and scientist have become its wage-laborers . . . it has left no other bond between man and man . . . but crude self-interest and unfeeling 'cash payment.' " No genuine culture can thrive in a society in which malnutrition is a natural cause of death, the exploitation of man by man the natural cause of wealth, and foreign war and domestic terror the natural means of retaining political power. It is capitalism which is destructive of all culture and Communism which desires to save civilization and its cultural heritage from the abyss to which the world crisis is driving it.

The intellectual worker is confronted on all sides by the massed unity of capitalism—chaotic and benighted in itself, yet organized enough when it works with its pawns—enforcing its own needs, confining them to its own limited and sterilizing program. How long will he suffocate within this narrow house? When will he attempt to break through this closed circle by alliance with the only militant force which seeks renovation?

In the interests of a truly human society in which all forms of exploitation have been abolished; in behalf of a new cultural renaissance which will produce integrated, creative personalities, we call upon all men and women—especially workers in the professions and the arts—to join in the revolutionary struggle against capitalism under the leadership of the Communist Party.

Vote Communist—For Foster and Ford—on November 8.

4

Toward a Soviet America
William Z. Foster

The year he ran for President, Foster presented his program for America. The Soviet paradigm may strike us as perverse in the extreme, but, as we have noted, it had some appeal in depression-ridden America.

THE AMERICAN SOVIET GOVERNMENT

When the American working class actively enters the revolutionary path of abolishing capitalism it will orientate upon the building of Soviets, not upon the adaptation of the existing capitalist government. Capitalist governments have nothing in common with proletarian governments. They are especially constructed throughout to maintain the rulership of the bourgeoisie. In the revolutionary struggle they are smashed and Soviet governments established, built according to the requirements of the toiling masses.

The building of Soviets is begun not after the revolution but before. When the eventual revolutionary crisis becomes acute the workers begin the establishment of Soviets. The Soviets are not only the foundation of the future Workers' State, but also the main instruments to mobilize the masses for revolutionary struggle. The decisions of the Soviets are enforced by the armed Red Guard of the workers and peasants and by the direct seizure of the industry through factory committees. A revolutionary American working class will follow this general course, which is the way of proletarian revolution.

The American Soviet government will be organized along the broad lines of the Russian Soviets. Local Soviets, the base of the whole Soviet State, will be established in all cities, towns and villages. Local Soviets combine in themselves the legislative, executive and judicial functions. Representation, based on occupation instead of residence and property, comes directly from the shops, mines, farms, schools, workers' organizations, army, navy, etc. The principle of recall of representatives applies throughout. Citizenship is restricted to those who do useful work, capitalists, landlords, clericals and other non-producers being disfranchised.

The local Soviets will be combined by direct representation into county, state, and national Soviets. The national Soviet government, with its capital in Chicago or some other great industrial center, will consist of a Soviet Congress, made up of local delegates and meeting annually, or as often as need be, to work out the general policies of the government. Between its meetings the government will be carried on by a broad Central Executive Committee, meeting every few months. This CEC will elect a small Presidium and a Council of Commissars, made up of the heads of the various government departments, who will carry on the day-to-day work.

The American Soviet government will join with the other Soviet governments in a world Soviet Union. There will also be, very probably, some form of continental union. The American revolution will doubtless carry with it all those countries of the three Americas that have not previously accomplished the revolution.

The Soviet court system will be simple, speedy and direct. The judges, chosen by the corresponding Soviets, will be responsible to them. The Supreme Court, instead of being dictatorial and virtually legislative, as in the United States, will be purely juridical and entirely under the control of the CEC. The civil and criminal codes will be simplified, the aim being to proceed directly and quickly to a correct decision. In the acute stages of the revolutionary struggle special courts to fight the counter-revolution will probably be necessary. The pest of lawyers will be abolished. The courts will be class-courts, definitely warring against the class enemies of the toilers. They will make no hypocrisy like capitalist courts, which, while pretending to deal out equal justice to all classes, in reality are instruments of the capitalist State for the repression and exploitation of the toiling masses.

The American Soviet government will be the dictatorship of the proletariat. In Chapter II we explained this dictatorship as the revolutionary government of the workers and toiling farmers. In the proletarian dictatorship the working class is the leader by virtue of its revolutionary program, superior organization and greater numbers. Toward the farmers, the attitude of the government will vary from an open alliance with the poor farmers and cooperation with the middle farmers, to open hostility against the big, exploiting landowners. Toward the city intelligentsia and petty bourgeoisie generally, its attitude will be one of friendliness and cooperation, insofar as these elements break with the old order and support the new. The new Workers' government, as part of its task of building Socialism, necessarily will have to hold firmly in check the counter-revolutionary elements who seek to overthrow or sabotage the new regime. To suppose that the powerful American capitalist class and its vast numbers of hangers-on will tamely submit to the loss of their power to the workers would be to ignore the whole history of that class. The mildness or severity of the repressive measures used by the workers to liquidate this class politically will depend directly upon the character of the latter's resistance. While the whole trend of the revolutionary workers is against violence, they always have an iron fist for counter-revolution.

In order to defeat the class enemies of the revolution, the counter-revolutionary intrigues within the United States and the attacks of foreign capitalist countries from without, the proletarian dictatorship must be supported by the organized armed might of the workers, soldiers, local militia, etc. In the early stages of the revolution, even before the seizure of power, the workers will organize the Red Guard. Later on this loosely constructed body becomes developed into a firmly-knit, well-disciplined Red Army.

The leader of the revolution in all its stages is the Communist Party. With its main base among the industrial workers, the Party makes a bloc with the revolutionary farmers and impoverished city petty bourgeoisie, drawing under its general leadership such revolutionary groups and organizations as these classes may have. Under the dictatorship all the capitalist parties—Republican, Democratic, Progressive, Socialist, etc.—will be liquidated, the Communist Party functioning alone as the Party of the toiling masses. Likewise will be dissolved all other organizations that are political props of the bourgeois rule, including chambers of commerce, employers' associations, rotary clubs, American Legion, YMCA, and such fraternal orders as the Masons, Odd Fellows, Elks, Knights of Columbus, etc.

A Soviet government will provide the workers and poor farmers with the political instrument necessary to defend their interests. The whole purpose of such a government will be to advance the welfare of those who do useful work. This is not the case with the present government of the United States. It is dominated by the Morgans, Mellons and other big bankers and industrialists. Its function is to protect the interests of the capitalist class—in first line finance capital—at the expense of the working masses. Every piece of legislation, every strike, every demonstration of the unemployed illustrates this afresh. In no matter what field, wherever the interests of the workers are involved, they find the powers of the government arrayed against them. The American government is as much the property of the capitalists as their mills, mines, factories and land. Only a Soviet government can and will represent the will of the workers.

The establishment of an American Soviet government will mark the birth of real democracy in the United States. For the first time the toilers will be free, with industry and the government in their own hands. Now they are enslaved: the industries and the government are the property of the ruling class. The right to vote and all the current talk about democracy are only so many screens to hide the capitalist autocracy and to make it more palatable to the masses. Consider the economic and political gulf between the Southern textile workers slaving for $5 a week and the rich Southern capitalists; between the hungry unemployed workers in the Northern cities and the fat capitalist parasite masters lolling the winters through at Palm Beach;

between the semi-slave Negroes in the South and their exploiters; between the outrageous treatment visited upon Mooney and Billings, Sacco and Vanzetti and many other class war prisoners and the protection given to the Falls, Daughertys and the whole clique of capitalist robbers of the poor— then one gets the true measure of the American capitalist "democracy" and "freedom." Ambassador Gerard blurted out the truth that the American government is a capitalist dictatorship when he declared that 59 bankers and captains of industry are the real rulers of the United States . . . .

BUILDING A NEW WORLD

The proletarian revolution is the most profound of all revolutions in history. It initiates changes more rapid and far-reaching than any in the whole experience of mankind. The hundreds of millions of workers and peasants, striking off their age-old chains of slavery, will construct a society of liberty and prosperity and intelligence. Communism will inaugurate a new era for the human race, the building of a new world.

The overthrow of capitalism and the development of Communism will bring about the immediate or eventual solution of many great social problems. Some of these originate in capitalism, and others have plagued the human race for scores of centuries. Among them are war, religious superstition, prostitution, famine, pestilence, crime, poverty, alcoholism, unemployment, illiteracy, race and national chauvinism, the suppression of women, and every form of slavery and exploitation of one class by another. Already in the Soviet Union, with the revolution still in its initial stages, the forces are distinctly to be seen at work that will eventually liquidate these handicaps to the happiness and progress of the human race. But, of course, only a system of developed world Communism can fully uproot and destroy all these evils.

The objective conditions, in the shape of scientific knowledge and the means of creating material wealth, are already at hand in sufficient measure to do away with these menaces to humanity. But the trouble lies with the subjective factor, the capitalist order of society. Capitalism, based upon human exploitation, stands as the great barrier to social progress. Communism, by abolishing the capitalist system, liquidates this subjective difficulty. It releases thereby productive forces strong enough to provide plenty for all and it destroys the whole accompanying capitalist baggage of cultivated ignorance, strife and misery. Communism frees humanity from the stultifying effects of the present essentially animal struggle for existence and opens up before it new horizons of joys and tasks. The day is not so far distant when our children, immersed in this new life, will look back with horror upon capitalism and marvel how we tolerated it so long.

Communist society, in its battle onward and upward, will attack and carry through many profound measures besides those mentioned. Among these will be the organization of the economics of the world upon a rational and planned basis, the systematic conservation and increase of the world's natural resources, the development of a vast concentration upon all the great problems now confronting science, the beautification of the world by a new and richer artistry, the liquidation of congested cities and the combination of the joys and conveniences of country and urban life, and the solution of many other great problems and tasks now hardly even imagined.

Communist society, however, will not confine itself simply to thus developing the objective conditions for a better life. Especially will it turn its attention to the subjective factor, to the fundamental improvement of man himself. Capitalism, with its wars, wage slavery, slums, crooked doctors, etc., undermines the health of the race and destroys its physique. Communism, with its healthful dwellings and working conditions, its pure food, physical culture, etc., will make good health, like thorough education, the property of all. Already this is becoming so in the Soviet Union. But this will be only a beginning. Communist society will go further. It will scientifically regulate the growth of population. It will especially speed up the very evolution of man himself, his brain and body. Capitalism has checked the evolution of the human species, if it has not actually brought about a process of race degeneration. But Communism will systematically breed up mankind. Already the scientific knowledge is at hand to do this, but it is at present inapplicable because of the idiocy of the capitalist system, its planlessness, its antiquated moral codes, its warp and woof of exploitation. . . .

Literary Currents

1

DRAFT MANIFESTO
John Reed Clubs

In April 1932 representatives of the various John Reed Clubs and Party literary figures met in Chicago to take stock and draw up a statement of purpose. It came out in the June 1932 New Masses.

The proletarian revolution has its own philosophy developed by Marx, Engels and Lenin. It has developed its own revolutionary schools, newspapers, and magazines; it has its worker-correspondence, its own literature and art. In the past two decades there have developed writers, artists and critics who have approached the American scene from the viewpoint of the revolutionary workers.

To give this movement in arts and letters greater scope and force, to bring it closer to the daily struggle of the workers, the John Reed Club was formed in the fall of 1929. In the past two and a half years, the influence of this orga-

throughout the country. These organizations are open to writers and artists, whatever their social origin, who subscribe to the fundamental program adopted by the international conference of revolutionary writers and artists which met at Kharkov, in November 1930. The program contains six points upon which all honest intellectuals, regardless of their background, may unite in the common struggle against capitalism. They are:

1. Fight against imperialist war, defend the Soviet Union against capitalist aggression;
2. Fight against fascism, whether open or concealed, like social-fascism;
3. Fight for the development and strengthening of the revolutionary labor movement;
4. Fight against white chauvinism (against all forms of Negro discrimination or persecution) and against the persecution of the foreign-born;
5. Fight against the influence of middle-class ideas in the work of revolutionary writers and artists;
6. Fight against the imprisonment of revolutionary writers and artists, as well as other class-war prisoners throughout the world.

On the basis of this minimum program, we call upon all honest intellectuals, all honest writers and artists, to abandon decisively the treacherous illusion that art can exist for art's sake, or that the artist can remain remote from the historic conflicts in which all men must take side. We call upon them to break with bourgeois ideas which seek to conceal the violence and fraud, the corruption and decay of capitalist society. We call upon them to align themselves with the working class in its struggle against capitalist oppression and exploitation, against unemployment and terror, against fascism and war. We urge them to join with the literary and artistic movement of the working class in forging a new art that shall be a weapon in the battle for a new and superior world.

2
The Great Tradition
Granville Hicks

Hicks had graduated from Harvard (with both bachelor's and master's degrees) intending to be a minister. But he turned to literature instead and discovered Marxism, then Communism, becoming literary editor of the New Masses. *His most notable work, a sort of vade mecum of the proletarian school, was* The Great Tradition, *published in 1933, from which the following is excerpted.*

We have attempted to view American life of the industrial age as the artist might view it. We have understood why some writers turned away in boredom, disgust, or fear, and we have walked along the paths they chose to follow. With other writers we have marched out upon the field of battle, sympathizing with their hopes and recording their defeats as well as their victories. The achievements of the first group have sometimes gratified us, but we have realized that their limitations were of the sort that must in the long run be fatal. After all, surveying the whole of literary history, one can scarcely think of any writer, commonly recognized as great, who did not immerse himself in the life of the times, who did not concern himself with the problems of his age—even when he chose some other time or place as the setting of his poem or his play. As we have seen, industrialism became more and more important in American life, the implications of capitalism grew clearer and clearer, the lines of the class struggle were drawn more and more sharply, and consequently the cost of evasion grew greater and greater. Comparing Edith Wharton with Henry James, or Willa Cather with Sarah Orne Jewett, or Robert Frost with Emily Dickinson, we have realized that it has been increasingly difficult for those who ignore industrialism to create a vital literature.

On the other hand, as we looked at the writers who tried to understand American life, we have found a steady growth. William Dean Howells made a beginning in the early seventies. His first sketches were simple realistic descriptions, but his novels came to embrace more and more of American life, and in such books as *A Hazard of New Fortunes* he came closer than any of his contemporaries to portraying the complicated changes that were going on in America. He was, it is true, quite as prudish as any other Victorian American, and he could no more understand the changes he described than could the kind of persons he wrote about. Yet he succeeded, as Hawthorne and Melville had not done, as James and Mark Twain did not do, in founding a school, and it was the men who followed his example who dominated our fiction at the end of the century. These men—Crane, Fuller, Garland, Norris—did something toward the breaking down of taboos, and they brought literature closer to the mainstream of American life. Their successors, the muckrakers, turned their attention directly to urgent problems of industrialism and politics. And the writers of the middle generation—Dreiser, Lewis, and Anderson—completed the liberation of literature from the stranglehold of prudishness and hypocrisy, and at the same time wrote out of a wider and deeper knowledge than their predecessors had possessed.

But the problem of intelligent mastery remained. Critics sometimes dwell on the failure of American writers to achieve order, form, significance. They do not realize that the question is not exclusively literary. One cannot achieve form by fiat; one has to understand the significance of the materials one uses, as Howells pointed out in *Criticism and Fiction*, if one is to make that significance felt in their literary organization. And that is what Dos Passos and

some of the other radicals have done. They stand in the major tradition of our
literature, for they deal with representative American men and women in
representative situations; and in their work, moreover, the tradition moves
toward its consummation. Equipped with a many-sided knowledge of contemporary life and unhampered by conventional reticence, so that their work
is quite as honest and quite as comprehensive as the work of any of their predecessors, they are also feeling their way toward an interpretation of the
American scene that enables them to bind together in satisfying forms its
diverse phenomena.

The tradition of realistic fiction of contemporary life has been, of course,
dominant in the literature of most nations in the last century, but it has been
faced with peculiar obstacles in the United States, and has had a peculiar
importance. We plunged into the maelstrom of industrialism before we had
developed any indigenous culture. Life was not organized for the American
artist. Industrialism was not sapping away an established order; it was boldly
creating a new civilization. The artist could not rely, even temporarily, on
pre-industrial traditions; struggle was the only alternative to abject flight.
Moreover, such pressure as American culture could exert on the writer was
all in this direction: men were crying out for an interpretation of the apparent chaos in which they lived. Slowly, as we have seen, our writers
responded, and now comes the promise of success.

The writer, if he is accurately and intelligently to portray American life, if
he is to express whatever is vital and hopeful in the American spirit, must ally
himself with the working class. Again and again we have seen the question
raised: what is the relationship between the existing social order and the
highest hopes and deepest desires of mankind? If a writer settled that problem, it scarcely mattered where he found his themes, for he could see them
in true perspective. But if the problem remained unsolved, the failure to contemplate industrial development became a fundamental evasion. To that
question Karl Marx long ago provided an answer: the machine is potentially
a source of good; it is, however, in fact a source of evil so long as it is operated for private profit; its full benefits can be realized only when it is socialized, and that can be accomplished only when the exploited overthrow the
exploiters. For decades that answer seemed inapplicable to America, where
the existence of the frontier gave meaning to the doctrine of self-reliant individualism; but the passing of the years has shown that America is no exception, and that, here as elsewhere, the only clue to the tangled web of life in
the last century is the Marxian analysis.

It has become increasingly clear, even to those who do not want to see,
that the central fact in American life is the class struggle. The writer has a
series of choices. If he ignores the class struggle, he surrenders all hope of
arriving at a clear interpretation, out of which a significant formal pattern
may be devised, and he commits himself to evasion after evasion. If he
assumes the role of impartiality, he merely deceives and confuses himself,

since impartiality is impossible. If he accepts the existing order and assumes that it operates for the best interests of mankind, he becomes an apologist, and dishonesty and misrepresentation follow. If he recognizes the existing order for what it is and nevertheless accepts it because he profits by it, he avoids the weakness of evasion, but he cuts himself off from a large part of the human race, and callousness is substituted for the sympathy which is so important an attribute. If, however, the writer allies himself with the proletariat, there is no need of evasion or self-deception. He may be tempted to exaggerate the faults of capitalists or the virtues of workers, but if he is wise he will find in facts his all-sufficient bulwark. Moreover, as this way of looking at life becomes an integral part of his imaginative equipment, he can not only perceive the operation of underlying forces; he can also rejoice in their play because of his confidence in what they will eventually accomplish.

In John Dos Passos and in his like-minded colleagues we find the modern expression of the spirit that moves in the noblest creations of the past. What stirs us in Emerson is his confidence in the common man, his courageous appeal for action, his faith in the future. He and Thoreau were rebels against the shams and oppressions of their day. Their rebellion inevitably took an individualistic form, but they spoke for all the oppressed, and some of their words remain a call to arms. Whitman, though no less an individualist, felt more deeply his kinship with the workers and farmers, and in later years was not unaware of the wisdom of curbing the individual for the collective good. Howells, too, taught himself to think in terms of a new order, and he and Bellamy tried to create, in imagination and in fact, a better world. Garland and Norris denounced oppression; Herrick and Phillips worked for reform; Sinclair and London called themselves socialists.

This is the great tradition of American literature. Ours has been a critical literature, critical of greed, cowardice, and meanness. How can authors refuse to strike at the sources of the evils they have so constantly attacked? It has also been a hopeful literature, touched again and again with a passion for brotherhood, justice, and intellectual honesty. How can authors refuse to struggle against an order based upon falsehood, oppression, and the division of mankind into exploiters and exploited? The issue is now so clearly drawn that evasion is almost impossible: on the one hand lies repudiation of the best in the American literary past, on the other the fulfillment of all that was dreamed of and worked for in the past and the beginning of struggle for more than the past could ever have hoped. Not every writer can make the choice that his ideals demand, but many can and will break the ties that bind them to the bourgeoisie, and give their support to the class that is able to overthrow capitalism.

Let no one be deceived; difficult years loom before us and the very existence of art may seem to be imperiled. Revolutionary writers will have obstacles of their own to overcome and peculiar temptations to resist. But certainly we cannot despair of the eventual outcome, and even in the days of stress revolutionary writers will have a kind of courage that others cannot share. For they will know that what is struggling for utterance on their pages is the spirit, not of an isolated individual, not of some literary clique, not of some decadent tradition, but the spirit of that class with which the future rests and into whose hands the highest hopes of mankind are entrusted. They will know that, whatever destruction the future may bring, they are allied with the forces of construction. They will know they are participating in a battle that, in the long run, is for civilization itself, and they will have no doubt of the outcome.

3
PROBLEMS AND PERSPECTIVES IN REVOLUTIONARY LITERATURE
Philip Rahv and Wallace Phelps

A different view of the "Great Tradition" appeared in the June–July 1934 issue of the Partisan Review, *organ of the New York John Reed Club. It was a statement distinguishing true proletarian literature from mere "leftism" and was written by its two young editors. Three years later they left the Party and launched the magazine anew according to the principles they espoused below.*

The last year has seen a quickening in the growth of revolutionary literature in America. The maturing of labor struggles and the steady increase of Communist influence have given the impetus and created a receptive atmosphere for this literature. As was to be expected, the novel—which is the major literary form of today—has taken the lead. Cantwell, Rollins, Conroy and Armstrong have steered fiction into proletarian patterns of struggle. In the theater, *Peace on Earth*, *Stevedore* and *They Shall Not Die* show a parallel growth. The emergence of a number of little revolutionary magazines, together with the phenomenal success of the weekly *New Masses*, has provided an outlet for the briefer forms of writing. *The Great Tradition*, by Granville Hicks, has launched us on a revaluation of American literary history.

This new literature is unified not only by its themes but also by its perspectives. Even a casual reading of it will impress one with the conviction that here is a new way of looking at life—the bone and flesh of a revolutionary sensibility taking on literary form. The proletarian writer, in sharing the moods and expectations of his audience, gains that creative confidence and harmonious functioning within his class which gives him a sense of responsibility and discipline totally unknown in the preceding decade. Lacking this solidarity with his readers, the writer, as has been the case with the esthetes of the twenties and those who desperately carry on their traditions today, ultimately becomes skeptical of the meaning of literature as a whole, sinking into the Nirvana of peaceful cohabitation with the Universe. Indeed, it is largely this intimate relationship between reader and writer that gives revolutionary literature an activism and purposefulness long since unattainable by the writers of other classes.

CONFLICTING CURRENTS IN REVOLUTIONARY LITERATURE

However, despite the unity of outlook of revolutionary literature, it contains a number of trends embodying contradictory aims and assumptions. It would be strange indeed, if the class struggle did not operate *within* revolutionary literature, though it is most clearly defined in the fight against bourgeois literature. The varying backgrounds of revolutionary writers and the diverse ways through which they come to Marxism set the frame for this inner struggle. Moreover, since forms and methods of writing do not drop like the gentle rain of heaven, but are slowly evolved in creative practice conditioned by the developing social relations, it is only natural that sharp differences of opinion should arise. To a Marxist such differences are not personal and formal, but actually reflect the stress of class conflict. Thus, the development of revolutionary literature is not unilinear; its progress is a process unfolding through a series of contradictions, through the struggle of opposed tendencies, and it is the business of criticism[*] to help writers resolve these contradictions. Unless criticism fulfills this task, the progress of revolutionary literature is retarded and certain writers may even be shunted off their revolutionary rails.

Thus far Marxian criticism in this country has not faced the problem squarely, nor has it stated the diverse tendencies. The illusion has been allowed to spread that revolutionary writers constitute one happy family, united in irreconcilable struggle against capitalism. To a considerable extent, therefore, an atmosphere of empiricism has resulted, where writers clutch at the nearest method at hand without conscious selection, unfortified by criticism with the Marxian equipment necessary for coping with the problems of creative method. Some incidental pieces of criticism have helped to guide writers and readers, but on the whole no attempt has been made to place such theoretical work in the center of our discussions.

Neither have critics given writers adequate guidance in their quest of realistic revolutionary themes. Many young writers have declared themselves for Communism, and have joined the John Reed Clubs, but with few exceptions, they have not shown as yet a sufficient understanding of the meaning of such declarations in practice. What does the present paucity of authentic revolutionary short stories prove? Most of our writers have not grasped the fact that workers' struggles cannot be written about on the basis of inven-

---

[*]By "criticism" we do not mean the body of formal analysis alone. Throughout this editorial most of our references to "critics" and "criticism" are meant to include the whole organizational and editorial leadership of revolutionary literature, the writer's critical attitude to himself and to others, as well as formal analysis.

tiveness or a tourist's visit. The profile of the Bolshevik is emerging in America, heroic class battles are developing, new human types and relations are budding in and around the Communist Party; obviously, therefore, revolutionary fiction cannot be produced by applying abstract Communist ideology to old familiar surroundings.

The assimilation of this new material requires direct participation instead of external observation; and the critic's task is to point out the dangers inherent in the *spectator*'s attitude. The critic is the ideologist of the literary movement, and any ideologist, as Lenin pointed out "is worthy of that name only when he marches ahead of the spontaneous movement, points out the real road, and when he is able, ahead of all others, to solve all the theoretical, political and tactical questions which the 'material elements' of the movement spontaneously encounter. It is necessary to be critical of it [the movement], to point out its dangers and defects and to aspire to *elevate* spontaneity to consciousness" (*A Conversation with Defenders of Economism*).

PULLING IN OPPOSITE DIRECTIONS

The most striking tendency, and the most natural one in a young revolutionary literature, is what is commonly called "leftism." Though it has seldom been explicitly stated in literary theory, its prejudices and assumptions are so widespread that at this time its salient features are easily recognized. Its zeal to steep literature overnight in the political program of Communism results in the attempt to force the reader's responses through a barrage of sloganized and inorganic writing. "Leftism," by tacking on political perspectives to awkward literary forms, drains literature of its more specific qualities. Unacquainted with the real experiences of workers, "leftism," in criticism and creation alike, hides behind a smoke-screen of verbal revolutionism. It assumes a direct line between economic base and ideology, and in this way distorts and vulgarizes the complexity of human nature, the motives of action and their expression in thought and feeling. In theory the "leftist" subscribes to the Marxian thesis of the continuity of culture, but in practice he makes a mockery of it by combating all endeavors to use the heritage of the past. In criticism the "leftist" substitutes gush on the one hand, and invective on the other, for analysis; and it is not difficult to see that to some of these critics Marxism is not a science but a *sentiment*.

"Leftism" is not an accidental practice, nor can it be regarded merely as youthful impetuosity. Its literary "line" stems from the understanding of Marxism as mechanical materialism. In philosophy, mechanical materialism assumes a direct determinism of the whole superstructure by the economic foundation, ignoring the dialectical interaction between consciousness and environment, and the reciprocal influence of the parts of the superstructure on each other and on the economic determinants. The literary counterpart of mechanical materialism faithfully reflects this vulgarization of Marxism. But its effects strike even deeper: it paralyzes the writer's capacities by creating a dualism between his artistic consciousness and his beliefs, thus making it impossible for him to achieve anything beyond fragmentary, marginal expression.

At the other extreme we find a right-wing tendency, which is equally unsuccessful in imaginatively re-creating the proletarian movement. The right-wing writer is usually very productive, but his work differs but slightly from that of liberal bourgeois writers. His acceptance of the revolutionary philosophy is half-hearted, though he makes sporadic use of it. The source of his attitude and practice is political fence-straddling, disinterest in Marxism, and lack of faith in the proletariat. . . .

LOOKING AHEAD

These problems cannot be solved by decree or dogma. Solutions will be made step by step, in the course of the continuous interaction of literary theory and literary practice. In this editorial, however, we wish to indicate several means of approach.

The very existence of two main types of revolutionary writing, the more intellectual and the more popular, shows that there is a division in our audience in terms of background and class composition. Workers who have had no literary education prefer the poetry of Don West to that of S. Funaroff, whereas intellectuals reverse this choice. The proletarian writer should realize that he is functioning through his medium within the vanguard of the movement as a whole. As such, his task is to work out a sensibility and a set of symbols *unifying* the responses and experiences of his total audience. Insofar as this cannot be done overnight, his innovations must be constantly checked by the responses of his main audience, the working class, even while he strives to raise the cultural level of the masses.

The question of creative method is primarily a question of the imaginative assimilation of political content. We believe that the sensibility is the medium of assimilation: political content should not be isolated from the rest of experience but must be merged into the creation of complete personalities and the perception of human relations in their physical and sensual immediacy. The class struggle must serve as a premise, not as a discovery. This the "leftist" does not do on the grounds that such a method dilutes the political directness that he aims at; actually, however, he defeats his purpose, inasmuch as he dissolves action and being in political abstractions. To a Marxist the bourgeois claims of universality are an empty concept; those elements in art that have been called universal are merely those that have recurred so far. The problem of the revolutionist is not to seek universals but usables, for his task is to create a synthesis and not merely an innovation. Ultimately, of course, the question of usables involves, first, the retaining of the cultural acquisitions of humanity as a *background of values*, and second, a selection of specific contributions by individual bourgeois writers.

Unless we are acutely aware of the body of literature as a whole, no standards of merit are possible. The measure of a revolutionary writer's success lies not only in his sensitiveness to proletarian material, but also in his ability to create new landmarks in the perception of reality; that is, his success cannot be gauged by immediate agitational significance, but by his re-creation of social forces in their entirety. This becomes specific literary criticism when applied to choice of theme, character and incident. And here it is necessary to stress what many writers tend to forget: literature is a medium steeped in sensory experience, and does not lend itself to the conceptual forms that the social-political content of the class struggle takes most easily. Hence the translation of this content into images of *physical life* determines— in the esthetic sense—the extent of the writer's achievement. . . .

Partisan Review, of course, cannot presume to solve these questions single-handed. Together with the *New Masses*, which is the central organ of the cultural movement, and with the numerous regional magazines, we hope to develop a critical atmosphere that will strengthen the most vital forces in our young literary tradition.

This is a perspective which can be realized only when the readers and the writers work with the editors toward this common aim. We invite all revolutionary writers and fellow-travelers, and especially the writers in the John Reed Clubs throughout the country, to contribute to the magazine; and we welcome readers and writers alike to use our columns for stating their reactions to our policy and to the contents of each issue. Only in the course of such collective discussion and reciprocal influence can a revolutionary literature reach maturity.

4

You Can Make Out Their Voices
Whittaker Chambers

Among the talented young writers drawn to Communism was one Whittaker Chambers. The piece he wrote for the March 1931 New Masses *about rebellious Arkansas farmers attracted a good deal of attention and praise, and a bright future was foreseen for him. The literary life was not for him, however. He was destined for other great things, but that is a story we cannot pursue here.*

Most of the men had driven over in flivvers. A heavier car drew up. A heavier man got out and came over.

Purcell had been a colonel in the war. "Talking about the drought?" he asked, eyeing each face in turn.

"Wardell's John killed a rattler in front of the house," said Davis. "The folks came over to find out just what a dead snake looks like. Would *you* like to see?"

A voice as vibrant and deep as Purcell's was a surprise, issuing from the small slit of his lips, while his full angular jaws worked up and down. He spoke deliberately, with his own emphasis.

"This 'drowt,' or 'drooth' as Wardell calls it, has been a lucky break for you, Wardell. You were running pretty low in your line of knocks when this bad luck came along." Little gray eyes glared gleefully on either side of his small, fighty wedge of turned-up nose.

"The 'general' 's got his chip on his shoulder," one of the Wardell boys whispered to the other.

"On his face, you mean, to keep his eyes from running together," John Wardell said aloud, staring at Purcell's nose.

"Some of us call it 'drowt' and some of us call it 'drooth,' " said Wardell, "but they both mean that the crops are done for, water and forage are dried up, the cattle are dying, and we'll be needing food when our credit gives out at the stores in town. Unless, of course, the banks want to make us long-term loans."

Purcell, the richest farmer in the district, had a finger in the Bank of Paris, of which his son-in-law was cashier.

"The trouble with Wardell is," Purcell said, preserving his good temper, but talking rather to the gathering than to Wardell, "the trouble with him is that he spends too much time nights reading those books he has in the house, and looking up the long words in the dictionary. So he gets sleepy and sore at the world, don't you, Jim?" The men smiled, being let in on the joke by the big boss. "What was that book, in that package of yours that came undone in the post office that time?" Purcell was also post-master. " 'Socialism *Yew*topian and Scientific!' " He laughed. "Well, every man's got a right to read what he wants to in his own house, I guess, if he don't try to force others to think his crazy ways, too. But I went to school with Jim Wardell, didn't we, Jim, and I know he's still the same wild Jim, wild ideas, but a heart of gold. So if you get hungry, and he tries to feed you Socialism *Yew*topian and Scientific, if you don't feel full, and I guess you won't, I think the Red Cross will do more for you all. I got to go. So long, Jim. So long, boys."

"The Red Cross!"

"The Red Cross!"

"They did fine work in the Mississippi flood!"

"The Red Cross!"

They began to drift away from Wardell's to town or home.

"So it's the Red Cross next," thought Wardell. "I know you dirt farmers! You've got to find out for yourselves. So it's the Red Cross you'll find out about now! And when you have, and I guess you'll get your chance this time, you'll be ready to show them a few things—"

"Say, Frances," he said when they were the last two left, "we can spare some of our milk for a baby, I guess. While the cow's still giving any. Drop in after milking. Throw that snake off the path, boys," he called from the porch, not to hear the young man's thanks. . . .

Frances used to come a little early and sit in the kitchen a few minutes in the evening while Wardell was milking the cow.

"And how's the baby and how is Hilda today?" Mrs. Wardell would ask.

"It's very bad up there. Since she lost her milk, it's terrible. And then the cow dying. Yours is the only cow left around here, except Purcell's."

"Take this home to them," she would say when he went, his milk can full. Wardell never asked her what was in the nameless parcels. But even the boys were going oftener to bed hungry, after eating everything there was. Sometimes there was no milk on the Wardells' table.

"The cow won't last much longer at this rate," said Wardell to his wife one night. Such a ridiculous sentence to make her heart almost stop beating!

One evening Ann Wardell thought Frances looked as if he hadn't eaten for two days, so she set some boiled dried beans, part of supper's only dish, before him. Wardell came in without the dribble of milk, and sat down. "Don't you think the time is coming, Frank," he said, "when the poor farmers, people like you and me and the Davises and Wiggens and Drdla, will have to go and take the food out of the store windows in Paris? There's always plenty of it there."

"You're a Socialist, ain't you?" Frank asked, ever so slyly, over his spoonful of beans.

(*"The branding reproach of Communism!"*)

"I'm a Communist, Frank."

"What does that mean?—" the beans suspended midway to the mouth.

"In this case, it means that I'm for unlimited free groceries and meat to all poor farmers. No rent for two years. Free seed. Free milk for babies."

"I guess you Reds want everything free," said Frank.

"I guess you will, too, before the baby's dead." Hard and bitter to hammer it home.

"Jim!"

"I know what I'm telling him, Ann. We're both dirt farmers, poor men, both come from the same class, so there's no reproach in your taking something from me when you need it, Frances. And there's no reproach meant, in my telling you that your kid would be dead but for your getting the milk from my cow. You couldn't buy it. Not from me, I wouldn't sell it to you. And you couldn't buy it from Purcell because he *would* sell it to you, and you haven't got the money to buy it. Well, my cow's dying. Now what do you think about having milk *free?*"

"Dying? Your cow's dying?" Frances was the color of milk himself.

"She'll be dead by morning. Now I'm going out to see what I can do for her. There won't be any milk tonight or from now on. But don't forget that it was the dirty Communist, the Red, the Bolshevik who wants everything free for every poor farmer, who kept the kid alive 'til now."

Frances stumbled, with the empty milk can, out the door Wardell had left open, past the barn where he saw a light, and the cow lying on her side, and Wardell bending over her.

"Jim's cruel, but Jim's right," said Mrs. Wardell. Her husband did not come back into the house, and she waited half an hour before she slipped out and across the field paths, with another milk-can. . . .

The deep snow separated the farms, but it made starvation general.

At first they burned the fence posts, those who had them; the others, the floor boards in the barns. Those who had no barns burned their hen coops. But after charcoal, what?

The men took out their guns, the pretext being to hunt jackrabbits, though most of them had died in the drought. But the women had no pretext and no will to escape the wailing of the babies, for whom there was no milk, and the whimpering and gaunt eyes of the older children.

The men made an honest search for game, but by afternoon most of them drifted into Paris, with their guns under their arms.

Many of them passed the bank windows, never suspecting what was going on within. Purcell saw them as he leaped to his feet in the fury of wrangling with his son-in-law, the cashier, and old Dr. Jesperson, the president, and walked to the front window of the Bank of Paris.

"They're walking around the streets with guns now, and you talk about closing the bank! I knew you'd do this," he screamed, shaking his fist at his son-in-law, the heavy jaws turkey red. "I knew you'd do this, I knew you would! You and your damn fool farm mortgages! And now the bank will crash, and so will you, and so will the Doc! But I won't! I took care of that!"

The main road entered Paris after turning a right angle, around an osage hedge, and crossing a creek, dried up in the drought, on a wooden bridge. It passed the double row of store fronts, and returned to the prairie on the other side. Two tracks led south and north to scattered farms. The latter had once been busy when Purcell worked his ground-level mines in the hills, twenty miles to the north. They had been closed down for years.

Wardell and Davis found about thirty armed men on the main street.

"I don't know what to do," said a little man named Shays, "my baby's dying. He's dying all right, dying. And we haven't got milk."

"Neither have we!"

"We haven't had any for two days. My baby's dying."

"We got some but my credit's gone. We can't even get any food. But milk comes first."

"There's only one place you can get milk around here," said Wardell.

"Where's that?"

"At Purcell's."

"We know that! Where are we going to get the money? He's not giving it away, and he don't trust now."

"Did you say your kid was dying, Dan?" Wardell asked Shays.

"Yes, he'll die if I don't get him milk."

"I'm glad you got your rifle with you. Will you come with me to Purcell's and make them give you milk?"

The little man blenched. "Take it from Purcell, you mean?"

"That's what I mean. Will anyone else come with us? Will you, Doscher?"

"No, I won't. I know your Socialist ideas! What do you think I am, a thief?"

"Will you lend me your gun, Doscher?" asked Davis. "I'd like to go with Jim and Shays. You know, our farms are too near together, and I can't stand listening to your baby scream itself to death, even if you can."

"I'll go!"

"I'll go!"

"I'll go!"

In the end, Doscher went, too.

They tramped out the western side of the town, fighting their way through the snow, and, in half an hour, were at Purcell's.

Wardell led them to the back door.

"Lilian," he said, "some of these men have babies, and all of us have children. None of us have any money. If those babies don't get their milk tonight, some of them will die. They'll all die in a week or two. Will you give us milk?"

"*Give* it to you? How can I give it to you, Jim Wardell? You're crazy!"

"You've got to give it to us."

"How can I give it to you? To *all* of you?"

"You've got to give it to us. We know how to milk cows just as well as you do. If you don't give it to us, we'll go down to the barn and take it."

She screamed. "I won't."

"In other words, you want us to take it. All right, we'll take it!"

"Wait, wait a minute, wait!" She flew into the house.

All three men sat stiff and terrified as the phone rang in the bank. "Well, then, I'll answer it," said Purcell.

"They want you to *give* it to them?" he shouted. "*Guns?* Oh, I see," he said, "Wardell! I see. Well, give it to them! Give it to them! *Give it to them!*" He missed the hook as he slammed the receiver against the case. . . .

Before noon the little house was so packed with men and women's bodies, you couldn't walk a foot. The heat rose perceptibly and with the smell of cow and horse manure and humans.

"We can't talk in here," Wardell called out. "Everybody outside!"

"Line up those cars in a half dozen rows," he said, "and sit in them." His own car was standing in front of the house. It was open and the top was down. His wife got in, and Davis. Wardell stood on the front seat and talked.

"I'm glad to see that there are so few of us here," he said. "It means that only the most reliable and the most needy are here. It means we can move together easier, and have more confidence in each other. And we need that."

"I'm glad to see, too, that you women have brought your babies with you. It's another sign that you're not afraid, and it means that we'll never lose sight of why we're going to Paris.

"And we're going down to Paris. We're starving, and we're going to Paris to get food. I hear that the Red Cross is going to give it to us. Now I want to tell you *how* they're going to give to us.

"First of all, before they give us anything, we've got to prove that we're not 'imposters.' That's what they're calling some of us now. In other words, we've got to prove that we really are starving to death. Can you prove it?"

Growls.

"Then, when we've proved that we're starving, I want to tell you *what* they'll give us."

"How do you know what they're going to do?" asked a voice. Other voices: "Ssh! Ssh!"

"Never mind, Ar Crocker, just remember that we *did* tell you, when the time comes," Davis bawled back.

"They're going to give us *one* loaf of bread! Not one apiece, but one to each family! One bag of flour—the same! Maybe some bacon!"

"How much milk?" called a woman.

"Enough for two days."

"What good does two days do? We had a day's before, and we made it last three. Now if they give us two day's, and we make it last five, what'll we do when it's gone?"

"It's the same with all the rest of the relief. It will last two days. What are you going to do when it's gone? There's food enough in the stores of Paris to last us for weeks. But they won't give it to us, because the Red Cross will only give a little money for a place like Paris, and most of that went to buying Purcell's milk for today's relief. Never mind how I know!

"The thing for us to do now, is to force them to give some food today. And to do that, we've got to all go down together. If we go in one by one, they'll cheat us, or they'll say we're not starving, and we won't get any relief at all.

"Now before we go, I want to ask you something. How many of you have guns in your cars? Nine, ten, eleven. You, too, Doscher? Good! Every man who brought his gun today was with us when we forced Purcell to give us milk. Those men learned something. But you've got to be doubly careful today not to use your guns unless somebody starts shooting at you first, I'll tell you why. We're starving. But they don't want to give us food. They give us food only to keep us quiet. You men with guns are the leaders in forcing them to give us food. Because they're afraid of guns. But they'll kill you if some of you keep on fighting. They'll kill you, because you're outnumbered. And when you're dead, Purcell and the rest will be boss here, and your babies will go just as hungry, but there'll be nobody to get them food. The time is not quite ripe for shooting. Do you understand?"

"Yes."

"We can threaten them today, we can force them, we may even *have to* shoot, but don't fire a gun if you can help it. Not today!

"Now, the cars with guns in the lead! Let's go!"

The grating of thirty gears, slipping from first to second, to high.

"I don't see how he can possibly claim to be starving," said Lily Purcell to the Red Cross supervisor: (The milk Frances did not buy!) "His baby died two days ago, and nobody knows where his wife is!"

"Well, at least he can't have any milk. That settles that right off!"

Frank Frances had not gone to the meeting. He was one of the first outside the relief store doors when they opened. For fifteen minutes he had been attempting to establish his status as a starving man. Meanwhile the line grew behind him, at first grumbling, then shouting, "Give him something!"

"This is no way to begin!" The supervisor scanned their heads disapprovingly. "Too many eye sockets!" he thought. He was unwilling to cede ground at once, and would not give Lily Purcell the order, "Let him have some bread."

Suddenly there was a shout from the edge of the crowd. "They're coming! They're coming!"

From the west the line of thirty cars swept into the town, two abreast. They stopped in the middle of the street. The men and women got out, the men with their guns, the women with their babies.

The crowd opened for thirteen men with guns. "Now we'll get some food!"

Wardell and Davis stopped where Frances stood suspended in an act of appeal. Lily Purcell and her supervisor stared.

Shays, Doscher, Drdla, staring back over the ends of their guns, which they rested on the floor.

Mrs. Wiggens with a baby in her arms had pressed to the front.

"Yes, what are you going to give us?" asked Mrs. Wiggens. "What are you going to give us?" said Davis.

"I don't know that we're going to give you anything. At least until you put those guns down," he said, tonguing his lips that were like earthworms that have been out too long in the rain.

"Give that man some bread," said Wardell.

"I don't think he deserves any. And I'm not taking orders here, I'm giving them!"

Several men laughed.

"And you, Lily, give Mrs. Wiggens some flour."

"She *certainly* don't need any. I know her well. She's a regular troublemaker." She appealed to the Red Cross knight.

"Give her some flour!"

"Don't give her flour!" said the supervisor. "These people are not ready for relief. They don't know how to take it. *This place is closed! Get out!*"

"Take it, men," said Wardell. "Don't hurt anybody. See that everybody gets a bag, Mrs. Wiggens."

"Oh! Oh! They're stealing our flour! They're stealing our flour!" Lily continued to scream until the store was stripped and empty. Mrs. Wiggens, who had been passing out the bags, was the last to leave. As she took up her own bag, Lily tried to stop her.

"You can't have that, you *can't* steal it!" She hung on to the bag with the grip of a kind of death she felt freezing her. Finally Mrs. Wiggens wrenched it loose. The girl's nails had torn the bag.

"Sow!" cried Mrs. Wiggens, seeing the waste. She struck Lily Purcell across the lower face with the bag. The flour whited her face like a clown's. Her glasses fell off and smashed. She screamed.

"She's killing me! She's killing me! She's stealing! She's killing me! She's stealing!" She was sobbing, a gulping blubber that shook her breasts.

"Shut up!" Mrs. Wiggens herself screamed. "Shut up! I'm sorry I hurt you!" Picking up the baby, she ran out of the store.

"Into the stores, men!" cried Davis and Wardell at opposite ends of the street. Some of the storekeepers tried locking up.

"If you don't open that door, we'll come in through the window," shouted Drdla.

The doors opened.

It was dark before all the milk had been taken from Purcell's cows, and the food apportioned and piled in the cars.

They started on a signal from Wardell, moving more consciously together as a mass than ever before. As they left the village, they were grim, still. Once outside it they began to laugh. They felt strong. They also felt afraid.

By then it had begun to snow again, fat, heavy flakes.

"How long do you think this lot will last?" asked Davis in the head car with Wardell.

"The food about two weeks, the milk, of course, only a few days."

"Then?" asked Davis.

"Well, they'll never *let* us do this again."

"You mean—shooting?"

"I suppose so. Everything depends on quick organization now, Mort. Shays and Doscher and Drdla and Mrs. Wiggens, and Frances, and any others we're sure about. You can be sure Purcell sent the SOS over the wires by now. Tomorrow or the day after, they'll have the troops here."

"I've been wondering about Purcell's old mine shafts in the hill."

"Oh, you have?"

Later Davis said, "I think you're wrong about Frances, Jim. I don't trust him."

"Of course, you may be right. It's true he's weak. It takes a lot to bring him over, and a lot to keep him going. But he's been through a lot by now. We've got to make the most of what we've got."

The cars moved slowly, so close together that the lights, many of them dim or missing, cast a blurred glare from the rear ends on the snow.

A car appeared, moving in the other direction. It stopped. They came abreast and stopped also.

"Mister Ooardel?"

"It's your Mex," said Davis. Wardell got out.

"I hear in the town ten miles away, there is fighting in Paris. Everybody is much excited." He was excited himself. "Everybody says he will take food, too. So I came back, Companero, I thought you need men."

"Them greasers have a long nose for food," said Shays. "They can smell a jumping bean no matter where it hops."

"Go get your own, Mex," said Drdla, "there ain't any here for you."

"He ain't asking you for food!" Drdla's eyes blinked before Davis turned away. "He's asking you if you'll allow him to shoot a gun shoulder to shoulder with you. I suppose you know you may be needing him. You come up to my place, Carrillo. You and your reti*noo*." He looked at the battered Ford.

It stopped the laughter. The cars dropped away one by one.

"I'm sending my boys away tomorrow, Mort," said Wardell.

"Where to?"

"East, to the comrades. I want them to be gone before the troops come. I'm driving them to the main road, at Tyrone, in the morning."

"Yes, I suppose you're right. Though I guess I couldn't do it."

"Anyway, out there they'll be learning something. What is there for them here—shooting, lynching? That's our business yet. Theirs is to learn more about Communism first."

"Tell the comrades what we are doing," Wardell said as he stopped the car at the crossroads the next morning. "Tell them we're organizing. Tell them that already there are many of us. Tell them we've got the dirt farmers here in motion. And make them understand that what we need above everything else, what we must have, is a hectograph.

"Try to get jobs and stick together.

"Now go along. I think you can hitch; if you can't, be careful on the freights. We've got no use for dead men or cripples. Come back alive in the spring, there's nothing here for you now but hunger."

The snow was fine and dry, and blew in little lifting spirals on the asphalt of the highway, which was comparatively open.

The boys got out and walked off together toward the east. The road followed the roll of the prairie. Coming to the top of the first rise, they turned and, standing together, waved.

They shouted. The cold wind preserved the ring of their voices that the snow might have muffled, blowing their words to the silent man and woman beside the Ford.

"We'll be back in the spring!"

"Could you make out both their voices?" she asked.

5

WOMEN ON THE BREADLINES
Meridel LeSueur

Meridel LeSueur was a young mother who lived in Minneapolis with her two children and had already published stories in reputable magazines. The direction her literary career took—its commitment to Communism—is prefigured in this piece for the January 1932 New Masses. Though the editors liked it, they had misgivings. They called it "defeatist in attitude" and "lacking in revolutionary spirit." But it is exactly the absence of rhetoric and ideological posturing that makes the story so compelling.

I am sitting in the city free employment bureau. It's the woman's section. We have been sitting here now for four hours. We sit here every day, waiting for a job. There are no jobs. Most of us have had no breakfast. Some have had scant rations for over a year. Hunger makes a human being lapse into a state of lethargy, especially city hunger. Is there any place else in the world where a human being is supposed to go hungry amidst plenty without an outcry, without protest, where only the boldest steal or kill for bread, and the timid crawl the streets, hunger like the beak of a terrible bird at the vitals?

We sit looking at the floor. No one dares think of the coming winter. There are only a few more days of summer. Everyone is anxious to get work to lay up something for that long siege of bitter cold. But there is no work. Sitting in the room we all know it. That is why we don't talk much. We look at the floor dreading to see that knowledge in each other's eyes. There is a kind of humiliation in it. We look away from each other. We look at the floor. It's too terrible to see this animal terror in each other's eyes.

So we sit hour after hour, day after day, waiting for a job to come in. There are many women for a single job. A thin sharp woman sits inside the wire cage looking at a book. For four hours we have watched her looking at that book. She has a hard little eye. In the small bare room there are half a dozen women sitting on the benches waiting. Many come and go. Our faces are all familiar to each other, for we wait here everyday.

This is a domestic employment bureau. Most of the women who come here are middle-aged, some have families, some have raised their families and are now alone, some have men who are out of work. Hard times and the man leaves to hunt for work. He doesn't find it. He drifts on. The woman probably doesn't hear from him for a long time. She expects it. She isn't surprised. She struggles alone to feed the many mouths. Sometimes she gets help from the charities. If she's clever she can get herself a good living from the charities, if she's naturally a lick-spittle, naturally a little docile and cunning. If she's proud then she starves silently, leaving her children to find work, coming home after a day's searching to wrestle with her house, her children.

Some such story is written on the faces of all these women. There are young girls too, fresh from the country. Some are made brazen too soon by the city. There is a great exodus of girls from the farms into the city now. Thousands of farms have been vacated completely in Minnesota. The girls are trying to get work. The prettier ones can get jobs in the stores when there are any, or waiting on table, but these jobs are only for the attractive and the adroit, the others, the real peasants have a more difficult time. . . .

Sitting here waiting for a job, the women have been talking in low voices about the girl Ellen. They talk in low voices with not too much pity for her, unable to see through the mist of their own torment. "What happened to Ellen?" one of them asks. She knows the answer already. We all know it.

A young girl who went around with Ellen tells about seeing her last evening back of a cafe downtown outside the kitchen door, kicking, showing her legs so that the cook came out and gave her some food and some men gathered in the alley and threw small coin on the ground for a look at her legs. And the girl says enviously that Ellen had a swell breakfast and treated her to one too, that cost two dollars.

A scrub woman whose hips are bent forward from stooping with hands gnarled like water-soaked branches clicks her tongue in disgust. No one saves their money, she says, a little money and these foolish young things buy a hat, a dollar for breakfast, a bright scarf. And they do. If you've ever been without money, or food, something very strange happens when you get a bit of money, a kind of madness. You don't care. You can't remember that you had no money before, that the money will be gone. You can remember nothing but that there is the money for which you have been suffering. Now here it is. A lust takes hold of you. You see food in the windows. In imagination you eat hugely; you taste a thousand meals. You look in windows. Colors are brighter; you buy something to dress up in. An excitement takes hold of you. You know it is suicide but you can't help it. You must have food, dainty, splendid food and a bright hat so once again you feel blithe, rid of that ratty gnawing shame.

"I guess she'll go on the street now," a thin woman says faintly and no one takes the trouble to comment further. Like every commodity now the body is difficult to sell and the girls say you're lucky if you get fifty cents.

It's very difficult and humiliating to sell one's body.

Perhaps it would make it clear if one were to imagine having to go out on the street to sell, say, one's overcoat. Suppose you have to sell your coat so you can have breakfast and a place to sleep, say, for fifty cents. You decide to sell your only coat. You take it off and put it on your arm. The street, that has before been just a street, now becomes a mart, something entirely different. You must approach someone now and admit you are destitute and are now selling your clothes, your most intimate possessions. Everyone will watch you talking to the stranger showing him your overcoat, what a good coat it is. People will stop and watch curiously. You will be quite naked on the street. It is even harder to try and sell one's self, more humiliating. It is even humiliating to try and sell one's labor. When there is no buyer.

The thin woman opens the wire cage. There's a job for a nursemaid, she says. The old gnarled women, like old horses, know that no one will have them walk the streets with the young so they don't move. Ellen's friend gets up and goes to the window. She is unbelievably jaunty. I know she hasn't had work since last January. But she has a flare of life in her that glows like a tiny red flame and some tenacious thing, perhaps only youth, keeps it burning bright. Her legs are thin but the runs in her old stockings are neatly mended clear down her flat shank. Two bright spots of rouge conceal her pallor. A narrow belt is drawn tightly around her thin waist, her long shoulders stoop and the blades show. She runs wild as a colt hunting pleasure, hunting sustenance.

It's one of the great mysteries of the city where women go when they are out of work and hungry. There are not many women in the bread line. There are no flop houses for women as there are for men, where a bed can be had for a quarter or less. You don't see women lying on the floor at the mission in the free flops. They obviously don't sleep in the jungle or under newspapers in the park. There is no law I suppose against their being in these places but the fact is they rarely are.

Yet there must be as many women out of jobs in cities and suffering extreme poverty as there are men. What happens to them? Where do they go? Try to get into the YW without any money or looking down at heel. Charities take care of very few and only those that are called "deserving." The lone girl is under suspicion by the virgin women who dispense charity.

I've lived in cities for many months broke, without help, too timid to get in bread lines. I've known many women to live like this until they simply faint on the street from privations, without saying a word to anyone. A woman will shut herself up in a room until it is taken away from her, and eat a cracker a day and be as quiet as a mouse so there are no social statistics concerning her.

I don't know why it is, but a woman will do this unless she has dependents, will go for weeks verging on starvation, crawling in some hole, going through the streets ashamed, sitting in libraries, parks, going for days without speaking to a living soul like some exiled beast, keeping the runs mended in her stockings, shut up in terror in her own misery, until she becomes too supersensitive and timid to even ask for a job. . . .

Mrs. Grey, sitting across from me is a living spokesman for the futility of labor. She is a warning. Her hands are scarred with labor. Her body is a great puckered scar. She has given birth to six children, buried three, supported them all alive and dead, bearing them, burying them, feeding them. Bred in hunger they have been spare, susceptible to disease. For seven years she tried to save her boy's arm from amputation, diseased from tuberculosis of the bone. It is almost too suffocating to think of that long close horror of years of child bearing, child feeding, rearing, with the bare suffering of providing a meal and shelter.

Now she is fifty. Her children, economically insecure, are drifters. She never hears of them. She doesn't know if they are alive. She doesn't know if she is alive. Such subtleties of suffering are not for her. For her the brutality of hunger and cold, the bare bone of life. That is enough. These will occupy a life. Not until these are done away with can those subtle feelings that make a human being be indulged.

She is lucky to have five dollars ahead of her. That is her security. She has a tumor that she will die of. She is thin as a worn dime with her tumor sticking out of her side. She is brittle and bitter. Her face is not the face of a human being. She has born more than it is possible for a human being to bear. She is reduced to the least possible denominator of human feelings.

It is terrible to see her little bloodshot eyes like a beaten hound's, fearful in terror.

We cannot meet her eyes. When she looks at any of us we look away. She is like a woman drowning and we turn away. We must ignore those eyes that are surely the eyes of a person drowning, doomed. She doesn't cry out. She goes down decently. And we all look away.

The young ones know though. I don't want to marry. I don't want any children. So they all say. No children. No marriage. They arm themselves alone, keep up alone. The man is helpless now. He cannot provide. If he propagates he cannot take care of his young. The means are not in his hands. So they live alone. Get what fun they can. The life risk is too horrible now. Defeat is too clearly written on it.

So we sit in this room like cattle, waiting for a nonexistent job, willing to work to the farthest atom of energy, unable to work, unable to get food and lodging, unable to bear children; here we must sit in this shame looking at the floor, worse than beasts at a slaughter. . . .

6
DENOUEMENT
Kenneth Fearing

Though he marched to his own drummer and kept aloof from the hurly-burly of politics, Fearing was squarely in the Communist camp in the 1930s. He can be counted among the proletarian poets but there was nothing hackneyed or obvious in his work, as the example below illustrates. It is from his 1935 collection, Poems. *He was to become well known for his novels, beginning with* The Big Clock, *which in 1946 was made into a hit movie of the same name.*

Leaflets, scraps, dust, match-stubs strew the linoleum that leads upstairs to
the union hall, the walls of the basement workers' club are dim and
cracked and above the speaker's stand Vanzetti's face shows green,
behind closed doors the committeeroom is a fog of smoke,

Who are these people?

All day the committee fought like cats and dogs and twelve of Mr. Kelly's
strongarm men patrolled the aisles that night, them blackjack guys
get ten to twenty bucks a throw, the funds were looted, sent to
Chicago, at the meeting the section comrade talked like a fool,
more scabs came through in trucks guarded by police,
workers of the world, workers of the world, workers of the world,

Who are these people and what do they want, can't they be decent, can't
they at least be calm and polite,
besides the time is not yet ripe, it might take years, like Mr. Kelly said,
years,

Decades black with famine and red with war, centuries on fire, ripped wide,

Who are these people and what do they want, why do they walk back and
forth with signs that say "Bread Not Bullets," what do they mean
"They Shall Not Die" as they sink in clouds of poison gas and fall
beneath clubs, hooves, rifles, fall and do not arise, arise, unite,
never again these faces, arms, eyes, lips,

Not unless we live, and live again,
return, everywhere alive in the issue that returns, clear as light that still
descends from a star long cold, again alive and everywhere visible
through and through the scene that comes again, as light on moving
water breaks and returns, heard only in the words, as millions of
voices become one voice, seen only in millions of hands that move
as one,

Look at them gathered, raised, look at their faces, clothes, who are these
people, who are these people,
what hand scrawled large in the empty prison cell "I have just received
my sentence of death. Red Front," whose voice screamed out in the
silence "Arise"?

And all along the waterfront, there, where rats gnaw into the leading platforms, here, where the wind whips at warehouse corners, look,
there, here,
everywhere huge across the walls and gates "Your party lives,"
where there is no life, no breath, no sound, no touch, no warmth, no light
but the lamp that shines on a trooper's drawn and ready bayonet.

1

MANIFESTO

First National Workers Theater Conference

Delegates from more than a hundred theater groups met in New York City early in 1932 for this conference, whose statement of intentions and purposes was published in the May 1932 issue of Workers Theater *magazine, put out by the pioneer Workers Laboratory Theater.*

BASIC TASKS

... 9 The basic tasks of the Workers Theater now are to spread the idea of the class struggle, to participate actively in the class struggle by raising funds for campaigns and for the revolutionary press, and by recruiting workers into the revolutionary unions and mass organizations, and especially to arouse the workers for the defense of the Soviet Union, against the coming Imperialist attack.

SHORTCOMINGS

10 The main shortcomings of the Workers Theater in America today are

- that there are not enough contacts between groups.
- that there are not enough plays being written to meet the growing need.
- that the more developed groups outside New York City do not assist the weaker groups in their locality.
- that the groups underestimate the necessity for cooperation.
- that there is no systematic attempt to build theater groups in the revolutionary unions and in most of the mass organizations.
- that international contacts are very weak.

TASKS: GENERAL

11 To overcome its weakness and to accomplish its important tasks, the Workers Theater must undertake the systematic political and artistic training of its members. It must increase and improve its Agit-Prop work. It must go out to the masses—into the streets, to the factory gates, to the farms. It

must reach the rank and file of the American Federation of Labor and the Socialist Party.

It must build and make use of the stationary Workers Theater wherever there are possibilities for its effective utilization.

It must experiment with forms in order to find the most effective methods of presenting its subject matter. It must use music and the dance and all other cultural forms, in order to make its material more attractive. It must take over from the bourgeois theater whatever can be used for revolutionary aims.

It must expose and fight anti-working-class propaganda of the bourgeois theater and its "socialist" stepchild. It must expose the deception of the slogan, "Art for Art's Sake."

It must draw in large numbers of workers and farmers. It must draw in sympathetic artists and intellectuals.

TASKS: REPERTORY

12 It must more quickly catch up with, and dramatize, the day-to-day struggles of the American working class.

It must present the most important developments of the class struggle in other countries.

It must popularize the tremendous achievement of the workers and farmers of the Soviet Union.

It must make clear that the great vitality of the Soviet Theater today was only made possible by the proletarian revolution in that country.

It must win workers and farmers, including those in the armed forces, for the tactic of turning the coming imperialist war against the Soviet Union into a civil war against the imperialists.

TASKS: ORGANIZATIONAL

13 To correct serious shortcomings in its organizational work

—it must establish the closest contact with, and help build, Agit-Prop troupes in the revolutionary unions and mass organizations.

—it must stimulate the growth of the Workers Theater in the important industrial sectors and in the rural districts.

—it must establish closer contact with the organizations of revolutionary writers, particularly to help solve the problem of adequate repertory.

—it must establish a national Workers Theater organization as the United States section of the International Workers' Dramatic Union.

The national organization must include federations of all Workers Theaters in the various languages, building federations where they do not

exist. The national Workers Theater organization will be a tremendous stimulus to the further growth of the revolutionary Workers Theater. . . .

2
The Artef
Samuel Kreiter

*The Artef stands for the Arbeiter Teater Verband, or Workers Theater Group. Radical Yiddish
language writers, actors, directors, et al., rallied to it as an alternative to the New York
Yiddish theater, which was as hackneyed and sentimental as it was popular with the Jewish
masses. Sustained by the Party's Jewish Bureau, the Artef itself grew increasingly popular,
thanks to its improvisatory talents, its ability to combine a multiplicity of genres. Much of
this is explained in the following article by a writer for the New Theatre magazine (successor to the Workers Theatre), in whose November 1934 issue it appeared.*

The Artef is one of the main stems in Yiddish proletarian culture. Going on
its ninth year, it bids fair to survive the once lively art of the now decadent
Yiddish histrionics.

In 1926, when the rank and file of American Jewish labor were junking
bureaucratic leadership, a group of class-alert shop workers with a passion
for the theater formed a dramatic studio under the guidance of the actor-
poet-regisseur, Jacob Mestel. For three years they rehearsed and studied the
manifold subtleties of stage technique. Following the period of strenuous
training, the studio matured into a compact artistic players ensemble under
the more resourceful direction of Beno Schneider, a student for years under
Vakhtangov. Besides the thirty-eight active players, the Artef maintains a studio for workers who desire dramatic training.

The Artef has successfully staged twelve productions which averaged
thirty performances each, a good average considering that its playing time is
confined to weekends and that the Artef operates without fat subsidies from
big-hearted donors. Of the twelve productions three dealt with the
American scene: *The Third Parade* by Paul Peters and Charles R. Walker, based
on the bonus march to Washington; *In the Roar of the Machines*, an original play
of American shop conditions by the Yiddish writer, F. Chernet; and *Drought*,
adapted by N. Buchwald from Hallie Flanagan's *Can You Hear Their Voices*. The
others were importations from Soviet repertory.

Though Jewish life is in a state of constant change, the Yiddish bourgeois
theater has not seen fit to change its threadbare pattern of inane mushy melodrama and Hasidic "romance" for a form of social art. As such it has failed to
identify itself with the varied and multiple problems that face the masses
today, an oversight which is fast becoming its downfall. The Artef, on the
other hand, arrived as a robust instrument in the class conflict. It reflects
mass struggle in place of mass suffering, which was a woebegone feature in

the "social problem play" that served early radical immigrants as a means of registering passive protest.

Furthermore, the Yiddish bourgeois plays are wanting in creative and technical imagination, in live humor, in fresh acting talent, in good lines. Even the most simple-minded of playgoers are no longer entertained by the facial and vocal acrobatics of a Ludwig Satz, the good-natured crooning and spoofing of the elfish Molly Picon, the prostrate unreal dilemmas of a Jennie Goldstein. The better front of the trade, the Yiddish Art Theater, fell upon evil days after sixteen years of near-heroic efforts on behalf of the finer play. Some of its disbanded troupers are now on the Coast doing earnest but ineffectual revivals. Others in New York have instituted themselves as the Yiddish Folk Troupe and premiered this season under Joseph Bulov in a Soviet melodrama, *The Verdict*, now playing at the Yiddish Folk Theater. Meanwhile, their lost leader, Mr. Maurice Schwartz, is in Hollywood trying to ease into film work.

Defying the confusion in the Yiddish theatrical world, the Artef dramatizations of dominant revolutionary forces are fearless and uncompromising, and transcend the old smug conception of what constitutes dramatic effectiveness.

Nearly one hundred thousand people saw Artef productions in seven months last year. In the same time it provided workers' clubs with mass recitations, readings, and improvisations. The Artef is still in the stage of development. It has an ambitious schedule for this season and plans to go on "the road."

The artistic development of the Artef is evident in its current production of *Recruits*, which had its premiere at the new Artef Theater on West 48th Street (the first workers' theater on Broadway). The play creates, in nine impressive scenes, a stirring re-creation of life under the Czar. The method Beno Schneider employs in directing is a synthesis of Reinhardt's expressionism and Stanislavsky's naturalism. He had to undo the corrosive tradition of Second Avenue exhibitionism, to steer clear of sentimental realism, in order to get at the inner dramatic pathos and intense truth that underlies mass struggle, without deviating from character portrayal. This he achieved through remarkable restraint, through subtle coordination of line and movement reaching often into symbolism. *Recruits* is unforgettable in its picture of primitive conflict between the poverty-ridden workers of a Russian-Polish village and its handful of rich Jewish proprietors. The central theme, going back to 1828 under Czar Nicholas I, revolves around the bitter system whereby the children of the poor were impressed into long years of servitude in the army. The havoc created in the village by the arrival of the Czar's decree calling for Jewish conscripts, how the decree was met by the community elders who seek to shift the obligation of supplying the Czar with recruits upon the poor, how they finally trick Nachmen, leader of the happy-go-lucky artisans, into signing himself away for the army, the running thread of romance, superstition, and suffering, the vivid impersonations against the richly toned, slightly grotesque back-drops prepared by Mr. Solotaroff, make a moving, artistic comedy.

NEWSBOY

V. J. Jerome and Gregory Novikov

Jerome originally wrote this as a poem. Novikov adapted it for the stage, that is, for a per-
formance by the Workers Laboratory (the "Shock Troupe") before a meeting of the American
League Against War and Fascism in 1934. Newsboy was an immediate hit and went on to
become one of the most popular skits seen by leftist audiences at the time.

The Scene

The entire action takes place on the stage which has been draped in black so that we
cannot distinguish its limitations. Before the black backdrop there are three two-foot
platforms, which serve as elevations for certain scenes and certain characters. However,
these too must be covered with a black fabric, so that they are not seen by the audience.
A street lamp is optional.

When the curtain rises, the stage is dark but the shuffling of many feet are heard.
Slowly a light is thrown along the street surface which lights up only the feet of the
passersby. We see all types of feet, well-shod, and poorly-shod, walking, strolling, and
running back and forth. In the center stands the Newsboy, in the dark.

NEWSBOY: Extry, read all about it! Love nest raided on Park Avenue,
            Extry! Marlene Dietrich insures legs for fifty thousand
            dollars! Extry! Mrs Vanderbilt calls Mrs Whitney a liar!
            Read all about it! Babe Ruth joins Boston Braves . . .
            Extry . . . College student murders his professor's mis-
            tress. Get your papers. American, News and Mirror.
            Morning papers!

(Slowly a spotlight creeps over the Newsboy's face and spreads until it covers the entire
stage with a sickly amber glow. Now we see the crowd in full, passing back and forth in
front of the newsboy. Occasionally someone stops to buy a newspaper. We see the fol-
lowing episodes as the newsboy continues his shouts.)

1. An attractive girl, evidently a stenographer, walks across the stage, fol
   lowed by a well-dressed man. She stops to buy a paper which the man
   pays for. They go off together.
2. A blind woman comes tap, tap, tapping across the stage, wailing: "Alms
   for the poor blind . . . Ain't no one goin' to help the blind . . . Alms for
   the blind!" A pompous man with a mustache drops a coin in her cup, and
   then stops to enter an item in his budget book.
3. Two shabbily dressed radicals cross the stage talking earnestly.

4. A nice young girl walks tearfully across the stage followed by a pleading young man.

(*The murmuring of the crowd grows louder. The strollers now appear like some mad ballet, forming various patterns behind the newsboy as they buy their papers. The headlines of the newspapers scream out the words MURDER, SUICIDE, and DIVORCE. A piano has joined the medley of voices and the effect is of a discordant babble. Above it all we hear the newsboy.*)

NEWSBOY: Read all about it! Murder . . . Rape . . . Scandal . . . All the latest sports events . . . morning papers . . .

(*The crowd is chanting Murder, Rape, Scandal, Suicide. The symphony of sound reaches a climax when suddenly we hear the booming voice of the Black Man, as yet offstage. At the first sound of his voice the murmur begins to die.*)

BLACK MAN: Hey, there, Newsboy, how long you goin' ter stand there under the "L," yellin' yer guts out? How long yer goin' to keep yellin' that workers should be murdered and strikes outlawed?

(*Crowd continues soft chant.*)

BLACK MAN: Because somewheres in a hotel room in "Frisco a Follies" girl shot the brains out of the old rip that kept her? Don't you ever get tired, Newsie, shoutin' about hold-ups, and murders, and raids on Love Nests? Come into the light, Newsboy, come into the light! . . .

(*As he speaks he advances into the sphere of light. The crowd pays no attention to him but the newsboy watches him carefully out of the corner of his eye, as if he senses a menace.*)

NEWSBOY: JAPAN WANTS WAR WITH THE UNITED STATES . . . SOVIET RUSSIA INSULTS UNITED STATES CONSUL . . . GERMAN OFFICIALS ATTACK AMERICAN GIRLS . . .

CROWD: (*as the chant changes in nature, their attitudes change from apathy to hatred*) Japan wants war . . . Soviet wants war . . . Germany wants war . . . Down with the Soviet . . . Down with the Soviet . . .

NEWSBOY: Eight thousand boys join CCC camps . . . Make professors swear loyalty to government . . . Bill passed in Congress to outlaw strikes . . . Japan prepares war . . . Germany arms 100,000 men . . . Italy masses troops on her border . . . attack on Abyssinia . . . Mrs Vanderbilt

calls Mrs Whitney a liar . . . Mary Pickford granted her
final decree . . . read all about it!

BLACK MAN: Why don't yer stop kiddin' yerself, Newsboy? Don't yer
see yer drunk with the poison gin of lies? All this talk of
CCC camps and Boy Scout parades and International
insults . . . you've got poison in yer bellies and it's eatin'
yer guts and rottin' away yer minds. Yer linin' up fer war
. . . that's what! Ye gettin' ready to fight again and kill
again, and slaughter again . . .

CROWD: (*growing louder*) We need another war. War brings out the
best in men. We need another war. War is natural. We
need another war—

BLACK MAN: They're chloroforming yuh with lies, I tell yuh. Lies!

(*The noise grows again to a crescendo as the crowd repeats the last speech and as the
Black Man keeps shouting "Lies." The scene fades off. A corner of the stage is brightened
with a white spotlight, slightly above the level of the crowd. In the spotlight we see a
man at a telephone. Behind him on the wall are the title streamers of the New York
American, Mirror, and Journal. It is William Randolph Hearst.*)

HEARST: (*into phone*) Rush through the following scare heads. Very
boldest type. "Six Million Starve to Death in Soviet Russia."
"Communism Must Go." "Down with American Reds."
"USA Spends One Billion Dollars on Armaments to be
Vested as Airplane Bombers, Cannon, Gas Bombs" . . .

(*The voice fades with the spotlight. A light fades in on the other side of the stage. We
see a man making a speech before a mob of people. Behind him is draped the bunting
of red, white, and blue. It is Huey Long.*)

LONG: Every man is a king. That's my motto. Share the wealth.
Every man is entitled to his rights, but no man should
make over a million dollars. Every man a king, that's the
motto of the Kingfish. A war wouldn't be such a bad
thing. Boys, ha, ha, ha—every man a king . . .

(*The lights and voice fade. A light on center of stage shows a man behind a microphone,
in priest's clothes. It is Father Coughlin.*)

COUGHLIN: . . . But our country, right or wrong. Of course, I am not
a militarist . . . (*sweetly*) No man of Jesus can be a militarist . . . Our Lord Jesus Christ teaches humility and
pacifism . . . BUT on the other hand, if our nation is in
danger of an attack by a foreign nation who is after our

gold—or, more particularly, our greatest asset, our silver supply . . . it is the God-ordained duty of every American citizen to fight and die for its protection. Our Government will be only as safe from without her borders as she is from within. Let us stamp out this ugly stain of communism with its militant peace policies. I can only repeat the words of that other great American, Chauncey Depew—"Our Country, right or wrong . . ."

(*The light and voice fade out, and again we see William Randolph Hearst speaking.*)

HEARST: Our country right or wrong. Japan insults US envoy. Russia plans to attack the USA. US steel up 40 points. Anaconda copper up 23 points. Du Pont powder works rises 82 points . . . Soviet Union plans to attack . . .

(*Voice dies away and spot fades. Murmuring of the crowd has begun again and grows louder. Sound of drums and martial music is heard in the distance, growing louder. As the lights reveal them, the people in the crowd line up in army formation, with rolled newspapers carried like rifles. They march back and forth and finally march straight front, and unroll their papers, revealing War Scare Headlines. The Black Man runs up and down the line trying to make them listen to him. They pay no attention; the Black Man is shouting over the music.*)

BLACK MAN: Come into the light, comrades, come into the light. You're being chloroformed. Your heads are full of lies, and you're gettin' ready to be killed. Cain't you see they're fixin' you for the slaughter. Cain't you see . . .

(*They pay no attention. Black Man goes over and sits on the curb, his head in his arms. An Unemployed Man in ragged clothes comes in and stops a Well-dressed Man.*)

UNEMPLOYED
MAN: How about a nickel for a cup of coffee, buddy?

WELL-DRESSED
MAN: Why don't you get a job?

UNEMPLOYED
MAN: Why don't I get a job? Ha, ha. That's rich. Why don't you get a job? Where do you suggest I look for one—in the White House?

WELL-DRESSED
MAN: Why don't you go to a CCC Camp?

UNEMPLOYED
MAN: Thanks, buddy, but I can starve here just as well as there.

(*The Well-dressed Man goes on, and the Unemployed Man approaches a dignified Old Gentleman.*)

Can you spare a nickel for a cup of coffee, sir? I've got to eat.

OLD
GENTLEMAN: I don't believe in it.

UNEMPLOYED
MAN: I don't get you.

OLD
GENTLEMAN: I don't believe in charity. Why don't you join the army? It would make a new man of you. (*Feels his muscles*) A man with a body like yours should be in the service. It would build up your morale.

UNEMPLOYED
MAN: I want to hang on to my arms and legs for a while, thanks. I'm not anxious to have them blown off in a war.

(*Old Gentleman goes on. Unemployed Man accosts a Kindly Old Lady.*)

UNEMPLOYED
MAN: Lady, can you spare a nickel for a cup of coffee?

KINDLY
OLD LADY: (*opening her purse*) Here you are, my good man. Always glad to help the unfortunate. But why don't you join the army? That would keep you off the streets.

UNEMPLOYED
MAN: (*throwing nickel back at her*) Thanks for the charity.

KINDLY
OLD LADY: It was only a suggestion.

UNEMPLOYED
MAN: A good suggestion. Why don't you join the army?

UNEMPLOYED
MAN: And get blown to bits!

WELL-DRESSED
MAN: (*coming back to him*) Or why don't you join the CCC camps?

UNEMPLOYED
MAN: And starve!

(*The cry of "Why don't you join the army?" and the answer, "And get blown to bits," and the other cry of "Why don't you join the CCC camps?" "And starve," are taken up by the crowd. They surge forward, and the chant becomes rhythmic. The Black Man jumps to his feet. The left entrance of the stage lights up. From offstage left is heard the voice of a Second Newsboy, quieting the other sounds.*)

SECOND
NEWSBOY: Fight against War and Fascism. Learn the truth about the munitions racket.

(*He enters with a magazine bag at his side. He is holding aloft a handful of papers, spread fanwise, so we cannot see their title.*)

Fight against War and Fascism. Fight NOW against that racket of the death manufacturers. The CCC camps are preparing men for war! Learn the truth! (*The First Newsboy belligerently steps forward to bar his way, but the Black Man and the Unemployed Man place themselves before the Second Newsboy as a shield. They hoist him to the top of a box stage center, and he gives them a stack of papers, which they distribute to the crowd. The First Newsboy slinks away. The crowd reads.*)

MAN IN CROWD:	(*as he reads*) Think of it. Eight and a half million men killed in the last war.
GIRL IN CROWD:	(*as she reads*) Ten million will probably die in the next war.
ANOTHER MAN IN CROWD:	(*as he reads*) Eight and a half million men killed for the profits of the munition-makers.
CROWD:	(*taking up the cry*) Eight and a half million men. Eight and a half million men. Killed—wounded—shell-shocked—millions more. Eight and a half million men murdered in war—murdered in war.

(*The crowd is huddled in the center, near the Second Newsboy, with their backs to the audience, continuing this chant. The First Newsboy runs on the stage, shouting his slogans, and wheeling each person of the crowd around so they face the audience. He is faced by a solid wall of "Fight" (the paper of the American League against War and Fascism), displayed to the audience. Above the wall, like a banner, the Second Newsboy waves his copy of "Fight." The First Newsboy runs up and down the line, shouting his slogans, but gets no response.*)

FIRST NEWSBOY:	Japan insults the USA—Germany insults the USA—Soviet Russia insults the USA—William Randolph Hearst says—Marlene Dietrich insures her legs—Soviet Russia wants war with USA.

(*He runs angrily off the stage, having gotten no response. The crowd is still chanting "Eight and a half million men" and so on. The tableau is something like the following:*)

Newsboy

Fight

Fight   Fight   Fight   Fight   Fight   Fight   Fight

Black Man   Unemployed Man

BLACK MAN:	(*exultantly*) Get yourself a trumpet, buddy, a big red trumpet, and climb to the top of the Empire State building, and blare out the news . . . Now is the time to fight war and Fascism. (*Comes center and speaks to audience.*)

Black men, white men, field men, shop men—it's time
to fight war. It's time to fight Fascism . . . Get yourself a
trumpet, buddy, a big red trumpet . . . and blare it out
. . . time to fight war . . . time to fight Fascism . . .

CURTAIN

Film

INTERVIEW
John Howard Lawson

*When he left New York for Hollywood in 1932 Lawson was an established playwright with a
number of hits to his credit. He was also a dedicated Communist, and so before long he was
organizing the Screen Writers Guild. Joining him later was a bevy of other Communists,
actors, directors, and technicians, as well as writers, most of them involved in union activities
and Party affairs. In 1973 two film scholars, Dave Davis and Ned Goldberg, interviewed
Lawson, age eighty, for a documentary. It appeared in* Cineaste *magazine the following year.*

I was back working at MGM at a reduced salary, but very happy to get the
money. At the same time, however, I was very disgusted with the conditions
in Hollywood. Then came the election of Roosevelt and its impact on the
whole social situation in the country—his inauguration, the closing of the
banks, and the stopping of all money transactions in the United States. This
was not a move which presaged a revolution, by any means; it was a practical measure to stabilize the banking system and to avoid failures of banks. But
it was used by the studios as the occasion to cut the salaries of all creative personnel by one-half. At MGM and the other studios, meetings were held of all
the creative personnel—all the actors, writers, technicians and directors—
and at these meetings the fifty percent cut was explained. Louis B. Mayer
presided over that meeting. I was sitting not very far from him and I saw that
as he talked about the cut in salaries—his salary was being cut one-half, too,
he said—tears streamed down his face as he explained what a sacrifice it was.
Well, I and most of my friends among the actors, writers and others did not
think it was such a sacrifice for MGM. We knew very well that they were
making profits and would go right on making profits, and that Louis B. Mayer
was retaining his enormous assets in terms of stock in MGM. About that time
I had begun to hold meetings regarding a writers' guild or union. When the
fifty percent cut came, it seemed obvious that the writers in Hollywood—
several hundred of them, many of them unemployed and others being cut
one-half regardless of the terms of their contract—that the time had come
when it was possible to really organize a union, although writers were afraid
of the word union, so we called it the Screen Writers Guild.

I was very active in the preparations for the first open meeting of the Guild. At the time of the first open meeting—I think in March or April of 1933, shortly after Roosevelt's inauguration—nobody in Hollywood knew anything about the Guild. But the word had gotten around to writers, and there was a turnout of several hundred writers that night. I had taken such a leading role in the preparations, and in the study of the legal questions in regard to the organization of the Guild, that it was unanimously agreed by the steering committee that I should make the main report, and that I should be elected without opposition as president of the new guild, which I was very proud to do.

I was interested in a Screen Writers Guild for two reasons: in the first place, from an economic point of view; and in the second place, to make better pictures, to make some sense of the production of pictures within the industry. Now I didn't labor under the delusion that the writer could control his material, which is supposedly the situation in the theater, although in the theater, too, there are all sorts of factors which determine what the writer can do with a play which is in production and under all the pressures of production. But I did think that writers should have more participation in production, that they should be part of a team which would include the director and the producers of the picture. The producer, the director and the writer, in my opinion, should work together in a collaborative effort to make a motion picture. Whether this was practical or not, I would wonder now, but anyway this was very important to us at that time, the whole question of the treatment of writers. Not only their physical treatment, their physical inability to function effectively as writers but also the custom of having four or five writers or ten or twelve writers work on the same story, and the confusion about credits. During the time I'd been at MGM I got some very big credits, and I got some fairly good credits at RKO afterward, but the credits did not correspond in any way to the actual work I had done on those pictures, because friends of the producers were put in for subordinate credits, and the credits were juggled in all sorts of ways.

So I was very much concerned with the writer's role in relation to the industry, and I still am. When I made the opening speech at the writers meeting—I opened with the words: "The *writer* is the creator of motion pictures." I think people have failed to recognize the significance of those words which foreshadowed by many years the development of the auteur theory which developed in France and which identified the director as the creator of the motion picture. Nowadays I wouldn't know whether it's the director or writer, but I would be very doubtful if the writer is the creator unless he and the director are the same person, or so close that they can really work in some sort of effective artistic collaboration. . . .

What happened to me personally was that I was definitely blacklisted in the industry, as were many other people, too, because of their known record as supporters and activists in the Screen Writers Guild. The blacklist was very loosely organized, however, because nobody was very worried as far as the producers were concerned. Zanuck was really the leader of the producers in suppressing the Guild, and he was very open and very frank about it. There were a great many full-page advertisements, many of them very insulting, in *Variety* and the *Hollywood Reporter* stating the positions of writers, pro and con, on the Guild. But as far as the blacklist was concerned, it really worked more or less automatically and it wasn't anything where there was a definite person or group of people to whom you applied to clear yourself or anything of that sort, as it was later. My friend Francis Faragoh, who was very successful in the industry at that time and who was Vice President of the Guild at the time it was broken up, was convinced that his fate in Hollywood was determined by his connection with the Guild and that the blacklist operated against him and against a great many other people with whom he was associated. In any case, that struggle in 1936 and 1937 marked the first stage in the rather naive effort to create a Screen Writers Guild in Hollywood.

Meanwhile, the creation of the Screen Writers Guild was responsible for the parallel and almost immediate creation of the Actors Guild, which was founded in 1933 just a few weeks after we founded the Screen Writers Guild. The Actors Guild was founded very largely with my advice and under my guidance. I sat with the committee and we talked over all the arrangements; their basic contract, and their agreement with their members, were really modeled directly on the arrangement of the Writers Guild. The Actors Gould had one thing in their favor, though. The Actors Guild was not feared in relation to the control of the material, because the only people who were a threat were the very powerful stars who were in a position to dictate what was written, but even these powerful stars were not independent enough to constitute any real threat to the power of the producers. At the same time, the actors had an advantage in that they were essential immediately to production. If actors walked off the set, that meant a loss of hundreds of thousands of dollars that very day, whereas the connection of writers with production was much more remote, and much less immediate in terms of a threat. . . .

An Illustration

Four Horsemen of the Apocalypse
Hugo Gellert

When Hugo Gellert joined the Communists in the early 1920s he was already a noted cartoonist of the Left. In 1935 he brought out a collection of his recent work entitled Comrade Gulliver, An Illustrated Account of Travels into that Strange Country the United States of America. *The horsemen in the following are (left to right) General Hugh Johnson, ex-head of the National Recovery Administration, on whom is perched a desiccated bird (the Blue Eagle being the NRA symbol); publisher William Randolph Hearst, dressed as a medieval knight, complete with an oriflamme bearing a swastika; Huey Long, in KKK outfit, swinging his manacles; and Father Charles E. Coughlin, the "radio priest," with his grim reaper on which a microphone is mounted.*

TWO COMMUNIST FRONTS

1

Manual
International Workers Order

Though the IWO began in 1930, it was not until 1935 that it put out a comprehensive manual of purpose and structure, from which the following is taken.

The International Workers Order is a workers' fraternal organization. It provides its members with sick, disability and death benefits, as well as with medical aid and other forms of help. It accepts members irrespective of sex, nationality, color, creed or political beliefs.

Workers' fraternal mutual benefits serve the purpose of meeting the problems of the economic insecurity of the workers. But they cannot solve the problem. The IWO therefore considers it its duty as a workers' organization to aid all other of the workers' efforts to liquidate their economic insecurity.

The workers depend for their living on wages. They cannot get wages when they are unemployed, sick, too old or otherwise disabled. Mutual aid supplies help in some of the emergencies. But it cannot solve the problem. To solve the problem the workers must make organized efforts for more effective economic security.

The workers need and must make continuous efforts to get decent wages to assure an adequate standard of living as the only possible guarantee for their health and physical ability.

The workers require and must demand sanitary and safe working conditions in the shops, mills, mines and factories.

The workers are entitled to the protection of effective social hygiene.

In addition to all this the workers must have and must do everything to get adequate unemployment and social insurance.

Organized efforts of the workers to achieve these needs are as necessary for the achievement of economic security as efforts to provide mutual benefits. The support of such organized efforts is, therefore, as much the duty of a workers' fraternal organization as is the payment of mutual benefits.

The International Workers Order recognizes this duty. Therefore it will organize its life, its activities and its services with the aim of developing among its members workers' solidarity and unity as the first necessity for effective workers' struggles. It will carry on educational and cultural work designed to break down the artificial barriers of race, creed and color which now divide the workers. As far as it is within its power, it will endeavor to win its members for participation in the efforts of the workers to end their economic insecurity.

By such efforts the IWO everywhere, and at all times, shall make itself a part of the forces that make for the continuous improvement of the living conditions of the workers. . . .

GENERAL PROGRAM

The International Workers Order was chartered by the Insurance Department of the State of New York in April 1930. The IWO has since then and is now securing charters in the many states in which we have branches and where we are making efforts to build our organization.

The IWO was built by five thousand workers, former members of other fraternal organizations. They set themselves the goal of building a new workers' fraternal order, the guiding principle to be that of *service to the working class*.

The "Declaration of Principles" embodies the aims and ideals of the International Workers Order—of *proletarian fraternalism*.

Most fraternal organizations in the field appeal to the workers of the same nationality, of the same religion, of the same political faith or of the same color. The International Workers Order appeals to all workers irrespective of their religion, race, color, sex or political beliefs.

Insecurity is a problem faced by *all* workers. The more workers are united, the more effective will be their mutual aid efforts. It is for this reason that the IWO strives to break down the artificial barriers which today serve to separate the workers along lines of race, color, nationality, religious or political beliefs.

The most harmful barrier is that of white chauvinism (theory of white supremacy) which is designed to separate the white workers from the Negro workers.

The IWO strives to break down this barrier by uniting in its ranks both Negro and white workers.

In order to meet the needs of foreign-born workers who speak in their mother tongue, the IWO has language branches in addition to the English-speaking branches.

The members of the IWO receive direct help in meeting the problems arising out of insecurity, in the form of life insurance, sick benefits, tuberculosis benefits, medical service and other forms of benefits.

As a workers' organization, it strives to maintain a maximum of benefits at a minimum of cost.

Creating a Bond of Solidarity

The Order strives to establish the closest fraternal relationship between the membership; to create among the members a genuine interest in each other's welfare, sharing in each other's joys, and coming to each other's assistance in times of trouble and stress—a real brotherly relationship, based on mutual understanding, on mutual efforts in meeting mutual problems. The Order strives to make its branches real centers for the social and cultural advancement of the membership.

Community Centers

To provide the facilities for the social, cultural and sport life of the membership, and to make these a factor in the neighborhoods, the IWO establishes IWO Community Centers. These centers, and their facilities, are open to the

IWO membership and to the workers in the neighborhood. Special emphasis in these centers is placed on providing the needs of youth.

Social Insurance

The IWO recognizes that at best a fraternal organization can only supply a minimum of self-help in meeting some of the emergencies which arise.

Only society as a whole can adequately meet the problem. That is why the Order endorses and fights for a system of unemployment and social insurance; a system of government aid to cover the needs of the unemployed, the disabled, the aged, widows and orphans and others in need.

Bourgeois vs. Proletarian Fraternalism

The masses join fraternal organizations to secure protection and to find a solution to the problem of insecurity. Yet many fraternal orders are under a leadership that uses the fraternal movement to further the interests, not of the workers but of the moneyed class.

Such leaders are continuously making efforts to line up the fraternal organizations behind an anti-working-class program; to use the fraternal movement in curtailing the civil rights of the workers, in breaking strikes and in suppressing every effort of the workers to improve their conditions. This constitutes bourgeois fraternalism.

As against such fraternalism, the IWO offers its program of *proletarian fraternalism*; the practice of workers solidarity, not only in the payment of mutual benefits but in support of the worker's efforts to protect himself against sickness, against accidents, against unsanitary and unsafe working and living conditions and against an insufficient standard of living. . . .

The Trade Unions

The International Workers Order supports the efforts of the workers to build trade unions for the purpose of using their united strength in fighting for better conditions.

The International Workers Order is seeking legislation that will insure safety for workers in the mines, mills and shops; to promote measures for the betterment of the health and working conditions of workers in our country; to secure a system of unemployment and social insurance.

The workers organized into trade unions are a most effective and most important factor in the fight for these conditions.

That is why the International Workers Order urges its membership to become members of their respective trade unions. That is why the IWO cooperates with the trade unions and asks in return the cooperation and unity of the trade unions with the IWO in these struggles. . . .

The proper development of the educational and social activities by the branch will bring with it a real fraternal relationship, with a maximum of attendance at branch meetings. It will bring new members actively into the life of the Order. Education will make it possible to get the members to act shoulder to shoulder in efforts to solve the burning problems of the day.

Interesting and educational meetings will become a source of steady recruitment for the branch. Every affair, every branch meeting should be used as a source of new members. Appeals for new members should be made. Where possible, arrangements should be made to have a doctor present to examine new prospects.

The social and educational features must be well planned and must include the widest variety of features which are of interest and are the concern of the membership of the IWO.

The Educational Director and his committee are responsible for planning the social and educational activity of the branch. The committee should consist of a minimum of three and should be enlarged as the branch grows and this activity broadens. Particular functions shall be assigned to members of the committee; one member in charge of dramatics, one for choruses, one for study circles and classes, one for publicity and press agent, etc.

The following is a list of the major educational and social features which come under the scope of the committee:

1. Discussions and question box at branch meetings.
2. Sale and distribution of literature—branch library.
3. Bulletin Boards and wall newspapers—branch publications.
4. Classes and study circles.
5. Writing for, reading and spreading our official organ, *The New Order*.
6. Movies, slides, etc.
7. Open Forums, lectures, symposiums, mass meetings, etc.
8. Dramatics.
9. Music and choruses.
10. Sports.
11. Dances, house parties, theater parties, concerts, etc.

2

MANIFESTO AND PROGRAM
The American League Against War and Fascism

The League was the Party's most successful front after its birth in 1933, attracting as it did well-known public figures who could never be called Communists— for example,

Norman Thomas, the Socialist leader, and Roger Baldwin, founder and for decades to come head of the American Civil Liberties Union. It went without saying that quite a few fellow travelers of note joined the League, notably Protestant ministers and theologians. It was so successful because it tapped into the prevailing antiwar sentiment, the bitter distrust of the arms makers and the military establishment.Wisely, the Party remained in the background.

The United States prepares for War. The government of the United States in spite of peaceful professions is more aggressively than ever following policies whose only logical result is War. The whole program of the Roosevelt administration is permeated by preparedness for War, expressed in the extraordinary military and naval budget, mobilization of industry and manpower, naval concentration in the Pacific Ocean, aid—direct and indirect—to Chiang Kai-shek against the Chinese Soviets, the initiation of currency and tariff Wars—all of which give the lie to the peaceful declarations of the United States Government.

Under the guise of public works, the NRA has diverted immense funds from the care of starving millions to the building of a vastly larger navy and to mechanization of the army. The widespread unemployment has been utilized to concentrate young men in so-called reforestation camps, which the War Department is using for trial military mobilizations. The military training of youth in the schools and colleges is being further developed. More and more, national holidays and specially prepared demonstrations are being used to glorify the armed forces and to stimulate the War spirit among the masses. Hundreds of factories are working overtime to produce munitions and basic War materials for shipment to the warring countries in South America and the Far East. The revelations of the Senate Committee investigating the munitions industry reveal the governments of our own and other countries as participating in a gigantic game of mass murder for profits.

A centralized War control of industry, along the lines of the War Industries Board of 1917, is being established. As in 1917, it is drawing the upper leadership of many trade unions into active collaboration in the War machine.

THE WORLD MOVES TOWARD WAR

. . . Never did mankind see such preparations for War. The greatest naval race in history is now on between the United States, England and Japan. To this is added the struggle for supremacy in the air. The World Disarmament Conference adjourns, confessing its complete failure. This is the reflection of the inability of the profit system to meet the economic needs of the masses. Unable to give them the means of life, it prepares for them the instruments of death.

The War danger arises inevitably out of the very nature of monopolistic capitalism—the ownership of the means of production by a small capitalist class and the complete domination of the government by this class. The imminent War danger is only another expression of the fundamental crisis of the capitalistic system, which continues its existence only at the cost of the intensification of exploitation and oppression of the masses at home and in the colonies, and of the struggle among the imperialist powers for a redivision of the markets and sources of raw materials.

Only in the Soviet Union has this basic cause of War been removed. There are no classes or groups which can benefit from War or War preparations. Therefore the Soviet Union pursues a positive and vigorous peace policy, and alone among the governments proposes total disarmament. Serious struggle against War involves rallying all forces around this peace policy and opposing all attempts to weaken or destroy the Soviet Union.

FASCISM BREEDS WAR

The rapid rise of the Fascist state increases the War danger. Fascism means forced labor, militarization, lower standards of living, and the accentuation of national hatreds and chauvinist incitements as instruments for the "moral" preparations for War. Its economic nationalism is an increased source of conflicts. It sets the people of one country against the people of another, and exploits the internal racial and national groups within each country in order to prevent them from uniting in joint action to solve their common problems. War and Fascism spring from the same source, the inability of the capitalist system to solve its economic problems. They are organized by the same people, for the same purpose—the preservation of the power and privilege of the ruling class. They must be fought together, by the same forces, using the same weapons. Stop the growth of Fascism and we check War. Make it impossible for the Fascist state to wage War successfully and its power is broken.

FOR MASS RESISTANCE

We can effectively combat War only by arousing and organizing the masses within each country for active struggle against the War policies of their own imperialist governments, whether these governments are working individually or through the League of Nations. The anti-War movement allies itself with the masses in the colonial and semi-colonial countries against imperialist domination, and gives full support to their immediate and unconditional independence, particularly to the Philippines and Cuba.

The Congress declares that the basic force in the imperialist countries for struggle against the War danger and the Fascist menace is the working class, organizing around it in close alliance all of the exploited sections of the population, working farmers, intellectuals, the oppressed Negro people, all toiling masses and all organizations and groups which are generally opposed to War on any basis or engaged in resisting any aspect of Fascism.

3

PROCEEDINGS OF SECOND U.S. CONGRESS
The American League Against War and Fascism

By the time of its second congress, which met in Chicago in 1934, the League claimed to represent an astronomical number of people, 1,807,201 to be exact. An exaggeration obviously, but the number must have been impressive whatever it actually was. The highlight of the congress was the surprising appearance of an army officer in uniform whose short speech roused the audience of almost four thousand delegates and guests. Included here, too, are Roger Baldwin's remarks on the delicate matter of working with Communists; he was founder and head of the American Civil Liberties Union.

First Lieutenant of the United States Army: The revolutionary soldiers of the 6th Corp area, which includes the regular army in Michigan, Wisconsin and Illinois, extend revolutionary greetings. The troops of this area have just completed in Camp Custer, Michigan, war maneuvers on a larger scale than ever since the last war. The reserve officers of this area have worked out all the details of their mobilization plans, while training has been intensified here. For the machines of destruction the capitalists pay dearly, but to the general staff the lives of workers are cheap. Our participation in this Congress is our militant answer to those preparations.

These are not preparations for an imperialist war alone. Special equipment has been issued and troops at Fort Sheridan have been called out on "riot duty." These troops can be brought into Chicago within one hour of call.

The treatment of the working class of Rhode Island, Toledo and San Francisco points out the significance of this fact, but at the same time today in ever greater numbers, soldiers and some officers are realizing that their function is not to defend the people, no—as part of the government machinery their function is to defend the profits of the capitalists against the interests of the people, at home as well as abroad.

We, who know this, believe that only by unity with all the sincere opponents of war and fascism within the civil population, can war be prevented. Our roots lie deep within the people, we in uniform are workers and farmers. We call upon you to let this fact be impressed. Only through much fraternization, only through your friendship can the soldiers realize their interest as workers. You must defeat the attempts to isolate the armed forces from the toiling masses. We ask you to cooperate in this task with our work from the inside. At the same time, from this mighty demonstration we take new courage and we therefore resolve and pledge to this Congress our support in the struggle against war and fascism within the armed forces. We will struggle relentlessly until the workers democracy has removed this dangerous development and if the capitalists call upon us to wage war, we will wage war, but it will be a war against the war makers. (*Loud and continuous applause*) . . .

Roger Baldwin: Now my friends, there is a good deal of criticism of this League in a good many quarters, that the League is a Communist organization, taking in all sorts of innocents to make it look respectable. I am supposed to be one of the innocents. They say that the Communists use these innocents. All right. But we use the Communists. I think that the non-Communists who think that the Communists are dominating the organization should come in and increase the non-Communist ranks. The real trouble is that the Communists have almost a monopoly on militancy. I would like to see other delegates outside of the Communist movement match them with equal spirit. That is a sufficient answer, it seems to me, to those critics from the minority groups, and others, who have regarded us as an organization politically dominated by the Communists. The task of all of us, Communists and non-Communists, is to try to get those who are not yet with us, into this great struggle against war and fascism. . . .

THE SAN FRANCISCO STRIKE

THE STRIKE
Tillie Lerner

The San Francisco longshoremen's strike of 1934, which captured the whole country's interest, including the Roosevelt administration's, as it persisted, violently, month after month, was a great Communist victory and a harbinger of further such victories to come. Twenty-one-year-old Tillie Lerner was an observer-participant. She was born in Omaha into a large Russian-Jewish family and in her teens joined the Young Communist League. By the time she settled in San Francisco, she had had quite a bit of experience as an organizer. Though she had been writing constantly, this piece, for the September–October 1934 Partisan Review, *was the first she published. And not until 1956, as Tillie Olsen (her married name), was she discovered. Since then she has come to be recognized as a major writer who has kept faith with the insurgencies of her youth by her involvement in recent ones, from civil rights and the antiwar movement to feminism.*

Do not ask me to write of the strike and the terror. I am on a battlefield, and the increasing stench and smoke sting the eyes so it is impossible to turn them back into the past. You leave me only this night to drop the bloody garment of Todays, to cleave through the gigantic events that have crashed one upon the other, to the first beginning. If I could go away for a while, if there were time and quiet, perhaps I could do it. All that has happened might resolve into order and sequence, fall into neat patterns of words. I could stumble back into the past and slowly, painfully rear the structure in all its towering magnificence, so that the beauty and heroism, the terror and significance of those days, would enter your heart and sear it forever with the vision.

But I hunch over the typewriter and behind the smoke, the days whirl, confused as dreams. Incidents leap out like a thunder and are gone. There flares the remembrance of that night in early May, in Stockton, when I walked down the road with the paper in my hands and the streaming headlines, "Longshoremen Out. Riot Expected"; "Longshore Strike Declared." And standing there in the yellow stubble I remembered Jerry telling me quietly, ". . . for 12 years now. But we're through sweating blood, loading cargo five times the weight we should carry, we're through standing morning after morning like slaves in a slave market begging for a bidder. We'll be out, you'll see; it may be a few weeks, a few months, but *we'll be out*, and then hell can't stop us."

H-E-L-L C-A-N-T S-T-O-P U-S. Days, pregnant days, spelling out the words. The port dead but for the rat stirring of a few scabs at night, the port paralyzed, gummed on one side by the thickening scum of prostrate ships, islanded on the other by the river of pickets streaming ceaselessly up and down, a river that sometimes raged into a flood, surging over the wavering shoreline of police, battering into the piers and sucking under the scabs in its angry tides. HELL CAN T STOP US. That was the meaning of the lines of women and children marching up Market with their banners—"This is our fight, and we're with the men to the finish." That was the meaning of the seamen and the oilers and the wipers and the mastermates and the pilots and the scalers torrenting into the river, widening into the sea.

The kids coming in from the waterfront. The flame in their eyes, the feeling of invincibility singing in their blood. The stories they had to tell of scabs educated, of bloody skirmishes. My heart was ballooning with happiness anyhow, to be back, working in the movement again, but the things happening down at the waterfront, the heroic everydays, stored such richness in me I can never lose it. The feeling of sympathy widening over the city, of quickening—class lines sharpening. I armored myself with that on National Youth Day hearing the smash and thud of clubs around me, seeing boys fall to their knees in streams of blood, pioneer kids trampled under by horses. . . .

There was a night that was the climax of those first days—when the workers of San Francisco packed into the Auditorium to fling a warning to the shipowners. There are things one holds like glow in the breast, like a fire; they make the unseen warmth that keeps one through the cold of defeat, the hunger of despair. That night was one—symbol and portent of what will be.

We League kids came to the meeting in a group, and walking up the stairs we felt ourselves a flame, a force. At the door bulls were standing, with menacing faces, but behind them fear was blanching—the people massing in, they had never dreamed it possible—people coming in and filling the aisles, packing the back. Spurts of song flaming up from downstairs, answered by us, echoed across the gallery, solidarity weaving us all into one being. Twenty thousand jammed in and the dim blue ring of cops back in the hall was wavering, was stretching itself thin and unseeable. It was *our* auditorium, we had taken it over. And for blocks around they hear *our* voice. The thunder of our applause, the mighty roar of it for Bridges, for Caves, for Schumacher. "That's no lie." "Tell them Harry" "To the Finish" "We're with you" "Attaboy" "We're solid." The speeches, "They can never load their ships with tear gas and guns," "For years we were nothing but nameless beasts of burden to them, but now. . . ." "Even if it means . . . GENERAL STRIKE," the voices rising, lifted on a sea of affection, vibrating in 20,000 hearts.

There was the moment—the first bruise in the hearts of our masters—when Mayor Rossi entered, padding himself from the fists of boos smashing around him with 60 heavyfoots, and bulls, and honoraries. The boos had filled into breasts feeling and seeing the tattoo of his clubs on the embarcadero, and Rossi hearing tried to lose himself into his top-coat, failing, tried to puff himself invincible with the majesty of his office. "Remember, I am your chief executive, the respect . . . the honor . . . due that office . . . don't listen to me then but listen to your mayor . . . listen," and the boos rolled over him again and again so that the reptile voice smothered, stopped. He never forgot the moment he called for law and order, charging the meeting with not caring to settle by peaceful means, wanting only violence, and voices ripped from every corner. "Who started the violence?" "Who calls the bulls to the waterfront?" "Who ordered the clubbing?"—and in a torrent of anger shouted, "Shut up, we have to put up with your clubs but not with your words, get out of here, GET OUT OF HERE." That memory clamped into his heart, into the hearts of those who command him, that bruise became the cancer of fear that flowered into the monstrous Bloody Thursday, that opened into the pus of Terror—but the cancer grows, grows; there is no cure. . . .

It was after that night he formed his "Citizens Committee," after that night the still smiling lips of the Industrial Association bared into a growl of open hatred, exposing the naked teeth of guns and tear gas. The tempo of those days maddened to a crescendo. The city became a camp, a battlefield, the screams of ambulances sent the day reeling, class lines fell sharply—everywhere, on streetcars, on corners, in stores, people talked, cursing, stirred with something strange in their breasts, incomprehensible, shaken with fury at the police, the papers, the shipowners . . . going down to the waterfront, not curious spectators, but to stand there, watching, silent, trying to read the lesson the moving bodies underneath were writing, trying to grope to the meaning of it all, police "protecting lives" smashing clubs and gas bombs into masses of men like themselves, papers screaming lies. Those were the days when with every attack on the picket lines the phone rang at the ILA— "NOW—will you arbitrate?"—when the mutter GENERAL STRIKE swelled to a thunder, when everywhere the cry arose—"WE'VE GOT TO END IT NOW." Coming down to headquarters from the waterfront, the faces of comrades had the strained look of men in battle, that strangely intense look of living, of feeling too much in too brief a space of time. . . .

Yes, those were the days crescendoing—and the typewriter breaks, stops for an instant—to Bloody Thursday. Weeks afterward my fists clench at the remembrance and the hate congests so I feel I will burst. Bloody Thursday— our day we write on the pages of history with letters of blood and hate. Our day we fling like a banner to march with the other bloody days when guns spat death at us that a few dollars might be saved to fat bellies, when lead battered into us, and only our naked hands, the fists of our bodies moving together could resist. Drown their strength in blood, they commanded, but instead they armored us in inflexible steel—hate that will never forget. . . .

"It was as close to war . . . as actual war could be," the papers blared triumphantly, but Bridges told them, "not war . . . MASSACRE, armed forces massacring unarmed." Words I read through tears of anger so that they writhed and came alive like snakes, you rear in me again, "and once again the policemen, finding their gas bombs and gas shells ineffective poured lead from their revolvers into the jammed streets. Men (MEN) fell right and left." " . . . And everywhere was the sight of men, beaten to their knees to lie in a pool of blood." "Swiftly, from intersection to intersection the battle moved, stubbornly the rioters refused to fall back so that the police were forced. . . ." "and the police shot forty rounds of tear gas bombs into the mob before it would move. . . ."

Law . . . and order . . . will . . . prevail. Do you hear? It's war, WAR—and up and down the street "A man clutched at his leg and fell to the sidewalk" "The loud shot like that of the tear gas bombs zoomed again, but no blue smoke this time, and when the men cleared, two bodies lay on the sidewalk, their blood trickling about them"—overhead an airplane lowered, dipped, and nausea gas swooned down in a cloud of torture, and where they ran from street to street, resisting stubbornly, massing again, falling back only to carry the wounded, the thought tore frenziedly through the mind, war, war, it's WAR—and the lists in the papers, the dead, the wounded by bullets, the wounded by other means—W-A-R.

LAW—you hear, Howard Sperry, ex-serviceman, striking stevedore, shot in the back and abdomen, said to be in dying condition, DEAD, LAW AND ORDER—you hear and remember this Ben Martella, shot in arm, face and chest, Joseph Beovich, stevedore, laceration of skull from clubbing and broken shoulder, Edwin Hodges, Jerry Hart, Leslie Steinhart, Steve Hamrock, Albert Simmons, marine engineer, striking seamen, scaler, innocent bystander, shot in leg, shot in shoulder, chest lacerated by tear gas shell, gassed in eyes, compound skull fracture by clubbing, you hear—LAW AND ORDER MUST PREVAIL—all right Nick, clutching your leg and seeing through the fog of pain it is a police car has picked you up, snarling, let me out, I don't want any bastard bulls around, and flinging yourself out into the street, still lying there in the hospital today—

LAW AND ORDER—people, watching with horror, trying to comprehend the lesson the moving bodies were writing. The man stopping me on the corner, seeing my angry tears as I read the paper, "Listen," he said, and he talked because he had to talk, because in an hour all the beliefs of his life had been riddled and torn away—"Listen, I was down there, on the waterfront, do you know what they're doing—they were shooting SHOOTING—" and that word came out anguished and separate, "shooting right into men, human beings, they were shooting into them as if they were animals, as if they were targets, just lifting their guns and shooting. I saw this, can you believe it, CAN YOU BELIEVE IT? . . . as if they were targets as if . . . CAN YOU BELIEVE IT?" and he went to the next man and started it all over again. . . .

I was not down . . . by the battlefield. My eyes are anguished from the pictures I pieced together from words of comrades, of strikers, from the pictures filling the newspapers. I sat up in headquarters, racked by the howls of ambulances hurtling by, feeling it incredible the fingers like separate little animals hopping nimbly from key to key, the ordered steady click of the typewriter, feeling any moment the walls would crash and all the madness surge in. Ambulances, ripping out of nowhere, fading; police sirens, outside the sky a ghastly gray, corpse gray, an enormous dead eyelid shutting down on the world. And someone comes in, words lurch out of his mouth, the skeleton is told, and goes again. . . . And I sit there, making a metallic little pattern of sound in the air, because that is all I can do, because that is what I am supposed to do.

They called the guard out . . . "admitting their inability to control the situation," and Barrows boasted, "my men will not use clubs or gas, they will talk with bayonets" . . . Middlestaedt . . . "Shoot to kill. Any man firing into the air will be courtmartialed." With two baby tanks, and machine guns, and howitzers, they went down to the waterfront to take it over, to "protect the interests of the people."

I walked down Market that night. The savage wind lashed at my hair. All life seemed blown out of the street; the few people hurrying by looked hunted, tense, expectant of anything. Cars moved past as if fleeing. And a light, indescribably green and ominous was cast over everything, in great shifting shadows. And down the street the trucks rumbled. Drab colored, with boys sitting on them like corpses sitting and not moving, holding guns stiffly, staring with wide frightened eyes, carried down to the Ferry building, down to the embarcadero to sell out their brothers and fathers for $2.00 a day. Somebody said behind me, and I do not even know if the voice was my own, or unspoken, or imagined, "Go on down there, you sonovabitches, it doesn't matter. It doesn't stop us. We won't forget what happened today. . . . Go on, nothing can stop us . . . now."

Somehow I am down on Stuart and Mission, somehow I am staring at flowers scattered in a border over a space of sidewalk, at stains that look like rust, at an unsteady chalking—"Police Murder. Two Shot in the Back," and looking up I see faces, seen before, but utterly changed, transformed by some inner emotion to faces of steel. "Nick Bordoise . . . and Sperry, on the way to punch his strike card, shot in the back by those bastard bulls. . . ."

OUR BROTHERS

Howard S. Sperry, a longshoreman, a war vet, a real MAN. On strike since May 9, 1934, for the right to earn a decent living under decent conditions.
. . .
Nickolas Bordoise, a member of Cooks & Waiters Union for ten years. Also a member of the International Labor Defense. Not a striker, but a worker looking to the welfare of his fellow workers on strike. . . .

Some of what the leaflet said. But what can be said of Howard Sperry, ex-serviceman, struggling through the horrors of war for his country, remembering the dead men and the nearly dead men lashing about blindly on the battlefield, who came home to die in a new war, a war he had not known existed. What can be said of Nick Bordoise. Communist Party member, who without thanks or request came daily to the embarcadero to sell his fellow workers hot soup to warm their bellies. There was a voice that gave the story of his life, there in the yellowness of the parched grass, with the gravestones icy and strange in the sun; quietly, as if it had risen up from the submerged hearts of the world, as if it had been forever and would be forever, the voice surged over our bowed heads. And the story was the story of any worker's life, of the thousand small deprivations and frustrations suffered, of the courage forged out of the cold and darkness of poverty, of the determination welded out of the helpless anger scalding the heart, the plodding hours of labor and weariness, of the life, given simply, as it had lived, that the things which he had suffered should not be, must not be. . . .

There were only a few hundred of us who heard that voice, but the thousands who watched the trucks in the funeral procession piled high with 50c and $1.00 wreaths guessed, and understood. I saw the people, saw the look on their faces. And it is the look that will be there the days of the revolution. I saw the fists clenched 'til knuckles were white, and people standing, staring, saying nothing, letting it clamp into their hearts, hurt them so the scar would be there forever—a swelling that would never let them lull.

"Life," the capitalist papers marveled again, "Life stopped and stared." Yes, you stared, our cheap executive, Rossi—hiding behind the curtains, the cancer of fear in your breast gnawing, gnawing; you stared, members of the

Industrial Association, incredulous, where did the people come from, where was San Francisco hiding them, in what factories, what docks, what are they doing there, marching, or standing and watching, not saying anything, just watching. . . . What did it mean, and you dicks, fleeing, hiding behind store windows. . . .

There was a pregnant woman standing on a corner, outlined against the sky, and she might have been a marble, rigid, eternal, expressing some vast and nameless sorrow. But her face was a flame, and I heard her say after a while dispassionately, as if it had been said so many times no accent was needed, "We'll not forget that. We'll pay it back . . . someday." And on every square of sidewalk a man was saying, "We'll have it. We'll have a General Strike. And there won't be processions to bury their dead." "Murder—to save themselves paying a few pennies more wages, remember that Johnny . . . We'll get even. It won't be long. General Strike."

Listen, it is late, I am feverish and tired. Forgive me that the words are feverish and blurred. You see, If I had time, If I could go away. But I write this on a battlefield.

The rest, the General Strike, the terror, arrests and jail, the songs in the night, must be written some other time, must be written later. . . . But there is so much happening now. . . .

CHAPTER FOUR

The Popular Front Against Fascism, 1935–1945

I

By mid-1934 the Communist world, the Soviet Union in particular, could no longer hide from itself the fact that Third Period militancy had done nothing to arrest, still less diminish, the enveloping malignancy of Fascism. The danger was growing by the minute. Early in the year a Fascist regime had triumphed in Austria after suppressing the Left with fire and sword. France for a while seemed close to suffering a similar fate following a political scandal (the Stavisky affair) that brought down the government; it was disheartening to see how enormous were the right-wing and pro-Fascist crowds that filled the streets of Paris and elsewhere. Mussolini, having already ruled as dictator (*Il Duce*) for twelve years, was never so completely in charge as now and was thus ready, as he boasted, to turn his attention to foreign climes and the restoration of the Roman Empire. For their part, Japan's warlords were obviously preparing for further adventures abroad now that Manchuria (Manchukuo) had been integrated in her ever expanding empire. And above all, Hitler, far from collapsing and thereby paving the way for Communism, had relentlessly consolidated his dictatorial authority, eliminating step by step his enemies on the Left (liberals and Socialists as well as Communists) and his Nazi rivals. And he never stopped proclaiming Germany's great mission in behalf of Aryanism and Western civilization: to destroy "Jew-Bolshevism" root and branch.

In America, too, Communists saw signs of danger. They routinely condemned the New Deal as incipient Fascism and Roosevelt as its charismatic embodiment. But in 1934 the real thing appeared on the horizon. Conservative business interests, led by the DuPonts, launched an organization, the Liberty League, to fight government regulations and higher taxes and public debts in the name of property rights, bulwark of the Constitution. At the same time two other charismatic figures, each with large national constituencies, launched organizations of their own to promote their ideologies, their visions of the good life: Father Charles E. Coughlin's National Union of Social Justice and Senator Huey P. Long's Share Our Wealth clubs. Why Communists, and the Left in general, might have heard the tumbrels of Fascism in the distance is entirely understandable. The millions of working- and lower-middle-class people who quickly joined the National Union and Share Our Wealth clubs were obviously looking to strong leaders to save them, leaders who would redistribute the wealth and make money easily available by taking America back from Wall Street and the international bankers. It gave Communists pause to realize that what Coughlin and Long and the Liberty Leaguers had in common was their hatred of Roosevelt because he and his New Deal either went too far in the direction of reform or not far enough, because he was, beneath the fraudulent charm, either the forerunner of Bolshevism or the champion of the status quo. For Moscow, then, this much was certain: Roosevelt was decidedly not the enemy. Given his popularity, he might in fact be the only force capable of preventing Fascism from conquering America as well.

As early as 1934 Communist movements everywhere were retreating from Third Period confrontationism and entertaining the feasibility of "united front" arrangements with other leftist groups, even those they had been regularly denouncing as "social Fascists." The transition quickened as the year wore on. The American Party served notice of what it had in mind by dissolving the Trade Union Unity League and dropping the whole subject of class struggle. The member unions, representing perhaps 100,000 workers, found places for themselves, it will be recalled, in whatever other union would have them.

In 1935 the united front evolved into the "Popular Front." The difference between the two fronts, trivial to anyone unschooled in Party dialectics, was significant. It was the difference between the Party's willingness to form ad hoc alliances of convenience in which it maintained a critical distance and its willingness to take a back seat or at least play an inconspicuous role in the collective attempt to resist an all-devouring evil. As for the willingness of potential allies—liberals and progressives of every stripe and even some conservatives—to work with the Party, that depended on many variables, the most important of which was the magnitude of the evil. Here the Party had time on its side, for the evil kept growing. That terrifying fact outweighed or at least militated against such reservations as they might have had about working with Communists.

Even before the Comintern, at its Seventh World Congress in August 1935, formally replaced Third Period Communism with Popular Front Communism, the American Party was taking the necessary steps to implement the change. It disbanded the John Reed clubs and shut down their magazines, to the consternation of the aspiring writers and artists who had come to depend on them. It ordered the other cultural groups—theater, dance, music, film and photography, and others—to soften their image and reach out to anyone who was not opposed to Communism as against opposing anyone who did not accept its leadership. They were encouraged to spread the Popular Front gospel wherever they could, in Hollywood, on the radio and in other popular media, and in the multifarious and well-funded New Deal (WPA) arts programs. Foreign-language affiliates and their publications emphasized the virtues of pluralism, the contributions of immigrants and ethnics to American life and not merely to the working class. The same applied to Negroes. No longer did black self-determination come up as a solution to second-class citizenship. Instead, Negro workers were to collaborate with the other Negro outfits that the Party had once anathematized—the churches and the enlightened bourgeoisie—to advance the cause of integration. Toward that end the Party established the National Negro Congress, which was to be an omnium-gatherum of all tendencies within the community. And the Party allowed the Unemployed Councils to go by the boards, merging with the much smaller Socialist and Musteite equivalents to form a new entity, the Workers Alliance, which in effect constituted the left wing of the New Deal's massive WPA jobs program. The Workers Alliance was a model Popular Front, since the Communists maintained a discrete and collegial presence in the act of dominating it.

A new Party leader emerged with the inauguration of the Popular Front. In 1934 Earl Browder became General Secretary. He was a perfect choice in that he had avoided its factional conflicts—largely because he was abroad in the late 1920s working for the Comintern—enjoyed good relations with Comintern boss Georgi Dimitrov, and had an impeccable *American* background: descent from an old Virginia family that settled in Kansas where he was born in 1891 and grew up. It was as a bookkeeper in Kansas City that he was drawn to radicalism (he spent two years in Leavenworth for opposing the war) and then Communism. More a follower than a leader, he was ideally suited for rising up in the Party. But he was no mere yes-man of the kind who survived in the Soviet apparatus. He spoke his mind clearly and to the point and had a sound working knowledge of Marxist texts. To Earl Browder, then, fell the responsibility of articulating the Popular Front rationale, being forever identified with it as its avatar during the ten years of his stewardship, when Communism in America reached its zenith. With some justification he could claim that his fall—a subject of later discussion—not accidentally coincided with the Party's.

In one speech and article after another (which he seemed effortlessly to churn out) he sounded a single basic theme, endlessly varied, contained in the remark that became his signature: "Communism is the Americanism of the twentieth century." The Communist movement, he meant, was the legatee, the modern embodiment, of a proud radical tradition. It kept faith with colonial dissenters and rebels (here Browder would allude to his own lineage), the revolutionaries of 1776, the Civil War abolitionists (including Lincoln), and the countless other insurgents since, who nourished that tradition. No longer did the Party regard itself as the vanguard merely of the working class: it was the vanguard of the *people*, the masses as a whole, and the best of their heritage.

This appreciation of America had a liberating effect on the Party's many institutions, its affiliates, auxiliaries, and fronts, and above all those among its sympathizers and friends who felt uncomfortable with the antagonistic mode that underlay its Third Period strategy. Especially in the propagation of culture was the effect liberating. In art, music, theater, dance, literature, the emphasis now was on affirming a usable past, discovering the germ of Communism in America's richly variegated culture, its land, its folk wisdom, its art. On the way out were the dark tones, the unrelieved descent into reality, of the proletarian genre. The mood now was celebratory and upbeat, even patriotic. The movement eagerly appropriated America's icons, chief among them Lincoln and Jefferson, both of whom, had they lived in the 1930s, would presumably have gone over to Communism or belonged to a Popular Front alliance with it.[*]

2

Communists could not help noting the irony implicit in one of their greatest accomplishments, the part they had in the spectacular rise of the industrial unions.

The irony involves none other than their inveterate foe, John L. Lewis, long-time president of the United Mine Workers (UMW). Besides being very conservative and very Republican, he had beaten off successive Communist (and other) challenges to his control of the union. He had once been vulnerable because the UMW had deteriorated so badly in the 1920s, but through guile and ruthlessness he had held on to what had been the largest labor organization in the country. The New Deal was his, and the union's deliverance. The 1933 National Industrial Recovery Act enabled the UMW in a matter of months to swell from around fifty thousand to more than five hundred thousand members. Suddenly Lewis, a man of boundless

---

[*]Browder would bring up the correspondence between Lincoln and Marx. As secretary of the Workingmen's International, Marx in 1864 congratulated Lincoln for the Emancipation Proclamation. Thanking him, Lincoln stated that free labor everywhere had the greatest stake in a Union victory.

ambition, could entertain thoughts of organizing the unorganized in the mass production industries: steel, autos, rubber, electrical equipment, and so on. Doing so, however, required that he also take on the AFL chieftains, who, content with the status quo (for there were small AFL craft unions in each industry), resisted any further insurgencies, especially if those insurgencies were led by radicals, most especially by Marxist-Leninists. The 1934 strikes convinced Lewis that the time had come to make the big push for industrial unions, which his ample treasury would finance. When at their 1935 convention the AFL chieftains rejected his offer to go ahead, he and several lesser union heads walked out and formed the Committee of Industrial Organizations (CIO), over which he of course presided. And then, in an about-face of Comintern proportions, he extended the hand of solidarity to the Communist Party. The CIO needed Communist organizers, who were most numerous precisely in those communities, that is, among foreign-language groups, where heavy industries were most concentrated and where their prior experience with the TUUL stood them in good stead. In return, Lewis promised to support Communist union leaders, and he appointed Communists to positions of authority in the CIO apparatus. Once the Party got over its qualms about Lewis, it threw itself wholeheartedly into the Popular Front collaboration with the Socialists and union bureaucrats it had once reviled so mercilessly.

Communists at the same time were discovering that they could do useful work as New Deal functionaries. In advancing this domestic cause or that through this government agency or that, Communists, thanks to their far-flung network, often proved effective indeed. Did they thus act conspiratorially? Yes, if by conspiracy is meant a shared commitment mediated through or managed by the Party. So it was, for example, that highly placed Communist lawyers for the National Labor Relations Board, a New Deal centerpiece, were instrumental in handing down decisions favorable to CIO unions, Communist-run or not, in jurisdictional disputes with AFL ones. Emphatically no, if by conspiracy is meant a secret cabal aimed at seizing power by stealth or, should circumstances allow, force or violence. This, the familiar canard, is unworthy of serious discussion.[*]

Having acknowledged a Communist presence, and yes, influence within

---

[*]Which is not to say that Communists in government would not have acted illegally if conditions, in their view, necessitated it. To the extent that such a charge can be made against them at all, it applied solely to those whose government work bore directly on the Soviet Union. The spy trials of the late 1940s and early 1950s, it should be emphasized, did not implicate the Party in any way. As for the trials of Party leaders accused of advocating the overthrow of the government by force and violence, the operative word is *advocacy*; in no instance, out of more than a hundred convictions, did the government present evidence of their committing a single violent act or even an act whose consequences could be regarded as violent (this despite the Supreme Court's decision upholding the convictions [until another decision undid that one]). And it should also be emphasized that the case against Communists rested on their alleged advocacy of force and violence *after* 1945—long after the influential Communists in government service were gone from the scene.

the New Deal, we must add that it was, all in all, a very limited presence or influence, and of short duration. The Roosevelt administration's conservative opponents immensely exaggerated the presence/influence syndrome not in order to discredit Communists—little could be gained by that—but to discredit the New Deal and liberalism in general. The motive was political opportunism and had no basis in fact.

While the Party fielded its own presidential candidate in the 1936 election (Browder)—the election that would ratify or repudiate the New Deal—it pulled every stop in Roosevelt's behalf; its candidate merely kept up appearances. The Party thought it imperative that Roosevelt not only defeat the Republicans but destroy the quasi-Fascist ticket—so general consensus had it—offered by the Union Party, Father Coughlin's creation and stalking horse. Huey Long was dead (felled by an assassin's bullet), but it was conceivable that the Union Party might pick up support from his defunct Share Our Wealth movement.

Communists adroitly utilized the Popular Front aspect of the election to their advantage. Wherever sizable liberal-left third parties backed Roosevelt, Communists, visible or not, played a role. This they did in Minnesota's powerful Farmer-Labor Party and to a lesser degree in Wisconsin's equally powerful Progressive Party. And in New York State they threw in their lot with the American Labor Party (ALP), which the Socialist leaders of the Ladies Garment Workers Union had organized so as to avoid having to vote for Roosevelt on the corrupt Democratic line. By receiving as many votes as it did—as Roosevelt did—on its first try, the ALP suddenly became an institution to reckon with in New York, hence in national politics. It became, in short, a valuable prize for whoever possessed it.

The 1936 election was what the Party hoped it would be. By the immensity of his triumph, Roosevelt did destroy the Union Party (though Coughlin still had his radio audience) and the Liberty League and marginalized the Republican Party. Progressives and Farmer-Laborites triumphed, too, in their states. The results totally vindicated the Popular Front strategy, so far at any rate.

3

The three years that followed, 1937 to 1939, were the glory years for American Communism. Rarely in American history had a movement so far to the left of the mainstream attained such prominence. And its votaries had every reason to believe that its prominence would grow and indeed become "the Americanism of the twentieth century."

The optimism, perversely enough, derived from the enveloping gloom of world affairs, that is, the increasing danger of Fascism. A brief rundown of international events in those critical years will explain why so many troubled Americans looked to Communism for solace.

The Communist rationale for the Popular Front, intimated to the public at large but taken for granted by the faithful, was that Germany, Italy, and Japan were building a cordon sanitaire around the Soviet Union with the intention of obliterating Communism there and everywhere and ultimately democracy, too. That the Soviet Union and world Communism provided the first line of defense against such an eventuality was the dogma underlying the Popular Front. True, Mussolini's bloody conquest of Ethiopia in 1935 could not be construed as part of the encirclement, but Mussolini made a point of including Italy among the anti-Comintern powers. The seriousness of his commitment could no longer be questioned when, in 1936, he and Hitler collaborated in supplying men and heavy weapons, including modern aircraft, to the Spanish army, led by General Francisco Franco and his Fascist cohorts, that rose up against the democratically elected republican government. That civil war seemed to prove, as nothing had before, the Communist argument that only Communists could be trusted to resist Fascist aggression. For it was the Soviet Union, not the Western democracies, and certainly not the United States, that assisted Spain's legitimate—and manifestly Popular Front—government, and it was Communist International Brigades, one of them being America's own, named for Abraham Lincoln, that went over and fought side by side with government forces at tremendous cost to themselves (half the Lincoln Brigade never returned).[*]

The hecatombs of Spain deeply saddened everyone concerned for the fate of democracy, but the really terrifying drama was unfolding elsewhere. Despite Versailles Treaty provisions to the contrary, Hitler occupied the Rhineland in 1936 even as he defiantly expanded Germany's military-industrial complex. A year later Japan, in blatant disregard of the world community, seized the Chinese coast and moved inland, gratuitously massacring untold thousands of civilians in the process. Soon after, Hitler swallowed Austria without firing a shot, and the democracies scarcely complained. Six months later, in the early fall of 1938, came the most disconcerting blow of all: the Munich accords, in which France and England allowed Hitler to take part of Czechoslovakia (Sudetenland) in return for his promise of peace, that is, of no further acquisitions. Never, in consequence, did the Communists argue so persuasively, so plausibly, that the democracies succumbed because Hitler promised *them* peace but was obviously preparing to attack the Soviet Union. The argument seemed irrefutable when a few months later he

---

[*]This is not to deny that non-Communists served in Spain too, and heroically—George Orwell (*Homage to Catalonia*) comes to mind—but compared to the Communist contribution their numbers were extremely small.

marched into the rest of Czechoslovakia, and they again stood by. That spring (of 1939) was also when Franco took Madrid and brought the Spanish Civil War to its tragically inevitable close. For those of the liberal-left inclination, the Communist argument seemed to carry everything before it, namely, that the Soviet Union was the only trustworthy opponent of Fascism on earth— it made much of the fact that Stalin had offered to join France and England in defense of Czechoslovakia, which offer they turned down cold—the express target of the "anti-Comintern" alliance, better known later as the Axis, comprising the three outlaw nations of the world.

As *the* preeminent anti-Fascist movement, Communism in the Popular Front era attracted an incalculable number of adherents to its standard. We say incalculable because although the number of Party members can be determined, the number of fellow-travelers, sympathizers, hangers-on and the like cannot. Nor will it do to estimate the ratio of the latter to the former by the usual rule-of-thumb formula of three to one. The Party stated that it had about thirty-five thousand members in 1934; by 1939, according to chairman Browder, the number approached a hundred thousand. By then, the trauma of Hitlerism must have raised the ratio well beyond three to one, swelling the ranks of the movement into the many hundreds of thousands, upwards of half a million perhaps. Communism in America was producing a thriving subculture of its own.

A considerable proportion were Jews. Why Jews flocked to the move- ment—not necessarily to the Party—needs no elaboration. They had long since designated Hitler as one of the greatest anti-Semites who ever lived— and this with no premonition (of which anyone today is aware) that a Holocaust was in the offing. One must imagine the gratitude even the anti- Communists among them felt toward the Soviet Union and their disappoint- ment with the pusillanimous democracies. But the surprising truth is that although Jews constituted the largest ethnic group within the Party, their ratio actually dropped, as did the ratio of foreign to native born. By 1939 an organization which the former had always dominated was now weighted two to one in favor of the latter. The Communist ideal of being an *American* Party and movement was coming to pass.

Other membership data further encouraged Party officials. The turnover rate, an important measure, changed dramatically; the revolving door had definitely slowed down. When the decade began, five members quit or aban- doned the Party for every two who stayed. In 1939 two stayed for every one who left. And whereas the number of union members belonging to the Party—another important measure—had been insignificant, embarrassingly so, they were now a considerable presence: some 40 percent of the vastly increased membership consisted of trade unionists. And all the labor that had gone into cultivating Negro support was at last paying off. Nearly seven thousand Negroes were enrolled in the Party, a ratio comparable to the ratio of Negroes to society as a whole. But with this obvious difference: Society ruthlessly kept Negroes down, but as Communists they enjoyed a unique solicitude. The Party went out of its way to publicly demonstrate its egalitarianism, its fraternal regard for them (even though the traces of "white chauvinism" were still not totally expunged). Negroes of every persuasion looked more kindly on Communism now that the chimera of black nationhood had been laid to rest. Party leadership, however, failed to reflect the increasingly pluralistic character of its rank and file. The Political and Central Committees were overwhelmingly white male and disproportionately Jewish. Criticism of the Party's shortcomings, especially its hypocrisies, is certainly in order—unnecessary advice for its army of critics—but it still deserves high marks, given what America was like at the time, in matters of race, ethnicity, gender, and so on.

Meanwhile, the rest of the Far Left went into a tailspin. Hoping to present an alternative to the Stalinists, Musteites had joined the Trotskyists in 1934. Two years later the combined group (A. J. Muste himself having dropped out and returned to pacifism) entered the Socialist Party, which in membership growth had so far kept pace with Communists. But this marriage was soon annulled, leaving trails of bitterness. With the international situation deteriorating, both entities, Trotskyists and Socialists, concentrated their energies on the class struggle while blaming Communists for concentrating their energies on defense of the Soviet Union, that is, for selling out the proletariat in the course of negotiating Popular Front arrangements with the bourgeoisie.

These anti-Communists also publicized the preposterous show trials of most leading Bolsheviks—Lenin's comrades, makers of the Revolution—that preoccupied Moscow between 1934 and 1938 and were followed by their execution or imprisonment in Siberia. American Trotskyists set up a blue-ribbon tribunal, chaired by philosopher John Dewey, to examine the charge that he, Trotsky, acting in concert with Soviet, German, and Japanese military officers, organized the conspiracy to overthrow the Soviet regime and kill its leaders. Not guilty was the verdict of course, the "evidence," absurd on its face, having been tortured out of the victims. Trotskyists and others were not only completely justified in crying out against Stalin's crimes, they performed a service in doing so, but the interested public tended anyway to gravitate toward the Popular Front view that the Soviet Union and Communism, the international situation being what it was, should have the benefit of the doubt, that nothing should interfere with the emergent anti-Fascist coalition. Socialists and Trotskyists ended up opposing, in the name of radical or revolutionary change, both Fascism (this went without saying) and the Popular Front response to it. The strategy proved disastrous. By 1939 the Socialists had dwindled to a fraction of their former size; the Trotskyists had remained a sect (and a divided one at that), their one source of strength being the gifted and prospering Minneapolis teamster local; and the Lovestonites, never more than a corporal's guard, had disbanded altogether. Outside of the Communist movement, then, the Far Left had precious little to boast of. For all intents and purposes *it* was the Far Left.

Within only two years of its formation in November 1935, the CIO's member unions had traveled a great distance toward attaining its ambitious goal: the unionization of America's mass production industries, a minor revolution in itself. And here the Communists had been instrumental. It was as though all their failures had prepared them for the breakthrough that coincided with, or could be attributed to, their Popular Front coalition with the likes of John L. Lewis.

The 1936–37 make or break sit-down strike against General Motors was their doing by and large. They planned and executed the tactical maneuvers that outwitted the world's biggest and richest corporation, forcing it to recognize and bargain with the United Auto Workers (UAW). Communists could probably have taken over the union had they chosen to, but out of deference to the Popular Front coalition they led, they chose not to try. The point is that the choice rested with them, and if they made a mistake—it would later haunt them—it was theirs alone to make.

At any rate the UAW's incredible victory over General Motors, soon repeated by a victory over Chrysler, emboldened labor militants throughout the country. It also persuaded many employers to accept the inexorability of unionization, particularly after the Supreme Court, in the midst of the general turbulence, ruled in favor of the National Labor Relations, or Wagner, Act, which (as administered with the indispensable help of Communist lawyers for the government) prohibited employers from interfering with the right of a majority of their employees to join whatever union they wished as the bargaining agents for all of them. So it was that another industrial giant, United States Steel, gave in without a fight to another CIO union, the Steel Workers Organizing Committee (SWOC). If the Communists had cause to celebrate because their foreign-language affiliates figured so enormously in the SWOC campaign, the celebration was tempered by the exclusion of their cadre from the union's higher leadership positions. But the U.S. Steel settlement was the exception, not the norm. Usually union recognition would come (if it came at all) after a drawn-out strike involving the police, vigilantes, a hostile press, and so on. In fact, SWOC lost its strike against the "little steel" companies; it was a stinging defeat in which ten workers were killed (the 1937 "Memorial Day massacre"). Remarkable nonetheless, when all is said and done, were the number and variety of unions the Communists not only organized but ran. A list of them will give some idea of what they wrought: Fur and Leather Workers; International Longshoremen and Warehousemen; Shoe Workers; Federation of Architects, Engineers, Chemists, and Technicians; Furniture Workers; Farm Equipment Workers; Screen Writers Guild; American Communication Association; Marine Cooks and Stewards; Transport Workers; Newspaper Guild; Packinghouse Workers;

Mine, Mill, and Smelter Workers; United Electric, Radio, and Machine Workers; International Woodworkers of America; National Maritime; State, County, and Municipal Workers; United Cannery, Agricultural and Packing, and Allied Workers; plus the numerous locals in non-Communist unions within both the conservative AFL and the left-oriented CIO.

What practical consequences followed from the existence of so many Communist unions? Few indeed despite the insensate fears aroused at the time by those who detested all unions, whatever their ideology, and by the AFL, which conducted a virulent anti-Red campaign of its own in hopes of smearing the rival CIO. Now Communist union leaders, it is true, stayed close to the Party line; not only were they committed to Communism and its worldview, they owed their success largely to the Party's supporting network. They rejected the ethos of business unionism that lay at the heart of the AFL craft tradition. Business unionists accepted a status quo that rewarded them, however racist, nativist, and xenophobic it might be, however indifferent to the plight of disadvantaged Americans, workers among them. Communist leaders invested their unions with a vanguard function, seeking to raise rank-and-file social consciousness on the important questions of the day, attempting to inculcate the Communist values to which they, the leaders, subscribed. But above all else they had to be good trade unionists, and if that required backing off from unpopular didacticisms or calls to political action they did so. Nor could they always avoid succumbing to the lure of business unionism. What Communists who headed unions and other mass organizations tried to do was reconcile their politics and Party loyalty with the quotidian obligations of their office, but where conflicts arose they usually gave the obligations priority. The Party understood this and acted accordingly.

The rise of the CIO had far-reaching residual consequences. Led by strong unions, many with a leftist bent, ordinary folk could for the first time challenge the power that the industrial elite had wielded with an iron hand over their communities. Democracy began at last to take root where previously it had been a sham, where elections and public discourse had been rigged. The change brought a breath of fresh air to those communities. Not so, however, where the familiar despotism reigned unchecked, for example, in the textile mill towns of the South, the "little steel" enclaves of Pennsylvania, Ohio, and elsewhere, the plantation counties of California—where labor had fallen short or failed altogether in their organizing drives. The contrast between the two Americas, union and open shop, could not be more glaring.

In the political realm, too, Communists had little to complain about. A dramatic left turn in California surprised and delighted them. From their Los Angeles and San Francisco redoubts, they entered into a formidable coalition with New Deal liberals and assorted radicals in the state Democratic Party. In 1938, to everyone's astonishment, the Democrats not only won the gubernatorial election, they installed a Popular Front administration; Culbert Olsen, the new governor, immediately freed Tom Mooney, a San Francisco labor activist who had spent twenty-two years in jail on a murder charge, whose poignant cause Communists had been championing with great effectiveness. True, the Republican tidal wave of 1938 swept two Popular Front third parties out of office, the Minnesota Farmer-Laborites and the Wisconsin Progressives, but the results in some ways redounded to Communist advantage. Both of them began to move into their respective Democratic Parties, giving the Popular Front more elbow room and leading perhaps to repetitions of California. The New York situation was very different. There the Democrats remained hopelessly bound to the Tammany machine. The American Labor Party thus continued to grow, and increasingly it reflected its Communist rather than its Socialist base of support.

Its accomplishments were impressive indeed. Some of New York's most notable liberal-left politicians—Mayor Fiorello LaGuardia (already a legend, yet vulnerable because he was a Republican), East Harlem Congressman Vito Marcantonio (most intimate of fellow travelers), and Governor Herbert H. Lehman (trying for a fourth term)—owed their re-elections to the margins the ALP supplied. Communists thus found themselves high-stake players in the biggest city and state in the nation. Compelling testimony, as if any were needed, to the success of their Popular Front strategy.

The genius of that strategy was nowhere brought out more clearly than in the Party's front organizations, organizations, as we have seen, that were designed to accommodate non-Communists of every kind who were willing to cooperate with Communists in the furtherance of specific objectives. Such organizations were as old as the Party itself, but they came of age in the Popular Front era, when they attracted hundreds of thousands of supporters, an amalgam of Party members, unaffiliated sympathizers, the mildly interested, the curiosity seekers. Of these, some inevitably were politicized, then got drawn into the movement and ended up as Party faithful. Fronts, in other words, served two purposes: they advanced foreign and domestic policies favored by the Party and they helped recruit persons whom the Party deemed worthy. Communists took their chosenness for granted.

Fronts fell into two main categories, large and small, which is to say, those of a general and comprehensive nature and those targeted for a specific and specialized audience. The large ones in turn consisted of two types, the directly and indirectly political (of course at bottom everything Communists did was political). Examples of the indirectly political were the International Workers Order, with its hundreds of thousands of insurance policy holders (providing as it did the cheapest and best coverage extant), the Workers Ex-Servicemen's League (America's only leftist veterans' group), and the Labor Sports Union (which offered members cheap or free athletic and gymnastic facilities). Three of the directly political fronts deserve brief discussion. One of them, the American League Against War and Fascism, predated the

Popular Front and has already been mentioned. It was an ideal organization of its kind for the Party because it resonated so well among Americans fed up with war and militarism and arms manufacturers (the particular scourge of the 1930s). Pacifist groups, especially religious ones, signed on and attended the League's huge congresses and subscribed to its publications, Communists keeping discretely in the background. But as the Fascist threat intensified, so its original mission changed into a Popular Front need for greater involvement in struggles abroad, aiding, for instance, the Spanish Republic or China. So the Communist Party saw to a change in its name—which change symbolized the underlying policy change—and it became the American League for Peace and Democracy.

Another political front was the National Negro Congress, chaired by the great A. Philip Randolph, president of the Sleeping Car Porters and a leading figure in the Socialist Party. He, along with Negro ministers, fraternal orders, newspaper publishers, and such popular entertainers as Paul Robeson and such public figures as Ralph Bunche, locked arms with Communists, whose finances and personnel enabled the Congress to put up a good fight for issues affecting blacks (anti-lynching laws, a wages and hours act, housing for the poor, no racial discrimination in hiring or in trade unions, etc.). Yet another front with mass political appeal was the American Student Union, by 1939 some twenty thousand strong on college campuses, whose Youth Congress and Southern Negro Youth Congress relentlessly kept up the pressure on government, national and local, to increase or maintain student assistance programs, guarantee the right of protest on campuses and off, actively promote racial equality, and of course support a vigorously anti-Fascist foreign policy.

From this run-through we can see why the boundaries separating the fronts were so porous, why belonging to any implicated the others as well. And indeed a rough correspondence can be drawn between the intensity of an individual's involvement in the movement and the number of fronts in which he or she participated. A good Communist was engaged at some level with every aspect of Party business appropriate to his or her place on the hierarchy.

Of the more narrowly specialized fronts two may be singled out for mention here. The National Lawyers Guild arose in 1937 as a radical alternative to the American Bar Association. First class lawyers, many recent graduates of top law schools, joined the Guild because they believed that the Constitution and the legal system in general should expand along New Deal lines by upholding human rights, community needs, and social welfare over the claims of property and privilege. More and more they supplanted the aggressively insurgent International Labor Defense. Then there were the writers' and artists congresses, which also represented professionals who were at odds with the institutions that dominated their fields. Particularly impressive was the American Writers Congress, whose hundreds of new members compensated for the departure from the movement of such erstwhile sympa-thizers as Edmund Wilson, John Dos Passos, and James T. Farrell, for the demise of the John Reed clubs (one of whose magazines, *Partisan Review*, was resurrected as an important purveyor of avant garde culture and criticism and anti-Communist radical politics), and for the increasing indifference to proletarian literature. The Popular Front now cultivated established artists and intellectuals in their respective disciplines—established and friendly to Communism—rather than bring along a flock of young and unknown rebels.

4

Whether Communists in authority were aware of the danger lurking in the Popular Front strategy we have no way of knowing; if any of them were they naturally said nothing in public. That danger, as we said, had undone the Party's leftist rivals and accounted for its prosperity. And that danger, unseen until too late, was the foreign connection—the identification of Party and movement with the welfare of the Soviet Union. That identification gave Communism its singular advantage over its rivals because the Soviet Union alone stood up to Hitler, and Hitler it was who made Fascism such a dread-ful menace to civilization. But in international affairs, ideology, however sig-nificant, yields to power politics, that is, national interests. So it has always been and so it was then, in the summer of 1939, at the height of Popular Front success.

This is not the place to explore the pros and cons of the Hitler-Stalin (or Ribbontrop-Molotov) nonaggression pact. According to the logic of power politics, Stalin may have had every reason to enter into a covenant with his hated enemy, the Western democracies having let down the Soviet Union again and again in the obvious hope—obvious to Stalin and Communists and many others too—that Hitler, thus appeased, would carry out his promise to destroy Bolshevism at its source and leave it at that. But Stalin's reasons, how-ever justified from the standpoint of national interest, certainly did not com-port with the logic of Popular Front anti-Fascism, and it was that logic that gave American Communism its specific appeal. Could the Comintern have better prepared the Party and its army of sympathizers by warning it before the blow struck at the end of August 1939? The Party faithful at least might have avoided the embarrassment of flip-flopping so egregiously, renouncing today the position ardently embraced yesterday. But, then again, many of the people who gravitated toward the movement out of loathing for Fascism could never have been mollified. The enormity of the betrayal stunned and enraged them. Imagine: Hitler and Stalin signing a pact!—their disillusion-ment was complete.

Had it been just a nonaggression pact the task of confronting the Party would have been difficult enough. What immediately followed made it insuperable.

In addition to the pact, as the world learned on September 1, when Germany invaded Poland, thus setting off World War II—in addition, Hitler and Stalin had also agreed that the Soviet Union would get the eastern third of Poland, giving the impression that he, Stalin, was as guilty as Hitler. He went on to reinforce that impression. While Germany was busy with France and England—busy is too strong a word: it was the period of the "phony war"—the Soviet Union ingested the three Baltic states and fought a mini-war against tiny, democratic Finland, after Finland refused to hand over the piece of land the Soviet Union demanded.

At about the time Finland conceded defeat in the spring of 1940 Germany launched the blitzkrieg that made it the master of Europe. Literally within weeks, by mid-June, the Wehrmacht had taken Norway, Denmark, the Netherlands, Belgium, and Luxembourg and had brought France to its knees; England alone survived the onslaught. That summer began Germany's massive air assault on English cities preparatory to an invasion. In other words, Hitler was on the way to winning the war and, with Mussolini as his junior partner, dominating the whole of Europe from the British Isles to the Vistula, from the Baltic to the Aegean, an empire already larger than Napoleon's. And his military might had scarcely been tested.

Such was the situation that confronted the United States. To its everlasting credit the Roosevelt administration sided with England within the limits prescribed by public opinion. A majority of Americans might go along with Roosevelt's attempt to provide England with more and more military and economic help, but only on the condition that they not be drawn into the war. A persuasive minority felt that unless America remained completely neutral and refused to provide the help Roosevelt asked for, it must sooner or later get drawn in. Roosevelt, however, proved more persuasive. Or rather Hitler did. He revealed in the Luftwaffe's brutally indiscriminate bombings—shown extensively in photographs and newsreels and described daily on the radio and in print—just how beastly he was. America could not stand idly by and watch the carnage and so Roosevelt got his way.

For Communists the course of events could not have been more topsy-turvy. In order to conform to Soviet policy they had to take a strictly neutral line toward the belligerents. But strict neutrality under the circumstances meant siding with the brutes, Germany and Italy, against the victim, England, which was holding on by the skin of its teeth. And in fact the Party directed its animus at Roosevelt, now metamorphosed into a warmonger acting in the interests of Wall Street. "The Yanks are not coming" was the clever slogan it came up with, its riposte to Roosevelt. This non-neutral neutrality, moreover, put Communists in bed with strange company indeed: Socialists of the Norman Thomas school, Trotskyists of both the Cannon and Shachtman schools, secular and religious pacifists, a phantasmagoria of Fascist and anti-Semitic groups—merely to enumerate them would require pages—the millions of "isolationists," most of them Republicans, who, like the great aviator Charles A. Lindbergh (he also happened to be a Nazi apologist), believed that the United States should withdraw into its continental or hemispheric bastion of security and leave the Europeans (and Asians) to their own devices, no matter how sordid and unpalatable they may be. Only an evil genius with a whimsical sense of humor could have invented the Popular Front to which the Communists now belonged.

For the Party and movement the effects were calamitous. The largest of the front organizations—the National Negro Congress, the American Student Union, the American League for Peace and Democracy—withered away. Liberal-left sympathizers not only quit the movement, they vehemently turned against the Party, and the Party reciprocated, Third Period style. The foreign-language affiliates, especially those representing nationalities under Nazi rule—and Soviet as well—went into sharp decline. Jews in particular were embittered and took to calling Communists "Communazis," the ultimate epithet. Numerous artists and intellectuals broke away and their Popular Fronts—the various congresses—dissolved. The Party itself suffered a sharp drop in membership.

But it can also be argued that the effects could have been much more calamitous than they were. Membership stabilized in early 1941 at seventy thousand. Few of the cadre, truest of believers, vanguard of the vanguard, abandoned the Party. They assumed as always that the preservation of the Soviet Union was humanity's abiding hope, the more so now that the capitalist order seemed on the verge of collapse; it was, after all, a war between capitalist nations. The Party may even have picked up new adherents from among the left-leaning isolationists and pacifists who were uncomfortable with their reactionary bedmates.

In addition to its internal perturbations the Party had to face mounting external difficulties—nothing less in fact than another red scare. The public lumped Communists and Fascists together as un-American and wanted them both suppressed. Eager to oblige, politicians seized the opportunity to settle old accounts with leftists, Communists most of all. President Roosevelt had authorized the FBI to resume its surveillance of radicals, its gathering of political dossiers (the practice had ceased in 1924). This was Director J. Edgar Hoover's passion, loathing radicals as he did, and he turned his agency loose on the Party. The various Red Squads around the country followed suit. Congress entered the fray too, passing the Smith Act, which allowed the Justice Department to prosecute individuals belonging to groups that advocated the overthrow of the government by force or violence, an express invitation to go after the Party. Before the government took that arduous route it went after Earl Browder, jailing him for four years on a technical violation: he once had falsified his passport. Meanwhile, the Dies Committee, predecessor of and model for the House Un-American Activities Committee of the McCarthy period, continued to hold its well-publicized hearings whose purpose was to discredit Communist and fellow traveling union leaders, Hollywood actors, and government programs, and impugn liberals, preferably those in the Roosevelt administration, for carrying out policies favorable to Communists and their friends. Nor were state governments wanting in their response to the perceived threat. Most notorious was New York's Rapp-Coudert hearings, so named for the two legislators who headed the committee that conducted them in 1940–41. Their intention was to root out "subversives" from New York City public schools, the colleges to begin with. Eventually, some twenty college teachers were summarily fired because of their alleged Communism and one went to prison on a perjury charge.

The Party interpreted all this as incipient Fascism, and it prepared for a return to the underground life, complete with concealment, false identities, clandestine meetings, emergency flights—techniques Communists had learned wherever the extreme Right had taken power.

But there was no need to employ those techniques. The red scare suddenly ran out of steam after June 22, 1941, and ended altogether after December 7. When Hitler invaded the Soviet Union the Roosevelt administration extended to it the same helping hand it gave England. With Pearl Harbor, followed by Hitler's (and Mussolini's) declaration of war against the United States, the Soviet Union became an ally and comrade. The repression of American Communists ceased forthwith, Roosevelt pardoned Browder, thoughts of going underground vanished, and Communists again were Americans in good standing.

5

So it was that the Popular Front was revived as suddenly as it had collapsed. Communists immediately resumed their adoration of Roosevelt, fighter against Fascism and isolationism, and friend of the Soviet Union. Front organizations emerged again to attract all non-Communists now, not only those of the Left but those of the Center and, yes, of the Right, too. Typical was the American/Slav Congress, with its numerous affiliates (Serbian, Polish, Ukrainian, et al.), and the National Council on Soviet Relations (or American-Soviet Friendship Society), chaired by Corliss Lamont, which flourished as news of Soviet heroism and sacrifice filled the media.

In retrospect, the wartime Popular Front has a surreal aspect about it. Communists could freely, openly, conduct their business in the knowledge that few opponents dared attack them in public; they were the American surrogates of the valiant ally Americans admired so much. The Popular Front redivivus received the extraordinary protection that authorized opinion always receives in war, authorized meaning the public's, and therefore the government's overwhelming sanction. Never had Communists enjoyed such a privileged status. Surreal may not even be the word for it.

The case against the Trotskyists brought home the surreality of the situation. In 1941 the government invoked the aforementioned Smith Act to prosecute and imprison eighteen of them on the spurious charge of advocating/conspiring to overthrow—etc., etc., and in the process to wrest from them—this being the real object of the travesty—the Minneapolis teamster local they had run with such exemplary skill and regard for the members since 1934. Neither the Justice Department nor certainly the Party had cause to feel proud of their roles in the wretched affair. Like Banquo's ghost, the case of the "Minneapolis 18" would come back to haunt the Communists.

During World War II Communists stood out as supremely patriotic Americans because they were indefatigably loyal Communists. No crusade was holier than this one in their estimation. No one went further than they in doing whatever the government asked of citizens—giving blood, serving as air raid wardens, collecting scrap metal, turning in black marketeers, working themselves to the bone in defense plants, buying bonds and, most important of course, being courageous soldiers. Translated into policy, this attitude meant one thing: the subordination of every issue, no matter how worthy, how historically identified with the Party, to the immediate object of defeating Hitler. Here was where tensions did arise between Communist trade union leaders and the workers who chafed under wartime controls as wages remained flat while corporate profits and executives' income rose vertiginously despite the heavy taxes on both, and also as workers were subject to a steady diet of speedups, overtime requirements, abuses, and so on. The Party condemned such inequities in the abstract, but it refrained from doing much about them concretely. It resolutely opposed any labor action that might have hindered production. It used every epithet in its vast repertory to denounce the mighty John L. Lewis, its former collaborator in the building of the CIO, for repeatedly defying the government by taking coal miners out on strike for higher wages. Critics of the Left later accused the Party of betraying the workers and playing the capitalists' game, so obsessed was it with defending the Soviet Union.

There is a large grain of truth in the accusation. And it is also true that a number of rank-and-file workers resented their Communist leaders' lack of militancy, their failure to be more like John L. Lewis. But two things should be kept in mind. Communist-led unions were hardly alone in taking the wartime no-strike pledge; anti-Communists like the United Auto Workers' Walter Reuther (then head of the General Motors division) were quite as determined as the Party in pushing for higher production goals, unfair as the wage rates may be. And the impartial observer, while conceding the justice of the Party's critics, must conclude that workers did very well indeed during the war, particularly the unionized ones, whose ranks swelled to a third of the labor force. Most of them, for the first time in their lives, were saving money; with wives working, too, their family income rose far beyond living costs, which remained modest through the war. Also, how many workers were *grateful* to their union leaders, Communist and non-Communist alike, compared to those who were dissatisfied with them is impossible to ascertain, but the number must have been considerable. Communist-run CIO unions emerged from the war stronger and more confident of their future than ever.

A similar accusation concerning Negroes had been made against the Party because it consigned racial issues to a back burner for the duration. Instead of playing up racial conflicts, as it once did, it tended to play them down in the name of wartime unity. It continued, of course, to plump for racial equality and attack Jim Crow practices, but with a restraint that offended not a few Negro members (and some white as well). Just as it had been Sleeping Car Porter Chief A. Philip Randolph, not the Communists, who in 1941 had forced President Roosevelt to sign an executive order promising to end racial discrimination in defense plants—Randolph had done so by threatening to lead a gigantic "March on Washington"—so now it was the historically moderate and much reviled National Association for the Advancement of Colored People that called for immediate government remedies for the intolerable mistreatment of black servicemen and workers and their families. Communists, moreover, were slow to respond to the race riots that broke out in 1943, most violently in Detroit, where scores died before the military restored a semblance of peace. When it came to defending Negro rights, Eleanor Roosevelt, the president's wife, was bolder than the Communists.

On one vital issue the Party did challenge the Roosevelt administration for a while. Getting the United States and England to create a Second Front against Hitler was the issue, and it came to a head in the fall of 1942, a dark moment for the Allies. German armies were on the attack, headed for the Caucasus, which were rich in oil and were the gateway to the Middle East. Meanwhile, there, in the Middle East, Rommel's crack army (the Desert Corps) had advanced to within striking distance of the Suez Canal after capturing all of Libya. Stalin was pleading with the United States to do something that would compel Hitler to let up long enough for Soviet forces to regroup. And so demands for a Second Front became a Party mantra at its frequent rallies and among its extensive agitprop network. A sinister imputation underlay its campaign: the reactionaries within the administration (never Roosevelt), in concert with their English brethren (Churchill?), really wanted the Germans and Russians to kill each other as long as possible while the Western allies dawdled on the sidelines. At any rate, the Allies, in November 1942, did finally launch a Second Front, a miniature one to be sure, to relieve the pressure on the Soviets when they invaded French North Africa. This did placate Stalin and the Communists somewhat, but what ended the campaign was the battle of Stalingrad, which turned back the German assault on the Caucasus and marked the beginning of Hitler's fatal retreat from Russia.

A rich paradox surrounds the whole Second Front brouhaha. If the United States and England held back from invading France longer than they should have, for sinister or any other motives, the paradox becomes that much richer. Rare was the person who in 1942 imagined that the Soviet Union would come roaring back after Stalingrad and go on to liberate not only the European segment of the Soviet Union (about one million square miles) but Hungary, Bulgaria, Romania, Poland, and parts of Czechoslovakia, Germany, and Austria. Would the United States and England have delayed the Normandy invasion as long as they did—until June 1944—had they anticipated the rapidity and magnitude of Soviet success? And did Stalin not have reason to be grateful for their unwillingness, or inability, to do as he had asked? We will leave it at that.

During the war, too, "Browderism" came into its own as the weltanschauung of American Communism. Party chairman Earl Browder built it on the "Communism as twentieth-century Americanism" theme he propounded with such good effect in the initial Popular Front era (1935–39). It was after the "Big Three" (Roosevelt, Churchill, and Stalin) met for the first time at Teheran in late November 1943—by then the war was definitely in their favor—that Browder began to articulate his vision of a postwar domestic and global order, a vision for which the Teheran conference served as the metaphor.

Browder had come to believe that an accord could be reached between American Communism and New Deal capitalism, enlightened big business regulated by a liberal welfare state. The Popular Front, that is, could be a permanent institution because it included powerful economic interests that were willing to make concessions to labor, the poor, Negroes, and so on, and go along with a modest but inexorable re-distribution of the wealth and enlargements of rights. Where was revolution in this scheme of things? Browder recast it to mean significant, but evolutionary, change for the better. A Communist future there would be, but it would come to pass in the fullness of time, according to its own invincible logic. Browderism could be called evolutionary Communism.

Browder's global vision was a projection of his domestic one. In it the Soviet Union and the United States, Stalin and Roosevelt (and their successors), would cooperate to emancipate the unemancipated, the peoples subjugated by colonial rule, and provide a sort of Popular Front reconstruction program to increase living standards for the nine-tenths of humanity condemned to poverty and squalor and disease. America had the resources to underwrite the effort, the greatest in history, one that would usher in the epoch of peace and happiness. Browder's utopian ideal obviously reflected the euphoria that he and all Communists felt now that Fascism was about to be destroyed and Communism planted well beyond the Soviet Union. If the Big Three (or rather two) could collaborate so beautifully to undo the evil, why should they not be able to collaborate to bring about the good?

Browder had every reason to assume that he was not merely speaking for himself. In 1943 Stalin had dissolved the Comintern, the gesture that pointed convincingly to the very thing Browder was formulating and would soon spring on his comrades. Moscow no doubt gave him the go-ahead or encouraged him to think it did; he had highly placed friends there. Nor could there be any doubt that the American Party overwhelmingly approved his Teheran, or Popular Front, approach to the emergent world order. His critics, Foster chief among them, toiled against Browder behind the scenes, but stayed in line publicly, good Communists that they were. They might have envied his popularity, for he received a respectful hearing from many middle-class Americans whose admiration of the Soviet Union rubbed off on him. There was nothing threatening—"Communist"—about the man. Women's organizations and chambers of commerce saw someone who looked and sounded and comported himself like the prototypical Midwesterner (and one-time bookkeeper) that he was. He made it seem as if Communism was indeed only another kind of Americanism, and that was fine with his Party associates.

So Browder met with little opposition when he got the Party to take the next bold step—to follow the Comintern example and dissolve itself; the Party, that is, not the movement, with its enormously complex network of institutions and outreach programs. Instead of a Party, vying with other parties for a chance to govern, Communists, he urged, should constitute themselves a "political association," an interest group operating within the existing political structure, and support either of the major parties on this issue or that in a framework defined by the Popular Front world order. Not since 1921, when Communists surfaced and became a legal party, had anything so far-reaching been advanced—but now from a position of strength and self-assurance—and the Party resoundingly went along with his proposal.

As the year 1945 dawned, the surviving Axis powers, Nazi Germany and Imperial Japan, were near defeat. The Big Three were meeting in Yalta, with Stalin as host, to conclude the war and begin laying the basis for the post-Fascist and newly expanded Communist world. In this setting Browderism sounded exactly the right chord.

LAUNCHING THE POPULAR FRONT

1
PROCEEDINGS
The Seventh Comintern Congress

It was a foregone conclusion that the 371 delegates from parties in every country would adopt a Popular Front strategy when they met in Moscow on July 25, 1935, for the Seventh Comintern Congress. A few weeks later they unanimously approved the following resolutions.

In face of the towering menace of fascism to the working class and all the gains it has made, to all toilers and their elementary rights, to the peace and liberty of the peoples, the Seventh Congress of the Communist International declares that at the present historic stage it is the main and immediate task of the international labor movement to establish the united fighting front of the working class. For a successful struggle against the offensive of capital, against the reactionary measures of the bourgeoisie, against fascism, the bitterest enemy of all the toilers, who, without distinction of political views, have been deprived of all rights and liberties, it is imperative that unity of action be established between all sections of the working class, irrespective of what organization they belong to, even before the majority of the working class unites on a common fighting platform for the overthrow of capitalism and the victory of the proletarian revolution. But it is precisely for this very reason that this task makes it the duty of the communist parties to take into consideration the changed circumstances and to apply the united front tactics in a new manner, by seeking to reach agreements with the organizations of the toilers of various political trends for joint action on a factory, local, district, national and international scale.

With this as its point of departure, the Seventh Congress of the Communist International enjoins the communist parties to be guided by the following instructions when carrying out the united front tactics:

1. The defense of the immediate economic and political interests of the working class, the defense of the latter against fascism, must be the starting point and form the main content of the workers' united front in all capitalist countries. . . .

2. Without for a moment giving up their independent work in the sphere of communist education, organization and mobilization of the masses, the communists, in order to render the road to unity of action easier for the workers, must strive to secure joint action with the social-democratic parties, reformist trade unions and other organizations of the toilers against the class enemies of the proletariat, on the basis of short- or long-term agreements. At the same time, attention must be directed mainly to the development of mass action in the various localities, conducted by the lower organizations through local agreements.

Loyally fulfilling the conditions of the agreements, the communists must promptly expose any sabotage of joint action by persons or organizations participating in the united front, and if the agreement is broken, must immediately appeal to the masses while continuing their tireless struggle for the restoration of the disrupted unity of action.

3. The forms in which the united proletarian front is realized, which depend on the condition and character of the labor organizations and on the concrete situation, must be varied in character. . . .

5. Joint action with the social-democratic parties and organizations not only does not preclude, but, on the contrary, renders still more necessary the serious and well-founded criticism of reformism, of social-democracy as the ideology and practice of class collaboration with the bourgeoisie, and the

patient exposition of the principles and program of communism to the
social-democratic workers.

While revealing to the masses the meaning of the demagogic arguments advanced by the right social-democratic leaders against the united front, while intensifying the struggle against the reactionary section of social-democracy, the communists must establish the closest cooperation with those left social-democratic workers, functionaries and organizations that fight against the reformist policy and advocate a united front with the communist party. The more we intensify our fight against the reactionary camp of social-democracy, which is participating in a bloc with the bourgeoisie, the more effective will be the assistance we give to that part of social-democracy which is becoming revolutionized. And the self-determination [crystallization] of the various elements within the left camp will take place the sooner, the more resolutely the communists fight for a united front with the social-democratic parties.

The attitude to the practical realization of the united front will be the chief indication of the true position of the various groups among the social-democrats. In the fight for the practical realization of the united front, those social-democratic leaders who come forward as lefts in words will be obliged to show by deeds whether they are really ready to fight the bourgeoisie and the right social-democrats, or are on the side of the bourgeoisie, that is, against the cause of the working class.

6. Election campaigns must be utilized for the further development and strengthening of the united fighting front of the proletariat. While coming forward independently in the elections and unfolding the program of the communist party before the masses, the communists must seek to establish a united front with the social-democratic parties and the trade unions (also with the organizations of the toiling peasants, handicraftsmen, etc.), and exert every effort to prevent the election of reactionary and fascist candidates. In face of fascist danger, the communists, while reserving for themselves freedom of political agitation and criticism may, in election campaigns, declare for a common platform and a common ticket with the anti-fascist front, depending on the growth and success of the united front movement, and on the electoral system in operation.

7. In striving to unite, under the leadership of the proletariat, the struggle of the toiling peasants, the urban petty bourgeoisie and the toiling masses of the oppressed nationalities, the communists must seek to bring about the establishment of a wide anti-fascist people's front on the basis of the proletarian united front, supporting all those specific demands of these sections of the toilers which are in line with the fundamental interests of the proletariat. It is particularly important to mobilize the toiling peasants against the fascist policy of robbing the basic masses of the peasantry. . . .

If with such an upsurge of the mass movement it will prove possible, and necessary in the interests of the proletariat, to create a proletarian united front government, or an anti-fascist people's front government, which is not yet a government of the proletarian dictatorship, but one which undertakes to put into effect decisive measures against fascism and reaction, the communist party must see to it that such a government is formed. . . .

In so far as the united front government will really undertake decisive measures against the counter-revolutionary financial magnates and their fascist agents, and will in no way restrict the activity of the community [communist] party and the struggle of the working class, the communist party will support such a government in every way. The participation of the communists in a united front government will be decided separately in each particular case, as the concrete situation may warrant.

2

WHO ARE THE AMERICANS?
Earl Browder

In 1934 Browder became the Party's General Secretary and as such presented its official views to the public. Above all he was identified with the Popular Front line that was now the order of the day. It was he who invented the catchy and very effective saying, "Communism is the Americanism of the twentieth century"—it was the Party's Popular Front signature—the meaning of which he explains below in an essay that appeared in his collection, published in 1936, What Is Communism?

The question asked of Communists more frequently than any other, if we can judge from the Hearst newspapers, is this:

"If you don't like this country, why don't you go back where you came from?"

The truth is, if you insist on knowing, Mr. Hearst, we Communists like this country very much. We cannot think of any other spot on the globe where we would rather be than exactly this one. We love our country. Our affection is all the more deep in that we have watered it with the sweat of our labor—labor which made this country what it is; our mothers nourished it with the tears they shed over the troubles and tragedies of rearing babies in a land controlled by profit and profit-makers. If we did not love our country so much, perhaps we would surrender it to Wall Street.

Of course when we speak of our love of America, we mean something quite different from what Mr. Hearst is speaking about in his daily editorial diatribes. We mean that we love the masses of the toiling people. We find in these *masses* a great reservoir of all things admirable and lovable, all things that make life worth living. We are filled with anger when we see millions of these people whom we love being degraded, starved, oppressed, beaten and jailed when they protest. We have a deep and moving hatred of the system, and of those who fatten on the system which turns our potential paradise into a living hell.

We are determined to save our country from the hell of capitalism. And most of us were born here, so Hearst's gag is not addressed to us anyway. But workers in America who happen to have been born abroad are just as much Americans as anybody else. We all originated across the waters, except perhaps a tiny minority of pure-blooded American Indians. The foreign-born workers have worked harder for less wages on behalf of this country than anybody else. They deserve, at a minimum, a little courtesy from those who would speak of Americanism. There is less historical justification in America than perhaps in any other major country for that narrow nationalism, that chauvinism, which makes a cult of a "chosen people."

We in America are a mongrel breed and we glory in it. We are the products of the melting pot of a couple of hundred nationalities. Our origin as a nation acknowledged its debt to a Polish Kosciusko, a German Von Steuben, a French Lafayette and countless other "foreigners."

Furthermore, let's be careful not to get snooty about pedigrees; half the names in the American social register were originally borne by men who were transported from Europe after conviction of crime or who in the new country became bold bandits and buccaneers. It was the more aggressive and violent types who rose to the top most quickly in our early days and laid the foundations of the great American fortunes. They were the Al Capones of their day, with no income-tax department to bring them to grief.

We love the past history of America and its masses, in spite of the Astors and Vanderbilts. We find in it a wealth of tradition striped in the purple tints of glory—the glory of men and women fighting fearlessly and self-sacrificingly against the throttling hand of a dead past, for those things upon which further progress depended.

Around the birth of our country as an independent nation cluster such heroic names as those of Patrick Henry, whose famous shout, "As for me, give me liberty or give me death!" re-echoes down the corridors of time; of Thomas Paine, whose deathless contribution to our national life of a militant anti-clericalism has long survived the many pamphlets with which he fought, the form of which alone belongs to a past age; of Thomas Jefferson, whose favorite thought revolved about watering the tree of liberty with the blood of tyrants (he thought this "natural manure" should be applied to the tree about every twenty years!); of all the founding fathers, whose chief claim to glory lies in their "treason" to the "constitutional government" of their day, and among whom the most opprobrious epithet was "loyalist."

These men, in their own time, faced the issues of their day, cut through the red tape of precedent legalism and constitutionalism with a sword, made a revolution, killed off a dying and outworn system, and opened up a new chapter in world history.

Our American giants of 1776 were the "international incendiaries" of their day. They inspired revolutions throughout the world. The great French Revolution, the reverberations of which filled Europe's ears during the entire nineteenth century, took its first steps under the impulse given by the American Revolution. The Declaration of Independence was for that time what the Communist Manifesto is for ours. Copy all the most hysterical Hearst editorials of today against Moscow, Lenin, Stalin; substitute the words America, Washington, Jefferson; and the result is an almost verbatim copy of the diatribes of English and European reactionary politicians in the closing years of the eighteenth century against our American founding fathers. Revolution was then "an alien doctrine imported from America" as now it is "imported from Moscow."

After the *counter-revolution* engineered by Alexander Hamilton had been victorious and established itself under *the Constitution* in 1787, a period of reaction set in. There was, as in our modern days since the World War, a period marked by oppressive legislation which went down in history as the "Alien and Sedition Laws." But the American masses had not been mastered; those who rode high and mighty with their eighteenth-century counterparts of criminal syndicalism laws, deportations, Palmers, Dicksteins and McCormicks, were driven out of power in a struggle, often bloody and violent, which again for a period placed the representatives of the masses (then predominantly agrarian) in control of government.

The greatest figure of them all in the American tradition, Abraham Lincoln, became great because he, despite his own desire to avoid or compromise the struggle, was forced by history to lead to victory a long and bloody civil war whose chief historical significance was the wiping out of chattel slavery, the destruction of private property rights in persons, amending the Constitution in the only way it has ever been fundamentally amended. Lincoln's words, which still live today among the masses, are those which declared: "This country, with its institutions, belongs to the people who inhabit it. Whenever they shall grow weary of the existing government, they can exercise their constitutional right of amending it, or their revolutionary right to dismember or overthrow it."

These words of Lincoln are but a paraphrasing of the Declaration of Independence. Our national holiday, July 4, is in memory of that immortal document of American history. The very heart of the Declaration, that which gives it life, without which all else becomes empty phrases, are these lines, the memory of which had grown dim until the Communists rescued them from the dust of libraries:

> Whenever any form of government becomes destructive of these ends [life, liberty and the pursuit of happiness], it is the right of the people to alter or to abolish it and to institute a new government, laying its foundations on such principles and organizing its powers in such forms, as to

them shall seem most likely to effect their safety and happiness . . . When a long train of abuses and usurpations, pursuing invariably the same object, evinces a design to reduce them [the masses] under absolute despotism, it is their right, it is their duty, to throw off such government and to provide new guards for their future security.

This is the heart of the American tradition. Without this revolutionary kernel, the whole history of the origin of our country becomes only the strutting of marionettes and stuffed shirts, the spread-eagle oratory of the Fourth of July under imperialism, the vulgar yappings of the Hearst press. Without this, patriotism becomes, as that acid critic of the British bourgeoisie, Dr. Johnson, described it, the last refuge of the scoundrel.

The revolutionary tradition is the heart of Americanism. That is incontestable, unless we are ready to agree that Americanism means what Hearst says, slavery to outlived institutions, preservation of privilege, the degradation of the masses.

We Communists claim the revolutionary traditions of Americanism. We are the only ones who consciously continue those traditions and apply them to the problems of today.

We are the Americans and Communism is the Americanism of the twentieth century. . . .

Americanism, in this revolutionary sense, means to stand in the forefront of human progress. It means never to submit to the forces of decay and death. It means constantly to free ourselves of the old, the outworn, the decaying, and to press forward to the young, the vital, the living, the expanding. It means to fight like hell against those who would plow under the crops in our fields, who would close down and scrap our factories, who would keep millions of willing toilers, anxious to create the good things of life, living like beggars upon charity.

Americanism, as we understand it, means to appropriate for our country all the best achievements of the human mind in all lands. Just as the men who wrote the Declaration of Independence had been nurtured upon the French Encyclopedists and the British classical political economists, so the men who will write our modern declaration of independence of a dying capitalist system must feed themselves upon the teachings of Marx, Engels, Lenin and Stalin, the modern representatives of human progress.

In the words of a famous American whose memory we love, we say to Mr. Hearst and all the Red-baiting cohorts of Wall Street: "If this be treason, make the most of it."

This is how we American Communists read the history of our country. This is what we mean by Americanism. This is how we love our country, with the same burning love which Lenin bore for Russia, his native land. Like Lenin, we will fight to free our land from the blood-sucking reactionaries, place it in the hands of the masses, bring it into the international brotherhood of a World Union of Socialist Soviet Republics, and realize the prophetic lines of Walt Whitman:

> We have adhered too long to petty limits . . . the time has come to enfold the world.

NEW INSURGENCIES

Turmoil in Akron

DANGEROUS SCOT
John Williamson

We encountered Williamson earlier in connection with his leadership of the Chicago Unemployed Councils. By 1936 he was head of the Ohio Communist Party and so took part in the first of the great sit-down strikes, against Goodyear, out of which arose the United Rubber Workers of the CIO. In his memoir he tells of the Communist role.

At three A.M., February 14, 1936, the tire-builders in Good-year Plant Two shut off the power and started a sit-down strike in protest against the layoff of 70 men, which they interpreted as the preparation for the introduction of the eight-hour day in their department also. This was the start of one of the greatest class battles in America's history, and the first major test of industrial organization as advocated by the CIO.

After rejecting a company ultimatum to go back to work, the sit-downers were fired. But they still were in the plant. The next day the local union leaders, guided by John House, the president, took the sit-downers out of the plant. The company had agreed to cancel the dismissals. But the men refused to return, because no provision was made to rehire the 70 men who had been laid off originally.

The entire factory was astir. The local union leaders, especially House, were not only inexperienced but afraid of responsibility. Thousands of men, union and non-union, were flocking into the big union hall. The Communist Party issued mimeographed leaflets calling for union action against the eight-hour day, wage-cuts and speedup and distributed them widely. . . .

In this situation, our party put all our experience at the disposal of the 14,000 strikers and the newly established trade union. We met with our own party members and all other key forces in the strike apparatus and conferred with the local leaders of the Rubber Union, including some members of the international executive board. We had regular meetings with Wilmer Tate, the left-wing president of the Central Labor Union.

I moved into Akron from Cleveland and, together with Jim Keller, lived through every minute of the strike. The first step was to get a program of demands adopted by the strikers. After the first 12 hours of picket duty, we met with the half-dozen party members who were most influential in the strike.

We worked out a leaflet which dealt with what was happening in the plants—the eight-hour day, the speedup, wage-cuts—and the swollen company profits. We brought to the foreground the question of unity and the possibility of the workers' responding with a general strike if violence and terror were used against the strikers. We called for total union organization and for union endorsement of the strike and then projected the following demands: The six-hour day; no layoffs; no wage-cuts; a wage increase of 10 percent over the base rate; the end of speedup, and a signed agreement. This leaflet was on the picket lines and in the Goodrich, Firestone and General factories by five o'clock that day.

House was still saying the strike was not union-endorsed and "just happened" and that the only issue was the reinstatement of the 70 discharged tire-builders. That night all the picket captains unanimously endorsed and adopted as their own all the demands in the party leaflet.

At the party meeting we had concluded that the key force in the strike were the picket captains. The chief picket captain was a party leader. These picket captains were the nerve center. They knew all the trends, reactions, fears and rumors. And, through them, action could be effectively organized at decisive moments.

The picket captains met on the second day, and again fulfilling the role of the absent leaders of the local's executive committee, decided that the work stoppage must be turned into a legal strike, and that all strikers must be signed up in the union and given voting rights. Negotiations were to be opened with the company on the five demands. Picket lines were to be held solid, irrespective of injunctions, police or National Guard, and efforts were to be made to win public opinion to the strikers.

Goodyear said it would never negotiate. Tension rose as the company appealed for court injunctions and armed intervention. The Central Labor Union voted full support and promised "to take all measures within our power to defeat" any injunctions. President Sherman Dalrymple of the International Rubber Union threatened "industrial paralysis affecting the entire city" if injunctions were issued. But the full court of six judges issued a sweeping injunction prohibiting mass picketing. Fortunately the police chief and the sheriff disagreed on shooting their way into the picket line. The company was still able to rally 2,500 workers against the strike, and these men were used in every way. The strikers christened them "Red Apples," and that term became a permanent part of the rubber worker's vocabulary to describe company-minded men.

At this point John L. Lewis and the CIO moved in. The steps they advised—making the strike official and signing up everybody into the union—were carried out. . . .

On the 23rd day, the company finally realized it had to negotiate. After several days of talks between the company and union leaders, Goodyear declared that its final proposals for a settlement were as follows: (1) All employees of the Goodyear Tire and Rubber Company, as of February 12, 1936, shall return to work without discrimination or interruption of service record; (2) management of the company will meet with any and all employees individually or through their chosen representatives; (3) notice will be given to representatives of the employees affected of changes in wage rates before they are posted; (4) in the tire division, the company has adopted the 36-hour week, six-hour shifts. Any change in these hours per week or per day below 30 hours or above 36 hours a week will be by arrangement with the employees in the departments or divisions affected; (5) lists of contemplated layoffs will be made in duplicate by the department foreman, one copy will be retained by the foreman and the other copy will be kept in the office of the labor department; both lists will be available for inspection.

These proposals were accompanied by a big barrage from the newspapers, the radio, ministers and civic officials who insisted that now was the time to settle. And four weeks of strike had had a negative impact on some of the less active strikers and their families.

The party leaders then met with all our comrades who were active in the strike. At the beginning there were sharp disagreements on what to do about the company proposals. After long discussions and much talk by Jim Keller, myself and Bill Ricketts, the head of the picket captains, it was decided that we could not advise an out-of-hand rejection of the company proposals, unsatisfactory as they were. We must prevent public opinion from being turned against the strikers.

Bill Ricketts said, "Instead of just voting 'no' to Litchfield's offer, why, we accept some of the points, the harmless ones, and the others we reject. Then we adopt a resolution saying the committee should go back to the Goodyear Co. and talk it over some more. That way the newspapers will say in their headlines. 'Union Wants More Parleys,' or something like that. Akron will see that sounds sensible, and the union won't be blamed for prolonging the strike."

It was decided that we would propose that the union accept the second and the third points. The company had already given the union a signed memorandum that they recognized the right of union committees as well as the International Union president to negotiate on questions of hours and wages as applying to the second point. On the first point, it was decided to add a clause that the men return within seven days. On the fourth, the amendment called for the six-hour day to apply to all workers. It was stipulated that the fifth point state specifically that one of the triplicate copies goes to the union.

The picket captains endorsed these proposals. Then came the local union meeting, with 4,000 inside and at least another thousand crowding around

outside. Our inside information was that the CIO and the rubber union leaders were divided among themselves on what to do. They had finally decided
not to speak, but to leave things in the hands of the strikers.

As they waited for the negotiating committee to arrive and report, the
workers from the Southland sang hymns, and patriotic and popular songs.
Finally, the committee arrived and reported on what the company said was
their final offer. Silence greeted the report, until Bill Ricketts got the floor
and submitted a resolution indicating what was to be accepted and what
amended. With great cheers, the meeting unanimously adopted Bill's
motion.

The first newspaper headline was "Two Points of Peace Plan Accepted.
Company Terms Partially Met." Later editions revealed the next moves of the
enemy. The company broke off negotiations and declared the strikers had
rejected their proposals in full. That night they organized a vigilante outfit
called the "Akron Law and Order League." On its behalf, ex-Mayor Sparks
went on the radio and called on all citizens "to gang up upon the out-of-town
radical and Communists leaders," saying, "It is this handful . . . of labor agitators, radicals, Communists, red orators . . . [that] . . . came into Akron
determined to make the rubber city 100 percent union or to wreck the
industry." Goodyear contributed $15,000 to the Law and Order League.

In the lynch atmosphere that was being created, it was decisive to maintain the unity of the strikers' ranks and the common front between ourselves
and the CIO leaders. I made it my business to talk to Central Labor Union
president Tate, CIO leaders John Ownes, Leo Krzyski and Rose Pesota and
various leaders of the United Rubber Workers of America.

Tate went on the radio and answered Sparks. The union took the radio for
nine continuous hours, with National Secretary-Treasurer Frank Grillo in
command, all through one night, interspersing announcements, news,
music, warnings and speeches. These countermeasures subdued the company hoodlums. The next day the company resumed negotiations with the
union.

While the new negotiations were going on, two of our leading comrades
who were picket captains argued for letting all the picket captains see and
hear an official spokesman of the Communist Party. With great modesty,
these two comrades, who had carried the burden for five weeks, pointed out
that without party leadership the strike would have been lost. It wasn't fair
that the picket captains should get all the credit when actually the party leadership was in great measure responsible.

We finally decided that Jim Keller, our Akron organizer, would be the
speaker, if the picket captains accepted Bill Ricketts' proposal to invite him.
By a big majority, the invitation was extended. Keller spoke for about 20
minutes, congratulating them on their great victory. He said, "I have seen a
lot of strikes, but I have never seen men who went on the picket line in the
worst blizzard in the history of northern Ohio and stayed there for 32 days

in cold and rain and against threats of violence until they won a great victory." At this point he was interrupted and one captain said, "I thought you guys was against the settlement. I got a leaflet here where you Reds call this a sellout."

Keller explained this was a leaflet issued by the Trotskyites and repudiated it in its entirety. But the question opened the door for an explanation of our party's attitude toward the agreement, which was to be voted on next day. Keller explained it clause by clause and how, with union organization, it could be built on.

He not only showed what it meant to rubber workers but added. "They're waiting in steel and in auto. When they hear you've won, they will be on the march." He concluded, "I hereby predict that if—and I know you will—if you fellows take the picket line back to the tire machines and the mill room, the Goodyear strike will be America's new declaration of freedom. Your strike, which you fought so bravely, was the first page of CIO history. It will not be the last. You are the new pioneers."

The next day the strikers voted for an amended agreement. They marched in a massive public parade throughout Akron, past the Goodrich and Firestone plants, into the center of town and past the Mayflower Hotel, where the rubber officials held their luncheons and banquets, and then past the more humble Portage Hotel, the scene of so many union conventions. Across the street from the Portage Hotel, in the Everett Building, was the party office, flying a big banner outside the window congratulating the Goodyear workers on their victory.

With the strike won in Goodyear, the union took in thousands of new members. Within a year, and after another big strike at Firestone, 70,000 workers were in the rubber union. This was virtually complete organization. The great sweep in rubber resulted in expanded union crusades in Akron and in nearby Barberton. The workers of Babcock & Wilcox Boiler Co., the Columbia Chemical and the big Diamond Match Co. in Barberton all flocked into the unions, as did virtually every worker in Akron, including the girls in Woolworth's. . . .

The General Motors Strike

1
ORGANIZE!
Wyndham Mortimer

In Organize!, his autobiography published in 1971, Mortimer, a skilled automobile mechanic and longstanding Party member, describes how he and his fellow Communists led the great General Motors strike of early 1937—how the fledgling United Auto Workers defeated the most powerful corporation on earth and went on to become a powerful organization in its own right.

Early in June 1936, I went to Flint, the center of General Motors operations

Early in June 1936, I went to Flint, the center of General Motors operations and power. I registered at a cheap hotel (The Dresden) obtaining a room costing twelve dollars a week. I had barely time to remove my coat when the phone rang. A voice said, "You had better get the hell back where you came from if you don't want to be carried out in a wooden box!"

"How would you like to go to hell?" I shot back, but the person had hung up. I was fifty-two years old and nobody had taken me out in a box yet; I'd be damned if this was going to be the first time! I ignored the phone call, which I attributed to the Black Legion, and proceeded to plan my work.

I began by making a survey of the problem facing me. I spent a week asking questions and gathering information. To organize this town that was so completely under the control of General Motors would not be easy, to put it mildly. A cloud of fear hung over the city, and it was next to impossible to find anyone who would even discuss the question of unions. . . .

I bought a copy of the Flint Directory which contained the names, addresses, and occupations of all residents in Flint. From the directory, and also from the membership lists of the five defunct locals, I compiled a mailing list of about five thousand names. I composed a letter each week and mailed it to the homes of these five thousand workers. These letters were short, but to the point. Each letter dealt with a specific issue, and each letter hammered home the fact that the answer to this problem was the union.

Many of these letters found their way into the plant and were read along the assembly lines. They had a powerful impact. Applications were returned by some of the workers, who requested me to call on them. I did so and would ask the applicant and his wife to invite trusted friends to a house party. Only those they invited would be present. I would arrange with the wife to serve any refreshments she desired, and the union would take care of the expenses. Such parties became very frequent, and many applications were obtained in this way. . . .

THE BIG STRIKE BEGINS

On December 26, 1936, I was with Bob Travis and Henry Kraus in Travis's room in the Dresden Hotel in Flint, when Louis Spisak, President of the Fisher Body local in Cleveland, telephoned, very excited and obviously upset. He managed to tell me that Fisher-Cleveland was on strike, that they were sitting down. Spisak was a weak leader, and I realized immediately that unless responsibility was taken out of his hands, the whole strike could be lost. I assured him I was leaving for Cleveland at once and that he was to sit tight, make no commitments whatsoever to anyone until I arrived on the 6:00 P.M. train. Upon my arrival in Cleveland, I was surrounded by newsmen. They wanted to know if I had come to settle the strike. Would I meet with Mayor Burton? Would I meet with the Fisher Body management? "No! That is all out!" I told them. However, I was told that Louis Spisak had already met with Mayor Burton, and that he wanted to settle the strike. I said, "President Spisak does not have the authority to settle this strike. The whole matter is now in the hands of the international union."

I went at once to the Fisher plant on Coit Road. The building was surrounded by hundreds of mounted police, who refused entry to anyone. The workers were in possession of the plant, and their morale was exceedingly high. I spoke to them over a public address system, and told them the international union would support them all the way. I said, "Keep up the fight, fellows, we are going to win this one!" I arranged a meeting with the Executive Board of the local at once.

Present were Spisak, Charles Beckman, John DeVito, and Jerry Strauss who had all come out of the plant to attend. Paul Miley remained in the plant in charge of the strike. We lost no time in coming to a decision. We issued a press statement to the effect that the strike could and would be settled only as a part of a national agreement with the General Motors Corporation, and that there would be no talks with local management or city officials.

The die was cast. The strikers were elated. At long last, the discredited leadership of the AFL had been discarded. The auto manufacturers could no longer count on the collective dotage of a moribund AFL Executive Council to help them out. Now the accumulated grievances of half a century of the open shop would be fought out.

I called Bob Travis in Flint and told him to close down Fisher #I, as soon as possible. Before going to my daughter's home for the night (she was now Mrs. Duaine Stewart, and living in Cleveland; Margaret and I had moved to Detroit), I received a wire from John L. Lewis, congratulating me on the press statement and pledging all-out support.

GM GIVES US AN ASSIST

On December 29, 1936, the General Motors Corporation secretly began to remove important dies from Fisher #I. The purpose was to get them out of this union "hotbed." One of the workers on the night shift, John Ananich, called Travis and said, "They are going to move the dies out, Bob!" Travis, who was quick to make decisions, told Ananich to get some of the other union men and to stop the dies from being moved. Travis then called the office girl, Hazel Simon, and told her to put the flicker on. The flicker was a two hundred watt bulb over the union hall across the street from the plant. When it was on, it meant that something of importance was happening, so at lunchtime the workers came streaming across the street to the union hall.

The meeting was short and to the point. Travis told them that the dies meant their jobs, and if they permitted the dies to be taken away, many of them would be unemployed. The workers decided to strike the plant, and to sit in and protect their jobs. It was a crucial decision, since if the workers went home over the weekend, and New Year's Day following, they would be leaving their jobs unprotected and the dies could be moved without opposition. The workers went directly from the meeting and took over the plant. They shouted from the windows to Travis and Kraus, "She is all ours, Bob." The strike started in Cleveland had now been confirmed. Thus began the historic forty-four-day sit-down strike, on December 30, 1936. . . .

After several days of negotiations by remote control, with Lewis, Pressman, and me in one room of Judge Murphy's court, and the representatives of General Motors and the Du Ponts in another, Murphy came to us very much worried. It was about 1:00 P.M. and the Governor said, "They have not removed their hats or coats. They are demanding that the strikers vacate their plants. They told me you have a half-hour to decide, and if you do not comply, they are leaving."

"They will not leave, Governor, they wouldn't dare," Lewis replied. The half-hour passed and they were still there. An hour passed, and they did not leave. Lewis then said, "Governor, invite them in here, and let us talk to them man-to-man."

The Governor conveyed this invitation to them, and after a short period, they came in. Their whole demeanor revealed that they knew they had lost. We arose and shook hands with them, inviting them to sit down and remove their coats and hats.

We all sat around a long table, our union group on one side, and the corporation's on the opposite.

Knudsen sat across from me. He leaned over and said to me, "This is a hell of a committee."

"Why? What do you mean?" I asked.

"It is all lawyers and coal miners," he said with a smile, "and only two auto workers."

This was true, since only Knudsen and myself were familiar with the inside working of an automobile factory. The company lawyers were totally ignorant of the complicated procedures in the manufacture of automobiles. They were concerned solely with legalities and the fourteenth-century ideas of the Du Ponts.

Knudsen was quite a different person. I am sure that if matters were left in his hands, the strike would have been of short duration. He was impatient with all the nebulous legal theories advanced by the two company attorneys and, in private statements made to me, indicated that he wanted to get back to the task of making automobiles.

John L. Lewis was a tower of strength. He knew, as did we all, that to get these men's signatures on a contract with the union meant an enormous victory for the CIO and a shattering defeat for the open shop. The Du Pont-General Motors combine was the fortress that dominated the entire automotive industry, and we were at last face-to-face with the men whose decisions were final.

Governor Murphy withdrew and left us alone with these men for the first time. The three representatives of Du Pont-General Motors were now face-to-face with the representatives of their workers. It was an experience they did not enjoy and would not have endured had not grim necessity demanded it. We entered into serious discussions with them on the issues involved and made it crystal clear that the resumption of work depended entirely on their entering into a contract with the UAW-CIO. We finally agreed to the wording of an agreement with the exception of three items. These were: the duration of the agreement, the designation and number of plants to be covered by the agreement, and the workers' right to wear union buttons on the job.

The last point may seem trivial, but the corporation's attorneys did not consider it so. They insisted that wearing union buttons constituted intimidation against other workers. Heated arguments occurred also over the corporation's intention to arrest and punish a number of workers for violence during the strike. I strongly opposed this. "Let us get one thing straight, gentlemen," I said. "Everyone goes back to work without reprisals, or nobody goes back. If we are going to end this strike, it must be on the basis of letting bygones be bygones."

"But what shall we do with a man who strikes his foreman?" Knudsen demanded.

"What shall we do with the foreman who calls a worker a son-of-a-bitch?" I replied.

"What foreman did that?" Knudsen asked.

"I am not naming names, Mr. Knudsen," I said. "But I think it is time the corporation understood that the union is here to stay. Over the years the General Motors Corporation has built up a supervisory staff, trained to drive the workers to the point of exhaustion, and at less than a living wage. You must begin to rearrange the furniture of your minds or this strike will become only the first of many more to follow."

Lewis raised the question of the Gadola injunction, still unenforced. He demanded that the injunction be withdrawn and all legal action initiated by the corporation against the union be halted. The corporation attorneys argued about whether or not Judge Gadola would agree to nullify the injunction, but they finally agreed.

It was now 2:00 A.M., February 10, 1937. We decided to meet at 2:00 P.M. in the Statler Hotel. President Lewis had developed a cold, and was running a temperature, so he went to bed and called a doctor to attend to him. We met as planned at 2:00 P.M. At 4:00 P.M. we moved over to Lewis's suite. He was still confined to his bed and his wife had flown in from Washington.

I got a call from Travis in Flint, telling me that the corporation had shut off the heat, and it was unbearably cold in the Chevrolet #4 plant. Over the phone we decided that he should get all the men over into the heat treat department, turn on the gas in the furnaces, then open the windows in plant

#4. I said, "Bob, I think this will bring a quick reaction." In about ten minutes, Governor Murphy came to me and said, "Mr. Mortimer, your people have opened the windows in plant #4, and the sprinkler system will freeze."

"Governor, it appears to me the corporation is showing very bad faith in shutting off the heat just when we are so close to a settlement," I replied. "We cannot tolerate their jeopardizing the health of our people. If the corporation will turn on the heat, we will close the windows."

The Governor shook his head. "Mr. Mortimer, don't you think it is asking a lot to have the corporation furnish heat while your people occupy their property?"

He left me and went to talk to Knudsen about the matter. Knudsen promised to turn the heat back on. Thereupon I called Travis, and said, "Bob, they are going to turn the heat on, so when you hear it come back into the radiators, be sure to close the windows." Travis promised to do so. Fifteen minutes later, the Governor again came to me and said, "Mr. Mortimer, the heat has been turned on but the windows are still open." I phoned Travis once more and asked him why the windows were still open. "The damned chain slipped off the pulley," Bob explained, "but a man is fixing it." Thus ended the episode of the open windows.

There were still three remaining matters in the dispute to be handled. About 5:00 P.M., corporation attorney Smith came to Lewis's bedside and once again raised the question of a thirty-day contract. Lewis arose on his elbow, and in his most sonorous voice asked, "But, you want your plants to reopen, do you not?" Smith replied, "Yes, yes, of course!" "Well, then, it is six months!" Lewis said, turning his back on Smith. The latter stood looking at Lewis for a few moments. "Very well, then, Mr. Lewis," he said, and left the room.

Mr. Knudsen and I went into an adjoining room, and before we sat down, he said to me, "Mr. Mortimer, let your people wear a button, ten buttons, a hundred buttons, a thousand buttons, I don't care a damn. Let us get back to making automobiles."

Knudsen was thoroughly disgusted with all the interminable legal arguments. He wanted to get back to the practical things of life. After consultation with Bob Travis and Henry Kraus, I had prepared a list of the seventeen plants to be included in the contract. There was some slight argument about Guide Lamp, but this was quickly decided in our favor. Knudsen readily agreed to the list I gave him, and the negotiations were over. The great victory of the GM sit-downers was officially sealed. . . .

2
THE MANY AND THE FEW
Henry Kraus

Kraus, a writer affiliated with the Communist Party, was deeply involved in the planning and execution of the Flint sit-down strike. The account of it he wrote years later (the fol-

lowing passage is from the second edition of 1985) is the best we have. The fascinating details he provides fleshes out Wyndham Mortimer's synoptic view. Kraus was for a while editor of the United Auto Workers newspaper.

Everybody liked Bob Travis, a personable young organizer from Toledo. Though still on the bright side of thirty, he had close to a decade of automobile production experience behind him. Strictly the extrovert, the depression had given Travis a serious turn, sobering his get-rich-quick dreams which had prior to 1929 inspired so many American youths. During the violent Toledo-Autolite strike in 1934, though employed at the Chevrolet factory, Travis had gone down to the other plant to have a look. When he arrived a fight was on with the militia who had driven the pickets from the factory gates. Darting from behind telephone poles, the pickets whipped stones down the hill. The troops retreated and the pickets ran forward. Travis knew little about the issues of the strike but suddenly the resentment of blasted hopes, of five years of misery and inadequacy, rose up in him and he began running with the strikers toward the factory.

He was a union man thereafter, becoming active in the organization of his own plant and in the strike there the following year, when the first unequivocal victory against a General Motors unit by a union was recorded. It was a fitting background for his new assignment and the young organizer soon proved that the general good opinion that was had of him was not misplaced. But the Flint stool-pigeons were given a rude awakening when on Travis's arrival he immediately let it be known that Mortimer's entire organization plan—including the methods of secrecy to which they so strenuously objected—would be retained intact. . . .

The secret union nucleus at Fisher One . . . included an exceptional group of men whose presence in the plant at the particular time was one of those lucky "breaks" which helped bring the union's stupendous task into the realm of possibility. At the center of the group were three friends—Bud Simons, Walter Moore and Joe Devitt—political left-wingers who would undoubtedly have been barred from membership as "Reds" if President Minzey and the old union clique had been allowed to "investigate" them. Fortunately for the union's future this did not occur.

Like the majority of Flint workers the three friends stemmed from the land, all being sons of small farmers. Simons came from southern Indiana, Devitt from South Dakota and Moore from Montcalm County, Michigan. Later events threw Simons into greatest prominence but the other men always remained a strong support to their excitable friend, Moore particularly often pulling him out of hot water. Part of Simons's difficulty with people was his pride. It was a trait that had early manifested itself and finally launched him on a wayward career. . . .

Bud Simons and his friends greeted the opening of the union drive in Flint with a burst of activity. Working fervently though carefully, they laid the union foundations in their own departments and moved slowly outward. Included with the early converts were Harry Van Nocker, Jay Green, Clayton Carpenter, Vic Van Etten and others, all later active in the strike. Among the women Marie Schlacter and Pat Wiseman were promptly involved. First steps were confined to such things as pasting stickers on the bodies. Foremen tried to spot these and scraped them off but that in itself was a dramatic admission of the union's existence in the plant. And often one of the stickers with a leading slogan on it would go down the entire line, silently regarded by the workers.

The first break in the shop occurred among a group of non-union tinners. The management by a typical speedup procedure that was very much used that season had withdrawn one man from a team of five and told the four remaining men that they would have to turn out the same amount of work. Bud Simons got wind of this and began working quietly on the tinners. Finally they hung up their torches and went into the office to protest. Simons arranged to see them outside at lunch time. He took a flyer.

"Now look," he told them, "I don't know any of you guys from Adam but I think I can trust you. I'm the union organizer in this shop."

Immediately they wanted to know more about it.

"Well, to be frank with you we aren't so strong yet but we're building right along," Simons went on. "Our idea is to work on grievances just like yours. You know as well as I do that things aren't what they ought to be in this plant. The bosses do anything they please and we've got to take it. That's all going to change when the union comes in here."

The four fellows agreed to come to a meeting at Simons's home the next day. He had most of the other union men from the shop there to make an impression. At a second meeting the original four boys brought eleven others with them. Bob Travis thought the number was getting too big to be safe, so he called the next meeting in some fellow's basement. To disarm any spies that might have got in, the place was kept dark except for a single candle which added more romance than visibility. The men really went for the atmosphere of mystery.

Travis talked to them at length about their problems, about the speedup and the other conditions. Then he told them in concrete detail what had been done in his plant, Toledo-Chevrolet, and how. The men were deeply interested, especially in the story of the 1935 strike in Travis's plant. The "atmosphere" undoubtedly helped also. They listened as though hypnotized. . . .

When the two Perkins boys came to work the next evening they found their cards missing from the rack. In their places were tell-tale notices: "Report to the employment office." They went and sure enough there was their money waiting for them. But the union had anticipated this contingency. The committee had talked the situation over with Travis the night before, after the end of the shift. It was decided that this would be an excellent opportunity to come out into the open. If anyone was victimized over the little stoppage the entire "body-in-white"* department must be closed down.

When the two brothers showed Simons and the other committee members their red cards the latter ran up to the department and spread the word:

"The Perkins boys were fired! Nobody starts working!"

The whistle blew. Every man in the department stood at his station, a deep, significant tenseness in him. The foreman pushed the button and the skeleton bodies, already partly assembled when they got to this point, began to rumble forward. But no one lifted a hand. All eyes were turned to Simons who stood out in the aisle by himself.

The bosses ran about like mad.

"Whatsamatter? Whatsamatter? Get to work!" they shouted.

But the men acted as though they never heard them. One or two of them couldn't stand the tension. Habit was deep in them and it was like physical agony for them to see the bodies pass untouched. They grabbed their tools and chased after them. "Rat! Rat!" the men growled without moving and the others came to their senses.

The superintendent stopped by the "bow-men."

"You're to blame for this!" he snarled.

"So what if we are?" little Joe Urban, the Italian, cried, overflowing with pride. "You ain't running your line, are you?"

That was altogether too much. The superintendent grabbed Joe and started for the office with him. The two went down along the entire line, while the men stood rigid as though awaiting the word of command. It was like that because they were organized but their organization only went that far and no further. What now?

Simons, a torch-solderer, was almost at the end of the line. He too was momentarily held in vise by the superintendent's overt act of authority. The latter had dragged Joe Urban past him when he finally found presence of mind to call out:

"Hey, Teefee, where you going?"

It was spoken in just an ordinary conversational tone and the other was taken so aback he answered the really impertinent question.

"I'm taking him to the office to have a little talk with him." Then suddenly he realized and got mad. "Say, I think I'll take you along too!"

That was his mistake.

"No you won't!" Simons said calmly.

"Oh yes I will!" and he took hold of his shirt.

Simons yanked himself loose.

And suddenly at this simple act of insurgence Teefee realized his danger.

---

*Where the main welding and soldering work of the assembly process takes place.

He seemed to become acutely conscious of the long line of silent men and felt the threat of their potential strength. They had been transformed into something he had never known before and over which he no longer had any command. He let loose of Simons and started off again with Joe Urban, hastening his pace. Simons yelled:

"Come on, fellows, don't let them fire little Joe!"

About a dozen boys shot out of the line and started after Teefee. The superintendent dropped Joe like a hot poker and deer-footed it for the door. The men returned to their places and all stood waiting. Now what? The next move was the company's. The moment tingled with expectancy.

Teefee returned shortly, accompanied by Bill Lynch, the assistant plant manager. Lynch was a friendly sort of person and was liked by the men. He went straight to Simons.

"I hear we've got trouble here," he said in a chatty way. "What are we going to do about it?"

"I think we'll get a committee together and go in and see Parker," Simons replied.

Lynch agreed. So Simons began picking the solid men out as had been prearranged. The foreman tried to smuggle in a couple of company-minded individuals, so Simons chose a group of no less than eighteen to make sure that the scrappers would outnumber the others. Walt Moore went with him but Joe Devitt remained behind to see that the bosses didn't try any monkeyshines. The others headed for the office where Evan Parker, the plant manager, greeted them as smooth as silk.

"You can smoke if you want to, boys," he said as he bid them to take the available chairs. "Well, what seems to be the trouble here? We ought to be able to settle this thing."

"Mr. Parker, it's the speedup the boys are complaining about," Simons said, taking the lead. "It's absolutely beyond human endurance. And now we've organized ourselves into a union. It's the union you're talking to right now, Mr. Parker."

"Why that's perfectly all right, boys," Parker said affably. "Whatever a man does outside the plant is his own business."

The men were almost bowled over by this manner. They had never known Parker as anything but a tough cold tomato with an army sergeant's style. He was clearly trying to play to the weaker boys on the committee and began asking them leading questions. Simons or Walt Moore would try to break in and answer for them.

"Now I didn't ask you," Parker would say, "you can talk when it's your turn!" In this way he sought to split the committee up into so many individuals. Simons realized he had to put an end to that quickly.

"We might as well quit talking right now, Mr. Parker," he said, putting on a tough act. "Those men have got to go back and that's all there is to it!"

"That's what you say," Parker snapped back.

"No, that's what the men say. You can go out and see for yourself. Nobody is going to work until that happens."

Parker knew that was true. Joe Devitt and several other good men who had been left behind were seeing to that. The plant manager seemed to soften again. All right, he said, he'd agree to take the two men back if he found their attitude was okay.

"Who's to judge that?" Simons asked.

"I will, of course!"

"Uh-uh!" Simons smiled and shook his head.

The thing bogged down again. Finally Parker said the Perkins brothers could return unconditionally on Monday. This was Friday night and they'd already gone home so there was no point holding up thousands of men until they could be found and brought back. To make this arrangement final he agreed that the workers in the department would get paid for the time lost in the stoppage. But Simons held fast to the original demand. Who knew what might happen until Monday? The Perkins fellows would have to be back on the line that night or the entire incident might turn out a flop.

"They go back tonight," he insisted.

Parker was fit to be tied. What was this? Never before in his life had he seen anything like it!

"Those boys have left!" he shouted. "It might take hours to get them back. Are you going to keep the lines tied up all that time?"

"We'll see what the men say," Simons replied, realizing that a little rank-and-file backing would not be out of the way. The committee rose and started back for the shop.

As they entered, a zealous foreman preceded them, hollering: "Everybody back to work!" The men dashed for their places.

Simons jumped onto a bench.

"Wait a minute!" he shouted. The men crowded around him. He waited until they were all there and then told them in full detail of the discussion in the office. Courage visibly mounted into the men's faces as they heard of the unwavering manner in which their committee had acted in the dread presence itself.

"What are we going to do, fellows," Simons asked, "take the company's word and go back to work or wait 'til the Perkins boys are right there at their jobs?"

"Bring them back first!" Walt Moore and Joe Devitt began yelling and the whole crowd took up the cry.

Simons seized the psychological moment to make it official.

"As many's in favor of bringing the Perkins boys back before we go to work, say Aye!" There was a roar in answer. "Opposed, Nay!" Only a few timid voices sounded—those of the company men and the foremen who had been circulating among the workers trying to influence them to go back to work. Simons turned to them.

"There you are," he said.

One of the foremen had taken out pencil and paper and after the vote he went around recording names. "You want to go to work?" he asked each of the men. Finally he came to one chap who stuck his chin out and said loudly: "Emphatically not!" which made the rest of the boys laugh and settled the issue.

Mr. Parker got the news and decided to terminate the matter as swiftly as possible. He contacted the police and asked them to bring the Perkins boys in. . . .

With the Cleveland plant struck, the union's strategy problems were very much simplified. A further lucky "break," coming this time also on a silver platter from the company, facilitated the confirmation of the second main feature of the strike plan. On the evening of December 30, or only two days following the beginning of the Cleveland strike, Bob Travis received a phone call from "Chink" Ananich, one of the Fisher One boys. "Chink" was working on the swing shift and had slipped out of the plant to make his important announcement.

"They're moving dies out, Bob!" he said excitedly.

"You sure?"

"Yeah! The boys in the press room working near the doors by the railroad dock say they got crank press dies on some trucks and they're loading a flock of freight cars."

Travis made his mind up instantaneously.

"Okay! They're asking for it!" he said almost gayly. "Tell the boys stewards' meeting at lunch time. Bring everybody down."

There is hardly anything about which a unionist is more sensitive than on the subject of the "runaway shop." It is one of the oldest of tactics used against organization efforts. In Travis's own experience, besides, the memory was fresh of how General Motors had slipped two-thirds of the jobs right from under his co-workers at Toledo-Chevrolet in revenge for the defeat it had sustained in May 1935. Present always to his mind were the confusion and suffering and despair that this act had caused, and the picture of fathers of families coming to the union office and pleading that the organization do something to get their jobs back. Those who were still working felt as though they were taking the bread out of the others' mouths. The role played by Travis in the Flint strike and by many volunteers who later came up from his local to engage in it was directly traceable to this tragic experience and to the desire of the victims to pay off the responsible corporation in the coin of union solidarity.

After "Chink" Ananich hung up, Travis called the Fisher One union office.

"Put the flicker on," he told the girl.

There was a big red 200-watt bulb over the front of the office which was right across from the plant. The boys near the windows inside the factory had instructions to give a look over every so often. If the flicker was on that meant something was up and that there would be a meeting. At 8 P.M. the workers streamed out of the plant for "lunch hour." In four minutes the union hall was filled with an excited crowd of men. The report of the moving of the dies had evidently spread everywhere by this time. Everybody's mind seemed made up before even a word was spoken. Travis got right down to brass tacks.

"Boys, we'll make this snappy," he said. "I understand there's something happening over there on the press room dock."

"That's right," one of the men called out, "they're taking dies out of the press room. They got four or five cars lined up there."

The men from the die room substantiated this.

"Well, what are we going to do about it?" Travis asked, looking slowly about the room.

There was a cold sort of pause. A chap raised his hand and stood up.

"Well, them's our jobs," he said quietly. "We want them left right here in Flint."

"That's right!" several others exclaimed.

"Boys," Travis said, still holding himself back, "I'm not going to tell you what you ought to do. That ought to be plain enough to you if you want to protect your jobs. In my plant in Toledo, General Motors walked off with 1,500 jobs a year ago and in Cleveland the Fisher Body boys struck just Monday to save theirs. What do you want to do?"

"Shut her down! Shut the goddam plant!"

The cry was taken up by the whole room until it was nothing but one big shout.

"Okay, fellows, that's what I wanted to hear you say. Now the important thing to remember from here on out is—discipline. You can't have too much of it in a strike, especially at the beginning. Roy and I will come in after you've got the plant down and help you get everything organized. Bud and the rest of the committee will be in charge. You'll have to enlarge the committee so as to get representation on it from all departments. Remember, absolutely no liquor. And tell the girls in cut-and-sew to go home and come around to the Pengelly headquarters tomorrow morning. We'll have plenty of work for them to do. Okay, good luck!"

"Everybody stays in till the warning whistle!" I yelled from the door.

"That's right," Travis said. "We don't want any stooges tipping the company off ahead of time."

The men stood still facing the door. It was like trying to chain a natural force. They couldn't hold back and began crowding forward. Then suddenly they broke through the door and made a race for the plant gates, running in every direction toward the quarter-mile building front which bordered the main highway from Detroit.

We waited outside, anxiously watching the windows. The starting whistle blew. We listened intently. There was no responsive throb. Was it right? we asked ourselves, looking at each other. Had they pulled it off?

"Here's where the fight begins," Travis said between tight lips as we stamped nervously on the cold pavement.

But there was no sign of any untoward activity inside the plant. Several minutes passed. Then suddenly a third-floor window was flung open and there was "Chink" Ananich waving his arms.

"Hooray, Bob! She's ours!"

Then other windows went up and smiling workers gathered about them.

"Was there any trouble?" we shouted.

"Naw!"

A little later the girls came out, wearing overalls and working caps. And there was a straggling male here and there. But the vast majority of the three thousand men remained voluntarily inside the plant that first night. . . .

A number of women workers at Fisher One heeded Bob Travis's call and came down to union headquarters at the Pengelly building the morning after the strike started. But not so Pat Wiseman who had wanted to sit in like the men and was angered at the discrimination of being ordered out. Heck, for six years she had done men's work in the plant, most of the time as a striper when she had carried the heavy apparatus on her hips like any man, working near the baking furnaces where even those "superior males" had sometimes toppled over in a faint. Feminine? Pat knew it was all hokum but one day she got the few other girls who were strong enough to do this work to try some of that sentiment stuff on the superintendent. Every time he passed nearby they would start weeping—tears came easy amid the heat and fumes and pain of excessive physical exertion—but it took a long time before the superintendent's heart was touched.

Pat, whose deep voice was eventually to command as much respect as that of any male in the union's councils, spurned such womanish work as kitchen duty during the strike. If she couldn't sit in she'd picket outside and she never missed a day. Once a male companion on the token line which was maintained throughout the strike asked her jokingly what she expected to get out of it, a union job?

"I never see a woman take such a lead before," he said.

"I'll tell you why I'm doing it," Pat snapped back, her nostrils flaring. "You're getting fifteen dollars a week more than I am for the same number of hours and I'll be damned if I don't work as hard as you do!"

Other Fisher One women, including many wives of strikers, accepted assignments in the kitchen without complaint. Donna Devitt, Hazel Simons and a few others had union backgrounds to go by. But many more could look back only at church or social activities, the Ladies' Aid and sewing clubs. It was often difficult to make the transition to the new type of organization where responsibility was so much greater, where so much more depended on one's efforts.

Bessie Taylor, whose husband, Lawrence, worked at Fisher One, and their friends the Brubakers and the Parrishes had all become interested in the union at the same time. Taylor himself had long been union conscious, having worked as a youth in the mines of Indiana. After coming to Flint he judged the General Motors city as "the scabbiest hole in the country" and for years he talked of leaving it. But where to? When he stayed in the plant that first night, his wife came down the following morning to see what it was all about.

Bessie asked if he couldn't come home that night at least since it was New Year's Eve and they had invited some friends.

"No," Lawrence replied firmly. "Tell them to accept my hospitality but that I have some important work on." He smiled. "You can tell them to save one toast for me."

The forbearance was like a symbol of a new existence, in which immediate pleasure must give way to the demands of loyalty and self-sacrifice. But it was the goal that made such relinquishment meaningful. Lawrence Taylor foresaw a time of dignity and self-respect under the aegis of the union.

"Honey," he would tell his wife, "when I walk out of this factory it'll be through the front door."

And Bessie Taylor, fully agreeing, took her place among those working for the prideful vision. . . .

Communism and the CIO

LABOR RADICAL
Len DeCaux

In this memoir of 1970, a Communist who rose to high place in the nascent CIO—editor of its newspaper—tells the extraordinary tale of how the United Steel Workers Union came to dominate the industry. (SWOC refers to the Steel Workers Organizing Committee, the embryo from which the union was formed.) In the process DeCaux gives a useful rundown of the Communist contribution to the union movement of the period.

The GM strike victory made its impact on all fronts. The UAW knocked off Chrysler, and hundreds of thousands joined its ranks. Workers everywhere—AFL, CIO, and unorganized—began sitting down. Early in 1937, sitdowns were pulled by hosiery, shoe, hotel, restaurant, steel, transport, tobacco workers; by seamen, shipbuilders, clerks, printers, pressmen, janitors, electricians; by Woolworth store girls, rug weavers, watchmakers, garbage collectors; by Postal and Western Union messengers, farm hands, bedmakers, food packers, movie operators, gravediggers.

Biggest beneficiary of the GM victory was SWOC. Myron Taylor began

secret talks with John L. Lewis during the GM sit-down. The outcome of
these talks strongly influenced Wall Street strategists then consulting on
overall policy toward unionism. Once GM had accorded union recognition
in mid-February, U.S. Steel followed, on February 28; and on March 2,
1937, it signed an agreement with SWOC.

This opened still wider the union floodgates opened by the GM strike.
Hundreds of thousands more workers joined CIO's now million-man ranks,
and employers everywhere started signing up. The U.S. Supreme Court
caught the spirit, and, in April 1937, upheld the Wagner Labor Relations act.

Many AFL and independent unions—prompted by their lefts—began
swinging into CIO. National Maritime Union; AFL Fur Workers; Transport
Workers (from Machinists to CIO); also machine workers (from Machinists
to UE), hosiery, leather, boot-shoe, office, optical workers, technicians,
retail clerks, inland-boatmen. West coast longshoremen and wood-workers
were also on the way.

Then, late in May 1937, when it seemed nothing could stop the CIO, a
mighty capitalist counteroffensive was mounted—not against the militant
leftish rank-and-file unions, but against CIO's richest, most respectable,
most from-on-top, most collaborating of new unions, the SWOC.

Steel had a background of labor struggle unmatched by the infant auto indus-
try—from Homestead to the 1919 national strike led by William Z. Foster.
But in drafting some of the first declarations of CIO's steel drive—before
SWOC's own setup took over—I found 1919 was out of bounds.

There were a number of reasons. That drive had failed to establish a permanent union; SWOC was to be a Success Story. AFL craft leaders had
divided and betrayed the last campaign; this one was CIO—all together in
one industrial union. The earlier drive had led to a national strike; SWOC
hoped to organize without strikes—and did in fact sign U.S. Steel without
one. The 1919 effort had been a regular class struggle with Wall Street,
Washington, state, and city governments using armed force, police, press,
scabs, goons. SWOC frowned on the class struggle idea. Were not labor's
friends in power? Franklin D. Roosevelt in the White House, his pal Mayor
Kelly in Chicago City Hall, New Deal governors and mayors all around.

SWOC leaders particularly wanted to liquidate the memory of the last
drive's leader, William Z. Foster. He was now at the head of the Communist
party, which some of his ablest steel organizers had also joined. Communists
had kept alive some union activity. They had influence among foreign-born
steelworkers, some following among the black. They had promoted a short-
lived Steel & Metal Workers Industrial Union and been active in 1933–35
efforts to organize through the AFL.

The SWOC leaders, coming mostly from coal, had little background and
few contacts in steel. They found the ready help of the communists invaluable. Foster, who should know, wrote later that 60 of the first organizers

hired by SWOC were members of the Communist party. Bill Gebert, a party leader, was liaison man and in charge of mobilizing foreign-born groups.

Rallying all their supporters and contacts, the communists threw themselves into the campaign more unconditionally and self-effacingly than is usual in politics. SWOC used their help and, rather underhandedly, tried to rub out their faces completely. It put communist steelworkers on the payroll, if needed, but each one was a marked man, closely watched at all times and dispensed with as soon as possible. Any move he might seem to make to win personal following would be countered quickly by undercover redbaiting or slander, by transfer to other territory, or by firing. . . .

Labor bureaucracy had closed the door to the young in spirit, the questioning, the rebellious. It co-opted dull schemers, who did as they were told and watched their step—so domesticated that some of the now toothless old tigers who raised them from cubs could blush for them.

CIO upset this closed-door pattern. It "opened the door to the communists"—as John P. Frey put it. Not in older-line unions like UMW, ACW, ILGWU, nor in their SWOC and TWOG. But in newcomer unions—more on their own—new-type leaders were everywhere on top.

Those of UE were typical. Young men like brainy Julius Emspak; nervous, restless, organizing Jim Matles; lively, showy Jimmy Carey. UAW's Homer Martin was more oddball than new-type—a Fidgety Phil who couldn't sit still. But Wyndham Mortimer was of the new type. So too, in different ways, darkly shy George Addes and that great big, new-boy Dick Frankensteen. Walter Reuther, a new-typer too, then leftish like Carey, was not yet on top—though on his way.

From the west, and from the left, a handsome Harry and a hardnosed one: Harold Pritchett of Woodworkers, Harry Bridges of Longshoremen. Big Joe Curran of Maritime was another lefty—red-rough to the eye, slick-smooth to the right touch. More colorfast, sailor Blacky (Ferdinand N.) Myers, eager, alert, outer.

"Red Mike" Quill of Transport personalized redness to the crowd. More so than soft-spoken Ben Gold of Fur, the most advertised communist. Quill featured Irish wit and blarney, with a blackthorn cane for shillelagh. His fiery retorts to redbaiters delighted the left. "I'd rather be a red to the rats," said he, "than a rat to the reds." Flanking Quill and also on the left, solid Austin Hogan and fluid John Santo—the latter with Irish-American brogue imposed on native Hungarian accent.

New-typers too, and on the left, were Don Henderson of Cannery, Mervyn Rathborne and Joe Selly of Communications, Reid Robinson of Mine-Mill. Soon to come from Organizing Committees were Grant Oakes, Joe Weber, Gerald Fielde, of Farm Equipment; Don Harris and Henry Johnson (one of CIO's rare black leaders) from Packinghouse.

The white-collar leaders differed little from the blue collars. Some college was now more common for all, and the mental strife of leftism did more than formal education to sharpen wits and broaden horizons. Big, bearlike Broun of the Newspaper Guild was different from anyone anywhere, but not his slim sidekick Jonathan Eddy. Jake Baker, of Federal Workers, was a bit tweedy, but Eleanor Nelson (rare woman CIO leader), Art Stein, Henry Rhine, of Federal, were typical new-unionists. So too Abe Flaxer and Henry Wenning, of State-County-Municipal; Lewis Alan Berne, of Architects-Engineers; Napoleonic little Lewis Merrill, of the Office Workers—in some ways a ringer for less officy Arthur Osman, head of Retail's wholesale empire in New York.

Up to Osman, I've listed only international or national union leaders who were, or might have been, at CIO's 1937 conference. There were hundreds of other new-typers and leftists on other levels—heads of state or local movements, or of parts of all but CIO's most old-line unions.

Many of these new-typers were trained in the communist movement as I knew it—a movement, that is, of militant unemployed; of union pioneers before New Deal permitted or CIO paid salaries; of rebels against corrupt inaction or reaction in AFL unions. Like many new radicals of the sixties, they were young-minded persons coming out of their shells and relating to the whole world around.

Not all the new-typers were communists, or sympathetic, though many were. Not all were leftist enough to work with the communists, though most did. Some were in-again-out-again, on-again-off-again, some factionally hostile. All were close enough to the left to know the score. . . .

An Illustration

AMERICAN TRAGEDY
Philip Evergood

After the 1937 Memorial Day massacre of ten striking steel workers in East Chicago, Evergood intended to paint a picture à la Guernica to commemorate it. "American Tragedy" was never done, but he left this extraordinary pencil study of it.

American Writers' Congress

It was clear at the October 1934 convention of the John Reed Clubs that their days were numbered, that the Party intended to replace their militancy with something like a Popular Front approach. And so in January 1935 the call for a writers' congress went out above the names of such eminent non-Communists (sympathizers though they were) as Theodore Dreiser, Lincoln Steffens, James T. Farrell, and Erskine Caldwell. Four months later more than two hundred writers met in New York to hear speeches, hold discussions, and create a permanent organization. Following are excerpts from three of the talks they heard. Kenneth Burke's talk, we should note, came in for a good deal of criticism from Communist literary spokesmen because of his suggestion that the Party could broaden its appeal by agitating in the name of the people rather than in that of the working class alone. This brilliant iconoclast was a step ahead of the Party.

1

THE WRITER AS TECHNICIAN
John Dos Passos

At this particular moment in history, when machinery and institutions have so outgrown the ability of the mind to dominate them, we need bold and original thought more than ever. It is the business of writers to supply that thought, and not to make of themselves figureheads in political conflicts. I don't mean that a writer hasn't an obligation, like any other citizen, to take part if he can in the struggle against oppression, but that his function as a citizen and his function as a technician are different, although the eventual end aimed at may in both cases be the same.

To fight oppression, and to work as best we can for a sane organization of society, we do not have to abandon the state of mind of freedom. If we do that we are letting the same thuggery in by the back door that we are fighting off in front of the house. I don't see how it is possible to organize effectively for liberty and the humane values of life without protecting and demanding during every minute of the fight the liberties of investigation, speech and discussion that are the greatest part of the ends of the struggle. In any organization a man gives up his liberty of action. That is necessary discipline. But if men give up their freedom of thought what follows is boss rule thuggery and administrative stagnation. It is easy to be carried away by the temporary effectiveness of boss rule, but it has always ended, in small things and in great, in leaving its victims stranded bloodless and rotten, with all the problems of a living society of free men unsolved. The dilemma that faces honest technicians all over the world today is how to combat the imperial and bureaucratic tendencies of the groups whose aims they believe in, without giving aid and comfort to the enemy. By the nature of his function as a technician, the writer finds himself in the dangerous and uncomfortable front line of this struggle.

In such a position a man is exposed to crossfire and is as likely to be mowed down by his friends as his enemies. The writer has to face that. His only safety lies in the fact that the work of an able technician cannot be replaced. It is of use and a pleasure to mankind. If it weren't for that fact, reluctantly recognized, but everywhere and always recognized, the whole tribe of doubters, inventors and discoverers would have been so often wiped out that the race would have ceased to produce types with those peculiar traits.

It's an old saying, but a very apt one, that a writer writes not to be saved but to be damned.

I feel that American writers who want to do the most valuable kind of work will find themselves trying to discover the deep currents of historical change under the surface of opinions, orthodoxies, heresies, gossip and the journalistic garbage of the day. They will find that they have to keep their attention fixed on the simple real needs of men and women. A writer can be a propagandist in the most limited sense of the word, or use his abilities for partisan invective or personal vituperation, but the living material out of which his work is built must be what used to be known as the humanities: the need for clean truth and sharply whittled exactitudes, men's instincts and compulsions and hungers and thirsts. Even if he's to be killed the next minute a man has to be cool and dispassionate while he's aiming his gun.

There is no escaping the fact that if you are a writer you are dealing with the humanities, with the language of all the men of your speech of your generation, with their traditions of the past and their feelings and perceptions. No matter from how narrow a set of convictions you start, you will find yourself in your effort to probe deeper and deeper into men and events as you find them, less and less able to work with the minute prescriptions of doctrine; and you will find more and more that you are on the side of the men, women and children alive right now against all the contraptions and organizations, however magnificent their aims may be, that bedevil them; and that you are on the side, not with phrases or opinions, but really and truly, of liberty, fraternity, and humanity. The words are old and dusty and hung with the dirty bunting of a thousand crooked orations, but underneath they are still sound. What men once meant by these words needs defenders today. And if those who have, in all kinds of direct and devious ways, stood up for them throughout history do not come out for them now to defend them against the thuggery of the bosses and the zeal of the administrators, the world will be an even worse place for men, women and children to live in than it is at present. . . .

2

REVOLUTIONARY SYMBOLISM IN AMERICA

Kenneth Burke

When considering how people have cooperated, in either conservative or revolutionary movements of the past, we find that there is always some unifying principle about which their attachments as a group are polarized. I do not refer to such mere insignia as tricolor, hammer and sickle, swastika, crucifix, or totem pole—but to the subtle complex of emotions and attitudes for which such insignia are little more than the merest labels.

From a strictly materialistic point of view, such symbols are pure nonsense. Food, tools, shelter, productive technique—these things are the "realest" part of our vocabulary; they correspond to objects that can be seen and felt, and to operations that can be clearly and obviously performed. But the communal relationships by which a group is bound, do not possess such primary reality. However vital they are in promoting historic processes, they are "myths," quite as the gods of Homer were myths. To search for them critically is to dissolve them, while a few rudimentary "realities" take their place. If you find a man attached to some cause, and keep pressing him with questions, he will not be able to point out the nature of his attachment in the way he might if you asked him to point to his house. Yet for all the illusive character of his attachment, we know that it may be a genuine social motive behind his actions.

"Myths" may be wrong, or they may be used to bad ends—but they cannot be dispensed with. In the last analysis, they are our basic psychological tools for working together. A hammer is a carpenter's tool; a wrench is a mechanic's tool; and a "myth" is the social tool for welding the sense of interrelationship by which the carpenter and the mechanic, though differently occupied, can work together for common social ends. In this sense a myth that works well is as real as food, tools, and shelter are. As compared with the reality of material objects, however, we might say that the myth deals with a *secondary* order of reality. Totem, race, godhead, nationality, class, lodge, guild—all such are the "myths" that have made various ranges and kinds of social cooperation possible. They are not "illusions," since they perform a very real and necessary social function in the organizing of the mind. But they may look illusory when they survive as fossils from the situations for which they were adapted into changed situations for which they are not adapted. . . .

The Communists generally focus their scheme of allegiance about the symbol of the worker, which they would put in the place of a misused nationalism as the polarizing device about which our present attempts at historic cooperation should cluster. Accordingly, my paper will discuss this symbol, and to what extent it fulfills the conditions of attachment. I should also emphasize the fact that I shall consider this matter *purely from the standpoint of propaganda*. It may be that the needs of the propagandist are not wholly identical with the needs of the organizer. Insofar as a writer really is a propagandist, not merely writing work that will be applauded by his allies, convincing the already convinced, but actually moving forward like a pioneer into outlying areas of the public and bringing them the first favorable impressions of his doctrine, the nature of his trade may give rise to special symbolic requirements. Accordingly, it is the *propaganda* aspect of the symbol that I shall center upon—considering the symbol particularly as a device for spreading the areas of allegiance.

In the first place, I assume that a symbol must embody an *ideal*. The symbol appeals to us as an incentive because it suggests traits which we should like to share. Yet there are few people who really want to work, let us say, as a human cog in an automobile factory, or as gatherers of vegetables on a big truck farm. Such rigorous ways of life enlist our *sympathies*, but not our *ambitions*. Our ideal is as far as possible to *eliminate* such kinds of work, or to reduce its strenuousness to a minimum. Some people, living overly sedentary lives, may like to read of harsh physical activity (as they once enjoyed Wild West fiction)—but Hollywood knows only too well that the people engaged in such kinds of effort are vitalized mainly by some vague hope that they may some day escape it. "Adult education" in capitalist America today is centered in the efforts of our economic mercenaries (our advertising men and sales organizations) to create a maximum desire for commodities consumed under expensive conditions—and Hollywood appeals to the worker mainly by picturing the qualities of life in which this commercially stimulated desire is gratified. The question arises: Is the symbol of the worker accurately attuned to us, as so conditioned by the reactionary forces in control of our main educational channels?

I tentatively suggest that it is not. By this I do not mean that a proletarian emphasis should be dropped from revolutionary books. The rigors of the worker must certainly continue to form a major part of revolutionary symbolism, if only for the reason that here the worst features of capitalist exploitation are concentrated. But the basic symbol, it seems to me, should be focused somewhat differently. Fortunately, I am not forced to advocate any great change—though I do think that the shift I propose, while minor in itself, leads in the end to quite different emphases in our modes of propaganda. The symbol I should plead for, as more basic, more of an ideal incentive, than that of the worker, is that of "the people." In suggesting that "the people," rather than "the worker," rate highest in our hierarchy of symbols, I suppose I am suggesting fundamentally that one cannot extend the doctrine of revolutionary thought among the lower middle class without using middle-class values—just as the Church invariably converted pagans by making the local deities into saints. I should also point out that we are very close to this symbol of "the people" in our term "the masses," which is embodied in the title of the leading radical magazine. But I think that the term "the people" is closer to our folkways than is the corresponding term, "the masses," both in spontaneous popular usage and as stimulated by our political demagogues. I should add that, in an interview published recently in the New York *World-Telegram*, Clarence Hathaway frequently used a compound of the two in the form: "the masses of the people."

The symbol of "the people," as distinct from the proletarian symbol, also has the tactical advantage of pointing more definitely in the direction of unity (which in itself is a sound psychological tendency, for all that it is now misused by nationalists to mask the conditions of disunity). It contains the *ideal*, the ultimate *classless* feature which the revolution would bring about—and for this reason seems richer as a symbol of allegiance. It can borrow the advantages of nationalistic conditioning, and at the same time be used to combat the forces that hide their class prerogatives behind a communal ideology. . . .

I believe that the symbol of "the people" makes more naturally for such *propaganda by inclusion* than does the strictly proletarian symbol (which makes naturally for a *propaganda by exclusion*, a tendency to eliminate from one's work all that does not deal specifically with the realities of the workers' oppression—and which, by my thesis, cannot for this reason engage even the full allegiance of the workers themselves). And since the symbol of "the people" contains connotations both of oppression and of unity, it seems better than the exclusively proletarian one as a psychological bridge for linking the two conflicting aspects of a transitional, revolutionary era, which is Janus-faced, looking both forward and back. I recognize that my suggestion bears the telltale stamp of my class, the petty bourgeoisie. And I should not dare to make it, except for a belief that it is vitally important to enlist the allegiance of this class. But I should point out, in closing, that there are really two features in my present paper, and although I think that they *tend* to be interconnected, they may not *necessarily* be. I make this point because I hope that, even if my hearers may resist my first suggestion (and I see many just grounds for their doing so), they may still accept the second. The first was that we take "the people" rather than "the worker" as our basic symbol of exhortation and allegiance. The second was that the imaginative writer seek to propagandize his cause by surrounding it with as full a cultural texture as he can manage, thus thinking of propaganda not as an oversimplified, literal, explicit writing of lawyer's briefs, but as a process of broadly and generally associating his political alignment with cultural awareness in the large. I consider the first suggestion important primarily because the restricted proletarian symbol *tends* to militate against the full use of propaganda by inclusion. But I should not like to make your acceptance of the second absolutely dependent upon your acceptance of the first. Some writers may be able to

dissociate them, and to surround the strictly proletarian symbol with sufficient richness of cultural ideals to make it appealing even as a symbol of allegiance for people who do not think of themselves primarily within the proletarian framework. But I still insist that their function as propagandists will
not be complete unless they do thus propagandize by inclusion, not confining themselves to a few schematic situations, but engaging the entire range
of our interests, even such interests as we might have at a time of industry
and peace.

3
To Negro Writers
Langston Hughes

There are certain practical things American Negro writers can do through
their work.

We can reveal to the Negro masses, from which we come, our potential
power to transform the now ugly face of the Southland into a region of peace
and plenty.

We can reveal to the white masses those Negro qualities which go beyond
the mere ability to laugh and sing and dance and make music, and which are
a part of the useful heritage that we place at the disposal of a future free
America.

Negro writers can seek to unite blacks and whites in our country, not on
the nebulous basis of an interracial meeting, or the shifting sands of religious
brotherhood, but on the *solid* ground of the daily working-class struggle to
wipe out, now and forever, all the old inequalities of the past.

Furthermore, by way of exposure, Negro writers can reveal in their novels, stories, poems, and articles:

The lovely grinning face of Philanthropy—which gives a million dollars
to a Jim Crow school, but not one job to a graduate of that school; which
builds a Negro hospital with second-rate equipment, then commands black
patients and student-doctors to go there whether they will or no; or which,
out of the kindness of its heart, erects yet another separate, segregated, shut-
off, Jim Crow YMCA.

Negro writers can expose those white labor leaders who keep their unions
closed against Negro workers and prevent the betterment of all workers.

We can expose, too, the sick-sweet smile of organized religion—which
lies about what it doesn't know, and about what it *does* know. And the half-
voodoo, half-clown, face of revivalism, dulling the mind with the clap of its
empty hands.

Expose, also, the false leadership that besets the Negro people—bought
and paid for leadership, owned by capital, afraid to open its mouth except in
the old conciliatory way so advantageous to the exploiters.

And all the economic roots of race hatred and race fear.

And the Contentment Tradition of the O-lovely-Negroes school of American fiction, which makes an ignorant black face and a Carolina head filled with superstition appear more desirable than a crown of gold; the jazz-band; and the O-so-gay writers who make of the Negro's poverty and misery a dusky funny paper.

And expose war. And the old My-Country-'Tis-of-Thee lie. And the colored American Legion posts strutting around talking about the privilege of dying for the noble Red, White and Blue, when they aren't even permitted the privilege of living for it. Or voting for it in Texas. Or working for it in the diplomatic service. Or even rising, like every other good little boy, from the log cabin to the White House.

White House is right!

Dear colored American Legion, you can swing from a lynching tree, uniform and all, with pleasure—and nobody'll fight for you. Don't you know that? Nobody even salutes you down South, dead or alive, medals or no medals, chevrons or not, no matter how many wars you've fought in.

Let Negro writers write about the irony and pathos of the *colored* American Legion.

"Salute, Mr. White Man!"

"Salute, hell! . . . You're a nigger."

Or would you rather write about the moon?

Sure, the moon still shines over Harlem. Shines over Scottsboro. Shines over Birmingham, too, I reckon. Shines over Cordie Cheek's grave, down South.

Write about the moon if you want to. Go ahead. This is a free country.

But there are certain very practical things American Negro writers can do. And must do. There's a song that says, "the time ain't long." That song is right. Something has got to change in America—and change soon. We must help that change to come.

The moon's still shining as poetically as ever, but all the stars on the flag are dull. (And the stripes, too.)

We want a new and better America, where there won't be any poor, where there won't be any more Jim Crow, where there won't be any lynchings, where there won't be any munition makers, where we won't need philanthropy, nor charity, nor the New Deal, nor Home Relief.

Second American Writers' Congress

Anti-Fascism was the theme of the Second Congress, which met in New York in May 1937. Party officials remained in the wings, content to see the number of writers who signed up with the League of American Writers swell into the hundreds. Hemingway, back from the Spanish front, was of course the star of the proceedings. Besides Hemingway, we have included two other speakers: *Newton Arvin, a scholar of American literature (his study of Melville is a classic), and Malcolm Cowley, literary critic and historian (his* Exile's Return *is still the best work on the expatriate American writers of the 1920s). We have also included an exchange with a Trotskyist writer who at the end bravely asked the audience a very pointed question.*

1
THE DEMOCRATIC TRADITION IN AMERICAN LETTERS
Newton Arvin

These Congresses represent a break, certainly, with the American tradition of individual action on the part of literary men or of action on their part simply in their general capacity as citizens. It is a break with that tradition, and a necessary break, for not until today—but today at last—have the things which as writers we stand for been quite flagrantly, quite undeniably, and quite disastrously threatened by the forces working toward coercion and inequality. A new and higher stage of the literary consciousness has been reached now that, for both defensive and constructive ends, American writers have come to recognize the advantages of common action; and we need neither expect nor wish to find precedent for it in the letter of our national inheritance.

The *spirit* of that inheritance is another matter, and if the form of these meetings and the organizations that emerge from them are without the verbal sanction of our history, the essential purposes that have led us to meet and to organize are purposes that, however modified and enlarged by time and experience, we have in common with a long series of men and women in all the generations of American literature. This is not the real reason, I know, why these purposes are worth struggling for: they are worth the struggle because they are good things in themselves. Yet it has become a commonplace in progressive literary circles—and it ought to have become a commonplace—that every ally must be pressed into service, that some of the most dependable allies are the writers of the past, and that our present aims are the culmination of a long native development. One could wish that the knee tribute paid to these commonplaces were more frequently paid than it is in solid and substantial ways. Liberal and radical writers as a group have not yet taken the lesson to heart, and the exploration of the national past is still too largely left to the takers of notes, to the G-men of scholarship, and to fascist-minded patrioteers. It is not a sentimental provincialism that we are asking for: it is certainly not for a romantic nationalism: it is only for the sort of native cultural consciousness without which, as our European fellow-writers so profoundly understand, a true internationalism is impossible. We ought to hear much from left-wing writers, as we do, of Pushkin and of Dostoevski, of Rimbaud and of Proust, of Goethe and of Thomas Mann. We have not yet heard quite enough—or have heard too largely from the wrong quarters—of Thomas Hooker and John Woolman, of Joel Barlow and Frances Wright, of Parker, of Howells, of Hamlin Garland.

There is a negative reason, if no other, why we who affiliate ourselves with a Congress such as this should regard it as part of our responsibility to deepen our familiarity with the literary record of the American experience. We are already hearing about that record from the Right and from the Center that bends toward the Right, and we shall hear more and more in the months and years that are approaching. We are hearing and shall hear American writers cited like Scripture—sometimes justly, oftener distortedly—in support of illiberal principles, of the spirit of caste, of distrust toward the people, or at the least of indifference and what is called poise. What knowledge we may have of Stendhal or of Strindberg will avail us precious little when these things are said. . . .

2

The Seven Years of Crisis
Malcolm Cowley

Some day—but it is still too soon—I hope to compile a calendar of important events in the literary world since 1930. I think it would show that these events were of two different types. At first they were chiefly literary in their nature—they were books on trends or critical arguments—but after 1933 most of them were social or political. The literary world had lost even the pretense of being independent and autonomous. It was part of the world at large, and as such it was being directly affected by world events—by Hitler's rise to power (the exiling of German writers, the burning of the books), by the New Deal (the devaluation of the dollar, which brought the expatriates home from Europe, as well as the Federal Writers' Projects), by the CIO (the rise of trade unionism in the arts), by the Moscow trials and the Spanish civil war. In 1936, people had quit even joking about the Ivory Tower. Almost all writers were "politicalized," even the conservatives—and perhaps one should say the conservatives most of all.

This was a new situation, and yet it did not represent a complete break with tradition, even with the tradition of the 1920s. All during the Jazz Age and the Coolidge Era, writers had been revolting against American business (in those days they did not call it capitalism). They had tried to escape from it by fleeing to Paris or Majorca or the South Seas, or into the world of pure art, but essentially their flight had led them nowhere. The depression taught them that American capitalism was not invincible. Instead of running away, they ought to stay home and fight.

Their fight, in the early days, was joyous and almost as irresponsible as a

literary shindig. There was a great deal of wild talk about revolution tomorrow. But after 1933, the talk died away. After 1933 it became evident that the
real fight was against the fascism that was beginning to spread from Italy and
Germany, and that this fight was one in which liberals and radicals could act
together.

That, briefly, is the intellectual background of many books written during
the years from 1930 to 1936. During that period many new tendencies
appeared. There was, for example, an obvious tendency toward autobio-
graphical writing; people were trying to explain the ideas that had determined their careers. There was a tendency toward historical fiction that was
perhaps even stronger among readers than among writers; the two most
popular books since 1930 have both been historical novels. There was a new
growth of regionalism in America; some of it was doctrinaire but some of it
was healthy and produced good books. Finally, coloring everything else,
there was the interest in social problems that showed itself primarily in proletarian novels and dramas and in Marxist criticism.

This interest has not produced the great books that we hoped from it.
Many of the proletarian novels have been too narrow in scope and too theoretical. Their authors haven't been certain of the audience for which they
were writing—whether it was middle-class or working-class, and whether it
demanded simple, entertaining books or was willing to work at its reading.
Many of the Marxist critics have got themselves involved in the old and sterile opposition between form and matter, style and message, without realizing that the two cannot be separated. Yet during this period there has been a
great deal of sound work, a great broadening of subject matter; and dozens
of promising new writers have appeared. The critics have learned a great deal
more about the problems with which they are dealing.

At the present time American literature seems richer and more vigorous
than at any other time since Anderson, Sandburg, Brooks and Eliot first
appeared and Dreiser first became popular. But, as we said in the call to this
congress, literature also seems to be more directly threatened. What would
happen to it during another world war is not pleasant to contemplate. Of
course there is always the chance that we could stay out of such a war; certainly
we shall fight against going into it. But that does not mean that America would
remain a haven of peace and culture in a world that has reverted to barbarism.
There is no use clinging to the theory of "democracy in one country." For the
truth is that democracy and education are threatened not only in Europe but
also here at home. The new Barbarians, who are the Fascists, are here, within
the gates, with us all the time. If Europe goes under, this country won't be able
to stay afloat—or at least it won't retain the sort of liberties that it has today.

Recently I was reading a damned good article by an Englishman named
John Sommerfield, who has been fighting in the International Brigade. One
of his jobs was to defend the Hall of Philosophy, in University City, against

the Fascists in the Clinical Hospital. In order to protect themselves, Sommerfield's comrades had to build barricades of books from the library. He found that the very best barricades were built with volumes of nineteenth-century German philosophy, because absolutely no machine-gun bullets could get through them. I think that one of our jobs today is to see that our own books aren't used as barricades to stop the fascist bullets.

3

The Writer and War
Ernest Hemingway

A writer's problem does not change. He himself changes, but his problem remains the same. It is always how to write truly and having found what is true, to project it in such a way that it becomes a part of the experience of the person who reads it.

There is nothing more difficult to do, and because of the difficulty, the rewards, whether they come early or late, are usually very great. If the rewards come early the writer is often ruined by them. If they come too late he is probably embittered. Sometimes they only come after he is dead, and then they cannot bother him. But because of the difficulty of making true, lasting writing, a really good writer is always sure of eventual recognition. Only romantics think that there are such things as unknown masters.

Really good writers are always rewarded under almost any existing system of government that they can tolerate. There is only one form of government that cannot produce good writers, and that system is fascism. For fascism is a lie told by bullies. A writer who will not lie cannot live or work under fascism.

Because fascism is a lie, it is condemned to literary sterility. And when it is past it will have no history except the bloody history of murder that is well known and that a few of us have seen with our own eyes in the last few months.

A writer, when he knows what it is about and how it is done, grows accustomed to war. That is a serious truth which you discover. It is a shock to discover how truly used to it you become. When you are at the front each day and see trench warfare, open warfare, attacks, and counterattacks, it all makes sense, no matter what the cost in dead and wounded, when you know what the men are fighting for and that they are fighting intelligently. When men fight for the freedom of their country against a foreign invasion, and when these men are your friends, some new friends and some of long standing, and you know how they were attacked and how they fought, at first almost unarmed, you learn, watching them live and fight and die, that there are worse things than war. Cowardice is worse, treachery is worse, and simple selfishness is worse.

In Madrid, where it costs every British newspaper fifty-seven pounds, or say 280 dollars, a week to insure a correspondent's life, and where the American

correspondents work at an average wage of sixty-five dollars a week uninsured,
we of the working press watched murder done last month for nineteen days. It
was done by German artillery and it was highly efficient murder.

I said you grow accustomed to war. If you are interested enough in the science of it, and it is a great science, and in the problem of human conduct
under danger, you can become so encompassed in it, that it seems a nasty sort
of egotism to even consider one's own fate.

But no one becomes accustomed to murder. And murder on a large scale
we saw every day for nineteen days.

The Totalitarian fascist states believe in the Totalitarian war. That put simply means that whenever they are beaten by armed forces they take their
revenge on unarmed civilians. In this war since the middle of November, they
have been beaten at the Parque del Oeste, they have been beaten at the
Pardo, they have been beaten at Carabanchel, they have been beaten on the
Jarama, they have been beaten at Brihuega and at Cordoba. Every time they
are beaten in the field they salvage that strange thing they call their honor, by
murdering civilians.

If I described it, it would only make you vomit. It might make you hate.
But we do not want hate. We want a reasoned understanding of the crimi-
nality of fascism and how it should be opposed. We must realize that these
murders are the gestures of a bully, the great bully of fascism. There is only
one way to quell a bully and that is to thrash him and the bully of fascism is
being beaten now in Spain as Napoleon was beaten in that same Peninsula a
hundred and thirty years ago. The fascist countries know it and they are desperate. Italy knows her troops will not fight outside of Italy, nor, in spite of
marvelous material, are they the equal as soldiers of the new Spanish regi-
ments. There is no question of them ever equaling the fighters of the
International Brigades.

Germany has found that she cannot depend on Italy as an ally in any sort
of offensive war. I have read that von Blomberg witnessed an impressive
series of maneuvers recently with Marshal Badoglio, but it is one thing to
maneuver on the Venetian plain with no enemy present and another to be
outmaneuvered and have three divisions destroyed on the plateau between
Brihuega and Trijueja, by the Eleventh and Twelfth International Brigades and
the fine Spanish troops of Lister, Campesino and Mera. It is one thing to
bombard Almeria and take an undefended Malaga given up by treachery and
another to lose seven thousand troops before Cordoba and thirty thousand
in unsuccessful assaults on Madrid.

I started to discuss the difficulty of trying to write well and truly and the
inevitable reward to those who achieve it. But in a time of war, and we are
now in a time of war, whether we like it or not, the rewards are all suspended. It is very dangerous to write the truth in war and the truth is also
very dangerous to come by. I do not know just which American writers have
gone out to seek it. I know many men of the Lincoln Battalion. But they are

not writers. They are letter writers. Many British writers have gone. Many German writers have gone. Many French and Dutch writers have gone and when a man goes to seek the truth in war he may find death instead. But if twelve go and only two come back, the truth they bring will be the truth and not the garbled hearsay that we pass as history. Whether the truth is worth some risk to come by, the writers must decide themselves. Certainly it is more comfortable to spend their time disputing learnedly on points of doctrine. And there will always be new schisms and new fallings off and marvelous exotic doctrines and romantic lost leaders, for those who do not want to work at what they profess to believe in, but only to discuss and to maintain positions, skillfully chosen positions with no risk involved in holding them. Positions to be held by the typewriter and consolidated with the fountain pen. But there is now, and there will be from now on for a long time, war for any writer to go to who wants to study it. It looks as though we are in for many years of undeclared wars. There are many ways that writers can go to them. Afterward there may be rewards. But that need not bother the writers' conscience. Because the rewards will not come for a long time. And he must not worry about them too much. Because if he is like Ralph Fox and some others he will not be there to receive them.

SUMMARY

. . . The Sunday afternoon session was divided into two parts, of the first of which Leane Zugsmith was chairman, and of the second Richard Wright. The first part began with a discussion of Albert Rhys Williams's paper, for which there had not been time on Saturday afternoon. Mr. Williams was asked a number of questions by Harry Roskolenko, one of which was: "Why has Leon Trotsky's book *Literature and Revolution* been removed from public circulation in the Soviet Union?"

This question was answered by H. W. L. Dana, who said: "This morning I attended the drama commission, which I found was getting rather critical, and I was told the critics' commission was getting very dramatic, so I left. Here I find some of the Trotskyites, who feel at home in any critical session. I am interested in observing how up-to-date that criticism is. Max Eastman talks about artists in uniform. It is nothing to the uniformity of the criticism of the Soviet Union. Trotsky's book *Literature and Revolution* is out of date. It has become out of date because of the creative work of Soviet writers. In the Soviet Union things are going forward, and I notice that these critics here object to going forward because, in doing so, certain things are left behind."

Eli Siegel remarked that such questions were like those "awful back seat drivers" who in Spain "are now impeding the work." He said that in the face of what the Soviet Union is doing for literature such questions are petty. "If you want to look at little things," he continued, "you can say, as I know some people have said, 'Look what happened to this man. In 1919 he was such-and-such. In 1927 he is so-and-so.' Well, that happens wherever there is change. For instance, a man named Burke was thought a good deal of in 1776 by the Americans. Yet Paine, who at that time also thought a good deal of him, had to attack him in 1793, when Burke got old, successful, confused and reactionary.." . .

American Artists' Congress

Inspired obviously by what the writers were doing, an insurgent group of artists supported by the Party organized a well-publicized meeting of their own in February 1936 at New York's Town Hall and the New School for Social Research. Presiding was the Cubist virtuoso Stuart Davis. Among the speakers were such other reputable artists as Peter Blume and Max Weber, both leftists but not of the proletarian school. What the congress sought is evident from the text below.

WHY AN ARTISTS' CONGRESS?
Stuart Davis

The American Artists' Congress is unique in the history of American art. That it takes place now is no accident. For it is the response of artists to a situation facing them today. How can we describe this situation?

Its immediate background is a depression unparalleled in the history of this country. The cracks and strains in the general social fabric resulting from the economic crisis inevitably reached the world of art, shaking those psychological and esthetic certainties which had once given force and direction to the work of artists.

In order to withstand the severe shock of the crisis, artists have had to seek a new grip on reality. Around the pros and cons of "social content," a dominant issue in discussions of present day American art, we are witnessing determined efforts by artists to find a meaningful direction. Increasing expression of social problems of the day in the new American art makes it clear that in times such as we are living in, few artists can honestly remain aloof, wrapped up in studio problems.

But the artist has not simply looked out of the window; he has had to step into the street. He has done things that would have been scarcely conceivable a few years back.

Nearly two years ago prominent New York artists started a campaign through the Artists' Committee of Action for a Municipal Art Gallery to provide a badly needed outlet for the artists of this city.

When the city administration finally took up the idea, without recognition of the Artists' Committee of Action, it opened a gallery in a remodeled pri-

STUART DAVIS, WHY AN ARTISTS' CONGRESS?

vate house early in 1936, on a basis of discrimination against non-citizens and censorship of art disapproved by the administration. Such reactionary ideas could never have been introduced under a truly democratic management of the Municipal Gallery by the artists themselves, which the Artists' Committee of Action had repeatedly called for.

What's more, leading New York artists, together with the Artists' Union, showed that they would not stand for such practices by making a prompt and emphatic protest. The result was an immediate victory! Both citizenship and censorship clauses were speedily withdrawn.

Sharp necessity likewise drove the most hard-pressed artists into organized efforts for Federal Government support. Their opportunity had come through the initiation of a limited Government art project in December 1933. This project was no more than a liberal gesture, employing a select few, and ignoring the dire distress of the great majority of American artists.

But that move of the liberal New Deal Government awakened artists to the realization that they had every right to go to the Government when all other resources and prospects had been exhausted, to demand support for their continued functioning as creative workers.

Artists at last discovered that, like other workers, they could only protect their basic interests through powerful organizations. The great mass of artists left out of the project found it possible to win demands from the administration only by joint and militant demonstrations. Their efforts led naturally to the building of the Artists' Union.

The relatively greater scope of the present art projects is due, in large measure, to the militant stand of the various artists' unions, on behalf of all unemployed artists.

The unions have also gone a long way toward showing that the best American art cannot be developed by merely encouraging a hand-picked few. Their insistence on a democratic extension of Government support to young and unknown artists has brought out a vast variety of talent completely ignored by private patronage and commercial galleries. For the young generation of American artists there is no visible hope except continuation and expansion of Government art projects.

Growing economic insecurity cannot be ignored by even the most firmly established American artists, those who contribute regularly to the big museum exhibitions. Now they are organizing to gain at least a minimum compensation for their important contributions through the loan of contemporary art to museums. They are requesting that the museums pay a small rental fee for the use of their work.

The hostility of most museum officials, and their boards of trustees, to the proposals of the American Society of Painters, Sculptors and Gravers is indicative of their indifference to the needs of artists.

In the struggle around the rental policy, the American Society has found its campaign can only be advanced through the active cooperation of other artists' societies and the Artists' Union. Here is a concrete instance of how great numbers of American artists are drawing together on an ever widening front for mutual support against exploitation. . . .

The members of this Congress who have come together to discuss their problems in the light of the pressing social issues of the day are representative of the most progressive forces in American art today. The applicants for membership were accepted on the basis of their representative power, which simply means that they had already, achieved a degree of recognition and esteem as artists in the spheres in which they function.

We, members of the Congress, have recognized that we are not alone in this fight. We recognize that our basic interests are not remote from those who do the work of the world. And with this recognition comes the realization that if we are to be serious, we can only attack even the most highly specialized problems that confront us, in relation to our main objective, which is to build a bulwark for the defense of intellectual freedom, for economic security.

Even if we were to rally all the American artists to our cause, we would achieve little working as an isolated group. But we have faith in our potential effectiveness precisely because our direction naturally parallels that of the great body of productive workers in American industrial, agriculture and professional life.

The Congress will enable us to focus our objectives.

To realize them, we plan to form a permanent organization on a national scale.

It will not be affiliated with any political group or clique of sectarian opinion.

It will be an organization of artists which will be alert to take action on all issues vital to the continued free functioning of the artist.

It will be alert to ways and means for extending this freedom and for making contact with a broader audience.

It will be a strengthening element to the whole field of progressive organization against War and Fascism.

It will be another obstacle to the reactionary forces which would rob us of our liberties.

I call on all artists of standing to join the permanent organization which will carry out the program planned by the succeeding sessions of the Congress.

2
THE ART MUST CHOOSE
Peter Blume

A few years ago, no one could ever have gotten the artists of America together to discuss anything. There never was, in fact, a common basis that many artists could get together on. They would have been prejudiced against the idea of holding a congress to talk about esthetic problems, for instance, because they considered this a private matter for individual artists to solve for themselves. Yet that was about the only thing they could have found to talk about. As a class they were broken into mutually antagonistic little groups, each trying to defend [its] own interests.

The astonishing thing is that American artists have changed in the past five years. This Congress Against War and Fascism would have been impossible before. Now they have come together, almost spontaneously, from every part of the country because they fear that their integrity as artists is being threatened and because they realize that their whole existence is tied up with the economic crisis of the entire world.

Many artists today, even in the face of these conditions, still view the fundamental problem with apathy and distrust. They consider themselves immune to the conditions in society. But as a matter of fact, all their peculiarities, their traditions, their general social outlook, are symptoms of how social conditions have molded them. Changes in the order of society have not only affected their style and technique, but have actually caused them to take sides in the economic struggle and to develop peculiar class prejudices.

The economic changes are clearly recorded in their work. The history of art and esthetics can be taken as a guide to the history of mankind, as everybody knows. If we had no other evidence of European civilization during the past 500 years, we could get a very good picture of this whole period through its art. It would give us not only a visual sense of how people lived, dressed, and were governed, but also the most subtle interpretations of how they thought and felt. . . .

We were afforded a concrete example of how our old ideas worked out in real life—what a return to medievalism was like in a modern state—during the reign of terror when the Nazis came into power in Germany. We could not remain complacent at the sight of a government persecuting its artists and sending them into exile and imprisonment. It shamed us to think how near we once came to being Fascists ourselves, and how we had cherished a belief in the choice place we would have in an established aristocracy with its perfectly balanced social hierarchies.

We became aware of the threat of Fascism as an international menace. We could see its economic impulses operating everywhere, under the stress of economic crisis; its brutality, its racial and religious prejudices parading under the flag of reaction. We recognized it as the real enemy of culture, and we saw its portentous beginnings right here in the United States, in the violations of civil liberties, in acts of censorship and in the destruction of works of art.

We are aware that these violations of human liberties can no longer be minimized. These are not mere scarecrows invented by radical propagandists to mislead loyal Americans, but the recognizable symptoms of incipient Fascism, increasing daily in frequency and boldness and condemned by every decent civil and religious organization in America.

We have called this Congress Against Fascism and War to discuss the threat that has arisen to our liberties and our future as artists, and to add our weight in the united struggle against it. We know that there is no retreat for the artist, no ivory tower we can hide away in for protection, and no promise, as we have seen in the countries where Fascism has triumphed, that our sensitivity will be in any way regarded. Fascism is a desperate method of making us mute automatons in a dying order. Fascism means the death of culture. We must oppose it now, or be destroyed by it. There is no other choice.

A few years ago, the advent of Fascism seemed inevitable. We now know that it cannot triumph against a united opposition; that Fascism can be and has been stopped. The world we live in is a modern world, torn by opposing forces and moving with ever greater intensity and violence toward a crisis— a crisis culminating with Fascism and war. We must fight against both for our own salvation. We, as artists, must take our places in this crisis on the side of growth and civilization, against barbarism and reaction, and help to create a better social order.

3

The Artist, His Audience and Outlook
Max Weber

It seems to me, my comrades and fellow artists, regardless of what innate talent or gifts we were favored with by the gods, in order to obtain a hearing and a return reasonably commensurate with our creative gifts, we must live in discarded places, lose our reason, cut off our ears and noses and finally commit suicide, if we hope for a considerable audience—half a century after our flight from this planet. (But it is tragic enough to starve and suffer the pangs of anxiety and fear in the midst of plenty.)

The causes of the neglect of the artist, and his limited audience are numerous, but the outstanding cause is economic. For how many in the population of a given area can find the time and leisure for cultural pursuits? How pitifully few people can visit galleries and the out-of-the-way museums. The art dealer who deals in work by living artists is, by reason of the overhead expense and general maintenance, confined to small and cramped stuck-away quarters. He is compelled to curtail his exhibitions. His as well as the artists' activities and genuine ambitions are stifled and their programs minced and hectic. The palatial spacious day-lit galleries in prominent cosmopolitan centers are for the great dead and the masters of old.

The comedian, the hooligan, the wise-crack has an audience in the millions upon millions every hour, every day. The reason for this is simple and obvious. The joker is the Novocain in the struggle and agony of the daily existence of the great multitude. Indirectly he sells all sorts of trash and announces tainted news and fraudulent commodities.

Compare the number of art lectures, art courses and publications, the number of art schools, with the carloads of pulp, variety and sex magazines and the bulk of the Sunday newspapers, the funnies, the radio propaganda of toothpaste, hair tonic, cereals, macaroni and shoe polish, and the cheap, lewd movies, the pool rooms and other demoralizing institutions.

Why, with so many vacant skyscraper lofts, armories and other spacious, unoccupied and centrally located buildings, should artists be driven to show their work and offer it for sale on the sidewalks of Greenwich Village? What impression can such a showing make on even the most sympathetic and understanding spectator? Pictures guillotined on iron railings, tossed by the wind, soiled by the dust and shouted out, as it were, by harsh out-of-door lighting; the grandest work of art would be mightily dimmed and its glow tarnished and cheapened, placed under similar conditions. These open-air art marts, while received good-naturedly, nevertheless call to mind the horror and sadness of the scenes of evictions in the slums.

High-domed edifices, veritable palaces in size and proportion, called banks, are built in the hundreds of thousands all over the land, of marble, granite, glass and brass for the mere counting of pennies and pieces of green paper, called money; for the housing in their cellars of military forts called safes, and a few desks and counters with clerks that look like ants in these vacant, space-wasted interiors, while art exhibitions, lectures, and musicals, with few exceptions, are relegated to improvised, dingy, cramped interiors.

Then we have the annual Independent Artists' Exhibition. Another makeshift. At such unimpressive, temporary exhibition places, the yellow journals and their reporters find it expedient and easy to display or give vent to their cheap vulgar wit at the expense of the bewildered, beaten and dispossessed artist and art student.

We do not seek the 57th Street gallery, robed in royal purple plush and trimmed with modern chromium, furnished with wrought-iron lamps and cushioned lounges. You don't see the staid art dealers display their pictures on iron railings, on dilapidated stoops, or in doorways over ash-cans. No! They must have their plush, shaded light, uniformed attendants like Pullman porters, little hot-house evergreens, tropical plants in private nooks and cozy corners. A hushed atmosphere, a sanctimonious, ecclesiastical environment, engraved catalogues with introductions and forewords by French critics for greater prestige, a stamp of imported goods from abroad—such surroundings are more conducive to the sale of their wares to the industrial magnates.

In these palatial, life-lacking galleries, the art critic enters with humility and reverence. He is awed. A two or three column article with 6-inch square illustrations, headlines, captions follow. He is eloquent in his praise of the foreign and the dead, although truly bored and nagged with having to write and rewrite on the same subjects season after season. These grand, staid merchants of art have a special genius for resurrecting the dead and know how to keep the dead living. Only the profit system can breed such commercial wizards, parasites and opportunists. What chance have we? Where and how shall the living find an audience? . . .

At this crucial moment, even more than ever before, we workers in the field of the fine arts owe to this and future generations a legacy of as perfectly balanced a vision as our talents will afford. We must show the way from malady to health, from psychiatry and obscurantism to clarity. We must impress it upon the artist and layman in no mincing terms that this is no time for mental squander and debauch, no time to play with distractions, pantomimic graphics, with fossils or seashells, machine parts of no machines, with geometric forms that cannot conform, with immobile dynamics, with distortions of the convex and concave lens, with distorted perspective, with the occult and perversions of all sorts.

And while it would be ludicrous to prescribe or insist on a proletarian art technique and curriculum, nevertheless, may we not aspire to create an art eloquent and unfailingly clear in its social import, as clear as is the religious meaning and decorative beauty in the frescoes of Giotto and Francesca or Uccello—an art so evocative and illuminating that it will not fail to bring new light and hope to the masses?

A truly modern art is yet to come, but not until the new life is here, and not before the imminent emancipation of mankind that we envisage.

By reason of the great and impending dangers we are morally obligated to look to the needs of the neglected and spiritually impoverished manual and mental workers in all fields, if we hope ever to link life with art inseparably.

In our effort at renewal let us also deviate from the academic and insipid nudes, and aristocratic madonnas of past centuries and tastes and ideals foreign to us in the twentieth century. Let us, instead, turn to the gladiatorial heroism, ambition, and tempo of modern beneficent and yielding industry, science and technology, to scenes of joy and verve of happy toilers in their own made environments, to the new home life, nursery and school, to the new comradeship and brotherhood hitherto unknown.

For, our own palaces of art and industry and social and cultural intercourse we must build, and adorn them in conformity with our own conception and aspirations of freedom, justice and happiness. And who can deny or doubt that we already have our feet on the only path that leads resolutely to the new edifice (to the new arena); but we must not falter or fail to bring with us an art, a literature, a music, a philosophy compatible and consistent with our renaissance and its potential revelation and liberation. From obscurity and vagary to the opulent light of the very heavens we must turn.

And now my dear colleagues, I hope that I have been able, if only in a slight way, to point out some of the difficulties that confront us, as well as the unlimited satisfactions that await us, in solving the problems of subject matter in our respective arts; and in that effort, how to gain closer contact with, and how to avail ourselves of the new social and spiritual resources and ideology, so that our arts will spring from, interlock with, and serve the new humanity.

To reach this goal is our task and only hope, and not until we reach it can we afford to rest.

STATEMENT
The American Music League

Not to be outdone, radical composers and musicians established the American Music League early in 1936; it was associated with the three-year-old Composers Collective. The League set forth its principles in the May 1936 issue of Unison, *its magazine.*

THE LEAGUE LOOKS AHEAD

Seven years of economic crisis have cut deeply into the American standard of living and proportionately into our musical culture. No longer can the average man afford to give his child the five dollar piano lessons of yesterday; no longer can he indulge in a dollar-fifty Victrola record or a fifty cent song sheet, nor is there the annual birthday visit to the opera or symphony concert. One after another, our great musical institutions have either to retrench, lower their standards, or shut down altogether. This past season, for the first time in years, the Metropolitan mounted no new opera, and recently Mssrs Warburg, Mackay and Marshall Field, pleading insufficient funds, announced that next years's Philharmonic season would be six weeks shorter. In fact, the Philharmonic narrowly missed cracking up when the trustees attempted to install the Nazi Furtwaengler as conductor, an action averted only by the pressure of public opinion.

If the music consumer has found it ever more difficult to satisfy his needs, the producer (the composer) has been faced with a problem equally acute. The few opportunities the American composer once had to have his works performed are becoming fewer. Writing for a cultured minority, America's leading composers have found even this group dwindling to ever rarer proportions. Composers began to think about "the problems of the audience" in all seriousness.

Simultaneously, the vitality of various sorts of modern music began to be questioned by the really vital part of the audience of young composers. Although they were confronted by new themes, to write of the stirring conflicts of the day, to mirror in their music the new thoughts that were beginning to agitate large segments of the American people, those composers remained for the most part isolated. They were either unwilling or unable to turn to these new tasks, continuing instead to turn out their quota of quarters, concertos and sonatas, and concerning themselves only with so-called "pure" musical problems.

Thus, on the one hand, big business, by wage cuts, speedups and replacement of men by machines are slashing the American standard of living, thereby forcing millions out of the class of those who could afford to study and hear good music; on the other hand, it still dangled enough prizes and fellowships to keep the best musicians on the path of "pure art" and thus functionally out of contact with the real American scene.

Witnessing the gradual impoverishment of musical life in this country and believing that the future of music will remain uncertain as long as music is controlled by big financial and banking interests which now dominate our leading operas, orchestras, conservatories, publishing houses and radio stations, the American Music League, on the occasion of its first festival, issues the call to musicians and music lovers everywhere, *For the Development of Music as a People's Art in America.* Music should be controlled by those who create and by those who enjoy it. . . .

The following has been proposed as the objectives toward which the *American Music League* will work in its building of a people's music movement in this country:

1. to encourage the development of the highest type of amateur musical activities among wide numbers of people; and to draw into active participation in these activities those who have been denied the benefits of musical education and culture.

2. to encourage the presentation of, and to create organized audiences for, concerts presenting the best music of the past and present at prices within the reach of everyone.

3. to bring composers and other professional musicians into close contact with amateur musicians and with working people who form the bulk of the potential American music audience.

4. to guide and further the development of an American music addressed to the people, reflecting their lives, interests and problems.

5. to collect, study and popularize American folklore and its traditions.

6. to defend musical culture against fascism, censorship and war.

While artists, writers and actors have for some time begun to see that the only solution of the crisis now affecting all the arts lies in organizing action and closer contact with the masses, composers have for the most part been clinging to the old shibboleths of rugged individualism and our expression—this in spite of the fact that the depression has hit the composers with particular force. Retrenchment by wealthy patrons who have in the past supported modern music concerts, has deprived him of practically the only means of having his music played and of effecting contact with his audience. This isolation has caused the composer of today to write music which is complex, introspective, remote from reality and understandable to fewer and fewer people.

Three years ago a small group of American musicians put into action their conviction that if the art of composition is to go forward, composers must abandon their isolated position and address themselves to the broad mass of workers and professional people for whom music is not a luxury but a thing of immense personal and social concern. On the initiative of Jacob Schaefer, Leon Charles and Henry Cowell, a seminar on the writing of mass music was organized which became the *Composers Collective of New York*. It set itself the task of writing music in all forms to meet the needs of the mass working class movement.

Among the main task of the Collective has been the writing of (1) mass songs, dealing with immediate social issues (United Front, Scottsboro Boys, Herndon, etc.) to be sung at meetings, on parades and on picket lines; (2) choral music for professional as well as nonprofessional choruses, dealing in a broader way with the social scene (Song of the Builders, Ballad of Harry Simms, etc.); (3) solo songs on social themes, to be sung at meetings and concentrate the attention on the subjective, private emotions to the exclusion of the realistic social questions . . . ; (4) instrumental music, to carry on the best musical traditions of the past, now threatened by the collapse of bourgeois culture, and to create, in the words of Romain Rolland, "A music of the masses, a sort of musical freso, in broad strokes and sweeps—a music which arouses the people to joy and fury."

In addition to its regular concerts, the Composers Collective now has available a Performers Unit, which consists of the composers themselves and other performing musicians who desire to bring the music heard in the Collective programs, as well as that of sympathetic composers and those working in the same field in other countries (Aaron Copland, Henry Cowell, Hanns Eisler, Davidenko, Shostakovich) out of the concert hall and into workers' and professional organizations. The Performing Unit is available for programs lasting anywhere from one half hour to an hour and a half, such performances to take place in the headquarters of the group or the organization concerned. At least two to three weeks' notice is required for the arrangement of such programs, and a small fee is charged.

Three Poems

1

SUNDAY: OUTSKIRTS OF KNOXVILLE, TENN.
James Agee

That young writers like Agee were willing to write for and be published by the New Masses *(its September 14, 1937, issue) speaks volumes about the intellectual ambience of that era. Readers of the magazine must have wondered what in the world the poem had to do with Communism, but there it was.*

There, in the earliest and chary spring, the dogwood flowers.
Unharnessed in the friendly sunday air
By the red brambles, on the river bluffs,
Clerks and their choices pair.

Thrive by, not near, masked all away by shrub and juniper,
The ford v eight, racing the chevrolet.
They can not trouble her:
Her breasts, helped open from the afforded lace,
Lie like a peaceful lake;
And on his mouth she breaks her gentleness:
Oh, wave them awake!
They are not of the birds. Such innocence
Brings us whole to break us only.
Theirs are not happy words.
We that are human cannot hope.
Our tenderest joys oblige us most.
No chain so cuts the bone; and sweetest silk most shrewdly strangles.
How this must end, that now please love were ended,
In kitchens, bedfights, silences, women's pages,
Sickness of heart before goldlettered doors,
Stale flesh, hard collars, agony in antiseptic corridors,
Spankings, remonstrances, fishing trips, orange juice,
Policies, incapacities, a chevrolet,
Scorn of their children, kind contempt exchanged,
Recalls, tears, second honeymoons, pity,
Shouted corrections of missed syllables,
Hot water bags, gallstones, falls down stairs,
Stammerings, soft foods, confusion of personalities,
Oldfashioned christmases, suspicious of theft,
Arrangements with morticians taken care of by sons in law,
Small rooms beneath the gables of brick bungalows,
The tumbler smashed, the glance between daughter and husband,
The empty body in the lonely bed
And, in the empty concrete porch, blown ash
Grandchildren wandering the betraying sun
Now, on the winsome crumbling shelves of the horror
God show, God blind these children!

2
AMERICAN RHAPSODY (5)
Kenneth Fearing

Here is another by Fearing, this one from his 1938 book Dead Reckoning.

Tomorrow, yes, tomorrow
    there will suddenly be new success, like Easter
    clothes, and a strange and different fate
        and bona fide life will arrive at last, stepping

from a nonstop monoplane with chromium
doors and a silver wing and straight, white
staring lights

There will be the sound of silvery thunder again to stifle
the insane silence
a new, tremendous sound will shatter the final unspoken question and
drown the last, mute, terrible reply
rockets, rockets, Roman candles, flares, will
burst in every corner of the night, to veil with
snakes of silvery fire the nothingness that waits
and waits
there will be a bright, shimmering, silver
veil stretched everywhere, tight, to hide
the deep, black, empty, terrible bottom of
the world where people fall who are alone,
or dead
Sick or alone
alone or poor
weak, or mad, or doomed, or alone

Tomorrow, yes, tomorrow, surely we begin at last to live
with lots and lots of laughter
solid silver laughter
laughter, with a few simple instructions,
and a bona fide guarantee.

3

LET AMERICA BE AMERICA AGAIN
Langston Hughes

Born in 1902 in Lawrence, Kansas, and raised in Cleveland, Hughes settled in Harlem long enough to take part in its renaissance as a very promising young poet. Having spent a year in the Soviet Union, he nailed his flag to the Party mast and wrote extensively for its publications. For example, the poem below, perhaps his best known, is from A New Song, *a collection brought out in 1938 by the International Workers Order. (In his introduction to the book Mike Gold tells an amazing story. In 1925, at a fancy Washington, D.C., hotel, Vachel Lindsay was reading poems to a distinguished audience. Among the poems were three by the unknown Langston Hughes, who happened to be working just then as a "busboy in that white man's hotel.")*

Let America be America again.
Let it be the dream it used to be.
Let it be the pioneer on the plain
Seeking a home where he himself is free.

(America never was America to me.)

Let America be the dream the dreamers dreamed—
Let it be that great strong land of love
Where never kings connive nor tyrants scheme
That any man be crushed by one above.

(It never was America to me.)

O, let my land be a land where Liberty
Is crowned with no false patriotic wreath,
But opportunity is real, and life is free,
Equality is in the air we breathe.

(There's never been equality for me,
Nor freedom in this "homeland of the free.")

Say who are you that mumbles in the dark?
And who are you that draws your veil across the stars?

I am the poor white, fooled and pushed apart,
I am the Negro bearing slavery's scars.
I am the red man driven from the land,
I am the immigrant clutching the hope I seek—
And finding only the same old stupid plan.
Of dog eat dog, of mighty crush the weak.

I am the young man, full of strength and hope,
Tangled in that ancient endless chain
Of profit, power, gain, of grab the land!
Of grab the gold! Of grab the ways of satisfying need!
Of work the men! Of take the pay!
Of owning everything for one's own greed!'

I am the farmer, bondsman to the soil.
I am the worker sold to the machine.
I am the Negro, servant to you all.
I am the people, humble, hungry, mean—
Hungry yet today despite the dream.
Beaten yet today—O, Pioneers!
I am the man who never got ahead,
The poorest worker bartered through the years.

Yet I'm the one who dreamt our basic dream
In that Old World while still a serf of kings,
Who dreamt a dream so strong, so brave, so true,
That even yet its mighty daring sings
In every brick and stone, in every furrow turned

That's made America the land it has become.
O, I'm the man who sailed those early seas
In search of what I meant to be my home—
For I'm the one who left dark Ireland's shore,
And Poland's plain, and England's grassy lea,
And torn from Black Africa's strand I came
To build a "homeland of the free."
The free?

Who said the free? Not me?
Surely not me? The millions on relief today?
The millions shot down when we strike?
The millions who have nothing for our pay?
For all the dreams we've dreamed
And all the songs we've sung
And all the hopes we've held
And all the flags we've hung,
The millions who have nothing for our pay—
Except the dream that's almost dead today.

O, let America be America again—
The land that never has been yet—
And yet must be—the land where *every* man is free.
The land that's mine—the poor man's, Indian's, Negro's, ME—
Who made America,
Whose sweat and blood, whose faith and pain,
Whose hand at the foundry, whose plow in the rain,
Must bring back our mighty dream again.

Sure, call me any ugly name you choose—
The steel of freedom does not stain.
From those who live like leeches on the people's lives,
We must take back our land again,
America!

O, yes,
I say it plain,
America never was America to me,
And yet I swear this oath—
America will be!

Out of the rack and ruin of our gangster death,
The rape and rot of graft, and stealth, and lies,
We, the people, must redeem
The land, the mines, the plants, the rivers,
The mountains and the endless plain—

All, all the stretch of these great green states—
And make America again!

An American Bard

1
WNEW
Woody Guthrie

WNEW was a New York City radio station in which Guthrie had a program for a while. Here, in the course of asking his listeners to send in their comments, pro and con, he gives a fine precis of his life and work over the years. It is included in a collection of songs, drawings, and remarks brought out posthumously (in 1967) as Born to Win.

I've followed all kinds of big work jobs all over the country, like the oil fields, coal mines, big timber jobs, the Grand Coolee Dam, the TVA in the state of Tennessee, the harvesting of all kinds of crops like cotton, wheat, spuds, beets, and grapes and fruits and berries and vegetables. I've followed the building of the big highways like the Lincoln and the Sixty-Six. And the hard rock tunnels and the WPA roads and streamlined speedways, and the building of the big ships, and the places where ferryboats land and where the subway trains and all of the other trains load up full of people, and I sang in road houses, hotels, messrooms, churches, union halls, saloons and night clubs and taverns, and have always sung for twelve or fourteen hours a day and sometimes twenty-four. And now to try to sing these same kinds of songs on a little old fifteen-minute spot here on the radio, well, it cramps me just a little bit. Sort of slows me down. I ain't got elbow room. Ain't got room enough to breathe in.

I need thirty minutes at the very least. If you write me a card or a letter, then the owner will see that you want thirty minutes, too, and then we'll be getting something done.

I sing all kinds of tales and stories that the people sing while they work or while they're looking for work. I sing old-time songs about love and fights and so forth and so on, and about the big jobs that have made this country what it is.

I don't sing any songs that are not real. I don't sing any silly or any jerky songs, nor any songs that make fun of your color, your race, the color of your eyes or the shape of your stomach or the shape of your nose. I don't sing any songs of the playboys and the gals that get paid for hugging the mikes and wiggling their hips. I sing songs that people made up to help them to do more work, to get somewhere in this old world, to fall in love and to get married and to have kids and to have trade unions and to have the right to speak out your mind about how to make this old world a little bit better place to work in. I sing songs about people that are fighting with guns to win a world where you'll have a good job at union pay, and a right to speak up, to think, to have honest prices and honest wages and a nice clean place to live in and a good safe place to work in. I even sing songs about getting nursery schools for little kids too young to play in the streets, and schools where all of the other kids can go to keep from playing their games under the garbage trucks. I don't sing any songs about the nine divorces of some millionaire playgal or the ten wives of some screwball. I've just not got the time to sing those kind of songs and I wouldn't sing them if they paid me ten thousand dollars a week. I sing the songs of the people that do all of the little jobs and the mean and dirty hard work in the world and of their wants and their hopes and their plans for a decent life.

I happen to believe that songs and music can be used to get all of these good things that you want. Maybe you never did hear a song that you figured was of much help to you in getting the job and the pay and the mate and the home that you want. Maybe you never did hear a song that you thought was a help to you in paying off your debts.

I hate a song that makes you think that you're not any good. I hate a song that makes you think that you are just born to lose. Bound to lose. No good to nobody. No good for nothing. Because you are either too old or too young or too fat or too slim or too ugly or too this or too that. . . . Songs that run you down or songs that poke fun at you on account of your bad luck or hard traveling.

I am out to fight those kinds of songs to my very last breath of air and my last drop of blood.

I am out to sing songs that will prove to you that this is your world and that if it has hit you pretty hard and knocked you for a dozen loops, no matter how hard it's run you down nor rolled over you, no matter what color, what size you are, how you are built, I am out to sing the songs that make you take pride in yourself and in your work. And the songs that I sing are made up for the most part by all sorts of folks just about like you.

I could hire out to the other side, the big-money side, and get several dollars every week just to quit singing my own kind of songs and to sing the kind that knock you down still farther and the ones that make fun of you even more, and the ones that make you think that you've not got any sense at all. But I decided a long time ago that I'd starve to death before I'd sing any such songs as that. The radio waves and your jukeboxes and your movies and your song books are already loaded down and running over with such no-good songs as that anyhow. . . .

I sing religious songs. I sing union songs. I sing all kinds of songs about people that are supposed to be mean, or vulgar, low down, no money, no good, and I sing songs that tell who the racketeers are and how they rob you and how they work and how they would like to keep you as their slave. And I sing the songs about robbers and about outlaws and people that try to take it from the rich and give it to the poor. I sing songs that tell you just why you can't help the people that are poor just by grabbing a club or a knife or a gun and going out to be an outlaw. I sing songs about the outlaws that the people loved and the ones that the people hated. I sing any song that was made up by the people that tells a little story, a little part, of our big history of this country, yes, or that tells a part of the history of the world.

The folks all around the world have been fighting now for a hundred centuries to all be union and to all be free and I sing the songs that tell you about that. I tell you about the hired thugs and the hired sluggers and the gas-bomb deputies.

I tell you the tall tales of the champion workers and the fights they had to see who could do the most work. I tell you the tales of the world's champion drinkers and the world's champion thinkers and the world's champion horses and the best argufiers and shooters of the bull. I tell you about the fastest horses and the fastest lovers and the biggest eaters and the fastest travelers. . . .

I speak for the union people that see a union world and that fight for a one big union all around the world. I speak as a singer for the AF of L, CIO, Brotherhoods and Sisterhoods and all of the kids and childhoods and all of the other hoods but I fight against the white hood of the Ku Klux Klan because I hate them and their gizzards and their whizzards and their lizzards and I hate their hot tar and their feathers and their beatings and killings and hangings of union men and women all over the country. I speak for the human beings of this human race and when anybody quits being a human and goes to fighting against the union right then I jump on them with all of my teeth and toenails. And I grab me a root and I growl. And I hang on and I keep on singing and yelling and singing and yelling and singing and yelling and reading and writing and hollering and fighting and everything else. . . .

2

I Don't Feel at Home on the Bowery No More
Woody Guthrie

We can do no better than quote Guthrie on where and when he came to write these wonderful verses (they are also included in Born to Win*): "Written February eighteenth of nineteen-forty in the City of New York, on West Fifty-Sixth Street, in Will Geer's house in the charge of his wine and in the shadow of his kindness. . . . I dedicate this song to the Geer family and to the bum situation up and down every Skid Row and Bowery Street in this country. This bum situation is a big situation."*

I'll sing you a song of the place that I stay
  Once on this Bowery I use to be gay
  Carefree and rambling in days of yore
But I don't feel at home on the Bowery no more

The flops they are lousy, the men are so thick,
  You can't go to sleep and you can't sleep a wink

They mumble and grumble, they snarl and they snore
I don't feel at home on the Bowery no more.

The beds are so small that your feet touch the wall
    The bedbugs so big that they swallow you whole
    The lice are so thick that they cover the floor
I don't feel at home on the Bowery no more.

I seen an apartment on Fifth Avenue
    A penthouse and garden with a skyscraper view
    The carpets so soft with a hardwood floor
So I don't feel at home on the Bowery no more.

I like my good whiskey, I like my good wine,
    And good-looking women to have a good time
    Cocktail parties and a big built-in bar
So I don't feel at home on the Bowery no more.

The girls on the Bowery have all advanced
    They're dancing for nickels at the old ticket dance
    I like pretty gals as I told you before
So I don't feel at home on the Bowery no more.

I got disgusted and I wrote this song
    I may be right and I may be wrong
    But since I seen the difference 'tween rich and the poor
I don't feel at home on the Bowery no more.

THE MOSCOW TRIALS

1

THE TROTSKY-ZINOVIEV ASSASSINS BEFORE THE BAR OF THE WORKING CLASS
P. Lang

By the Summer of 1936 the Moscow show trials were putting on display Lenin's oldest and closest associates, chief among them Zinoviev and Kamenev. Hideously tortured, they and other scarcely less notable heroes of the Revolution confessed to their involvement in a plot, led by Trotsky and German and Japanese Fascists, to overthrow the Soviet government, etc. Typical of the Party's response to the widespread criticism of the trials was this article from the October 1936 issue of Communist.

The trial of the Trotsky-Zinoviev terrorist center was conducted for five days by the Supreme Court of the USSR. This center was accused of the gravest crime, namely, the murder of Comrade Kirov and the preparation of a number of terrorist acts against the leaders of the Communist Party of the Soviet Union and the Soviet government. At the open public sessions of the trial the accused were allowed every possibility for defense. They fully utilized the possibilities offered them with the skill of cunning politicians. If they refused the right to invite counsel and call witnesses it was for the simple reason that they knew that it was impossible to deny the facts of their crimes. At the same time every one of the accused in every way strove, both at the preliminary investigation and at the trial, to minimize, at the expense of the others, their role in the crimes they jointly committed. The chiefs of the center in particular tried in every way possible—in the words of the other accused—"to hide behind the backs of the others."

But, with the existence of indisputable proofs incriminating all the criminals, the whole of this struggle led to the fact that not a single one of the terrorists was in a position to deny his guilt. All of the accused right up to Smirnov himself, who stubbornly not only defended himself but was anxious to conceal the remaining fragments of his terrorist group, were obliged to admit the complete justice of the charges against them.

By the end of the trial not a single one of the terrorists was able to deny the fact that the Trotsky and Zinoviev counter-revolutionary groups, who were active in the territory of the Soviet Union, in 1932, following an instruction sent by Trotsky from abroad, united on the basis of the use of individual terror against the leaders of the CPSU and the Soviet government. Nobody, not even Zinoviev and Kamenev, with all their unsurpassed cynicism in denying established facts, could conceal that on their hands lies the blood of Comrade Kirov. No evasions could shake the truth of the charge against the members of the terrorist group that, simultaneously with the preparations of the murder of Comrade Kirov, and after this murder, they time and again tried to assassinate Comrades Stalin, Voroshilov, Zhdanov, Kaganovich, Orjonikidze, Kossior and Postishev.

Not all the provocation and hocus-pocus of the Fascists and cunning efforts of other defenders of Trotsky will be able to whitewash the absolutely established fact that Trotsky not only demanded of his representatives by every available channel that they speed up terrorist murders but, apart from this, personally, at different times, sent terrorists from abroad to the USSR. Five of them were in the dock and had, with the direct knowledge of Trotsky, worked directly with the agents of the German secret police in carrying out terrorist acts, or were paid agents of the Gestapo. . . .

Why is it then they did not even mention a single political program of their own, or any kind of political views? For the simple reason that the Trotsky-Zinoviev terrorists had no political program, that they did not even take the trouble to invent such a program. Why? The accused themselves clearly answered this question.

At the trial, they declared that their terrorist activity needed no program.

"We had nothing in our group," stated the accused Reingold. "All we had was a gun." To such an extent have the Trotsky-Zinoviev adventurers lost all semblance to political leaders! In the dock are "has-beens," degenerates, criminals who, carrying on an unprincipled struggle simply for power, had nothing to show the Soviet people but their fascist face distorted with rage.

In the struggle against the Communist Party, against the Soviet power, against the Soviet people, the Trotsky-Zinoviev center passed from one means of criminal counter-revolutionary struggle to ever more criminal forms of struggle. They began with internal Party discussion which had the object of forcing their will on the Party. Then, they unsuccessfully tried to carry their counter-revolutionary agitation into the masses who cast them off. They ended up with gangster terrorism.

Those of the accused who were formerly members of the Communist Party could not but mention at the trial the patience and leniency with which the Bolshevik leadership treated them, how the leadership repeatedly tried to save them from final disgrace. Even Kamenev, when he spoke of the depths to which he had fallen, had to state that the Party many times had warned him, forgiven him, had given him the possibility of atoning for his crimes, believed his statements, promises, and oaths.

But the Trotsky-Zinoviev adventurers made use of the leniency of the Party, and afterward of the proletarian court, not in order to come to their senses and to leave the path of crime. On the contrary, they used ever more cunning means of evading the vigilance of the Soviet government. They fell so low that they became gangsters of the counter-revolutionary underworld, knowing no bounds to their bloody plans. They joined up with the Gestapo.

The question may be asked, why did people who had fallen so low hold on so firmly to the mask of revolutionaries and Marxists?

The court proceedings showed that they needed this mask *not only in order to avoid punishment for crimes committed, but also in order to have the possibility of continuing their crimes in the future.*

Camouflage was the most necessary element in all the terrorist work of the Trotsky-Zinoviev criminals. They knew that once the mask was torn from their faces they would lose the particular value they had in the eyes of international reaction.

Zinoviev, Kamenev and their associates did not fraudulently make their way into the Bolshevik Party because of any kind of ordinary careerist aims. No! They made their may in because, under cover of a stolen Party card, they calculated on assassinating the leaders of the Party. . . .

But the condemned gangsters have found defenders. Who are the defenders? First and foremost the Fascists themselves.

The help which the Trotsky-Zinoviev gang are getting from fascism is of two kinds. First, and this the trial has clearly shown to the whole world, the Trotsky-Zinoviev band of terrorists rely on the material forces of fascism. If

Trotskyism had not the forces of international reaction behind it, its pernicious work would not be a danger to the working-class movement.

Second, the Fascists are giving real assistance to the Trotskyists by helping them to disguise themselves and to appear as revolutionaries. The Fascists know the value of Trotsky's lies and his pretended hostility to fascism, and they pay him in the same coin. They present the Trotskyists, their agents and collaborators, as their uncompromising enemies.

Before the beginning of the trial, when they saw they had been found out, the fascists hastened to speak of the "persecution" of Trotsky.

The fascists of Norway, where Trotsky has now set up his fascist headquarters, have taken even more demonstrative action: a few days before the beginning of the trial a group of young fascists played the comedy of an arbitrary search of the "revolutionary" Trotsky's house.

In view of this house searching, *Der Angriff* and the *Voelkischer Beobachter*, which have nourished the German Trotskyists, have raised the cry that the revolutionary work of Trotsky threatens the peace of fascism.

After the trial Goebbels and Rosenberg did not withdraw their support from Trotsky. The *Voelkischer Beobachter* prints Trotsky's picture and underneath it in black type a biography in which Trotsky is shown as a "permanent revolutionary" who, from youth up, has devoted himself to the "service of the revolution."

But now that Trotsky is exposed before the whole world as the direct ally of the Gestapo, that, in the public sessions of the court, people have appeared who are at the same time agents of Trotsky and of Himmler, and that the names of others of the same kidney were mentioned, the disgraceful Trotskyist *Bulletin* and Goebbels' *Angriff* can no longer keep up the comedy of mutual attack and their game of provocation. . . .

The trial has shown the friends as well as the foes of the Soviet Union that there is no place on Soviet soil for cowardly terrorists and fascist mercenaries.

It has shown the international proletariat that the renegades, the double-crossers, the miscreants in the ranks of the working class, who, like Trotsky, play with radical phrases, are carrying on fascism's dirty work.

2

IT HAD TO BE REVOLUTION
Charles Shipman

Charles Phillips was born in 1895 into an upper-middle-class New York German-Jewish family. After going to Columbia he fled to Mexico during World War I; there as Jesus Ramirez he helped found the Communist Party. He returned to the United States as Manuel Gomez and got involved in the Party's cultural activities, among them the John Reed Clubs and the Theater Union. He differed with Party leaders over the Moscow tri-

als, and that was his undoing as a Communist. In 1987, under the name Charles Shipman, he wrote his memoir, which Cornell University Press brought out posthumously five years later.

In the latter part of 1936 the New York newspapers featured Edward VIII's insistence on marrying the divorced "Wallie" Simpson at the cost of his throne, and pushed the Spanish Civil War to one side. Coinciding with this first stage of the fighting in Spain was a new Stalinist horror in "the Socialist homeland" at the other end of Europe. Imprisoned after a secret trial for "complicity" in the 1934 murder of Kirov,[1] Zinoviev, Kamenev, and I. N. Smirnov now had to be prosecuted in public—for "treason"—and, of course, executed. The charges included plotting (with Trotsky, and Nazi agents, and agents of the Western powers) to murder the entire Bolshevik leadership, bring down the Soviet regime, and restore Russia to capitalism. The shock of this first of the Moscow "show trials" was indescribable. All the past Stalinist indignities had not prepared observers for the transparent absurdity of these allegations, the hypnotic atmosphere of the courtroom, the dazed Old Bolsheviks stumbling through their extorted confessions, the prospect of Kamenev (about to be executed) begging his sons to devote their lives to "our great Stalin."

I felt that I could no longer piddle around with the John Reed Club, the Theater Union, and such. There was bound to be latent opposition to Stalinism inside the Communist Party, USA, and someone had to organize it. I had been indulging myself at the Theater Union up to then, showing more interest in theater as theater than as weapon.

For the formidable task of "boring from within" I had one exceptional resource. Bill Dunne was a front-rank Party leader, wise in its ways, uncowable, and my best friend. I had never ceased criticizing the Party to Bill—as well as to Thurber Lewis and a few others. All of them disliked the Browder regime. But what about Stalin? The fantastic trial of Zinoviev, Kamenev, and fellow Old Bolshevik leaders shocked Bill and the others as much as me. Their initial responses encouraged me, but the only one who would hear a word against Stalin was Liston Oak, and he would not commit himself. I tried and tried, but the shell refused to crack. The second show trial of illustrious Old Bolsheviks (Karl Radek, Iu. L. Piatakov, et al.), the "confessions," the swift executions—none of this made any difference. In the meantime, invited by Intourist (the official Soviet tourist agency), Liston led a group of

---

[1] Sergei Kirov was a key Stalin protégé, closer to him than any other collaborator, with the possible exception of Molotov. His assassination on December 1, 1934, became the excuse for the succession of wholesale arrests, persecutions, and Party "purges" that followed. It is now widely believed that Stalin himself arranged Kirov's assassination as a pretext for his assault against the Old Bolshevik cadres.

American sightseers on a tour of Russia. The visit completed his disillusion with Stalin, and he went to Spain to serve the Loyalists in the foreign press division. I tried to reach him in Barcelona, but he never received my letter. Ubiquitous Stalinist censors must have waylaid it, because it fell into the hands of the New York *Daily Worker*. With it they "unmasked" Manuel Gómez as a vicious renegade, a paid counterrevolutionary long known to be in the service of Wall Street. The ineffable Mike Gold ran a column denouncing "four Trotskyites of the defunct Theater Union: Charles Walker, Adelaide Walker, Liston Oak, and Manuel Gómez."

This was October 9, 1937. A day or two later I received a missive signed William F. Dunne, severing all relations with me. Lofty, verbose, oratorical, it wound up: "In that sector of the barricades where I command you will be shot on sight." Bill's communication must have been eight pages long. Soon thereafter I received a short one from Albert Maltz, dismissing me with a condemnatory quotation from Lenin which I had taught him. A bit later, Liston, who had stopped off in London on his way home, attacked the Party and the Comintern publicly, much to my surprise—and disapproval. At this Nemo and Juanita, who were practically family, came to Sunnyside with an ultimatum: they rejected the *Daily Worker*'s characterization of me, but they would stop seeing Sylvia and me unless we broke with Liston. We told them "too bad"; we loved them dearly but . . . Other comrades cut us off without bothering to inform us. The Party was now definitively closed to me.

Without access to the party of Lenin, how could a conscientious Leninist carry on? I considered turning to the Trotskyites, but only for a moment. They were a futile sect, going nowhere. So I waited, without knowing what I was waiting for. I was still waiting in 1938 when the third—and most bizarre—of the Moscow show trials struck. On the prisoner's bench sat the last of Lenin's old comrades in arms—Bukharin, Rykov, N. N. Krestinsky—plus a conglomeration of alleged Trotskyites, physicians, and G. G. Yagoda (who as head of the NKVD had set up the first show trial). Charges included the medical murder of Maxim Gorky and a 1918 plot to assassinate Lenin. All but Krestinsky "confessed." Most were shot.

This ultimate phantasmagoria—and the acquiescence of the Communist parties throughout the world—forced me to reexamine the structure of my beliefs. Things that had disturbed me since my first contact with Bolshevik reality came to mind one after the other: . . .

Against lingering emotional resistance and with great pain, I recognized that the seeds of Stalinism lay in Leninism, that the Leninist ideology and methods that had made the October Revolution possible were also responsible for its corruption. My disillusion was stupefying. It left me incapable of believing in anything.

That year, 1938, was the first one in which neither May Day nor November 7 gave me a lift.

1

ON THE AMERICAN DEAD IN SPAIN

Ernest Hemingway

The February 1939 New Masses *featured this dirge by Hemingway for the death of republican Spain, particularly for the Lincoln Brigade volunteers who were buried there.*

The dead sleep cold in Spain tonight. Snow blows through the olive groves, sifting against the tree roots. Snow drifts over the mounds with the small headboards. (When there was time for headboards.) The olive trees are thin in the cold wind because their lower branches were once cut to cover tanks, and the dead sleep cold in the small hills above the Jarama River. It was cold that February when they died there and since then the dead have not noticed the changes of the seasons.

It is two years now since the Lincoln Battalion held for four and a half months along the heights of the Jarama, and the first American dead have been a part of the earth of Spain for a long time now.

The dead sleep cold in Spain tonight and they will sleep cold all this winter as the earth sleeps with them. But in the spring the rain will come to make the earth kind again. The wind will blow soft over the hills from the south. The black trees will come to life with small green leaves, and there will be blossoms on the apple trees along the Jarama River. This spring the dead will feel the earth beginning to live again.

For our dead are a part of the earth of Spain now and the earth of Spain can never die. Each winter it will seem to die and each spring it will come alive again. Our dead will live with it forever.

Just as the earth can never die, neither will those who have ever been free return to slavery. The peasants who work the earth where our dead lie know what these dead died for. There was time during the war for them to learn these things, and there is forever for them to remember them in.

Our dead live in the hearts and the minds of the Spanish peasants, of the Spanish workers, of all the good simple honest people who believed in and fought for the Spanish Republic. And as long as all our dead live in the Spanish earth, and they will live as long as the earth lives, no system of tyranny ever will prevail in Spain.

The fascists may spread over the land, blasting their way with weight of metal brought from other countries. They may advance aided by traitors and by cowards. They may destroy cities and villages and try to hold the people in slavery. But you cannot hold any people in slavery.

The Spanish people will rise again as they have always risen before against tyranny.

The dead do not need to rise. They are a part of the earth now and the earth can never be conquered. For the earth endureth forever. It will outlive all systems of tyranny.

Those who have entered it honorably, and no men ever entered earth more honorably than those who died in Spain, already have achieved immortality.

2

APPEASEMENT
William Gropper

The following cartoon is Gropper's acidulous comment on the world situation in 1938. British Prime Minister Neville Chamberlain is the one on his knees; the umbrella was his signature.

1

THE RISE AND FALL OF EARL BROWDER
Philip J. Jaffe

Because Jaffe was such a close associate of Earl Browder we have him to thank for this remarkable cable from Moscow—sent in code in late September 1939—on the "new tactical line" expected of the American Party in the wake of the Hitler-Stalin nonaggression pact. It first appeared in the Spring 1972 issue of Survey, *a British magazine specializing in Communist affairs.*

Tasks now are bringing united militant action of working class, strengthening alliance with farmers by independently mobilizing against reaction and exploitation. Must cease to trail in wake of F.D.R., adopt independent position on all fundamental questions. Against entering war, because we do not want people to die for imperialist exploiters. But this is not identical with "neutrality" of American bourgeoisie, which is not anti-imperialistic but is dictated by rapacious strivings to use European war to strengthen its own positions, thrust competitors out of markets, become predominant on oceans, sovereign over other states exhausted by war. . . . New tactical lines: (a) Imperialist war, unjust, equally reactionary both sides. Not war of democracy against fascism, but of reactionary imperialist Germany against the reactionary imperialist states of Britain, France and Poland. Question of who first attacked is of no importance; main thing is, it is war for imperialist domination. (b) War is continuation of the struggle between rich states (England, France, USA) which are backbone of capitalist system, and the "wronged" states (Germany, Italy, Japan), which by their struggles for redivision are deepening and sharpening the crisis of the capitalist system. (c) Bourgeoisie of Britain and France cover up their war of plunder with legend of "anti-fascism"; Germany with story it is fighting remnants of unjust Versailles. (d) Poland was reactionary multi-national state, built on oppression of Ukrainians, Byelo-Russians, Jews, disintegrated by corruption of ruling classes. International working class had no interest in existence of such a parasitic state. (e) Soviet Union, by coming to the aid of working people of West Ukraine and Byelo-Russia, has extricated eleven million people from hell of capitalism, linked them up with socialism, freed their national and cultural development, rid them of the danger of foreign enslavement. (f) War created new international situation, United Front and People's Front lose significance. Tasks, bold struggle against war, no credits, fire against bourgeois dictatorship of own country, ruthlessly expose Social Democracy which has joined the camp of reaction; expose bourgeoisie as war speculators and freebooters; hold high the banner of proletarian internationalism.

AMERICA AND THE INTERNATIONAL SITUATION
Communist Party Political Committee

On October 13, 1939, the Party's Political Committee met in special session to work out a formal resolution justifying the nonaggression pact. The fight against Fascism now gave way to a pox on both your houses, the war being an imperialist one. It appeared in the November 1939 Communist.

Events since the outbreak of the present imperialist war have fully confirmed the correctness of the analysis and position of the National Committee of the Communist Party of the USA on the imperialist war as set forth in its declaration of September 18. On the basis of this declaration and in view of the latest developments internationally and within the country, the Political Committee wishes to reemphasize and further develop the following central political conclusions and tasks flowing from the present political situation:

1. The present war is an imperialist war for which the bourgeoisie of all belligerent powers are equally guilty. With the invasion of Poland, predatory Nazi imperialism has continued to follow the path of armed conquest in its efforts for world domination. Reactionary British imperialism, together with the French monopolists, which helped bring German fascism to power, which initiated the policy of appeasement to the former Rome-Berlin-Tokyo Axis at the expense of the national integrity and existence of the peoples of China, Ethiopia, Austria, Czechoslovakia, Spain and Poland, and at the risk of the national interests of Britain and France—strove and still endeavors to incite and divert Nazi armed forces eastward against the Soviet Union. Balked in this objective as a result of the peace policy and strength of the land of socialism which brought about the Soviet-German Non-Aggression Pact, the British ruling class has entered the robber war against German imperialism in order to weaken the German bourgeoisie, to consolidate British imperialist hegemony in Europe and the world, and to try to bring to power in Germany that section of the bourgeoisie which will immediately engage in military intervention against the USSR.

Thus, the current imperialist war for world domination and the forcible redivision of empires, nations, colonies and spheres of influence is an imperialist war on both sides, expressing the deepest and sharpest crisis of world capitalism. This is deepening and accentuating to an unprecedented degree the rivalries and contradictions between and within all imperialist powers. This is also rendering more acute the struggle between the systems of decaying, predatory capitalism and victorious, liberating socialism. In short, the present imperialist war signifies that the crisis of disintegrating world capitalism is entering a new and more acute phase, marked by the opening of a new series of wars and revolutions of a protracted nature.

Therefore, the working class and exploited peoples of all countries should not and must not support either side of the predatory imperialist war which is being waged by the ruling classes of Germany and of Britain and France for the dismemberment and enslavement of nations and peoples, for monopoly profits and for greater class oppression of the working people in their own countries. Keep America out of the imperialist war must be the foremost slogan of the American people....

4. Under the cynical mask of "neutrality" the American bourgeoisie, despite certain inner tactical differences, is united in its greed for huge war profits and imperialist aggrandizement. It is preparing to involve the USA in the imperialist war under conditions most favorable to strengthening the world hegemony of American imperialism. Important sections of the American bourgeoisie are encouraging and stimulating hostility toward the Soviet Union, supporting the British plan of converting the present imperialist war into a counterrevolutionary war against the land of socialism. Pressed by the imperialist bourgeoisie, the Roosevelt government, despite its avowed intentions of "keeping America out of war," more and more takes a course which threatens to involve the USA in the imperialist war. But the overwhelming mass of the people are definitely opposed to United States involvement in the imperialist war.

Therefore it is imperative for the American working class and toiling people to pursue an independent policy and to resist and defeat the policy and influence of the reactionary Wall Street monopolists and their agents upon the government's foreign and domestic policy. It is necessary to organize and register the people's opposition to America's involvement in the imperialist war....

3

NOT MY PEOPLE'S WAR
Richard Wright

Wright was still a devoted Communist when he wrote this piece for the June 17, 1941, issue of New Masses—*it was based on a talk he gave to a recent meeting of the Writers Congress (what was left of it)—despite the chilly reception the Party had given his great book* Native Son, *which had come out a few months earlier. In 1944 he quit the Party and soon after settled in Paris.*

Some of you may wonder why a writer, at a congress of writers, should make the theme of war the main burden of a public talk. Some of you may be expecting to hear writers discuss and compare books and stories. Others of you may be expecting to hear what writers think of what has been recently written, or of what other writers are now engaged in writing. Well, I, for one, find such an order impossible to fill. My eyes are drawn toward war. Frankly and unfortunately, there is not much else in this world tonight that means one-half as much as war. Every single human aspiration is dwarfed by

the forces of war that grip and restrict the movement of men today. War
overshadows and dominates all other meanings and activities. War is hourly
changing the look of reality. War is creating a new and terrifying subject matter for writers.

It is, however, with reluctance that we think, feel, and talk of war. But we
have no choice. Our preoccupation with war and destruction constitutes a
sort of invidious tribute which we writers must pay to the men who rule the
so-called Western world, the men who deceived the peoples of the earth in
the first world war by fabricating their Fourteen Points of Peace, the men
who deluded hundreds of millions of people by pledging that all covenants
would be openly arrived at, the men who naively and proudly declared only
a few short years ago that all peoples would have the right to determine their
own destinies, the men who declared so comically only a few short months
ago that we would enjoy "peace in our time." And today we continue to pay
invidious tribute to the men who are conjuring up another program, the
Four Freedoms, for another war, and who are today blindly plunging the
world into another protracted conflict whose outcome is not in sight.

So the nature of my remarks here tonight is in the form of a report to you
upon a new array of subject matter which the war is bringing into view in
Negro life in the United States. The texture of what I have to say deals with
the state of feeling that exists among the Negro people in this country toward
the current war. That state of feeling is so clear and unmistakable that the war
leaders of our nation recognize and fear it. It is the *one* thing on the war horizon which they cannot "explain away." Indeed, the Negro's experience with
past wars, his attitude toward the present one, his attitude of chronic distrust, constitute the most incisive and graphic refutation of every idealistic
statement made by the war leaders as to the alleged democratic goal and aim
of this war.

Against the background of Hitler's treatment of the Jews, the Negroes'
plight in this country is what even labor-baiting Westbrook Pegler quaintly
calls an "embarrassment" to the efforts of the war leaders! Throughout the
high, ruling circles of the nation, the attitude toward the Negro is: Oh, why
should we be bothered with this old Negro question? Or, The Negro issue is
a dead issue. Or, Listen, all you do in bringing up the Negro issue is to make
things worse for them. Or, Oh, the Negroes. . . . Why, they're getting along
all right. And so on. The Negro people are aware of this, and their attitude
toward this war is conditioned by it.

The dogged reluctance on the part of the Negro people to support this
war is undeniably justified and is rooted deep in historical background. Bitter
and obstinate memories separate 15,000,000 Negroes from this war, memories of hypocrisy, of glib promises easily given and quickly betrayed, of cynical exploitation of hope, of double-dealing, memories which are impossible
to forget or ignore. . . .

Parenthetically, I'd like to ask this audience a question: If the United States is really anxious to stop Hitler; does it not seem logical that the morale of the Negro and white troops of the International Brigade, who beat back the fascists from the gates of Madrid, is a good morale for our troops? I'd like to ask, has there ever fought a more determined army than that wall of men, black and white, who, standing side by side for many months, endured all that Germany and Italy had to hurl at them? Evidently, that is *not* the kind of morale they are planning to instill into the United States Army, which is being created allegedly to fight fascism and spread the Four Freedoms.

The White House secretary went on to state the "democratic" policy of the crusade for the Four Freedoms:

"For similar reasons, the War Department does not contemplate assigning colored reserve officers other than those of the Medical Corps and Chaplains to the existing Negro combat units of the regular army."

In view of the above fascist statement, one must conclude that, insofar as the Negro is concerned, it *is* an imperialist war, a war which continues and deepens discriminatory tactics against the Negro people, against progressive people, against labor unions, professionals, and intellectuals. Such a statement reduces Roosevelt's Four Freedoms to a metaphysical obscenity!

How is it possible for any sincere or sane person to contend that the current war, World War II, is a crusade for freedom, for the "majesty of the human soul," for a full life, in the face of official utterances which categorically reject the very concept of freedom and democracy? . . .

Hourly the radio assures us of the nobility of England's mission in the world, and they would have us believe that India would be better off under England's rule than under the Nazis.' It never seems to occur to them that perhaps the Indians would like to be let entirely alone. England waged a successful fight recently against Italian imperialism in Ethiopia, but she still has to grant the Ethiopian people their independence.

The cry of the Negro people today is for peace. The cry of America today is for peace. The cry of the common people of the world today is for peace.

The Soviet Union and its leaders stand today as living testimony to the profound hatred of war and to the sincere love of peace that resides in the hearts of the common people of the world. Here is a nation that owes its very existence to the fact that its common people dared lift their voices for peace.

Writers, artists, educators, all men who exert or wield influence in the world should proceed diligently and fearlessly to prepare the minds of millions of people caught in the mesh of war to answer the call for peace when it comes.

And that call is surely coming. The universal demand for peace is the secret weapon of the masses of the common people! It is a weapon which Hitler, Churchill, and Roosevelt fear more than any bomb! Do not all of you remember the futile rage and despair with which the English and American press greeted the treaty of peace signed by the Soviet Union and Finland after a brief spell of fighting? There was a sinister meaning behind that rage; the

desire of the British government and the United States government was for
a continuance of that war! The panic, the hate, the uneasiness which informs
the chancelleries and the state departments of the governments of the world
today is added testimony to the fear that exists among those who dread to
hear the call for peace sound throughout the world.

The voice of the common man has not yet been heard in this war, and the
common people have something to say about what happens in this world. A
Hitler victory will not end this war. An English victory will not end this war.
And America's entrance into this war will not decide its ultimate outcome.
Those facts comprise the most optimistic aspect of this war; it is what sepa-
rates this war from all other wars. And that is why the warring nations dare
not mention their war aims, save in but the most general terms. They are
afraid.

When the voice sounds for peace, the Negro people will answer it.

WOMEN

1
WOMEN ARE HUMAN BEINGS
Ruth McKenney

*By 1940 the Party was finally giving women a public voice. Prominent among them was
Ruth McKenney, who began writing a "Mostly Personal" column for the* New Masses, *one
of which, from the December 17, 1940, issue, is excerpted here. McKenney was already
famous as the author of* My Sister Eileen, *about her sister who had died in a car crash
with her husband, novelist Nathanael West. (*My Sister Eileen *became a long-running
Broadway play and was the basis for Leonard Bernstein's musical* Wonderful Town.*)
McKenney's 1939 study of Akron rubber workers,* Industrial Valley, *is still very much
worth reading. In 1946 the Party expelled her for factional reasons. She died in 1972.*

The question arises: but if the machine is supposed to set women free, why
hasn't it? And the answer is that it has in one country of the world, the Soviet
Union. I believe nobody can write about the "woman question" today in good
faith without stating the fact that women have been completely and unconditionally emancipated in the Soviet Union. It is a fact. It is the truth. It cannot be denied even by people who dislike Russian foreign policy to the point
of hysteria. . . .

So why isn't it that way in the United States? We still have better machinery that they do in the Soviet Union, although the Russians, from being in the
last place in modern development are now second, next to us. We still have
larger schools, better hospitals, more libraries than the Soviet Union,
although again, that nation has come from bottom to top in twenty years.

We're still the richest, most developed nation in the world. Why haven't American women been able to make themselves free and happy?

The answer is, the profit system. Perhaps that seems far-fetched, blaming the anomalous position of women in America on the capitalist class. But look at the facts. Everybody knows we have over 9,000,000 unemployed in the midst of a war boom. Suppose to this 9,000,000 were added at least another 25,000,000 women seeking jobs in industry. If you think this over, you will have the answer to the strange, heart-breaking training of women in modern American society. The power-driven tool, once capitalism's great force, has now become its Frankenstein. Machinery cannot be used for profit now and still employ all available labor power in the working class. Gradually, the gap between what the manufacturer pays his workers and what manufactured articles the workers can afford to buy with their wages grows larger; the market shrinks—and unemployment, the great tragedy, the rotting, fatal disease of capitalism, marches on the scene.

And in the midst of this shifting scene stands the woman. She is trained to work because the capitalist needs her labor—in industries where the employer can pay her rock bottom wages, for instance, or in case of war when available manpower diminishes. It is one of the searing ironies of this too-ironic economic system that war, which brings the woman untold personal agonies, also liberates her from her long dull life in the kitchen and parlor. The women in Great Britain today have come up out of the slavery of the home to do honest, socially necessary work. But the new-found freedom must be gall in their mouths and wormwood to their hearts, for another generation of their husbands and sons and fathers and this time their babies, is being killed off, even while they celebrate their right to work.

But capitalism, which educates the modern woman to do productive work, rarely needs her labor power. Indeed, in the past twenty years, every capitalist nation in the world has suffered from a dreadful surfeit of productive workers. So the woman, trained for an emergency, is fed a whole library of ideas to keep her safe in the grueling unpaid labor of the home. Her husband is carefully taught to despise intelligent, able women; the movies and the novels and the magazines feed her the dreams of romantic love. Out of the need to keep women safely off the already glutted labor market comes the stream of nauseous propaganda: married women must not work; keeping house is fun; doing housework is scientific; be a "home-manager"; a man likes to come home to find a pretty girl keeping his slippers warm; if you work, he'll leave you.

And so on. And so forth. This is the reason for the whole fetish of super-housekeeping, promoted in a hundred women's magazines, a thousand newspaper women's pages. This is the reason for the entire beauty cult, the mad business of super-self-decoration. Women have to have something to do; they have to be cajoled and kidded and forced into staying home, everlastingly home, until they are needed. Every woman knows that all this business about housekeeping is just pure plain hooey except perhaps the women who write the blithe articles for the papers about it; and no wonder, they have an amusing job, exhorting other women to do beauty exercises while sweeping under the bed! Ha!

STAY-AT-HOME PROPAGANDA

As a matter of fact, if women were needed in the labor market, the capitalists, in their press and magazines, through their advertising and over their radio, would suddenly reverse the current stay-at-home propaganda. Overnight, the real truth would appear. "Ladies," the women's pages would thunder, "send your laundry out, it's cheaper if you count in your own labor time!" Why should a house be kept so so frightfully clean it jumps at you, a dulcet-voiced lady commentator would mew over the airwaves. Stern newspaper editorials would argue that two-thirds of the current scrubbing and waxing and polishing that women do is something to keep them busy and sell soaps and waxes and polishes. And in very truth why should a meal take all day to get with Bird's-Eye foods and canned specialties and good bakeries around every corner? If a woman likes to cook for fun (a few do, and I among them), why shouldn't she do her fancy cooking on Sunday, *pour le sport*? And for the children, every expert knows that nurseries and preschools are the ideal training for children. No mother, no matter how well educated or intelligent, can possibly give her children at home what they would get in a group of youngsters carefully supervised. If women were ever needed to work, the majority of women, I mean, in this country, you would see an overnight reversal in the silly propaganda forced down women's throats today. Men would be told that the correct thing is to encourage your wife's ambitions, help her to clean and cook, doing share and share alike. And the crazy notion that it takes a woman's full time in a modern machine-age society to keep house, take care of the children, and toady to her husband would evaporate into thin air.

If! I wish I could say that I thought the time would ever come, in this system of society, when women would have a chance to be normal human beings. I'm afraid that matters are getting worse for women, not better. Hitler "solved" unemployment by taking the youth for his immense army, stray labor for concentration camps and road gangs, and finally forcing all women out of schools and factories, offices, and professions, back to the middle ages and the purdah. Today, in this country, important men writers appearing in respectable magazines have the gall to suggest the identical solution for America's staggering unemployment problem. Even famous women columnists' urge women back to the home—as though they had ever been able to get out of it, in any appreciable numbers. The rising, bumbling tide of obscurantist literature on the woman question engulfs feminine America. In proportion to the increasing gravity of the unemployment problem, which stubbornly refuses to disappear in the face of vast profits for steel and armament corporations, the anti-woman propaganda grows, often fed, to their everlasting shame, by bought-off women themselves. I say bought-off, using the phrase literally. The exceptional woman, who through gall, luck, money, or advantages of education manages to make a place for herself in this man's world, is often the first to kick her humbler sisters in the teeth for the greater glory of the system which so handsomely supports her.

So must women sit back and resign themselves to a long dreary period of reaction against the struggle for women's place in society? Must the next generation of girls content themselves with sewing and basting the turkey and hanging out the wash and keeping an absurd little bookkeeping system under the delusion they are "home-managers"? Must the working women docilely give up their jobs and march uncomplainingly back to their dreary "woman's work"?

I, for one, think not. Absolutely not. The women must fight back, and fight back hard against this tide which threatens to destroy even the few paltry gains they have made. And they must fight harder still to bring the day when women can work side by side, as free human beings, with their husbands and brothers. And I don't mean the word fight poetically; I mean practically. For even the woman cooped up in her home, a prisoner to her dustmop, can help in this all-important battle. How? well, for a beginning, by writing into newspapers and answering every letter which complains about married women working, with the battle cry: "What do you mean women shouldn't work? Why not? We have as much brains, as much training—find us jobs! We want to work!" Be a propagandist for the rights of women from your kitchen table! Write to every women's magazine you read and ask for realistic stories, recipes for the working woman, and so on. And train your children—not just your daughter, but your son, too—to understand that women are human beings. . . .

And finally, in politics, I am frankly an avowed Red. But I urge you to consider the Communist Party as a means of expressing yourself politically, not because of my admitted bias, but because it is the only organization I honestly know in this country which energetically, consistently, and as a matter of principle, fights for the complete—and I mean complete—emancipation of women. The major parties are even chary of lip-service, and lip-service is cold comfort after the elections are over. And most of the existing women's organizations are either dismal little playgrounds for the bored leisure classes, or adjuncts of local and national machine politics. . . .

Sometimes, when I think about being a woman in America today, I have a sort of daydream. Think of how great and strong and beautiful 65,000,000 American men have made this land! And now suppose that the energies, the skills, the brains, the hearts, the courage of 65,000,000 women were added to the labor power of our country. What a world we women could build, side by side with our men, if only we had the chance!

And I believe we can make that chance for ourselves, or at least for our daughters. Forward!

I Love My Comrade Organizers
Elizabeth Gurley Flynn

When Elizabeth Gurley Flynn joined the Party in the late 1930s she already had quite a career as a labor radical bred up in the Anarcho-Syndicalist school of the IWW. She was a fiery public speaker who had been prominent in famous IWW-led strikes at Lawrence and Paterson. Pleased with such a valuable catch, the Party gave her a twice-weekly column in the Daily Worker. *There and in her other writings Flynn occasionally discussed women's issues, for example, in the selection below, which she composed in 1940 but did not publish; it is among her papers at New York University's Tamiment Library.*

I love my comrade organizers and speakers—but I don't envy their wives,
I've been a wife myself and I'm a comrade too,
I know the strain we are!
The skipped meals, the broken dates, the unpaid bills, the hard lives
The clothes you can't have, the worries you do have,
We come late or not at all! You wait and watch
Are we in jail or mobbed or just the car broke down?
The endless meetings, trips, committees, calls,
To go here and run there, this comrade needs advice, this one is fired—the
    Party must attend.

I love my comrades—but, dear wives, I don't envy you
At home, alone, and waiting for your men,
I know them in their work, I talk with them, laugh, meet, eat drink, travel
    day and night, with them,
Sleep in the same houses, run risks together, have endless discussions with
    them
They are great and I admire them tremendously and collectively,
But you wash their shorts and shirts, lay out their ties and socks,
You pack their suitcases, and have their shirts pressed,
I see your loving care in their nice blue shirts and matching vest and clean
    handkerchiefs!
I don't envy you!

I love my comrades 'deed I do, I love them one and all,
But I don't envy you dear wives, the care they are,
How good they are, how uncomplaining, devoted we know well,
But careless of their health sleep and food and rest,
Now impatient to stop a while and think of self,
So you must do it for them; make them dress warm, take a pill;
Put on their rubbers and their mufflers, make them get a haircut and a
    shave.

They love you, you should hear them tell what grand girls you are!
But they forget to tell you, I'm afraid. NO—I don't envy you!
But I do envy them the comradeship of understanding love you give to
    them
Because you so unselfishly serve our cause in taking care of them,
You forget self to keep them free from personal tasks and fit, healthy and
    strong
And I do envy them the sweetness of your love,
Don't worry their devotion to their task absorbs and consumes them
Keeps them true to you, dear wives, beyond all other men,
Yes I do envy them having someone to really care so much,
I fear I envy you one thing only dear wives,
Their love when I am lonely!
and some one man—to do all that for me!
I guess I need a wife!

3
EVERY DAY SHOULD BE MOTHER'S DAY FOR US
Elizabeth Gurley Flynn

Flynn wrote this piece for the May 11, 1941, Sunday Worker.

The Philadelphia lady who first proposed Mother's Day meant well. Her suggestion was that everyone should wear a carnation on the second Sunday of May, in honor of their mother—a red carnation if she was living, a white carnation if she was dead.

Out of this modest gesture has grown a million-dollar business. Mother is the least and last beneficiary. The day has been seized upon by telegraph companies, florists, confectioners, and department stores for nationwide exploitation. The universal sentiment which surrounds motherhood is debased by their profane, pioneering hands. Signs are displayed for weeks, "Give Mother This—or That—or the Other!" Leftovers from Christmas are unloaded on dutiful, filial purchasers. Mother's Day becomes a money-making mockery. Real feeling for Mother is smothered in a sugary sentimentality which comes from the radio, drips from greeting cards, and makes of this day a sort of maternal Valentine's Day.

People who love their mothers don't need a special day to be reminded of it. What our mothers have done for us or mean to us should be in our hearts and minds at all times. The trouble is, we're apt to take Mother too much for granted, like the sun and the stars, day and night, she's always there. It's nice to remember your mother with an occasional gift—a few flowers, a pretty scarf, some handkerchiefs, a pair of stockings. But not just once a year, to do penance for indifference the rest of the time. Not just to make a Roman holiday for merchants. It's thoughtful to take your mother to a restaurant and to a show, so she won't have to cook. But not just once and leave her to the tiresome round of monotonous tasks the rest of the year. A good way to neutralize the crass commercializing of Mother's Day is to spread our attentions to Mother. Make every day Mother's Day. It is for her—she's always on duty.

All of the mothers who work in industry carry a double burden—their job and their own work at home. The thousands of domestic day workers who first clean somebody else's home must then do their own. The thousands who work in laundries go home to do their own washing. The thousands who work in hotels rush home to tidy up their own rooms. The thousands who work in restaurants go home to stand several more weary hours to prepare food for their own families.

They do not get equal pay for equal work in industry. Nor is there equalization at home where all domestic work is still "woman's work." Only the most progressive and intelligent men lend a hand at home to lighten this double burden capitalism places on working mothers. On Mother's Day, resolve to do this.

The ones who stay home to care for their children are neither useless nor idle. They handle the finances, do the buying and budgeting. They see the cost of living rise before the statisticians plot the curve. The methods used in the home are antiquated and individualistic. Mother is the last to get modern appliances for her work. On farms with cars and tractors, women will carry water from outdoors.

Mothers need union hours, modern methods of work, relief from worry; peace and security. With the threat of war manacling her, how can any mother enjoy this day under capitalism? Socialism is the way out for mothers when every day will be truly a mother's happy day. Mothers can only be happy when their children are safe and happy.

WAR YEARS

1

NO DELAY IN OPENING THE WESTERN FRONT
The Communist

This editorial in the August 1942 issue of the Party's theoretical organ sums up the desperate message it broadcast far and wide demanding an immediate Allied invasion of Europe. The Red Army was on the ropes.

The continued delay in the full and immediate implementation of the agreement for launching the Second Front is endangering the position of all of the United Nations, and is working to Hitler's advantage.

Because of this, it must be noted, in recent days an element of doubt bordering on cynicism has crept into the thinking of some people—namely, that a Second Front can no longer be realized this year. Hence, questions arise as to why we do not withdraw the slogan of "Smash Hitler in 1942."

To all these doubtings and questionings the answer should be given that there is no need for panic, though there is need for deep concern and action. . . .

What explains this restricted approach to the Second Front as well as some of the hesitation and delay? It represents the failure to appreciate fully the danger of not acting swiftly and decisively; it is the last pitiful remnant of the theory of a long war—as if the war hasn't been going on long enough already. And what is the explanation for this thesis if not the mistake of seeing the apparent as the real—the overestimation of the strength of the enemy and the underestimation of the ability of the people, who, when given bold leadership and a real people's program, can rapidly turn the tide of battle—can smash Hitler before this year is over.

We need a Second Front, not as a mere token action, not as a mere diversion, but as a major offensive. Any front opened in Western Europe, however, will have its own logic of development and will swiftly become a major offensive, which can, in conjunction with the mighty Red Army and the Soviet counter-offensive, speedily crush Hitler and the fascist Axis. . . .

The Communists, on their part, must strive today more than ever to work in a manner that will aid in cementing the broadest unity of labor and the people, for the single objective—to win the war. By their work in the factories and trade unions, by their work in the communities, by their efforts to strengthen every phase of our country's war efforts, in the armed forces, in the preparations for realizing the Second Front, in the Congressional and State elections, they must set an example and thereby rouse labor and the people to the understanding and course of action in line with the following words of Comrade Browder:

With full faith in the justness of the United Nations' cause, as a Peoples' War of National Liberation; with full faith that our own true national interests coincide with those of other peoples; with pride and confidence in American labor's mighty contributions to our nation's war; with strict adherence to principle as the only sure guide to effective solution of all domestic and international problems; with the inspiration of the glorious achievements of our Soviet ally in this war; with confidence that British and American arms will earn their full share of the glory of final victory—we join our voices to the call to all Americans:

Unite for victory!
Open the Western Front now and smash Hitler in 1942!
Everything for the destruction of the Nazi-Fascist Axis!

HOLD THE HOME FRONT
Earl Browder

The Party's hostility to anything that might hinder the war effort and the growth of labor productivity is here officially enunciated by Browder in the July 1943 Communist. *His logic is to equate any demand for a wage increase with John L. Lewis's lack of patriotism, his repeated threats to take the coal miners out on strike.*

The most acute and difficult of our problems are epitomized in the Lewis insurrection against the war. It has become clear that we must characterize the campaign of John L. Lewis and his long list of helpers in these past weeks as nothing less than an insurrection against the war. John L. Lewis has become the key figure and the spearhead of the anti-war diversion, and for this he is manipulating the miners' union, of which he has, over the years, become the unchallenged autocrat. There is not the slightest doubt that Lewis is working and has worked during the past two years at least, as an integral part of the pro-Nazi fifth column, aiming at a negotiated peace with Hitler at the expense of Britain and the Soviet Union, and, in a deeper sense, at the Nazi subjugation of the United States itself. There is no doubt that the miners' strike was developed consciously as a part of that conspiracy. There is no doubt that this is treason against the miners, against the labor movement, against our own country and against the United Nations. . . .

Lewis's stooges, especially the Trotskyites and Norman Thomas Socialists, the Social-Democratic Federation and the George Sokolskys, have raised the cry that strikes must always be supported, and especially by the Communists. They are trying to convince us that we are renegades from the principles of Lenin and Stalin in condemning the strike movement; that it is against the laws of nature for Communists to be against strikes. Yes, they go so far as to quote Lenin against us and for John L. Lewis. Such references to Lenin are beneath contempt and are an obvious cover for treason to trade unionism as well as to the nation. Even in the days when strikes were in the main progressive acts and to be supported, Lenin never failed to warn, and on this he had the agreement of all sound trade union leaders, that not all strikes can be supported, that the consequences of a strike must always be taken into consideration before a strike is advocated, planned, carried out or supported. The consequences of an act are the determining factor of the class attitude toward it. That is a basic rule of all sound trade unionism. Way back in 1902 Lenin had occasion to criticize a program that had been advocated by one of the organizations in Russia and which extolled strikes as the best means of struggle. The strike, Lenin replied,

is only one of the means, not always even one of the best. It is enough to indicate the necessity to give leadership to economic struggles in general; sometimes this leadership must be expressed by restraining strikes. (*Collected Works*, vol. 5, p. 130, Russian edition)

Today in the United States it has become an imperative duty of all sound labor leadership to restrain strikes and to do everything to dissolve the strike movement. You cannot have strikes and win the war. . . .

The problem before us is to carry the issue of the incentive wage over from the stage of discussion to the stage of action, by having it applied in life by the trade unions in collaboration with the government and with those sections of the enlightened employers who are ready to welcome it. It is necessary to break down the resistance and sabotage of this issue within the labor movement which come from people with special interests, most of them linked up with Lewis, and to overcome that section of the employers whose resistance is based upon shortsightedness, greed and inertia, as well as that section of the employers whose resistance is political, caused by their connection with the defeatist conspiracy.

In general, we can sum up our tasks in relation to the Lewis insurrection against the war in a few simply stated aims which we must set for all conscious and honest men in the labor movement and outside. These provide the key to the solidification of the home front for the next crucial period in the military struggle. . . .

3

AMERICAN NEGROES IN THE WAR
Paul Robeson

That prominent black Communists, or pro-Communists, among them the great singer and actor Paul Robeson, refused to sweep the race issue under the rug for the duration of the war is brought out in these remarks by Robeson before the prestigious Herald-Tribune Forum in New York and disseminated to a wide audience when the paper printed them on November 21, 1943.

World War II has been repeatedly and eloquently described as a war in the interest of the common man, the little man—a people's war of liberation. Americans who have not known through personal experience the meaning of fascist oppression may be prone to think of such characterizations of the war as only fine rhetorical and idealistic expressions.

But the Chinese, the Ethiopians, the Russians, and all the peoples of Europe upon whom the axis forces have heaped murder and destruction know full well what it is they are fighting for. *They* understood—in their hearts and in every conscious moment of their existence—what a people's war of liberation means.

Other peoples however, besides the direct victims of axis aggression, also have a genuine awareness of the democratic significance of the present conflict. Their awareness is born of their yearning for freedom from an oppression which has pre-dated fascism and their confidence that they have a stake in the victory of the forces of democracy.

The American Negro has such an outlook. It dates from the fascist invasion of Ethiopia in 1935. Since then, the parallel between his own interests and those of oppressed peoples abroad has been impressed upon him daily as he struggles against the forces which bar him from full citizenship, from full participation in American life.

The disseminators and supporters of racial discrimination and antagonism are to the Negro, and are *in fact*, first cousins if not brothers of the Nazis. They speak the same language of the "Master Race" and practice, or attempt to practice, the same tyranny over minority peoples.

There are three things in American life which today arouse the bitterest resentment among Black Americans and at the same time represent the greatest handicap upon his full participation in the national war effort. First is their economic insecurity which they know to be the result of continuing discrimination in employment even now, coupled with other forms of economic exploitation and social discrimination in urban communities such as Harlem.

Second is the segregation and inferior status assigned to Negroes in the armed forces and their complete exclusion from most of the women's auxiliary services. Added to this are the insults and acts of physical violence nurtured by the segregation policy which have been inflicted upon them in many of the camps and camp communities. . . .

Third is the poll-tax system of the South, which operates to maintain undemocratic elements in places of authority not only below the Mason Dixon line but in our national life as a whole.

Some progress has been made in righting these wrongs. The most positive action has been in the accomplishments of the President's Committee on Fair Employment Practice. . . . But these gains are pitifully small indeed when measured against the loss of manpower, the lowered morale, the interracial friction and national disunity which characterize America at war.

And yet there are some who deplore the Negro's present-day struggle for democracy and equality as *endangering* national unity and our war effort. They point to the trouble (so they say) that the FEPC has stirred up in the South and to the disgraceful race riots—insurrections or pogroms would be more accurate—in Detroit and other industrial centers which resulted (so they say) from Negro militancy.

Such people are looking at the world upside down or hind-parts forward. They believe the wagon is pushing the horse. They are the people who believe Hitler's lie that Nazism and fascism were and are necessary in order to save the world from Communism. . . .

The great majority of these peoples, especially in Africa, are on the sidelines of the war. They have not been mobilized to any appreciable extent by their colonial administrators in either the military or production services. Their participation *now* in the United Nations' war effort—just as in the case of the American Negro—is the measure of the kind of victory and the kind of peace that is in store for them.

Let me read to you something that a Negro leader in South Africa recently said: "I know like anybody else that although we are fighting for Democracy, we do not enjoy democratic rule in this country, but I look with hope to the influence that will be exerted by America and Russia toward our rights, as I think that if the Allies win, a new order of government will be brought about."

Those words represent the thought of millions of colonial peoples throughout the world.

A few days ago, Americans honored the Soviet Union on the occasion of the 10th anniversary of the establishment of friendly diplomatic relations between that great nation and ours. We honored the heroic fight which the people of that nation have made against Hitler's erstwhile invincible legions. Two years ago, many Americans, like Hitler, expected the Soviet Union to crumble under the treacherous blitz attack. Now Americans are beginning to know something of the great power of the Russian people—a power born of unity, of legally enforced equality, of opportunity for all the many millions within its wide borders, regardless of race, creed, nationality or sex. No other nation on earth has achieved such a thing. And no other nation has stated with such explicitness its war aims: "abolition of racial exclusiveness; equality of nations and integrity of their territories; the right of every nation to arrange its affairs as it wishes."

The United States and Great Britain must learn from their Soviet ally the true meaning and application of democracy to minority and colonial peoples. Upon these three great powers rests the primary responsibility, accepted by them jointly in the recent Moscow Conference decisions, of turning military victory into enduring peace and security for all peoples. America and Britain must prove to the world that they are in truth waging a people's war of liberation, or they must face the shame and scorn of the world.

4

TEHERAN AND AMERICA
Earl Browder

Browder presented his extraordinary views on the postwar future—a future based more or less on class reconciliation within the United States and national reconciliation between the United States and the Soviet Union—that is, on a permanent Popular Front—in a speech before the Party's plenary session on January 7, 1944. It was included in a pamphlet published later in the year.

Churchill, Stalin and Roosevelt in Teheran expressed the determination to
"work together in the war and in the peace that will follow."

Dealing with the war and the peace thus in a single sentence was surely not accidental. It reflected the insuperable difficulties in waging a joint war without having a joint perspective for the peace to follow, and the impossibility of any perspective for a long peace unless the war is jointly fought and jointly won.

Both phases of this declaration must be taken with equal seriousness. We cannot accept one and reject the other. They stand together in their very nature, like Siamese twins who, if severed, are in the gravest danger of immediate death.

When Churchill, Stalin and Roosevelt can say they "have surveyed the problems of the future," and that they "are sure that our concord will make it an enduring peace"; when they hold out a perspective of a future which will "banish the scourge and terror of war for many generations"—then we may be sure that these three men have found a path to which, as realists, they expect to win not only the great majority of their own people, but the "overwhelming masses of the peoples of the world." They were not playing with diplomatic phrases. They were projecting a practical policy.

The difficulties which stood in the way of such agreements are not secrets. The whole thinking world knows what they were. And knowing this, we can begin to formulate for ourselves on a much more extensive scale than the official communiqués give us, the nature of the common policy, the "concord," which was begun in Teheran.

Not so widely appreciated as the difficulties, there was operative in Teheran a motive for agreement for the post-war period equally as forceful as the motive for agreement on the joint war.

Where the overriding consideration for a joint coalition war against Hitlerism is the alternative of a Hitler-dominated world, which means the extinguishing of civilization for generations to come, it must be recognized that for the coalition peace, after Hitlerism has been destroyed, there is the equally strong motive that without it the alternative is the spread of civil wars over vast areas, culminating finally and inevitably in a new world war between nations.

Those who have said, lightheartedly, that it was Hitler who forced the Anglo-Soviet-American coalition but as soon as Hitler is gone the coalition will fly apart overnight were but shallow thinkers who underestimated the depth of the world crisis through which we live. Likewise they underestimated the amount of effective intelligence that has been achieved by mankind. Roosevelt, Stalin and Churchill at Teheran were the representatives of the collective intelligence of mankind facing the threatening supreme catastrophe of history and determined to avert it. . . .

It would be the greatest single contribution to wartime national unity, therefore, if we could seriously establish the prospect that this unity will be continued in the post-war period, that it will not explode into a chaos of inner struggles at the moment war hostilities cease.

Further, this expectation of unlimited inner conflict threatens to destroy also the perspective of international unity held forth at Teheran. If we wish to uphold and realize the Teheran perspective, we must find the way to minimize, and to place definite limits upon, the settlement of inner differences in the country by conflict in the post-war period. The perspective of inner chaos within the United States is incompatible with the perspective of international order.

These two basic considerations are sufficient to establish the supreme responsibility upon all who support the Teheran policy, to work for such policies within the country that will lead toward, and give realistic promise of, the continuation of national unity into the post-war period for a long term of years. . . .

It will be necessary for us to be very harsh and unyielding to this insistent demand for post-war plans on our part. We must put a few questions and demand clear answers to them from all who aspire to make plans for America.

The first question is, what kind of America are the plans for, a socialist or a capitalist America?

No one can suspect me of holding any prejudices in favor of capitalism, whether in America or elsewhere. I have been an advocate of socialism during all of my adult life, of socialism for America. The Communist Party is the only party of socialism in this country. But I have not the slightest hesitation in declaring that any plans for American post-war reconstruction which are based upon the introduction of socialism are in effect a repudiation of the aim to unite the majority of the nation behind the Teheran policies.

It is my considered judgment that the American people are so ill-prepared, subjectively, for any deep-going change in the direction of socialism that post-war plans with such an aim would not unite the nation, but would further divide it. And they would divide and weaken precisely the democratic and progressive camp, while they would unite and strengthen the most reactionary forces in the country. In their practical effect, they would help the anti-Teheran forces to come to power in the United States.

If the national unity of the war period is to be extended and even strengthened in the post-war period, then we must recognize that in the United States this requires from the Marxists the reaffirmation of our wartime policy that we will not raise the issue of socialism in such a form and manner as to endanger or weaken that national unity. . . .

Now our country is entering a new period, in which, with the successful conclusion of the war, all issues will be subordinated to the supreme aim of realizing the promise of Teheran, of maintaining an orderly world which will give us some generations of peace.

Obviously, to realize the promise of Teheran the broadest democratic-progressive united front must be maintained in the United States. Equally obviously, the Communists will be a part, and a small minority part, of that united front. The Communist organization will be in a long-term alliance with forces much larger than itself.

It follows from this fact, that in the peculiar American sense of the word, the Communists will not be operating as a "party," that is, with their own separate candidates in elections, except under special circumstances when they may be forced to act through "independent candidates."

This is already our practical situation; and we are now extending the perspective of national unity for many years into the future. It is no longer an "emergency situation" but is merging into a "normal" situation.

All these considerations point to the expediency of a decision that the Communist organization in the United States should adjust its name to correspond more exactly to the American political tradition and its own practical political role.

Such a decision would be that, instead of being known as "The Communist Party of the United States," our organization should call itself something like "American Communist Political Association."

It is the recommendation of our Political Committee that this meeting of the National Committee should endorse such a proposal, referring it to our 1944 National Convention for final action.

Under such a name we will find it much easier to explain our true relationship with all other democratic and progressive groupings which operate through the medium, in the main, of the two party system, and take our place in free collaboration at their side. . . .

We are independent, in the same way as the great bulk of America's independent voters who make up fully one-third of the total voting strength of the country and who are not committed to either of the major parties, though most of them are registered with one or the other. As a part of this independent voters' group, we may find our members registering wherever they think will best advance the progressive cause. That is one of the rights of citizenship and our organization would not think of denying to any American the full exercise of all his rights as an American citizen. But our organization is not and will not be an organization committed to any party; and that is necessarily the case because of the nature of the two major parties. These two parties are essentially institutionalized channels, semi-governmental in their nature, through which the citizenry groups and regroups itself from election to election according to the leadership that is thrown up and the issues that are thereby developed.

In the general relationship of forces in the country, for us there can be no commitment to party because that would be to commit ourselves to an institutionalized structure which stands for nothing in particular in the political sense. Therefore we have to concentrate our attention exclusively on issues, and on men who represent issues within the various party structures, and choose freely among them on their merits without regard to party label.

This is the major point that I thought necessary to bring forward in these summary remarks, as a sort of continuation of the discussion, because it seems to me that while there is general acceptance of the course on which we are going, there is perhaps not the same complete and general understanding that this new course is not in any way an identification with any of the old party structures. If we are identifying ourselves with any general, big political grouping in the country, in the narrower electoral sense, it is with the great body of independent voters of America who in the electoral struggle will choose whom they support on the basis of their judgment of the character of men and of the issues for which they stand, and nothing else.

I have the general feeling that in these three days we have welded together such a common body of opinion so firmly grounded in our own experience, in the objective reality of the world outside, and in our capacity to understand—a collective capacity which is our great strength—that we can go from this meeting of the National Committee with a greater confidence than ever before that we will meet and solve the problems facing us with honor to our great movement, to our organization and with a full meeting of our responsibilities to the nation and to the working class.

5

BLACK BOLSHEVIK
Harry Haywood

Here is a summary of the anti-Browder, anti-collaborationist sentiment within the Party. It has special interest because it comes from one of its leading blacks of those years, a forerunner in his militancy of the radical nationalist tendencies within the civil rights movement of the 1960s. In 1978 Haywood wrote the memoir from which the following passage is taken.

[The] Party entered the war period with a reputation as the leading fighter for equality and Black liberation. Yet as Browder's line developed, it continually pushed us into a position of tailing after Black reformist leadership. In the thirties, the Communist Party had often been looked upon as "the Party of the Negro people"; in the forties, however, our line led to repeated betrayals of the struggle. For a broad assortment of Black reformists, it was just the opportunity they had been waiting for. Still smarting from defeat in the Scottsboro campaign, they jumped in to fill the tremendous void left by our retreat.

When A. Philip Randolph called for a dramatic march on Washington to protest discrimination, the Party leadership backed away from the issue and urged "unity" in the face of the fascist enemy. The Party declared that the march would create "confusion and dangerous moods in the ranks of the Negro people." Black newspapers and the NAACP popularized a mass of the "Double V" (Victory over Hitler abroad and over Jim Crow at home), but the Party leadership rejected the slogan on the grounds that it detracted from the war effort!

Occasionally the Browder revisionists would give lip service opposition to discrimination and segregation in the armed forces. When it came down to a concrete situation, however, their support was considerably less vigorous. For example, four Black WACs at Fort Devens, Massachusetts, were court-martialed for protesting their commanding officer's demand that they should "do all the dirty work." Outraged churches, unions, newspapers and civil rights organizations quickly organized and forced the Army to reverse itself.

The Party leadership, however, reprimanded the WACs. Ben Davis stated, "The U.S. general staff has on many occasions . . . proved that they deserve the full confidence of the Negro people . . . we cannot temporarily stop the war until all questions of discrimination are ironed out.." . .

The Party's work in the trade union movement also suffered from Browder's opportunist distortions of the united front. In 1939, the Party dissolved its system of trade union fractions, factory nuclei and shop papers as a concession to the CIO's leadership, a move which seriously weakened the Party's strength in basic industry. This move also accentuated the tendency to hide the Party's face. In the UAW and TWUA (Textile Workers' Union of America), the Party retreated from situations where it had the support to elect one or more of its members to leadership and supported other candidates.

During World War II, the Party supported the no-strike pledge. While it was a generally correct policy for the situation, the Party refused to fight for reciprocal pledges from business to curb war-profiteering and ensure the workers' standard of living. Browder opposed any struggle to extract such agreements from business, viewing them as a disruption to war production. He attacked slogans like "equality of sacrifice"—which was being raised by some Party trade unionists—as stemming from narrow factional considerations. Thus, the Party found itself tailing behind the labor bureaucrats on the day-to-day issues of safety, speedup and overtime pay for overtime work.

Browder's revisionist theories extended into the field of foreign policy, resulting in nothing less than his approval of American imperialism. He argued that the peoples of Latin America should place their trust in the Roosevelt administration and the continuance of the "good neighbor policy." He urged the Chinese communists to "trust America" and in 1945 openly endorsed U.S. foreign policy as "pressing toward the unity and democratization of China." Browder abandoned support for the struggles of the oppressed and colonized peoples, arguing that they should rely on the good intentions of the great nations to gain their liberation.

The ascendancy of Browder's revisionism was based upon both objective and subjective factors within the Party. Objectively, bourgeois ideology had long penetrated the working class movement in the United States, had been nurtured during the reformist years of the Roosevelt era and had thrived in an atmosphere of inadequate Marxist-Leninist training of Party members and leaders. . . .

CHAPTER FIVE

Cold War and Demise, 1945–

With the luminous clarity of hindsight we can see why Browder's vision came to naught, why Communism itself went into decline and, except in name, practically disappeared from the American scene. The further the Cold War period recedes into the distance, the more the fall of Communism strikes us as predestined and ineluctable.

I

We still do not know precisely why, in the early spring of 1945, while the battle of Berlin raged, Moscow decided that Browder had gone too far in relegating the Party to a mere association, though Moscow left unsaid how far he should have gone in pursuit of his vision. After all, the Big Three were slated to meet again after Germany's defeat; the Soviet Union would then enter the war against Japan; and, soon after, United Nations delegates would convene in San Francisco to draw up a charter. According to polls, Americans trusted the Soviet Union to be as much America's partner in maintaining the peace as it was its great ally in winning the war. Perhaps Moscow did not regard the rebuke to Browder as a serious one and took it for granted that he would accept it and make the adjustment—restore the Party, for example—and that would be that.

He refused to accept it, however. He stuck to his guns and denied there was any need for an adjustment. Attacking him pitilessly, his longtime adversaries, led by William Z. Foster, then carried the dispute—now that it *was* a dispute, open and unavoidable—to its ideological extreme, as a conflict between Marxism-Leninism and "revisionism," code word for rank betrayal. By the summer of 1945 Browder had been deposed from his chair and the Communist Political Association replaced by the Communist Party. Eventually he and his followers were expelled. An unrepentant "Browderite" he remained to his death twenty-seven years later, never in that time having succumbed to an anti-Communism that surely would have brought him personal rewards and general approbation. He quietly watched the locomotive of history leave the station without him.

But did his fall mean that *Browderism* had to die? Not at all. Marxist-Leninists, Foster included, could be perfect revisionists if that was what they had to be, though they would no more use that dread word than Browder ever did. Global events determined the fate of Browderism, as he had predicted it would. In short, the Cold War doomed it from the start, and but for his courageous refusal to bend, he himself might have written its epitaph.

2

To recount the history of the Cold War would be an exercise as tedious as it is unnecessary. Suffice it to say that the conflict between the United States and the Soviet Union, the Communist and anti-Communist worlds, became a way of life in both societies, each demonizing the other as a mortal threat to its existence, each embarking on a course of repression against its putative internal enemies whom it accused of subverting the national will in the other's behalf—which is emphatically not to say that the repressions were equivalent. To even suggest such a thing would be a moral travesty. Compared to the purges that swept through the Soviet Union and the other Communist countries bound to it, filling grave sites and gulags without end, and this to the day Stalin died in March 1953, the American experience was paradisal. America was a democracy where public opinion, usually humane and tolerant, ultimately decided government policies. But here exactly is the nub of the issue. The proper comparison is not between entirely different social and political systems; it is between one period and another of American history—between America before the Cold War set in and after. And by that standard, judged by its own democratic values, America wrote a very dark chapter in its history.

The vast majority of Americans, shadowed by fear, easily submitted to the lure of McCarthyism. Named for the Wisconsin Senator whose outrageous violations of elementary fairness and decency made him man of the hour for a while—he was hailed as the honest zealot, his excesses justified by the cause he served—McCarthyism has become a catchword for this worst of all red scares. Worst because for one thing it lasted so long, having gotten under way in 1947, three years before McCarthy himself emerged from obscurity,

and continued well after he died in 1957; and because, for another thing, its
reach was so extensive, so all-embracing, combining as it did the features of
an inquisition, a witch hunt, a purge, and a blacklist. For what had seemed an
eternity anti-Communists, antiradicals, antiliberals, anti-New Dealers had
been waiting for this moment to arrive. And although McCarthyism killed
few and condemned none to slave labor camps, hundreds went to jail, some
for eight years, and thousands lost their careers and/or suffered the humiliation and ignominy of public censure. That McCarthyism was, all in all, infinitely less brutal than Soviet repression hardly consoled its many victims or
brightened the historical record.

Communist Party leaders, it goes without saying, were its paramount victims. More than a hundred of them, beginning with the General Secretary
(Eugene Dennis) and ten other members of the Political Committee (ill-
health excused Foster), were convicted under the vague provisions of the
1940 Smith Act and sent away for five years, some longer because they broke
bail and fled to far-off mountains. To imagine these aged hierarchs in New
York and other cities plotting the violent overthrow of the United States government is ludicrous, even after taking into account the prevailing psychosis.
Only its diminutive size and distance from the Kremlin distinguished the
American Party from its sister parties in other democracies. Yet no other
democracy dared to prosecute and imprison their Communists. As for the
atomic spies, the government offered no evidence in their trials that they had
anything to do with the Party. (Incidentally, the government sent the
Rosenbergs, husband and wife and parents of young children, to the chair for
espionage while a much greater atomic spy, Klaus Fuchs, the English put
behind bars for only fourteen years!) At any rate, what happened to
American Communist leaders was symptomatic of what happened to the
movement as a whole. It steadily shrunk and withered away, as the pressure
on front organizations, affiliates and auxiliaries, that is, on the individuals
who belonged to or were even remotely associated with them, became too
tremendous to withstand. For those who continued to affirm their allegiance, along with those who quit the movement but continued to sympathize with it and even support it (albeit surreptitiously), the results were the
same: the loss of a public voice, marginalization, irrelevance.*

History demonstrated its cruelty toward Communists in yet another way.
It denied them the satisfaction that their Marxist-Leninist faith, their understanding of the laws of capitalism, should have brought them. It made them
martyrs without making them prophets. Their martyrdom, so commendable
in itself, they suffered in vain.

---

*The foreign-language groups, once bulwarks of the Party, succumbed completely to the Cold War. The hun-
dreds of thousands of Eastern European and Southern Europeans who came to the United States after World
War II, many or most of them deeply hostile to Communism (not a few were out-and-out Fascists), utterly
transformed the character of the émigré population.

One reason the Party ousted Browder was the prevailing belief that the economic crises would resume after the war, that the contradictions of the system would intensify because of the gigantic wartime investments in "constant capital" (heavy industry, raw materials, everything but labor or "variable capital") and the gigantic national debt. How could such an economy, which was about to contract, survive the return of eleven million servicemen? Nor were the Communists alone in their dire anticipations. The Great Depression of a few years ago was burned into the national psyche: it was the norm; war prosperity was only an interregnum. And no sooner did the war end in early September 1945 than massive unrest followed. Strikes convulsed the major industries—coal, autos, railroads, steel, and so on—well into the next year, and President Truman, no epigone of the sainted Roosevelt, appeared to side with management rather than labor. But the crisis never came. Labor won most of the strikes. (How unlike 1919!). And instead of depression, an incredible boom got under way that lasted through the ensuing Cold War decades. By the time it ran its course in the 1970s—though nothing like a major depression followed—American Communism was in no position to do anything about it.

3

In the midst of that enduring prosperity, and with McCarthyism still riding high, came the Khrushchev revelations. It was, to be exact, in the winter of 1956 that the Soviet Communist Party Secretary, one of Stalin's favorite lieutenants, informed the Twentieth Party Congress that the horrors ascribed to Stalin by Western anti-Communists were true. Nor, hour after hour, for the speech ran on into early morning, did Khrushchev spare the grisly details, many surpassing anything Stalin's detractors claimed. News of the speech, delivered in secret but broadcast to the world through the good offices of the CIA, traumatized the American Party as it did every other Communist Party. A fierce internal debate erupted into the open for the first time since the Party was Bolshevized thirty-five years earlier over how democratic and how independent of Moscow it should be; the two were of course inseparable. The debate ended in 1957 with differences unresolved; that is, with the status quo ante more or less holding sway. By then, thousands of Party stalwarts had resigned, including many of the middle and upper levels of the apparatus. They comprised its bone and sinew; they were the veterans of a hundred difficult campaigns that went back to their youth, some fought on foreign battlefields, others against domestic authorities bent on punishing them.

The memoirs they wrote belong to a literature of disillusionment, a literature of failed idealistic movements that once inspired ordinary people to transcend themselves and accomplish extraordinary things. Their memoirs express the pathos of their contradictory feelings toward the Party: on the one hand, gratitude for allowing them to sacrifice so much in behalf of the insulted and injured, the abandoned and disenfranchised, this during the prime of their lives and when the survival of civilization hung in the balance; and, on the other, resentment for having prevented them, by its hard-bitten authoritarianism and its subservience to Moscow, from contributing even more than they did and being even more successful than they were. These memoirists reaffirm the ideals that brought them to Communism and made them such devoted Party members. Theirs is a collective portrait of a Party, spent and demoralized, that failed *them*.

Mysterious, however, are the ways of Providence. All at once there were the 1960s. An insurgent mood took hold and spread quickly, among young people in particular. They seemed to call everything into question, traditional norms, roles, conventions, institutions, and they did so aboveboard, flaunting their irreverence, acting out their protestations in rallies, marches, and demonstrations and challenging laws they regarded as unjust and oppressive. We will not try to discuss a subject as complex and multifarious as the 1960s. What interests us is the continuity, such as it was, between the moribund Communist movement and the new insurgencies.

In some respects there was little continuity. In matters of sexual conduct and experimental lifestyles, for example, Communists hardly distinguished themselves, publicly at least. When it came to political activism the "New Left" differed markedly from the old. The New Left saw scant merit in the Soviet or Bolshevik model and reflected the wide open, ingenuous, novelty-seeking qualities of the burgeoning counterculture. Absent from the New Left was anything like the "Old Left's" commitment to the working class and trade unionism and the primacy of economics.

But continuity there was in other respects. A generational continuity existed as measured by the number of "red diaper babies," the children of the Old Left (i.e., Communists and their sympathizers), who joined the New, some becoming leaders of this or that insurgency (campus free speech, antiwar, civil rights, etc.). A new crop of very talented folk singers—Bob Dylan, Judy Collins, Joan Baez, Tom Paxton, Arlo Guthrie, Phil Ochs, among many others—modeled themselves on Woody Guthrie, who had recently died, and Pete Seeger, whose career took off again. There were strong filaments of continuity in the way young historians, social and natural scientists, and professionals and intellectuals generally dealt with the Cold War. They may have been unaware of the similarity between their view and the Old Left's—the view, in brief, that military-industrial capitalism invented the Communist bogeyman in order to win over the American people and impose its imperial will on peoples throughout the world, especially on the poor and colored peoples who struggled to free themselves from colonial subjugation. Overwhelming resistance to the Vietnam War gave that view broad credibility. What remained of the Party could take comfort in its vindication.

And continuity there certainly was with another insurgency that roiled America's waters in the 1960s. The civil rights revolution, it can be said, was the end result of work that had, as we saw, passionately engaged Communists for decades, nor did it cease to engage them in the years of their decline. Their moral courage on the issue—and here they truly fulfilled their vanguard calling—must not go unremarked. On civil rights the country caught up with them.

Soon after World War II the Party sought to reestablish its bona fides with the black community. The time was ripe for it, what with countless black veterans facing an uncertain future along with the countless other blacks who had settled in the industrial cities, scenes of persistent racial tensions. Regrouping, the Party created the Civil Rights Congress, an amalgam of two defunct organizations that had achieved much in their day, the National Negro Congress and the International Labor Defense. That the new outfit, the CRC, was having an effect became quickly apparent. It repeatedly embarrassed the government by its propaganda campaign against a country that preached democracy to a world made up mostly of colored peoples while segregating and otherwise humiliating its own colored people. The CRC went so far as to present its case—it spoke of genocide—before the United Nations. Its notoriety, and membership, rose sharply with its defense of black men victimized by Southern lynch laws, for instance, when in 1951 Mississippi executed Willie McGee on the blatantly false charge of raping the white woman with whom he had been having an affair, or when, four years later, a Mississippi mob killed a Chicago boy, Emmett Till, because, they claimed, he got "fresh" with a white woman.

In the meantime, on another front, the Party was definitely influencing policy at the highest government levels. In 1948 it provided the impetus behind a major new third party that adopted the venerable name Progressive. Its presidential candidate, whose credentials enabled him to vie with Truman, the incumbent, for the liberal-left or New Deal vote, was Henry A. Wallace, Roosevelt's third-term Vice President and for eight years before that the popular Secretary of Agriculture. Mainly Wallace promised to make friendship, not enmity, the basis of America's relations with the Soviet Union. Without saying so, of course, he was giving the Browderite vision of international and domestic politics (to which the Communist Party now fully subscribed, but not in so many words). A central feature of the Progressive Party was abolition of segregation, complete equality for blacks, and so on. Alarmed by the Wallace candidacy and the stir it was causing, Democrats made a left turn. At their nominating convention they adopted a civil rights plank, the first time either of the major parties had done so in this century, thereby driving out the "Dixiecrats," uncompromising Southern segregationists, who then formed a fourth party. President Truman accordingly was able to run as a civil rights proponent and an enthusiastic New Dealer. He took the wind out of Wallace's sails.

The election justified the wisdom of the Democratic left turn. Wallace did poorly, receiving only a fraction of the votes (just over a million, concentrated in a few states) he and the Communists had expected. It was in the midst of the campaign, not accidentally, that the administration decided to prosecute American Communists (under the Smith Act). The election committed the Democratic Party to a civil rights program, gradual to be sure, out of fear that the considerable black vote might go elsewhere. And so Truman, following up the convention mandate, desegregated the armed forces over the objections of top military brass, from General Eisenhower down.

As for the civil rights revolution itself, there too the Communists played a part worth mentioning. It should be noted that the revolution started with the 1956 bus boycott in Montgomery, Alabama, not far from where Communists had planted the seed two decades before, some of the boycott tacticians having been in or around the movement, specifically the Civil Rights Congress. Martin Luther King, Jr., who happened to have a ministry there, joined the boycott as it was being planned. Becoming leader of the nascent revolution, King wisely employed some old Communist organizers and brain trusters. To J. Edgar Hoover, the FBI boss who considered any kind of insurgency as treason, whose hatred of anything tainted by Communism was pathological, all of this proved that the civil rights movement was subversive through and through, that King represented an acute danger to the republic. This was why President Kennedy insisted that King purge such Communists, actual and alleged, from his ranks as the government might reveal to him. Fearful of alienating Kennedy, King reluctantly complied. By then the revolution was irreversible, thanks in no small measure to the contribution made by the most despised of America's dissenting minorities, obsolete as it had become.

4

When the ultimate blow to American Communism struck it scarcely mattered, given its marginality. An organization of several thousand, denuded of resources, subject to factional struggles and breakaways, the Party's activities and positions went unnoticed even by its detractors, those for whom Communism remained the symbol, otherwise void of meaning, for every moral failing. Its sole distinction as a radical group was its peculiar attachment to the Communist world at large or that portion of it allied with or dependent on or under the control of the Soviet Union, namely, East Germany, Poland, Czechoslovakia, Romania, Bulgaria, Vietnam, Cuba, Ethiopia, Angola, and Mozambique; the other Communist states—China, North Korea, Yugoslavia, Albania—lay outside the pale. The blow in question, struck between 1989 and 1991, brought the whole Soviet world to an end, leaving only China, North Korean, Cuba, and Vietnam, as keepers of the faith, but it was a faith lacking conviction in the era of triumphal capitalism. That the American Party to this day persists in its faith is rather touching. In keeping its name—most of the other parties having changed theirs—it reminds us, much as an artifact would, of the Communist Party of bygone days, when it figured so prominently in the history of American radicalism.

BROWDER'S DOWNFALL

1

ON THE DISSOLUTION OF THE COMMUNIST PARTY OF THE U.S.A.
Jacques Duclos

Duclos, a warhorse of the French Communist Party, wrote a seemingly innocuous piece in the April 1945 Cahiers du Communisme, *mildly chastising Browder's program. That it was neither innocuous nor mild was evident from the fact that the* Daily Worker *reprinted it in a headline story on May 24. The fat was in the fire.*

Many readers of *Cahiers du Communisme* have asked us for clarification on the dissolution of the Communist Party of the USA and the creation of the Communist Political Association. . . .

The reasons for dissolution of the Communist Party in the USA and for the "new course" in the activity of American Communists are set forth in official documents of the Party and in a certain number of speeches of its former secretary, Earl Browder. . . .

The Teheran Conference served as Browder's point of departure from which to develop his conceptions favorable to a change of course of the American CP. However, while justly stressing the importance of the Teheran Conference for victory in the war against fascist Germany, Earl Browder drew from the Conference decisions erroneous conclusions in nowise flowing from a Marxist analysis of the situation. . . .

Earl Browder declared, in effect, that at Teheran capitalism and socialism had begun to find the means of peaceful co-existence and collaboration in the framework of one and the same world; he added that the Teheran accords regarding common policy similarly presupposed common efforts with a view of reducing to a minimum or completely suppressing methods of struggle and opposition of force to force in the solution of internal problems of each country.

To put the Teheran policy into practice, Earl Browder considers that it is necessary to reconstruct the entire political and social life of the U.S. . . .

Such are the facts. Such are the elements of understanding which permit passing judgment on the dissolution of the American Communist Party. French Communists will not fail to examine in the light of Marxist-Leninist critique the arguments developed to justify the dissolution of the American Communist Party. One can be sure that, like the Communists of the Union of South Africa and of Australia, the French Communists will not approve the policy followed by Browder for it has swerved dangerously from the victorious Marxist-Leninist doctrine whose rigorously scientific application could lead to but one conclusion, not to dissolve the American Communist Party, but to work to strengthen it under the banner of stubborn struggle to defeat Hitler Germany and destroy everywhere the extensions of fascism. . . .

We too, in France, are resolute partisans of national unity and we show that in our daily activity; but our anxiety for unity does not make us lose sight for a single moment of the necessity of arraying ourselves against the men of the trusts.

Everyone understands that the Communist Party of the United States wants to work to achieve unity in their country. But it is less understandable that they envisage the solution of the problem of national unity with the good will of the men of the trusts, and under quasi-idyllic conditions as if the capitalist regime had been able to change its nature by some unknown miracle.

In truth, nothing justifies the dissolution of the American Communist Party, in our opinion. Browder's analysis of capitalism in the United States is not distinguished by a judicious application of Marxism-Leninism. The predictions regarding a sort of disappearance of class contradictions in the United States correspond in nowise to a Marxist-Leninist understanding of the situation. . . .

2

MARXISM-LENINISM VS. REVISIONISM
William Z. Foster

The vehemence Browder's enemies felt toward him is manifest in the report Foster presented to a special convention of the Communist Political Association called in late July 1945 to repudiate Browderism and bring the Party back to its traditional revolutionary (Marxist-Leninist) stance. The special convention went on to depose Browder and make Foster General Secretary. The report later appeared as a tract from which the following is an excerpt.

Browder's line is a rejection of the Leninist theory of imperialism as the final stage of capitalism. Comrade Browder, in his books and speeches, paints a utopian picture of a world capitalist system, not moribund, but vigorous and progressive, especially in its American section—a world capitalist system about to enter into a period of unprecedented expansion. It is a denial of the general crisis of the capitalist system. Browder believes that under the leadership of his "enlightened" American monopolists, the imperialist ruling classes in this and other capitalist countries will peacefully and spontaneously compose their differences with each other, with the USSR, with the liberated countries of Europe, and with the colonial and semi-colonial countries, without mass struggle. This is the bourgeois liberal notion that the epoch of imperialism is past. It conflicts fundamentally with the Leninist theory of imperialism as the last stage of a decadent capitalist system. . . .

Our Party discussion has made it clear that Comrade Browder's revisionism has exerted a weakening effect upon our wartime policy. Many of our comrades still believe that Browder's policy was necessary during the war. It was not. It was definitely a detriment in our war work, as I have shown in detail in my article in *The Worker* of June 19 [1945]. And not a few believe that Browder worked out our policy of all-out support of the war, of strengthening the United Nations coalition, of the fight for the Second Front, of maximum war production, of the no-strike pledge, etc. But this is not true. Browder was in Atlanta [penitentiary] when this correct general war policy was developed and he had nothing whatever to do with its formulation. Almost as soon as he was released from prison, however, he began to undermine our correct policy with his enervating revisionism. He did not succeed, however, in completely destroying our otherwise correct wartime policy. Despite his revisionism, our Party may well be proud of its record during the war. The full destructive force of Browder's revisionism would have been felt, however, if we had attempted to extend his policies over into the postwar period. . . . Browder's line is a rejection of the Marxian principles of the class struggle. Comrade Browder denies the class struggle by sowing illusions among the workers of a long postwar period of harmonious class relations with generous-minded employers; by asserting that class relations no longer have any meaning except as they are expressed either for or against Teheran; by substituting for Marxian class principles such idealistic abstractions as the "moral sense," "enlightenment," "progressivism," and "true class interests" of the big monopolists, as determining factors in establishing their class relations with the workers. Browder's theories of class collaboration and the harmony of interest between capital and labor are cut from the same opportunistic cloth as those of Bernstein, Legien and Gompers, except that his ideas are more shamelessly bourgeois than anything ever produced by those notorious revisionists of the past.

Browder's line is a rejection of the Marxian concept of the progressive and revolutionary initiative of the working class and with it, the vanguard role of the Communist Party. The very foundation of Marxism-Leninism is that the working class, with the Communist Party at its head, leads the democratic masses of the people in the amelioration of their conditions under capitalism and also in the eventual establishment of Socialism. But Comrade Browder has thrown this whole conception overboard. His books *Victory—and After* and especially *Teheran: Our Path in War and Peace*, present the thesis of a progressive capitalist class, particularly American finance capital, leading the peoples of this country and the world to the achievement of the great objectives of the Moscow, Teheran, Yalta and San Francisco Conferences and the building of a peaceful, democratic and prosperous society. Browder sees only a secondary, non-decisive role in the present-day world. . . .

3
War or Peace with Russia
Earl Browder

Here is Browder's explanation, in a book that came out in 1947, of why he was correct in his analysis. He sees himself as having provided the rationale, of which Roosevelt was the exemplar, for a rapprochement between enlightened and responsible capitalism and Soviet Communism.

The Roosevelt policy of Soviet-American co-operation has a base broader than any ideology or creed. It provides for the continuation of the American capitalist system, yet it commands the support of socialists and Marxists. It provides a platform of unity for the heterogeneous majority of American progressives "from Center to Left." But it puts every ideology to the test, for any system of ideas which obstructs a durable peace has something basically wrong with it.

I myself approach the present crisis in American history from the background of a lifetime of activity as an American Marxist. But I unhesitatingly say that the non-Marxist policy hammered out by Roosevelt represents the only present salvation for America.

My right to be heard on this issue has been challenged from Right and Left. On the one hand I have been denounced as a "Soviet agent," therefore a prejudiced witness, and one who serves another country rather than his own; on the other hand I have been called a renegade from Marxism, therefore not to be trusted by the Left.

Such attacks as these are immaterial and irrelevant to the validity or otherwise of the argument of this book. In the past I have refused to discuss them. I mention them now only in order to establish this point—that to attain a durable peace America must learn how to unite persons of the most diverse ideological views and interests. . . .

The arguments of this book do not rest upon any prejudice in favor of the Soviet Union or of its system of life. But it should be read with the knowledge that the author long studied the Soviet Union precisely because of being predisposed in its favor. I viewed the Soviet Union, from the moment of its emergence from the Russian Revolution, as a frontier in humanity's struggle for a better world, for better ways of living. It is the same sort of frontier my own parents and grandparents followed so eagerly on the American continent since the seventeenth century.

When I grew up on the plains of Kansas this frontier, after having dominated the progressive minds of the world for two centuries, was fading out of America, leaving a void and a frustration of spirit. The Russian Revolution rediscovered that frontier for me, and I felt a deep kinship for the new Russia from its first days. I have studied the Soviet Union constantly as one of its American friends, and visited it many times. All this has given me a prejudice in favor of Soviet-American co-operation, at the same time that it has qualified me to speak on the issue.

My only remark to the charge made by some of the American Left that I am a renegade is that I have reneged on nothing (can they say as much?) and that better Marxists than they continue to call me friend. They have been forced by events to take the same course which I have taken from foresight, even while they have denounced me.

I speak for peace and co-operation between America and Russia. I say this is possible without the Soviet Union abandoning its socialism and without the United States abandoning its capitalism. . . .

In this book I am speaking only for myself, an individual without present organizational ties. But I know America and her people, her workers in mines, factories, railroads, highways, shops, and offices, with their great and complex trade unions; I know the farmers of the plains and the people of the small towns, as well as the crowds of the great cities. I even know a little of what goes on in the minds and hearts of men and women in our business circles. And I know that a large majority of my countrymen and women, although they would disagree with me on a thousand other things, are of one mind with me in seeking unity under the banner of Roosevelt. I know they will gather with enthusiasm around any leadership which restates the Roosevelt policy for a stable peace clearly and boldly.

This is Roosevelt's great legacy to America.

4
REQUEST TO BECOME A COMMUNIST
Theodore Dreiser

It was in the midst of the anti-Browder campaign that the great novelist, long a Party sympathizer (despite his religiosity, his anti-Semitism, etc.), formally applied for admission. It was no accident that he addressed this letter, dated July 25, 1945, to his friend Foster. The convention that ousted Browder was just then in session and cheered its approval of Dreiser's application. On July 30 the Daily Worker *printed the letter.*

William Z. Foster
New York, N.Y.

Dear Mr. Foster:

I am writing this letter to tell you of my desire to become a member of the American Communist organization.

This request is rooted in convictions that I have long held and that have been strengthened and deepened by the years. I have believed intensely that the common people, and first of all the workers—of the United States and of the world—are the guardians of their own destiny and the creators of their own future. I have endeavored to live by this faith, to clothe it in words and symbols, to explore its full meaning in the lives of men and women.

It seems to me that faith in the people is the simple and profound reality that has been tested and proved in the present world crisis. Fascism derided that faith, proclaiming the end of human rights and human dignity, seeking to rob the people of faith in themselves, so that they could be used for their own enslavement and degradation.

But the democratic peoples of the world demonstrated the power that lay in their unity, and a tremendous role was played in this victory by the country that through its attainment of socialism has given the greatest example in history of the heights of achievement that can be reached by a free people with faith in itself and in all the progressive forces of humanity—the Soviet Union. The unity of our country with the great Soviet Union is one of the most valuable fruits of our united struggle, and dare not be weakened without grave danger to America itself. . . .

In the United States, I feel that the Communists have helped to deepen our understanding of the heritage of American freedom as a guide to action in the present. During the years when Fascism was preparing for its projected conquest of the world, American Communists fought to rally the American people against Fascism. They saw the danger and they proposed the remedy. Marxist theory enabled them to cast a steady light on the true economic and social origins of Fascism; Marxism gave them also a scientific understanding of the power of the working people as a force in history which could mobilize the necessary intelligence, strength and heroism to destroy Fascism, save humanity and carry on the fight for further progress. . . .

More than 11,000 Communists are taking part in that struggle as members of the armed forces of our country. That they have served with honor and patriotism is attested to even by the highest authorities of the Army itself.

More and more it is becoming recognized in our country that the Communists are a vital and constructive part of our nation, and that a nation's unity and nation's democracy is dangerously weakened if it excludes the Communists. Symbolic of this recognition was the action of the War Department in renouncing discrimination against Communists in granting commissions. A statement signed by a number of distinguished Americans points out that "the Army has apparently taken its position as a result of the excellent record of Communists and so-called Communists, including a number who have been cited for gallantry and a number who have died in action."

It seems to me that this ought to discredit completely one of the ideological weapons from the arsenal of Fascism that disorients the country's political life and disgraces its intellectual life—red-baiting. Irrational prejudice against anything that is truly or falsely labeled "Communism" is absurd and dangerous in politics. Concessions to red-baiting are even more demoralizing in the field of science, art and culture. (If our thinkers and creators are to fulfill their responsibilities to a democratic culture, they must free themselves from the petty fears and illusions that prevent the open discussion of ideas on an adult level. The necessities of our time demand that we explore and use the whole realm of human knowledge. . . .

These historic years have deepened my conviction that widespread membership in the Communist movement will greatly strengthen the American people, together with the anti-fascist forces throughout the world, in completely stamping out Fascism and achieving new heights of world democracy, economic progress and free culture. Belief in the greatness and dignity of Man has been the guiding principle of my life and work. The logic of my life and work leads me therefore to apply for membership in the Communist Party.

ART AND CULTURE

The Great Debate Redivivus

1

WHAT SHALL WE ASK OF WRITERS?
Albert Maltz

Before coming to Hollywood in the late 1930s Maltz had made something of a name in New York as a writer of plays and short stories. A faithful Communist, he was a leader of the left faction of the Screen Writers Guild. It was surprising that he would criticize the Party, in the February 12, 1946, New Masses, for its constrictive attitude toward art. Not that the points he raised were novel. Almost since the inception of American Communism they had been debated repeatedly. (See, for example, the Mike Gold–Floyd Dell exchange in the 1920–21 Liberator.) Surprising, too, was the reception to Maltz's piece. In subse-

quent numbers of the magazines, the Party took aim at him with such big guns as novelist | **351**

Howard Fast and screenwriter Alvah Bessie. What effect their firepower had on the hapless

Maltz is evident from his embarrassingly abject recantation.

We should note that Maltz, along with Bessie (and John Howard Lawson, who also attacked him), were among the "Hollywood Ten" who in 1947 defied the House Un-American Activities Committee by refusing to testify about their beliefs and associations and went to jail for contempt of Congress. They were all blacklisted, of course.

Left-wing writers have been confused, yes. But why?

The answer, I believe, is this: *Most* writers on the Left have been confused. "The conflict of conscience," resulting in wasted writing or bad art, *has been induced in the writer by the intellectual atmosphere of the left wing*. The errors of individual writers or critics largely flow from a central source, I believe. That source is the vulgarization of the theory of art which lies behind left-wing thinking: namely, "art is a weapon."

Let me emphasize that, properly and *broadly* interpreted, I accept this doctrine to be true. The ideas, ethical concepts, credos upon which a writer draws consciously or unconsciously are those of his period. In turn, the accepted beliefs of any period reflect those values which are satisfactory to the class holding dominant social power. To the degree that works of art reflect or attack these values, it is broadly—not always specifically—true to say that works of art have been, and can be, weapons in men's thinking, and therefore in the struggle of social classes—either on the side of humanity's progress, or on the side of reaction. But as interpreted in practice for the last fifteen years of the left wing in America, it has become a hard rock of narrow thinking. The total concept, "art is a weapon," has been viewed as though it consisted of only one word: "weapon." The *nature* of art—*how* art may best be a weapon, and how it may *not* be, has been slurred over. I have come to believe that the accepted understanding of art as a weapon is not a useful guide, but a strait-jacket. I have felt this in my own work and viewed it in the works of others. In order to write at all, it has long since become necessary for me to repudiate it and abandon it.

Whatever its stimulating utility in the late twenties or early thirties, this doctrine—"art is a weapon"—over the years, in day to day wear and tear, was converted from a profound analytic, historic insight into a vulgar slogan: "art *should be* a weapon." This, in turn, was even more narrowly interpreted into the following: "art should be a weapon as a leaflet is a weapon." Finally, in practice, it has been understood to mean that *unless* art is a weapon like a leaflet, serving immediate political ends, necessities and programs, it is worthless or escapist or vicious.

The result of this abuse and misuse of a concept upon the critic's apparatus of approach has been, and must be, disastrous. From it flow all the constrictions and—we must be honest—stupidities—too often found in the earnest but narrow thinking and practice of the literary left wing in these past years. And this has been inevitable. . . .

II

From this narrow approach to art another error also follows rather automatically. If, in actual practice (no matter how we revere art), we assume that a writer making a speech is performing the same act as writing a novel, then we are helpless to judge works written by those who make the "wrong" sort of speeches. Engels was never bothered by this problem. For instance, he said of Balzac (I paraphrase) that Balzac taught him more about the social structure of France than all of the economists, sociologists, etc., of the period. But who was Balzac? He was a Royalist, consistently and virulently anti-democratic, anti-socialist, anti-communist in his thinking *as* a citizen.

In his appreciation of Balzac, Engels understood two facts about art: First, as I have already stated, the writer, *qua* citizen, making an election speech, and the writer, *qua* artist, writing a novel, is performing two very different acts. Second, Engels understood that a writer may be confused, or even stupid and reactionary in his thinking—and yet, it is possible for him to do good, even great, work as an artist—work that even serves ends he despises. This point is critical for an understanding of art and artists! An artist can be a great artist without being an integrated or a logical or a progressive thinker on all matters. This is so because he presents, not a systematized philosophy, but the imaginative reconstruction of a *sector* of human experience. Indeed, most people do not think with thoroughgoing logic. . . . Writers must be judged by their work and *not* by the committees they join. It is the job of the editorial section of a magazine to praise or attack citizens' committees for what they stand for. It is the job of the literary critics to appraise the literary works only. . . . And, if Engels gave high praise to the literary work of Balzac—despite his truly vicious position—is this not a guide to the *New Masses'* critics in estimating the literary work of a whole host of varied writers—Farrell, Richard Wright, someone else tomorrow? What is basic to all understanding is this: There is not always a commanding relationship between the way an artist votes and any particular work he writes. *Sometimes* there is, depending upon his choice of material and the degree to which he consciously advances political concepts in his work. (Koestler, for instance, always writes with a political purpose so organic to his work that it affects his rendering of character, theme, etc. He must be judged accordingly.) But there is no inevitable, consistent connection.

Furthermore, most writers of stature have given us great works *in spite* of philosophic weaknesses in their works—Dostoyevsky, Tolstoy, Thomas Wolfe, are among many examples. All too often narrow critics recognize this fact in dealing with dead writers, but are too inflexible to accept it in living writers. As a result it has been an accepted assumption in much of left-wing literary thought that a writer who repudiates a progressive political position (leaves the intellectual orbit of *New Masses*, let us say) *must* go downhill as a creative writer. But this is simply not true to sober fact—however true it may be in individual cases. . . .

Those artists who work within a vulgarized approach to art do so at great peril to their own work and to the very purposes they seek to serve.

2

ART AND POLITICS
Howard Fast

What then is the core of Maltz's article? Not the charges he levels against criticism, for even he himself admits that those charges are of a tactical rather than a theoretical nature; *criticism* is one of the chief straw men he poses, and there his position is a comfortable one; for who is there in the literary left-wing who has not recognized and protested certain critical failings of the Marxist press? Of course, we are not free from critical mistakes, vulgarity, incompetence; this we know, and the reasons for the situation are manifold. Some of these critical failings we have corrected; others we will correct. And if Maltz had merely intended to add his voice to the many that are already raised against our critical failings, no one could have had a real difference with him. Indeed, such criticism is healthy.

But Maltz's attack on left-wing criticism is merely a cover for his theoretical approach to left-wing creative writing. When you come to his estimation of the Marxist as an artist, there are no straw men to confuse the issue. Flatly and baldly, Maltz says: "Engels understood that a writer may be confused, or even stupid and reactionary in his thinking—and yet it is possible for him to do good, even great, work as an artist—work that even serves ends he despises. *This point is critical for an understanding of art and artists!*"

The italics are mine. But the sentence italicized is the core of Maltz's position, and the word *critical* is the peg upon which he hangs his entire premise.

Why, we must inquire, is this point which Maltz singles out *critical* to our understanding of art and artists? If it is critical—and that is a term of absolute usage—to our understanding, then we are at least led toward presuming that confusion, stupidity, and a reactionary position are all qualities of art. And, conversely, clarity and understanding are detrimental to art.

We note in passing that Maltz does not quote Engels, but hinges his statement on his own interpretation of what Engels understands. This is a fallacious and opportunistic method of supporting a premise. But once embarked on that premise, Maltz goes on to state:

"An artist can be a great artist without being an integrated or a logical or a progressive thinker on all matters."

But who has denied that? And to take two ends of a historic pole, when has the Left claimed that either Shakespeare or Dreiser was an integrated, logical, and progressive thinker on all matters, and when has the Left denied that either of them was a great artist? One must look deeper than the obvious to understand why Maltz indulges in platitudes and truisms, and why he puts them forth with such a thunderous crash. . . .

Webster defines politics as the art of government; but when we speak of politics in terms of the average citizen, we refer to that citizen's relationship to both the state and the class which uses the state as its instrument. And in the broadest sense, the relationship of the twentieth-century American to society is a political one. To ask that a writer divorce himself from politics is to ask that he exile himself from civilization; to ask that he be unaffected by changes in the political weather is to ask that he relinquish his sensitivity to life. To do either is to abandon art, for art and life do not exist separately. . . .

From all of this, one cannot help but draw some unpleasant conclusions. It is no simple and straightforward attack upon left-wing criticism that Maltz puts forward. Underlying all of his arguments is a rejection of the whole progressive movement in America. It is no accident that he singles out Farrell, Wright, and Koestler to bolster an inherently reactionary point of view; nor is it an accident that he ignores the fact that for fifty years now, from Jack London to young Arthur Miller, almost every American writer of stature has drawn strength, sustenance, and a living philosophy from the left-wing movement.

Left-wing art is the result of a conscious use by the artist of a scientific understanding of society, of an identification with the working class, that class which is vital and in the ascendancy, and of a sharing of the vital ideology of that class. Such art is always a weapon—a weapon in the struggle for a better world.

Unhappily, the art which Maltz enthrones is the art of rejection, and, in the end, of annihilation. His own books, however, are a direct refutation of the theory he now propounds. He himself provided the best of arguments, in his work, for left-wing writing.

Yet he must be reminded that the road he charts here leads to sterility— whether it be the sterility of the esthete, the mediocrity, or the neo-fascist.

3
What Is Freedom for Writers?
Alvah Bessie

What is so astonishing about Maltz's article, after he has disposed of this moth-eaten straw man, is the fact that his basic contentions are not only un-Marxist, but actually anti-Marxist. Perhaps I do Maltz a disservice in thus associating him with Marxism, for he nowhere identifies himself in his article as anything more than "a working writer," whatever that may be. He nowhere states his frame of reference or identifies the point of departure from which he launches what is, objectively, not only an attack on Marxism but a defense of practically every renegade writer of recent years who ever flirted with the working-class movement: Farrell, Wright, Fearing. (And why not John Dos Passos?)

The un-Marxist character of Maltz's approach is revealed in the almost endless series of idealist categories into which he divides writers and writing: "artistic activity" and "journalism"; the "social novelist," the "political novelist" and perhaps, by extension, the "working" novelist; the writer "*qua* artist"; the writer "*qua* citizen"; works written for an "immediate political end" and works written, presumably, for eternity.

I think a Marxist would contend that these categories are idealist, unreal and basically reactionary. I think a Marxist would contend that when Steinbeck wrote *The Grapes of Wrath* he was at least under the influence of working-class ideas—*and people*; that these served him as powerful inspiration, gave him a certain clarity and offered him a springboard into a work that served both "an immediate political end" and the questionable standards of "eternity."

Maltz quotes us Engels on Balzac, who was a great writer and a "reactionary" at the same time. Well, what about Balzac? He was a monarchist at a time when the rising bourgeoisie of France was the historically progressive class; that made him a reactionary, for his time. He loathed, hated and despised the power of money *and* the corruption of his own beloved aristocracy, whom he castigated more bitterly than the shopkeepers, merchants and bankers themselves. That makes him for us (and for Engels) a progressive. What is more, to quote Engels's famous letter to Miss Harkness: "And the only men of whom he speaks with undisguised admiration are his bitterest political antagonists, the republican heroes of the Cl¥tre Saint-Marie, the men who at that time (1830–1836) were indeed the representatives of the popular masses." If this is true then it is not enough to catalog Balzac as a reactionary and thus "prove" that it is possible to be a reactionary and a great writer at the same time, Q.E.D. To do so is to remove Balzac from his historical context and to isolate the word *reactionary* as though it were a constant, equally applicable to all times and persons. For it has frequently happened that what was progressive yesterday is reactionary today and vice versa.

Balzac was a monarchist in a period when the modern industrial proletariat was practically nonexistent. Can Maltz cite us a monarchist writer today who could at the same time be a "great" writer? Today's ultra-reactionaries are fascists. The proletariat rules a country covering one-sixth the land surface of the globe. Can Maltz cite us a fascist writer who is "great." Will he contend that it is even possible for a fascist to write a great novel when the mere fact of being a fascist premises an attitude toward human beings that makes it categorically impossible for a person to see or write the truth about anything? . . .

For if we should accept Maltz's contention that all we need ask of writers is that they work "deeply, truly, honestly re-creating a sector of human experience" within "the great humanistic tradition of culture" (whatever that may be), then surely there is no need for a Communist Party so far as writers are concerned, and certainly there is no need for them to join it, for it would only cramp their style. By the same token, there is no need for the Party or even for a trade union, so far as workers are concerned, if we only ask them to behave themselves, keep their noses clean, live deeply, truly and honestly—and if they will only do so.

I do not mean to vulgarize Albert Maltz's approach to this complicated problem or offer ready-made solutions for it. But this is what he seems to be asking for in his article—"freedom" for the artist to "create" irrespective of party or working-class needs, aspirations and criticism. "Let them leave us alone," he seems to say, "to work deeply, truly and honestly, and we will be on their side, and we will automatically write the truth." This is nonsense, but it follows inevitably from the separations Maltz makes between the artist *qua* artist and the artist *qua* citizen.

No. We need more than "free" artists. We need *Party* artists. We need artists deeply, truly and honestly rooted in the working class who realize the truth of Lenin's assertion that the absolute freedom they seek "is nothing but a bourgeois or anarchist phrase (for ideologically an anarchist is just a bourgeois turned inside out). It is impossible to live in a society and yet be free from it. The freedom of the bourgeois writer, artist, or actress is nothing but a self-deceptive (or hypocritically deceiving) dependence upon the money bags, upon bribery, upon patronage." Lenin wrote these words in 1905 and they still touch the very heart of the liberal dilemma.

We need writers who will joyfully impose upon themselves the discipline of understanding and acting upon working-class theory, and *they* are the writers who will possess the potentialities of creating a truly free literature.

4

MOVING FORWARD
Albert Maltz

I

I published an article in the *New Masses* some weeks ago which was greeted by severe criticism. The sum total of this criticism was that my article was not a contribution to the development of the working cultural movement, but that its fundamental ideas, on the contrary, would lead to the paralysis and liquidation of left-wing culture.

Now these are serious charges, and were not rendered lightly, nor taken lightly by me. Indeed, the seriousness of the discussion flows from the fact that my article was not published in the Social Democratic *New Leader* (which, to my humiliation, has since commented on it with wolfish approval), but that it was published in the *New Masses*.

In the face of these criticisms, I have spent the intervening weeks in serious thought. I have had to ask myself a number of questions: Were the criticisms of my article sound? If so, by what process of thought had I, despite earnest intentions, come to write the article in the terms I did?

Intimately connected with these personal questions were broader matters demanding inquiry by others as well as by myself. If the criticisms of my article were sound, why was it that a number of friends who read the manuscript prior to publication and whose convictions are akin to mine had not come to such severe conclusions? And why was it that the *New Masses* accepted the article without comment to me, indeed with only a note of approval from the literary editor? And why was it that even after the criticisms of my article appeared, I daily received letters which protested the "tone" of the criticisms of me, but considered that at worst I only had fallen into a few "unfortunate" formulations?

I have come to quite a number of conclusions about these questions. And if I discuss the process of my arriving at them with some intimacy, I hope the reader will bear with me, since I know of no other way of dealing honestly with the problem involved. I particularly invite those who have written me letters of approval to consider whether some of the remarks I have to make about myself may not be also appropriate to them.

II

I consider now that my article—by what I have come to agree was a one-sided, non-dialectical treatment of complex issues—could not, as I had hoped, contribute to the development of left-wing criticism and creative writing. I believe also that my critics were entirely correct in insisting that certain fundamental ideas in my article would, if pursued to their conclusion, result in the dissolution of the left-wing cultural movement.

The discussion surrounding my article has made me aware of a trend in my own thinking and in the thinking of at least some others in the left-wing cultural movement: namely, a tendency to abstract errors made by left critics from the total social scene—a tendency to magnify those errors and to concentrate attention upon them without reference to a balanced view of the many related forces which bear upon left culture—and hence a tendency to advance from half-truths to total error. . . .

The total truth about the left-wing is therefore the only proper foundation and matrix for a discussion of specific errors in the practice of social criticism and creative writing. It was in the omission of this total truth—in taking it for granted—in failing to record the host of writers who have been, and are now, nourished by the aspirations of the left-wing—and that I presented a distorted view of the facts, history and contributions of left-wing culture to American life. This was not my desire, but I accept it as the objective result. And, at the same time, by my one-sided zeal in attempting to correct errors, etc., I wrote an article that opened the way for the *New Leader* to seize upon my comments to support its unprincipled slanders against the left.

Of all that my article unwittingly achieved, this is the most difficult pill for me to swallow. My statements are now being offered up as fresh proof of the old lie: that the left puts artists in uniform. But it is a pill I have had to swallow and that I now want to regurgitate. . . .

IV

At this point I should like to ask a question particularly of those who read my earlier article with approval, or with only sketchy criticism: What is the aim of what I have been saying up until now?

It seems clear to me, as I hope it is already clear to them, that I have been discussing and illustrating revisionism, and that my article, as pointed out by others, was a specific example of revisionism in the cultural field.

For what is revisionism? It is distorted Marxism, turning half-truths into total untruths, splitting ideology from its class base, denying the existence of class struggles in society, converting Marxism from a science of society and struggle into apologetics for monopoly exploitation. . . . The intense, ardent and sharp discussion around my article, therefore, seems to me to have been a healthy and necessary one—and to have laid the foundation whereby a new clarity can be achieved, a new consciousness forged, and a struggle undertaken to return, deeply, to sound Marxist principles. . . .

For now, certainly, the times call for moving ahead. We have in America today the flowering of a profound art, one that will deeply enrich the great traditions we inherit. If this flowering comes to pass, it will be based upon a passionate, honest rendition of the real, mutual relations in society; it will be a true art, based upon the real lives, the disappointments, the struggles, the aspirations, of the American people. Such an art, being realistic, will be socially critical; this follows as night follows day. But, by being tied to life as the source of true artistic inspiration, it will not substitute slogans for rich events, or substitute mechanical selectivity for a description of real mutual relations in society. Marxism will be the interpretive guide; the raw material will be the facts of life, faced absolutely, with burning honesty. . . .

If the writer is to retain inner firmness, if he is not to sink into cynicism and despair, if he is to maintain his love for people, without which true art cannot flourish, then he must understand that events have a meaning, that history has a direction, that the characters he portrays are part of a social web

based upon the life and death struggle of classes. For this understanding, for
inner firmness, for the spiritual ability to retain faith in people and faith in
the future, he must turn to Marxism in this epoch.

THE 1948 ELECTION

COMMUNIST PARTY PLATFORM

*At its August 1948 convention the Party adopted this platform at the same time as it threw
its support behind—eventually it took a leadership role in—Henry Wallace's newly
established Progressive Party. Defeating President Truman in the upcoming election was the
main object. Weeks earlier, the administration, as part of its campaign, had indicted twelve
top Communists for plotting the violent overthrow of the government.*

In this crucial 1948 election the American people have a fateful decision to
make: Shall America follow the path of peace or war, democracy or fascism?

Our boys returned from World War II with the hope that their wartime
sacrifices had not been in vain.

Remember the promises:

- Fascism would be wiped out.
- The great-power unity that brought war victory would bring enduring
  peace.
- An economic bill of rights would provide every American with security.

These promises have been broken.

Instead of peace, there is war—in Greece, in China, in Israel.

Instead of peace, we witness feverish preparations for a new world war.

Instead of peace, American boys are being regimented for war with the
enactment of the peacetime draft.

Instead of security and abundance, we have sky-rocketing prices, lowered
living standards and the shadow of an impending economic crash with mass
unemployment. Farmers fear the inevitable collapse of farm prices. After
three years our veterans are still denied housing. Our youth face a future of
insecurity and new wars.

Instead of greater democracy, we have lynch law, mounting Jim-Crowism
and anti-Semitism, and a conspiracy to undermine our sacred democratic
heritage. We have anti-Communist witch-hunts, the arrest and conviction of
anti-fascist leaders, the harassment and intimidation of writers, artists and
intellectuals. We have phony spy scares, the hounding of government
employees and former Roosevelt associates, the persecution of foreign-born
workers, and the adoption of anti-labor legislation, attempts to outlaw the

Communist Party through Mundt-Nixon Bills, and now the indictment of the twelve Communist leaders on the trumped-up charge of "force and violence." These are the methods by which the American people are step by step being driven down the road to a police state and fascism.

These are the chief issues of the 1948 elections.

We are today threatened by no outside force. We are in no danger of attack from any nation. Why then the war hysteria?

The answer lies in this simple fact—250 giant corporations, operating through a handful of banks, control the economic life of the United States. These in turn are largely owned by a few plutocratic families—Morgan, Rockefeller, Mellon, du Pont and Ford.

The nation's industries are not operated for the public welfare, but for the private gain and power of the multi-millionaire ruling class. Prices continue to rise because of vast military expenditures and because the monopolies, through price-fixing agreements and other devious devices, extract exorbitant profits.

They make huge profits from war and from armaments. They extract super-profits abroad by forcing other nations into economic dependence upon Wall Street. This drive for foreign markets, for Wall Street domination of the world, is at the bottom of the war hysteria and war preparations. Big Business strives to crush the growth and advance of democracy and Socialism throughout the world, in order to protect and swell its profits.

Big Business seeks to re-establish the old Nazi cartels and to use Germany and Japan as military bases for new aggression. But the failures of the bipartisan policy to achieve its main aim of world conquest have increased the frenzy with which Wall Street seeks to plunge the nation into fascism and World War III.

WAR AND PEACE

Neither the American people nor the Soviet Union is responsible for the sharpening tension in international relations. The responsibility rests squarely on Wall Street and the bipartisan Truman-Dewey atomic diplomacy. Only the capitalist trusts want war. The Soviet Union is a socialist country. It has no trusts, no I. G. Farben or du Pont cartels to profit from wars. That is why the Soviet Union is the most powerful force for peace in the world.

The Communist Party calls upon the labor movement and all progressive, peace-loving Americans to struggle for the realization of the following peace program:

- End the "cold war," the draft, and the huge military budget.
- Restore American-Soviet friendship, the key to world peace and the fulfillment of the peoples' hope in the United Nations.

- Conclude a peace settlement for a united, democratic Germany and Japan based on the Yalta and Potsdam agreements. Guarantee the complete democratization and demilitarization of these countries.
- Stop military aid and intervention in China, Korea and Greece.
- Break diplomatic and economic ties with Franco-Spain.
- Scrap the Marshall Plan and the Truman Doctrine. Furnish large-scale economic assistance to the war-ravaged victims of fascist attack. Give this aid through the United Nations without political strings.
- Lift the embargo on, and extend full recognition to, Israel.
- Give immediate, unconditional independence to Puerto Rico.
- Aid the economic development of the colonial and semi-colonial countries of Asia, Africa and Latin America on the basis of full support to their fight for their national independence. Defeat the Truman Arms Standardization Plan.
- Abandon economic, political and military pressures on the countries of Latin America.

THE ATTACK ON LABOR AND OUR LIVING STANDARDS

The trusts have inflated prices and battered down the real wages of American workers to 16 percent below 1944.

Huge war expenditures amount to 15 billion dollars this year—one-third of the entire national budget! The American people are already paying dearly for this "cold war economy," through a heavy tax burden, speedup and reduction in real wages. We will pay still more heavily as the inflationary boom speeds the day of the oncoming economic bust.

Big Business has decreed that labor's hands be tied and its rights destroyed. The Taft-Hartley Law and strike-breaking injunctions are weapons against the people's resistance to the monopoly drive toward war and fascism.

To defend the labor movement and the vital economic interests of the overwhelming majority of the American people, labor and all progressives should unite in stubborn and militant struggle for the following demands:

- Repeal the Taft-Hartley Law and end strike-breaking injunctions. Adopt a code of Federal labor legislation, including the best features of the Wagner Act and the Norris-LaGuardia Anti-Injunction Law.
- Restore price control and roll back prices, without any wage freeze.
- Enact an extensive program for federally financed low-rent public housing, minimum wage legislation, old-age pensions, adequate health insurance, and increased aid to education.
- Provide increased security for the working farmers through up-to-date parity price and income guarantees, based on unlimited farm produc-

tion. Such income guarantees require farm subsidies, effective crop insurance and sharp curbs on the giant food trusts and their marketing agencies. Carry out a program of planned conservation and River Valley projects. Extend the federal minimum wage and social security laws to agricultural workers, including seasonal and migratory labor.

We call for heavier taxation on high incomes and excess profits, with increased exemption for the low brackets. We demand a capital levy on big fortunes and corporations to finance essential social legislation.

We support all steps to curb the power of the trusts, the source of reaction, fascism and war. The American people can make gains, even under capitalism, by mass resistance to the monopolies.

We support measures to nationalize the basic industries, banks and insurance companies, but point out that such measures can only be useful as part of the fight to realize a people's democratic government in the United States. Democratic nationalization of trustified industries requires guarantees of democratic controls and the right of labor to organize, bargain collectively and strike. This can only be accomplished by a people's government dedicated to curbing the power of the trusts.

We point out that capitalism cannot become "progressive" even by curbing the excesses of the monopolies. The basic causes of unemployment, economic crisis, fascism and war can only be removed by the establishment of Socialism through the democratic will of the majority of the American people.

CIVIL RIGHTS

The destruction of the rights of the Communists is the classical first step down the road to fascism. The tragedy of Germany and Italy proves this. Therefore, it is incumbent upon the working class and all Americans who hate fascism to defend the rights of the Communists, and to help explode the myth that Communists are foreign agents or advocate force and violence.

We Communists are no more foreign agents than was Jefferson who was also accused of being a foreign agent by the Tories of his day. We follow in the best traditions of the spokesmen of labor, science and culture whose contributions to human progress knew no national boundaries. We follow in the tradition of Abraham Lincoln, who said: "The strongest bond of human sympathy, outside of the family relation, should be one uniting the working people of all nations and tongues and kindred."

It is the monopolists who advocate and practice force and violence, not the Communists. Reaction has always resorted to force and violence to thwart the democratic aspirations of the peoples. In 1776, force and violence were the weapons of King George against the American colonists seeking national independence. in 1861, force and violence were used by the

Southern slave owners in an attempt to overthrow the democratic republic headed by Lincoln. Today the people suffer the violence of the KKK, the lynch mobs, the fascist hoodlum gangs and police brutality.

We are Marxists, not adventurers or conspirators. We condemn and reject the policy and practice of terror and assassination and repudiate the advocates of force and violence. We Communists insist upon our right to compete freely in the battle of ideas. We Communists insist upon our right to organize and bring our program to the people. Let the people judge our views and activities on their merits.

We call upon the American people to fight with all their strength against the danger of fascism, to resist every fascist measure, to defend every democratic right.

- End the witch hunts, loyalty orders and phony spy scares.
- Abolish the Un-American Committee. Withdraw the indictments against the twelve Communist leaders and the contempt citations against the anti-fascist victims of Congressional inquisitions.
- Stop the campaign of terror and intimidation against labor leaders, intellectuals and people of the professions.
- End persecution and deportation of the foreign born and lift the undemocratic bars to citizenship.
- Outlaw all forms of anti-Semitism, anti-Catholicism, and every other expression of racial and religious bigotry.
- End all discrimination against the Mexican-American people in the Southwest.
- The Communist Party calls for an end to any and all political, social and economic inequalities practiced against women and demands the maintenance and extension of existing protective legislation.
- Extend the suffrage. Remove the bars directed against minority parties. Lower the voting age to 18 years in every state.

NEGRO RIGHTS

The hypocrisy of the democratic pretensions of Wall Street and the Administration are shattered by the reality of the Jim-Crow system in America. The most shameful aspect of American life is the Jim-Crowism, the terror and violence imposed upon the Negro people, especially in the South. Discrimination in employment, only slightly relaxed during the war, is once again widespread.

The Communist Party, which has pioneered in fighting for full political, economic and social equality for the Negro people, calls for an end to the policies of the Federal and state governments which give official sanction to the Jim-Crow system in the United States.

We call upon all progressives, especially white progressives, to carry on an unceasing day-to-day struggle to outlaw the poll tax, lynchings, segregation, job discrimination and all other forms of Jim-Crowism, official and unofficial, and to give their full support to the rising national liberation movement of the Negro people. This is vital to the Negro people, to the white workers, and to the whole fight for democracy in America.

- We demand a national F.E.P.C. law, to be vigorously and fully enforced.
- We demand that the Ingram family be freed and adequately compensated for the ordeals to which they have been subjected.
- We demand that the Ku Klux Klan and all other hate-and-terror organizations be outlawed.
- We condemn President Truman's cynical evasion of the issue of segregation in the armed forces. We demand that he immediately issue an Executive Order ending every form of segregation and discrimination in the armed forces and the government services.
- We defend the right of the Negro people to full representation in government, and demand Federal enforcement of the 13th, 14th and 15th Amendments, so that the Negro people, North and South, may participate freely and fully in the 1948 elections, and all elections thereafter.
- We call for a democratic agricultural program which will give land and other forms of assistance to millions of Negro and white tenants and sharecroppers in the South, and thereby help put an end to the semifeudal plantation system.

Such reforms will help provide the material basis for the Negro people's advance toward full liberation from their national oppression, toward their full political, economic and social equality. . . .

THE NEW PARTY

Millions of Americans, disillusioned with the two-party system, have joined to found a new people's party.

The new Progressive Party is an inescapable historic necessity for millions who want a real choice now between peace and war, democracy and fascism, security and poverty.

The Communists, who support every popular progressive movement, naturally welcome this new people's party. We supported the progressive features of Roosevelt's policies, domestic and foreign. We helped organize the CIO in the 1930s. We have supported every democratic movement since the Communists of Lincoln's generation fought in the Union cause during the Civil War.

On most immediate questions before the people of the country the

Progressive Party has offered detailed platform planks around which all for-ward-looking people can unite. Our support of the Progressive Party poli-cies and campaign does not alter the fact that we have fundamental as well as some tactical differences with Henry Wallace and related third-party forces.

The Communist Party is not nominating a Presidential ticket in the 1948 elections. In 1944 we Communists supported Roosevelt to help win the anti-Axis war. Similarly, in 1948 we Communists join with millions of other Americans to support the Progressive Party ticket to help win the peace. The Communist Party will enter its own candidates only in those districts where the people are offered no progressive alternatives to the twin parties of Wall Street.

The Progressive Party is by its very nature a great coalition of labor, farmers, the Negro people, youth, and professional and small business people. It is anti-monopoly, anti-fascist, anti-war. By its very nature it is not an anti-capitalist party. It is not a Socialist or a Communist Party and we are not seeking to make it one. It is and should develop as a united front, broad, mass people's party.

There is only one Marxist Party in America, one party dedicated to replac-ing the capitalist system with Socialism—and that is the Communist Party.

Our firm conviction that only a Socialist reorganization of society will bring permanent peace, security and prosperity is no barrier to cooperation with all other progressive Americans, in helping create a great new coalition in order to save our people from the twin horrors of war and fascism.

We seek no special position in this movement and will, of course, oppose any attempt to discriminate against us because of our Socialist aims.

We Communists are dedicated to the proposition that the great American dream of life, liberty and pursuit of happiness will be realized only under Socialism, a society in which the means of production will be collectively owned and operated under a government led by the working class. Only such a society can forever banish war, poverty and race hatred. Only in such a soci-ety can there be the full realization of the dignity of man and the full devel-opment of the individual. Only such a society can permanently protect the integrity of the home and family. Only a Socialist society can realize in life the vision of the brotherhood of man.

THE GREAT AMERICAN RED SCARE

1

THE ORDEAL OF JOHN GATES
John Gates

Gates, one of the top eleven Communists (he was editor of the Daily Worker), tried and con-victed in 1949, gives the best account of the torturously surreal nature of the year-long experience. The selection is from his autobiography, which he wrote after he left the Party.

Rarely has a case received as much publicity as ours; rarely has the public known so few of the actual facts about a major trial. The average person thought—and still thinks—that we were tried and found guilty of espionage, sabotage, treason and planning to overthrow the government by force. None of these crimes was even charged against us. We were actually accused of "conspiracy" to organize a political party which would teach and advocate the duty and necessity of the violent overthrow and destruction of the United States government. We were not accused of practicing force and violence, or of advocating it, or of forming a party which so advocated, but of "conspiracy to organize" a party—meaning getting together in a convention to form a party which would so advocate at some time in the future. The "conspiracy" charge is a highly technical one, having nothing to do with being conspirators in the cloak-and-dagger sense. In every anti-trust suit, corporations are accused of "conspiring" to violate the law—but they are not therefore pictured in the press, as we were, as conspirators.

The actual charge in our case was thrice removed from acts of violence and had nothing whatsoever to do with espionage, sabotage or treason. Moreover, the government did not even have to prove that the individual defendants themselves taught or advocated the forbidden doctrine (and the record shows the government did not prove this); the charge of conspiracy is so loose that it made any such proof entirely unnecessary.

The case hinged around the reconstitution of the party in 1945 which, according to the prosecution, meant the return to a policy of advocating force and violence. The reconstitution of the party meant a return to mistaken policies that finally destroyed the organization as an effective political instrument; but this had nothing to do with force and violence. We had not advocated it prior to 1944, so we could not "return" to it in 1945.

Three of the defendants, Henry Winston, Gus Hall and myself, were not even present at the convention which reorganized the party; at the time we were members of the armed forces of the United States. This fact alone should have resulted in our eventual acquittal if the present standards established by the Supreme Court had been applied in our case.* For that matter, under the present standards, *all* the original defendants would have been acquitted.

The idea that the small, weak, uninfluential Communist Party of 1948 represented a threat of violent overthrow of the most powerful government in the world, even if the party so desired, was ludicrous. As the main evidence of this charge, the government introduced the classic works of Marx, Engels, Lenin and Stalin, and pointed to the well-known fact that these were used as textbooks in Communist schools.

---

*In its decision reversing the California Smith Act case, the Supreme Court ruled that "we should follow the familiar rule that criminal statutes are to be strictly construed and give to 'organize' its narrow meaning, that is, that the word refers only to acts entering into the creation of a new organization, and not to acts thereafter performed in carrying on its activities, even though such acts may loosely be termed organizational" (*Yates v. U.S.*, June 18, 1957).

Years later, in 1957, the Supreme Court ruled that this type of evidence was insufficient to convict under the Smith Act; proof was needed that each defendant actually incited to violent action. No such evidence was presented against us in our trial. I challenge anyone to find one piece of testimony to this effect in the 20-volume record of the case.

The real reasons behind our indictment revolved around entirely different matters from force and violence. One of these was the cold war and the Truman Administration's determination to suppress all opposition to its international policies—what Dean Acheson at the time euphemistically called "total diplomacy" and which later, at least with respect to the government's loyalty program, he conceded was a major mistake.

The other purpose was simple enough: to demonstrate in an election year that the Democrats were not "tainted," that they could be as tough on Communists as the GOP claimed that only Republicans could be. As though being a victim of the cold war were not enough, the Communist Party also had the misfortune to be caught in the crossfire of big-time partisan politics.

The anti-Communist hysteria was so intense, and most Americans were so frightened by the Communist issue, that we were convicted before our trial even started. We would have been found guilty of any charge brought against us, I am sure, and it was a foregone conclusion that we would get the maximum sentence. When at the end of the trial Judge Medina said he wished he could give us more than the five years permitted by law, I had no doubt that if death had been permitted, death is what we would have received.

There have probably been few judges in American jurisprudence who have received more awards and citations than Judge Medina. Surely this could not have been in response to a display of impartial conduct on his part; after all, this is the simple duty of any judge and is seldom rewarded. The conclusion is inescapable that Medina has been showered with honors because, to put it bluntly, he "did a job" on the Communists. The judge has been enshrined in the public eye as a hero and martyr, for which there is little justification. I grant I am hardly an impartial judge in the matter, but then it is my contention that neither was Medina. One would think from the fuss raised by the judge that he was the victim and that he, rather than we, served five-year prison sentences. Medina has been pictured (chiefly by himself) as terribly harassed by the defense lawyers, but it was the lawyers who went to prison for contempt and, in some cases, suffered disbarment.

On his perennial tour of the lecture circuit, Judge Medina tells and re-tells the story of how he felt his life was threatened by the defendants and how he dreamed of suicide. If His Honor actually felt this way during the trial, he could hardly have been impartial, unbiased and unprejudiced toward us; it was his duty to bring his feelings of persecution out into the open and turn the case over to a judge who would not feel that the defendants before him were trying to murder him.

Judge Medina not only bore a marked resemblance to actor Adolphe

Menjou; like Menjou, he was a consummate actor. From the outset he assumed the star role in the proceedings. Evidently believing that the prosecution could not produce any evidence to back up the charge on which we were indicted, he proceeded to prosecute us on a charge which he dreamed up himself: we and our lawyers were supposed to be conspiring to obstruct justice by dragging out the trial—a charge which the U.S. Supreme Court rejected.

Although our case was a hopeless one under the circumstances, the defendants made every mistake in the book. We permitted the trial to become a duel between judge and defense; it is difficult enough to get a federal jury to vote against the government prosecutor, it will never vote against the judge. Medina baited and provoked our lawyers and they fell into the trap. With the press solidly behind the judge and against us, no matter what we did was reported in a bad light, and our defense tactics often made a bad situation worse. A good picture of the proceedings and of Medina's conduct can be found in the opinions written by Justices Frankfurter and Douglas in the contempt case of one of our lawyers, Harry Sacher.

Justice Frankfurter wrote:

> The particular circumstances of this case compel me to conclude that the trial judge should not have combined in himself the functions of accuser and judge. For his accusations were not impersonal. They concerned matters in which he personally was deeply engaged . . . No judge should sit in a case in which he is personally involved . . . At frequent intervals in the course of the trial his comments plainly reveal personal feelings against the lawyers . . . Truth compels the observation, painful as it is to make it, that the fifteen volumes of oral testimony in the principal trial record numerous episodes involving the judge and defense counsel that are more suggestive of an undisciplined debating society than of the hush and solemnity of a court of justice. Too often *counsel were encouraged* (my emphasis—J. G.) to vie with the court in dialectic, in repartee and banter, in talk so copious as inevitably to arrest the momentum of the trial and to weaken the restraints of respect that a judge should engender in lawyers . . . Throughout the proceedings . . . he failed to exercise the moral authority of a court possessed of a great tradition.

To which Justice Douglas added:

> I agree with Mr. Justice Frankfurter that one who reads the record will have difficulty in determining whether members of the bar conspired to drive a judge from the bench or whether the judge used the authority of the bench to whipsaw the lawyers, to taunt and tempt them, and to create for himself the role of the persecuted. I have reluctantly concluded that

neither is blameless, that there is fault on each side, that we have here the spectacle of the bench and the bar using the courtroom for an unseemly discussion and of ill will and hot tempers.

While the Supreme Court upheld the contempt convictions of the defense lawyers, it threw out Medina's charge that the attorneys had engaged in a conspiracy to subvert the administration of justice and to undermine his health. Since the judge announced early in the trial that he believed that such a conspiracy existed, this also must have prejudiced his conduct. Despite the higher court's finding, the judge has continued in his innumerable speeches and voluminous writings to insist on the existence of this conspiracy.

Unless the reader has had occasion to be the defendant in a political trial, cooped up in a courtroom for nine months, it will be difficult for him to imagine our frustrations—especially when we had to sit and listen while witnesses swore to imaginary conversations which could not be disproved and which, under the Smith Act, could usher us straight into prison.

One of the prosecution witnesses alleged that a Communist leader, not on trial, had stated that the Red Army would march down on the United States via Alaska and Canada. Several of us could not refrain from smiling broadly. I had been in the Aleutians and knew the utter impossibility of such a march, except perhaps by sea-lions. Medina interrupted the proceedings to remark that he noticed the defendants were smiling and rebuked us.

I arose and inquired whether the judge was ordering us never to smile in the course of the trial. "It is bad enough that we are on trial for our right to think," I said, "without forbidding us now even the right to smile." This helped to break our tension and relieve our frustration. But it can hardly be said to have advanced our case or impressed the jurors, if any were in a frame of mind to be impressed by anything we might have done or left undone.

It must be said in justice to our lawyers that they not only performed miracles of courage and zeal in our behalf; they were not chiefly to blame for our ill-conceived tactics. Time and again they advised against doing certain things, but since we were the clients, they would defer to our wishes.

Something was even more seriously wrong, however, than our day-to-day tactics; this was our futile attempt to prove that the classics of the Marxist writers meant what we said they meant, instead of what they plainly did mean, if taken literally. It is clear now that instead of becoming involved in doctrinal disputes which nobody could understand, we should have concentrated on the civil liberties aspects of the case: the right to read, write, say and think any political thoughts we pleased—as set forth as a sacred right in the First Amendment to the United States Constitution—even the right to say and think things which we never dreamed of saying and of which we were accused by perjurious witnesses. . . .

2

LET US MARCH FORWARD
Eugene Dennis

*Just before going to prison with the other Party leaders Dennis, the General Secretary, had
this to say to his comrades, many of whom would end up in jail too.*

As you have already heard this evening, I shall be leaving you for a while. I
leave, so to say, as a prisoner of war, as a prisoner of Wall Street's "cold war."
And as I am about to go, I want you to know that I regret that I have not done
more for our Party, that I haven't worked more effectively. Above all, I regret
that I shall not be in the operative leadership of our Party during the very
critical days ahead, at the time when the danger of war grows more imminent and the peril of fascism looms larger from day to day. . . .

Yes, there are many weaknesses in our work, and we have made some mistakes. But as Stalin said in 1910, in an article about the great German working-class leader, Bebel, "Only the dead do not make mistakes." However, we
are working to overcome our weaknesses and errors. We must overcome
them more speedily, strive not to repeat them, and endeavor to eliminate
weaknesses and errors from our work.

Finally in this connection, I would like to say that our Party has grown
stronger in these past years, because in the midst of the mass struggles we
have been waging a simultaneous fight on two fronts, against both Right and
Left opportunism. At the same time, we have been waging a ceaseless war
against reactionary Social-Democracy, against labor reformism, and especially against the malignant ulcer and treachery of the Tito clique which
attracts to itself in the United States the Anna Louise Strongs, the John
Rogges, the Trotskyites, and the Browderites.

Yes, comrades, I leave the operative ranks of our Party and our leadership
for a while with keen regrets, yet certain that our Party is in good hands. It
is in *your* hands. . . .

I would like to stress briefly a few major questions which I consider
imperative to insure the further progress and Bolshevization of our own
Party, our own American Marxist-Leninist party—questions that are decisive in equipping our Party for its vanguard leadership of the working
masses. I want to raise these questions, although not necessarily in the order
of their importance.

First, we must nurture and develop our Party further as the vanguard
party of the working class and of all exploited. This requires the maximum
political and organizational initiative of our Party on all levels—of each organization, each committee, each member. To be the vanguard, however, means
neither to lag behind nor to run ahead. This must particularly be borne in
mind today, in the central struggle of this period, in the fight for peace. We

must stimulate, organize, and lead struggles, taking the initiative and even going it alone when it is necessary, but always with the aim of setting into motion not only the host of friends and sympathizers of the Party but the tens of millions throughout the country. This is necessary, if we are to live up to our responsibilities and help to impose the American people's will for peace upon the war makers.

Next, we must safeguard the purity of Marxism-Leninism. We must wage a relentless war against all deviations, be they Right or Left opportunism, whether they are manifested in our trade union work, in our election campaigns, in the fight for Negro rights, in national group work, or in any other field of our mass activities. To do this, we must open up on a wider scale a merciless, relentless, and sustained struggle against Browder and Browderism, against the traitorous Tito camp.

Third, we must close ranks and establish a greater Communist discipline, guarding the unity of our Party as never before, as our indispensable weapon. Bear in mind, comrades, that precisely while the enemy attacks us from without, while he attacks us frontally, he will also redouble his efforts to weaken and disrupt us from within. We saw this in 1945 and 1946. We have seen it since. Now, with your National Chairman seriously ill, and your General Secretary going away for a while, be on guard against the efforts of the enemy to disrupt our Party. The enemy will seize on all weaknesses and shortcomings. He will try to utilize all differences and shadings of opinion, as well as to exploit personal ambitions, personal weaknesses of comrades. We must defeat the enemy on this front, as well as on all other fronts, and we must preserve and strengthen at all costs the unity of our Party.

Fourth, it is incumbent on us to raise to new heights the struggle for proletarian internationalism, the touchstone of which, for Communists and non-Communists, is the attitude to the Soviet Union, to the land of socialism. We know, and we must help other workers and progressives to realize, that the Soviet Union is *not just another country*. It is the land of socialism, the land of the workers, of the farmers, of all the peoples and nationalities that make up the USSR. It is the land where the workers rule and live today free from exploitation, from mass unemployment, free from the insecurities and the oppression of capitalism. It is the land of freedom and culture, the land of true democracy, the democracy of socialism. . . .

3

PROCEEDINGS
Eleventh CIO Convention

Following are portions of the debate at the 1949 convention over expelling Communist-led unions from the organization which those unions—i.e., their leaders—had been instrumental in creating. The Communists did not stand a chance of course and the purge went ahead without a hitch. The vehemence displayed by CIO spokesmen may be explained

by the fact that two of them, Quill and Curran, had until recently been Communists themselves, and the other, Reuther, had worked closely with the Party in the early days of the
United Auto Workers, which he now headed.

The Committee recommends that the Constitution of the CIO adopted in
Portland, Oregon, on November 25, 1948, be re-adopted by this Convention
as of this date, November 1, 1949, with the following changes:

(A) Page 10: Article IV concerning Officers and Executive Board is
amended by the insertion of a new Section 4 which reads as follows:
"Section 4. No individual shall be eligible to serve either as an officer or as
a member of the Executive Board who is a member of the Communist
Party, any fascist organization, or other totalitarian movement, or who
consistently pursues policies and activities directed toward the achievement of the program or the purposes of the Communist Party, any fascist
organization, or other totalitarian movement, rather than the objectives
and policies set forth in the constitution of the CIO." . . .

JOSEPH SELLY, PRESIDENT OF THE AMERICAN COMMUNICATIONS ASSOCIATION

Several speakers have referred to the fact that this proposed amendment to
the constitution represents a fundamental and basic change in the character of
this labor organization, of this Federation. I don't think that point can receive
too much emphasis. It is my humble opinion that the adoption of this resolution so completely reverses the fundamental policies of CIO on which it was
founded as to make the organization unrecognizable, as to give it a character
not only different but the opposite of the character it formerly enjoyed.

And what was the fundamental characteristic of CIO which endeared it to
millions of workers throughout this country, which made it possible to conduct effectively an organizing job among all the groups in this country, which
made it the hope and made it express the aspirations of the Negro group and
other minority groups, the people of my own faith, the Jewish faith, and all
other peoples? That characteristic was that CIO, unlike the organizations that
preceded it, was founded on the principle of the democratic rights of the
rank and file of the organizations affiliated to it.

We have spoken much at one convention after another on civil rights resolutions and other resolutions about our devotion to the fundamental
American principle of freedom of thought and expression. Let me remind
you gentlemen that that is pure demagogy unless we agree such freedom of
thought and expression, freedom of opinion and differences must be granted
to the minority group; and I will go further and say unless we learn the les-

son that there must be tolerance not merely of a minority but a minority of unpopular opinions, unless that remains the policy of CIO we will have surrendered one of the most cherished heritages of the American people. . . .

All of us, of course, get up and say we are in favor of the enforcement of the Constitution of the United States and of the Bill of Rights. All of us have engaged in many struggles in order to make this a reality, and I urge upon those who support this resolution that they consider carefully what they are doing, because they are here now proposing an amendment to the CIO constitution which they are at the same time arguing is in violation of the Constitution of the United States of America and of the Bill of Rights. We are considering here the enactment of a loyalty oath, a purgatory oath. . . .

WALTER REUTHER, PRESIDENT OF THE UNITED AUTO WORKERS

Every time you get into this basic question as to whether or not free people, through their democratic organizations, have a right to protect themselves and their freedoms, these people raise pious, hypocritical slogans, they talk about unity, they talk about autonomy, they talk about the democratic rights of the minority, they raise the civil rights issue, and they do everything they can to becloud the real issues involved in this debate. . . .

The Communist minority in our organization, like the disciplined Communist majority throughout the world, want the rights and privileges without the obligations and responsibilities, and we are saying here and now that those people who claim the rights and privileges must also be prepared to accept the responsibilities and the obligations.

There is room in our movement for an honest difference of opinion. Sincere opposition is a healthy thing in the labor movement. But there is a fundamental difference between honest opposition and sincere difference of opinion and the kind of obstructionism and sabotage carried on by the Communist minority, because the Communist minority is a trade union opposition group who disagree with CIO policies, because they believe that there are other policies that ought to take the place of our current policies. They are not a trade union group. In one sense they are to be pitied more than despised, because they are not free men, they are not free agents working in this movement. Their very souls do not belong to them. They are colonial agents using the trade union movement as a basis of operation in order to carry out the needs of the Soviet Foreign Office. And when you try to understand the basic characteristics of the Communist minority opposition group you have got to begin to differentiate between the kind of a minority opposition group of that kind and a minority opposition group that has a basic, honest trade union opposition in their differences with the official policies of their organization. . . .

When Harry Bridges says Communism is not the issue here—Harry, you are lying like hell and you know you are. And you are not leaving CIO because you could not keep your membership for one month after leaving CIO. You see, it was a nice, soft business up until now. As long as they could stay in CIO and peddle the Party medicine, as Walter Reuther said, with the label of CIO, it was easy, but when they are forced out and have to take off their outer coat and really show their red underwear, then they will not be able to hold their membership. And that is why they are split. . . .

JOSEPH CURRAN, PRESIDENT OF THE NATIONAL MARITIME UNION, CHAIRMAN OF THE RESOLUTIONS COMMITTEE

Now therefore be it resolved that:

1. This Convention finds that the Certificate of Affiliation heretofore granted to the United Electrical, Radio and Machine Workers of America has fallen into the control of a group devoted primarily to the principles of the Communist Party and opposed to the constitution and democratic objectives of the CIO, and in particular to the following declaration in the Preamble of the Constitution of the CIO:

> In the achievement of this task we turn to the people because we have faith in them and we oppose all those who would violate this American emphasis of respect for human dignity, all those who would use power to exploit the people in the interest of alien loyalties.

and in conformance with the provisions of Article III, Section 6, of our Constitution, this convention hereby expels the United Electrical, Radio and Machine Workers-of America from the Congress of Industrial Organizations and withdraws the said Certificate of Affiliation.

2. This Convention recognizes that overwhelming majority of the membership of the United Electrical, Radio and Machine Workers of America are not members of the Communist Party, and further recognizes the desire of the working men and women in the electrical and allied industries for a free and autonomous union affiliated with the CIO and devoted to the constitutional principles and policies of the CIO.

3. This Convention hereby authorizes and directs the Executive Board immediately to issue a Certificate of Affiliation to a suitable organization covering electrical and allied workers which will genuinely represent the desires and interests of the men and women in those industries.

The resolution, I notice, deals with a series of charges. There are four pages of the resolution in hysterical language setting forth reasons why the Union is so-called Communist dominated, and that its officers are serving as agents of a foreign union. And yet when I look at the charges I don't find one single charge that says the Union has not done a job for its members and has not organized hundreds of thousands of workers in an important basic industry, that the Union has not struggled to advance hours, wages and conditions—not a single economic charge is levied against the Union.

I look and I see that the resolution states that the charges are that they are Communist controlled, conceived and dominated—No. 1, in that the Union opposed the Marshall Plan. No. 2, the Union is against the Armament Pact, and so on down the line, the Atlantic Pact, etc. It goes on to say that the Union has disagreed with the CIO in matters of critical affairs, that the Union disagreed with the CIO in their action to repeal the Taft-Hartley law, that the Union accepted into its ranks the Farm Equipment Workers.

I have here the minutes of the ILWU convention last April and a copy of a telegram sent by the CIO. It says here that any action taken with respect to the merger of the Farm Equipment Workers with another Union shall be by the voluntary action of its membership, and if the membership of the Farm Equipment Workers want to join the UE, I would think that it's their business. However, the resolution speaks for itself in that respect. There is not one single charge that this Union has not organized, has not improved wages and obtained seniority, union security, welfare plans, and other things.

So now we have reached the point where a trade union, because it disagrees on political matters with the National CIO can be expelled. And yet we say we are not a political organization. Who is guilty of not following basic trade union policies and principles? In the Union that I represent, wages, hours, conditions, and the economic program come first. It has no loyalty to any political programs or any political party or any government except the American government. Neither does its membership nor its officers take second place to any union in their Americanism and their patriotism.

CIVIL RIGHTS

1

DEFENDING WILLIE MCGEE

Jessica Mitford

Jessica Mitford belonged to the California Communist Party and was an active member of the Civil Rights Congress, which took up the case of Willie McGee, executed in 1951 after four trials for alleged rape of a white woman (actually he had had an affair with her), and made it an international cause célèbre. Here, in her 1977 memoir, Mitford recounts the incident and how the anti-Communist press treated it at a time when the Cold War was at its height.

On the eighth of May, Willie McGee was executed. That the execution was indeed a surrogate lynching, for the Laurel mob was next best to the real thing, can be inferred from the Jackson *Daily News*, which devoted eight pages of news stories, photographs, and feature articles "to the event." To ensure that local would-be lynchers would not be cheated of this long-awaited moment, the electric chair had been transported to the Laurel courthouse from Parchman Penitentiary, 150 miles away.

A crowd of a thousand, or one out of every twenty Laurel residents, gathered outside the courthouse. For those unable to attend, the *News* re-created the festive atmosphere, compounded of blood lust and jollity, what James Baldwin described in his short story about a lynching as "a very peculiar, particular joy":

> Teenage boys did some laughing and there were a few girls and women in the throng. A patrolman shouted, "Let's everyone be nice. We want no demonstrations. You've been patient a long time." Everybody shouted as he said Willie was going to die. . . . A 70-year-old plumber perched atop a 30 foot cedar tree overlooking the courtroom where the execution took place. The nimble old man excitedly related the events to the eager crowd below as they took place. . . . When the execution was finally completed, witnesses were rushed by hundreds of people asking such questions as "Is he dead?" "How did he look?" and "What did he say?"
> A big cheer arose as the body was driven away.

A few days after McGee's death, the *News* had this editorial comment:

> The recent Willie McGee case was a striking illustration of the desperate tactics Communists use to gain ground for their cause. They spent at least $100,000 in defense of Willie McGee, a proven rapist, not because they cared anything whatever about the defendant, but they were boldly and impudently seeking to create disrespect for law and order among Negroes throughout the nation, and especially in Southern states. . . . The Communists tell the Negro's plight in all the far corners of the earth. It is their greatest weapon against the Marshall Plan and places us in a false light, especially to the yellow and black races.

Time and *Life* picked up the theme, rounding on the CRC and the

Communists, denouncing them for "using" the McGee case to further the cause of international Communism and foment racial strife. Thus *Time* of May 14, 1951:

To Communists all over the world, "the case of Willie McGee" had become surefire propaganda, good for whipping up racial tension at home and giving U.S. justice a black eye abroad. Stirred up by the Communist leadership, Communist-liners and manifesto-signers in England, France, China and Russia demanded that Willie be freed. . . . Not only Communists took up the cry. In New York, Albert Einstein signed a newspaper ad protesting a miscarriage of justice. Mrs. McGee, a captive of the Communists, addressed party rallies.

And *Life* a week later:

There was a bare chance that this sentence might never have been carried out on the reasonable ground that he, a Negro, had been condemned to death for a crime no white man has ever been executed for in Mississippi. But something very unfortunate happened to Willie. His case fitted too well into the strategy of the Communist International. . . . Money was raised to reopen Willie's defense and to prolong his propaganda value. . . . As the Communists moved in, such groups as the NAACP drew back. . . . Five years and five months later, after numerous appeals, six stays of execution and three Supreme Court refusals to review the case, the Communists had worked Willie McGee for all they could.

The liberal weeklies, ever alert for an opportunity to prove their own political purity and lack of any taint of subversion, followed in Luce's wake to launch their own peculiar kind of flank attack against McGee's defenders. John Cogley wrote in *Commonweal*:

The Communists vigorously espoused McGee's cause, but their support nowadays is rather a kiss of death. . . . The Communists and fellow travelers have been so thoroughly and rightfully discredited that no decent American wants to have any share in their crocodile tears and phony indignation.

Mary Mostert, writing in *The Nation*, also bought the "kiss of death" theory. While deploring "the new and most dangerous element, conviction by association," she proceeds to buttress the element in her own way:

After the Civil Rights Congress, a so-called Communist Front organization, took up the fight, people seemed no longer to care about any evidence presented by either prosecution or defense. . . . Willie McGee was convicted because he was black and supported by Communists, not on any conclusive evidence.

Thus did *The Nation* and *Commonweal* end up in a cozy, safe alliance with the Jackson *Daily News* and the Luce press. Neither magazine had printed one word about the case when it was being fought through the courts, when there might still have been time to mobilize liberal opinion for a nationwide effort to halt the execution. Gripped by the prevailing hysteria, they joined the chorus: Communism, not racism or injustice, is the issue. There is not a word of criticism of a Supreme Court that tacitly gave its blessing to institutionalized racism, and upheld the double standard of justice by three times refusing to review the case. Nor is there a word of recognition for the inconvenient truth: that had it not been for CRC and the Communists, the McGee case and the issues it raised would have gone unnoticed outside Mississippi, his execution just another local bloodletting in the violent history of black repression.

Evidently Willie McGee perceived his case as part of the continuum of that history. The day before his death, he wrote to his wife:

Tell the people the real reason they are going to take my life is to keep the Negro down in the South. They can't do this if you and the children keep on fighting. Never forget to tell them why they killed their daddy.

I know you won't fail me. Tell the people to keep on fighting.

Your truly husband, Willie McGee

2

WE CHARGE GENOCIDE
Civil Rights Congress

In 1951 the Congress laid before the United Nations a formal charge, from which this an extract, that the United States was practicing genocide against its black population. Most of the charge consisted of harrowing case studies. It received no response from the UN, but the American press, by damning it, brought it to the public's attention.

Out of the inhuman black ghettos of American cities, out of the cotton plantations of the South, comes this record of mass slayings on the basis of race, of lives deliberately warped and distorted by the willful creation of conditions making for premature death, poverty and disease. It is a record that calls aloud for condemnation, for an end to these terrible injustices that constitute a daily and ever-increasing violation of the United Nations Convention on the Prevention and Punishment of the Crime of Genocide.

It is sometimes incorrectly thought that genocide means the complete and definitive destruction of a race or people. The Genocide Convention, however, adopted by the General Assembly of the United Nations on December

9, 1948, defines genocide as any killings on the basis of race, or, in its specific words, as "killing members of the group." Any intent to destroy, *in whole or in part*, a national, racial, ethnic or religious group is genocide, according to the Convention. Thus, the Convention states, "causing serious bodily or mental harm to members of the group" is genocide as well as "killing members of the group."

We maintain, therefore, that the oppressed Negro citizens of the United States, segregated, discriminated against and long the target of violence, suffer from genocide as the result of the consistent, conscious, unified policies of every branch of government.

The Civil Rights Congress has prepared and submits this petition to the General Assembly of the United Nations on behalf of the Negro people in the interest of peace and democracy, charging the Government of the United States of America with violation of the Charter of the United Nations and the Convention on the Prevention and Punishment of the Crime of Genocide.

We believe that in issuing this document we are discharging an historic responsibility to the American people, as well as rendering a service of inestimable value to progressive mankind. We speak of the American people because millions of white Americans in the ranks of labor and the middle class, and particularly those who live in the southern states and are often contemptuously called poor whites, are themselves suffering to an ever-greater degree from the consequences of the Jim Crow segregation policy of government in its relations with Negro citizens. We speak of progressive mankind because a policy of discrimination at home must inevitably create racist commodities for export abroad—must inevitably tend toward war.

We have not dealt here with the cruel and inhuman policy of this government toward the people of Puerto Rico. Impoverished and reduced to a semi-literate state through the wanton exploitation and oppression by gigantic American concerns, through the merciless frame-up and imprisonment of hundreds of its sons and daughter, this colony of the rulers of the United States reveals in all its stark nakedness the moral bankruptcy of this government and those who control its home and foreign policies.

History has shown that the racist theory of government of the USA is not the private affair of Americans, but the concern of mankind everywhere.

It is our hope, and we fervently believe that it was the hope and aspiration of every black American whose voice was silenced forever through premature death at the hands of racist-minded hooligans or Klan terrorists, that the truth recorded here will be made known to the world; that it will speak with a tongue of fire loosing an unquenchable moral crusade, the universal response to which will sound the death knell of all racist theories.

We have scrupulously kept within the purview of the Convention on the Prevention and Punishment of the Crime of Genocide which is held to embrace those "acts committed with intent to destroy in whole or in part a national, ethnical, racial or religious group as such."

We particularly pray for the most careful reading of this material by those who have always regarded genocide as a term to be used only where the acts of terror evinced an intent to destroy a whole nation. We further submit that this Convention on Genocide is, by virtue of our avowed acceptance of the Covenant of the United Nations, an inseparable part of the law of the United States of America.

According to international law, and according to our own law, the Genocide Convention, as well as the provisions of the United Nations Charter, supersedes, negates and displaces all discriminatory racist law on the books of the United States and the several states.

The Hitler crimes, of awful magnitude, beginning as they did against the heroic Jewish people, finally drenched the world in blood, and left a record of maimed and tortured bodies and devastated areas such as mankind had never seen before. Justice Robert H. Jackson, who now sits upon the United States Supreme Court bench, described this holocaust to the world in the powerful language with which he opened the Nuremberg trials of the Nazi leaders. Every word he voiced against the monstrous Nazi beast applies with equal weight, we believe, to those who are guilty of the crimes herein set forth.

Here we present the documented crimes of federal, state and municipal governments in the United States of America, the dominant nation in the United Nations, against 15,000,000 of its own nationals—the Negro people of the United States. These crimes are of the gravest concern to mankind. The General Assembly of the United Nations, by reason of the United Nations Charter and the Genocide Convention, itself is invested with power to receive this indictment and act on it. . . .

Your petitioners will prove that the crime of which we complain is in fact genocide within the terms and meaning of the United Nations Convention providing for the prevention and punishment of this crime. We shall submit evidence, tragically voluminous, of "acts committed with intent to destroy, in whole or in part, a national, ethnical, racial or religious group as such,"—in this case the 15,000,000 Negro people of the United States.

We shall submit evidence proving "killing members of the group," in violation of Article II of the Convention. We cite killings by police, killings by incited gangs, killings at night by masked men, killings always on the basis of "race," killings by the Ku Klux Klan, that organization which is chartered by the several states as a semi-official arm of government and even granted the tax exemptions of a benevolent society.

Our evidence concerns the thousands of Negroes who over the years have been beaten to death on chain gangs and in the back rooms of sheriff's offices, in the cells of county jails, in precinct police stations and on city streets, who have been framed and murdered by sham legal forms and by a legal bureaucracy. It concerns those Negroes who have been killed, allegedly for failure to say "sir" or tip their hats or move aside quickly enough, or, more often, on trumped up charges of "rape," but in reality for trying to vote or otherwise demanding the legal and inalienable rights and privileges of United States citizenship formally guaranteed them by the Constitution of the United States, rights denied them on the basis of "race," in violation of the Constitution of the United States, the United Nations Charter and the Genocide Convention.

ECONOMIC GENOCIDE

We shall offer proof of economic genocide, or in the words of the Convention, proof of "deliberately inflicting on the group conditions of life calculated to bring about its destruction in whole or in part." We shall prove that such conditions so swell the infant and maternal death rate and the death rate from disease, that the American Negro is deprived, when compared with the remainder of the population of the United States, of eight years of life on the average.

Further we shall show a deliberate national oppression of these 15,000,000 Negro Americans on the basis of "race" to perpetuate these "conditions of life." Negroes are the last hired and the first fired. They are forced into city ghettos or their rural equivalents. They are segregated legally or through sanctioned violence into filthy, disease-bearing housing, and deprived by law of adequate medical care and education. From birth to death, Negro Americans are humiliated and persecuted, in violation of the Charter and the Convention. They are forced by threat of violence and imprisonment into inferior, segregated accommodations, into jim crow busses, jim crow trains, jim crow hospitals, jim crow schools, jim crow theaters, jim crow restaurants, jim crow housing, and finally into jim crow cemeteries.

We shall prove that the object of this genocide, as of all genocide, is the perpetuation of economic and political power by the few through the destruction of political protest by the many. Its method is to demoralize and divide an entire nation; its end is to increase the profits and unchallenged control by a reactionary clique. We shall show that those responsible for this crime are not the humble but the so-called great, not the American people but their misleaders, not the convict but the robed judge, not the criminal but the police, not the spontaneous mob but organized terrorists licensed and approved by the state to incite to a Roman holiday.

We shall offer evidence that this genocide is not plotted in the dark but incited over the radio into the ears of millions, urged in the glare of public forums by Senators and Governors. It is offered as an article of faith by powerful political organizations, such as the Dixiecrats, and defended by influential newspapers, all in violation of the United Nations charter and the Convention forbidding genocide.

This proof does not come from the enemies of the white supremacists but from their own mouths, their own writings, their political resolutions, their racist laws, and from photographs of their handiwork. Neither Hitler nor Goebbels wrote obscurantist racial incitements more voluminously or viciously than do their American counterparts, nor did such incitements circulate in Nazi mails any more freely than they do in the mails of the United States.

There was a time when racist violence had its center in the South. But as the Negro people spread to the north, east and west seeking to escape the southern hell, the violence, impelled in the first instance by economic motives, followed them, its cause also economic. Once most of the violence against Negroes occurred in the countryside, but that was before the Negro emigrations of the twenties and thirties. Now there is not a great American city from New York to Cleveland or Detroit, from Washington, the nation's capital, to Chicago, from Memphis to Atlanta or Birmingham, from New Orleans to Los Angeles, that is not disgraced by the wanton killing of innocent Negroes. It is no longer a sectional phenomenon.

Once the classic method of lynching was the rope. Now it is the policeman's bullet. To many an American the police are the government, certainly its most visible representative. We submit that the evidence suggests that the killing of Negroes has become police policy in the United States and that police policy is the most practical expression of government policy.

Our evidence is admittedly incomplete. It is our hope that the United Nations will complete it. Much of the evidence, particularly of violence, was gained from the files of Negro newspapers, from the labor press, from the annual reports of Negro societies and established Negro year books.

But by far the majority of Negro murders are never recorded, never known except to the perpetrators and the bereaved survivors of the victim. Negro men and women leave their homes and are never seen alive again. Sometimes weeks later their bodies, or bodies thought to be theirs and often horribly mutilated, are found in the woods or washed up on the shore of a river or lake. This is a well-known pattern of American culture. In many sections of the country police do not even bother to record the murder of Negroes. Most white newspapers have a policy of not publishing anything concerning murders of Negroes or assaults upon them. These unrecorded deaths are the rule rather than the exception—thus our evidence, though voluminous, is scanty when compared to the actuality. . . .

We plead as patriotic Americans, knowing that any act that can aid in removing the incubus of United States oppression of the American Negro people from our country is the highest patriotism. The American Dream was for justice, justice for all men, regardless of race, creed, or color. He who betrays it, betrays our country, betrays the world itself since the United States is a power in it for good or for evil.

We speak, too, as world citizens, certain that if the forces of predatory reaction are allowed to continue their present policies, are allowed to continue a profitable genocide against Americans, the time will not be long removed, the world being what it is, that the same forces will practice genocide on a wider scale against the nationals of other nations. So we plead not for ourselves alone but for all mankind. We plead not only for an end of the crime of genocide against the Negro people of the United States but we plead, too, for peace.

If the General Assembly acts as the conscience of mankind and therefore acts favorably on our petition, it will have served the cause of peace, the protection of which is the fundamental reason for its being. We recall the words of Mr. Justice Jackson at the Nuremberg trial of the Nazi war criminals when he declared that silence in the face of such crimes would make us a partner of them. We cannot believe that the General Assembly will not condemn the crimes complained of in this petition.

We ask that the General Assembly of the United Nations find and declare by resolution that the Government of the United States is guilty of the crime of Genocide against the Negro people of the United States and that it further demand that the government of the United States stop and prevent the crime of genocide.

We further ask that the General Assembly by resolution condemn the Government of the United States for failing to implement and observe its solemn international obligations under the Charter of the United Nations and the Genocide Convention and that the General Assembly also demand that the United States immediately take effective steps to carry out and fulfill its international obligations under the Charter and the Genocide Convention. . . .

3
REQUEST TO JOIN THE PARTY
W. E. B. DuBois

DuBois, the great social scientist, author of such classics as Souls of Black Folks *and* Black Reconstruction, *who had helped found the NAACP, tells in this letter why at the age of ninety he wished to become a card-carrying Communist. Shortly after, he left for Ghana, the first of the African colonies to be free, where he settled and died two years later.*

To Gus Hall,

Communist Party of the USA
New York, New York

On this first day of October 1961, I am applying for admission to membership in the Communist Party of the United States. I have been long and slow in coming to this conclusion, but at last my mind is settled.

In college I heard the name of Karl Marx, but read none of his works, nor heard them explained. At the University of Berlin, I heard much of those thinkers who had definitively answered the theories of Marx, but again we did not study what Marx himself had said. Nevertheless, I attended meetings of the Socialist Party and considered myself a Socialist.

On my return to America, I taught and studied for sixteen years. I explored the theory of Socialism and studied the organized social life of American Negroes; but still I neither read or heard much of Marxism. Then I came to New York as an official of the new NAACP and editor of the *Crisis Magazine*. The NAACP was capitalist orientated and expected support from rich philanthropists.

But it had a strong Socialist element in its leadership in persons like Mary Ovington, William English Walling and Charles Edward Russell. Following their advice, I joined the Socialist Party in 1911. I knew then nothing of practical Socialist politics and in the campaign of 1912, I found myself unwilling to vote the Socialist ticket, but advised Negroes to vote for Wilson. This was contrary to Socialist Party rules and consequently I resigned from the Socialist Party.

For the next twenty years I tried to develop a political way of life for myself and my people. I attacked the Democrats and Republicans for monopoly and disfranchisement of Negroes; I attacked the Socialists for trying to segregate Southern Negro members; I praised the racial attitudes of the Communists, but opposed their tactics in the case of the Scottsboro boys and their advocacy of a Negro state. At the same time I began to study Karl Marx and the Communists; I read *Das Kapital* and other Communist literature; I hailed the Russian Revolution of 1917, but was puzzled at the contradictory news from Russia.

Finally in 1926, I began a new effort: I visited Communist lands. I went to the Soviet Union in 1926, 1936, 1949 and 1959; I saw the nation develop. I visited East Germany, Czechoslovakia and Poland. I spent ten weeks in China, traveling all over the land. Then, this summer, I rested a month in Rumania.

I was early convinced that Socialism was an excellent way of life, but I thought it might be reached by various methods. For Russia I was convinced she had chosen the only way open to her at the time. I saw Scandinavia choosing a different method, half-way between Socialism and Capitalism. In the United States I saw Consumers Cooperation as a path from Capitalism to Socialism, while England, France and Germany developed in the same direction in their own way. After the depression and the Second World War, I was disillusioned. The Progressive movement in the United States failed. The Cold War started. Capitalism called Communism a crime.

Today I have reached a firm conclusion:

Capitalism cannot reform itself; it is doomed to self-destruction. No universal selfishness can bring social good to all.

Communism—the effort to give all men what they need and to ask of each the best they can contribute—this is the only way of human life. It is a difficult and hard end to reach—it has and will make mistakes, but today it marches triumphantly on in education and science, in home and food, with increased freedom of thought and deliverance from dogma. In the end Communism will triumph. I want to help to bring that day.

The path of the American Communist Party is clear: It will provide the United States with a real Third Party and thus restore democracy to this land. It will call for:

1. Public ownership of natural resources and of all capital.
2. Public control of transportation and communications.
3. Abolition of poverty and limitation of personal income.
4. No exploitation of labor.
5. Social medicine, with hospitalization and care of the old.
6. Free education for all.
7. Training for jobs and jobs for all.
8. Discipline for growth and reform.
9. Freedom under law.
10. No dogmatic religion.

These aims are not crimes. They are practiced all over the world. No nation can call itself free which does not allow its citizens to work for these ends.

4

AN AUTOBIOGRAPHY
Angela Davis

That the Party had not entirely lost its ability to attract talented young radicals is evident from Davis's 1974 Autobiography. She became a Communist (as she describes below) while studying philosophy at the University of California at Los Angeles with Herbert Marcuse, aging doyen of the New Left; eventually she taught there. A few years later she was indicted for helping a black inmate of Soledad Prison in his attempt to break out, during which he and several others, including a judge, were slain. She had then fled, been captured, tried, and acquitted. It went without saying that she was, and remains, America's most celebrated Communist (this despite the fact that she and the Party's official leadership have fallen out).

I tried to acquire the information I needed in order to decide whether I wanted to become a member of the Communist Party. At this stage in my life and my political evolution—even more than during the San Diego days—I needed to become a part of a serious revolutionary *party*. I wanted an anchor, a base, a mooring. I needed comrades with whom I could share a common ideology. I was tired of ephemeral ad-hoc groups that fell apart when faced with the slightest difficulty; tired of men who measured their sexual height by women's intellectual genuflection. It wasn't that I was fearless, but I knew that to win, we had to fight and the fight that would win was the one collectively waged by the masses of our people and working people in general. I knew that this fight had to be led by a group, a party with more permanence in its membership and structure and more substance in its ideology. Confrontations were opportunities to be met; problems were entanglements to be sorted out with the right approach, the correct ideas. And I needed to know and respect what I was doing. Until now all our actions seemed to end, finally, in an ellipsis—three dots of irresolution, inconsistency and ineffectiveness.

During that depressing time, I reread Lenin's *What Is To Be Done*, and it helped me to clarify my own predicament. I read DuBois again, particularly his statements around the time he decided to join the Communist Party.

Since Frankfurt, since London, since San Diego, I had been wanting to join a revolutionary party. Of all the parties that called themselves revolutionary or Marxist-Leninist, the Communist Party, in my opinion, alone did not overstate itself. Despite my criticisms of some aspects of the Party's policies, I had already reached the conclusion that it would be the Communist Party or, for the time being, nothing at all.

But before I could make my decision I had to examine it, study it. The Che-Lumumba Club, the Black cell of the Party in Los Angeles, was the section of the Party which interested me. I wanted to know what its role and responsibilities were within the Party and how it maintained its identity and consistency as its cadres involved themselves in the Black Liberation Movement. As with all the other Communist parties, the basic unit of the CPUSA was and remains the "club" (or cell, as it is called in other countries). In general, the club is composed of from five to twenty members. There are sections, districts, states, regions, and finally the national leadership, which carries out policy which is made by periodic national conventions. Insofar as the democratic centralist structure of the Party was concerned, the Che-Lumumba Club was just like any other club. Yet it did have a special role, originating from the fact that Black Communists in Los Angeles had fought within the Party for a club that would be all Black and whose primary responsibility would be to carry Marxist-Leninist ideas to the Black Liberation struggle in L.A. and to provide leadership for the larger Party as far as the Black movement was concerned.

The club had been established in 1967—at a time when the Black movement was approaching its zenith. The Communist Party was bound to be affected by the stirrings in the ghettos from Harlem to Watts. Because L.A. was the scene of one of the first recent, full-scale Black uprisings, it seemed inevitable that the Che-Lumumba Club would come into existence in that city.

The knowledge I gained about the Che-Lumumba Club did not satisfy me completely, because I had little firsthand knowledge of the larger Party. Kendra and Franklin, therefore, introduced me to some of the white comrades. I began to pay visits to Dorothy Healey, who was then the District Organizer of Southern California. We had long, involved discussions— sometimes arguments—about the Party, its role within the movement, its potential as the vanguard party of the working class; its potential as the party that would lead the United States from its present, backward, historically exploitative stage to a new epoch of socialism. I immensely enjoyed these discussions with Dorothy and felt that I was learning a great deal from them, regardless of whether I ultimately decided to become a Communist myself.

In July 1968, I turned over my fifty cents—the initial membership dues—to the chairman of the Che-Lumumba Club, and became a full-fledged member of the Communist Party, USA. . . .

5

RADICAL PERSPECTIVES ON EMPOWERMENT FOR
AFRO-AMERICAN WOMEN
Angela Davis

Davis wrote this piece for the August 1988 issue of the Harvard Educational Review.

During this decade we have witnessed an exciting resurgence of the women's movement. If the first wave of the women's movement began in the 1840s, and the second wave in the 1960s, then we are approaching the crest of a third wave in the final days of the 1980s. When the feminist historians of the twenty-first century attempt to recapitulate the third wave, will they ignore the momentous contributions of Afro-American women, who have been leaders and activists in movements often confined to women of color, but whose accomplishments have invariably advanced the cause of white women as well? Will the exclusionary policies of the mainstream women's movement—from its inception to the present—which have often compelled Afro-American women to conduct their struggle for equality outside the ranks of that movement, continue to result in the systematic omission of our names from the roster of prominent leaders and activists of the women's movement? Will there continue to be two distinct continuums of the women's movement, one visible and another invisible, one publicly acknowledged and another ignored except by the conscious progeny of the working-class women—Black, Latina, Native American, Asian, and white—who forged that hidden continuum? If this question is answered in the affirmative, it will mean that women's quest for equality will continue to be gravely deficient. The revolutionary potential of the women's movement still will not have been realized. The racist-inspired flaws of the first and second waves of the women's movement will have become the inherited flaws of the third wave.

How can we guarantee that this historical pattern is broken? As advocates and activists of women's rights in our time, we must begin to merge that double legacy in order to create a single continuum, one that solidly represents the aspirations of all women in our society. We must begin to create a revolutionary, multiracial women's movement that seriously addresses the main issues affecting poor and working-class women. In order to tap the potential for such a movement, we must further develop those sectors of the movement that are addressing seriously issues affecting poor and working-class women, such as jobs, pay equity, paid maternity leave, federally subsidized child care, protection from sterilization abuse, and subsidized abortions. Women of all racial and class backgrounds will greatly benefit from such an approach.

For decades, white women activists have repeated the complaint that women of color frequently fail to respond to their appeals. "We invited them to our meetings, but they didn't come." "We asked them to participate in our demonstration, but they didn't show." "They just don't seem to be interested in women's studies."

This process cannot be initiated merely by intensified efforts to attract Latina women or Afro-American women or Asian or Native American women into the existing organizational forms dominated by white women of the more privileged economic strata. The particular concerns of women of color must be included in the agenda. . . .

Black women scholars and professionals cannot afford to ignore the straits of our sisters who are acquainted with the immediacy of oppression in a way many of us are not. The process of empowerment cannot be simplistically defined in accordance with our own particular class interests. We must learn to lift as we climb.

If we are to elevate the status of our entire community as we scale the heights of empowerment, we must be willing to offer organized resistance to the proliferating manifestations of racist violence across the country. . . .

Black women have organized before to oppose racist violence. In the nineteenth century the Black Women's Club Movement was born largely in response to the epidemic of lynching during that era. Leaders like Ida B. Wells and Mary Church Terrell recognized that Black women could not move toward empowerment if they did not radically challenge the reign of lynch law in the land. Today, Afro-American women must actively take the lead in the movement against racist violence, as did our sister-ancestors almost a century ago. We must lift as we climb. As our ancestors organized for the passage of a federal antilynch law—and indeed involved themselves in the woman suffrage movement for the purpose of securing that legislation—we must today become activists in the effort to secure legislation declaring racism and anti-Semitism as crimes. Extensively as some instances of racist violence may be publicized at this time, many more racist-inspired crimes go unnoticed as a consequence of the failure of law enforcement to specifically classify them as such. A person scrawling swastikas or "KKK" on an apartment building may simply be charged—if criminal charges are brought at all—with defacing property or malicious mischief. Recently, a Ku Klux Klanner who burned a cross in front of a Black family's home was charged with "burning without a permit." We need federal and local laws against acts of racist and anti-Semitic violence. We must organize, lobby, march, and demonstrate in order to guarantee their passage.

As we organize, lobby, march, and demonstrate against racist violence, we who are women of color must be willing to appeal for multiracial unity in the spirit of our sister-ancestors. Like them, we must proclaim: We do not draw the color line. The only line we draw is one based on our political principles. We know that empowerment for the masses of women in our country will never be achieved as long as we do not succeed in pushing back the tide of racism. It is not a coincidence that sexist-inspired violence—in particular, terrorist attacks on abortion clinics—has reached a peak during the same period in which racist violence has proliferated dramatically. Violent attacks on women's reproductive rights are nourished by these explosions of racism. The vicious antilesbian and antigay attacks are a part of the same menacing process. The roots of sexism and homophobia are found in the same economic and political institutions that serve as the foundation of racism in this country and, more often than not, the same extremist circles that inflict violence on people of color are responsible for the eruptions of violence inspired by sexist and homophobic biases. Our political activism must clearly manifest our understanding of these connections. . . .

I want to suggest, as I conclude, that we link our grassroots organizing, our essential involvement in electoral politics, and our involvement as activists in mass struggles to the long-range goal of fundamentally transforming the socioeconomic conditions that generate and persistently nourish the various forms of oppression we suffer. Let us learn from the strategies of our sisters in South Africa and Nicaragua. As Afro-American women, as women of color in general, as progressive women of all racial backgrounds, let us join our sisters—and brothers—across the globe who are attempting to forge a new socialist order—an order which will reestablish socioeconomic priorities so that the quest for monetary profit will never be permitted to take precedence over the real interests of human beings. This is not to say that our problems will magically dissipate with the advent of socialism. Rather, such a social order should provide us with the real opportunity to further extend our struggles, with the assurance that one day we will be able to redefine the basic elements of our oppression as useless refuse of the past.

1

Cult of the Individual
Nikita Khrushchev

On the evening of February 25, 1956, Chairman Khrushchev spoke for six hours to the Twentieth Congress of the Soviet Communist Party. The delegates were dumbstruck when they heard him detail Stalin's crimes, this from one of Stalin's intimates. The extraordinary speech was supposed to be secret, but the CIA of course got hold of a copy and published a translation of it on June 5th (the day the New York Times *printed it in full). That was also when the American Party learned of it, with what effect can be imagined.*

At the present we are concerned with a question which has immense importance for the party now and for the future—[we are concerned] with how the cult of the person of Stalin has been gradually growing, the cult which became at a certain specific stage the source of a whole series of exceedingly serious and grave perversions of party principles, of party democracy, of revolutionary legality. . . .

When we analyze the practice of Stalin in regard to the direction of the party and of the country, when we pause to consider everything which Stalin perpetrated, we must be convinced that Lenin's fears were justified. The negative characteristics of Stalin, which, in Lenin's time, were only incipient, transformed themselves during the last years into a grave abuse of power by Stalin, which caused untold harm to our party.

We have to consider seriously and analyze correctly this matter in order that we may preclude any possibility of a repetition in any form whatever of what took place during the life of Stalin, who absolutely did not tolerate collegiality in leadership and in work, and who practiced brutal violence, not only toward everything which opposed him, but also toward that which seemed to his capricious and despotic character, contrary to his concepts.

Stalin acted not through persuasion, explanation, and patient cooperation with people, but by imposing his concepts and demanding absolute submission to his opinion. Whoever opposed this concept or tried to prove his viewpoint, and the correctness of his position, was doomed to removal from the leading collective and to subsequent moral and physical annihilation. This was especially true during the period following the XVIIth Party Congress [1934], when many prominent party leaders and rank-and-file party workers, honest and dedicated to the cause of Communism, fell victim to Stalin's despotism. . . .

It was precisely during this period (1935–1937–1938) that the practice of mass repression through the government apparatus was born, first against

the enemies of Leninism—Trotskyites, Zinovievites, Bukharinites, long
since politically defeated by the party, and subsequently also against many
honest Communists, against those party cadres who had borne the heavy
load of the Civil War and the first and most difficult years of industrialization
and collectivization, who actively fought against the Trotskyites and the
rightists for the Leninist Party line.

Stalin originated the concept "enemy of the people." This term automatically rendered it unnecessary that the ideological errors of a man or men
engaged in a controversy be proven; this term made possible the usage of
the most cruel repression, violating all norms of revolutionary legality,
against anyone who in any way disagreed with Stalin, against those who
were only suspected of hostile intent, against those who had bad reputa-
tions. This concept, "enemy of the people," actually eliminated the possibility of any kind of ideological fight or the making of one's views known on
this or that issue, even those of a practical character. In the main, and in
actuality, the only proof of guilt used, against all norms of current legal science, was the "confession" of the accused himself; and, as subsequent probing proved, "confessions" were acquired through physical pressures against
the accused.

This led to glaring violations of revolutionary legality, and to the fact that
many entirely innocent persons, who in the past had defended the party line,
became victims.

We must assert that in regard to those persons who in their time had
opposed the party line, there were often no sufficiently serious reasons for
their physical annihilation. The formula, "enemy of the people," was specifically introduced for the purpose of physically annihilating such individuals.
. . .

It was determined that of the 139 members and candidates of the Party's
Central Committee who were elected at the XVIIth Congress, 98 persons,
i.e., 70 percent, were arrested and shot (mostly in 1937–1938). (*Indignation
in the hall*) . . . The same fate met not only the Central Committee members
but also the majority of the delegates to the XVIIth Party Congress. Of 1,966
delegates with either voting or advisory rights, 1,108 persons were arrested
on charges of anti-revolutionary crimes, i.e., decidedly more than a majority. This very fact shows how absurd, wild and contrary to common sense
were the charges of counterrevolutionary crimes made out, as we now see,
against a majority of participants at the XVIIth Party Congress. (*Indignation
in the hall*) . . .

Facts prove that many abuses were made on Stalin's orders without reckoning with any norms of party and Soviet legality. Stalin was a very distrust-
ful man, sickly suspicious; we knew this from our work with him. He could
look at a man and say: "Why are your eyes so shifty today?" or "Why are you
turning so much today and avoiding to look me directly in the eyes?" The

sickly suspicion created in him a general distrust even toward eminent party workers whom he had known for years. Everywhere and in everything he saw "enemies," "two-facers" and "spies."

Possessing unlimited power he indulged in great willfulness and choked a person morally and physically. A situation was created where one could not express one's own will.

When Stalin said that one or another should be arrested, it was necessary to accept on faith that he was an "enemy of the people." Meanwhile, Beria's gang, which ran the organs of state security, outdid itself in proving the guilt of the arrested and the truth of materials which it falsified. And what proofs were offered? The confessions of the arrested, and the investigative judges accepted these "confessions." And how is it possible that a person confesses to crimes which he has not committed? Only in one way—because of application of physical methods of pressuring him, tortures, bringing him to a state of unconsciousness, deprivation of his judgment, taking away of his human dignity. In this manner were "confessions" acquired. . . .

Some comrades may ask us: Where were the members of the Political Bureau of the Central Committee? Why did they not assert themselves against the cult of the individual in time? And why is this being done only now?

First of all we have to consider the fact that the members of the Political Bureau viewed these matters in a different way at different times. Initially, many of them backed Stalin actively because Stalin was one of the strongest Marxists and his logic, his strength and his will greatly influenced the cadres and party work. . . .

Later, however, Stalin, abusing his power more and more, began to fight eminent party and government leaders and to use terroristic methods against honest Soviet people. As we have already shown, Stalin thus handled such eminent party and government leaders as Kossior, Rudzutak, Eikhe, Postyshev and many others.

Attempts to oppose groundless suspicions and charges resulted in the opponent falling victim of the repression. This characterized the fall of Comrade Postyshev.

In one of his speeches Stalin expressed his dissatisfaction with Postyshev and asked him, "What are you actually?"

Postyshev answered clearly, "I am a Bolshevik, Comrade Stalin, a Bolshevik."

This assertion was at first considered to show a lack of respect for Stalin; later it was considered a harmful act and consequently resulted in Postyshev's annihilation and branding without any reason as a "people's enemy."

In the situation which then prevailed I have talked often with Nikolai Alexandrovich Bulganin; once when we two were traveling in a car, he said, "It has happened sometimes that a man goes to Stalin on his invitation as a friend. And when he sits with Stalin, he does not know where he will be sent | **393**

next, home or to jail."

It is clear that such conditions put every member of the Political Bureau in a very difficult situation. And when we also consider the fact that in the last years the Central Committee plenary sessions were not convened and that the sessions of the Political Bureau occurred only occasionally, from time to time, then we will understand how difficult it was for any member of the Political Bureau to take a stand against one or another unjust or improper procedure, against serious errors and shortcomings in the practices of leadership. . . .

[We must] restore completely the Leninist principles of Soviet socialist democracy, expressed in the Constitution of the Soviet Union, to fight willfulness of individuals abusing their power. The evil caused by acts violating revolutionary socialist legality, which have accumulated during a long time as a result of the negative influence of the cult of the individual, has to be completely corrected. Comrades! The XXth Congress of the Communist Party of the Soviet Union has manifested with a new strength the unshakable unity of our party, its cohesiveness around the Central Committee, its resolute will to accomplish the great task of building Communism. (*Tumultuous applause*) And the fact that we present in all their ramifications the basic problems of overcoming the cult of the individual which is alien to Marxism-Leninism, as well as the problem of liquidating its burdensome consequences, is an evidence of the great moral and political strength of our party. (*Prolonged applause*)

We are absolutely certain that our party, armed with the historical resolutions of the XXth Congress, will lead the Soviet people along the Leninist path to new successes, to new victories. (*Tumultuous, prolonged applause*)

Long live the victorious banner of our party—Leninism! (*Tumultuous, prolonged applause ending in ovation. All rise.*)

2

Steve Nelson, American Radical
Steve Nelson

Nelson, most stalwart of Communists for decades, who had fought in many battles and had suffered much in the process (e.g., jail), tells in his interesting autobiography, published in 1981, why the Khrushchev revelations had such an impact on him. He soon after left the Party.

At the end of April I traveled to New York for a National Committee meeting. Until then we had heard only rumors concerning the last speech at the Soviet Party's Twentieth Congress, which Khrushchev had delivered in a closed session. Now someone from the National Board announced that a comrade had just returned from England with the text of the speech and that because of the document's length, it would occupy the entire afternoon agenda. As we adjourned people filed out, chattering nervously. We ate lunch with queasy stomachs, and most people returned early from the break, a rarity at such conferences.

The National Committee itself consisted of about 65 people, but this meeting was a plenum, which meant that many of the key people at the district level—trade union and Party organizers, for example—were invited. I was elected to chair the session, and took my seat at a table facing about 120 people, the collective backbone of the Party. I'd never enjoyed chairing meetings. It meant always keeping one eye on the clock and sometimes cutting people off when they exceeded their allotted time, but it was especially uncomfortable to chair this session. The air buzzed with 120 variations of the same question: What's going on? Someone from the administrative committee that made the arrangements for the meeting asked that we remove all notebooks, pens, and pencils. There were to be no notes taken. This had never happened before at a National Committee meeting. Everyone sat up, waiting for something extraordinary to happen.

The comrade who brought the speech rose and proceeded to read it in its entirety, which took an hour and a half. For twenty years we'd labeled the stories of Stalin's atrocities as lies and distortions. We'd suppressed every doubt, feeling that a Communist Party could never have perpetrated such crimes. Now the secretary general of the Communist Party of the Soviet Union confirmed all these accusations and added documentation of many more. Of 1,966 delegates to the 1934 Seventeenth Congress of the Soviet Party, 1,108, including many members of the Central Committee, were arrested, and many of them executed by 1936. Seventy percent of the 139 members and candidates for the Party Central Committee elected at the Seventeenth Congress, a group comparable in stature and experience to the comrades sitting before me, were arrested and shot, not by the guns of the class enemy but by those of other Communists! An entire generation of leadership—the cream of the Bolsheviks, the men and women who made the Revolution— was wiped out. You might prove that one guy was a rascal, that he had dealings with the White Guards, that he had been stealing from the people. Perhaps you could prove this about two or even a dozen, but 70 percent of the Central Committee? This was a massacre. As the speech was read, the list of atrocities seemed endless. Even the idea of Stalin allocating millions of pounds of copper for a giant statue of himself seemed monstrous to anyone who realized that thousands of Russian workers were homeless at the time.

The words of the speech were like bullets, and each found its place in the hearts of the veteran Communists. Tears streamed down the faces of men and women who had spent forty or more years, their whole adult lives, in the movement. I looked into the faces of people who had been beaten up or jailed with me and thought of the hundreds that I had encouraged to join the Party. My head was swimming. I thought, "All the questions that were raised along the way now require new answers, and there's no longer one seat of wisdom where we can find them. We're on our own."

As chairman, I broke the deafening silence that followed the last sentence of the speech. I had made my sacrifices voluntarily and never thought of myself as a martyr, but now I felt betrayed. I said simply, "This was not why I joined the Party." The meeting ended in shock. I found myself in a car heading across town with friends and comrades I had known for years, but not one of us could bring him- or herself to speak. I spent the next couple of days discussing the implications of the speech with those to whom I felt closest, Spanish veterans like Bill Lawrence and George Watt and other comrades like Sid Stein, Dorothy Healey, George Charney, Mike Russo, Fred Fine, and Martha Stone. I wanted to call Margaret, but how could I break this sort of news over the phone?

Above all, I was angry, not with the Russians or Foster or even Stalin, but with myself and others who had been so blind in our adherence to Soviet policy and so mechanical in our application of Marxism. All of our lives we had pointed to the Soviet Union as the model for what we were trying to achieve. This was the sort of system we were asking people to fight for in place of capitalism. I, and I'm sure many others who were at the meeting, vowed that our Party would change in order that nothing like this could ever happen again.

The most astounding thing was that some people were so rigid that not even this shock could move them. Foster and others acknowledged that it was a terrible thing but insisted that we were still on the right track and that the Soviet leaders would overcome the problem. A few even defended Stalin, arguing that he should still be respected for his great accomplishments. The emotion produced by the shock seemed to harden the division that had been growing for some time in the national leadership, and for the first time I feared there might be a split. . . .

3
TIME FOR A CHANGE
John Gates

Gates, most loyal of Party hierarchs, became one of the chief advocates of radical reform in the wake of the Khrushchev speech and the general perturbations throughout the Communist world. That the Party might be opening up was demonstrated when it allowed Gates to present his views in the pages of Political Affairs *(the November 1956 issue), its theoretical organ.*

The present Party discussion is undoubtedly the most crucial in our history. I believe we are in a profound crisis. This situation did not come about just in the last few months, but is the accumulation of many factors, some of which operated during the entire history of our Party and were brought to a head by recent events.

The protests against those who feel that their lives have been wasted miss the point, in my opinion. Of course we have made vital and lasting contributions to the progress of our country, and this is a legitimate source of pride for all of us. But that is exactly why so many of our members are so deeply disturbed. Why, despite our contribution to making our country and the world a better and safer place to live in, is our Party at such a low point? Just because of our past achievements, we must give frank and honest answers to where we are, how did we get there, and where do we go from here.

The crisis we are in is a deep and many-sided one. We have suffered great losses in membership and even more in influence. We are isolated almost entirely as a Party from the labor movement, the Negro people, and the farmers. The confidence of many people in us that we built up over many years has been largely dissipated. Even the confidence of our own members in the Party and its leadership has been severely shaken. Those of our members who are in the popular mainstream are doing fine work as progressive trade unionists and Negro militants, but not in most cases as known and organized Communists. We are still compelled to function largely as an illegal or semi-legal organization. Although the country is emerging from the reaction of the past decade, our decline in numbers and influence has still not been halted. The labor and Negro people's movements successfully resisted the reactionary offensive of the cold war years and are advancing with seven-league boots, but we who pioneered in the struggle for labor unity, industrial unionism, and equal rights for the Negro people are largely outside of this advance. . . .

ON MARXISM-LENINISM

The first change that is necessary is our approach to Marxist-Leninist theory. I voted with the majority of the National Committee to recommend to the convention that we delete the phrase "Marxism-Leninism" from the preamble to our Party constitution. I think this is necessary because the government has successfully made use of this phrase to distort what we American Communists really believe and stand for, to isolate us from the American people, and to virtually illegalize us. Instead of tying ourselves to a phrase which can so easily be distorted and misused against us, we need to spell out in our own language the theories we base ourselves on and our true program and policy. Does this mean throwing out and abandoning all the work of Marx, Engels and Lenin? Of course not. But if anyone asks me whether I base myself on the principles of Marx and Lenin, I want to be able to answer which of those principles I believe in and which I do not. Theory is the generalization of experience, and since experience is always changing, theory must change with it. . . .

ON THE USSR

The second change necessary concerns our approach to the Soviet Union. The historic role of the USSR in blazing the trail for Socialism, and in transforming the world situation to where lasting peace is now possible, has fully justified the high regard we have always had for the Soviet Union and its Communist Party. Humanity will be forever indebted to the Soviet Union for those services. We played our own modest part in bringing this about, and our defense of the Soviet Union against the efforts of world capitalism to destroy it by force has proved to be in the best patriotic interests of our country. . . .

The revelations of Stalin's mistakes and crimes, though shocking and brutal, and the process of correction by the Communist Party of the Soviet Union since Stalin's death, have had a liberating effect on world Communism, in my opinion, and were absolutely essential for the further progress of Socialism not only in the USSR but everywhere. They have laid the foundations for a new leap forward in healing the historic breach between Socialist and Communist Parties, the achievement of working-class unity in general, and important new successes in the fight for peace. They are making possible big new strides in socialist democracy, justice and morality which were seriously compromised under Stalin's leadership. They are helping each country to find and to travel its own national path to Socialism.

All this is a gigantic process which is not proceeding evenly and smoothly, but it is inexorable. There is no turning back from it. It will be facilitated and speeded to the extent that we learn the fullest lessons from the Stalin mistakes. The discussion precipitated by the 20th Congress in world Communist ranks was healthy and constructive. In my opinion it must be continued and developed further in order to extract the maximum benefits. The questions of many Communists concerning the adequacy of the explanations for Stalin's misleadership are fully justified. History is not made primarily by heroes or gods, nor by villains or devils. The violations of democracy and justice in the USSR cannot be explained by the deficiencies of Stalin alone. How could one man have achieved the power he did and why was a whole country powerless before him? How could such flagrant violations of socialist ideals take place for such a long time in a socialist country? . . .

SOCIALISM AND DEMOCRACY

The great lesson we must learn is that the expansion of democracy is not automatic under Socialism but must be fought for. Socialism creates the material conditions for the fullest expansion of democracy, much higher than in the most advanced capitalist democracies, but it must be built just as socialist economy must be. Violations of democracy are not inherent in Socialism but on the contrary come into conflict with it and must be eliminated as is now taking place, but we also know now that neither is it inherent in Socialism that democracy cannot be suppressed, restricted and violated. Better controls by the people over their leaders and institutions must be devised than up until now in order to make impossible any future violations of democracy.

We Americans must guarantee that American Socialism will be a fully democratic Socialism. I am confident we will be able to achieve that, partly as a result of the pioneering efforts and enormous sacrifices of the Soviet Union and the other socialist countries, partly because we will be on guard against repeating the mistakes of the Soviet Union if we master all the lessons of it, and especially because of our own more favorable circumstances and historical traditions.

FOR A CHANGED PARTY

The third change we must make is to build a different kind of a party. To make our most effective contribution to the achievement of the broadest type of American socialist democracy, superior in every respect to our present democracy, requires the most democratic kind of Communist Party. The present concept of our Party may have been necessary for a period in which war was inevitable and peaceful constitutional transition impossible but this is no longer the case.

We are in a new era which requires new programs and forms of organization. In my view this requires that we take a new look at the concept of democratic centralism. Our experience has been the tendency for this to become transformed into maximum centralization and minimum democracy. Whether this is inherent in the concept or not I do not know but it very well may be. The essential thing at this time is to make our Party fully democratic from top to bottom. I think it is necessary to separate democracy from centralism, else the former becomes subordinate to the latter. This is not to deny the need for centralism but it must be made subordinate to democracy. Democratic centralism apparently results in a semi-military type of organization which is clearly not valid for our country in this period. . . .

In my opinion the name of the Party ought to be changed. I have no illusions that such a change will automatically and miraculously solve all of our problems, but if we make the serious changes described above, it will dramatize to the American people that our Party is making profound and genuine changes, and under such circumstances help us in the fight for legality, not only in the courts but more important in our relations with the American people.

I think too that we must give the most serious consideration to whether we should retain the party form of organization. Our resolution correctly states that this is not a matter of principle. Political principles are primary and forms of organization are subordinate to and flow from them. Form and structure of organization can vary greatly and must be determined by what can most effectively carry forward our political objectives under given circumstances. We are not a political party as the American people understand it. Political parties in America are electoral organizations primarily. We must admit we are not that today if we are honest with ourselves. . . .

The test as to whether we shall succeed in becoming a truly independent American working-class organization dedicated to the immediate struggles of the American people and Socialism lies right now in the kind of atmosphere we develop in the discussion, and ultimately of course in the policies we adopt. If we develop an atmosphere of respect for and consideration of each other's views on their merits, do not stifle the discussion, avoid name calling and emotionalism, learn how to live together in the same Party despite differing and opposing views, and increase our mass work as we discuss, I think we will make significant headway. I am confident that such will be the case, and that our Party will emerge strengthened and in a better position to go forward.

4

Marxism-Leninism and "American Prosperity"
William Z. Foster

Speaking for the Old Guard, Foster answered Gates a few months later (February 1957) in Political Affairs.

At the present time there is a militant drive on in the Communist Party against Marxism-Leninism, on the grounds that it is essentially Left-sectarian and, as such, unadaptable to American conditions. . . .

Even after the heavy losses suffered by the Communist Party under the fierce attack by the Government during the cold war years, the CP is still numerically stronger than all the other Left groups put together—Socialist Party, Social-Democratic Federation, Socialist Labor Party, Socialist Workers Party, the Industrial Workers of the World, and the Sweezy and Cochran groups. Besides, over the years, the CP has made a record of struggle and achievement that dwarfs those of the other Left groups combined. All this constitutes living proof of the greater adaptability of Marxism-Leninism to class struggle conditions in this country. . . .

The present proposal of Comrade Gates and others to transform the Communist Party into a so-called political action association is based upon the assumption that from here on to Socialism in the United States there will be a minimum of class struggle. In his article in the November number of *Political Affairs*, Comrade Gates paints an idyllic picture in this general respect. He ignores the existence of the general world crisis of capitalism and the certainty of serious repercussions of it in the United States, and he foresees a relatively smooth evolutionary development to Socialism.

This line is much akin with that promulgated by Browder a dozen years ago and by Lovestone in the latter 1920s. It is essentially influenced by the "prosperity" illusions among the masses, as indicated above, and is an ideological weakening under the hammer blows of the Government's persecution of the Communist Party and its members. Browder and Lovestone, however, were fundamentally wrong in their no-class struggle perspective, and so is Comrade Gates.

In accordance with its generally incorrect perspective, the Gates tendency develops an attack upon the workers' fighting philosophy, strategy, and tactics—Marxism-Leninism—and precisely upon those active polities which made the Communist Party into a fighting organization and which were responsible for such successes as the Party scored. Thus, the Gates group would have us discard the Party form itself, the very incorporation of Marxism-Leninism; it cuts the heart out of our endorsement of Leninism in general by making such endorsement conditional and by abandoning the term Marxism-Leninism; it gives up the principle of democratic centralism; it casts aside the vital concept of the vanguard role of the Party; it ignores the policy of the united front, having in mind a perspective essentially of tailing after the leaders of mass organizations; it abandons the Leninist concept that labor leaders of the Meany type are lieutenants of the capitalists, etc., etc.

The proposed political action association would be primarily a propaganda organization for Socialism. This would be in line with the Gates conception that serious class struggle will be but a minor factor in the American future and that the Communists have no special vanguard role to play in it, except to advocate Socialism abstractly. The association, because of its bizarre form and limited functions, obviously could not be a mass organization. Besides, in the change-over from Party to association, involving the formal liquidation of the Party (just as in the Browder case), there would necessarily be a heavy loss of members. The whole project is highly liquidationary, despite the main Resolution's assertion to the contrary. . . .

The American working class needs imperatively a strong Communist Party, based firmly upon the principles of Marxism-Leninism. This would be true even if the perspective ahead of the American workers were such a smooth and struggle-less one as that foreseen by Comrade Gates. But his picture of the future is basically false. The workers of this country will certainly confront a perspective of sharpened class struggle. In such a situation, they must have a fighting Communist Party, acting as their vanguard. The need for this type of Party was graphically illustrated during the cold war years, when the big majority of the mass leaders tamely followed the imperialist lead of monopoly capital in its aggressive foreign policy.

Those who think that the present "boom" conditions in industry and the corresponding class collaboration relations between the top trade union leaders and the monopoly capitalists will last indefinitely are in for a rude awakening. The current post-war industrial boom is wearing to its end. American monopoly capital still has lots of fight left in it, as it will demonstrate once its general position, in the world and in an internal economic crisis, begins to deteriorate seriously under the inexorable workings of the general crisis of world capitalism, and when American workers face massive assaults against their living and working conditions. Such a perspective of struggle makes doubly necessary the building of a strong Communist Party. . . .

5

KEYNOTE ADDRESS
Eugene Dennis

At the Party's national convention, held in February 1957, the General Secretary— recently let out of jail—announced the settlement of the dispute between reformers and Old Guard—Gates versus Foster—by standing squarely in the middle. The effect was pretty much to drive the reformers out of the Party. His speech appeared in the March 1957 Political Affairs.

Comrades and Friends:

In the course of its 38 years of existence, our American Communist Party has weathered a good many storms, and more than one stormy convention.

This convention meets at an especially difficult moment in our Party's history. We have been engaged in a painful and searching effort to correct past errors, to surmount losses sustained during the cold-war decade, to overcome our relative isolation, as well as to probe a host of new problems arising out of the changing world in which we live. This already protracted endeavor is by no means over. But we anticipate that our convention will go forward, making some imperative changes and that we shall emerge a wiser, stronger, and a more united party. . . .

Starting with the April National Committee meeting, our party took some important first steps toward grappling with the most pressing of our many complicated problems. We correctly emphasized, among other things, the urgent need to eliminate from our ranks all dogmatic views and sectarian and bureaucratic practices. Shortly thereafter we laid the basis for further progress by approving the main political approach of the Draft Resolution, and submitted the Draft for general discussion and amendment.

But, during this same period, when the facts in the Khrushchev speech on Stalin became known in this country, and again after the tragic events in Hungary, important sections of the party at *all* levels were temporarily disoriented and demobilized. Some tried to start a stampede. Some wandered into strange pastures; while others exhibited a hardening of the political arteries.

Temporarily thrown off balance, the Party began to become enmeshed in a bitter and divisive internal struggle, and was in danger of being torn apart. In this situation, the struggle against doctrinairism and for effecting big and long overdue changes in our functioning and style of work, in our relationships with masses, as well as the fight against revisionist tendencies, became hampered by factional attitudes and extremism.

Without going into the matter fully, I believe all of us on the National Committee must share responsibility for this situation. But some of the N.C. members who, at least until recently, clung to inflexible polities and pursued extreme political objectives will perhaps take on themselves more than the common share.

Fortunately, as the zero hour approached and the danger of a split in the Party loomed as a possibility, substantial sections of our membership and some of the leadership rose to the occasion. As distinct from the conciliators of either the "Right" or the "Left," they began to intervene forcefully. They combined a resolute struggle to save the Party, defend Marxist-Leninist principles and make the necessary changes, *with* an all-out effort to preserve its unity. . . .

In emphasizing all of these questions, I do not mean to imply that we are already out of the woods of our internal difficulties, or that the crucial question of Party unity has already been settled.

On the contrary. We still have sharp and unresolved differences on a host of vital questions. We still face inflexible tendencies to crystallize an extreme polarization of views which foster dangerous divisions and factionalism.

Therefore one of the central questions before this convention is: What are some of the prerequisites for achieving that principled unity which is indispensable to the life and progress of our party, to enable us to enhance our contributions to our people and country?

Communist unity can be forged and maintained only on the basis of working class, Marxist-Leninist principles. These scientific and universally valid principles must be fought for firmly, and in a comradely spirit.

But it is not enough to recite or proclaim these Marxist principles. They must be grasped scientifically and applied creatively in accord with the concrete conditions of our country and the needs of the American working class. We need to study more deeply the science of Marxism-Leninism *and* American traditions and conditions. We need to synthesize and enrich these, bearing in mind the big and favorable changes in the world *and* the new trends developing in our own country. . . .

I believe too that what has happened in regard to Party unity and the lessons of the past decade underscore the great need for boldly refreshing our Party leadership at all levels, for effecting a united team which embodies the best of the old and the new, with special stress on Negro, shop, trade union, women, and youth representation.

FAREWELLS

1

THE STORY OF AN AMERICAN COMMUNIST
John Gates

Having failed in his quest to change the Party, Gates goes on to describe his unceremonious withdrawal from it, and his valiant refusal thereafter to join the anti-Communist crusade which was then in progress.

On New Year's Eve, 1957, I attended an office party at the national headquarters of the Party and told Elizabeth Gurley Flynn that when the *Daily Worker* went, I would go with it. The following Monday I was called in by Dennis and other leaders of the party and asked whether it was true I was going to leave the party. I said "Probably." I was then asked "when," and I replied I would let them know when I was ready. They then passed a motion to remove me from all posts. I told them mildly that they ought to examine the new party Constitution which stated that any member of the party could resign without prejudice, and that their action was obviously unconstitutional. [I walked out of the meeting after I had the pleasure of telling everyone present that "I have the utmost contempt for every one of you, the same contempt you have shown for the party's program and constitution."]

That was Monday, January 6. Time was running out. The evening of Thursday the 9th I wrote my letter of resignation after discussing it with my wife. She had long known of my feelings and was impatient for me to draw my conclusions. I called up Si Gerson, the executive editor of the paper, informed him I had written my letter of resignation and was calling a press conference at the Hotel Albert the following day to inform the public. I invited him to cover it for the *Daily Worker*. He said he was sorry about my decision, that he would not cover the event himself but would send another reporter. I then called Sid Stein, at that time the national secretary of party organization, read him my letter, told him about the press conference, and then I went out to mail the letter.

It read as follows: "I hereby submit my resignation from membership in the Communist Party of the United States, effective immediately. I have come to this decision, after 27 years in the Communist movement, because

I feel that the Communist Party has ceased to be an effective force for democracy, peace and socialism in the United States. The isolation and decline of the Communist Party have long been apparent. I had hoped, as a result of the struggle that has been going on in the party for the last two years, that the party could be radically transformed. The program adopted by the last National Convention gave some promise that this might happen. Not only has this program never been carried out, it has been betrayed. I have come to the reluctant conclusion that the party cannot be changed from within and that the fight to do so is hopeless. The same ideals that attracted me to socialism still motivate me. I do not believe it is possible any longer to serve those ideals within the Communist Party. Obviously, under these circumstances, my continued employment as editor-in-chief of the *Daily Worker* and the *Worker* will no longer be desirable to you. Consequently, my function as such ceases as of this moment."

It had taken me only a few minutes to write this letter. How many thousands had taken this step, without writing letters! How unthinkable it had seemed to us when we joined! Yet how inescapably events had left no other course. . . .

I did not quit the Communist Party to embrace the Un-American Committee.

About a month after my departure, the House Committee on Un-American Activities subpoenaed me and I appeared before it in executive session. I refused to answer any questions about my political views before or after I quit the party on the grounds that Congress had no constitutional rights to pry into political beliefs. If that was all they were interested in, I offered to sell them a copy of my pamphlet "Why I Quit the Communist Party," a compilation of my articles in the *New York Post*. They would not buy it. I stood on the First and Fifth Amendments to the Constitution and told the Committee I would use every amendment in the Bill of Rights if necessary, that the Founding Fathers had added the Bill of Rights to the Constitution to protect Americans from political inquisitions such as this Committee. When the Committee asked me what ideas I had to offer on curbing subversive activities, I advised the Un-American Committee to go out of business, saying it had proved to be a greater menace to American liberties than the Communist Party had ever been. At this point Rep. Scherer of Ohio jumped up and exclaimed, "That proves you are still a Communist!" and demanded that I be cited for contempt. This same Congressman said at a meeting sponsored by Aware, Inc., some weeks later that the Communist Party had a fifth column behind it of 25 million Americans. He evidently arrived at that figure by totaling the approximate number of Americans who had voted the Democratic ticket in the previous presidential election. Rep. Scherer, of course, is a Republican.

The Communists call me a traitor to the cause but the extreme Right insists I am still a Communist. It reminds me of the old *Daily Worker* cartoon of a cop beating a man over the head with his club at a demonstration. The man is protesting, "But officer, I am an anti-Communist." The cop replies "I don't care what kind of Communist you are," and continues to beat him over the head.

My prediction that J. Edgar Hoover and various congressional committees would claim the Communist Party was now stronger than ever was confirmed almost immediately. Indeed, this is the main thesis of Hoover's latest book, *Masters of Deceit*. He reaches the curious conclusion that the fewer members, the stronger and more dangerous the Communist Party becomes. By this standard, the high point of the menace of the Communist Party will come when it ceases to exist altogether. Many people must wonder whether the billions of dollars lavished by Congress on the FBI to combat communism were worthwhile if after 40 years of ceaseless FBI activity, the Party is more powerful than ever. Actually, the Communist Party of the United States has dwindled almost to the vanishing point and this alarms the FBI and certain other legislative committees whose main business has been built around the idea of a growing American Communist menace. There's no more gold in them thar red hills.

The most significant feature of the party's decline is the kind of people who have left in the last two years. These were not the Johnny-come-latelys or people on the fringes of the movement but the tried and tested cadre of the party. They went through every twist and turn of policy, veterans of 25 years standing who had dedicated their entire lives and made every conceivable sacrifice, in short, people whom the FBI called the "hard core" of the party. The fact that such people quit is proof that they were never like the picture that was painted of them but were sincere adherents of an ideal. They left because of fundamental reasons—what they once thought the party stood for could no longer be squared with reality. . . .

2

CAUSE AT HEART
Junius Irving Scales

Scales, who came from an elite North Carolina family, was the last of the Smith Act Communists to go free, thanks to President Kennedy's 1962 pardon. He quit the Party soon after. Here, in his 1990 memoir (which he wrote with author Richard Nickson), he explains why and praises it at the same time.

Learning to live outside the Party was an extremely painful adjustment. Gone was the sense of living each day with the utmost intensity in the selfless service of a great purpose. Gladys and I had anticipated that loss before leaving the Party and felt that we simply must face the truth as we saw it: the belief was dead and with it had gone the innocence and joy forever. The truth as we saw it was that the American Communist dream had become a cruel, convoluted hoax.

Facing that truth was not so simple. Though the lesson had been learned painfully, it was easy to adjust to the fact that Marxism-Leninism had become a Stalinist hodgepodge which meant at any moment precisely what the Soviet Politburo said it did. But so many years of mental and emotional conditioning had gone into determining my response to certain stimuli that for some time thereafter I continued to feel a warm response at the mere mention of the Soviet Union. Since my mind was once again on cordial terms with objective facts, I was bombarded with data which proved that my romantic dream of socialism in the Soviet Union was false; that the USSR was in a terrible state, lacking most democratic rights; that it was a country in which the government killed, persecuted, or regimented its artists and intellectuals; and that its government preyed on weaker neighbors as brutally as any imperialist power. But my mind and emotions resisted every fact, every bit of evidence. Deeply painful was the loss I felt as each encrusted illusion about socialism in the Soviet Union fell apart.

What was needed, I thought, was time to examine myself closely, to separate the phony from the genuine in my Communist past. Gladys gradually focused her altruism and her passion to better the world on one small, vital area: she would teach the children in her care, with all the love, gentleness, and skill she could command, how to be better people than those in the preceding generation.

But I couldn't sort myself out so easily. For one thing, I was still in grave danger of going to jail for six years. I thought that if my case could be won in the Supreme Court it would break the back of the Smith Act and provide a great victory for American civil liberties. The Party would be the first beneficiary because all the pending membership cases would be thrown out; that was fine with me. Although I'd separated my life from the Party, it never occurred to me to think of it as an adversary. John Gates, George Charney, Max Gordon, Doxey Wilkerson, Doc Blumberg, Joe Clark, and many another good friend had remained inside, fighting a good, if hopeless, fight to transform it into a democratic socialist organization.

Through months and years I mulled over my Party experience. Several years later, Dwight Macdonald gave me one of his books inscribed: "To one failed politician from another." I never got a chance to discuss with Macdonald, whom I admired, his reasons for the inscription. But I'd already arrived at that evaluation of my own political career.

My eighteen years in the Party had spanned military and political defeats for Fascism, significant improvements in the welfare of working people, and the beginnings of a Second Reconstruction of the South that ended the disfranchisement of Negroes and largely eliminated racism from the body of the law. In those historic achievements I had played a positive role as a Communist. In the effort to advance a foreign policy to oppose the cold war and the drift toward atomic war, I, with my Party, generally floundered. As for

advancing the principles of socialism (the heart of my political outlook), I had
seized blindly on an unworthy model, had mired myself in indefensible
dogma, and had often allowed the needs of the moment to betray the ideals
of my goal. Considering the strength and virulence of the opposition, some
excuses might be made for the failures of my Party as a whole.

Where I felt *my* real failure lay was in my lack of intellectual courage in
thinking out political and cultural questions for myself; my fear of trusting
my own conscience; my slavish, opportunistic following of the Party line
when I knew it was wrong or inadequate; my ineptitude in playing the Party
leader, a role I felt was unsuited to my temperament and abilities. I had, along
with some few achievements and some joyous and proud memories, enough
failures to provide me with grief and guilt for decades to come. Much of that
grief and guilt should be shared, I believe, by those who led our country during that same period.

(At this writing, even the "achievements" seem less solid: my native state
seems to be dominated politically by ultra-right-wing racists; the labor
movement in North Carolina and the nation is less substantial than it was
forty years ago; the poor are getting poorer and more numerous; blacks are
still at the bottom of the heap; the country is ruled by an administration
firmly gripped by the negative ideology of anti-Communism; fear of the
Soviet Union and Communism is offered as justification for any outrage, military or legal, foreign or domestic; the Bill of Rights—indeed, the Constitution—is under deadly attack; life on the planet is threatened both by pollu-
tion and by atomic war—and there are intellectuals in droves to defend and
praise the way things are going.)

Had my Communist experience been worthwhile, on balance? The
Communist Party made me keenly aware of the danger of Fascism, the misery of the Negroes, the plight of the workers, and the desirability of democratic socialism. Elsewhere I might have found a satisfactory way of opposing
Fascism, of aiding the organization of workers, or of promoting socialism.
But when it came to opposing white supremacy, there was nowhere else to
turn.

In my youth the most glaring injustice facing a southern white was the
mistreatment of Negroes. The horror of it was palpable and everywhere.
Because the Party showed me this horror firsthand, there was no alternative
for me but to fight it. Many principled southern whites were unaware of the
extent of the outrage that permeated every facet of their society, and they
could look the other way, deplore racism privately, while applying their talents in admirable and creative ways. Unfortunately, most southern white liberals found that they could live with a slightly altered version of the
Declaration of Independence: "All men are created [separate but] equal."
Thus they failed to attack the heart of Negro oppression, and abjectly helped
to perpetuate the most corrosive wrong of our time.

Had Bart Logan, my first Party leader, been an insensitive hack instead of a passionately feeling person, I might have stayed relatively sheltered and largely oblivious of my surroundings. And I might have become a liberal history professor. Instead, I joined the *only* organization committed to full economic, political, and social equality for Negroes; and that is still a matter of pride. For that, more than for anything else, I think my Communist experience was worthwhile. Gladys, who suffered the most, thought so too. . . .

3

A FINE OLD CONFLICT
Jessica Mitford

In this part of her engaging memoir, Mitford makes no apologies for having served in the Party.

"The Ex's," as they were called in Party parlance, suddenly freed from years of intense pressure and discipline, ran in a thousand directions, like schoolchildren when the dismissal bell rings. A minority, those tired of the struggle, or bitter and disillusioned, retreated altogether from the political arena to devote themselves to the pursuit of their own happiness. But for the most part the Ex's were endowed with an outsize sense of social responsibility and exceptional organizational skills, legacies from their years in the CP. In search of new outlets for these qualities they fled variously to the Unitarian Church, the Democratic Party, Women for Peace, the Co-op movement. These Ex's had, after all, joined the Party originally because of their vivid desire to improve the world and their conviction that this was possible, and on the whole they continued to be guided by what they had learned in the Party organization. For many of us, I think, the Party experience proved to have been a kind of adult Project Head Start that enabled us to function better than we otherwise might have in the new endeavors we now pursued. . . .

Since writing the above I have received some 350 Xeroxed pages of my FBI file, which I requested under the Freedom of Information Act. In an accompanying letter, Mr. Clarence Kelley, FBI director, explains that he has made some excisions from these documents "in order to protect materials which are exempted from disclosure." That he has, and with odd results. Some pages consist largely of heavy crossings-out: "xxxxx advised xxxxxxxx on xxxxxxx that the Subject was quite active in a union which had been formed among OPA employees in San Francisco. Xxxxxx advised xxxxxxxx that he was of the opinion that the union was endeavoring to promote Communism." Other pages have been almost entirely blanked out, leaving merely a tantalizing opener: "Subject was observed entering . . . " The government's charge of ten cents a page for these seems excessive; I am currently appealing the deletions. Nevertheless, what remains legible is a dizzy-

completely forgotten. Reading it was like seeing one's whole life flash before
one's eyes, as is supposed to happen to a drowning person:

"Subject seen at Fair Employment picket line. . . . Subject listed as outstanding worker in Twin Peaks Club of Communist Party. . . . Subject at
meeting to protest bombing murders in Florida. . . . Subject present at a
Rosenberg clemency rally. . . . Subject chairman of meeting of Committee
to Secure Justice for Morton Sobell. . . . Subject signer of Petition to Repeal
internal Security Act . . . " and so on, for day after day, year after year.

One memorandum, from the assistant attorney general, Internal Security
Division, to the FBI director, I found of more than passing interest. It is
headed EMERGENCY DETENTION PROGRAM," and offers a choice of two boxes
to be checked: "It has been determined that Subject's name should be
retained on security index" or ". . . removed from security index." In my case,
there is a large black "X" in the first box. The date of this memo is October
1, 1962, when Robert Kennedy was Attorney General, a creepy reminder
that McCarthyism did not die with McCarthy.

Reading on into the sixties, I learn that Subject was observed at anti-
Vietnam War demonstrations, was seen at meetings of the Northern
California Committee to Repeal the McCarran Act, was featured speaker at
a rally to raise $500,000 to appeal conviction of the University of California
Free Speech Movement defendants, was listed as a sponsor of the Spring
Mobilization Committee to End the War in Vietnam, was a member of the
Jeanette Rankin Brigade for Peace, was trapped by white rioters in a
Montgomery, Alabama, church at a meeting for the Freedom Riders, made a
speech at a National Lawyers Guild meeting to raise funds for the Student
Nonviolent Coordinating Committee, was mistress of ceremonies at a meeting of the Black Panther Defense Committee, was chairman of a meeting to
celebrate release of Morton Sobell from federal prison, was believed to be
writing a book about the trial of Dr. Spock. The very last entry, for March
1972, reports that "Subject is currently working on a book about prisons and
has won a Guggenheim fellowship for a year's study of the United States
penal system."

Subject must confess that, as she pored over this telescoped account of her
activities through the years, she felt an unbecoming surge of pride, not
unmixed with gratitude to the Communist Party for all it taught her, for the
avenues it opened up for her to take part in what she perceived as the crucial
battles of the day.

True, the CPUSA made some abysmal mistakes, mostly stemming from
its unshakable reliance on the Soviet Union for leadership and its resolute
blindness to developments in the Communist countries—to the fact that
Stalinism did not die with Stalin. Robert Scheer, one of the more perceptive
spokesmen of the New Left, writes: "Neither the Old Left nor the New took
the building of an indigenous popular radical organization as its main task.

And yet without such an organization, no revolution in the world could succeed." This is a telling observation. Preoccupied as we were with the day-to-day tactics of survival, we may well have lost sight of our overall strategic aims. But I do not believe we ever betrayed them. Did we not, in fact, leave something of a heritage—however limited, as Rita Baxter would say—for future radical movements to inherit? That is for new generations to decide.

4

DOROTHY HEALEY REMEMBERS
Dorothy Healey

Since she was a girl growing up in Oakland Healey had been a militant Communist. Adding charm to ideology, she became a leader of the California Party, the country's second largest. She left it rather late: 1973. Her criticisms, spelled out in her 1990 autobiography (written with Maurice Isserman), lack the bitterness one often finds among ex-Communists. That may be because she retained her faith in Marxism, but a Marxism resting on democratic principles, as she goes on to explain.

It was a tremendous relief to find myself for once with no organizational affiliations or responsibilities. Now, I thought, I could be like all those other "independent radicals" who enjoyed the luxury of standing above the fray, criticizing what other people on the Left were doing without actually having to do anything themselves. Although I had no intentions of plunging back into organizational work, I did join a discussion circle, which referred to itself jokingly as the "Forty Socialists Without a Party," made up for people who had been in or close to the Communist Party. . . . Marxism had been taught as a set of formulas, and most Party members had neither the time nor interest to look beyond those formulas. I know from my own case that it took nearly two decades of practical experience before it occurred to me that the "theory" I was reading in books by Marx and Lenin had much of anything important to do with my practical activity. That was in part my own fault, but it was also the fault of the intellectual atmosphere within the Party. We weren't encouraged to think of Marxism as a *methodology*, as an open system of thought that could change in a changing world.

There is an important lesson to be learned in the way that Marx dealt with contemporary thinkers. Marx is remembered as a fierce polemicist, which he was, but that's only half the story. Even when he dismissed other theories as nonsense or invalid, he was still able to extract some valid kernel of truth from what he was reading and make it part of "Marxism." The disciples and descendants who followed him, for the most part, lost that ability. Either we attacked our opponents at their weakest points, or ignored them completely. If they weren't Marxists—and Marxists of our own persuasion, for that matter—we felt we could just dismiss what they had to say with a wave of our hand, ignoring whatever empirical data or new theoretical conclusions they might have drawn. In contrast, treating Marxism as a methodology means having the ability to look dialectically at contemporary reality and not to be contented with one-sided arguments or formulas from the past. I still call myself a Marxist, although I respect other revolutionaries who do not. The Japanese Communists, for example, took the word Marxism out of their Party constitution. They say they are guided by "scientific socialism," which of course is what Marx and Engels called their own theory. I really don't care what it's called. When I say that I'm a Marxist, what I mean is I see the value in continuity in the spirit in which Marx approached his own world. . . .

I won't see socialism in my lifetime; I don't know if my son will see it in his, or even my grandchildren in theirs. There is no way to foretell what kind of political developments and issues will galvanize a future generation to turn toward socialism. The model I embraced in my youth, the vision of a vanguard party of the working class seizing power in the midst of a great social and political crisis like the one that had overtaken Russia in 1917, is no longer relevant. But I still believe that working people must be at the center of any real movement for socialism, for they are the majority for whose well-being that government "of, by, and for the people" should be concerned.

Ultimately I have faith that people, given the understanding of how they can help bring it about, want to live in a better world. People *can* change the world, but they can't do it as individuals alone. They have to join with others to do it. One thing I have not changed my views on over the years is the belief that organization is the key to winning victories for social change. That's why it was such a tragedy that so little in the way of organized radicalism survived the collapse of the New Left. . . .

I have never understood the bitterness that some former members of the YCL [Young Communist League] and the Communist Party feel about their years in the movement. As the poet Johann Schiller admonished Don Carlos, "Bear respect for the dream of one's youth." For all of my own criticisms of the Communist movement, I retain a great feeling of gratitude that those of us who were in it gained knowledge that we never could have gotten any other way. My respect for thousands of people with whom I worked in the Communist Party, including some who have remained in it, remains undiminished. But my loyalties are to a vision of socialism, not to a particular organization. There's a phrase I've always liked in the revolutionary anthem "The International." It goes, "No more traditional chains shall bind us." As Communists we argued that the survival of capitalism depended on the false consciousness of the majority of the people who weren't able to perceive the reality of their own lives. Ironically, the Communists also found themselves bound by "tradition's chains," and substituted a false consciousness for a real understanding of the world around them. The challenge that faces the Left in the future—if it is to have a future—is to base itself on the knowledge of what collective action by human beings can mean, rather than on faith in the infallibility of either its dogma or its leaders. If I were allowed just one piece of advice to give a new generation as to how to sustain a lifelong commitment, I would suggest the cultivation of those two essential virtues of a good revolutionary, patience and irony.

I

A discussion of the literature on American Communism requires a word about its historical context, the two—the literature and the historical context—roughly corresponding to the stages of the Party's career, its rise, decline, burial, and ascension.

I call the first stage "polemical" because it was characterized by a literature of apologetics and denunciations, hagiography and demonization. It emerged with the Party and more or less petered out when the Party did during the early Cold War years. Throughout those decades Communists were able to give as roundly as they got, thanks to the sizable audience it commanded for its countless books, magazines, pamphlets, newspapers, and so on. It would be bootless here even to touch on this vast literature of polemics, of life and death controversies between irreconcilable hosts, a literature unrelieved by what might pass as objective scholarship, fair and open-minded, or at least by dispassion, irony, distance.

By the 1950s American Communism could no longer defend itself in the marketplace of ideas. Its audience was rapidly dwindling, along with its publications. The polemicizing had become altogether one-sided, an increasingly shrill rhetoric of hatred and revenge. But in due course that rhetoric subsided: there was a sudden thaw in the Cold War. In January 1953 Eisenhower replaced Truman; six weeks later Stalin died; and five months after that the Korean War ended. Within a year, McCarthy the man, the bully, the demagogue was in disgrace and out of the political picture. To be sure,

McCarthy*ism* still held sway and the Cold War still dominated American life, but a change of national mood—less anxious, less combative—was clearly discernible.

In this environment there arose a new nonpolemical literature about the Communist experience that rendered increasingly preposterous such throwbacks as J. Edgar Hoover's *Masters of Deceit* (New York: Henry Holt, 1958). Thus was ushered in what might be called the "consensus" stage, the consensus school of historians and social scientists. It held that Communism represented not so much a satanic evil, an enemy to be vanquished by fire and sword, as a social pathology or psychic disorder to be rationally analyzed and understood if it, along with every other form of "extremism," was to be fought effectively.

This was the assumption behind an extraordinary project that a distinguished liberal foundation, the Fund for the Republic, launched in the mid-1950s, nothing less than an examination of the whole Communist phenomenon in America, its history, institutions, ethnic makeup, and so on, to be done by reputable scholars and published by established houses. And indeed the nine volumes in the series that came out (fewer than planned) did observe every canon of scholarship and therefore did pass the standard tests of objectivity. But that objectivity lay within the ideological parameters already indicated. Resolute anti-Communism defines even the best of the Fund for the Republic studies: Theodore Draper's *The Roots of American Communism* (New York: Viking, 1957) and *American Communism and Soviet Russia* (New York: Viking, 1960), Daniel Aaron's *Writers on the Left* (New York: Harcourt, Brace, and World, 1961), and Nathan Glazer's *Social Basis of American Communism* (New York: Harcourt, Brace, and World, 1961).

Deserving special notice is a work that was more *in* than *of* the consensus stage of literature. Irving Howe's and Lewis Coser's *The American Communist Party: A Critical History* (Boston: Beacon, 1957) presented itself as unashamedly political if not polemical. For years it was the widely accepted one-volume book on the subject because it was so well researched and written and carried its authors' high imprimatur; it simply had no competitors. Its politics, moreover, comported nicely with the liberal consensus scholars, for it attacked the Communist Party from the Left rather than the Right, condemning it as treasonable not to America but to the radical tradition to which they, the authors, proudly laid claim. In its omissions and emphases and jaundiced interpretations the book was no doubt a settling of old scores, but it is more than that and has much to recommend it.

And so, for that matter, do many of the older, uncompromising polemics, among them—to select two antithetical ones at random—Eugene Lyons's angry screed, *The Red Decade* (New York: Bobbs-Merrill, 1941), and William Z. Foster's triumphal march, *The History of the Communist Party of the United States* (New York: International, 1952). They are not merely period pieces.

Consensus was followed by dissensus, by the 1960s rebellion that surprised everyone, its practitioners included, and led to a "discovery" stage in the literature on American Communism that has continued unabated to the present.

From the standpoint of this bibliography the rebellion is interesting for the paradox it called forth. That it was a movement of the young is incontrovertible—of young people against racial segregation, against the Vietnam War and Cold War policies in general, against the conventional norms of family life, gender roles, sexual practices, and self-reliance through hard work, against repressive schooling, and on and on. The sixties also saw the largest increase ever in the college population (the burgeoning military and civilian economy demanded it) and with it the size of the faculty. It was perforce a faculty of young people, often the very people who had participated in these rebellions or identified with them. Before long, they were acquiring tenure and achieving autonomy and freedom unique in the history of higher education.

The paradox of rebels winning a place in an institution they reviled helps explain how the discovery stage came about, the discovery in question here being the American Communist movement. Young scholars uncovered enormously rich fields of research that consensus scholars had overlooked or examined with an indifferent eye. Especially rich were such fields as labor, popular culture, black and ethnic studies, and biographies of Party activists. Overwhelmingly, the books on American Communism that rolled off the university presses (themselves an expanding industry made to order for young scholars seeking advancement) and that were published by the commercial publishers (whose market was mostly college students) viewed their subjects sympathetically and brushed aside the charge of Communist subservience to the Soviet Union that so preoccupied the consensus generation. In any case the scholars of the discovery generation were doing the hard work, exhuming the archives, interviewing the old activists, and discovering fresh material, insights, and possibilities. They were creating a vast new literature on American Communism.

Its magnitude may be gauged by a recent bibliographical compilation (a rather critical one of Communism, incidentally) that already needs updating, by John Earl Haynes, *Communism and Anti-Communism in the United States* (New York: Garland, 1987). For what amounts to a continuous updating, see (where it can be found) the invaluable *Newsletter of the Historians of American Communism*.

How Theodore Draper, the most prominent of the consensus historians, felt about these goings-on he summed up in two sharply polemical essays for the May 1985 *New York Review*; later that year they appeared as the afterword to a new edition of *American Communism and Soviet Russia*. He flayed the "new historians" (and some documentary filmmakers) for their pathetic wish to discover a usable past, a rebelliousness enveloped in romance, nostalgia, myth. Conceding nothing, Draper still regarded American Communism as little more than the reflex of Soviet Communism. "'Americanized' American Communism," he wrote "has corresponded to the fluctuations of Russian policy; it has not obeyed a compelling need within the American Communists themselves." And Irving Howe gave the new historians the back of *his* hand, though not in so many words, by reciting the familiar theme— that Communism was a disaster for the American Left—in the book-length essay he brought out in 1985: *Socialism and America* (San Diego: Harcourt Brace Jovanovich, 1985). But these animadversions did nothing to stop the swelling tide of books and articles that sympathized with the things Communists had done, if not with Communism itself.

All the more conspicuous, then, have been the recently published studies that harked back to the consensus phase and even further back to a yet more virulent anti-Communism. The most impressive without question is Harvey Klehr's *The Heyday of American Communism* (New York: Basic Books, 1984), which picks up where Draper's works leave off. Another solid critique is Lowell K. Dyson, *Red Harvest: The Communist Party and American Farmers* (Lincoln: University of Nebraska Press, 1982). Aileen Kraditor deepens her indictment of the Left in American life as something alien to its nature and indeed to human nature and nature's God with *"Jimmy Higgins"* (Westport, Conn.: Greenwood, 1988). She has made a valiant but failed attempt to "explore . . . the mental universe" of average Communists ("Jimmy Higginses") who, out of misplaced idealism, allowed themselves to be manipulated by corrupt and designing leaders. Along the same lines is Guenter Lewy's *The Cause That Failed* (New York: Oxford University Press, 1990), a no-holds-barred assault on liberals and others ensnared in the Communist web. But it is these books, ironically, that convey nostalgia for a world where the lines were rigidly drawn—between right and wrong, friends and enemies, misfits and the normal—a lost world as far as the literature of American Communism is concerned.

2

Following is the bibliography proper, consisting of the other works that have helped me put this book together and that may help readers dig further into the history of American Communism.

Only a handful of books take in the whole Communist experience, the Foster and Howe and Coser ones included. Daniel Bell's *Marxian Socialism in the United States* (Princeton: Princeton University Press, 1967) does so brilliantly but rushes by the subject too cavalierly for anyone interested in finding out what actually happened. Three good synopses may be recommended: Paul Buhle, *Marxism in the United States* (London: Verso, 1987), which lays heavy emphasis on Communist contributions to cultural and ethnic life; Harvey Klehr and John Earl Haynes, *The American Communist Movement* (New

York: Twayne, 1992), which emphasizes the Party's subservience to Russia
and tends to blame it for the disasters that brought it down; and James
Weinstein, *Ambiguous Legacy* (New York: New Viewpoints, 1977), a well-
informed but all too perfunctory survey from a radical who wastes little
sympathy on the Party. A compendious, exhaustively researched study of
William Z. Foster, Edward P. Johanningsmeier's *Forging American Communism*
(Princeton: Princeton University Press, 1994), enables us to look at the
Party and movement through the career of its main player for almost four
decades; in short, a real contribution to the literature. An equally remarkable
overview, but of a different kind, is Joel Kovel's *Red Hunting in the Promised
Land* (New York: Basic Books, 1994), which turns the tables on historic anti-
Communism by locating the pathology in the anti-Communists (though it
does not completely exculpate the victims). Worth mentioning again in this
connection are the two encyclopedias on the Left alluded to in the preface.

To repeat: There is no better introduction to Communism in the 1920s—
its political institutional side at any rate—than the Draper volumes. In the
First Ten Years of American Communism (New York: Pathfinder, 1972) James P.
Cannon presents a fascinating account of the Party in its formative decade by
one of its founders and leaders at the time. An intensive history of its first few
years from the same (i.e., Trotskyist) standpoint is Farrell Dobbs, *Revolutionary Continuity* (New York: Monad, 1983). Valuable certainly are the recol-
lections of yet another Communist turned Trotskyist: Max Shachtman,
"Memoirs and Interviews," *Columbia Oral History Project* (1972). As for the
Trotskyist revolt inside the Party see Tim Wohlforth, *The Prophet's Children:
Travels on the American Left* (Atlantic Highlands, N.J.: Humanities, 1994). As
for Lovestone and his group and their travails, Robert S. Alexander provides
a tediously thorough study, *The Right Opposition* (Westport, Conn.: Greenwood, 1981). The lives of some notable Communists of the 1920s (who
became notable anti-Communists) is amply detailed in John Diggins, *Up from
Communism* (New York: Columbia University Press, 1994). The best discussion of Communist-led strikes in the 1920s remains Irving Bernstein, *The
Lean Years* (Boston: Houghton Mifflin, 1960).

An insider's view of *Liberation* and other intellectual currents of the day
can be gleaned from Max Eastman's accurately titled *Love and Revolution*
(New York: Random House, 1964) and Joseph Freeman's still valuable
American Testament (New York: Farrar and Rinehart, 1936). See also a fulsome
new biography by Douglas Clayton, *Floyd Dell: The Life and Times of an American
Radical* (Chicago: I. R. Dee, 1994) and the first part of James D. Bloom's fine
study, *Left Letters: The Culture Wars of Mike Gold and Joseph Freeman* (New York:
Columbia University Press, 1992). (A decent biography of Mike Gold, by
the way, is very much in order.)

The literature on Communism in the 1930s is huge, and so any selection
must be fairly ruthless. Harvey Klehr's previously cited *Heyday* is the obvious
point of departure. Somewhat friendlier to the Party and movement is a sig-

nificant addition to the literature: Fraser M. Ottonelli, *The Communist Party of the United States from the Depression to World War II* (New Brunswick: Rutgers University Press, 1991). Frank A. Warren's *Liberals and Communism: The "Red Decade"Revisited* (New York: Columbia University Press, 1994) does a fine job of refuting Eugene Lyons's wild exaggerations. A nice summary of the Popular Front at its height is Mark Naison, "Remaking America's Communists and Liberals in the Popular Front," in *New Studies in the Politics and Culture of United States Communism*, ed. Michael E. Brown, Randy Martin, Frank Rosengarten, and George Snedeker (New York: Monthly Review, 1993). Murray Kempton, *Part of Our Time: Some Ruins and Monuments of the Thirties* (New York: Simon and Schuster, 1955) is always entertaining, even when it is harsh and unforgiving in its ridicule. As implied earlier, Nathan Glazer's book, *supra*, has lost none of its relevance. Exceptional portraits of an urban Jewish subculture are Paul Lyons, *Philadelphia Communists, 1936–56* (Philadelphia: Temple University Press, 1982), Vivian Gornick, *The Romance of American Communism* (New York: Basic Books, 1972), and Kim Chernin, *In My Mother's House* (New Haven: Tickner and Field, 1983).

On the cultural front in general these are first rate: Richard H. Pell, *Radical Visions and American Dreams: Culture and Thought in the Depression Years* (New York: Harper & Row, 1973); James B. Gilbert, *Writers and Partisans: A History of Literary Radicalism in America* (New York: Wiley, 1968); the relevant chapters in Walter Rideout's excellent piece of scholarship, *The Radical Novel in the United States* (New York: Columbia University, 1993); Paula Rabinowitz, *Labor and Desire in Women's Revolutionary Fiction in Depression America* (Chapel Hill: University of North Carolina Press, 1991); Alan Wald, "Culture and Commitment: U.S. Communist Writers Reconsidered," in Michael Brown et al., eds., *supra*; Douglas C. Wixson, *Worker-Writer in America: Jack Conroy and the Tradition of Midwestern Literary Radicalism, 1898–1990* (Urbana: University of Illinois Press, 1994); the early chapters in Larry Ceplair and Steven Englund, *The Inquisition in Hollywood* (Garden City, N.Y.: Doubleday, 1980), and Nancy Lynn Schwartz, *The Hollywood Writer's War* (New York: Knopf, 1982); Mishra Kshamanidhi, *American Leftist Playwrights of the 1930s* (New Delhi: Classical, 1991); Morgan Yale Himelstein, *Drama Was a Weapon: The Left-Wing Theater in New York, 1929–1941* (New Brunswick, N.J.: Rutgers University Press, 1963); Leah Levenson, *Granville Hicks: The Intellectual in Mass Society* (Philadelphia: Temple University Press, 1993); naturally, Daniel Aaron's classic study, *supra*; and the best book about the Party and folk music: Robbie Lieberman, *My Song Is My Weapon* (Champaign: University of Illinois Press, 1989).

The literature on Communist involvement with labor in the 1930s fills a library. Irving Bernstein, *Turbulent Years* (Boston: Houghton Mifflin, 1969) is a good place to start. Then there is the work by an ex-Trotskyist who grudgingly admires what Party activists accomplished and does it with style and panache: Bert Cochran, *Labor and Communism: The Conflict That Shaped*

American Unions (Princeton: Princeton University Press, 1977). Highly recommended as well for the period is Harvey Levenstein, *Communism, Anti-*
communism, and the CIO (Westport, Conn.: Greenwood, 1981), a persuasively
devastating critique of the standard anti-Communist position advanced years
earlier by Max Kampleman, *The Communist Party vs. The CIO: A Study in Power*
Politics (New York: Praeger, 1957). The most interesting work by labor historians comes out of their probing, often microscopic inquiries into specific
unions, industries, events; for example, Joshua Freeman, *In Transit: The*
Transport Workers of New York City, 1933–1966 (New York: Oxford University
Press, 1989); the collection of essays in *The CIO's Left-led Unions*, ed. Steven
Russworm (New Brunswick: Rutgers University Press, 1992); Bruce
Nelson, *Workers on the Waterfront* (Urbana: University of Illinois Press, 1988);
Ronald Schatz, *The Electrical Workers* (Urbana: University of Illinois Press,
1983); and Roger Keeran, *The Communist Party and the United Auto Workers*
(Bloomington: University of Indiana Press, 1980). Communists and farmers
are explored in several first-rate books: Cletus E. Daniel, *Bitter Harvest: A*
History of California Farmworkers, 1870–1941 (Ithaca, N.Y.: Cornell University
Press, 1981); Lowell K. Dyson, *supra*; and three outstanding ones on the
Negro aspect of the same subject: Robin D. G. Kelley, *Hammer and Hoe:*
Alabama Communists during the Great Depression (Chapel Hill: University of
North Carolina Press, 1991), Theodore Rosengarten, *All God's Dangers: The*
Life of Nate Shaw (New York: Vintage, 1984), and Nell Irvin Painter, *The*
Narrative of Hosea Hudson: His Life as a Negro Communist in the South
(Cambridge, Mass.: Harvard University Press, 1970).

On Communists and Negroes, along with the last three above, the fol-
lowing are highly recommended: Mark Naison, *Communists in Harlem during*
the Depression (Urbana: University of Illinois Press, 1983); James E.
Goodman's enthralling tour de force, *Stories of Scottsboro* (New York:
Pantheon, 1994); Gerald Horne's biography of Benjamin Davis, *Black*
Liberation / Red Scare (Cranbury, N.J.: Associated University Presses, 1994);
and Charles Martin, *The Angelo Herndon Case and Southern Justice* (Baton
Rouge: Louisiana State University Press, 1976).

An important book, because it is the only thoroughgoing study we have of
Communists and students, is Robert Cohen, *When the Old Left Was Young:*
Student Radicals and America's First Mass Student Movement, 1929–41 (New York:
Oxford University Press, 1993).

The question of Communists and women remains to be explored; what
we have is rather impoverished, given the number of remarkable women in
the movement. But definitely see two recent studies: Helen C. Camp, *Iron in*
Her Soul: Elizabeth Gurley Flynn and the American Left (Pullman: WSU, 1995)
and Constance Coiner, *Better Red: The Writing and Resistance of Tillie Olsen and*
Meridel LeSueur (New York: Oxford University Press, 1995).

For the war years (1939– 45) the essential text is Maurice Isserman,
Which Side Were You On? (Middletown: Wesleyan University Press, 1982). But

see also George Sirgiovanni, *An Undercurrent of Suspicion* (New Brunswick: Transaction, 1990). How America felt about Communists during the Hitler-Stalin pact is told authoritatively by Leslie K. Adler and Thomas M. Paterson, "Red Fascism: The Merger of Nazi Germany and Soviet Russia in the American Charge of Totalitarianism, 1930–1950," *American Historical Review* (April 1970). Nelson Lichtenstein has written an important study: *Labor's War at Home: The CIO in World War II* (New York: Cambridge University Press, 1982). Philip J. Jaffe's *The Rise and Fall of American Communism* (New York: Horizon, 1975) is, alas, the only book we have on Earl Browder and Browderism. A good biography of the man is sorely needed. His papers, widely available on microfilm, reveal little.

And so we come to the last phase of American Communism, which set in as World War II gave way to the Cold War and America's (relatively) good feelings toward Communists and their friends gave way to rage and persecution, the movement then going into a tailspin from which it never recovered. Again Maurice Isserman is a dependable cicerone, this time with *If I Had a Hammer* (Urbana: University of Illinois Press, 1993). Philip Jaffe's book, *supra*, is useful in giving Browder's version of his fall. Ex-Communist Joseph R. Starobin's *American Communism in Crisis, 1943–1957* (Cambridge: Harvard University Press, 1972) provides a thoughtful analysis of the Party's grave miscalculations in this period. A far more sympathetic reading of its behavior, specifically its leadership role in Henry Wallace's 1948 presidential bid, is Norman D. Markowitz, *The Rise and Fall of the People's Century* (New York: Free Press, 1973). And the whole issue of Communism and liberalism during the Cold War is explored from two opposing perspectives: William L. O'Neill, *A Better World: The Great Schism* (New York: Simon and Schuster, 1982) and Mary S. McAuliffe, *Crisis on the Left: Cold War Politics and American Liberalism, 1948–1954* (Amherst: University of Massachusetts Press, 1978).

The effect of McCarthyism on Communism—and on the Left, and indeed on liberalism—has itself become a flourishing industry. Illuminating are the two studies on the government's prosecution of Communist leaders: Peter L. Steinberg, *The Great "Red Menace"* (Westport, Conn.: Greenwood, 1984) and Michael Belknap, *Cold War Political Justice* (Westport, Conn.: Greenwood, 1977). David Caute, *The Great Fear: The Anti-Communist Purges under Truman and Eisenhower* (New York: Simon and Schuster, 1978) is as indispensable as it is encyclopedic. Quite on target is Ellen Schrecker's brief article, "McCarthyism and the Decline of American Communism, 1945–1960," in Michael Brown et al., eds., *supra*. The ferocity of the assault on Communists and suspected friends in the labor movement is brought out in *The Cold War Against Labor* (Berkeley: Meiklejohn Civil Liberties Institute, 1987), ed. Ann Fagan Ginder and David Christiano; in David Oshinsky, "Labor's Cold War: The CIO and the Communists," in *The Specter*, ed. Robert Griffiths and Athan Theoharis (New York: Franklin Watts, 1974); and in Harvey Levenstein, *supra*.

Concerning blacks in particular see Gerald Horn, "The Red and the Black: The Communist Party and the African-Americans in Historical Perspective," in Michael Brown et al., eds., supra, for a trenchant summary of what McCarthyism wrought. Horne has also written a book about a front organization whose story is very much worth telling: *Communist Front?: The Civil Rights Congress, 1946–1956* (Rutherford, N.J.: Farleigh Dickinson University Press, 1988). And by all means see the relevant portions—those that refer to Communism—in three popular books of the late 1980s: Taylor Branch's masterful volume on Martin Luther King, *Parting the Waters: America in the King Years, 1954–1963* (New York: Simon and Schuster, 1988); Carl Bernstein's paean to his radical father, *Loyalties* (New York: Simon and Schuster, 1988); and Martin B. Duberman's poignant biography of the great and greatly maligned *Paul Robeson* (New York: Knopf, 1989).

The endlessly fascinating subject of Communism and Hollywood has provoked estimable studies, among them Larry Ceplair and Steven Englund, *supra*, Nancy Lynn Schwartz, *supra*, and above all, Victor Navasky, *Naming Names* (New York: Viking, 1980). For a defiantly unapologetic Communist's response to the blacklisting there is Lester Cole, *Hollywood Red: The Autobiography of Lester Cole* (Palo Alto: Ramparts, 1981).

I will conclude with a list of the better memoirs by ex-Communists, those who, after long, dedicated service, quit the Party in the years of its demise. Some of them I used as documentary sources for this book.

John Gates, *The Story of an American Communist* (New York: Thomas Nelson, 1958)

George Blake Charney, *A Long Journey* (Chicago: Quadrangle, 1968)

Al Richmond, *A Long View from the Left* (Boston: Beacon, 1972)

Jessica Mitford, *A Fine Old Conflict* (New York: Knopf, 1977)

Peggy Dennis, *The Autobiography of an American Communist* (Westport, Conn.: Lawrence Hill, 1977)

Steve Nelson, James R. Barrett, and Rob Ruck, *Steve Nelson, American Radical* (Pittsburgh: University of Pittsburgh Press, 1981)

Junius Irving Scales and Richard Nickson, *Cause at Heart* (Athens: University of Georgia Press, 1987)

Dorothy Healey and Maurice Isserman, *Dorothy Healey Remembers* (New York: Oxford University Press, 1990)

This section lists the sources, pages included, from which the documents have been extracted, and gratefully cites permissions for those still in copyright. I have been unable to track down several copyright holders. To them, should they come forward, and to any others I may have missed I apologize and will certainly make amends, for one thing by acknowledging them in the next edition. The following citations follow the exact order of the table of contents.

CHAPTER TWO

Louis C. Fraina, *Revolutionary Socialism* (New York: Communist Press, 1918), 218, 220–222.

Left Wing of the Socialist Party, "Manifesto," *Revolutionary Radicalism, Its History, Purpose and Tradition: Report of the Joint Legislative Committee Investigating Seditious Activities, in the Senate of the State of New York* (Albany: Lyons & Co., 1920), Part I, Vol. I, 716, 730–731, 735–736.

Communist Labor Party, "Platform and Program," *Revolutionary Radicalism,* Part I, Vol. I, 809, 816–817.

Communist Party, "Manifesto," *Revolutionary Radicalism,* Part I (I): 785–786, 791–792.

Zinoviev Letter, *Revolutionary Radicalism,* Part I (II): 1902–1907.

The United Communist Party, "Unity Convention," *Communist* (May 1921): 3, 5, 11.

Workers Party of America, *Program and Constitution* (Chicago: Lyceum and Literature Department, 1922), 6–10.

Workers Party of America, "Convention and Resolutions," *Fourth National Convention and Report of the Central Executive Committee* (Chicago: Daily Worker Publishing Co., 1925), 87–89, 91.

J. Peters, *The Communist Party: A Manual of Organization* (San Francisco: Proletarian Publishers, 1975), 23–26, 28, 108–109.

Benjamin Gitlow, *The Red Ruby* (New York: Workers Defense Conference, 1919), 4–8, 13–14.

Art Young, "American Liberty," *Liberator* (February 1920): 12.

Carl Sandburg, "The Liars," *Liberator* (May 1919): 1.

Claude McKay, "The Dominant White," *Liberator* (May 1919): 13.

Stuart Davis, "Theory and Practice," *Liberator* (July 1920): 39.

Crystal Eastman, "Now We Can Begin," *Liberator* (December 1920): 23–24.

Irwin Granich, "Toward Proletarian Art," *Liberator* (February 1921): 20–24.

Floyd Dell, "Explanations and Apologies," *Liberator* (June 1922): 25–26.

Robert Minor, "Evolution of the American Peasant," *Liberator* (January 1924): 18.

Joseph Freeman, *An American Testament* (New York: Farrar & Rinehart, 1936), 309–310, 313–315.

Mike Gold, "A New Continent," *New Masses* (July 1926): 28–30.

Max Eastman, Letter to the New Masses, *Love and Revolution* (New York: Random House, 1964), 492–494.

William Z. Foster, "Bankruptcy of American Labor," *Labor Herald* (October 1922): 1–2.

Benjamin Gitlow on the cloakmakers' strike: *I Confess* (New York: E.P. Dutton, 1940), 357, 359, 360–363.

Mary Heaton Vorse, *Passaic* (International Labor Defense, 1926), 5, 16–21, and *The Passaic Textile Strike* (New York: N.Y. General Relief Committee, 1927), 115–119.

Jay Lovestone, "Perspectives for Our Party," *Communist* (June 1927): 308–309.

Fred Ellis, "An Evening Affair," *Daily Worker* (August 9, 1927).

Michael Gold, "Lynchers in Frockcoats," *New Masses* (September 1927): 6.

James P. Cannon, "A Thriving Monument to Sacco and Vanzetti," *Labor Defender* (October 1927): 152–153.

James P. Cannon, *History of American Trotskyism* (New York: Pioneer Publishers, 1944), 51–55.

S. Mingulin, "Crisis in the United States and the Problems of the Party," *Communist* (June 1930): 500–502.

CHAPTER THREE

Sixth Comintern Congress, "Theses and Program," *The Communist International, 1919–1934: Documents,* edited by Jane Degras (London: Frank Cass, 1971), II, 455–456, 509–510.

William F. Dunne, "Immediate Effects of the Gastonia Struggle," *Gastonia: Citadel of the South* (New York: Workers Library, 1929), 41–42, 49–50, 54–55.

Ella May Wiggins, Two Ballads, in Margaret Larkin, "Ella May Songs," *Nation* (October 9, 1929): 382–383.

Fred Beal, *Proletarian Journey* (New York: Hillman-Curl, 1937), 345–346, 348–349.

William Z. Foster, *Organization and Program, Trade Union Unity League* (New York: Trade Union Unity League, 1931), 17–22.

James Matles and James Higgins, *Them and Us* (Englewood Cliffs, NJ: Prentice-Hall, 1974), 29–31.

William Gropper, "The Specter" (New York: ACA Gallery Publications, 1938).

Moritz Hallgren, *Seeds of Revolt* (New York: Alfred A. Knopf, 1933), 51–54.

Moritz Hallgren, "Ford Protest March," in *Seeds of Revolt,* 172–174.

Peggy Dennis, *The Autobiography of an American Communist* (Westport, CT: Lawrence Hill, 1977), 44–46.

Frank Spector, *The Story of Imperial Valley* (New York: International Labor Defense, 1930), 2–4.

Moritz Hallgren, "Mobilizing the Poor," in *Seeds of Revolt,* 192–193.

John Williamson, *Dangerous Scot* (New York: International Publishers, 1969), 81–85.

Kim Chernin, *In My Mother's House* (New York: Perennial Library: 1983), 96–98.

The Southern Worker (August 16, 1930): 1.

Hosea Hudson, *Black Worker in the Deep South* (New York: International Publishers, 1972), 36–43. With the permission of International Publishers.

Al Murphy, *Achievements and Tasks of the Sharecroppers Union* (New York: Workers Library, 1933), 6–7.

Lem Harris, *Farmers Unite Their Fight* (New York: Workers Library, 1934), 6–8.

The Yokinin Affair, in *Race Hatred on Trial* (New York: Workers Library, 1931), 24–25, 31–33, 38–39.

John Dos Passos, "Scottsboro's Testimony," *Labor Defender* (July 1931): 131.

James S. Allen, "Scottsboro," *Communist* (May 1933): 441–443, 446–448.

Muriel Rukeyser, "The Trial," in *Theory of Flight* (New Haven: Yale University Press, 1935), 40–42. With the permission of Louis Rukeyser.

Angelo Herndon, *Let Me Live* (New York: Random House, 1937), 344–348.

Edmund Wilson, "The Case of the Author," *American Jitters* (New York: Charles Scribner's Sons, 1932), 298–299, 302–303, 309–311.

V. F. Calverton, *For Revolution* (New York: John Day, 1932), no pagination.

League of Professional Groups for Foster and Ford, *Culture and the Crisis* (New York: Workers Library, 1932), 3, 5–5, 18–19, 23–24.

William Z. Foster, *Toward a Soviet America* (New York: International Publishers, 1932), 271–277, 338–341.

John Reed Clubs, "Draft Manifesto," *New Masses* (June 1932): 3–4.

Granville Hicks, *The Great Tradition* (New York: Macmillan, 1933), 301–306.

Philip Rahv and Wallace Phelps, "Problems and Perspectives in Revolutionary Literature," *Partisan Review* (June-July 1934): 3–10.

Whittaker Chambers, "You Can Make Out Their Voices," *New Masses* (March 1931): 7–16.

Meridel LeSueur, "Women on the Breadlines," *New Masses,* (January 1932): 5–6.

Kenneth Fearing, "Denouement," *Poems* (New York: Dynamo, 1935), 37–62.

First National Theater Conference, "Manifesto," *Workers Theater* (May 1932): 2–3.

Samuel Kreiter, "The Artef," *New Theater* (November 1934): 7–8.

V. J. Jerome and Gregory Novikov, *Newsboy* (from a copy in New York City's Lincoln Center Library Theater Collection), 1–5.

John Howard Lawson, "Interview," *The Cineaste Interviews: On the Art and Politics of the Cinema,* edited by Dan Georgakas and Lenny Rubenstein (Chicago: Lake View Press, 1983), 192–194, 197–198. With the permission of Lake View Press.

Hugo Gellert, "Four Horsemen of the Apocalypse," *Comrade Gulliver* (New York: G.P. Putnam's Sons, 1935), 41.

International Workers Order, *Manual* (New York: IWO, 1935), 3–9, 18–19.

The American League Against War and Fascism, *Manifesto and Program* (New York: American League Against War and Fascism, 1933), 2–7.

The American League Against War and Fascism, *Proceedings of Second Congress Against War and Fascism* (New York: American League Against War and Fascism, 1934), 23–25.

Tillie Lerner, "The Strike," *Partisan Review* (September–October, 1934): 3–9.

CHAPTER FOUR

The Seventh Comintern Congress, "Proceedings," *The Communist International, 1919–1943: Documents*, edited by Jane Degras (London: Frank Cass, 1971), III: 361–362, 363–365.

Earl Browder, "Who Are the Americans?" *What Is Communism?* (New York: International Publishers, 1936), Ch. 1.

Turmoil in Akron: John Williamson, *Dangerous Scot,* 114–121.

Wyndham Mortimer, *Organize!* (Boston: Beacon Press, 1971), 85–93.

Henry Kraus, *The Many and the Few* (Champaign: University of Illinois Press, 1985), 31–33, 38–39, 48–53, 86–90, 97–99. With permission of University of Illinois Press.

Len DeCaux, *Labor Radical* (Boston: Beacon Press, 1970), 278–279, 298–299. With permission of Jeryl Lacayo.

Philip Evergood, "American Tragedy," Lucy R. Lippard, *The Graphic Work of Philip Evergood* (New York: The Art Digest, Inc., 1966), 45.

American Writers' Congress, edited by Henry Hart (New York: International Publishers, 1935): John Dos Passos, 81–82; Kenneth Burke, 87–90, 93–94; Langston Hughes, 139–141.

Second American Writers Congress, *The Writers in a Changing World,* edited by Henry Hart (New York: Equinox Cooperative Press, 1937): Newton Arvin, 35–37; Malcolm Cowley, 44–47; Ernest Hemingway, 69–73; Summary, 228–229.

Artists Against War and Fascism: First American Artists Congress, edited by Matthew Baigell and Julia Williams (New Brunswick, NJ: Rutgers University Press, 1986): Stuart Davis, 65–67, 69–70; Peter Blume, 98–99, 101–102; Max Weber, 123–125, 127–129. With the permission of Rutgers University Press.

Bringing Music to the Masses, Statement by the American Music League, *Unison* (May 1936): 2–4.

James Agee, "Sunday: Outskirts of Knoxville, Tenn.," *New Masses* (September 14, 1937): 9.

Kenneth Fearing, "American Rhapsody (5)," *Dead Reckoning* (New York: Random House, 1938), 33.

Langston Hughes, "Let America Be America Again," *A New Song* (New York: International Workers Order, 1938), 9–11.

Woody Guthrie, *Born to Win,* edited by Robert Shelton (New York: Macmillan, 1965), 220–227, 236–237.

P. Lang, "The Trotsky-Zinoviev Assassins Before the Bar of the Working Class," *Communist* (October 1936): 938–940, 943–944, 948–950, 955.

Charles Shipman, *It Had to Be Revolution* (Ithaca, NY: Cornell University Press, 1993), 292–205. With permission of Cornell University Press.

Ernest Hemingway, "On the American Dead in Spain," *New Masses* (February 14, 1939): 13.

William Gropper, "Appeasement," *William Gropper* (East Brunswick, NJ: Associated University Presses and Cornwall Books, 1983), 104.

Philip J. Jaffe, *The Rise and Fall of Earl Browder* (New York: Horizon Books, 1975), 44–45.

Communist Party Political Committee, "America and the International Situation," *Communist* (November 1939): 995–996, 997–998.

Richard Wright, "Not My People's War," *New Masses* (June 17, 1948): 8–12.

Ruth McKenney, "Women Are Human Beings," *New Masses* (December 17, 1940): 9–10.

Elizabeth Gurley Flynn, "I Love My Comrade Organizers," Flynn Papers, Tamiment Institute, and "Every Day Should Be Mother's Day for Us," *Sunday Worker* (May 11, 1941): 12.

"No Delay in Opening the Western Front," *Communist* (August 1942): 579, 581–582, 591.

Earl Browder, "Hold the Home Front," *Communist* (July 1943): 582, 586–588.

Paul Robeson, "American Negroes in the War," *New York Herald Tribune* (November 21, 1943).

Earl Browder, *Teheran and America* (New York: Workers Library, 1944), 12–13, 16–17, 18–19, 40–41, 47–48.

Harry Haywood, *Black Bolshevik* (Chicago: Liberator Press, 1978), 534–536.

CHAPTER FIVE

Jacques Duclos, "On the Dissolution of the Communist Party of the U.S.A.," *Daily Worker* (May 24, 1945).

William Z. Foster, *Marxism-Leninism v. Revisionism* (New York: New Century Books, 1945), 4–8.

Earl Browder, *War or Peace with Russia* (New York: A. A. Wynn, 1947), 180–182, 188–189.

Theodore Dreiser, Request to Become a Communist, *Daily Worker* (July 30, 1945).

Albert Maltz, *New Masses* (February 12, 1946): 19–22.

Howard Fast, *New Masses* (February 26, 1946): 6–8.

Alvah Bessie, *New Masses* (March 12, 1946): 8–10.

Albert Maltz, *New Masses* (April 9, 1946): 8–9.

Communist Party Platform, *Political Affairs* (September 1948): 437–440.

John Gates, *The Story of an American Communist* (New York: Nelson Associates, 1958), 121–126.

Eugene V. Dennis, "Let Us March Forward," *Political Affairs* (July 1950): 15–17. "Proceedings," Congress of Industrial Organizations, Eleventh Constitutional Convention (Cleveland: 1949), 240, 262–263, 267, 273, 304–306.

Defending Willie McGee: Jessica Mitford, *A Fine Old Conflict* (New York: Alfred A. Knopf, 1977), 190–194. With permission of Alfred A. Knopf.

Civil Rights Congress, *We Charge Genocide* (New York: Civil Rights Congress, 1951), xi-xiii, 4–5, 8–9.

W. E. B. DuBois, Request to Join the Party, in *The Seventh Son,* edited by Julius Lester (New York: Random House, 1971), II, 721–723.

Angela Davis, *An Autobiography* (New York: International Publishers, 1988), 187–189. With permission of International Publishers.

Angela Davis, "Radical Perspectives on Empowerment for Afro-American Women," *Harvard Educational Review,* Vol. 58, 1988): 349–353.

Nikita Khrushchev, "Cult of the Individual," *New York Times* (July 5, 1956): 13–16.

Steve Nelson, James R. Barrett, and Rob Ruck, *Steve Nelson: American Radical* (Pittsburgh: University of Pittsburgh Press, 1981), 386–388. With permission of University of Pittsburgh Press.

John Gates, "Time for a Change," *Political Affairs* (November 1956): 39–40, 44–47.

William Z. Foster, "Marxism-Lenism and 'American Prosperity,' " *Political Affairs* (February 1957): 50–55.

Eugene V. Dennis, "Keynote Address," *Political Affairs* (March 1957): 4, 11.

John Gates, *The Story of an American Communist* (New York; Nelson Associates, 1958), 188–191, 203, 205.

Junius Irving Scales and Richard Nickson, *Cause at Heart* (Athens: University of Georgia Press, 1987), 318–320. With permission of University of Georgia Press.

Jessica Mitford, *A Fine Old Conflict* (New York: Alfred A. Knopf, 1977), 314, 318–320. With permission of Alfred A. Knopf.

Dorothy Healey and Maurice Isserman, *Dorothy Healey Remembers* (New York: Oxford University Press, 1990), 245–248, 253–255. With permission of Oxford University Press.